The Complete
Encyclopedia of Needlework

The Complete
Encyclopedia of Needlework

Thérèse de Dillmont

AN IMPRINT OF RUNNING PRESS
PHILADELPHIA • LONDON

Third Edition

9   8   7   6   5   4   3   2   1
Digit on the right indicates the number of this printing.

Library of Congress Cataloging-in-Publication Number 95–70675

ISBN 0-7624-0388-8

Cover photograph by Michael Weiss
Cover design by Ken Newbaker

Published by Courage Books, an imprint of
Running Press Book Publishers
125 South Twenty-second Street
Philadelphia, Pennsylvania 19103-4399

Foreword to the Third Edition

Thérèse Maria Josepha von Dillmont, the daughter of an aristocratic Viennese family, has perhaps contributed more to the development of fine needlework throughout the world than any other person. Her influence is as strong today as in 1884 when *The Complete Encyclopedia of Needlework* was published in France. *The Encyclopedia* was immediately translated and published in seventeen countries. In its first sixty-two years it sold more than 1.5 million copies.

Thérèse was born in 1846 and studied in Vienna at an embroidery school founded by the Empress Marie-Therese. After completing her schooling, she moved to Donarch, a village near Mulhouse, France, and founded her own embroidery school. At a time when aristocratic women confined their embroidery to their salons and boudoirs, Thérèse was a pioneer.

Mulhouse was also the home of Dollfus Mieg & Cie, a manufacturer (known today as DMC) of fine needlework threads and materials. DMC opened its doors in 1746. Dillmont had been acquainted with the grandson of DMC's founder, Jean Dollfus, and their businesses shared a close association for many years.

The success of the embroidery school in Mulhouse enabled Thérèse to open shops bearing her name in Vienna, Paris, London, and Berlin. She traveled extensively, studied needlework in many countries, collected outstanding pieces of embroidery, and became internationally known. Her research and studies paid off in 1884 with the publication of the 800-page DMC *The Complete Encyclopedia of Needlework*.

This is the book you hold in your hands today; a book that has never been equalled. What has made it popular for so long? First, it is comprehensive. If you're interested in pillow lace, macrame, knitting, crochet, tatting, gold embroidery, or mending this book will tell you how to do it. Every needlework skill imaginable is described in detail.

Second, the illustrations—originally steel engravings—are outstanding. Their detail and clarity is amazing. In most cases you can learn a skill just by following the illustration. They make every step look easy.

Many professional needleworkers have learned their art from Thérèse de Dillmont. For more than a century, her voice has spoken to new generations of needleworkers throughout the world.

Thank you, Thérèse, for your gift. We wish we had known you.

Rita Weiss and Jean Leinhauser
American School of Needlework, ® *Inc*
San Marcos, California

TABLE OF CONTENTS

Strip worked in running, herringbone, and buttonhole stitches.

CHAPTER I

Plain Sewing

Most people who open *The Complete Encyclopedia of Needlework* will say, on seeing the title of this chapter, that this information about sewing by hand is superfluous, especially in these days when the machine so often takes the place of the hand in sewing. But, in reality, among all the branches of needlework there is none more important than plain sewing. It is the basis of all other needlework.

A hand well trained in the execution of various kinds of plain sewing will easily surmount the difficulties encountered in any sort of fancywork. Further, in whatever circumstances of fortune one may be placed, the ability to sew well will always be useful. On the one hand, a practical knowledge of plain sewing enables one to appreciate other people's work at its true value, and on the other hand, it enables one to produce strong and lasting work should necessity arise.

Working Position.   Before proceeding to a description of stitches and methods of sewing, we would point out the importance of a correct posture of body and hand, no matter what work is being done. Long experience has proved that no kind of plain sewing or embroidery compels one to adopt an awkward attitude.

In order to avoid this inconvenience, the height of the chair should be well suited to that of the table. The work should be held at a height that will render it unnecessary to lower the head, which should be held as straight as possible and at most only slightly bent forward. Never fasten the work to your knee: the position which this entails is both ungraceful and unhealthy. Pin it, instead, to a leaded cushion heavy enough to resist the pull of the thread in working.

Needles.   Only the best quality needles of finely tempered steel should be used. To try the temper, break one between the fingers. If the steel is well tempered, a considerable resistance will be felt before it snaps, and the break will be a clean one. If, however, the needle is very brittle, or bends without breaking, the steel is poor and it should be discarded. Never sew with a bent needle—it makes ugly and irregular stitches—and see that the eye is well polished, so that it will not fray or cut the thread.

White work should be done with short or half-short needles; for other kinds of work long ones are best.

The needle should always be a little thicker than the thread, to ensure the latter an easy passage through the stuff.

To preserve needles from rust, put a little asbestos powder in the packets. People with damp hands, which oxidize the needles they touch, will do well to keep a small box of the powder by them, and occasionally dip their fingers in it. One can, further, make a small cushion, filled with fine emery powder, which will restore the polish to rusty needles if they are passed backward and forward through it.

Scissors. It is advisable to have two pairs of scissors for working: a large pair, with one pointed and one rounded end (the latter always to be above the material when cutting); and a small pair, with both ends pointed, for cutting threads and removing small portions of material, as in openwork embroidery and scalloping. The rings should be rounded and as large as possible: if at all tight they tire the hand and leave marks on the fingers. These two pairs of scissors will suffice for most of the various kinds of needlework described in the following chapters.

Thimble. Nickeled thimbles are the best; those of bone are very liable to break, and silver ones are not always deeply enough pitted to keep the needle from slipping. A good thimble should be light, with a slightly rounded top and a flat rim.

Length of Thread. A needleful of thread for sewing should never be more than twenty inches long; for tacking and basting, however, it may be longer.

Cotton should be cut rather than broken, as breaking weakens it.

Fastening the Thread into the Eye of the Needle (fig. 1). When the thread becomes inconveniently short, and you do not want to take a

Fig. 1. Fastening the thread into the eye of the needle.

fresh needleful, it may be held at the eye of the needle by means of a loop.

When knots have to be used in any kind of work, take pains to make them as neat and small as possible.

The end of the needleful to be threaded into the needle is more important than one might suppose: the end cut from the reel should be the one passed through the eye. If the other end is threaded, it is apt to fray and lose its gloss.

Materials. For tacking, use a loosely twisted cotton, such as DMC tacking cotton, obtainable on reels or in balls, and especially made for this purpose.

For plain sewing, use DMC Alsatian sewing cotton, which is sold on reels and in balls; DMC best 6 cord sewing machine cotton; DMC Alsa, nos. 40 and 60; DMC Alsatian twist, no. 50; and DMC Alsatian cordonnet, nos. 60 and 80, brilliant cotton threads which can be used as a substitute for sewing silk.

Position of the Hands When a Weighted Cushion is Used (fig. 2). The stuff, fastened to a leaded cushion, must be held with the left

Fig. 2. Position of the hands when a weighted cushion is used.

hand, which should not rest either on the table or on the cushion. The middle of the needle should be held between the thumb and forefinger of the right hand, while the middle finger, protected by the thimble, rests against the needle and pushes it far enough through the stuff for the thumb and forefinger to be able to take hold of it and draw it out, together with the thread, which will then lie between the third and fourth fingers in the form of a loop, which is allowed to slip gradually through the fingers to prevent it from knotting.

Position of the Hands Without Cushion (fig. 3). When a cushion cannot be used, the work must not be rolled over the forefinger of the left hand, but should merely be held between the thumb and forefinger and allowed to fall freely over the other fingers. However, should the material need to be slightly stretched, hold it between the third and fourth fingers.

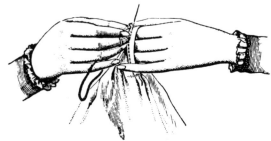

Fig. 3. Position of the hands without cushion.

This will prevent your sewing from getting puckered or dragged.

Stitches. Plain sewing comprises four varieties of stitches: (1) running, (2) back stitching, (3) hemming, and (4) top or oversewing (commonly called seaming).

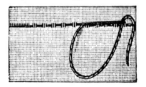

Fig. 4. Running stitch.

(1) *Running stitch* (fig. 4). This stitch, being the simplest of all, is also the first to be taught to children. It is made by passing the needle through the material from two to four threads ahead of the stitch just made, and bringing it out again the same number of threads farther on. When the nature of the stuff permits, several consecutive stitches are taken up on the needle at once, before the thread is pulled through. The running stitch is used for plain seams, for gathers, and for making up light materials.

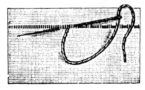

Fig. 5. Back stitching.

(2) *Back stitching* (fig. 5). Working from right to left, take up six threads of the material on the needle and draw it through; then insert the needle two threads back from where it was last drawn out, and bring it through again six threads beyond. Back stitching, as well as stitching, is generally done by machine.

Stitching (fig. 6). This is the name given to back stitching in which the stitches are made to meet exactly, without leaving any gap between them. The needle must always be inserted at the spot where it was previously drawn out, and brought out at an equal distance beyond the following stitch.

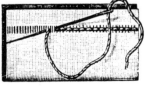

Fig. 6. Stitching.

This stitch must be executed with perfect regularity. This is achieved by counting the threads of the material, two or three threads according to thickness being taken up to make a stitch. For white work, a thread of the material should be drawn to mark the line of the stitching if it is to be done on the straight, the thread removed being replaced by the line of stitches. If you have to stitch on the cross, or if the stuff is too thick to allow a thread to be drawn, a tacking thread in a contrasting color should be run in first to serve as a guide.

Stitched hem (fig. 7). The stitch described above is used for this type of seam. Make a double turning, as for a hem, draw a thread two or three strands above the edge of the first turning, and do your stitching as described above through all three layers of material. The right side of the work is that on which the stitching is done.

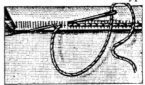

Fig. 7. Stitched hem.

(3) *Hemming and plain hem* (fig. 8). To make a good hem, the material must be cut by the line of the thread. Highly dressed fabrics, such as linen, muslin, and calico, should be rubbed in the hands to soften them before the hem is laid. Make the first turning not more than an eighth of an inch wide, down the whole length of the piece; then, starting from the same point, make a second fold of the same width. The

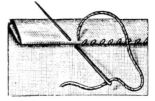

Fig. 8.
Hemming and plain hem.

cut or raw edge will thus be enclosed between two folds of the stuff. Only hems that are more than half an inch wide need to be tacked, and the first turning only needs to be just wide enough to prevent the edge from fraying.

Hemming is done by taking up the underneath layer of material at a distance of one thread from the hem, then inserting the needle through the upper layer, two threads above the fold, at a slight slant. A gap of two threads should be left between the successive stitches, always keeping these latter in a perfectly straight line. Some people draw a thread along the edge of the second fold to ensure the latter's being quite even, but this is unwise, as folding has already somewhat worn the material and removing threads weakens it still further.

Woollen materials will not keep a fold, and can rarely be prepared for more than a length of two or three tacks at a time.

In making what are called rolled hems—which are first turned down on the right side and stitched close to the edge, then turned double on the wrong side and tacked like other hems—the needle should be slipped in so as to pierce the stuff of the stitched fold and the hem edge only, so that no stitch shall appear on the right side.

Hems with ornamental stitches (figs. 9 and 10). In underclothing, where something more decorative than an ordinary hem is wanted, open-work hem stitch, as described in the chapter, ''Drawn Thread Work on Linen,'' may be used; or the edge of a plain hem may be overcast with em-

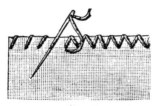

Fig. 9.
Hem with ornamental stitches.

Fig. 10.
Hem with ornamental stitches.

broidery stitches of various kinds worked in colors.

Make the hem first, as in fig. 8. Choose bright colors for the overcasting in order to heighten the effect. For stout materials, we recommend DMC pearl cotton, DMC special quality embroidery cotton, and DMC floss flax or flourishing thread in the thicker grades. For fine, transparent materials, the fine grades of DMC pearl cotton, DMC special quality embroidery cotton, DMC floss flax or flourishing thread, DMC rayon, DMC special stranded cotton, and DMC Persian silk. The last two may be divided into single or double strands, if so desired.

Figure 9 is worked thus: hold the material in your left hand, right side toward you—the hem turned upward—and, starting at the left, insert the needle into the edge of the fold and bring it out on the right side, skip six threads, take the needle over to the back of the work and, inserting it into the back of the material, bring it out in front. Skip six threads and continue in the same way to the end. Your hem will then be overcast with stitches slanting from left to right.

The second row of stitches is worked in the opposite direction, that is, from right to left, the needle entering and leaving the material at the same points as in the first row, so that the stitches cross each other at the edge of the fold and look the same on both sides of the hem.

In working fig. 10, hold the stuff as before, the right side toward you, and begin on the left. Insert the needle into the edge of the fold and make three buttonhole stitches (see figs. 40 and 41) meeting in the same hole at the bottom; skip eight threads, make another group of three buttonhole stitches, and so on. These little clusters are fan-shaped, as seen in the figure.

Three more decorative hems will be found in figs. 217–220 in the chapter, "Embroidery on Linen."

Flat seam (fig. 11). Lay your two edges, whether straight or on the cross, exactly even, tack them together with stitches one-half to three-

Fig. 11. Flat seam (stitch and fell).

quarters of an inch from the edge, then back stitch them together, following the tacking threads. Trim off half the inner edge very carefully with sharp scissors, turn the outer one as if for a plain hem, and fell it down. As you proceed, smooth the under part with the forefinger to prevent it from puckering. This hem, when finished, will lie quite flat. A novice is advised to smooth the seam with her thimble or the handle of the scissors before beginning to hem, as the wider edge is apt to get pushed up and bulge over in the sewing, which hides the stitches.

Rounded or whipped seam. Back stitch the two edges together, as directed above, then cut off the inner edge to a width of four threads, and roll the outer one with the left thumb in such a way as to enclose the cut edge. After securing the thread in the seam, make four or five hemming stitches; roll the fold, then make another series of stitches, and so on. This kind of work should form, on the wrong side, a very regular little roll, resembling a fine cord. It is used in making the daintier articles of underclothing.

Joining in a new thread (fig. 12). Knots should be avoided in white work. In hemming, the two ends are placed under the fold, which is then hemmed down. To begin a new needleful in back stitching or running, make one stitch with the fresh thread, then take both ends, lay them together to the left, and, holding them with the thumb, work over them so that they are wound in and out of the next few stitches.

Fig. 12. Joining in a new thread.

(4) *Top or oversewing (seaming) stitch for linen* (fig. 13). The seam stitch is used for joining selvedges together. As one edge or other is apt to slip out of place if merely held by the fingers, it is better to hold them together with tacking threads or pins placed close together.

Fig. 13. Top or oversewing (seaming) stitch for linen.

Insert the needle from the back under the first thread of the two selvedges and sew from right to left, setting the stitches not more than two or three threads apart. The thread must not be drawn too tight, so that the stitches may have a little play. When the seam is finished, flatten it out on the wrong side with your thimble; the two selvedges should lie side by side, touching without overlapping.

Dressmaking seam (fig. 14). For dress seams and patching, the stitches are also worked from right to left, but the needle is inserted first into the selvedge nearest to the worker. It is advisable to tack or pin the two edges together, as in oversewing, and to hold the material between the thumb and forefinger only, for fear of pulling one edge or the other.

Fig. 14. Dressmaking seam.

Antique seams (figs. 15 and 16). Tack or pin the selvedges together, as already described. Then, pointing the needle upward, insert it under two

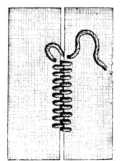

Fig. 15. Antique seam.

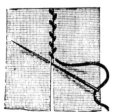

Fig. 16. Antique seam.

threads of the left selvedge; then, again pointing it upward, insert it under two threads of the right selvedge, and continue thus, setting the stitches two threads apart. In this manner the threads cross each other between the two selvedges and a perfectly flat seam is produced.

This kind of seam used to be employed whenever the material was not quite wide enough for the purpose to which it was destined, and the worker wished to conceal the joining of the breadths. In making sheets, the widths of linen are sometimes joined in a similar way (fig. 16), the only difference being that the stitches are set slightly slanting instead of straight.

Openwork seams (fagotting) (figs. 17, 18, 19). These are used for the same purpose as those illustrated in figs. 15 and 16, that is, in making bed and table linen from widths of fabric which are in themselves too narrow.

These stitches require a strong, closely twisted thread. Besides the thicker grades of DMC best 6 cord sewing machine cotton, we recommend DMC Alsatian sewing cotton, DMC flax lace thread, DMC cotton lace thread, and DMC special quality crochet cotton. The last two articles, available in colors in certain thicknesses, are especially suitable for working on colored materials.

Fig. 17.
Openwork seam.

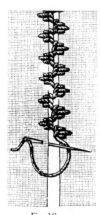

Fig. 18.
Openwork seam.

Lay the work straight before you, so that the two selvedges lie parallel. Fasten your thread onto the left hand strip, then insert the needle in the right hand one, two threads from the edge, and bring it out above the thread. Then make a small loop and, in drawing up the thread, close the loop, thus forming a knot. Returning to the left side, make a similar stitch there, at a distance of three threads from the starting point. Pass back to the right, skip three threads, make a knot as before, and so on. The stitches on the right are thus the counterpart of those on the left.

The seam shown in fig. 18 is formed from groups of three buttonhole stitches, placed alternately on the two edges to be joined. The first and the third stitch are worked over two threads, the middle one over four. The groups are five threads apart from each other.

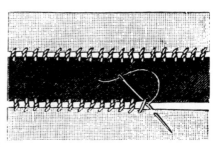

Fig. 19. Openwork seam.

The seam represented in fig. 19 is particularly suited for trimming colored underlinen. The width of the insertion may be increased at will by the addition of two or more bands of colored material on the edges of the white. These can be made of colored ribbon or of strips of material taken double, folded in at the edges, and joined to the selvedges of the material by two rows of little bars worked in overcast stitch, for which it is best to use DMC Alsatian sewing cotton, DMC Alsa, DMC Alsatian cordonnet, DMC cotton lace thread, or DMC flax lace thread. When working on colored materials, such as the fashion of today recommends for fine underwear and even for house and table linen, use DMC special quality crochet cotton and DMC cotton lace thread in plain or shaded colors. It is advisable to tack hem and insertion very carefully, parallel to each other, onto American cloth, to avoid the risk of getting either puckered in the working. The rows of bars should be begun on the left in the edge of the material itself, not in the edge of the band that is to be inserted. The needle must enter the insertion two threads from the edge and emerge to the right of the thread, then be passed once over the stretched thread, thus forming a bar of overcast stitch, and be brought out through the edge of the material on the right, three threads distant from the point whence the first stitch issued. The bars must all be at an equal distance from each other and quite vertical. The second side is worked in the same way.

Double or French seam (fig. 20). For joining materials liable to fray,

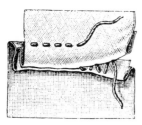

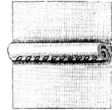

Fig. 20.
Double or French seam.

Fig. 21.
Hemming in lining.

Fig. 22. Open
hemmed double seam.

use a double seam. The two pieces of material are placed together, back to back, the edges exactly meeting. They are then joined with running stitches close to the edge. Then turn them over at the seam, so that the right sides come next to each other and the two raw edges are hidden. Another running seam is then made below the first, care being taken that no threads of the raw edge are visible on the outside of the seam. This seam is used chiefly in dressmaking, for joining light fabrics which cannot be kept from fraying by any other means.

Hemmed double seams (figs. 21 and 22). Turn in the two raw edges and lay them one upon the other so that the one next to the forefinger lies slightly higher than the one next to the thumb. Instead of upward from below, insert the needle first into the upper edge and then, slightly slanting, into the lower one. This seam is used in dressmaking for fastening down linings.

Fig. 22 shows another kind of double seam, where the two edges are laid together, turned in twice, and hemmed in the ordinary manner, with the sole difference that the needle has to pass through six layers of stuff.

Gathering (fig. 23). Gathering is used in all kinds of underwear and dressmaking. The gathers are made by means of a series of running stitches done very regularly in a straight line. Three or four threads of the material are always taken up on the needle, and the same number left beneath it, but the material, instead of being stretched with the left hand, is pushed onto the needle, and in this manner the gathers are produced. The needle is drawn through only after five or six gathers have been made.

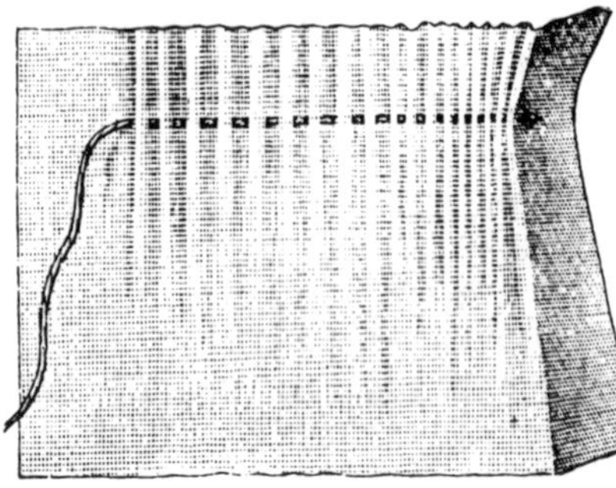

Fig. 23. Gathering, first row.

Stroking the gathers (fig. 24). When the gathering thread has been run in, draw up the gather almost tight and twist the thread round a pin put upright at the end. Holding the work between the thumb and forefinger of the left hand, take a strong needle and stroke it down vertically between the gathers so as to fix them evenly side by side. In doing this, push each gather under the left thumb to keep it in place, while the other fingers support the stuff at the back.

Running in a second gathering thread (fig. 25). When the gathers have been made even, run a second thread about one-quarter to one-half inch below the first, according to the nature of the material and the article. This thread serves to emphasize the gathers. In garments likely to require constant washing and ironing, such as children's frocks and pinafores, yet another line of gathering stitches may be added, and the extra rows overcast with a fancy thread, or a fine cord or silk thread whipped on. This keeps the gathers firm and straight, and is called biassing the gathers.

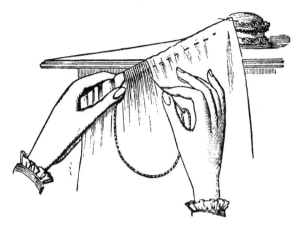

Fig. 24. Stroking the gathers.

Setting in gathers (fig. 26). To distribute the fullness equally, divide the gathered portion of the material, and the band onto which it is to be sewn, into equal parts, and pin the two together at corresponding distances, the material being slipped under the band so that the edge of the latter comes halfway between the two rows of gathering stitches. Before stitching on the band, see that the fullness of the gathers is evenly distributed along the whole length that they are to occupy. Hem

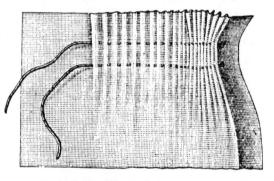

Fig. 25. Running in a second gathering thread.

each gather separately to the band through the upper threads only. Fasten off the gathering thread, turn the work, and set in the wrong side of the gathers to the back of the band in the same manner.

Smocking (figs. 27 and 28). The need to secure and at the same time ornament gathers in heavy materials has given rise to a special form of fancy gathering called smocking, which we here describe.

This kind of work occurs in the national costumes of the Hungarians, as well as in England, where it is still in vogue. "Smock" is an old English word for shirt or chemise, hence the term "smocking" came to be applied to the ornamental gathering of the necks of these garments and also to the elaborate, beautifully embroidered linen "smock-frock" of the field laborers. A great variety of patterns exists, but as they are executed in prac-

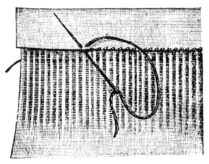

Fig. 26.
Setting in gathers.

tically the same way, one explanation will suffice for all.

Prepare the material .as described in figs. 23 to 25. After the first row of gathers, make as many parallel rows beneath it as the selected pattern requires, leaving rather less than half an inch of the material between them. This process is called gaging.

The three horizontal rows which form the heading of the pattern are worked from left to right. Begin with the third row from the top, carry the thread over two gathers and bring it back under one gather. Carry the thread again over two and back under one, and continue thus,

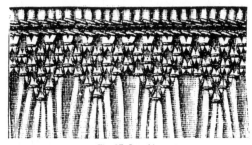

Fig. 27. Smocking.

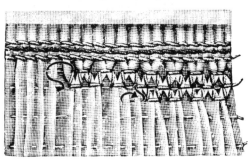

Fig. 28. Working detail of smocking.

taking care to bring out the needle above the stitch just made, so that the stitches may be slightly slanting.

Following upon these three rows of stitches comes the true smocking, done from right to left. At the next auxiliary thread, pass the needle under two gathers, then secure both these gathers together with a back stitch, bringing the needle out a quarter of an inch higher up on the material and passing under the next gather beyond the two already secured. Going back over two gathers, make another back stitch, bringing the needle level with the first stitch, but one gather beyond the last two secured. Continue in this way to the end of the row. The thread with which you are embroidering remains on the right side of the work all the time.

The second row is made close to the first, the third close to the second, and so on. From the second row downward, no back stitch is made in the upper line of stitches, the needle merely passing under the back stitch of the previous row. In the last row, make the points, which must be placed at regular intervals along the whole length of the embroidery. They are worked to and fro without the course of the stitches being interrupted, as fig. 27 shows.

The gathering threads must be pulled out when the embroidery is completed.

For working the embroidery, a strong and durable thread is used, such as DMC special quality embroidery cotton, DMC pearl cotton, DMC floss flax or flourishing thread, or DMC embroidery rayon.

Smocking in horizontal and oblique stitches (fig. 29 and 30). For this design, prepare a foundation of twelve rows of gathers, not quite half an inch apart. This smocking pattern is worked chiefly in horizontal stitches, sometimes joined by oblique stitches.

Begin with two rows of horizontal stitches, in the second row of which the lower back stitch holds the same two gathers as the upper back stitch of the first row (fig. 30). Next work a triple row, set in the same way, and completed by points. The top of the diamond requires two rows for working. Beginning exactly below the first point on the left of the work, and on the next line of gathering thread, make a horizontal stitch over two gathers. This is made by passing the needle under the gathers from left to

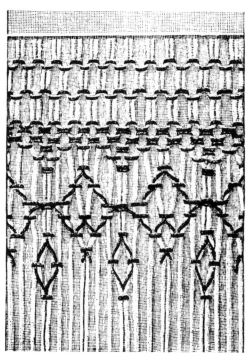

Fig. 29.
Smocking in horizontal and oblique stitches.

right, making a back stitch over the two (the thread thus going from right to left on the right side of the work), and bring the needle out again on the right of the second gather. Draw this stitch very tight. Then pass the thread over two gathers to the right, and pass the needle from right to left under the second of these two gathers, bringing it out so that the thread lies above the stitch just made. Pass the thread obliquely upward over this same gather, and pass the needle under the same gather, again from right to left, halfway between the thread on which the first two stitches were made and the next thread above. Pass the thread horizontally to the right over two gathers, pass the needle from right to left under the second gather, bringing it out immediately above the stitch just made, pass the thread obliquely upward over the same gather, pass the needle under the same gather from right to left, pass the thread horizontally to the right over two gathers at the upper gathering thread, pass the needle from right to left under the second gather, bringing it out immediately below the stitch just made. Work in the same way downward to the first gathering thread, then upward, and so on, to the end (fig. 29).

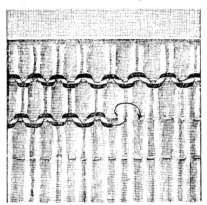

Fig. 30. Detail of working of smocking design shown in fig. 29.

The lower part of the diamond is done in the same way, but working first downward, then upward. The small diamonds below can be worked separately, or in conjunction with the lower halves of the larger diamonds.

Fig. 30 shows the method of working the horizontal stitches of this design. It shows how the horizontal stitch takes in two gathers and how the needle crosses the gather obliquely in order to work the next horizontal stitch. By inserting the needle once from above downward, and once from below upward, the stitches and gathers are arranged in alternating fashion.

Smocking in chain stitch (figs. 31 and 32).   This design is worked entirely in chain stitch, and requires four rows of gathers, a quarter to a half inch apart.

Begin the work at the top and to the left with two horizontal rows of chain stitch. Next, work the loop design between these two rows. The loop design consists of two waving lines of chain stitch, crossing each other at every seventh gather and forming regular ovals.

Fig. 32 shows on the one hand the working of these waving lines, and on the other hand the way in which the needle is inserted, to make the chain stitch, through the upper threads of the gather. The working of the chain stitch itself is explained in the chapter, "Embroidery on Linen" (see fig. 256). To work the pointed design in Fig. 31, begin with a waving line, which is cut at regular intervals by pointed scallops.

Whipping (fig. 33). Where very fine materials must be gathered, whipping is often used to replace the ordinary hem. With the thumb and forefinger of the left hand, roll the edge little by little into a very tight, thin roll, inserting the needle on the inside of the roll next to the thumb and bringing it out on the outside next to the forefinger, at regular distances. As in the run-ning stitch, the needle is

Fig. 31. Smocking in chain stitch.

drawn out only after several stitches have been made. By pushing the stuff back from time to time along the tightened draw thread, the gathers will be formed quite naturally.

Scalloped Hem (fig. 34). An ornamental hem on fine calico, muslin, or cambric can be made in the following manner: fold over the edge to a depth of from one half to one inch and run a thread up and down with small running stitches, as shown in fig. 34. When the thread is drawn up, little scallops are formed.

Sewing on a Round Cord (fig. 35). For sewing on round cords, use a very strong thread, such as DMC best 6 cord sew-ing machine cotton, DMC Alsatian sewing cotton, DMC cotton lace thread, and DMC

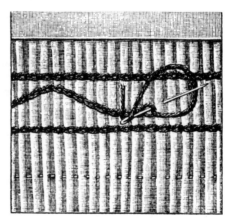

Fig. 32.
Detail of working of fig. 31. Smocking.

special quality crochet cotton, of medium thickness. Be careful not to stretch the cord, but rather to ease it on as you sew, because it invariably shrinks more than the material in the first washing. Hem it firmly with small close stitches to the edge of the turning. To avoid twisting it, always keep the plait formed by the threads of the cord in a straight line.

Binding with Braid or Galoon (fig. 36). These should be back

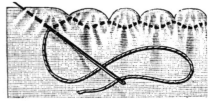

Fig. 33. Whipping.   Fig. 34. Scalloped gathers.

stitched onto the right side of the article to be bound, quite close to the edge, then folded in half and hemmed down on the wrong side. Like the cord, the

Fig. 35.
Sewing on a round cord.

braid must be eased on with the left hand during stitching, to allow for its shrinking in the wash without puckering the articles that it trims.

To save time, the first stitching is often done with the machine, or the braid is folded in half, the material to be bound being placed between the two edges, which are then stitched together. Though the stitching can be done more quickly by machine, it is much better done by hand, as fingers alone can ease the braid on properly.

Sewing on Tape Loops (figs. 37 and 38). These, where the commoner articles of household linen are concerned, are generally fastened to

Fig. 36. Binding with braid or galoon.

the corners. Lay the ends of your piece of tape, which should be five or six inches long, side by side, turn in the ends, and hem them neatly down to the article on three sides. The loop should be folded into a three-cornered point as shown in fig. 37. Join the two edges of the tape together in the middle with a few cross stitches, and stitch the edge of the article to the loop on the right side.

The tape loop may also be sewn onto the middle of an article, the tape being doubled and the two ends sewn down as described above; see fig. 38.

Strings and loops for fine underclothing (fig. 39). Sew these likewise onto the wrong side of the article, securing them by hemming round three sides, and making two crossing diagonal lines of back stitches on the right side, and a third line along the edge of the article.

Buttonhole Stitch and Buttonholes in Linen (fig. 40). Cut a perfectly straight slit in the material, large enough to allow the button to pass through easily, having previously marked out the length by means of two rows of running stitches on each side, two or three threads apart, the stitches in the second row taking up the threads of the material left in the first row.

Working from left to right, pass the needle through the slit, and insert it from behind so that the eye is toward the slit and the point downward. The thread is then passed round under the point of the needle from right to left, and the needle drawn through toward the other edge of the slit. The stitch is drawn tight, as close as possible to the edge of the slit.

When the first side has been finished, throw three or four threads across the end of the slit and buttonhole them over,

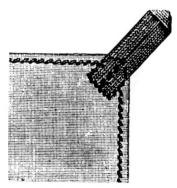

Fig. 37. Tape loop sewn on at the corner of the article.

thus making a little bar to prevent the end from splitting. Then do the second side of the slit like the first, with another buttonhole bar to finish off the other end.

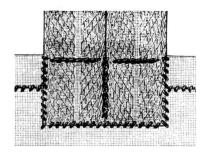

Fig. 38. Tape loop sewn onto the middle of the article in coarse linen.

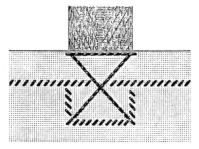

Fig. 39. Strings and loops for fine underclothing.

For making buttonholes in underwear, use DMC Alsatian sewing cotton, DMC best 6 cord sewing machine cotton, DMC cotton lace thread, DMC special quality crochet cotton, and DMC Alsa, which are strong, closely twisted threads. The last three are obtainable in colors and therefore are suitable for modern underwear.

Buttonholes in Dress Materials (fig. 41). Mark out and cut the slits as already described. If, however, the material is liable to fray, wet the freshly cut slit with a solution of gum arabic and let it dry before working.

Here only one traverse bar is made to complete the buttonhole. The end in which the button will rest must be rounded, and the stitches form a semicircle enclosing it. In thick cloths it is best to cut a very small piece right out. It is also a good plan to lay two threads of coarse silk, or a very fine

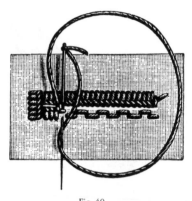

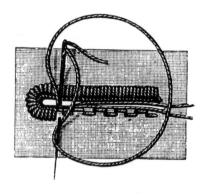

Fig. 40.
Buttonholes in linen.

Fig. 41.
Buttonholes in dress materials.

cord, around the buttonhole, work the stitches over this, and draw it up a little when the buttonhole is finished, in order to straighten the edges. This gives firmness and strength, while keeping the stitches from getting stretched in use. For this work we especially recommend DMC Alsa and DMC Alsatian cordonnet, which are made in a great variety of shades.

Sewing on Buttons (figs. 42 and 43). To sew linen or webbed buttons onto underlinen, fasten in the thread with a stitch or two at the place where the button is to lie, bring the needle up through the middle of the button and, from this central point, make a series of stitches, raying outward at equal distances.

Fig. 42.
Sewing on linen
buttons.

Fig. 43.
Sewing on webbed
buttons.

For other soft buttons, make a little circle of back stitches round the center; then bring the needle out between the button and the fabric, twist the cotton several times round the stitches to make a stem, and fasten off the end in the circle of back stitches.

Binding Slits (figs. 44, 45, 46, 47). Nothing is more apt to tear than a slit in lingerie, whether it is hemmed or bound. To obviate this trouble, make a semicircle of buttonhole stitches at the bottom of the slit, and a buttonhole bar above them to connect the two sides (fig. 44).

Fig. 45 represents a slit backed by a narrow bias strip of material; fig. 46 a slit backed by a wide straight piece.

When two selvedges form the slit, it is unnecessary to back them, but a small square of material called a gusset is inserted in the following manner: turn in the raw edges of the gusset and seam two sides of it to the selvedges of the slit; then fold over the other half of the gusset on the cross and hem

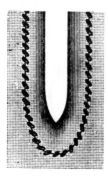

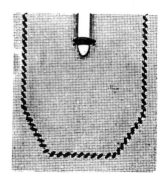

Fig. 44.
Slit bound with
hem.

Fig, 45.
Slit bound with narrow
crosspiece.

Fig. 46.
Slit bound with broad
band.

down on the wrong side exactly over the seam stitches, as shown in fig. 47.

Piping (fig. 48). Piping consists of a strip of material, three-quarters to an inch wide, cut on the cross and folded over a cotton cord, which is then stitched to the edge of an article to strengthen and finish it. On a bias edge, it is a good substitute for a hem or binding, as it prevents stretching.

Fig. 47.
Slit strengthened
with gusset.

Cut the narrow strips diagonally and very evenly across the web of the material and run them together end to end till the required length is obtained; lay the piping cord or bobbin along the strip on the wrong side, a fifth of an inch from the edge, fold the edge over and tack the cord lightly in. Then lay the prepared piping on the right side of the article, with all the raw edges away from you, and back stitch the piping to the material with small stitches, keeping close to the cord. Turn the article over, fold in the raw outside edge of the strip to cover the other edges, and fell it down like an ordinary hem.

Herringboning (fig. 49). To prevent certain materials from fraying, and to neaten seams which have a raw edge, these are covered with widely spaced overcasting, or with herringbone stitch. Herr-

Fig. 48. Stitching on piping.

ingboning is done from left to right and forms two parallel rows of small stitches, one of which is done through the turning and does not show upon the right side. Insert the needle from right to left in the folded-down part and

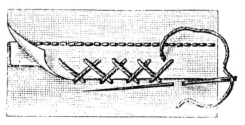

make a stitch first above and then below the edge, the threads crossing each other diagonally, leaving an eighth of an inch between the stitches; repeat to the end of the seam. When this stitch is done in the lining, the thread should never show on the right side of the work itself.

Fig. 49. Herringbone seam.

This same stitch is often used in fancywork as an ornament, and is then done in colors contrasting with the ground.

Ornamental Stitches for Underlinen (figs. 50, 51, 52, 53). A plain surface may be rendered more attractive by embroidering it with one of the

stitches described below, either in white or in colors.

The threads which we recommend for this purpose are DMC pearl cotton, DMC floss flax or flourishing thread, and DMC embroidery rayon.

Fig. 50 illustrates the single feather or coral stitch, which is worked vertically. The width of the stitch may be varied at will, but must be kept uniform throughout. Bring the needle up on the left, hold the thread lightly down with the left thumb, make a vertical stitch over three threads on the right hand side, keeping the needle always above the thread, and draw up the loop. Returning to the left, make another stitch under three threads the same distance lower down, and draw up the loop. Continue these stitches alternately on either side, fastening off the last with a back stitch.

Fig. 50.
Ornamental
stitches for underlinen, single
feather or coral
stitch.

Fig. 51.
Ornamental
stitches for underlinen, double
feather or coral
stitch.

Fig. 51 shows the working of double feather stitch, which is done in the same manner, but with two stitches to the left and two to the right.

The stitch in fig. 52 is worked horizontally: begin on the left with a horizontal stitch over four threads, go two threads back to the left—that is, bringing out the needle in the middle of the last stitch—make a slanting stitch to the right over four threads, then, passing the needle under two threads towards the left, the lower horizontal stitch is made; come back to the middle for the second slanting stitch upward and repeat the top horizontal stitch already described.

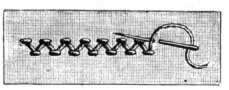

Fig. 52. Ornamental stitches for underlinen, chevron stitch.

The stitch shown in fig. 53 is made in two separate journeys. The first process consists of herringbone stitch (or Russian cross-stitch, see fig. 49), worked over eight threads in height and four in width. The second, which should be worked in thread of a color contrasting with that of the first, consists of horizontal stitches interlaced with the threads of the herringbone, as our illustration shows.

Fig. 53. Herringbone or Russian stitch with interlaced stitches.

Border worked in chain stitch.

CHAPTER II

The Sewing and Embroidering Machine
Machine Sewing and Embroidering

The first attempts to construct a sewing machine were made in the middle of the eighteenth century. In 1755 an Englishman, F. Weisenthal, took out a patent for an apparatus provided with a needle, pointed at both ends and with an eye in the middle, which could be worked backward and forward through material without being turned. From 1755 to 1846 the attempt to produce a sewing machine was carried on by Thomas Saint, J. Duncan, J.-A. Dodge, B. Thimonnier, and Walter Hunt. They patented various devices and each did something to bring the solution of the problem nearer, but without producing any very practical result. It was not until about 1850, with E. Howe and I.M. Singer, that the new machine, after many vicissitudes, became a practical thing and began gradually to come into general use.

Since then numerous alterations and improvements have made it the almost perfect machine which is an indispensable part of the equipment of every household today. We shall content ourselves here with a brief description of the machine and its accessories.

The Sewing Machine. Every sewing machine consists of two essential parts: the upper part, which includes the needle holder and the mechanism which imparts a vertical movement to the needle; and the lower part, which includes the shuttle and its mechanism. The thread, unwinding from the reel, runs through the needle after being subjected to a suitable degree of tension by means of a very important little apparatus called the tension regulator. The needle, on its downward journey, carries the thread through the material and brings it opposite the shuttle, where a slight vertical movement causes it to make a loop through which the shuttle passes with its thread. The needle, rising again, completes the stitch, while a claw moves the work on and regulates the length of the stitch.

The earliest machines worked with only one thread and without a shuttle, producing a chain stitch (fig. 54), the great disadvantage of which is that it comes undone very easily as soon as one stitch is broken. The shuttleless machine is seldom used nowadays, except for certain special types of embroidery, and for temporary seams which it is convenient to be able to unpick quickly. Modern machines work with two threads. They are provided with a shuttle containing a thread which, in conjunction with that of the needle, produces a lock stitch (fig. 55).

There are two kinds of shuttle: the long shuttle and the circular or central shuttle. The former contains a small, long bobbin round which the thread is wound; a horizontal movement to and fro drives the shuttle and thread through the loop made beneath the material by the needle, and a stitch is made each time the needle passes through. The long shuttle is still much used, but preference is usually given to the circular one, which contains a round bobbin large enough to hold a considerable quantity of thread; it is fixed on an axle, on which it turns, and as this is its only movement a much more regular tension of the lower thread is possible.

Accessories. As the sewing machine became more and more perfect, efforts were made to extend its usefulness, and several very ingenious accessories were successively invented for the purpose of facilitating certain preparatory work, such as laying hems, tacking on binding, and so forth. These appliances are fixed onto the machine in place of the shoe; with a little practice very good results can be obtained with them. The most generally used are:

The *hemmer,* which mechanically folds the material. There are hemmers of fixed width for wide or narrow hems, and adjustable hemmers with which hems of any width can be obtained by means of a regulator.

The *binder,* with which the edge of a material can be bound with braid or binding. The braid is folded and placed in the apparatus, then the material is laid in the fold of the braid so that it touches the bottom of the fold. The stitching is then done, great care being taken that the material does not slip out of the fold.

The *braider,* used for laying down braid flat along a design traced on the material. The braid is threaded into the apparatus and sewn to the lines of the design, the material being turned with the curves of the pattern so that the part to be braided is always in front of the worker.

The *gatherer,* by means of which material can, without any preliminary work, be gathered or sewn to a band or bias strip. The material to be gathered is placed under the gatherer, the band is slipped into the horizontal slot of the apparatus, and then the stitching is done.

Motive power. Sewing machines can be worked by hand, with a treadle, or by means of some extraneous power, without necessitating any alteration in their essential structure. The most convenient power is afforded by an electric motor, which can be used wherever electric lighting is available. The electric motor has the additional advantage of taking up very little space; the sewing machine can still be placed on a table or in some corner and can be moved when required without much effort. The mechanism to be operated is extremely simple: the machine is started by moving a lever, with which its speed can also be regulated, and the worker thus has both hands free for the work itself.

Machine Sewing. Machine sewing has become an absolute necessity of everyday life. Although hand sewing also is indispensable for certain kinds of work, the sewing machine is used for making clothes, all kinds of underwear, and common articles of fine or coarse material, leather, and so forth. It is very important for mending, patching, and darning, even for mending knitted articles or woven stockings.

While not wishing to embark here upon a complete course of instruction in the use of the sewing machine, we think a few practical hints may be of use to our readers, since the machine or the materials used are often blamed for bad results which are in reality due to ignorance of these details, to lack of experience, or to forgetfulness of certain principles.

Stitches. As we have already said, two different kinds of stitch can be produced by the machine: chain stitch (fig. 54) and lock stitch (fig. 55).

Chain stitch (fig. 54). This stitch is little used for sewing because it comes undone too easily; it is used for certain kinds of embroidery and

Fig. 54. Chain stitch.

decorative seams. On the right side of the material, chain stitch looks the same as lock stitch, while the true chain stitch appears on the wrong side. Therefore, when embroidery or a decorative seam is to be worked in this stitch, the pattern must be traced and the stitching done on the wrong side of the material so that the chain stitch may appear on the right side. The great elasticity of chain stitch is an advantage in the sewing of very elastic materials.

Lock stitch (fig. 55). This stitch, worked with two threads, is reversible, that is to say, it appears the same on both sides of the material. It is used

Fig. 55. Lock stitch.

in making clothing and underwear, and also for embroidery. With some machines, lock stitch must be worked with two threads of different thicknesses, of which the finer is used in the shuttle; with others, both threads may be of the same thickness.

Care of the Machine. A well-made machine, if properly cared for, should work easily and noiselessly; a machine which runs heavily and is noisy is tiring to use and wears out quickly. It is therefore important to keep it in good condition. To that end all parts of the machinery that are subject to friction must be regularly oiled; oiling holes are provided for this purpose. It is important to use only special sewing machine oil of the best quality. When not in use, the machine should always be protected from dust.

When the work is in progress, there is frequently a tendency, varying according to the kind of material used, for fluff to be produced. This fluff gradually penetrates into the mechanism of the machine and impairs its working. It also happens that during a long period of idleness the oil thickens. In either case, a thorough cleaning is necessary. First apply a little turpentine through the oil holes, then work the machine for a moment; then clean the driving gear with turpentine or paraffin, wipe, and lubricate afresh with the special oil.

Needles. Before beginning any piece of work, always make sure that the needle is sharp and free from any particle of rust. Spare needles should always be kept slightly greased to prevent them from rusting. The size of the needle should also be carefully chosen to suit the material and thread to be used.

Materials. Cotton threads wound on reels are usually used for machine sewing. These threads are usually either *6 cord sewing machine cotton* or *3 cord twist:* the former consists of six single threads twisted together two by two, then united and twisted the reverse way; the latter consists of three single threads twisted together in one direction. The six cord machine cotton is greatly superior to the three cord twist, on account of its greater regularity and strength; it is moreover preferred for all sewing which requires strong and regular stitches.

According to their outward appearance, threads can further be divided into *unglazed* and *glazed.* The former are more often used, being more supple and more readily adapted to every kind of sewing; glazed threads are stiffer, and are used for materials containing a great deal of dressing.

We particularly recommend for machine sewing DMC best 6 cord sewing machine cotton. For colored threads, use DMC Alsa, a very brilliant cotton thread which is dyed in fast colors and can often, thanks to its strength and silky appearance, take the place of sewing silk. The same may be said of DMC Alsatian cordonnet, a very supple two-ply twist, intended for sewing fine materials.

For machines requiring two threads, always use the same quality of thread for both, in a finer number for the shuttle if necessary.

Tension (figs. 56 and 57). It is most important that the tension of the thread should be correctly adjusted, as only in this way can good seams be obtained and the thread kept from breaking. The tension is regulated by means of a special screw placed on the

Fig. 56.
Tension of upper thread too tight.

side of the machine. In a lock stitch seam, the two threads should meet exactly in the middle of the thickness of the two layers of material, as in fig.

55; the seam then presents a good appearance and is both elastic and strong. If the upper thread is too tight (fig. 56) or too loose (fig. 57), the seam will be irregular in appearance and weak.

Fig. 57.
Tension of upper thread too loose.

If the tension is correct, breaks in the thread—which are so annoying, and too often attributed to the quality of the thread, whereas they are really due to incorrect tension—will rarely occur.

Embroidery and Darning by Machine. Machines with circular shuttles can be used for embroidery and darning. All that is necessary for this is the substitution of certain accessories. It is not our intention to give a complete treatise on machine embroidery and darning, since the necessary information can be obtained from the firm which supplies the machine. We will content ourselves here with a few instructions which will be supplemented later in other chapters.

How to adjust the machine for embroidery and darning. Remove the shoe and raise the bar which holds it as far as possible, so that it shall not interfere with the view of the work. Unscrew the claw and replace the needle plate with the special embroidery plate.

When all this has been done, the work, while in progress, can be turned in any direction. The stitch—lock stitch—is always the same; the length and direction of the stitches, and the relative tensions of the upper and lower threads, vary according to the kind of embroidery or lace to be worked.

Different kinds of embroidery and lace that can be worked with the machine. Embroidery by machine is being more and more perfected, and its use is spreading from the special and commercial workroom to the home. The uses of this kind of work are manifold, for besides being a pleasant pastime it enables those whose means are slender to gain a livelihood. Almost every kind of embroidery that can be done by hand can also be done with the sewing machine. It can be used for white work, that is to say, satin stitch embroidery and broderie anglaise; for the trimming of underwear, table and bed linen, curtains, blinds, and sash blinds; and for large articles requiring imposing ornamentation. The field of colored embroidery has been enormously extended. According to the thread chosen, embroidery may be done on any kind of material—linen, silk, or cloth. The use of the sewing machine for tapestry work is of comparatively recent origin and requires certain special appliances; it has not yet been perfected.

Filet lace and embroidery on net can be done by machine without any difficulty. They can be done easily and quickly and work so executed is attractive in appearance and very strong. It can be used—apart from small fancy articles—for trimming large household articles: curtains, blinds, bedspreads and cot covers. Designs worked in flat stitch and darning stitch are particularly rich and luxurious in effect. Finally we must mention openwork on linen worked with the machine, from simple drawn-thread strips to designs approaching the richness of needlemade lace. They are used in the same ways as openwork done by hand: to trim underwear, bed and table linen, etc.

With the exception of openwork strips, all these kinds of work must be done in a frame. This special frame is very much like the Swiss embroidery frame (fig. 103). It consists of two wooden hoops, one fitting into the other. They must be thin enough to slip with ease under the needle of the machine when the material has been stretched between them.

Apparatus. We have still to mention the various special and additional appliances recently invented to facilitate the use of the sewing machine for darning- and embroidery, ornamental stitches, and the embroidery of dresses. These are the darning spring; the darning shoe (which is also used for modern embroideries worked in coarse thread); the central shoe; the Kelim regulator, which is used in connection with the padding shoe; etc.

Materials. These should be selected according to the kind of embroidery or lace to be made. For work done in darning stitch or for openwork, use DMC Alsatian twist on reels, DMC Alsatian cordonnet, and DMC Alsa, in white or ecru. For embroidery on white materials, DMC special quality embroidery cotton will be found suitable. For fancy stitches, DMC Alsa, DMC Alsatian twist, and DMC Alsatian cordonnet, in colors.

The above threads should be used for the upper thread in embroideries with a right and wrong side. For the shuttle, DMC best 6 cord sewing machine cotton, no. 150, should be used. For reversible embroideries, both upper and lower threads must obviously be the same.

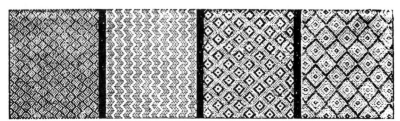

Examples of various twill and damask darns.

CHAPTER III

Mending

The mending of clothing, underwear, and house linen, though wearisome, is nevertheless very necessary, and no woman should be ignorant of the best methods of doing it. There is as much merit in knowing how to repair the damage caused by wear and tear, or by accident, as in the perfect making of new articles.

There are two ways of mending, both in general use—darning and patching. Darning consists of replacing the weakened threads of a material by new threads, variously intersecting to reproduce as faithfully as possible the weave of the damaged material. Patching consists of accurately fitting a piece, if possible of the same material, into a hole made in an article by a tear. When a fine repair has to be done, invisible mending may be required.

Darning. A darn is necessary when a part of the material has worn thin and is transparent, or when in some spots the threads have been destroyed by wear or accident, while the rest of the material is in good condition. When the worn area is extensive, it must be cut out. The actual darning can be done by hand or with the help of the sewing machine. When it is done by machine, we recommend in most cases the use of the darning shoe, which will usually greatly simplify the work.

Needles. There are special needles for darning, with long-shaped eyes to take the flat threads which are used for this kind of work.

Materials. Since the ideal darn is one which should melt imperceptibly into the surrounding material, the threads of the material itself are sometimes used for this purpose. This, however, is only possible when these threads are sufficiently strong and can be detached easily from the material. When the weakness of the threads makes this impossible, or the article to be darned is not worth so much trouble, a thread should be chosen which as nearly as possible matches the material. DMC special quality darning cotton, DMC superfine darning cotton, or DMC stranded darning cotton are used for most kinds of darning. DMC special quality darning cotton is obtainable in white in thirteen different thicknesses numbered from 8 to 100, as well as unbleached and in many colors in no. 25; while DMC superfine darning cotton in white, unbleached, and in colors is available in one thickness only. DMC stranded darning cotton can be had in white in nos. 1 to 10, and unbleached and in various colors in no. 3. Unbleached cotton is preferable for darning coarse articles of household linen which, owing to the uses to which they are put, are never the pure white of fine linen. These threads are composed of several strands, loosely twisted and merely laid together so that, if the exact thickness required is not obtainable, it can easily be produced by the addition or removal of a few strands.

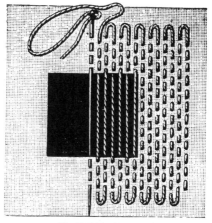

Fig. 58. Linen darning.
Running in the wrap threads.

For fine darns in damask linen or in cambric, where cotton threads would show too much against the linen ground, DMC floss flax or flourishing thread, nos. 25 to 150, will be found an excellent substitute.

The finer numbers of DMC special quality floss embroidery cotton will be found particularly

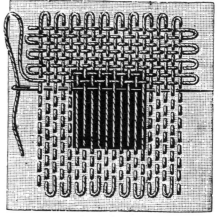

Fig. 59. Linen darning.
Running in the weft threads.

suitable for darning cotton cambric and other fine, transparent materials.

Different kinds of darning. There are four different kinds of darning: (1) linen darning; (2) twill darning; (3) damask or fancy darning; (4) invisible darning (sometimes called fine drawing).

(1) *Linen darning* (figs. 58, 59, 60). All darns should be done on the wrong side of the material. A row of threads forming a warp is first prepared. The thread should never be drawn too tight; on the contrary, a small loop should always be left at the end of each row of stitches so that the

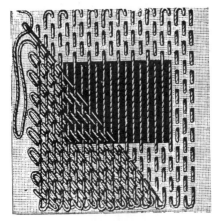

Fig. 60. Diagonal linen darning.

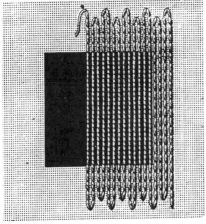

Fig. 61. Darning linen with the sewing machine.
Laying the warp threads.

new thread may not pucker the material when the article is washed.

The first stitches are begun about half an inch from the worn part; a series of little running stitches is made, taking up and leaving two, or at most three, threads of the material, and following the line of a thread. If the worn part has been cut away, the thread is carried across the space and the same number of similar stitches is made on the opposite side, following the same thread of the material. Returning, the needle takes up the threads which have been left in the first row and leaves those which have been taken up.

The weft is worked in the same way, but only one warp thread at a time is taken up or left. The threads of both warp and weft must be as close together as those of the material so that the finished darn shall be, in appearance and in thickness, so like the material itself as to be practically indistinguishable from it. In our illustrations the threads have purposely been placed farther apart in order to make the manner in which they are worked clearer. The weft is sometimes begun across one corner of the part to be mended. This produces a darn in which the straight threads of the warp are crossed by a diagonal weft.

Darning linen with the sewing machine (figs. 61, 62, 63). For household linen, darning by machine is to be preferred, as it not only produces strong and even work but also saves time and eyesight. For this, the work is done in a frame, but without using the darning shoe, and the same threads are used for both needle and shuttle. The actual darning is always done vertically, as in darning by hand; it is only necessary to turn the frame in order to change the direction of the threads and produce their intersection.

Fig. 61 shows, enlarged, the way in which the first threads are laid; fig. 62 shows the work turned and the laying of the second set of vertical threads, intersecting the first, which are now placed horizontally.

A method of simplifying linen darning, which requires the use of the frame and the darning shoe, consists of replacing the warp threads with a layer of DMC special quality darning cotton or DMC floss flax or flourishing thread of suitable thickness, first held in position by a zigzag line of stitching and then crossed with vertical threads as in ordinary linen darning; see fig. 63.

This kind of darning, being very quick to do, is eminently suitable where the surface to be darned is extensive. To fill holes in linen of medium coarseness or in cambric, use DMC Alsatian twist no. 1000, DMC Alsatian cordonnet no. 80, or DMC

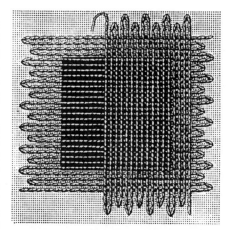

Fig. 62. Darning linen with the sewing machine. Laying the weft threads.

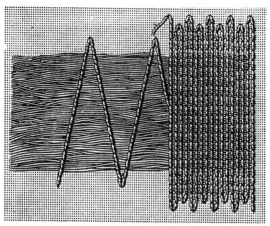

Fig. 63. Darning linen with the sewing machine over a layer of floss thread.

special quality embroidery cotton no. 120, on reels; for quiltings and coarse linen, DMC Alsatian twist no. 60, DMC Alsatian cordonnet no. 80, and DMC special quality embroidery cotton no. 100; for coarse damask and molleton, DMC Alsatian twist no. 50, DMC Alsatian cordonnet no. 60, and DMC special quality embroidery cotton, no. 80.

Twill darning (fig. 64). This kind of darning is used for repairing materials of twill or figured weave. These weaves vary greatly, and it would be impossible to describe them all; but if the directions which accompany fig. 64 are followed, it will be found possible to imitate the weave of any

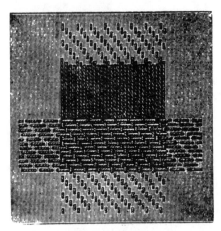

Fig. 64. Twill darning.

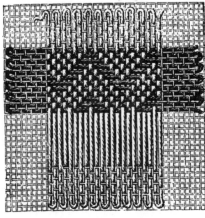

Fig. 65. Damask darning. Wrong side.

material without much difficulty.

After laying the warp, proceed with the weft, missing three threads of the warp and taking up one. Always take up the warp thread next to the one taken up the previous time, the fresh thread taken up being always on the same side of the previous one. Or one thread may be left and two taken up, advancing by one or two threads with each successive weft thread, as the weave of the material may require.

(3) *Damask darning* (figs. 65, 66, 67, 68, 69, 70). Begin by laying the warp as for the preceding darns. The design is produced by the variations in the number of warp threads taken up and left in the laying of the weft. Figs. 65 and 66 show respectively the wrong and right sides of a partly worked damask darn. Fig. 67 shows the finished darn. When the material is woven in several colors, a light shade is usually used for the warp and a colored thread for the weft, which follows the design of the material itself.

Figs. 68 and 69 show two specimens of darning as it was once done in convents. Both warp and weft are first laid with fairly fine thread, and the design is reproduced on this foundation with coarse or colored thread.

The darn shown in fig. 70 is worked in white and a contrasting color. A careful examination of this illustration will enable the reader to imitate checked materials.

(4) *Invisible darning* (fig. 71). This kind of darning is used for mending tears, the edges of which can be drawn together. The broken threads should not be cut away: they form the warp of the darn.

The two edges are tacked, wrong side out, onto a piece of waxed linen and joined with rows of small running stitches worked backward and forward across them.

Invisible darning by machine (fig. 72). For the execution of this kind of darning with the machine, the darning shoe is used, but the work is not mounted in a frame. For thin materials, the part to be darned is tacked onto a sheet of tracing paper, then the two edges are joined by means of very close rows of stitching worked backward and forward across the tear.

As materials, we recommend for colored work DMC Alsa no. 60; DMC Alsatian twist no. 50, on reels; or DMC Alsatian cordonnet no. 80.

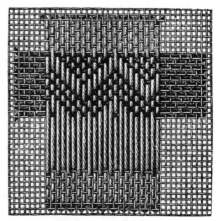

Fig. 66. Damask darning. Right side.

Invisible darning in cloth (fine drawing) (fig. 73). In spite of its undeniable usefulness and importance, the art of darning cloth invisibly is

Fig. 67.
Damask darning.

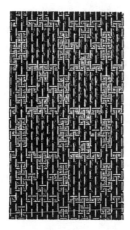

Fig. 68.
Damask darning on a
needlemade foundation.

Fig. 69. Damask darning:
another design worked on
a needlemade foundation.

known to only a few people. This kind of mending is very fine and requires great patience and care, but it is a very easy process to understand.

A very fine needle is used, threaded with hair, which is stronger than the threads drawn from the cloth itself and less visible than silk or any other

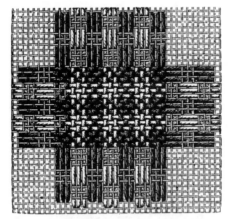

Fig. 70. Damask darning in colored threads.

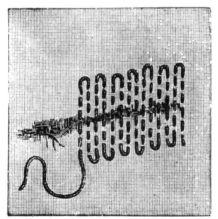

Fig. 71. Invisible darning.

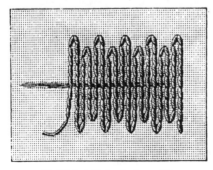

Fig. 72. Invisible darning by machine.

thread. Red or white hair is stronger than other colors. It is scarcely necessary to mention that the hair must be carefully cleaned before use, to free it from all trace of grease.

The cloth is first cut, on the right side, in an absolutely straight line, with a razor. Scissors would remove too much of the nap, which should cover and conceal the finished darn. When the edges have been thus prepared, the pieces to be joined are placed edge to edge and held in position by fairly widely spaced overcast stitches. Then a hair is threaded by the root into the needle, which enters the material about an eighth of an inch from the edge. The needle must not go right through the material and come out on the other side, but passes through the thickness of the cloth itself, emerging again on the same side of the material at about an eighth of an inch beyond the opposite edge of the join. The hair is thus embedded in the thickness of the material.

To make the next stitch, the needle re-enters the material exactly where it was drawn out, and the stitch is made slightly oblique, so that it shall not follow the same course as the preceding stitch, which would in that case be undone. Do not draw the hair too tight: it should be allowed some play.

When the join is finished, it is ironed on the wrong side, under a damp cloth, on a bare board of hard wood. A join made in this way is quite invisible.

Patching. As already described, any part of an article which is too badly worn to be mended by means of a darn must be cut away and replaced by a new piece. If the patch is to be applied to an article of underwear, the material used for the patch should be slightly thinner than that of the garment itself, for the latter will certainly have become thinner and weaker with wear. The new material should be washed before being used. The patch should be cut in exactly the same shape as the hole to be filled, and about an inch larger in every direction to allow for turnings.

The edges of the hole to be filled must be cut straight by the thread of the material, as in every kind of patching. The new piece can be applied by means of a flat seam or overcasting. The patching can be done by hand or with the machine; in the latter case, the ordinary sewing shoe will naturally be used.

Hemming down a patch (fig. 74). The patch is tacked to the article so that its edges lie a little beyond those of the hole. The patch is back stitched onto the article itself, which makes the turning of the corners much easier. Then the edges of the hole are

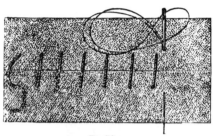

Fig. 73.
Invisible darning in cloth (fine drawing).

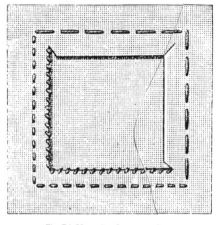

Fig. 74. Hemming down a patch.

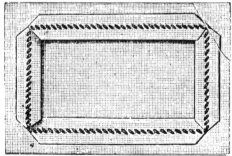

Fig. 75. Overcasting a patch.

turned down and hemmed to the patch. Care must be taken not to pucker the material at the corners; this is avoided by cutting away a snip of the material from the fold of the hem at the corners. The back stitching must be carried far enough beyond the corner for the last stitch of the finished side and the first stitch of the next to form a right angle.

Overcasting a patch (fig. 75).   When a patch is applied by means of overcasting, the edges of both patch and hole are turned in; they are then placed together and joined. To prevent the raw edges from fraying, buttonhole stitch (fig. 77) or herringbone stitch (fig. 49) can be worked all round them, or both the patch and the hole can be hemmed round beforethey are joined.

Drawing in a patch (fig. 76).   Take a piece of the material of which the damaged article is made, about two to two and a half inches larger than the

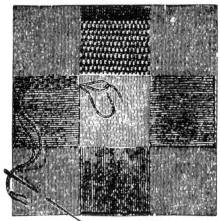

Fig. 76. Drawing in a patch.

hole to be filled. Remove threads from all four sides of this piece, until there remains in the center a piece consisting of the same number of threads as the part which is to be replaced. Tack this to the article, keeping it straight by the threads of the material.

Take a very fine needle, thread both ends of a needleful of silk into it, run it into the material at the corner of the part to be darned, exactly in line with the first of the free threads of the patch. Make a few running stitches outward, bring the needle out and draw half the length of the silk through. Into the loop formed by the silk pass the first of the loose threads of the patch, then draw the rest of the silk through the stitches, bringing with it the thread caught in the loop. Repeat the same process with each loose thread, until all the threads, on all four sides of the patch, have been drawn through.

Strip worked in broderie anglaise, satin stitch, and French knots.

CHAPTER IV

Embroidery on White Materials

The kind of embroidery we are about to describe was once known simply as white embroidery. Nowadays, however, this term has ceased to be strictly accurate, since this type of work is done in colored threads as often as in white. We have therefore given this chapter the more correct title of "Embroidery on White Materials."

This kind of embroidery is used not only for trimming lingerie and toilet articles, but also for bed and table linen and for household articles such as cushions, counterpanes, curtains, blinds, and so forth. According to the method of working, it can be divided into several classes. We shall begin with the simplest, which is raised embroidery in buttonhole and satin stitch. From that we shall proceed to Swiss embroidery, with its openwork fillings; then to Madeira, Renaissance, and Richelieu work, with their very much cutaway designs; then to Venetian embroidery, an imitation of Venetian lace, which may be considered the most artistic variety of embroidery on white. At the end of the chapter we shall introduce to our readers a Danish type of embroidery, known as Hedebo, the Wallachian embroideries of Moravia, and pique embroidery, much used in the eighteenth century for trimming underlinen and dresses.

All kinds of embroidery on white can be worked with the sewing machine. We particularly recommend the use of the machine, which is so much quicker, for large objects embroidered in satin stitch and broderie anglaise.

Preparatory Work. The material to be embroidered is usually mounted either on American cloth or in a frame. Only very skilled workers can undertake to do embroidery without mounting, as one who is not accustomed to this kind of work is very liable to pucker the material by drawing the stitches too tight.

If, however, the worker wishes to do without either of these aids, the part of the material which is to be worked should be placed, quite flat, on the first finger, care being taken to follow the line of the threads of the material, otherwise the finished design will be distorted. The other three fingers hold the material in position, while the thumb rests on the work itself, outside the outline of the design, which faces the worker. It is always the outer line of the design, when this is drawn with double lines, that should lie toward the palm of the hand.

Tracing of Designs. Designs can generally be bought already traced. However, since it is often necessary to repeat, enlarge, or reduce them, it is essential to be able to do such work, for which we therefore give all the necessary instructions in the last chapter.

Materials. The different types of embroidery on white require various materials, and we cannot do better than to recommend the articles bearing the DMC trademark. Raised embroidery should be worked in DMC embroidery cotton and DMC special quality embroidery cotton; in some cases DMC special quality floss embroidery cotton may be used. This is a more loosely twisted thread which, while covering the fabric rapidly, gives a perfectly even surface.

For embroidering underlinen and children's clothes, which often require the use of colored threads, use special quality DMC embroidery cotton, which is produced in a great variety of shades. We also recommend this cotton, in white, for work in which, in addition to the raised embroidery, ornamental stitches are used, as in the case of monograms, initials, etc. For kitchen towels and similar articles, which are usually marked in a simple stitch, we advise the use of DMC floss flax or flourishing thread, or DMC special quality marking cotton.

Swiss embroidery is worked in a specially fine thread, the raised parts with the fine grades of DMC special quality floss embroidery cotton, and the lace stitches with DMC 6 cord cotton lace thread, DMC Alsatian sewing cotton, or DMC flax lace thread.

The padding of the raised parts is done in special quality DMC darning cotton in the same shade as the embroidery.

Embroideries which consist of cut figures, outlined in buttonhole stitch or connected by buttonhole bars—such as Renaissance, Richelieu, and Venetian embroidery—require the use of several kinds of thread. The buttonhole outlining is done in DMC special quality embroidery cotton, while the connecting bars and the ornamental stitches, if there are any, are worked in DMC Alsatian sewing cotton and DMC 6 cord cotton lace thread.

For Madeira work, there is a special thread, DMC special quality embroidery cotton, Madeira shade. This thread is dyed a faint blue-green and gives the effect of original Madeira work.

Hedebo embroidery must be worked in linen thread; we recommend DMC floss flax or flourishing thread for the raised parts and DMC flax lace thread for the openwork parts.

Piqué embroidery can be worked just as well in cotton as in linen thread. For the filling stitches we recommend the use of a loose thread such as

DMC special quality darning cotton, DMC special stranded cotton, or DMC floss flax or flourishing thread; for the outlines, on the other hand, a well-twisted thread, such as DMC 6 cord crochet cotton or DMC flax lace thread is used.

Outlining and Padding of Designs. If the embroidery is to be a success, it is essential that the design should be accurately outlined. A careless appearance in the finished work is often due solely to the fact that the outlines have not been carefully followed with a line of small stitches. For this part of the work, a slightly coarser thread should be chosen than that which is to be used for the embroidery itself. It is fastened to the material by means of a few running stitches, never by a knot, and all the outlining is done in the same stitch.

The space between the two outlines is filled in with running stitches worked backward and forward as often as is necessary to ensure that the work will stand out in the required relief, and so arranged that it will be well rounded off toward the edges. This preparatory work is clearly shown in figs. 93 to 97.

If a fresh needleful of thread is required while the buttonhole stitch is being worked, the needle is brought through between the last two stitches, and the buttonholing, or any other kind of stitch, is continued over the two ends of thread.

Raised Satin Stitch Embroidery. This is the name given to embroidery in which well-padded designs are covered with straight or slanting transverse stitches, which are called flat or satin stitch. This kind of embroidery is used chiefly for flowers, leaves, initials, and monograms.

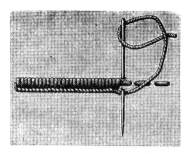

Fig. 77.
Buttonhole or blanket stitch.

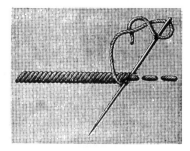

Fig. 78.
Slanting overcast stitch.

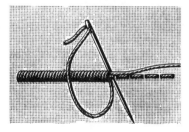

Fig. 79.
Straight overcast stitch.

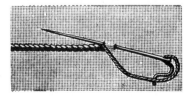

Fig. 80. Stem stitch.

Fig. 81. Back stitch or seed stitch.

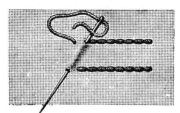

Fig. 82. Double or crossed back stitch.
Right side.

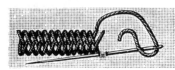

Fig. 83. Double or crossed back stitch.
Wrong side.

Fig. 84. Dot stitch or simple knot stitch.

Fig. 85.
Knotted knot stitch or close daisy stitch.

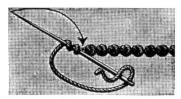

Fig. 86.
French knots or twisted knot stitch.

Buttonhole or Blanket Stitch (fig. 77). Buttonhole stitch is worked from left to right. The thread is passed under the thumb of the left hand, outside the traced outline. The needle enters the material above the outlining stitches and emerges below them. The stitch is drawn tight, without, however, puckering the material. The succeeding stitches, made in the same way, must be very regular and as close as possible to each other.

Slanting Overcast Stitch (fig. 78). This is also worked from left to right, over a single line of outline stitches. The needle enters above the outline, and emerges below it. When a very fine and delicate line is to be made, the needle must take up only those threads of the material which lie under the outline thread.

Straight Overcast Stitch (fig. 79). This stitch is also worked from left to right over a single line of outline stitches. To give it greater relief, a round, well-twisted thread may be laid along the outline and covered with straight stitches set side by side. This kind of overcasting is used chiefly for embroidering letters and monograms.

Stem Stitch (fig. 80). Stem stitch is worked without a foundation of running stitch. The needle is passed under one or two horizontal threads and four or six vertical ones, in such a way that the last stitch always extends half its length beyond the preceding one. The outlines of monograms, initials, numbers, and designs for tablecloths, napkins, etc., stamped on linen, are usually worked in this stitch.

Back Stitch or Seed Stitch (fig. 81). This stitch, worked from right to left, can also be used as a filling stitch in embroidery on fine materials, particularly on cambric. Worked as shown in the illustration, it is known as back stitching; when the stitches are separated from each other it is called seed stitch.

Double or Crossed Back Stitch (figs. 82 and 83). This stitch must be worked on very transparent material, so that the crossing of the threads at the back shows through to the right side.

The needle is inserted as for ordinary back stitching, and passed, at a slight slant, under the material to the second outline of the design. It emerges slightly ahead of the first stitch. After making a back stitch on the second outline, the needle is again passed under the material to emerge on the first outline, far enough in front of the first stitch to make the next back stitch. The crossing of the threads and another way of making this stitch are shown in fig. 83; the wrong side of this stitch can also in many cases be used for the right side.

We shall treat this double back stitch again in the chapters, ''Openwork on Linen'' and ''Embroidered Laces.''

Dot Stitch or Simple Knot Stitch (fig. 84). This stitch consists simply of two back stitches, side by side, in which the needle takes up the same threads twice.

Knotted Knot Stitch or Close Daisy Stitch (fig. 85). This consists of a chain stitch and a back stitch, and produces a similar effect to French knots. The thread having been fastened into the material, the needle is reinserted at the same spot

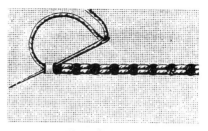

Fig. 87. Belgian stitch.

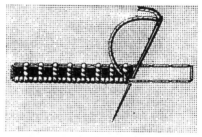

Fig. 88. Ladder insertion stitch.
First stage of the working.

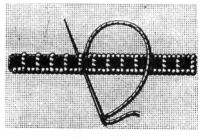

Fig. 89. Ladder insertion stitch.
Completion of the openwork.

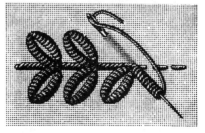

Fig. 90. Bullion or post stitch.

and brought out again a little further on, so that the little loop of thread is under the point of the needle. The loop is then secured by means of a small back stitch, and the stitch is complete.

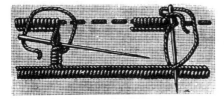

Fig. 91. Buttonholed bars.

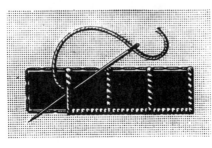

Fig. 92. Overcast bars.

French Knots or Twisted Knot Stitch (fig. 86). When the thread has been fastened on, the needle is placed close to the spot where the thread emerges from the material. The thread, held firmly by the thumb of the left hand, is twisted twice round the needle; then the point of the needle is turned round from left to right, as indicated by the arrow, and reinserted at the spot marked by the black dot.

Belgian Stitch (fig. 87). This stitch can be worked in straight or curved lines. It consists of a row of openwork formed by back stitches drawn very tight over a certain number of threads of the material.

Ladder Insertion Stitch (figs. 88 and 89). This stitch, like the last, can be worked in straight or curved lines. Prepare the outline by means of two parallel rows of running stitch; then work from left to right. The holes of the ladder are pierced with

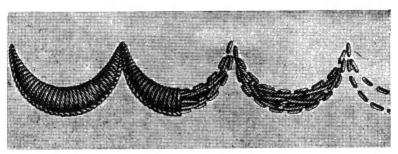

Fig. 93. Large round scallops.

the help of a special little knife. Pierce the first hole and overcast the lower edge with two vertical stitches; then pierce the second hole, thus making the first little bar of the ladder. Pass the thread upward, insert the needle into the upper edge, and work back over this thread with overcast stitches.

Make two overcast stitches in the lower edge of the shole, pierce the third hole, and continue in this way to the end of the row. Then finish the upper edge with two overcast stitches in each hole.

Bullion or Post Stitch (fig. 90). This stitch, much used in the working of small flowers and leaves, for which it often replaces satin stitch, has a certain resemblance to French knots. The illustration shows five completed leaves and a sixth in the process of working.

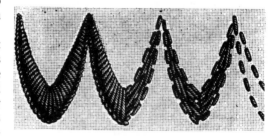

Fig. 94. Large pointed scallops.

Fig. 95. Small pointed scallops.

The needle is inserted at the point of the leaf and passed under the material toward the stalk, where half its length is brought out. The thumb of the left hand is placed on the eye of the needle and, with the right hand, the thread is wound round the point of the needle as often as it necessary to cover the space from the point of the leaf to the stem. The left thumb is then placed on these spirals and the needle, with the rest of the thread, is drawn through them. The

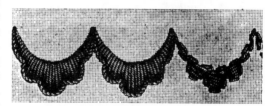

Fig. 96. Round-toothed rose scallops.

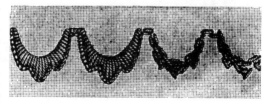

Fig. 97. Rose scallops with pointed teeth.

needle is then reinserted at the point of the leaf and brought out at the spot indicated for the next leaf.

Buttonholed Bars (fig. 91). When the design is to be ornamented with buttonholed bars, the first step is to outline in running stitch the outer buttonholed edges; then the whole of one edge is buttonholed. For the second side, the buttonholing is worked as far as the spot where a bar is to be made, then the thread is carried across to the first edge and brought up from below

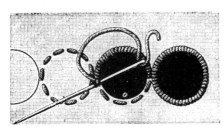

Fig. 98. Overcast eyelet holes.

through one of the loops of the stitches on that edge. The needle is then taken back to the second edge, where it passes through the last loop, and back again under the next loop of the first edge. In this way the two edges are connected by three threads, and the bar is completed by buttonhole stitches worked over these three threads, without penetrating the fabric, which is cut away from behind the bars when the work is finished. Buttonholed bars are used in Renaissance, Richelieu, and Venetian embroidery.

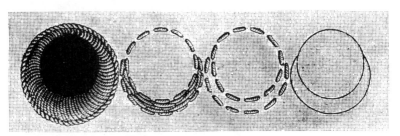

Fig. 99. Shaded eyelet holes worked in buttonhole stitch.

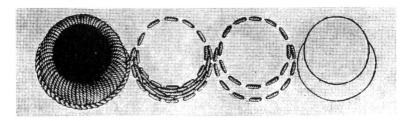

Fig. 100. Shaded eyelet holes worked in buttonhole stitch and overcasting.

Overcast Bars (fig. 92). This type of bar is used in the kind of embroidery known as broderie anglaise. It is worked like ladder insertion stitch, except that the whole of the openwork part is cut away, and the edges of the material are turned in on the wrong side. The bars are formed by laying three threads across the open space and covering them with overcast stitches, working back to the starting point.

Different Kinds of Scallops (figs. 93, 94, 95). These scallops are outlined and padded in the manner described at the beginning of this

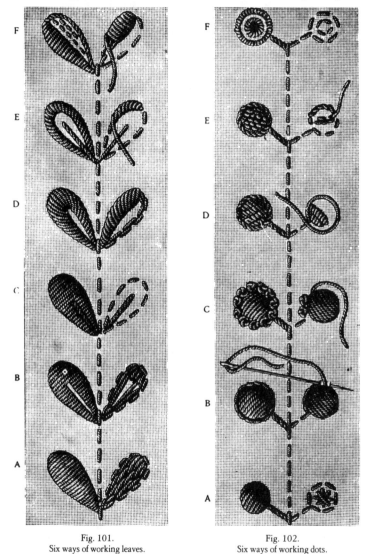

Fig. 101.
Six ways of working leaves.

Fig. 102.
Six ways of working dots.

chapter. The buttonholing is also done as already described, except that the length of the stitches varies with the shape and width of the scallops.

For pointed scallops it is necessary to set the stitches more closely on the

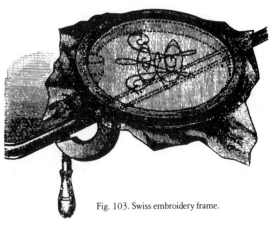

Fig. 103. Swiss embroidery frame.

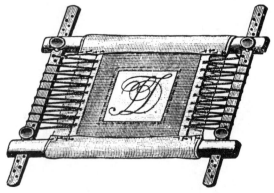

Fig. 104. Ordinary embroidery or tapesty frame.

inner edge and space them out a little at the outer edge, so they will be straight at the point, which must be very accurately shaped.

Rose scallops (figs. 96 and 97). These are large scallops made up of several smaller round or pointed scallops. Fig. 96 shows a series of

Fig. 105. Letter X.

Fig. 106. Letter B.

Fig. 107. Letter C.

round-toothed rose scallops; fig. 97 a series of rose scallops with pointed teeth, joined to each other at the top by a straight bar.

Eyelet Holes (figs. 98, 99, 100). First outline the eyelet hole with small running stitches, then cut out the fabric inside this outline with very pointed scissors and overcast the raw edge with very close stitches. When a whole row of eyelets is to be set close together, begin by outlining only half of each circle. Alternate between the upper and lower half, passing from one to the next at the point of contact of the eyelets. When the end of the row is reached, turn back and outline the other half of each in the same way. The overcasting is done in the same way as the outlining. In this way, there will be four threads crossing between the eyelets, which makes the latter much stronger than if each were worked separately and the thread merely passed under the material from one to the next.

Fig. 108. Letter P.

For shaded eyelets, the stitches are graduated in length, being very short at the top and longer at the bottom. This type of eyelet is often worked entirely in buttonhole stitch, or the lower half way be buttonholed while the upper half is overcast, as in fig. 100.

Six Ways of Working Leaves (fig. 101). After the design has been outlined, the inside is filled up with as many padding stitches as it will contain. Then the embroidery of the leaf is begun at the top (leaf A), the whole leaf being covered with flat stitches set very

Fig. 109. Vignette containing the monogram HB and a coronet.

close together and worked from right to left. Leaf B is divided down the middle and worked in straight satin stitch. Leaf C, divided like the preceding one, has a vein of overcast stitch. Leaf D is worked in wide slanting satin stitch. Leaf E is in very narrow slanting satin stitch, with a vein of overcast stitch, and leaf F is half in straight satin stitch and half in seed stitch, with an overcast edge. According to the type of design to be worked—whether naturalistic, conventional, or fantastic—one or another of these methods will be found appropriate.

Fig. 110. Letter O.

Six Ways of Working Dots (fig. 102). Well-made dots are particularly effective in embroidery, especially if the stitches are varied. Dot A is worked in plain satin stitch over a padding of stitches crossed in the center.

Dot B is also worked in satin stitch, framed in back stitch. Dot C is surrounded with French knots. Dot D consists of several bullion stitches surrounded by stem stitch. Dot E consists of seed stitch surrounded by overcast stitch, and dot F of a small eyelet hole with an outer ring of overcast stitch.

Fig. 111. Letter A.

Embroidery Frames (figs. 103 and 104). For initials, monograms, coronets, and all designs requiring fine, delicate lines, the use of a frame is almost indispensable if the work is to be perfect.

The type of frame most generally used is the round Swiss or tambour frame. It consists of two wooden hoops, one of which is attached to a support, by which it can be clamped with a wooden screw to a table edge. The second hoop is free. The material to be embroidered is placed on the frame with the design in the center of the hoop, then the free hoop is pressed down over the material so that the latter is held firmly between the two hoops. The Swiss frame is suitable only for small pieces of work; large objects require the use of the ordinary tapestry frame.

Fig. 112. Letter D.

A piece of very strong material, such as drill, is sewn to the frame and stretched very tightly and evenly; then a square opening is cut in the middle, large enough to show the whole of the design to be worked. The work is then placed beneath this opening, straight by the threads of the material, fastened with pins and then tacked into position with very close stitches. The rest of the material is then folded and pinned to the surface of the frame to prevent it from getting in the way.

Letters and Monograms. Raised Embroidery. Raised satin stitch embroidery, as we have already said, is much used for letters and monograms for marking linen. According to personal taste and the time that can be devoted to such work,

Fig. 113. Letter E.

the methods of embroidering monograms allow infinite variety.

For this work, we particularly recommend the use of DMC special quality embroidery cotton and DMC special quality floss embroidery cotton.

Letter X (fig. 105). This simple letter is worked in satin stitch over very thick padding.

Letter B (fig. 106). Though not much larger than the preceding letter, this lends itself to a much richer effect, which can be obtained by using, for instance, running stitch with satin stitch for the wide parts.

Letter C (fig. 107). Letters of this size allow the use of several different stitches, which divide the strokes of the letter into light and shadow. In the illustration, satin stitch, seed stitch, and overcast stitch can be seen.

Letter P (fig. 108). This letter, Italian in character, lends itself to the use of two colors, the lighter for the main lines worked in satin stitch, the darker for the ornamentation worked in straight overcast stitch.

Fig. 114. Monogram FV.

Vignette containing the monogram HB and a coronet (fig. 109). This illustration shows how monograms may be enriched by the addition of ornamental scrolls, etc. We have had this design, with its ribbon streamers, worked as a model from which others can easily be copied. The monogram, as can be seen from the illustration, is worked entirely in satin stitch, without ornament.

Letter O (fig. 110). Letters of this kind are more difficult to work than the preceding ones. The plain part is worked as far as the spot where the ornament separates from it. The thread is

Fig. 115. Monogram GU.

Fig. 116. Letter J.

Fig. 117. Letter R.

then carried to the point, and the work, beginning with small stitches, is continued back to the base of the ornament, where the stitches merge into those of the plain part.

Letter A (fig. 111).Here the embroidery is divided to leave small open diamonds, which are filled in with dot stitch. Unless the letter is entirely in white, two colors may be used with advantage.

Fig. 118. Letter K.

Fig. 119. Letter J.

Letter D (fig. 112). The outlines of this letter are worked in straight overcast stitch. The wide parts are ornamented with alternate triangles of flat stitch and seed stitch.

Fig. 120. Letter N.

Fig. 121. Letter M.

Letter E (fig. 113). This letter, a plain Roman capital, is placed against a background richly ornamented in a bright color. The letter itself is worked in satin stitch, in a light color; the ornamentation is in straight overcast stitch, in a deep color.

Monogram FV (fig. 114). In the days of Holbein, artists and tapestry weavers signed their work with initials, rarely with their names in full. We reproduce here a monogram composed of the letters F and V, taken from a document of that time. To suit the stiff character of the letters, the work is carried out in straight satin stitch with shadows in straight overcast stitch.

Monogram GU (fig. 115). Although of the same origin as that shown in fig. 114, this monogram is worked in a richer style. The letter U is in divided satin stitch, while the letter G shows outlines in stem stitch and filling in back stitch.

Letter J (fig. 116). This letter is worked in the Swiss style with open-work filling in the thick strokes of the letter. After working all the outlines in very close overcast stitch, cut away the material from the inside of the letter and fill up the spaces with a little insertion stitch (see fig. 938). Particular care should be taken to make the dots quite round and to give a graceful curve to the tendrils which ornament the letter.

Letter R (fig. 117). The filling which forms the body of this letter is composed of fine openwork. When the openwork is finished, the outlines are worked in straight overcast stitch. Then the material is cut away from behind the open work.

Letter K (fig. 118). This letter may also be classed among manuscript initials. In the illustration, the fabric of the background has been left bare. A fancy stitch, or double back stitch, could be substituted for the double frame of overcast stitch.

Letter J (fig. 119). Here both letter and ornament are worked in overcast stitch, the stitching of the letter and of the frame being bolder than that of the ornamentation. If the letter is worked on a white material, ecru or grey might be used for the seed stitch filling, with the rest in white.

Fig. 122. Letter J.

Fig. 123. Letter R.

Letter N (fig. 120). Our illustration shows how, by means of auxiliary stitches and finely executed designs, the simplest letters can be enhanced and enriched. The starred effect of the background of the letter N is produced by little eyelet holes where the design would seem to suggest satin stitch. Although the work requires more care and patience when executed with eyelet holes, we strongly recommend this method of treatment rather than plain satin stitch, as the solid letter will stand out in much stronger relief on the openwork ground.

Fig. 124. Letter O.

Letter M (fig. 121). This letter, with its ornamentation in the style of Holbein, would be just as effective in white on a dark ground as in the colors chosen for the model, which are a very soft pink for the letter; a dark red for the flowerets, bar, and frame; and a light blue for the filling.

Letter J (fig. 122). Initials of this size are usually found only in ecclesiastical books, missals, etc. Considering the richness of the design, the work may be very simple. Our illustration shows the initial worked in satin, overcast, and stem stitches.

Letter R (fig. 123). The outlines of this letter are worked in straight overcast stitch, and the body is filled with diagonal lines in the same stitch. The letter is surrounded by a double frame; the ground is covered with little satin stitch stars.

Letter O (fig. 124). In this letter, the dark outlines are embroidered in straight overcast stitch, the ornaments in satin stitch, and the filling of the letter in encroaching satin stitch, in white (see figs. 301 and 303), which stands out well against the ground of seed stitch.

Alphabet for Monograms (fig. 125 and 126). It is often difficult to find monograms for marking linen. To solve this difficulty, we give here an alphabet of simple letters which will make it possible to compose monograms containing any desired initials. The alphabet is of medium size; the letters can be reduced or enlarged at will. We again advise our readers to be guided, for such modifications, by the instructions which will be found in the last chapter.

We add several examples of monograms made with the letters of this alphabet and carried out in different ways.

Monogram composed of the letters P and M (fig. 127). Both letters are worked entirely in raised satin stitch.

Monogram composed of the letters L and B (fig. 128). The letter L is in raised satin stitch, and the letter B has corded outlines with a filling of satin stitch dots.

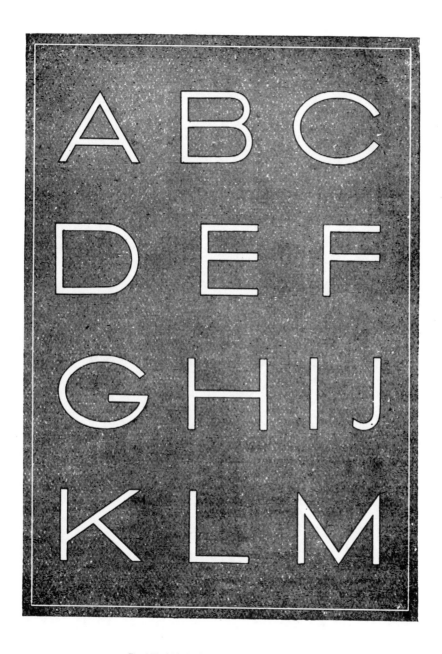

Fig. 125. Alphabet for monograms. Letters A to M.

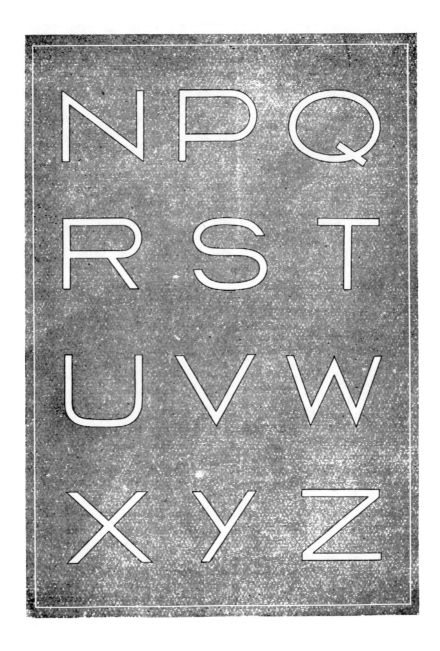

Fig. 126. Alphabet for monograms. Letters N to Z.

Monogram composed of the letters K and H (fig. 129). The letter H is worked in raised satin stitch, while the K consists of corded outlines with a filling of alternated back stitches.

Monogram composed of the letters D and N (fig. 130). Both letters are worked in wide corded outlines, separated by a line of back stitches in color.

Fig. 127.
Monogram composed of the letters P and M.

Fig. 128.
Monogram composed of the letters L and B.

Fig. 129.
Monogram composed of the letters K and H.

Fig. 130.
Monogram composed of the letters D and N.

Alphabets for Monograms (figs. 131, 132, 133, 134, 135, 136). These plates present two series of letters, the first purposely rather short, wide, and heavy in appearance, to frame the tall narrow letters of the second series. The interlacing of the letters requires some care. A study of the examples which follow the alphabets will show how this should be done and will also give some idea of the most appropriate stitches for this kind of work.

Monogram composed of letters A and D (fig. 137). In this case the letter A is embroidered in light blue, shadowed in red; the letter D is worked

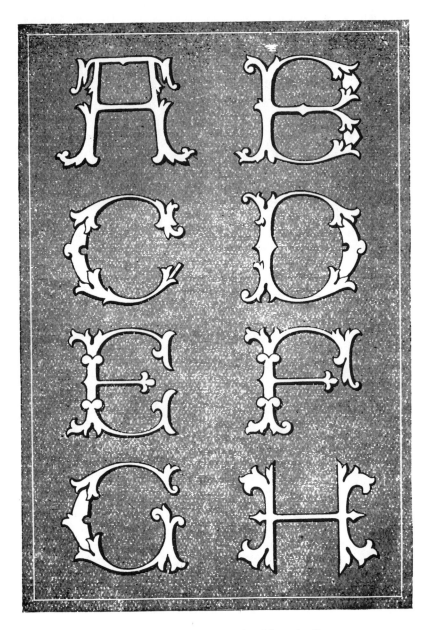

Fig. 131. Alphabets for monograms. Outside letters A to H

Fig. 132. Alphabets for monograms. Outside letters J to Q.

Fig. 133. Alphabets for monograms. Outside letters R to Y.

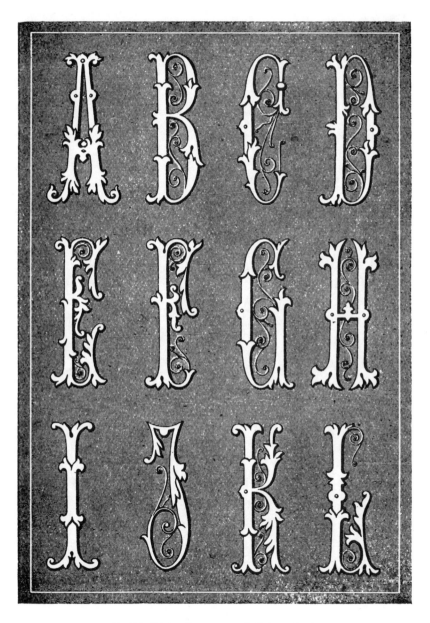

Fig. 134. Alphabets for monograms. Inside letters A to L.

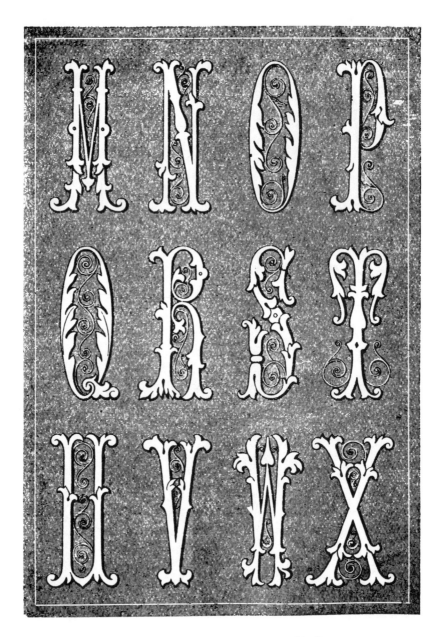

Fig. 135. Alphabets for monograms. Inside letters M to X.

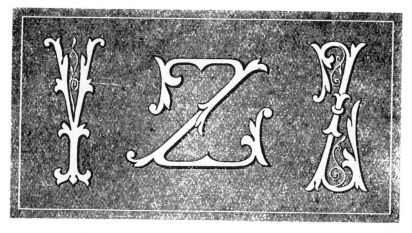

Fig. 136. Alphabets for monograms. Last inside letters and last outside letter.

in transverse stripes, the left half in light blue and white, the right half in light and dark blue. For the ornaments, either of the last two shades can be used equally well.

Fig. 137.
Monogram composed of letters A and D,
taken from the
alphabets for monograms.

Fig. 138.
Monogram composed of letters V and S,
taken from the
alphabets for monograms.

Monogram composed of the letters V and S (fig. 138). To show how mourning colors can be used, where full or half mourning prohibits the use of plain white handkerchiefs, the letters in this monogram have both been worked in grey and framed in black.

Monogram composed of the letters R and C (fig. 139). Here, the two letters are distinguished by the difference in the way or working. The letter R, embroidered in satin stitch, is outlined in slanting overcast stitch,

Fig. 139.
Monogram composed of letters R and C,
taken from the
alphabets for monograms.

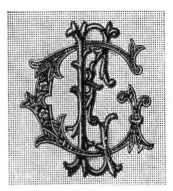

Fig. 140.
Monogram composed of letters G and E,
taken from the
alphabets for monograms.

Fig. 141. Nobleman's coronet.

Fig. 142. Baron's coronet.

whereas the C is devoid of outline and its widest part, between two very narrow bands of overcasting, is embroidered in slanting stripes of satin stitch and seed stitch.

Monogram composed of the letters G and E (fig. 140). The letter E has been worked in satin stitch in white; for the fancy stitches of the letter G, a fine grade of embroidery cotton has been used, in ecru, which makes the G stand out in contrast to the E.

Crowns and Coronets. To follow the initials and monograms, we give a few examples of crowns and coronets to go with them. These show the various ways of embroidering coronets, from the simplest to the most elaborate, making use of the stitches already described.

The details of these coronets must be worked with the utmost accuracy, particularly those parts which represent precious stones and pearls. Colors should be used for the coronet only when the monogram itself is embroidered in color.

Nobleman's coronet (fig. 141). This is worked in white. The balls should be thickly padded so that they stand out from the material in high relief like beads. The band which supports the balls is filled in with seed stitch.

Baron's coronet (fig. 142). This is worked entirely in satin stitch, in two boldly contrasted colors.

Earl's coronet (fig. 143). This is worked in one color, in satin stitch and straight overcast. The space between the circlet and the balls is filled with an openwork stitch.

Fig. 143. Earl's coronet.

Royal crown (fig. 144). The design of the royal crown is classic and is common to all countries. It can be worked all in white or in several colors, according to the article it is to adorn. The ground on which the ermine tails rest may be covered with dot stitch, seed stitch, or encroaching satin stitch (see figs. 81, 86, and 301).

Letters and Monograms in Fancy Embroidery. Simple, quickly done letters can be worked in chain stitch, stem stitch, or cross stitch, according to individual taste. This method of marking in the simplest stitches is par-

Fig. 144. Royal crown.

ticularly suitable for household articles for which elaborate work is out of place, especially for sheets and cloths of all kinds.

Letter J (fig. 145). When time is limited or no frame is available for working the initial,

Fig. 145. Letter J.

Fig. 146. Letter G.

it can be done in ordinary chain stitch (see fig. 256). The finer the cotton, the smaller and more regular the stitches, the better will be the effect of this very simple way of

Fig. 147.
Monogram GW.

Fig. 148.
Letter A.

marking linen, particularly if colored cotton is used.

Letter G (fig. 146). Here is an example that shows how large letters can be worked in lace stitches. The letter having been outlined with a double line of stem stitch, the inner space is filled with small darned wheels (see figs. 711 and 712), worked in DMC Alsatian sewing cotton or DMC cotton lace thread.

Monogram GW (fig. 147). All the letters of this type are extremely simple in composition and working, yet when reproduced in embroidery they are remarkably effective. We recommend simple chain stitch (fig. 256) or chain stitch with overcasting (fig. 257), for monograms of this kind.

Fig. 149. Letter A.

Fig. 150. Letter M.

Letter A (fig. 148). This letter belongs to the old Gothic type; it is worked in two colors. The lighter color is used for the stem stitch and double back stitch

Fig. 151. Letter A.

which fill the body of the letter, while the darker is used for the back stitches which are worked into the intersections of the double back stitch.

Letter A (fig. 149). This script letter is worked entirely in double back stitch (fig. 83), in colored thread.

Letter M (fig. 150). Our illustration shows an example of the modern Gothic type, worked in double back stitch and stem stitch.

Letter A (fig. 151). The outlines of this letter are worked in flat stitch in a medium shade, the filling is in encroaching satin stitch in white, while the interlaced ornamentation is worked in chain stitch in a dark shade.

Fig. 152. Narrow insertion in satin stitch with openwork strip.

Narrow Insertion in Satin Stitch with Openwork Strip (figs. 152 and 153). The leaves are worked first in raised satin stitch, then the stalks in slanting overcast stitch. The two lines which edge the openwork are in straight overcast stitch (see fig. 79).

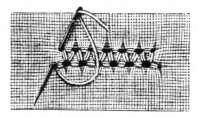

Fig. 153. How to do the openwork.

When all the rest of the embroidery is finished, the openwork is begun. There is no need to draw any thread for this: the openwork is produced by the tightening of the stitches. As can be seen in fig. 153, the openwork requires a width of six threads of the material. It is begun on the right, at the bottom, with two back stitches from left to right over six threads of the material; then follow two stitches over six horizontal and three vertical threads, sloping toward the right; then two horizontal stitches at the top; two sloping to the right downward to the first line, again over six horizontal and three vertical threads, that is to say, to the point of departure of the last sloping stitches. Continue in this manner, drawing the stitches very tight; in this way the openwork is produced.

Border in Satin Stitch and Seed Stitch with Openwork Wheels (fig. 154). In spite of the delicacy of the design, this border, intended for

Fig. 154. Border in satin stitch and seed stitch with openwork stitch.

handkerchiefs, is not difficult to work. The small six-petalled flowers which surround the openwork wheel are worked in straight satin stitch; those with five petals, in the sprays, in slanting stitches with veins. The leaves are outlined in straight overcast stitch and filled with seed stitch, the latter also being used as a filling in the large flower. For the working of the wheels, which are also framed in straight overcast, we refer our readers to the chapter, "Needlemade Laces."

The illustration further shows little clusters of overcast eyelets.

Fig. 155. Flower design in raised satin stitch with openwork centers.

As materials for this embroidery we recommend DMC special quality embroidery cotton; and for the wheels, DMC Alsatian sewing cotton or DMC cotton lace thread in white.

Flower Design in Raised Satin Stitch with Openwork Centers (fig. 155). This kind of embroidery, in satin stitch and openwork, is known as Swiss embroidery.

Before the satin stitch is begun, the openwork centers are worked; instructions for these will be found in the chapter, "Openwork on Linen," figs. 821 and 823. These done, the eyelet holes are worked in overcast stitch. Only then is the padding for the satin stitch parts of the design begun.

As materials we recommend: for the openwork, DMC Alsatian sewing cotton or DMC cotton lace thread; for the padding, DMC special quality

Fig. 156. Border in Madeira work.

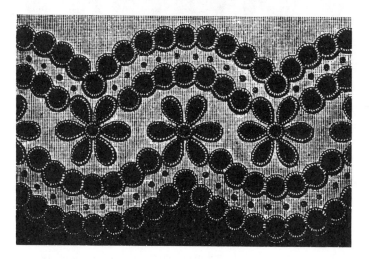

Fig. 157. Border in Madeira work.

floss embroidery cotton no. 35; and no. 70 of the same thread for the satin stitch.

Two Borders in Madeira Work (figs. 156 and 157). Embroidery consisting entirely of eyelet holes used to be called broderie anglaise; nowadays

nowadays it is usually known as Madeira work. The work executed in the island which gives its name to the style is, like broderie anglaise, done in simple overcast stitch, and is distinguished by the regularity of the stitches and the extreme care bestowed on the work. The edges of the material are so well caught by the stitches that, even after long use, the embroidery never becomes frayed.

Fig. 158. Square in broderie anglaise.

The design in fig. 156 is edged with small shaded eyelets; that in fig. 157 with plain eyelets, buttonholed on the outside edge. These two designs will be found particularly suitable for trimming pillowcases and lingerie.

Square in Broderie Anglaise (fig. 158). Openwork or "cutwork" embroidery in white in which the overcast outlines are joined by bars, also overcast, is known as broderie anglaise. For practical reasons, simple designs should not be too large.

At the time of the Renaissance this kind of embroidery on white was used to ornament plain linen surfaces in conjunction with motifs in needlemade lace or filet lace. Our square, fig. 158, is embroidered in satin stitch on a foundation of cambric, with openwork parts in broderie anglaise. It is intended to be used in combination with Reticella or Richelieu squares.

The satin stitch is worked first, then the openwork, according to the instructions accompanying fig. 92. For the outlining and the embroidery, DMC special quality embroidery cotton no. 60, in white, should be used.

Border in Renaissance Embroidery (fig. 159). This term is applied to cut embroidery worked entirely in buttonhole stitch, connected by buttonholed bars without picots. The buttonholing is worked over a single outline thread and is of the same width throughout, except at the outside edge, where it may be made a little wider.

Fig. 159. Border in Renaissance embroidery.

Fig. 160. Border in Richelieu embroidery.

Border in Richelieu Embroidery (fig. 160).   This kind of embroidery is similar to Renaissance work, except that the connecting bars are ornamented with picots. Both these types of embroidery are used principally for trimming bed and table linen, for which purpose they make an excellent substitute for pillow lace.

Border in Wallachian Embroidery (fig. 161).   The border shown in fig. 161 is a fine example of the work of the Wallachian peasants of Moravia. It is a scalloped edging used on the much-gathered linen of the peasant women's dresses, especially on collars and cuffs. The particular

peasant women's dresses, especially on collars and cuffs. The particular method used for this embroidery produces a most delicate effect. The fabric

Fig. 161. Border in Wallachian embroidery.

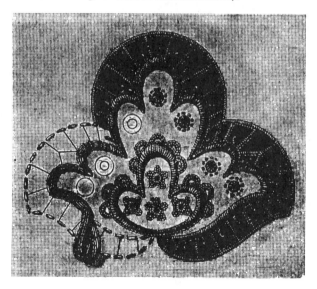

Fig. 162. Motif in Venetian embroidery.

is cut away from the openwork part and from the outside of the scallops only when the embroidery is completely finished. The design should be traced onto coarse cambric or fine, loosely woven linen. It is then outlined, and the connecting bars made, following the design, with a single thread of DMC special quality crochet cotton no. 15; these threads are left bare. The more solid parts are worked partly in overcast stitch and partly in buttonholing. Finally, the leaves are filled with seed stitch. The embroidery is worked in DMC special quality embroidery cotton no. 25, in white.

Motif in Venetian Embroidery (fig. 162). This work, in which thickly padded buttonholing is used, is a reproduction upon material of Venetian lace, a distinguishing feature of which is the high relief of its outlines. In the embroidery, the material takes the place of the needlemade openwork of the lace; occasionally the foundation is left bare. To increase the resemblance to the original, the interior of the design is covered with fancy filling stitches such as those shown in our illustration. The buttonholed bars can be made with or without picots. These latter are fully described in the chapter, ''Needlemade Laces'' (see figs. 918 to 923).

It is essential that the parts to be covered with buttonholing should be padded as thickly as possible. For this purpose, six or eight threads of DMC special quality darning cotton no. 25, should be taken and held in place with overcast stitches set a little

Fig. 163. Insertion in Venetian embroidery.

distance apart, so that they form a round cord laid along the lines of the design. Where the outlines become wider, and the number of threads no longer suffices for the padding, additional threads are added, one by one; and in the same way the number is reduced where the outline becomes narrower. The fabric beneath the bars should not be cut away until the embroidery is completed.

Insertion in Venetian Embroidery (fig. 163). In fig. 163 we show our readers an insertion in Venetian embroidery intended for the trimming of tablecloths, pillowcases, sheets, etc. The foundation for this should be

Fig. 164. Border in Danish Hedebo embroidery.

fine linen in which the threads can be counted. The padding of the raised parts is done with DMC special quality darning cotton, while the buttonhol-

Fig. 165. Border in piqué embroidery.

ing is worked in DMC special quality embroidery cotton. The bars and fill-ings require a twisted cotton, such as DMC Alsatian sewing cotton or DMC cotton lace thread.

The various stitches are explained in the chapter, ''Embroidered Laces.''

Border in Danish Hedebo Embroidery (fig. 164). Danish peasant women ornament their linen with rich openwork embroidery in white. This work, called Hedebo embroidery, is little known outside its country of origin since it is intended solely for the worker's own personal use and seldom appears on the market. Our illustration, fig. 164, shows the border of a towel. This design could, however, be used equally well for small tablecloths, runners, etc.

The little openwork squares are made first; they are done on counted threads and divide the whole of the border into diamonds and triangles. Then the design of the embroidered figures is traced onto the material. Here again the openwork fillings are worked first; a large selection of these will be found in the chapter, ''Embroidered Laces,'' figs. 851 to 866. Last of all, the satin stitch parts are padded and embroidered. A little openwork strip frames the border on all four sides.

Border in Piqué Embroidery (fig. 165).   This is the name given to a variety of embroidery on white, worked on a very strong, firm fabric, in which braid or overcasting is used for the outlines, while the fillings consist of various stitches imitating figured materials. It is generally used nowadays for trimming bed and table covers of all sorts, children's garments, etc.

In the border shown in the illustration, all the various parts of the design are filled with damask stitches, which are explained in the chapter, "Embroidered Laces," figs. 843 to 850. The braid with which the motifs are outlined is made of crochet chain.

The foundation used for our specimen is plain twill. The damask stitches are worked in DMC special stranded cotton no. 25, in ecru. The crochet braid is made with DMC 6 cord crochet cotton nos. 1 and 3; it has been sewn down with DMC Alsatian sewing cotton no. 100, these last two threads also in ecru.

Border in two-sided cross stitch.

CHAPTER V

Linen Embroidery

This kind of embroidery has been known for centuries as a domestic industry among the rural populations of many lands. The country of origin is easily recognized by the character of the design and the colors in which it is worked. Italian, Greek, and Spanish work of the sixteenth and seventeenth centuries is usually embroidered in a single color, purple red; those of Eastern origin, on the other hand, present a great variety of shades mingled with gold and silver threads. The embroideries of the Slavonic, Hungarian, and Swedish peasants are also distinguished by the richness of their colors, in which red, blue, and yellow predominate.

At the present day, linen embroidery adapted to modern tastes is in great favor among those who are interested in needlework, thanks to the great variety of stitches and designs, and the comparative ease with which they are worked. Linen embroidery may be divided into two classes: the first includes all kinds of embroidery in which the work is done on counted threads from an embroidered model or a design worked out on squared paper; the second, those in which the design is first traced onto the material and then worked freely, without thought for the threads of the material. The embroidery never covers the whole surface of the material, parts of which remain bare and form the background of the design.

Embroidery on linen can be worked with the sewing machine just as well as embroidery on white materials. For some kinds, the thread guide is used.

Fabrics. Most old embroideries, especially those of Italian origin, are worked on very fine linen. Such minute work requires more time and perseverance than most people nowadays are willing to give to fancywork. To meet modern requirements, materials are now manufactured with round, well-spaced threads, so that stitches can be counted and designs reproduced with greater ease.

Linen fabrics are manufactured in white, in cream, and unbleached. Cotton and linen fabrics can also be obtained in colors, which are often preferred to white or cream for work in stem stitch and satin stitch, for articles such as cushion covers, tablecloths, panels, blinds, etc.

Preparatory Work. Small pieces of linen embroidery, worked in short, simple stitches, can be carried out without being mounted in a frame. On the other hand, when the work is to contain complicated stitches, filling stitches covering large spaces, or stitches consisting of stretched threads and overcasting (overcast bars, etc.), the use of a frame is necessary (see fig. 104). The work will always be more accurate if a frame is used, and the material will not become puckered or crushed.

The method of mounting the work in the frame is as follows: a tape or a band of material is attached along two opposite sides of the work by means of back stitching; then on the other two edges a quarter-inch fold is made; the folded edges are then stitched with overcast stitch to the two bands of the frame, taking care to stretch the material taut. The frame is then set up by slipping the two stretchers, provided with holes, into the slots at the ends of the bars; the material is stretched very tight, and the stretchers fixed by means of wooden or metal pegs. The material is then stretched in the other direction. To do this, a piece of twine or fine string is threaded into a large needle and the work is fastened to the stretchers by stitches which pass through the tape or band sewn to the edge and over the stretcher.

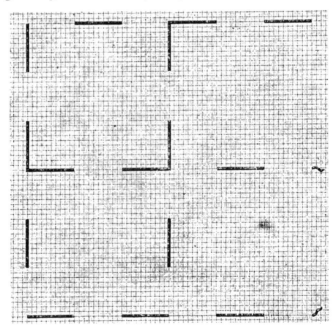

Fig. 166. Making the framework for the stitches.

Embroidery on Counted Threads. Making the Framework for the Stitches (fig. 166). Before beginning a piece of embroidery which is to be done on counted threads, a framework is made with colored thread. This is generally done, as shown in fig. 166, by running the thread alternately under and over ten threads, along two sides, in the length and width of the material. Then, the number of stitches having been counted and divided, two more threads are run, one horizontally and the other vertically, each starting from the middle stitch; their point of intersection will show the position of the center stitch. If, in addition, there is a central motif or a design to be reversed in the corners, diagonal lines should be run from the corners to the center. This framework, which will be of great help in working successive repeats of a design, should never be removed until at least half the work is finished.

Materials. As linen embroidery is used chiefly for articles which require frequent laundering, it is advisable to do it with materials which will stand as much washing as possible. For work in cross stitch, square Holbein stitch, and line stitch, to be carried out on hard, stiff material, a moderately twisted thread is usually chosen, such as DMC special quality embroidery cotton or DMC pearl cotton. For work on linen or washed congress canvas, which are soft and supple, in cross stitch, plait stitch, or flat stitch, a floss thread is to be preferred. For this purpose we recommend DMC embroidery twist, DMC floss flax or flourishing thread, and DMC embroidery rayon as well as DMC special stranded cotton and DMC Persian silk, which, being composed of six strands, can be divided or added to at will according to the thickness of the material.

Stitches. Plain cross stitch, as shown in fig. 167, is the most commonly used. It is, however, of less value than reversible stitches, which excite wonder and admiration whenever we see them in those beautiful embroideries which are still to be encountered here and there and are still one of our richest sources of inspiration. Besides cross stitch, with all its variations, line stitch or double running stitch and square ground stitch (also called Holbein stitch) can be worked so that they are reversible. Nowadays cross stitch designs are often worked in flat or satin stitch, which, passing over several threads at a time, covers the ground much more quickly than cross stitch and is therefore much used for fancy embroidery.

As can be seen from the illustrations which follow, a design is seldom worked all in one stitch. It is common to find cross stitch combined with line stitch, gobelin stitch, star stitch, plait stitch,

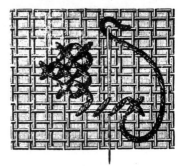

Fig. 167. Plain cross stitch worked over auxiliary canvas.

etc. The beauty of a design is greatly enhanced by the use of various kinds of stitches.

Plain Cross Stitch Worked over Auxiliary Canvas (fig. 167).   Plain cross stitch consists of two slanting stitches, one over the other and crossing

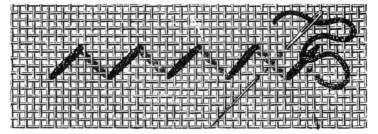

Fig. 168. Two-sided (reversible) cross stitch, worked in four journeys.
First journey completed, and auxiliary stitch for the second journey.

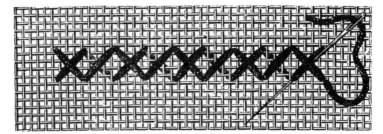

Fig. 169. Two-sided (reversible) cross stitch, worked in four journeys.
First three journeys completed, and auxiliary stitch for the last journey.

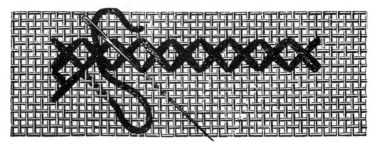

Fig. 170. Two-sided (reversible) cross stitch, worked in four journeys.
First row finished. Beginning of a new row.

in the center. If the material allows the counting of threads, the stitches can be worked directly onto it; if, however, it is too closely woven, it is covered with an auxiliary canvas, over which the design is worked. When the work is finished, the canvas is drawn out, thread by thread. It may be of use to add that when cross stitch is worked thus over an auxiliary canvas, the latter must be tacked into place quite straight, its threads following those of the material beneath, and a sufficient margin left to allow the easy withdrawal of the threads when the work is finished.

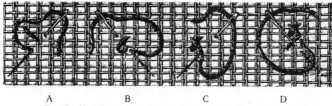

A   B   C   D
Fig. 171. Various positions of the needle for the formation of isolated stitches in two-sided (reversible) cross stitch.

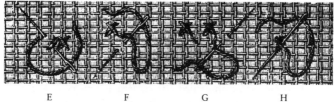

E   F   G   H
Fig. 172. Various positions of the needle for the formation of isolated stitches in two-sided (reversible) cross stitch.

To ensure the neatness of cross stitch, the needle should always enter and leave the material at the same points as on the previous journey.

Two-sided (Reversible) Cross Stitch (figs. 168, 169, 170, 171, 172). This form of cross stitch is worked in straight lines, taking four journeys to each line, that is to say, two journeys in each direction. Starting at the left, the thread is fastened on without a knot by means of a few little stitches which will be hidden by the first half of the first cross stitch. The stitches are worked from left to right and pass alternately upward over four horizontal and four vertical threads, and downward under the same number of threads, till the end of the row is reached.

Fig. 173. Two-sided Italian or arrowhead cross stitch. Fastening on the thread and position of the needle for the first stitch.

When the last stitch is reached, the needle is brought up again at the middle of the stitch, a half stitch is made to the right, and the needle is again brought up in the middle of the stitch, to re-enter the material to the left to complete the half stitch. The second journey is then completed in the same way as the first, but working from right to left. The two half stitches are often covered with a long stitch, as can be seen in figs. 169 and 170. After the last stitch of the second (return) journey, the thread is brought to the right for the beginning of the third journey, which forms the first half of the crosses in the spaces left by the two previous journeys.

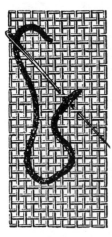

Fig. 174. Two-sided Italian or arrowhead cross stitch. Position of the needle for the second stitch.

In the auxiliary stitch which serves to begin the last journey, the thread will be double on both sides of the material. Fig. 170 shows how a new row is begun. This method of working reversible cross stitch cannot be used for designs in broken lines, which consist chiefly of single stitches.

Figs. 171 and 172 show the working of the stitches in this kind of embroidery. In fig. 171, detail A shows where the thread enters the material and the position of the needle for the first stitch; detail B shows the first half stitch of the cross completed, with an auxiliary stitch to the right, the thread emerging on the right, and the position of the needle for the third stitch, which will complete the cross. Detail C shows the stitch begun in B finished, and the position of the needle to reach a stitch to the right; detail D shows one cross stitch completed and the beginning of another beneath it. In fig. 172, detail E shows how to continue the stitches toward the left; detail F, an auxiliary stitch to reach an isolated cross to the right; detail G, auxiliary stitches between two isolated stitches; and detail H, the second and last auxiliary stitch to complete the cross.

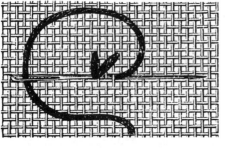

Fig. 175. Two-sided Italian or arrowhead cross stitch. Position of the needle for the third stitch.

This method of working reversible embroidery demands a certain amount of experience and, further, extreme care in the placing of the stitches in order to avoid superfluous stitches which would disfigure the work.

Two-sided Italian or Arrowhead Cross Stitch (figs. 173, 174, 175, 176). This consists of reversible cross stitches separated by horizontal and vertical stitches. The upper and lower stitches of each cross should all slant in the same direction, as in plain cross stitch. Italian cross stitch is worked in two journeys. Fig. 173 shows how the thread is fastened on, and the position of the needle from right to left for the first stitch. Fig. 174 shows the position of the needle from left to right to make the cross on the wrong side and the left-hand vertical stitch on the right side. Fig. 175, shows the position of the needle to make a two-sided horizontal stitch at the bottom of the cross. After this, the work proceeds again as in fig. 173. Fig. 176 shows the return journey, which completes the double crosses and the vertical lines between them, those which were not made in the first journey being filled in. In the next row, the horizontal stitches beneath the crosses will form the top of the row below.

Fig. 176. Two-sided Italian
or arrowhead cross stitch.
Second journey,
completing the cross stitch.

For the last row, the needle is passed from left to right under and over the threads of the foundation, starting from the last cross stitch, before passing under the vertical stitch as shown in fig. 176. This stitch, worked on a loosely woven material, produces a particularly happy effect of transparency, provided the thread is drawn fairly tight in the working.

Montenegrin Cross Stitch (figs. 177, 178, 179). The Slavonic races of the southeastern countries of Europe, and particularly the inhabitants of Montenegro, have a marked preference for the stitch illustrated in fig. 179, which does not appear to have been described until now in any book of needlework.

Here again we have cross stitches separated by vertical stitches, but this

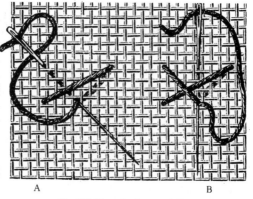

A   B

Fig. 177. Montenegrin cross stitch.
First and second oblique stitches and transverse stitch.
Right side.

time the crosses are made on the right side over two oblique stitches, while on the wrong side they present the appearance of ordinary cross stitches, separated, as on the right side, by vertical stitches. A coarse thread will enhance the beauty of this embroidery; it covers the threads of the material better, as well as the vertical stitch, which in Slavonic embroideries is completely lost between the cross stitches.

The stitch is begun, as can be seen at letter A in fig. 177, by a long stitch passing from left to right over four horizontal and eight vertical threads;

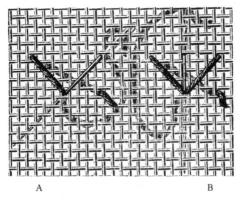

then the needle is brought back from right to left, under four threads and drawn out again to be reinserted from left to right under the first four threads of the canvas, as the illustration clearly shows. After these two stitches, the third, shown at B, is made: it crosses the first two stitches vertically. These three stitches are repeated to the end of the row.

Fig. 178. Montenegrin cross stitch.
First and second oblique stitches and traverse stitch.
Wrong side.

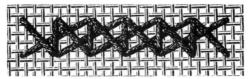

Fig. 179. Montenegrin cross stitch.
Row of stitches completed.

At the back, the threads form cross stitches separated by vertical stitches, and the regular interchanging of the threads makes the so-called wrong side of this stitch particularly charming.

Long-armed Cross Stitch or Plaited Slav Stitch (figs. 180, 181, 182, 183, 184, 185, 186, 187). This stitch is very similar to Montenegrin stitch, but it is easier and requires scarcely any more time

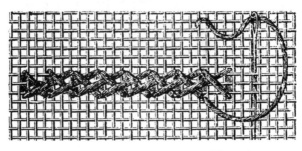

Fig. 180. Long-armed cross stitch or plaited Slav stitch.
Worked in a horizontal line.

and attention than ordinary cross stitch. It is usually worked over three and six threads, as can be seen in fig. 180; but if it is to be rounded, it must be worked from the outset over an even number of threads.

In working a straight row, the first stitch should be carried over eight vertical threads; if, however, it is to be rounded, the thread must, to begin with,

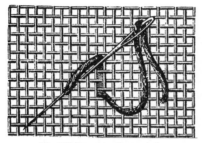

Fig. 181. Long-armed cross stitch or
plaited Slav stitch.
Left-hand frame stitch, half stitch for the
return and position of the needle for the next stitch.

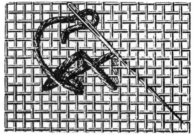

Fig. 182. Long-armed cross stitch or
plaited Slav stitch.
Position of the needle for the half stitch
and the right-hand frame stitch.

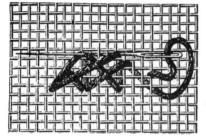

Fig. 183. Long-armed cross stitch or
plaited Slav stitch.
Right-hand frame stitch
and position of the needle for the upper
frame stitch.

Fig. 184. Long-armed cross stitch or
plaited Slav stitch.
Position of the needle for the return to
the lower line, with dotted line marking
the right-hand half stitch.

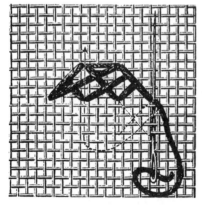

Fig. 185. Long-armed cross stitch or
plaited Slav stitch.
Right-hand frame stitch and beginning of the
second row of stitches.

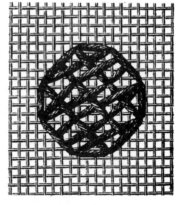

Fig. 186. Long-armed cross stitch or
plaited Slav stitch.
Circle surrounded with frame
stitches.

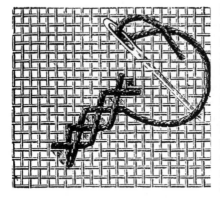

Fig. 187. Long-armed cross stitch or plaited
Slav stitch. Worked in a diagonal line.

Fig. 188. Oblique Slav stitch.
Worked in horizontal rows.

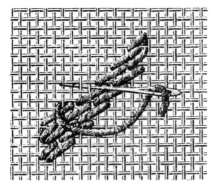

Fig. 189. Oblique Slav stitch.
Worked in diagonal rows.

be carried over only four threads in each direction (see fig. 181), thus making the first framing stitch to the left. This stitch is followed by a half stitch, after which the needle returns to the point at which the first stitch emerged. In fig. 182 the half stitch is completed and hidden by the succeeding stitches; the fifth stitch, which ends at the fifth thread, has been begun and the needle is directed obliquely from left to right under three threads of the material. In fig. 183 the needle is seen returning horizontally to the left under four threads, so that the right-hand framing stitch is completed as the needle passes to the top stitch. In fig. 184 the needle passes straight down under four threads; then, following the direction of the arrow, obliquely over two threads and out again under two. Fig. 185 shows first the position of the needle for the vertical framing stitch, and a dotted line marking one cross stitch and one long stitch to form the plait. Fig. 186 shows a circle completed and framed all round.

Plaited Slav stitch can also be worked in slanting lines and can therefore be used for broken wavy lines or for the stems of flowers and leaves. Fig. 187 shows how to work the stitch diagonally over two threads.

Oblique Slav Stitch (figs. 188 and 189). This stitch, which covers the background well and quickly, is often found on Slavonic embroideries. As its name suggests, it is worked obliquely, over two and four threads. According to the design to be filled, it can be worked in horizontal, vertical, or even diagonal lines.

Fig. 188 shows how to work it in horizontal rows: the stitches are carried over two horizontal and four vertical threads, two threads apart, and so arranged that each stitch overlaps the previous one by two threads.

To work the stitch in vertical rows, the thread is carried over four horizontal and two vertical threads. It sometimes happens, however, that this stitch can be more useful worked in diagonal rows. In this case also, each stitch is carried over two and four threads of the material, but on the wrong side the needle passes under two horizontal threads, as can be seen in fig. 189.

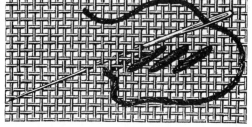

Fig. 190. Two-sided plaited Spanish stitch. First row.

Two-sided Plaited Spanish Stitch (figs. 190 and 191). This stitch has the double advantage of being quick to work and very effective. It can be used for work which, while producing a certain effect, must be done in a comparatively short time. The stitch is worked in two journeys. Any design for cross stitch embroidery can be worked in it, but the spaces left by the long stitches must be filled in with short ones.

Spanish stitch consists of stitches passing over five

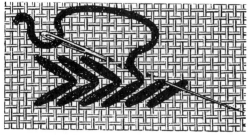

Fig. 191. Two-sided plaited Spanish stitch. Second row.

and three threads, each being set three threads further along. Figs. 190 and 191 show clearly how to work this stitch, which is as easy as it is pleasant to do.

Certain imitations of oriental carpets worked on coarse linen show a similar stitch in which, however, the stitches are set much closer together than in Spanish stitch: see the knitting stitch (fig. 407) in the chapter on "Tapestry."

Two-sided Square Holbein Stitch (figs. 192 and 193). Line (or stroke) stitch, double running stitch, and square stitch are all varieties of the Holbein stitch and are worked according to the same principles. Although all these reversible stitches belong to the same family and are comparatively

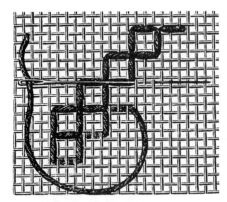

Fig. 192. Two-sided square Holbein stitch.
First row.

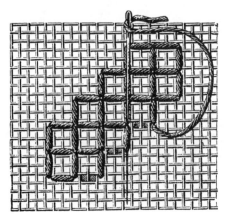

Fig. 193. Two-sided square Holbein stitch.
Second row.

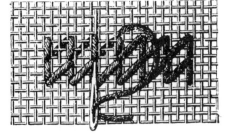

Fig. 194. Bosnian stitch.
Worked in horizontal lines.

easy to work, anyone new to this kind of work will find a little practise necessary before she can be sure of working the stitches in an order that will ensure their continuity.

Fig. 192 shows how the needle passes alternately over and under the threads of the material in zigzag fashion; while fig. 193 shows how, on the return journey, the threads left uncovered on both sides are covered. The great difficulty in Holbein stitch is placing the stitches in the first journey so as to ensure an unbroken line on the second journey, without unnecessary stitches on the wrong side. When the stitch passes diagonally over the material, as is often necessitated by the design, the course to be followed is the same as when it covers the straight threads.

Bosnian Stitch (fig. 194). This filling stitch is composed of straight and oblique stitches, and is worked in two journeys. The straight stitches are made on the first journey, the oblique stitches on the return journey.

Fig. 194 shows the vertical stitches laid over two threads of the material, two threads apart, for the horizontal row, and the working of the oblique stitches which connect them. When the design requires the stitches to be worked in vertical lines, the vertical stitches are naturally replaced by horizontal ones.

Triangular Two-sided or

Turkish Stitch (figs. 195, 196, 197, 198, 199, 200, 201). Among the many pretty stitches which distinguish Turkish embroideries, there is one in particular which appears at first sight to be very difficult but which is, in reality, very easy. Although it resembles stroke stitch worked on straight threads, in oriental embroideries it is usually worked in diagonal lines. Each row requires four journeys, two in each direction.

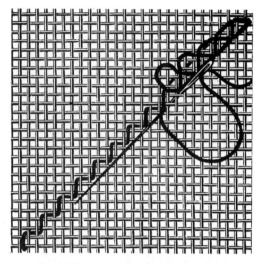

Fig. 195. Triangular two-sided or Turkish stitch.
First and second journeys, forming half a row of stitches.

In the first journey (fig. 195), the needle always passes over and under two horizontal and two vertical threads, in a diagonal line. On the return journey, the needle passes under the material and the stitch that appears on the right side, emerging at the bottom of the stitch; then a back stitch is made, slanting upward over two horizontal and two vertical threads; the needle passes horizontally over two threads to the left, to emerge at the top of the stitch above and re-enter at the top of the stitch

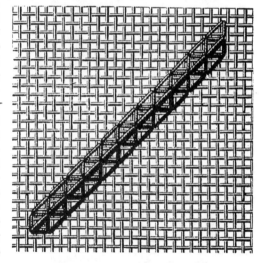

Fig. 196. Trianular two-sided or Turkish stitch.
The row completed in journeys.

below, thus forming a second slanting stitch, after which the thread is carried to the base of the vertical stitch. Four threads always meet at the hole formed by the passage of the needle. The third and fourth rows are done in a color contrasting with that of the first two rows and form, with the latter, a

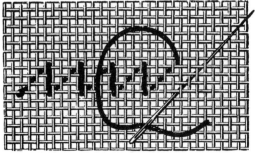

Fig. 197. Triangular two-sided or Turkish stitch,
worked in horizontal lines.
First journey.

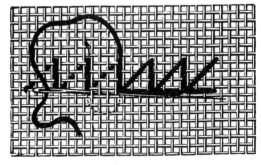

Fig. 198. Triangular two-sided or Turkish stitch,
worked in horizontal lines.
Second (return) journey.

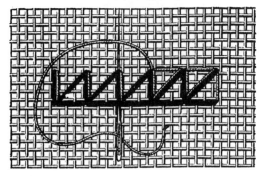

Fig. 199. Triangular two-sided or Turkish stitch,
worked in horizontal lines.
First three journeys completed, fourth journey
in course of execution.

complete row of the Turkish stitch.

Figs. 197 and 199 show the same stitch arranged in straight lines. In fig. 199 the first two rows of the working are shown in a dark thread, and the third and fourth in a light thread.

When this stitch is used as a filling stitch for extensive surfaces, the method of working is different. The parts to be filled are embroidered with a square stitch which, in turn, is covered with oblique stitches.

Fig. 200 shows the working of the square stitch, which differs from that shown in figs. 192 and 193 in that it produces, on the wrong side, oblique stitches. When the surface has been completely covered with this square stitch, the series of oblique stitches (fig. 201) is executed, producing the squared ground on the wrong side.

Oka Eyelet Stitch (fig. 202 and 203). In the peasant embroideries of Roumania and some Slavonic countries, we sometimes meet an interesting stitch called oka stitch, which means "eye" stitch. It is worked in two journeys. First comes a row of ver-

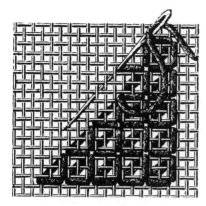

Fig. 200. Triangular two-sided or Turkish
filling stitch.
How to work the squares.

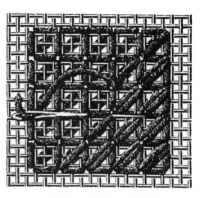

Fig. 201. Triangular two-sided or Turkish
filling stitch.
How to work the slanting stitches.

tical stitches over three threads of the material, set three threads apart and alternately above and below, so as to produce horizontal stitches on the wrong side; see fig. 202. On the second journey, these vertical stitches are interlaced with horizontal stitches so that several rows worked one above the other form a collection of eyelets; see fig. 203.

It is essential that the horizontal stitches on the right side should

Fig. 202. Oka eyelet stitch.
Working of the vertical stitches and of the
interlacing stitches.

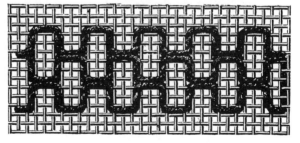

Fig. 203. Oka eyelet stitch.
Three rows of stitches completed.

be set in exactly the same order as those on the wrong side. When rows of some length are to be worked, the first and second journeys will be started from the same point, but for small designs the two journeys will be worked in opposite directions.

One-sided Insertion Stitch (figs. 204, 205, 206, 207, 208). This stitch is begun with a plain cross stitch over three threads in each direction, after which the needle is carried upward, three threads above the first stitch, and passed under the same number of threads (see fig. 204). Returning to

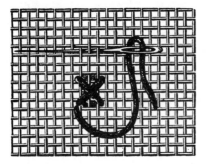

Fig. 204. One-sided insertion stitch.
First cross stitch
and position of the needle for the
upper stitch.

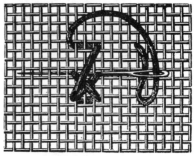

Fig. 205. One-sided insertion stitch.
Position of the needle for the completion
of the upper stitch and
the return for the second cross stitch.

Fig. 206. One-sided insertion stitch.
Second cross stitch
completed and position of the needle
for the lower stitch.

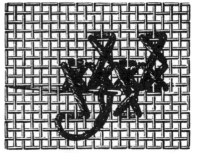

Fig. 207. One-sided insertion stitch.
Series of completed stitches
and position of the needle for the return
to the cross stitch.

the line of the first stitch, the needle is passed under six threads (fig. 205), and a second cross stitch is made, followed by a stitch downward (figs. 206 and 207). This is followed by another cross stitch, after which the series of stitches is begun again at fig. 204. Fig. 208 shows a section of the insertion worked in DMC special stranded cotton.

Two-sided Insertion Stitch with Square Stitch on the Wrong Side (figs. 209, 210, 211, 212, 213, 214, 215). Fig. 214 shows a two-sided insertion stitch, eminently suitable for the completion of embroideries worked in reversible stitches. Fig. 209 explains the first stitch and the passage of the thread from left to right under three vertical and three horizontal threads, together with the second stitch to the

Fig. 208. One-sided insertion stitch.

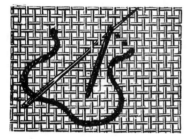

Fig. 209. Two-sided insertion stitch with square stitch on the wrong side. First stitch completed, position of the needle for the second stitch.

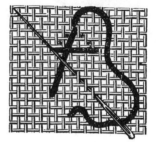

Fig. 210. Two-sided insertion stitch with square stitch on the wrong side. Second stitch completed, position of the needle for the third stitch.

left over six threads, and the position of the needle for the beginning of the third stitch. Figs. 210 and 211 show the second and third stitches finished, the course of the fourth stitch, and the return of the needle for the next; fig. 212, the first lower horizontal stitch worked over six threads and the return stitch under three threads; fig. 213, the eleventh stitch completed and the next step for the twelfth. Fig. 214 show a series of completed stitches on the right side, and fig. 215 the

Fig. 211. Two-sided insertion stitch with square stitch on the wrong side. Third stitch completed, position of the needle for the fourth stitch.

Fig. 212. Two-sided insertion stitch with square stitch on the wrong side. Fourth stitch completed, position of the needle for the fifth stitch.

wrong side of the work, presenting an entirely different design but one which will go with any kind of reversible embroidery.

These insertion stitches can be worked on any kind of material, but the stitches which form them must be worked in both directions over a number of threads divisible by three; thus the first stitch can be made over six, nine, or twelve threads, but never over eight, ten, or fourteen.

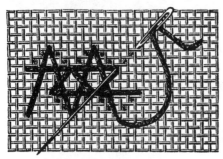

Fig. 213. Two-sided insertion stitch with square stitch on the wrong side.
Series of stitches completed, position of the needle for the twelfth stitch.

Buttonhole Insertion Stitch (fig. 216). Begin by making a buttonhole stitch upward over four threads of the material at a distance of six threads from the point where the needle emerged; draw this stitch fairly tight. Then make a similar stitch downward so that the two stitches meet in the same hole. After completing a group of these stitches, consisting of five upward and five downward stitches, carry the thread over six threads of the

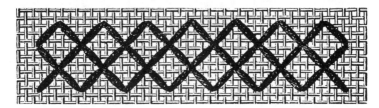

Fig. 214. Two-sided insertion stitch with square stitch on the wrong side. Right side.

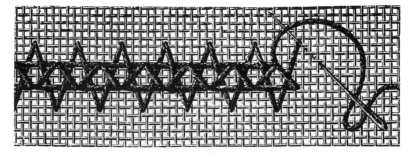

Fig. 215. Two-sided insertion stitch with square stitch on the wrong side. Wrong side.

material and make another group of buttonhole stitches.

Various Hems for Embroidery (figs. 217, 218, 219, 220). Pieces of colored embroidery are finished not only with openwork hems and strips but also with hems ornamented with various kinds of stitches. When the material has a good selvedge, the stitches can even be worked directly over it.

To work the two varieties of stitch shown in figs. 217 and 218 along a raw edge, an ordinary hem is first prepared, rolled on a fine material, flat on

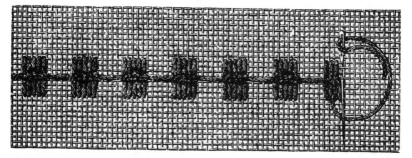

Fig. 216. Buttonhole insertion stitch.

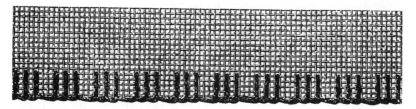

Fig. 217. Selvedge or hem ornamented with single blanket stitch.

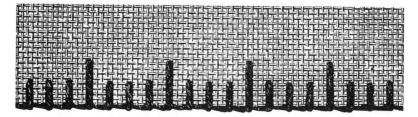

Fig. 218. Selvedge or hem ornamented with double blanket stitch.

a coarser one. This done, three buttonhole stitches are made, with a small space between them (this kind of spaced buttonhole stitch is usually known as a blanket stitch); in the illustration (fig. 217) the spaces consist of two threads. Then a space of double the number of threads is left and another group of three stitches is made. In fig. 218, the ornamentation of the hem is made by working two stitches over the width of the hem—if there is one— both into the same hole, followed by two longer ones, also worked into one hole, and separated from the first two by four threads; this group is followed by three groups of two stitches like the first ones and separated from each other by four-threads.

Another hem, as unusual as it is pretty, is reproduced in figs. 219 and 220. This is begun by rolling about three-eighths of an inch of the material as tightly as the fabric will allow. The thread is brought round from the back to the front, passing over nine threads, and nine stitches are made, one thread apart from each other. Each stitch must be drawn very tight and all must lie straight, side by side. It is advisable to draw out a thread along the hem to ensure an absolutely straight line. The material must be completely covered by the stitches; this can most easily be achieved by the use of a loosely twisted thread such as DMC special stranded cotton, DMC floss flax or flourishing thread, DMC embroidery rayon, or DMC Persian silk.

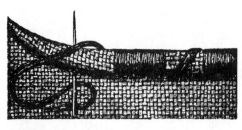

Fig. 219. Rolled and embroidered hem.

Fig. 220. Rolled and embroidered hem.

Cross Stitch Border. Gothic Design (fig. 221). We owe this delightful design, so truly Gothic in character, to a visit to the Munich National Museum, where we found it in a pile of old scraps relegated to the rubbish heap. The simple, graceful lines of the design make it suitable for reproduction on tablecloths, napkins, bedspreads, curtains, and a host of other articles. The embroidery should be finished off with a wide fringe made of the threads of the material itself or with a knotted fringe; see the chapters on ''Macrame'' and ''Needlework Trimmings.'' The design can be reproduced in a single shade, or equally well in two shades of the same color, as in fig. 221, where a darker shade has been used for all the outer stitches.

Cross Stitch Border in Shades of One Color. Chinese Design (fig. 222). This Chinese design, interpreted in cross stitch, comes from the border of a rich mandarin's robe. It is very interesting and sure of a warm welcome from our readers. It forms a charming motif for chair backs of all kinds, and we suggest that it be worked on soft congress canvas, slightly tinted, in three distinct shades of blue. The work can be finished off with narrow pillow lace.

Repeating Design and Border in Cross Stitch and Line Stitch. Roumanian Designs (figs. 223 and 224). These two delightful designs, of Roumanian origin, are remarkable for the particularly happy arrangement of the colors. Bright red stands out against a medium blue and a soft green, with here and there a few isolated stitches in bright yellow and golden yellow. In the repeating design (fig. 223), the flowers of every alternate diagonal row are worked in red, with decorative stitches in green or

Fig. 221. Cross stitch border. Gothic design.

blue; in the other rows, the flowers are alternately green or blue with decorative stitches in red, and in every motif there are four bright yellow stitches in the center. In fig. 224, which serves as an outside border to the work, deep golden yellow is used only for the stems of the fancy carnations, which, with the cross in the center, form a square.

These squares are separated from the lower border by an insertion, three crosses in depth, which can also be worked in vertical flat stitch over a cor-

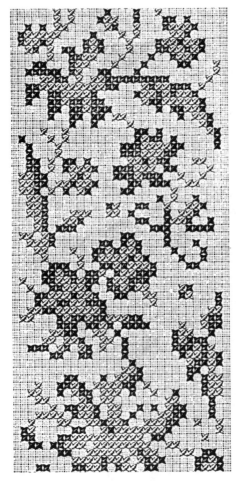

Fig. 222. Cross stitch border.

responding number of threads. The colors used for the body of the work have been alternated in the insertion, which is finished off with a line of double running stitch on each side. A little waving band of line stitch edges the insertion on both sides.

These two designs can be used to trim tablecloths. In this case, the border and insertion, fig. 224, will be worked all round the cloth; the center will be filled with the little repeating design, fig. 223. The work can be simplified, if desired, by separating the border from the inside by a strip of silk or dark velvet and adding another strip of the same material to the outside edge in place of the flowered design of the border.

Cross Stitch Border. Greek Design (fig. 225). For the execution of these simple, solid figures, the long-armed cross stitch illustrated in fig. 180 is the best suited. All those parts which appear darkest in the illustration are worked in black; the leaves, whose edges form steps, are worked, one in light red and one in dark red, as far as the beginning of the stalks, which can readily be recognized by the different types of crosses. There will consequently always be two light and two dark leaves facing each other.

In the original, the crossbars which connect the leaves are worked in brown, while the detached figure which separates them is embroidered in light blue. The outer part of this figure is filled in with brown stitches, except for the double cross stitches, which are worked in golden yellow DMC embroidery rayon. For the S-shaped figures of the little outer border, two shades of blue are used: dark blue for the outside stitches and light blue for the filling. The small bars which connect the S's are alternately edged with black and filled with light red, and then edged with dark red and filled with brown.

We especially recommend this border for trimming articles of dress, in which case the embroidery should be worked on a band of linen or canvas, which will make it much easier to handle.

Corner Designs in Line Stitch or Double Running Stitch (figs. 226 and 227). These two charming motifs with corners can be used to trim all

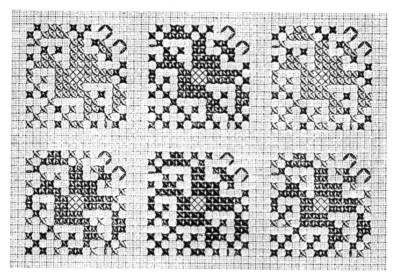

Fig. 223. Repeating design in cross stitch and line stitch. Roumanian design.

sorts of small objects made of linen—such as ladies' and children's collars, tea napkins, and fine linen handkerchiefs—and may be worked in a single color or in two, according to taste. We would repeat here the advice which accompanied figs. 192 and 193: the course of the stitches should be carefully studied so that it may proceed uninterrupted.

If the embroidery is done in two colors, the inner stitches should be done in the lighter one and the little outside borders in the darker.

Border in Line Stitch or Double Running Stitch (fig. 228). This delightful strip is taken from an exceptionally fine piece of Italian work, though, judging from the design, which resembles the rose, the thistle, and the shamrock, one might have supposed it to be of English origin. Everything indicates that the original was worked in the most brilliant purple-red, but this color has faded to such an extent that it now most resembles umber or Morocco red. This faded, yellowish red is so effective on the white linen that we strongly recommend its use in order to give the

Fig. 224. Border in cross stitch and line stitch. Roumanian design.

new work that quality of distinction characteristic of all old embroidery.

When this design is used for a sideboard or dresser cover, it would look well finished off with a wide openwork border, which can be chosen from the chapter, "Openwork on Linen."

Allover Design in Diagonal Lines Worked in Line Stitch or Double Running Stitch (fig. 229). This design can be worked in two-sided line stitch or in simple back stitch. The original, however, is in one-sided line stitch, worked in a very loosely twisted thread. Since the design, worked on coarse material, will be somewhat large, it can only be used for fairly large articles, such as cushions or panels, and in one color. It can, moreover, be varied by the addition of a second line of leaves on the upper side of the diagonal stem. In this case, the leaves should be made to turn upward in-

Fig. 225. Cross stitch border. Greek design.

stead of downward, and be alternated in such a way that a flower will be opposite a leaf and vice versa.

Repeating Design in Cross Stitch, Double Cross Stitch, and Line Stitch (fig. 230). In this design we have a charming combination of double cross stitch, line stitch, and plain cross stitch, which could be used on any article which lends itself to embroidery. For the cross stitch, in which all the solid parts of the design are worked, a single color should be used. Golden yellow should be used for the line stitch and the stars in double cross stitch.

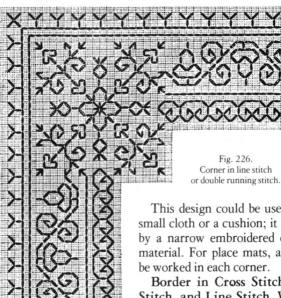

Fig. 226.
Corner in line stitch
or double running stitch.

This design could be used as the ground of a small cloth or a cushion; it should be completed by a narrow embroidered edging or a band of material. For place mats, a single motif should be worked in each corner.

Border in Cross Stitch, Square Holbein Stitch, and Line Stitch. Wallachian Design (fig. 231). A piece of Wallachian embroidery, worked on handwoven linen and unusual both in its forms and coloring, was the inspiration for the delightful design shown here. Softer shades have been substituted for the very vivid colors of the original.

The edging of square Holbein stitch and line stitch is worked in dark red and green. For the cross stitch filling, four colors are used in turn: indigo, garnet red, bright green, and golden yellow.

The design is here interpreted in cross stitch, square Holbein stitch, and line stitch, which are all easy to work and can be undertaken by those who have little experience. Those who wish to make it even more effective are advised to replace the cross stitch by oblique Slav stitch (figs. 188 and 189), changing the direction of the stitch according to the design.

We suggest working this design on a band of colored material—red or dark brown—which can then be used as a trimming on curtains, portieres, tablecloths, panels, valances, etc. The articles themselves will be made of cloth or plush, then the embroidery will be sewn on, and the whole can be further trimmed, if desired, with a fancy fringe.

Design in Assisi Work (fig. 232). This type of embroidery, worked in colors on linen, in which the design is left bare and outlined in a dark color against a cross stitch ground of a light shade, is derived from the ancient

Italian embroideries carefully preserved in the churches of Assisi from the thirteenth and fourteenth centuries. The production of this kind of embroidery has, since the beginning of the present century, become a local home industry of Assisi.

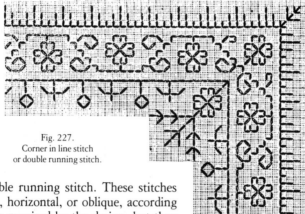

Fig. 227.
Corner in line stitch or double running stitch.

The work should begin with the ornamental outline in double running stitch. These stitches will be vertical, horizontal, or oblique, according to the direction required by the design, but they will always be worked over three threads of the material. The background consists of horizontal rows of cross stitch, worked backward and forward. When the outline stitches are horizontal and vertical only, the filling stitches are always whole cross stitches. However, where there are slanting stitches in the outline, there must obviously be gaps in the background between the cross stitches and the slanting stitches. These triangular gaps, which spoil the appearance of the work, are filled with small slanting stitches, as can be seen, for instance, round the head of the apocryphal beast in fig. 232.

Our model is worked on a ground of white linen with DMC special quality embroidery cotton no. 16, in black for the outlines and indigo for the filling of the background.

This motif, used singly, is suitable for trimming napkins, pincushions, shades, and bags of all kinds. Wide borders for tablecloths, panels, towels, etc., can also be made by repeating it and edging the whole with a border on either side.

Border in Flat Stitch. Italian Design (fig. 233). The beauty of Italian designs worked in flat stitch on fine linen consists in the happy choice of colors. In our model, the wavy line is embroidered in golden yellow and the little flowers which touch it in light yellow. The small crosses and trees are worked in red, green, and blue in turn.

We recommend this design for trimming articles of dress, such as aprons, collars, children's dresses, etc. It should be worked on a strip of linen or soft canvas, which can be edged with crochet picots.

Border in Flat Stitch and Line Stitch. Slovakian Design (fig. 234). The design shown here is copied from a cuff worn by the peasant women of Moravia. The motifs of the strip which edges the design are outlined in single faggot stitch; instructions for working this stitch will be

Fig. 228. Border in line stitch or double running stitch.

found in the chapter, "Openwork on Linen," fig. 775. The flower motifs are in line stitch, filled with horizontal or vertical flat stitch. The embroidery is worked on counted threads on cream linen. As materials, we suggest DMC Persian silk in two shades of green. For this silk one could substitute DMC embroidery rayon, DMC special stranded cotton, or DMC floss flax or flourishing thread.

When this design is used to trim articles of dress, it should be worked directly onto the article, over an auxiliary canvas, and not on a separate strip of material.

Fig. 229. Allover design in diagonal lines, worked in line stitch or double running stitch.

Coverlet in Moroccan Embroidery (figs. 235, 236, 237, 238). This kind of work, whose name reveals its origin, can also, according to the way it is worked, be classed under darned embroidery or damask embroidery.

Clear-cut designs, consisting of the material left bare and standing out sharply against a background of encroaching flat stitch, are characteristic of Moroccan embroidery.

Fig. 230. Repeating design in cross stitch, double cross stitch, and line stitch.

In working the design of the coverlet (fig. 235), the needle always passes over five threads and picks up the sixth. On the return journey, the third of the five stitches previously passed over is picked up, and the whole surface of the work is covered in this way, unless the lines of the design make a deviation from this rule necessary, as for instance, in certain parts of the border (fig. 237) where stitches can be seen occasionally passing over six

Fig. 231. Border in cross stitch, square Holbein stitch, and line stitch. Wallachian design.

threads, and in the border (fig. 238), where the stitches are arranged somewhat arbitrarily in order to make the design stand out clearly. Fig. 236 shows one quarter of one of the motifs of which the complete design in fig. 235 is composed.

Four of these sections must therefore be worked to make one complete motif, and the work, begun in the middle, is continued as far as the point at which one of the little borders (figs. 237 and 238) is to be added; for this the allover design can be interrupted at any point.

Most cotton and linen materials can be used as a foundation for this beautiful work; embroidery threads should be chosen to suit the material. DMC pearl cotton is suitable only for the coarser materials, while DMC em-

Fig. 232. Design in Assisi work.

broidery rayon, DMC special quality embroidery cotton, DMC special stranded cotton, and DMC floss flax or flourishing thread are to be recommended for finer materials.

Repeating Design in Rhodes Embroidery (figs. 239 and 240). Here again the name indicates the origin of the embroidery—the island of Rhodes, where it had a great vogue in the sixteenth and seventeenth centuries. It is worked in the same way as Moroccan embroidery (fig.

Fig. 233. Border in flat stitch, Italian design.

Fig. 234. Border in flat stitch and line stitch. Slovakian design.

235), but the motifs of the design are embroidered and it is the background which is left bare. The original embroideries are almost always worked in a single color, medium red, occasionally relieved by small motifs in light blue or green.

Fig. 239 shows, on a slightly reduced scale, part of a coverlet in Rhodes embroidery, worked on white linen in DMC pearl cotton no. 5, in medium red; this thread can, if desired, be replaced by DMC special stranded cotton no. 25, DMC floss flax or flourishing thread no. 16, or DMC embroidery rayon no. 30.

Fig. 235. Coverlet in Moroccan embroidery.

Fig. 240, which illustrates a detail of the repeating design of fig. 239, shows the frequent changes of direction of the stitches, which produce a peculiarly rich effect of light and shade.

Floral Design in Triangular Turkish Stitch (fig. 241). The triangular Turkish stitch explained in figs. 195 to 201 is applied in this floral motif, copied from an ornamented Turkish towel.

A very fine lawn has been used for the foundation. The embroidery is worked in DMC embroidery rayon no. 60. The large flower is worked in two shades of Morocco red; the stems, the narrow leaves, the center of the flower, and the small branches in bright green; the dark dots in red-brown and tangerine yellow; while the vase is in two shades of sky blue. These same two shades of blue are used for the little flowers surmounted by squares in slanting flat stitch worked in yellow.

Border in Arab Embroidery (figs. 242 and 243). The border in fig. 242 is an example of the rich, many-colored embroideries found on Algerian panels and curtains. The contours of the design are outlined in

Fig. 236. Moroccan embroidery.
One quarter of one of the motifs in fig. 235.

double running stitch in black. The filling is worked in a slanting stitch in bright colors. This stitch is worked like the first row of plaited Spanish stitch (fig. 190), and is also reversible.

The work is begun with the outlining, for which DMC embroidery rayon no. 60 in black should be used. We would point out that the oblique stitches of the filling are worked sometimes in horizontal and sometimes in vertical rows, and sometimes from left to right and sometimes from right to left; they are always adapted to the shapes to be filled. The explanatory detail (fig.

243) shows how a horizontal row, from right to left, is worked.

Choose DMC embroidery rayon no. 30 for the filling of the motifs. The deeply serrated leaves are worked in Turkey red, the large central motif in

Fig. 237. Moroccan embroidery.
Outer border and edging of fig. 235.

indigo, the small motif in the center in cream. The small leaf, pointing upward is embroidered in violet and the stems in bright green. The center of the six-petalled flower is in tangerine yellow; the petals themselves are worked in cream, hazelnut brown, and ash grey, in turn. These last three shades are also used for the remaining small motifs.

Fig. 238. Moroccan embroidery.
Narrow border suitable for finishing off fig. 235.

Border in Caucasian Embroidery (figs. 244, 245, 246, 247). Caucasian embroidery in several colors on fine linen is always characterized by black outlines in line stitch and square Holbein stitch. The inside of the motifs is completely covered by a filling stitch, so that the embroidery is almost like a fabric woven in colors. This kind of work therefore requires the most minute care, but the delicacy of the finished work and the richness of the coloring amply repay the worker for the trouble she has bestowed upon it.

The working of the border in fig. 244 is begun with the outlines in black silk, after which the ground is filled in with the stitch explained in fig. 245.

Fig. 239. Repeating design in Rhodes embroidery.

This stitch is worked in two journeys, one in each direction. It is begun by a horizontal stitch over five threads of the material, the sixth thread is picked up, the next stitch again passes over five threads and picks up the sixth, and so on. In the return row, the stitch is completed by a second row of horizon-

Fig. 240. Rhodes embroidery. Part of the repeating design in fig. 239.

tal stitches, also over five threads with one thread between, but this time the thread taken up is the third of those passed over on the first journey.

It should be further noted that on the second journey the needle enters as close as possible to the stitches of the first row. These two journeys done, the next row is begun one thread higher up on the material. This process is continued until the figure is completely filled. As can be seen in the illustration of the border, the filling stitch is worked, sometimes in horizontal and sometimes in vertical rows, according to the parts to be filled.

For the coloring we recommend green and rose for the large dark figures of the center and grey and gold for the centers of these figures; the four little squares in the middle of the intermediate figures are filled with grey and pale yellow, the light-colored triangles at the top and bottom with another shade of pale yellow, and the small detached leaves with violet. Indigo is used for filling the background of the wide central band, gold for the background of the narrow bands at each side. The little figures in these narrow bands are worked in violet, grey, and green, in turn.

Fig. 241. Floral design in triangular Turkish stitch.

This kind of border, combined with a more open ground, can be used to trim tablecloths, cushions, or panels.

In figs. 246 and 247, we give two other filling stitches, which are also found in Caucasian embroidery. The stitch in fig. 246 consists of horizontal stitches over five threads and one thread apart; in the rows which follow, the stitch is always set one thread farther to the left, so that the ground forms a design of oblique stripes. The stitch in fig. 247 completely covers the foundation; it is composed of horizontal rows of encroaching oblique stitches. It is worked over six vertical and one horizontal thread, the needle being brought back obliquely under two threads to begin again as described above. Stitches of the same kind are described in the chapter on "Netting"; see figs. 757 to 760.

Hungarian Border in Satin Stitch with Openwork Rows (fig. 248). This border, of Hungarian origin, formed the trimming of an unbleached linen sheet; the embroidery itself was worked in white flax thread. The openwork stitch which divides the band into squares and triangles is explained in the chapter, "Openwork on Linen"; see fig. 776.

Fig. 242. Border in Arab embroidery.

The triangles are filled with a half star in satin stitch and a band with little squares of the material left bare. The inside of the squares is ornamented with a star in satin stitch, with rays made of two rows of back stitch; round the star, eight little squares are worked to fill the empty space. To complete the band, a narrow openwork strip is worked at the top and bottom; the stitch used for this can be chosen from those given in the chapter, "Openwork on Linen."

Worked in white on a white material, this kind of embroidery is used for trimming bed linen; in white on an unbleached or yellowish foundation, for table linen.

Yugoslav Border in Satin Stitch (fig. 249). The Slavs are in the habit of making aprons and bags out of colored materials which they weave themselves by hand; the delightful designs of these materials can easily be reproduced in embroidery. In fig. 249 we give one of these borders, copied from a bag and reproduced in satin stitch on linen. It can be used for the trimming of bags, cushions, stools, etc. Our model is worked in vertical flat stitches over four threads of the material in four colors.

The darkest shade in the illustration represents dark blue; the medium, red; the light, green; and the very light, brown.

Border in Bulgarian Embroidery (fig. 250). The design illustrated here is a Bulgarian border taken from a woman's chemise at Doupnitza. The base consists of a narrow edging in oblique Slav stitch. The principal motifs, worked in the same stitch and outlined in double running stitch, are placed just above this edging. The minor motifs are worked in cross stitch and satin stitch.

Fig. 243. Working of the filling stitch of the border in fig. 242.

The work is begun with the narrow border in oblique Slav stitch (see figs. 188 and 189), worked in DMC special stranded cotton no. 25 in indigo and geranium red. The outlines of the large figures are worked next, in DMC pearl cotton no. 8 in black. Then the dark parts are filled with DMC special stranded cotton no. 25 in indigo, with geranium red for the light parts worked in oblique Slav stitch or satin stitch. The striped band which runs up the center of the motifs is worked in copper green and hazelnut brown; the latter shade is also used for the small, light-colored motifs.

This border, like other Slav embroideries, is especially suitable for the trimming of underlinen.

Loop Stitch Embroidery (figs. 251, 252, 253, 254). In Schleswig, in the Viöl region, cushions are to be seen, delightfully ornamented with designs of loops woven into the material, which can very easily be imitated in embroidery.

Fig. 251 represents a piece of work of this kind, carried out in DMC special stranded cotton no. 25 used fourfold on a foundation of yellow-green linen.

This stitch is worked very similarly to single Maltese or candlewick stitch

Fig. 244. Border in Caucasian embroidery.

(figs. 287 and 288) and single knotted stitch (figs. 408 to 410). It is worked over a mold or a thick knitting needle. The little loops are about a quarter of

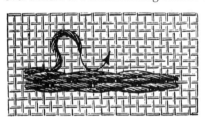

Fig. 245. Filling stitch used for the border in fig. 244.

an inch long, and the horizontal stitch which holds the stitch at the top should be about the same length; according to the material, these stitches will pass over six to eight threads. The rows of stitches are worked in succession, beginning at the bottom. The number of threads separating the rows should be the same as the number covered by each horizontal stitch. At the beginning and end of each row there will be a small end of thread which should not be any longer than the loop. Where there is a change of color in the row, there will perforce be two such ends side by side.

Fig. 252 shows how this stitch is worked over a mold, with the horizontal stitches covering eight threads and set with eight threads between the rows. Fig. 253 shows three rows of stitches completed, in two shades. Fig. 254 gives a working diagram of the design, showing the arrangement of the colors; each symbol represents one horizontal stitch.

Embroidery on Traced Linen. For embroidery which is to be worked independently of the threads of the material, the design is first traced onto the fabric; then, following the lines of the design, the various stitches required by the pattern are embroidered. According to its character, the design may be merely outlined, the motifs may be filled in, or the two styles may be combined in the same piece of work.

When the design is only to be outlined, one or other

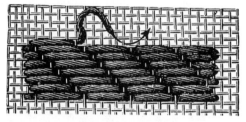

Fig. 246. Another filling stitch with horizontal stitches forming oblique lines.

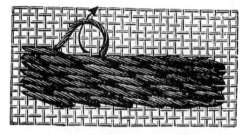

Fig. 247. Another filling stitch with encroaching oblique stitches.

of the various stitches which imitate a cord or braids should be chosen, unless a knotted or crocheted cord or a woven braid is preferred. If the design is to be entirely covered, flat or satin stitch can be used, or one of the various forms of herringbone or Russian stitch, Roman stitch, Cretan stitch, etc.

Examples with embroidered outlines and fillings combine every kind of stitch, as will be seen in the illustrations which follow. In a class by itself is Maltese or candlewick embroidery, in which the design is made up of little tufts.

Materials. For stem stitch, chain stitch, etc., a moderately twisted thread should be used, such as DMC pearl cotton, DMC embroidery twist, or DMC special quality embroidery cotton; in certain rare cases, as for instance for pearl stitch, use DMC crochet cotton, 6 cord, or DMC knotting cotton.

Satin stitch, herringbone stitch, and other filling stitches require a loosely twisted thread, such as DMC special stranded cotton, DMC floss flax or flourishing thread, DMC embroidery rayon, or DMC Persian silk. Very rich designs sometimes also require gold and silver threads.

Stitches. The stitch most used for traced embroidery on linen is flat or satin stitch, worked exactly as for raised satin stitch embroidery on white, except that the padding is omitted and the embroidery is consequently flat.

The chapter on "Embroidery on White Materials" also contains instructions for working stem stitch (fig. 80) and double back stitch (figs. 82 and 83). To these we add here a series of stitches which can be used for embroidering either outlines or fillings.

Raised stem stitch (fig. 255). Take a very strong thread, such as DMC pearl cotton no. 3 or the coarse numbers of DMC 6 cord crochet cotton, lay

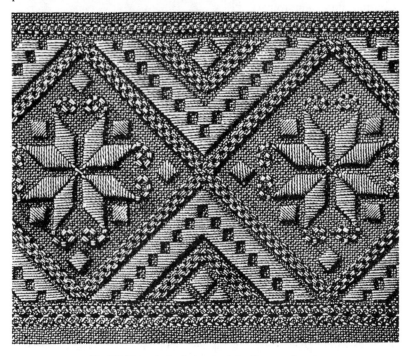

Fig. 248. Hungarian border in satin stitch with openwork rows.

it along the line of the design, and cover it with slanting overcast stitch (fig. 78). The thread chosen for the overcasting may be the same as that which is used as a foundation, or a finer number, according to the material.

Simple chain stitch (fig. 256). The thread having been brought out at the required point, the needle is reinserted at the same point, leaving a small loop on the right side of the work; it is then brought out again at a distance of three or four threads from the first point. The loop of thread is held with the thumb of the left hand and passed under the point of the needle. The thread is then drawn tight, and the stitch is complete. To make the next stitch, the needle is reinserted at the point where it was last drawn out, another loop is formed, and the same process repeated. The last loop is secured by a back stitch.

This stitch is used instead of stem stitch for small motifs composed solely of outlines, or to outline large motifs embroidered in satin stitch or other filling stitches. We shall frequently have occasion to return to this kind of stitch.

Fig. 249. Yugoslav border in satin stitch.

Whipped chain stitch (fig. 257). The chain stitch just described having been completed, it is overcast with a thread of contrasting color over each stitch, without penetrating the material beneath; see fig. 257. The finished stitch has the appearance of a rounded cord.

Cretan stitch (fig. 258). This stitch which, is sometimes called long-armed feather stitch, is not unlike the simple feather stitch shown in fig. 50;

Fig. 250. Border in Bulgarian embroidery.

like the latter, it is composed of two buttonhole stitches made one to the right and one to the left; the slanting outer stitches, however, are much

Fig. 251. Loop stitch embroidery.

longer, and the inner stitches form a straight vein instead of an undulating line. In embroidery on linen, Cretan stitch is most often used as a filling for leaves, for which purpose the central vein makes it particularly suitable.

Roman stitch (fig. 259). This consists of stitches worked across the width to be filled and intersected by a slightly slanting back stitch. It is used both for narrow bands and for filling larger spaces; see fig. 273.

Although the illustration is so clear that further instructions hardly seem necessary, we add here a detailed explanation of the course of the stitches. Bring out the needle to the left, two or three threads beyond the line which the embroidery is to follow, the exact distance depending on the nature of the material and thread used;

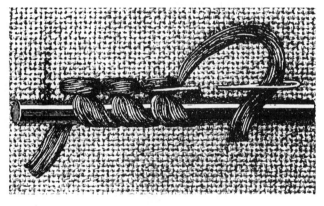

Fig. 252.
Loop stitch. How to make the loops.

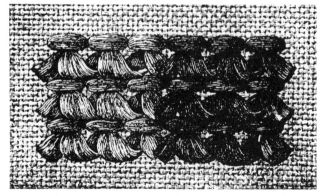

Fig. 253.
Loop stitch. Three rows of loops completed.

insert the needle again the same distance to the right of the line and bring it out in the middle of the stitch; then, passing the needle over the stitch just made, reinsert it one or two threads in advance of the point where it emerged and bring it out once more close to the starting point of the first stitch.

Pearl stitch (fig. 260). This is a stitch frequently found in old embroideries on linen. Unlike most stitches, pearl stitch is worked upward: several threads of the material are taken up on the needle and the thread is drawn through; then the needle, following the direction of the arrow, passes under the stitch just made and a tight knot is formed.

Italian link stitch (fig. 261). Begin with a slanting stitch upward from left to right and bring out the needle to the left below this stitch. Over this slanting stitch work two buttonhole stitches—without penetrating the material—then insert the needle to the right, at the same level and a little

Fig. 254. Diagram of the design in fig. 251.
Key to the colors: ■ Moss green, ▣ Indigo, ✖ Red brown,
▢ Cypress green, ⊡ Indigo, ▥ Smoke grey.

distance from the first slanting stitch. Return downward to the left and make two buttonhole stitches over the free thread, and so on.

This stitch can be used as an ornamental stitch, or to fill narrow bands which have previously been edged with stem stitch. Wider bands can be filled very quickly if the stitch is worked in a coarse thread used double.

Basket stitch on linen (fig. 262). This stitch bears a certain resemblance to long-armed cross stitch (fig. 180); it can be worked on any kind of material, on counted threads or following a wide or narrow tracing, with fine or coarse thread, and with stitches set very close together or further apart.

The needle is inserted into the material and a sloping stitch is made downward from left to right, passing under from three to six threads of the material, according to the nature of the material and thread used. Then, returning toward the right, a second stitch is made, slanting upward and of the same width as the first; then a third stitch, emerging at the same point as the first stitch to the right, then a stitch upward, and so on. The dotted line in the illustration clearly shows the course of the stitches.

Fig. 255. Raised stem stitch.

Three little borders in various stitches (figs. 263, 264, 265). We give here three narrow borders intended for the trimming of small napkins, aprons, and dresses, examples of the type of design known as line designs. Fig. 263 shows a little band worked in stem stitch in two colors; fig. 264 another design in simple chain stitch; and fig. 265, the same design in whipped chain stitch.

Flower motif in satin stitch (fig. 266). This flower motif is an example of the style of embroidery

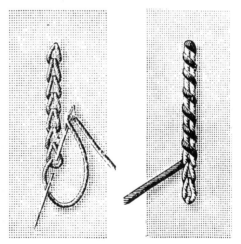

Fig. 256.
Simple chain
stitch.

Fig. 257.
Whipped chain
stitch.

known as Magyar embroidery. The peasant women of the Mezökövesed district use it to trim their clothing as well as their household linen. The foundation is of fine linen, the embroidery in bright red with a few leaves in yellow. The direction of the stitches is clearly shown in the illustration and no further instructions for the working are necessary.

Fig. 258. Cretan stitch.

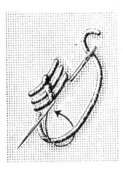

Fig. 259. Roman stitch.

Fig. 260. Pearl stitch.

This kind of flower motif, arranged along an undulating line or used as a corner, is suitable above all for the trimming of household and table linen, but can also be used on cushion covers, aprons, etc.

Border and flower motif in satin stitch, stem stitch, and chain stitch (fig. 267). This design is representative of the Slavonic embroideries of Moravia, which the peasant women use to trim their cuffs, shawls, and bonnets. It should be worked in red, black, yellow, blue, and cream, the characteristic colors of the embroidery of that country. The work is done on a foundation of dark blue linen.

The first step in the working is the overcasting of the eyelet holes in yellow cotton; then the petals of the flowers are worked in satin stitch in red. The upturned serrated leaves as well as the two small leaves at the base of the stalk are embroidered in cream. The flowers of the edging are alternately blue with black centers and red with blue centers; he leves are alternately yellow and cream.

When all the satin stitch has been worked, the filling stitch is done. The apple itself, and the heart below it, are outlined alternately in chain stitch and stem stitch in red; the center of the apple in black. All the other stem stitch and chain stitch parts of both flower and border are worked in yellow, with the exception of the veining of the yellow leaf in the edging, which is done in blue.

The eyelets in the flower are surrounded with three rows of chain stitch in black. Two rows of chain stitch—one blue and one black—frame the edging at the top, and three rows—blue, yellow, and black—at the bottom. For the working of the chain stitch, see fig. 256.

Border in Serbo-Croatian embroidery (fig. 268). The peasant women of Croatia often weave their aprons with colored thread mingled with threads of gold and silver. As an example of these designs we give the border in fig. 268, which was embroidered in DMC pearl cotton in blue, green, and red, and DMC embroidery rayon in yellow.

Each diamond is framed with two lines of stem stitch in color, separated

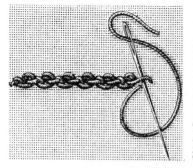

Fig. 261. Italian link stitch.

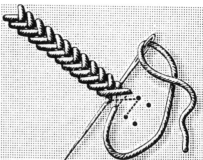

Fig. 262. Basket stitch on linen.

Fig. 263. Border in stem stitch.

Fig. 264. Border in simple chain stitch.

by a thread of golden yellow rayon held down with overcasting. Inside the diamonds are eyelet holes in yellow rayon, ornamented with French knots. Finally, the slanting bands are filled with small gold spangles.

Fig. 265. Border in whipped chain stitch.

The width of this border can be varied at will; it can be finished off with a toothed edge or made into an insertion and will in either case form a beautiful trimming for summer frocks or other articles of dress or fancy articles.

Border in Roumanian stitch (fig. 269). The stitch used in this kind of embroidery, which comes from Persia and is also known as oriental stitch, is very similar to the one explained in fig. 83. However, instead of bringing the needle out as shown in fig. 83, it is brought back, as can be seen in the illustration, between the outlines of the figure and behind the thread which forms the next stitch. Before the design is filled, it is outlined in stem stitch or with a fine cord held in place with overcasting, which should be invisible on the surface.

This delightful design, which can be adapted to the most varied uses, is composed of seven-lobed leaves, worked alternately in dark and light green; flowerets with three petals, worked in scarlet with golden yellow centers; and small leaves worked in raspberry. The whole of the design is outlined in black.

Fig. 266. Flower motif in satin stitch.

Fig. 267. Border and flower motif in satin stitch, stem stitch, and chain stitch.

Flower motif in Roumanian stitch (fig. 270). In this example the stitch can be worked according to the instructions for fig. 83 in the chapter, "Embroidery on White Materials." The stitches should be set far enough apart for the material of the foundation to show through between them.

As materials, we recommend DMC pearl cotton. This thread, in black and red, is used for the eight petals of the large flower at

Fig. 268. Border in Serbo-Croatian embroidery.

the top; in blue, for the three-petalled buds on each side of the stem. The small pointed leaves are worked in green, and the heart of the flower and of the buds in saffron. All the important figures are surrounded with gold cord, stitched invisibly to the material with DMC Alsa in golden yellow.

This kind of flower motif is suitable for the composition of large allover designs to trim panels, cushion covers, chair backs, etc.

Border in encroaching satin stitch and stem stitch (figs. 271 and 272). This design is typical of Croatian embroideries, which are carried out on fine linen in colored silks and are generally used for trimming the peasant women's shawls. The figures are filled with encroaching satin stitch, the working of which is shown in fig. 272. The outlining and stems are worked in plain stem stitch.

The darkest shade represents black; the lightest, pale yellow; the large petals of the flowers require red and green alternately. Blue, yellow, red, and green are equally distributed in the

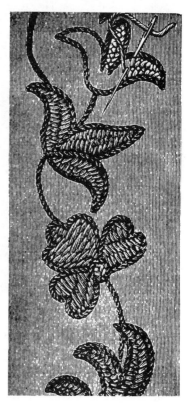

Fig. 269. Border in Roumanian stitch.

rest of the spray. This kind of flower motif, like the last, is suitable for allover embroidery.

Border in Roman stitch (fig. 273). Roman stitch (fig. 259) is used for the greater part of the design in fig. 273. The original, still very well preserved in spite of its great age, was worked in a fairly bright red on a slightly cream-tinted material. The use of DMC pearl cotton in garnet red will ensure a faithful copy of the ancient embroidery which served as a model.

Roman stitch is used wherever the lines of the design are

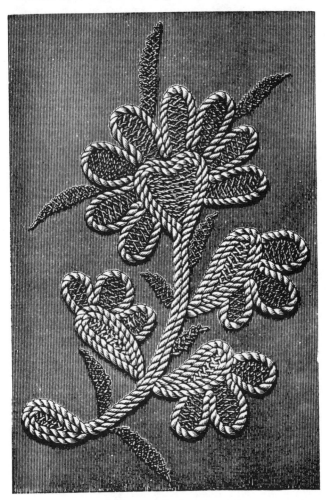

Fig. 270. Flower motif in Roumanian stitch.

wider apart; where they are narrow, as in the tendrils along the stems and the ends of the flower petals, satin stitch is used.

The detached motif may be used to compose a strip or an allover design; an effective strip can be made by taking the central flower motif and working it, with a rather longer stem, between the larger motifs. A very handsome border, eminently suitable for trimming curtains and all kinds of furnishing articles, can be made by placing the motifs base to base.

Bird in medieval embroidery worked in Roumanian couching or figure stitch (figs. 274 and 275). In southern Germany and Switzerland

Fig. 271. Border in encroaching satin stitch and stem stitch.

during the Middle Ages, a special kind of embroidery was cultivated, consisting of a sort of satin stitch overcast with long stitches, which, owing to the subjects for which it was used (people, animals, birds, figures of saints), was known as "figure stitch." Nowadays, however, it is better known under the name of Roumanian couching.

This embroidery was almost always used to ornament curtains. It was worked on linen with a white or unbleached flax thread, making very little contrast with the foundation, the effect of the embroidery being seen only when it is hung against

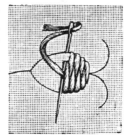

Fig. 272. Method of working encroaching satin stitch.

the light, when the figures stand out dark against the more or less transparent foundation.

This kind of embroidery was used to great advantage in compositions in the Romanesque style, in which detached figures of animals or birds are surrounded with a richly ornamented framework. At the present day, it has been adopted for embroidering panels and table covers for the dining room, smoke room, or garden room. Fig. 274 shows an example of a bird worked in this ancient style.

Fig. 273. Border in Roman stitch.

Fig. 274. Bird in mediaeval embroidery, worked in Roumanian couching or figure stitch.

The stitch itself—for which a coarse, loosely twisted thread should be chosen—is worked in two journeys, one in each direction. A thread is stretched right across the surface to be embroidered and then covered with long, slightly slanting stitches, making only very small stitches on the wrong side of the work. To make the method of working the stitch clearer, we have illustrated it in two shades. The thread which is stretched across on the first journey is shown in a light shade, and the slanting overcast stitches are shown in a darker shade; see fig. 275.

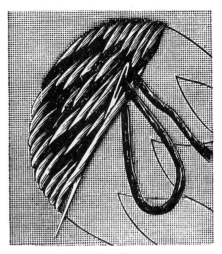

Fig. 275.
Method of working Roumanian couching.

The first and last of these latter stitches should never touch the outline. When the first series of stitches is complete, another thread is stretched, quite close to the previous one: this is

Fig. 276. Border with braided outline and various filling stitches.

covered with overcasting, and so on, until the whole figure has been filled. In fairly large spaces, such as, in this case, the wings and breast, the stitches can be fairly long; for the head, legs, and feet, on the other hand, short stitches are necessary. The effects of light and shade are produced solely by the varying direction and length of the stitches.

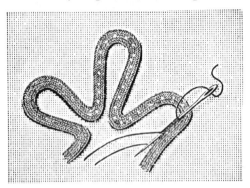

Fig. 277. Method of gathering the braid to form curves.

We urge readers to consult the illustration frequently in order to ensure that the stitches are correctly placed in all the various parts of the bird.

Embroideries Worked With Braid. The next two designs belong to the class in which embroidery is replaced by a narrow braid. In the border shown in fig. 276, braid replaces embroidery for the outlines, while in the bouquet in fig. 278 the flowers and ears of corn are entirely composed of braid.

Border with braided outline and various filling stitches (figs. 276 and 277). Following the tracing, DMC superfine braid is sewn down between the outlines with small back stitches worked in DMC Alsatian twist no. 50 and set, as invisibly as possible, in the center of the braid. Where the design follows a curve, the braid is stitched along the outside of the curve and then gathered along the inside. In this way the excess length of the braid is disposed of and the braid will lie flat; see fig. 277.

When all the outlines have been completed, the filling stitches are worked in DMC special quality embroidery cotton, no. 20. The flower petals and the leaves are filled with Cretan stitch (fig. 258), the stems with double back stitch (fig. 83); finally, a darned wheel is worked in the center of each flower.

This kind of embroidery, which should be worked in colors, is to be recommended for trimming table linen, towels, cloths, panels, etc. which have to stand frequent washing.

Bouquet in braid and embroidery (fig. 278). In the bouquet shown in our illustration, braid replaces flat stitch embroidery with advantage, since this method of working the flowers takes much less time.

To reproduce this bouquet (fig. 278), DMC superfine braid is used, in ecru and umber for the wheat ears, white for the marguerites, and blue for the cornflowers.

The actual working of the flowers is as simple as can be. Thread the braid into a crewel needle and pass it through the material from the wrong side to the right at the base of one of the petals. Meanwhile a sewing needle is put ready, threaded with thread of a thickness and color to match the braid; this is brought through from the wrong side at the point where the tip of the petal is to be; the braid is brought to this point and two stitches made over it; the braid is then brought back to the center of the flower, where it is passed back through the material, and is brought out again at the required

Fig. 278. Bouquet in braid and embroidery.

distance for the next petal. Thus each petal requires only three or four stitches.

It will be noticed that the braid petals of the marguerite are wider apart than those of the cornflower; in the latter it suffices to fold the braid back without passing it through the material and to fix it with a stitch on the right side at top and bottom. The wheat ears are even more quickly done: a single stitch in the folded braid imitates the beard of the ear; stem stitch con-

Fig. 279.
Special
thimble for
tambour
crochet.

ceals the point where the braids meet, and is continued to form the stalks.

French knots are used for the stamens, (fig. 86), in yellow cotton for the marguerites and dark blue for the cornflowers. The remaining small details of the design are worked in raised satin stitch or flat stitch.

This charming little design, so quickly worked, is suitable for the trimming of all sorts of articles, such as book covers, sachets, pincushions, mats, etc.

Crochet Worked in a Frame (Tambour Crochet) (figs. 279, 280, 281, 282). Large pieces of work requiring a wide range of colors are not worked in chain stitch with a sewing needle, but in crochet chain stitch. This can only be done in a frame of a size proportionate to the article to be embroidered.

Fig. 280. Hook for tambour crochet.

The crochet chain stitch produced in this way requires the use of a special implement, shown in fig. 280, in which the hook is screwed into the han-

Fig. 281. First position of the hands for tambour crochet.

dle, as in the stitching needle, to which we shall refer again later. A kind of thimble, shown in fig. 279, is worn on the first finger of the right hand. It consists of a small sheet of brass, rolled but not joined, so that it will fit any finger; it is open at the top, like a tailor's thimble, and has a small notch in the side, which is placed over the fingernail. The top being slightly slanted, the part which covers the back of the finger is a little longer than the inner side. This thimble greatly accelerates the upward and downward movements required by this work.

The thread having been fastened onto the material, the hook is passed

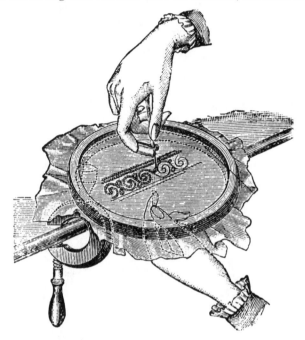

Fig. 282. Second position of the hands for tambour crochet.

through the stretched material, moving, as it were, in the notch at the top of the thimble, the screw being held towards the thumb; the thread, held in the left hand under the work, is passed over the hook, and the hook is brought out again on the right side, the material being at the same time pressed downward with the thimble, to prevent it from being pulled up by the hook, which, as it returns, brings to the right side a chain stitch; see figs. 281 and 282.

The only difficulty in this kind of work is the same as that encountered by beginners in tatting and macrame—a tendency to confuse the movements of the hands. If it is remembered that the two actions of withdrawing the hook and pressing down the material must be performed simultaneously, proficiency will soon be attained, and it will be found possible to produce delightful pieces of work in a comparatively short time.

For this kind of work, it is advisable to use a very tightly twisted thread,

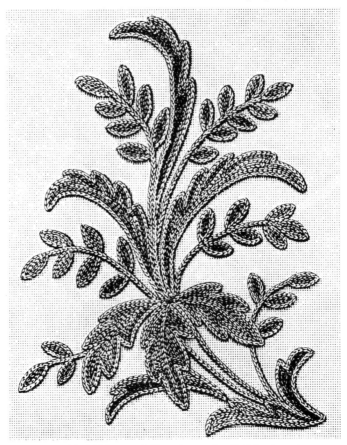

Fig. 283. Spray worked in tambour crochet. Turkish style.

so that it shall not be split by the hook. Among the DMC threads, those which we especially recommend are Alsatian sewing cotton, Alsa, Alsatian twist, cotton lace thread, and pearl cotton.

Spray in tambour crochet. Turkish style (figs. 283, 284, 285).   The original of this spray, consisting of leaves and wheat ears, was worked in gold and silver thread on a modern Turkish veil.

The method of doing crochet in a frame has just been explained; it remains to point out that the outlines must always be done first, then the veinings, if there are any, and last of all the filling.

Fig. 284 shows part of a wheat ear; the outlines are finished, and the filling has been begun. Fig. 285 shows how the serrated leaves are worked: the right-hand half of the right-hand leaf is finished; in the left-hand half of the same leaf, the way in which the filling is worked can be seen. It is done in two zigzag rows, following the line of the outer edge. The left-hand leaf shows once more the working of the outlines and veinings.

In the large leaves, the outlines are worked in DMC embroidery rayon no. 60 in tangerine yellow; the veins in grey; and the filling in DMC shaded pearl cotton no. 8 in scarab green and blue; and the small leaves with DMC shaded pearl cotton no. 8 in scarab green and grey. The wheat ears have outlines of DMC embroidery rayon no. 60 in tangerine yellow and grey alternately, with DMC shaded pearl cotton no. 8 in terra-cotta and grey for the filling. The shaded pearl cotton used for the filling affords a contrast with the brilliance of the outlines in embroidery rayon, and gives delicate shaded effects which it would be much more difficult to obtain

Fig. 284. How to work the wheat ears.

with a range of shades of the same color in plain pearl cotton.

This method of crocheting in a frame is used only for very rich articles. It can be used for narrow borders for veils, headdresses, collars, and jabots; or for larger designs for trimming shawls, fans, the fronts of dresses, etc.

Maltese Embroidery. There exists in Malta a very special type of embroidery which the inhabitants use to trim furnishing articles and which

Fig. 285. How to work the serrated leaves.

is variously known as Maltese stitch, single and double knotted stitch, and candlewick stitch.

The design consists of little tufts which can be made in two ways—single or double. The tufts of single Maltese stitch hang down over the material like little tassels, in low relief. The double form of the stitch, on the other hand, produces rows of fat, round loops, more like pompoms, ornamented with two short, full ends spreading out on either side of the central loop. We offer our readers two examples, illustrating the two different varieties of this stitch, together with all the necessary details and instructions.

Border and allover design in single Maltese or candlewick stitch (figs. 286, 287, 288). We recommend this type of work, with its hanging tufts, for curtains, portieres, panels, and similar large objects, for which the speed at which it can be worked seems to make it particularly suitable.

Fig. 286. Border and allover design in Maltese or single knotted stitch, also called candlewick stitch.

The material of the foundation should be very strong; a pale shade of pink or yellow is preferable to an unbleached material.

After tracing the design—which consists of a horizontal line marking the position of each tuft—has been done, the embroidery is begun at the bottom of the article. The working of the stitch, which is not unlike single Smyrna stitch (see the chapter on "Tapestry," figs. 408 and 409), is very easy. Each stitch, according to the coarseness of the material, requires from four to six threads width. The direction of the stitch itself, which holds the tuft at the top, is always horizontal.

The most suitable materials are DMC Alsatia or a loosely twisted thread such as DMC special stranded cotton, DMC floss flax or flourishing thread, or DMC embroidery rayon, of which from six to twelve threads are used in each needleful. The stitch is begun in the middle of the horizontal line traced on the right side of the work, where a loose end of thread, from one half to three quarters of an inch in length, is left hanging; the needle is then brought out again at a distance of two or three threads to the left, the thread is passed over the top of the loose end and the needle reinserted the same number of threads to the right of the starting point and, finally, brought out again at the center of the stitch; the thread is then cut off to the same length as the first loose end, and the stitch is complete.

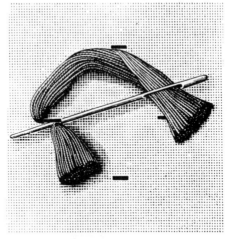

Fig. 287. Maltese or single knotted stitch, also called candlewick stitch. How to make the tufts.

Our illustration, fig. 287, shows how the little tufts are made; in fig. 288 four finished tufts can be seen. The border and the little triangles on the outside are worked in green and cream, and the straight lines which edge the border in blue and yellow. In the allover design, blue has been used for the large diamonds, yellow and green for the lilies, and cream and green for the small diamonds which fill the spaces.

Fig. 288. Maltese or single knotted stitch, also called candlewick stitch. Four completed tufts.

Border in double Maltese or candlewick stitch (figs. 289, 290, 291, 292, 293). Fig. 289 shows the border of a curtain embroidered on soft (washed) congress canvas in DMC special stranded cotton, the colors being golden yellow, scarab green, royal blue, and scarlet, arranged as follows: the horizontal lines which edge the border are done in green and yellow, the large diamonds inside are worked in the same colors, and the angles in blue and red.

Fig. 289.
Border in double Maltese or candlewick stitch.

To work the stitch, take a full needleful of DMC special stranded cotton and pass it under two or three vertical threads of the material from right to left (fig. 290). Bring the needle back to the right and pass it under the two or three threads in front of the first stitch. The needleful thus passes under the loose end already in place; the stitch must be drawn fairly tight.

Repeat the first stitch (fig. 291), making a loop in the middle over a mold and of the same length as the first loose end. Then repeat the second stitch, passing above the loop (fig. 292), and finally cut the end of the needleful to the same length as the loop. Fig. 293 shows four finished stitches.

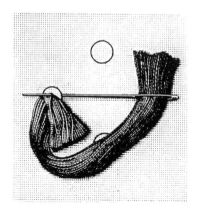

Fig. 290. Double Maltese or candlewick stitch.
First stage.

Fig. 291. Double Maltese or candlewick stitch.
Second stage.

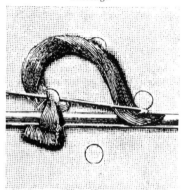

Fig. 292. Double Maltese or candlewick stitch.
Third stage.

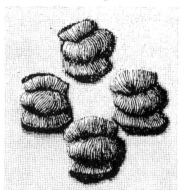

Fig. 293. Double Maltese or candlewick stitch.
Four stitches completed.

Border in satin stitch. Louis XVI style.

CHAPTER VI

Embroidery on Silk and Velvet

When we see rich silks, velvets, and plush fabrics, with their warm colors gleaming under the light, or materials brocaded with gold and silver, we are inclined to think that no ornamentation can increase their beauty. Yet the demands of worldy luxury, as well as those of religious pomp, have from the earliest times sought to enhance the effect of such materials by means of rich embroideries. In this chapter will be found the various kinds of work most often used for embroidery in colors on silk and velvet. They are, incidentally, not unlike those which have been described in the chapter "Linen Embroidery."

We will begin with the most familiar kind—flat or satin stitch embroidery, which can be subdivided into shaded and unshaded, reversible (also called Chinese), and needle painting. After these will come embroidery in knot and plait stitches, and Arab embroidery.

Although we introduce these various stitches under the heading of "Embroidery on Silk and Velvet," this must not be taken to mean that they cannot be used equally well on modern linen, cotton, and woolen fabrics. If, however, one of the examples in this chapter is to be worked on some material other than silk or velvet, the threads used in the working must naturally be in keeping with the material. Some of the stitches used have already been explained in previous chapters. We will, as occasion requires, give references to the appropriate illustrations.

All kinds of satin and knot stitch embroidery can be done with the sewing machine. With a little care, reversible satin stitch can be produced; a kind of seed stitch, worked spirally, takes the place of knot stitches.

Fabrics. The originals of all our designs are worked on a foundation of silk or velvet. We recommend, first and foremost, thick silk materials, such as satin, rep, and short-pile velvet. Thin materials should be avoided, owing to their tendency to stretch out of shape during working; so also should plush, in which the stitches are lost in the thick pile unless well padded.

Church embroidery is often worked on a foundation of gold and silver brocade. These materials are, nevertheless, to be avoided if possible, as the metal threads are very liable to damage the threads used for the embroidery. When the embroidery is to have a foundation of brocade, we suggest that the embroidery itself should be done on linen, and the embroidered figures then cut out and applied to the brocade in the way described in the chapter ''Appliqué Work.''

Materials. In the choice of materials it is important to take into account the type of embroidery to be executed and the delicacy of the design. Thus, satin stitch embroidery, Chinese embroidery, and needle painting require a loosely twisted thread, such as DMC Persian silk, which can be divided at will. Modern satin stitch embroidery and knot stitch embroidery, on the other hand, require a coarser thread, such as DMC embroidery rayon or DMC embroidery twist.

When the work is carried out on cotton or linen, real silk should be replaced by DMC embroidery rayon, DMC special stranded cotton, or DMC floss flax or flourishing thread; DMC special quality embroidery cotton, DMC pearl cotton, DMC embroidery twist, DMC Alsa, and DMC Alsatian twist can be used for knot stitch embroidery.

Frame and Mounting. Preparatory Work (fig. 294). We recommend the use of a strong frame of the type illustrated in fig. 294 for all embroidery of this type. When large pieces of embroidery are being worked,

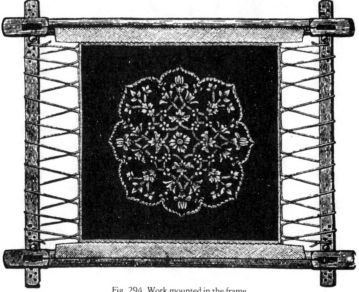

Fig. 294. Work mounted in the frame.

some of the material must be wrapped around the rollers of the frame. These should be well polished so that there will be no danger of the material being marked by unevenness in the wood.

A piece of white or unbleached material is mounted in the frame in the manner described in the preceding chapter. On this tightly stretched foundation the material to be embroidered is laid. It is placed straight by the threads and hemmed down to the lining, care being taken to stretch the upper material more tightly than the under, so that there shall be no danger of the former puckering when it is removed from the frame. Then the design is traced. Before beginning the embroidery, it is well to obtain a colored sketch from which to work the stitches. This sketch is essential for all inexperienced workers and saves them from making serious mistakes in the shading.

Fig. 295. Border in unshaded satin stitch.

Border in Unshaded Satin Stitch (figs. 295 and 296). This design is worked in ordinary satin stitch and stem stitch. Each figure should be begun at the point. The divided leaves are worked one half at a time, care being taken to make the vein even. The stitches are generally worked more or less obliquely, as can be seen in the explanatory illustration, fig. 296.

If the direction of the stitches forming a motif has to be gradually changed, it is wise to make a few short extra stitches from the outside edge toward the middle. These stitches, always partly hidden by the full-length stitches which follow them, enable curved shapes to be worked without the stitches overlapping at the inner edge.

The dots are begun exactly in the middle. One half is finished, then the other. It will be found easier in this way to make perfectly round dots.

Our border is worked in a single color, but in four shades. The stem stitch, shown again in fig. 296, is in very dark blue and the other three shades are used for the satin stitch flowers and leaves, as can be seen in the illustration.

Fig. 296. Working of the unshaded satin stitch embroidery of the borders in fig. 295.

This design is suitable for edging small tablecloths and coverlets to which much time cannot be given. In such cases it will be found best to work the border separately on a different material from that of the article itself.

Border in One-sided Chinese Embroidery (fig. 297). The whole of this design is filled in with unshaded satin stitch; the direction of the stitches is clearly shown in the illustration. As for the arrangement of the colors, it suffices to say that the large flowers are worked in four shades of pink, the leaves in dark blue and golden green and in five shades of bright green, evenly distributed. This design, worked on a silk ribbon, can be used to trim articles of clothing.

Fig. 297. Border in one-sided Chinese embroidery.

Bouquet in One-sided Chinese Embroidery (fig. 298). This design is worked in the same way as the border shown in fig. 297. The chrysanthemums are worked in three shades of red, as are the small round five-petaled flowers. The large flowers, resembling campanulas, are in three shades of ash grey, with red for the calyx. The leaves are in reseda green, parakeet green, and golden green, with a few points worked in dark ash grey. Various other shades are distributed among the small leaves and the stems. The light-colored spray, hanging downward, is embroidered in white.

Fig. 298. Bouquet in one-sided Chinese embroidery.

This bouquet could be used for a pincushion, sachet, or blotter. Four bouquets, one in each corner, make a charming trimming for cushions or small cloths.

Border in Two-sided Chinese Embroidery (fig. 299). Before describing shaded satin stitch, we give a specimen of two-sided Chinese embroidery. This type of embroidery comes to us from China and Japan, where it is used for trimming clothing. The original of our illustration is worked on a foundation of thick, dark silk; this work, however, which has no wrong

Fig. 299. Border in two-sided Chinese embroidery.

side—it is the same on both sides—can very well be used on transparent materials.

Fig. 300. Border in shaded satin stitch or long and short stitch.

This kind of embroidery is less difficult to work than one might think. All parts of the design are filled in with satin stitch, but great care must be taken to make the stitches very regular and close together. The worker should avoid either returning to parts already finished or passing from one part to another without first fastening off the thread.

To begin the work, the thread is fastened on by means of a few stitches inside one of the motifs to be filled; when this motif has been worked, the thread is fastened off in the embroidery without disturbing the stitches. The border is worked with DMC Persian silk, divided into single strands, in four shades of indigo; only a few very light-colored small leaves are worked in white.

These two-sided embroideries are wonderfully suitable for trimming articles of dress, in which the wrong side would be ugly. We suggest their use for such articles as shawls, jabots, collars and cuffs, and fans.

Border in Shaded Satin Stitch or Long and Short Stitch (figs. 300 and 301). The most elaborate form of stain stitch embroidery is shaded embroidery, by means of which the most complicated ornamentation can be reproduced, both conventional and naturalistic. Our illustration shows a border of conventional flowers worked with a lightly twisted thread on fine ribbed silk in encroaching satin stitch. The method of working the embroidery is shown in the explanatory illustration, fig. 301.

Fig. 301. Working of the shaded satin stitch embroidery for the border in fig. 300.

The embroidery is always begun with the lightest shade and, taking care to follow the outline very accurately, the figure to be worked is partly filled with flat stitches laid toward the inside of the figure. These stitches must be of varying lengths. The stitches of the next row, worked in a darker shade, encroach on the light stitches of the first row so that the shades melt into each other. In this way successive shades are added until the figure is entirely filled.

We advise beginners to consult the illustration frequently so as to place the stitches exactly as shown; this will contribute greatly to the success of the finished work. The stalks and tendrils are worked in stem stitch.

As regards coloring, red is used for the large flowers, blue for the calyx, and yellow and green for the stems and leaves.

Fig. 302. Japanese spray in needle painting.

Shaded satin stitch is most often used for trimming large tablecloths, bedcovers, panels, and curtains.

Japanese Spray in Needle Painting (figs. 302 and 303). This name is applied to shaded satin stitch embroidery which reproduces as accurately as the artist's brush all kinds of ornamentation, such as natural flowers, birds, etc.

The spray in fig. 302 is worked from a Japanese painting in DMC Persian silk, used two strands at a time. The stitches used are plain and encroaching satin stitch.

The work is begun with the lightest shade—in this case

Fig. 303.
Method of working a flower in the spray in fig. 302.

white—and successive shades are added, as already exeach stitch beginning in the part already covered and ending in the part still to be covered, till the whole figure is filled. To ensure that the stitches shall lie in the right direction, it is wise to begin each figure in the middle, and complete one half, then the other. The stamens are made of French knots; see fig. 86 in the chapter "Embroidery on White Materials." The large flower in the middle is in shades of red, the flower at the top in white and green with a calyx in red and blue. The buds are worked in blue and yellow, the stems in dull blue, and the leaves in bright green.

Fig. 304. Bouquet of wild flowers in needle painting.

This spray could be used for the same purposes as the one shown in fig. 298.

Bouquet of Wild Flowers in Needle Painting (fig. 304). This delightful design, which is particularly suitable for the adornment of sachets and trinket boxes, is embroidered in DMC Persian silk, using two strands at a time. The poppies are worked in purple, the carnations in pink; for the large leaves a golden green has been chosen, and a bright green for the grasses and stems; the wheat ears are shaded in yellow.

Butterfly in Needle Painting (fig. 305). In this case the embroidery is carried out in a single strand of DMC Persian silk, which allows a finer gradation of shades.

Fig. 305. Butterfly in needle painting.

The two large wings of the butterfly are shaded almost entirely in blue, from the lightest to the darkest shade, with a band of white along the upper

Fig. 306. Spray worked in French knots or twisted knot stitch.

edge, interrupted by stitches in black. Close to the body are a dark red dot and some triangular spots of pink, edged with white.

The small lower wings, worked in a complete range of red, are ornamented with black stripes, with white stitches and green crescents set close to the edge.

Fig. 307. Method of working a leaf in the bouquet in fig. 306.

The body of the butterfly is white with horizontal black bars; the legs are white; the eyes black; the proboscis red; and the antennae white oversewn with black stitches. We advise frequent reference to the illustration to ensure setting the stitches in the right direction, a detail of great importance in needle painting.

This butterfly can be used for the adornment of small fancy objects, work bags, bonbon bags, sachets, etc.

Spray Worked in French Knots (Twisted Knot Stitch) (figs. 306 and 307).

This type of work is met with most frequently in Chinese and Japanese embroideries. It lends itself admirably to the blending of shades and offers an easy method of producing shaded embroidery. In

Fig. 308. Border in Indian knot stitch.

Japanese embroidery we usually find the design in French knots surrounded by a gold thread, couched invisibly or visibly, with a thread of a contrasting shade. The method of working French knots is explained in the chapter "Embroidery on White Materials," fig. 86.

After following all the outlines with a fine gold thread secured by overcast stitches in DMC Alsa in golden green, the filling is carried out in French knots, all the knots being worked in the same direction. Where one shade touches another, a light knot and a dark knot are worked alternately, the better to conceal the change of shade; see the explanatory illustration, fig. 307.

The two large fruits are embroidered in red brown and umber, one in lighter and the other in darker shades; the various leaves in blues and greens mingled; the stems and tendrils all in pale blue; and the flowers in the lower left-hand corner in three shades of red.

This kind of embroidery is suitable for articles in which the work rests on a cardboard or wooden foundation, such as jewel boxes, glove boxes, cases, etc.

Border in Indian Knot Stitch (figs. 308 and 309). The garments of Hindu women are often trimmed with borders worked in knot stitch or flat stitch. In fig. 308 we offer our readers an example of this work, embroidered in Indian knot stitch. It can be seen from the illustration that these knots are not round, as in Chinese and Japanese work, but rather long-shaped.

Fig. 309 shows how the knot is made. The needle is brought out at the required spot, the thread is held with the left thumb, the needle is passed under the thread and turned upwards, then re-inserted into the material

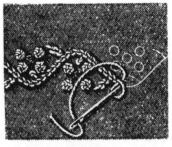

Fig. 309. Method of working the border in Indian knot stitch.

Fig. 310. Small flowers in bullion or post stitch.

about one-fifth of an inch from the spot where it emerged. It is then brought out again a little farther on, towards the right, and the next stitch is made in the same way. Little round knots are obtained, each preceded by an oblique stitch. The finished work has the appearance of having been done with braid, for it has a certain thickness and presents the appearance of regular stripes. The wrong side is covered with slightly slanting short stitches.

The embroidery is worked on a foundation of dark purple satin with DMC embroidery rayon no. 30. The body of the bird, certain of the dots, and the surrounding of the leaves are in violet; the stems, the bird's feet, and the zigzag line of the narrow border are in golden yellow; the eye, the beak, the dark part of the tail, and the dark veining of the upward-pointing leaves are in red-brown; the veins of the downward leaves and the dark dots are in emerald green. The wing is begun with a row of stitches in emerald

Fig. 311. Allover design in Maltese cross stitch and chain stitch.

green, continued with golden yellow, and is finally filled with red-brown
Small Flowers in Bullion or Post Stitch (fig. 310).   For small flowers to be worked singly or as an allover design on fancy articles, we recommend the use of bullion stitch, which is quick to do; see fig. 90 in the chapter ''Embroidery on White Material.''

In fig. 310 we show a little bunch of roses, the flowers of which are worked in bullion stitch with DMC shaded pearl cotton no. 5. We have used light pink for the pale rose on the left, raspberry for the dark rose on the right, and cerise for the lower flower. Begin at the center with the darkest part of the shaded thread and work in circles with stitches increasing in length until the flower is the required size.

The leaves are worked in simple flat stitch with DMC special shaded stranded cotton no. 25 in green, using two strands at a time. Begin at the point of each leaf with the lightest part of the shaded thread and work the left-hand half of the leaf first, then the right, so that the left is always lighter than the right.

Allover Design in Maltese Cross Stitch and Chain Stitch (figs. 311 and 312). This is one of the oldest

Fig. 312. Method of working Maltese cross stitch.

stitches. It was brought to Europe from Asia in the Middle Ages. It cannot be used for filling motifs, for it forms designs of itself, as can be seen in our illustration, fig. 311.

The stitches are made almost entirely on the right side of the material in two layers of interlaced stitches. Begin by laying a network of threads very carefully interlaced and overlapping slightly at the corners; see the left-hand side of fig. 312. The thread is next passed as for linen stitch or interlacing stitch (see fig. 701), with great regularity, over the threads of the network without penetrating the material of the foundation; see the right-hand side of fig. 312. The stems are worked in chain stitch with DMC embroidery rayon no. 60 in golden yellow.

When the method of working has been fully mastered, it will be found easy to work the charming allover design shown in fig. 311, which we have

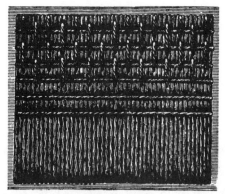

Fig. 313. First oriental stitch.

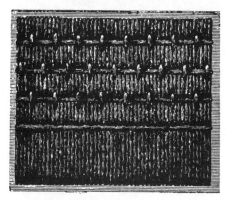

Fig. 314. Second oriental stitch.

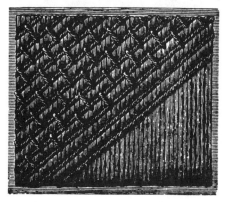

Fig. 315. Third oriental stitch.

copied from an Indian garment. We have worked it on garnet red satin with DMC embroidery rayon no. 30 in hazelnut brown for the light-colored stitches, indigo for the medium-dark stitches, and golden yellow for the dark stitches. This kind of embroidery, which produces a very supple result, is particularly suited for trimming articles of dress and underclothing.

Oriental Stitches (figs. 313, 314, 315). We have grouped the three following stitches under the heading of "Oriental Stitches" because they are found in the majority of oriental embroideries, and it is more than likely that we owe them to the Asiatic peoples who have from the earliest times excelled in the art of embroidery.

These stitches can only be used for fairly large designs and are worked with long, bold stitches. When they are done in one shade and then surrounded with a clearly marked outline, the embroidery thus obtained is called Arab embroidery. If, on the other hand, they are worked in graduated shades and the motifs are not outlined they are called Renaissance embroidery, which, however, must not be confused with Renaissance embroidery on white materials (fig. 159).

The stitches are first laid lengthwise. If the thread used is soft and silky, the needle can be brought out beside the last stitch in order to economize the thread and not make the embroidery too heavy. If, however, the thread is tightly twisted or has a tendency to twist, it must be brought back under the material to emerge beside the starting point of the previous stitch, so that all the threads which form the ground are laid in the same direction. The same process is to be used for figs. 314, 315, 316, and 317.

When all the vertical threads have been laid, a single thread is laid horizontally across them and held down by isolated stitches, with a space of six vertical threads between them. On the succeeding transverse threads, these isolated stitches alternate with those of the preceding row, as shown in fig. 313.

For the stitch shown in fig. 314, the work is begun by laying a foundation in the same way as for the preceding stitch. The horizontal threads are laid a little closer together than in fig. 313; the isolated stitches are laid across two horizontal threads. In fig. 315, the second set of stitches is laid diagonally, and the isolated stitches are also diagonal.

Plaited Stitch (fig. 316). The foundation by long threads having been prepared, a kind of braid is made by means of the second set of stitches. The thread is passed three times alternately under and over three threads of the foundation. To do this work correctly, the thread should always be brought back under the material to its starting point; the stitch is therefore always made from right to left.

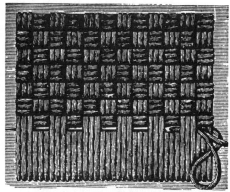

Fig. 316. Plaited stitch.

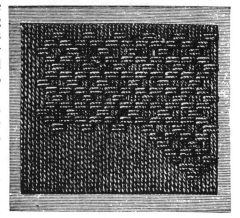

Fig. 317. Mosaic stitch.

Mosaic Stitch (fig. 317). In the very fine work of ancient embroideries, this stitch is often to be found covering spaces in place of applied material. The same preliminary work is required as for the last four stitches. Each stitch is worked separately and passes under the material of the foundation so that the threads forming the design may be slightly raised instead of lying flat as in the previous examples.

Border in Arab Embroidery (fig. 318). The design of this border is inspired by a modern Caucasian design. The embroidery is carried out in two different oriental stitches and plaited stitch; see figs. 314, 315, 316. It

Fig. 318. Border in Arab embroidery.

is worked on a foundation of dark blue velvet with DMC Persian silk and outlined with gold and silver cord.

The filling stitches are those shown in figs. 314 and 315 and are worked with three strands of silk for the foundation stitches; the second set of stitches is in gold thread, and the isolated stitches are in silver thread. The plaited stitch (fig. 316) is worked entirely in silk. For the arrangement of thestitches, consult the illustration.

The coloring is as follows: in the narrow edging the large flowers are in yellow-green, the small ones in rust-brown, and the two narrow bands in pale red-brown. The narrow braid which winds its way through the wide border is in yellow-green; the second braid, which forms motifs within the design, is in rust-brown; the small central leaf in dark green, and the large leaves, pointing downward, in pale green. The upright leaves are worked in pale red-brown and the small figure above them in light green; the calyx beneath the pale red-brown leaves is worked in white silk and rests on a dark green motif.

When all the filling has been done, the latticework is done with gold cord, and the design which ornaments it with silver cord. The small half circles are carried out in gold cord. To complete the work, all the motifs are out-

Fig. 319. Motif in shaded Renaissance embroidery.

lined with gold cord, which is held in place invisibly with DMC Alsa in golden yellow; see also the chapter "Gold Embroidery," fig. 324.

This handsome design, with its indented motifs, is especially suited to the adornment of hangings of all kinds. The narrow edging can be placed at the top, so that the scallops point downward.

Motif in Shaded Renaissance Embroidery (fig. 319). In southern Germany and Switzerland in the eighteenth century, church embroideries were often worked with stitches akin to those of Arab embroidery, in richly shaded silk, laid in long threads, held down with cross threads and stitches.

The shading was done in several shades of the same range of color. The surface was then covered with each successive shade, and the change of thread disguised by inserting the fresh thread into the stitches already made;

in addition, care had to be taken that the shades of the threads used for working over the foundation were exactly the same as those of the foundation itself. At the present time a large choice of shaded threads is obtainable, and the work is much less tedious and complicated. In fig. 319 we give a detached motif in which the filling is first done in DMC special shaded stranded cotton no. 25, and the overstitching in DMC shaded pearl cotton no. 8. The stitch which has been used is the one shown in fig. 313. It should be borne in mind, however, that when a new thread is introduced, the light part of the thread should never come in direct contact with the dark part, and vice versa, so that the finished effect should be even and present no contrasts of shade.

The outer petals of the large flowers and the central dot are worked in light pink; the middle leaf, the two side leaves, and the three dots touching the stem are in red; the five-lobed leaf is in brown and red; the stem, the center of the five-lobed leaf, and the large three-lobed leaf at the bottom are in grey.

Band embroidered with gold and silver threads, purl, and spangles.

CHAPTER VII

Gold Embroidery

If the various kinds of embroidery are compared from the point of view of their effectiveness, the first place must unquestionably be awarded to embroidery worked with gold and silver threads. Through the centuries we find frequent use made of sumptuous gold embroidery. It has held a place of honor in the Far East from the earliest times, and inimitable work of a very individual style is found there. The Byzantines used such embroidery profusely on their garments, both priestly and secular. It was, finally, very greatly appreciated by the peoples of India, Persia, and Asia Minor, and in the Balkans under Turkish rule.

In the seventeenth and early eighteenth centuries this difficult art was cultivated chiefly in Spain, Italy, France, and Germany, where gold embroidery was adopted for the adornment of church ornaments and vestments. Since the eighteenth century it has been practised only by those who have made it their profession. It was seldom done in private houses, for amateurs feared to attempt a style of work which, according to the opinion formerly held, required nine years of apprenticeship to attain perfection.

But since nowadays it has become usual to make use of several styles of embroidery at the same time and in the same piece of work, and gold is used in the same way as other materials, it is quite natural that there should be a revival of interest in gold embroidery, even when needlework is done as a pastime.

Some kinds of gold embroidery can even be done with the sewing machine. We hope that, with the help of our illustrations and explanations, our readers will be able to dispense with the five years of apprenticeship still deemed necessary by professional workers in some countries.

In gold embroidery the effect is produced by various ways of covering more or less thickly padded motifs with metal thread.

Fabrics. Gold embroidery requires as a foundation a strong, firm material. Various kinds of silk, velvet, and brocade are generally used, but cloth and leather can also be used, according to the purpose for which the work is intended.

Materials. For the working of this kind of embroidery, we recommend first of all the gold and silver threads which can be bought in various thicknesses. To make the outlines of the designs stand out more clearly, they are surrounded with gold or silver cord. Gold and silver purl, spangles, metal folioles (leaf-shaped spangles), and colored stones serve further to enhance the effect of the embroidery.

According to the stitch to be worked, a colored thread will be required in addition to the gold and silver threads to hold these latter in place; for this purpose we recommend DMC Alsa in golden yellow or ash grey. The same article can be used when the metal threads are to be held down with threads of a contrasting color.

Implements. The most essential accessory for gold embroidery is a really strong frame for mounting the work; see fig. 294. In addition, for some kinds of stitches a spindle is needed, on which the thread is wound, as well as a very fine stiletto and a tray divided into compartments to hold the purl and spangles.

The spindle (fig. 320). The spindle is an instrument made of hardwood, about nine inches long, on which the metal threads are wound and with which they are guided while the work is in progress so that they need not be touched by the hands.

The body and the lower part of the prongs are first covered with a double thread of DMC pearl cotton in yellow or grey, ending with a loop, to which the gold or silver thread to be wound onto the spindle is attached. The thread is usually wound double onto the spindle. In the course of the work the thread is passed backward and forward over the motif and secured by means of a stitch or two. The stiletto is also used.

The stiletto (fig. 321). This implement consists of a metal handle and a sewing needle screwed into the handle. The handle is hollowed to take the head of a needle of the required size. The needle is held firm by means of a screw, and the greater part of its length remains free. By means of this stiletto, the material is pierced at the point where the thread is to enter and a passage prepared for the needle used for the embroidery.

In soft materials, the stiletto can be dispensed with; but for brocaded materials, plush, and all kinds of leather, in which every false stitch leaves a disfiguring mark, it is essential to mark beforehand the spot where each stitch is to be made.

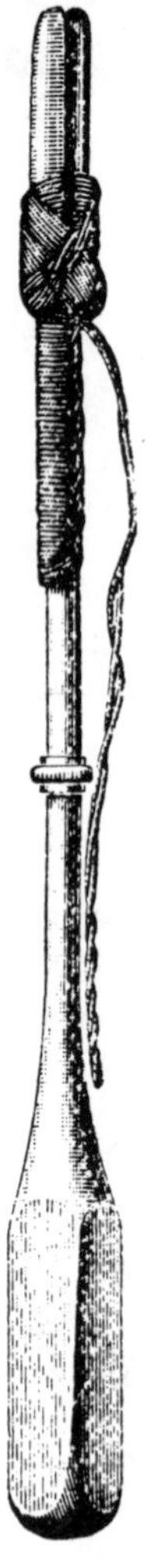

Fig. 320.
The spindle.

Tray for the materials. To make this, cut out of a piece of wood or thick cardboard as many compartments as there will be varieties of material in the work—gold and silver threads, beads of various shapes, spangles of different sizes and shapes, and matt or brilliant purl.

The purl alone will often require several compartments. It is cut into various lengths, according to the design to be worked, and pieces of each length are put together in a separate compartment. The bottom of the tray

Fig. 321. The stiletto.

should be covered with coarse, unmilled cloth; on this base, the materials will not slip about and can be picked up more easily with the needle than on a smooth, hard surface.

Preparatory Work.   Whatever kind of gold embroidery is to be worked and whatever material is used as a foundation, a piece of material must first be mounted in the frame to serve as a backing. To this is sewn the material to be embroidered, stretched as tight as possible, as we have already explained in the chapter ''Embroidery on Silk and Velvet.'' After the design has been traced, the embroidery can be begun immediately, if it is of a kind that does not need padding, that is to say, if it is one of the flat varieties of embroidery.

If the figures are to be in relief, the padding is done as explained in the chapter ''Embroidery on White Materials,'' for Venetian embroidery, fig. 162. A soft, loose thread should be used for this work, such as DMC special stranded cotton or DMC embroidery twist in yellow or grey; see also the illustration, fig. 328.

Instead of a padding of stitches, one can also use shapes cut out of cardboard or leather, but as the cutting out of these shapes requires great care and accuracy, we advise our readers to use embroidered padding, which requires much less work and trouble.

Different Kinds of Gold Embroidery.   These are classed as follows, according to the method of working:

(1) Chinese embroidery

(2) Embroidery on a cord foundation

(3) Piqué embroidery

(4) Laid embroidery

(5) Fancy embroidery, with spangles and purl.

(1) *Chinese embroidery* includes all embroideries in which the motifs are covered with threads of gold or siller laid side by side and secured, visibly or invisibly, by means of overcast stitches made in a thread of the same color as the metal thread or of a different color.

(2) *Embroidery on a cord foundation.*   In this type of embroidery, the metal threads are passed over padding made with a cord and are secured by means of overcast stitches, as in Chinese embroidery. These two kinds of

embroidery do not require large quantities of metal thread, as this thread always remains on the right side of the work.

(3) *Piqué embroidery.* This is the name given to gold embroidery in which all parts of the design are covered with flat stitches which, unlike the last two styles, pass under the material.

These first three kinds of gold embroidery can be worked with or without padding, according to the design.

(4) *Laid embroidery.* This type of embroidery always requires padding. The thread is passed backward and forward over the padding and secured at each turn by a back stitch close to the padding. For this type of embroidery, the thread is wound round the spindle, with which it can be more easily guided.

Fig. 322. Border in gold embroidery with cord and spangles.

(5) *Fancy embroidery, with spangles and purl.* Gold embroideries to which much time cannot be devoted are worked with spangles and purl; imitation pearls and precious stones are often introduced. Fancywork of this kind is sometimes met with in conjunction with true gold embroidery; thread remains on the right side of the work, such as Chinese embroidery, embroidery on a cord foundation, and laid embroidery.

Fig. 323.
Filling of the small flowers
of the border in fig. 322.

(1) *Chinese embroidery.* When the motifs are to be filled with a single thread, the gold thread can be used in the shuttle, and the fine thread with which the gold thread is secured is the upper thread. In this case the embroidery will be worked wrong side up. If, on the other hand, the motifs are to be filled with a fine gold thread used double, the securing thread will have to be used for both upper and lower thread, and the metal threads are passed freely over the material, on the right side.

whenever that occurs in our examples, we will give an explanation of the various stitches in question.

Gold Embroidery Worked with the Sewing Machine. The sewing machine can be used for all kinds of gold embroidery in which the metal

(2) and (3) *Embroidery on a cord foundation and laid embroidery* can only be worked on the right side of the article; for the latter type, we recommend the use of the thread guide.

Border in Gold Embroidery with Cord and Spangles (figs. 322, 323, 324). This border, copied from and eighteenth century embroidery, is typical of those embroideries in which the effect is produced by a thick

Fig. 324.
Method of working the veins of the leaves
for the border in fig. 322.

cord invisibly secured to the foundation; it may be considered the easiest of the various kinds of work in metal thread. The beauty of the work depends on the choice of design, which must be such that the motifs can be embroidered without interruption, as is the case in our example. If it were necessary to pass the thick cord frequently through thematerial, the latter might be damaged and the appearance of the work would suffer.

When the design has been traced, it is outlined with gold cord, each twist of the cord being secured to the foundation with an invisible overcast stitch in DMC Alsa no. 60 in golden yellow. At the beginning and end of every round, the cord is threaded into a crewel needle of suitable size and passed through to the wrong side. When the whole of the design has been outlined with gold cord, the inside of the little flowers is filled with single spangles, secured by a small piece of purl caught to the center of the spangle, as shown in our illustration, fig. 323.

Fig. 325. Insect in gold embroidery. Chinese style.

The veins of the leaves require more attention. The first spangle having been fixed with a back stitch, the needle is brought out close to the spangle; a second spangle and a piece of purl are threaded and the needle reinserted into the first spangle. In this way the second spangle will half cover the first. A third and a fourth spangle are added in the same way, and thus veins of spangles are made, as fig. 324 clearly shows.

The red stones, set singly in various parts of the work, are secured by means of two back stitches in red thread, worked through the two holes pierced in the stone, see fig. 323.

This wide border is suitable for adorning chasubles, copes, and other church vestments and ornaments.

Insect in Gold Embroidery. Chinese Style (fig. 325).   This motif, copied from the trimming of a Chinese woman's dress, is embroidered on a foundation of grey-blue silk with gold thread held down by overcast stitches in DMC Alsa no. 40 in tangerine yellow. The fairly thick gold thread is used in a single strand, and the stitches which secure it are set about one fifth of an inch apart. The gold thread is laid in rows at varying distances

Fig. 326. Butterfly and silver embroidery. Chinese style.

apart, from the outline towards the inside; see also the working detail in fig. 329. The eye is embroidered in raised satin stitch with DMC Alsa no. 40 in copper green.

Butterfly in Gold and Silver Embroidery. Chinese Style (fig. 326).   This butterfly is typical of Chinese gold embroidery, both in design and in execution. The whole of the design is embroidered in gold or silver thread, used double, and secured by overcast stitches in different colors, which soften the brilliance of the metal threads and give them a distinctive sheen.

For the actual working, we refer readers to figs. 329 and 336, which explain the method fully and clearly; we confine ourselves here to indicating the colors used in the embroidery. The body, antennae, and legs are worked in gold and copper green, the eyes in gold and black. The chief surfaces of the large upper wings are worked also in gold, caught down with red; the small part of the right-hand wing is in gold and tangerine yellow, the light part of the left-hand wing in silver and green. The lower right-hand wing is worked in silver and green, the left-hand wing in gold and tangerine yellow. The tail-like continuation of the wings is in gold and silver overcast with violet. The round spots in the gold wings are silver and green; those in the silver wings are gold and tangerine yellow.

Before beginning to work this butterfly, the illustration should be carefully examined, to ensure that the metal threads are set in the right directions.

This butterfly and the insect in fig. 325 can be used to complete designs or powderings in the Chinese style; they can also be used singly to adorn small blotters, spectacle or other cases, pincushions, fans, etc.

Border in Gold and Silver Piqué Embroidery (figs. 327, 328, 329). This border, an example of gold piqué embroidery, was inspired by

Fig. 327. Border in gold and silver piqué embroidery.

an old piece of seventeenth century embroidery. As we have already explained in the introduction to this chapter, this kind of embroidery consists of flat stitch worked in metal thread, usually over padding. This padding should be done with a coarse, supple cotton thread. In the original, we have used DMC special stranded cotton no. 25, held in place with overcast stitches in a single strand of the same thread. When the design has been covered with several layers of cotton—which should be made successively narrower in order to produce a rounded effect—any irregularities should be filled up by means of flat stitches worked with two strands of DMC special stranded cotton; then the whole is covered with satin stitch worked in the opposite direction from that of the gold stitching which is to follow; see fig. 328. The narrow parts of the design should be padded with only two strands of DMC special stranded cotton. Over this padding the gold embroidery is worked in the same way as unshaded satin stitch embroidery; see fig. 329. It is wise to use a thick needle which will make a fairly large hole for the metal thread to pass through and thus save the material, which is often fragile.

Fig. 328.
Method of padding for the border
in fig. 327.

In our border, fig. 327, the small leaves, the buds, and the wide parts of the undulating line are worked with a thick silver thread; the large leaves and the calyx of the flowers with a thick gold thread. As the illustration shows, all the stitches are set obliquely; only those of the lines forming the edge, worked in gold, are straight. To ensure that these bands shall be quite straight, a strip of stiff cardboard is pasted onto the material in place of padding.

The stems and tendrils are made of two parallel threads of gold, held down with overcast stitches in DMC Alsa no. 40 in golden yellow. Where a tendril or stem branches out from the main stem, one thread is carried to the end of the stem, bent back at the point, and brought back, lying close to the first, to the starting point, so that the embroidery appears to have been worked with a double thread, as fig. 329 shows. On the return journey, the overcast stitches

Fig. 329.
Method of working the piqué embroidery
and stems for the border in fig. 327.

which secure the thread must be placed side by side with those made on the first journey.

This border can be used to trim blotters, table mats, etc.

Motif in Gold and Silver Embroidery, Worked with Laid Threads and Cord Foundation (figs. 330, 331, 332, 333, 334). We give here an

Fig. 330. Motif in gold and silver worked with laid threads and cord foundation.

example of laid embroidery combined with embroidery on a cord foundation. This method requires less metal thread than piqué embroidery, because, as we have explained above, these threads remain always on the right side of the work.

The three-fold leaves are worked in silver with laid threads, used double; the method of working is shown in fig. 331. This type of embroidery is worked over cardboard molds, which the worker can prepare herself. The design is traced onto white cardboard and cut out with a very sharp knife, so that the edges shall be smooth; then it is pasted onto the material with strong glue. Where the embroidery is to be worked in gold thread, the cardboard should be yellow. If strips of cardboard of some length are needed, they should be further secured by single overcast stitches at intervals along the strip; smaller molds—those, for instance, for the small leaves—are held by a stitch at the point of the leaf; see figs. 331 and 332.

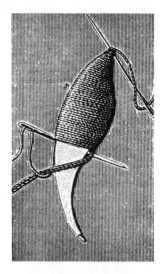

Fig. 331. Leaf worked in laid embroidery with double thread, for the motif in fig. 330.

The silver thread is wound double onto the spindle; then a large needle is threaded with Alsa, which is further strengthened by waxing. The silver thread and the Alsa having been fastened on at the point of the leaf, the embroidery is begun by laying the silver threads across the mold; they are secured at the opposite side by a back stitch, then again passed—always by means of the spindle— back to the first edge and again secured by a back stitch. This process is continued until the mold is entirely covered, as shown in fig. 331. The small, fine points are worked in flat stitch, as is also shown in the illustration. Where the leaves touch a stem, these points are not completed until the stem has been worked, to enable the joining of leaf and stalk, worked in different styles, to be more easily concealed. In our example, the petals of the flowers are worked in fine gold thread, used in a single strand, and laid across molds cut out of yellow cardboard; see fig. 332.

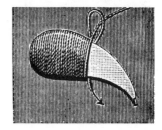

Fig. 332. Leaf worked in laid embroidery with single thread, for the motif in fig. 330.

The thick stems of the flowers and the leaves which spring from them are worked in coarse silver thread; the knot which unites the two sprays is of fine gold thread, used double, and worked over a foundation of cord. For this, before the gold thread embroidery is begun, the whole design is covered with horizontal stitches, separated one from another by a small space, and made with a thick twine or cord, over which the gold embroidery is subsequently worked. The method of placing the cord is shown in fig. 333; for this purpose, use DMC knotting cotton no. 15 in ecru, which should be carefully waxed to make it stiffer. It is then laid as shown in the illustration. When this has been done, the gold or silver thread is taken double, placed lengthwise over the cord, and caught down after every other cord with a back stitch in DMC Alsa no. 40 of the corresponding color, drawn very tight. When the end of the motif is reached, the thread is brought back; the stitches in the second row should alternate with those in the first. In order to cover the foundation properly, it is well to begin in the center and cover first one side, then the other; see also the explanatory illustration, fig. 334. In larger designs, charming grounds can be made by placing the back stitches in different ways.

Fig. 333.
Laying the cords for the motif
in fig. 330.

Fig. 334.
Method of securing the silver
threads over the cords
for the motif in fig. 330.

A single motif is often used to ornament small pincushions or blotters; repeated to form an all over design, it can be used for panels, church ornaments, banners, hangings, etc.

Border and Ground in Gold and Silver Embroidery, Chinese style, with Cord Foundation, Laid Threads, and Purl (figs. 335, 336, 337). This design, copied from a very rich Italian work of the seventeenth century, combines several types of gold embroidery and shows the varied effects of the different stitches.

The working of most of the stitches has already been explained; it remains only to describe the method of embroidering unpadded motifs with double thread, that is to say, the Chinese type of gold embroidery. The detail in fig. 336 shows a pointed leaf worked in this way. To make a neat point, the embroidery should be begun at one side of the leaf; the outer thread is taken right to the point, and the inner thread to a short distance from the point; then both threads are bent and brought back. The double threads are secured with stitches set at intervals, the length of the latter depending on the thickness of the threads. For these securing stitches DMC Alsa is used. The whole of the leaf is filled in this way, the securing stitches being set alternately in successive rows. When large motifs have to be filled, the design can be varied by means of different arrangements of the stitches.

Purl embroidery is rather more complicated. The motifs are first thickly

padded, in the way shown in fig. 328; then a very fine sewing needle is
threaded with DMC Alsa no. 40 and brought out close to the padded motif;

Fig. 335. Border with ground in gold and silver embroidery, Chinese style,
with cord foundation, laid threads, and purl.

the purl is then cut into short lengths corresponding to the width of the
motif to be covered. One of these lengths is threaded onto the needle, which
is inserted into the material on the other side of the motif and brought out

again on the first side, as shown in fig. 337. If the purl has been cut to the correct length, it will exactly cover the width of the motif. Those who are unaccustomed to this work will find some difficulty at first in cutting the pieces of purl to the exact lengths, but with a little practice it will soon be found quite easy.

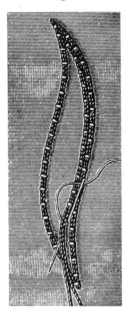

Fig. 336.
Method of filling a leaf in the ground in fig. 335.

In the border design in fig. 335, the scrolls are embroidered on a cord foundation in gold thread of medium thickness; the outer petals with the same thread, laid and used singly; the inner petal is covered with gold purl, and the two small hanging leaves with silver purl. The large leaves of the ground and the small light dots of the upper border are worked in coarse silver thread; the scrolls in coarse gold thread, in the Chinese manner; the small leaves are worked with laid threads in a single strand of gold thread of medium thickness.

The ornaments in relief, shown light in our illustration, are covered with silver purl. All the other lines and scrolls are embroidered with gold cord, invisibly secured with DMC Alsa.

We would recommend beginning with the parts to be embroidered in the Chinese manner; next should come those worked in laid embroidery and on cord foundation; next the cord embroidery; and last of all the purl embroidery, which is the most delicate part of the work.

Fig. 337.
Purl embroidery for the ground in fig. 335.

This large, handsome design is intended for church embroidery. The small border which edges it at the bottom can be used separately to trim articles of dress and furnishing.

Allover Design in Fancy Embroidery in Gold, with Pillow Lace and Leaf-shaped Spangles (fig. 338). The little rosettes composed of spangles are made first. They are made by fixing, first, the eight long spangles which form the outer circle, each one being secured by means of two stitches through the two holes pierced in the ends. It will be found easier to place these regularly if the two vertical ones are placed first, then the two horizontal ones, and finally the four diagonal ones; the small round spangle in the center is placed last.

Fig. 338. Allover design in fancy embroidery in gold, with pillow lace and leaf-shaped spangles.

When all the rosettes have been made, the picot-edged braid made of fine gold thread, which divides the ground into diamonds, is sewn down as invisibly as possible. It is advisable to tack on the braid first, to ensure that the lines shall be straight. Instructions for making this picot-edged braid will be found in the chapter ''Pillow Laces,'' fig. 1067; see also ''Needlework Trimmings,'' fig. 1120.

This design, being very easy to work, can be used for sofa cushions, veils, the fronts of dresses, and other articles of clothing.

Border in appliqué work, with cord outlines and ornamental stitches.

CHAPTER VIII

Appliqué Work

Appliqué work consists in laying pieces of one material on a foundation of a different material. This method of producing work of many colors was known as early as the middle ages, a time when the various materials for satin stitch embroidery now at our disposal were unobtainable.

The same term is also applied to a type of Persian embroidery from Recht, which is in reality a kind of incrustation. Designs of very complex outline are cut out and fitted into spaces cut in a foundation material to receive them. They are joined to this foundation by seams hidden by one or more rows of chain stitch. The latter stitch, worked in bright colors, is also used to emphasize the details of the encrusted designs. It is sometimes replaced by metal braids made of threads or narrow bands of gold or silver. The appliqué motifs are pasted to the foundation, then edged with cords sewn along the outlines, or with embroidery stitches which join the two layers of material. Gold and silver threads, spangles, and purl are sometimes used for the ornamental stitching and further enhance the effect of this kind of work.

We also give a reproduction in this chapter of a design in braid appliqué in which the design is made with braids of various widths instead of cutout material.

Appliqué work can also be done with the sewing machine. However, designs which are finished off with straight bands should be avoided as far as possible, as the mounting of these will present some difficulty to those who have not had much experience in this kind of work.

The process of securing the appliqués and surrounding them with braid or flat stitch embroidery is the same as when the work is done by hand. The finished appearance of the work done by machine is scarcely distinguishable from that done by hand.

Fabrics. Appliqué embroidery can be worked on silk, velvet, brocade, plush, linen, and leather. Since the materials used for the appliqués take the place of embroidery, they should be chosen to contrast as effectively as possible with the foundation. The effect of the embroidery can be further enhanced by the use of different kinds of fabric for the different parts of the design, as we shall show in the various examples we give.

Materials. As we have already pointed out, the appliqué materials are most frequently secured by means of cords, but outlines in flat stitch can also be used.

We recommend the use of the cord wheel, illustrated in fig. 1106, which will enable our readers to make the required cords in any thickness.

As materials for the cords (see the chapter "Needlework Trimmings" for the method of making cords and braids), a lightly twisted thread is used: DMC pearl cotton, DMC floss flax or flourishing thread, or DMC embroidery rayon. DMC Alsa is used for sewing on the cords, and for the ornamental stitches DMC Persian silk or DMC embroidery rayon. Silk and rayon are also used for outlines worked in flat stitch.

Preparatory Work. Most fabrics used for appliqué work need to be backed with very fine tissue paper before the work is begun. For this purpose, paste is made from wheat starch (this is the only kind that dries quickly enough). The paste is

Fig. 339.
Appliqué border, outlined with cord.

spread on the paper with a paintbrush, and any little lumps which may have been left in the paste are carefully removed. The paste should never contain more water than is necessary to ensure the perfect adherence of the material and the paper. It must never be moist enough for damp patches to appear on the former.

As soon as the paste has been evenly spread on the paper, the material is

Fig. 340. Allover design and border in appliqué work, with outlines in cord and ornamental stitching.

laid on the latter and gently smoothed down, following the direction of the warp, with a piece of clean linen, to expel any bubbles of air which might otherwise remain between the two and cause the material to bulge.

This first operation completed, the paper-backed material is laid on a straight, smooth piece of wood covered with several sheets of smooth paper. Several more sheets of paper are laid on top, and finally another board is placed over the whole and weighted with stones or other heavy objects. The material is left in this press until it is quite dry.

In this way even quite delicate materials can be used for appliqué work. Velvet and plush will not be injured in any way; there is no need to fear that their pile will be crushed in the pressing.

While the materials are drying, the complete design is traced onto the material which is to be used as the foundation. On the paper-backed material, when it is dry, only those parts of the design which are to be applied are traced. They are then cut out with very sharp scissors, for in no circumstance must their edges be frayed or uneven.

The foundation, mounted in a frame, is laid on a board or table in such a way that only the material itself rests on it. The frame projects over all four sides. The detached, cutout motifs are then covered on the wrong side with a second layer of paste and laid on the corresponding lines of the design. This second pasting should be done as quickly as possible, so that the whole can be pressed again under a board until it is dry.

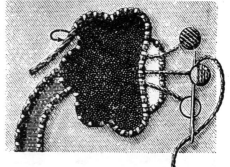

Fig. 341. Method of working a flower for the allover design and border in fig. 340.

Before the outlining of the appliqué motifs is begun, the edges of these latter are secured to the foundation with overcasting, which will subsequently be covered and hidden by the outlining.

The Outlining. The cords which outline the appliqué parts are secured along the edges by invisible stitches on the surface—the needle being passed between the twists of the cord—(see the chapter "Gold Embroidery," fig. 324), or by visible overcasting in a bright color. In either case, the cord should overlap the cut edges sufficiently to cover them completely and prevent them from eventually becoming frayed. A piece of appliqué work in which this occurs is badly made.

If the design is to be outlined with embroidery stitches, the needle must be brought out close to the cut edge, and the stitch carried a fraction of an inch toward the middle of the appliqué.

Appliqué Border, Outlined with Cord (fig. 339). Our illustration, fig. 339, shows an example of Spanish origin in which the foundation and the appliqué present the same design. The foundation is of blue silk, the appliqué in old gold velvet outlined in umber cord, invisibly secured. Alongside this brown cord, to soften the transition to the blue silk, is laid a

Fig. 342. Appliqué border with cord outlines and ornamental stitches.

fine blue cord, secured with overcast stitches in DMC Alsa of the same shade.

The cords are made with the cord wheel. For the brown cord, two double threads are used, of DMC pearl cotton no. 5, DMC floss flax or flourishing thread no. 8, or DMC embroidery rayon no. 30, in umber. The threads are twisted first to the right, then to the left. The blue cords are made with three single threads of DMC pearl cotton no. 8, DMC floss flax or flourishing thread no. 16, or DMC embroidery rayon no. 60, and should also be twisted first to the right, then to the left.

This design is particularly suitable for trimming furniture, tablecloths, portieres, and panels of all kinds.

Allover Design and Border in Appliqué Work with Outlines in Cord and Ornamental Stitching (figs. 340 and 341). The foundation of this design is ivory satin; in the border, the two horizontal bands and the curved leaves are cut out of dark garnet-red velvet; the light-colored calyx of

Fig. 343. Method of outlining and ornamental
stitches for the border in fig. 342.

the flower is of snow white satin; the inner
part of the flower and the cross- shaped stem
are of grey-green silk. All the motifs are
outlined with cords secured visibly with
overcast stitches. The red velvet is outlined
with black cord; the white satin with cream
cord; and the green silk with green cord.

As for the allover design, all the appliqué
flowers are of garnet-red velvet with white
satin centers; the stems and the oval,
spindle-shaped figures are of green silk.

When all the cutout motifs have been
secured to the foundation with a few overcast stitches, the herringboning which fills
the centers of the oval figures and the
horizontal band which joins the stems of the
flowers are worked with DMC embroidery
rayon no. 60 in golden yellow. Then the
outlining in cord is begun, the cord being
secured with overcasting, also in yellow.

Finally, the stalks of the stamens are embroidered in DMC Persian silk in green,
and the stamens themselves in yellow silk;
see fig. 341. Here, as in the border, the red
velvet motifs are outlined in black, the
white in cream, and the green in green.

The cords are composed of two single
threads of DMC pearl cotton no. 5, twisted
first to the right, then to the left.

This design can be used for table covers

Fig. 344.
Narrow appliqué border with
outlines in flat stitch.

Fig. 345.
Method of outlining in flat stitch
for the border in fig. 344.

of all kinds; to save work, the border alone can be worked and added to a foundation of material. The ground alone can readily be adapted for the adornment of cushions, chair covers, etc.

Appliqué Border with Cord Outlines and Ornamental Stitches (figs. 342 and 343). In this design the appliqué motifs in white, yellow,

Fig. 346. Allover design in appliqué work, with outlines in back stitch.

and red satin stand out boldly against the ground of black velvet.

The outlining consists of golden yellow and ivory white cords, invisibly secured. These two shades can easily be distinguished in the illustration. The cord which outlines the figures is in its turn outlined with a full thread of DMC Persian silk in dark red, held down by overcast stitches, also in red, which helps to make the design stand out against the velvet; see fig. 343.

The wide stems, made of yellow satin, are ornamented with veinings of stem stitch worked in yellow silk; the large red leaves with veinings of red silk. The velvet ground is enriched by isolated stitches in DMC embroidery rayon no. 30 in golden yellow. The cords are made of DMC floss flax or flourishing thread no. 8, with three single threads, twisted first to the right, then to the left.

This border is suited for the trimming of church ornaments and articles of domestic furnishing. When the article to be embroidered is large, the border should be worked separately and then, when it is finished, applied to the article it is to trim.

Narrow Appliqué Border with Outlines in Flat Stitch (figs. 344 and 345). We have here an example in which the appliqué motifs are outlined in flat stitch. The foundation is of red velvet, the design in old gold satin.

When all the motifs have been invisibly secured, the outlining is worked in flat stitch, as shown in fig. 345. Care should be taken that the stitches are of the same length throughout the embroidery. The stem is embroidered in green and the leaves in red, in DMC Persian silk. When the outlines are completed, the veinings of the leaves, which are slightly padded, are worked.

The uses of this little border are very varied. It would be effective as a trimming on blotters, glove boxes, magazine covers, etc.

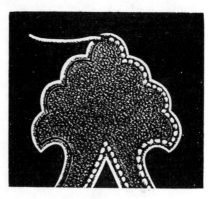

Fig. 347.
Detail of back stitch outlining for the allover design in fig. 346.

Allover Design in Appliqué Work, with Outlines in Back Stitch (figs. 346 and 347). In this example we have a new variety of appliqué work. The foundation is emerald green velvet and the appliqué of yellow leather, secured with back stitching in glossy green thread.

The design is traced onto yellow (Danish) leather, and the motifs are cut out a little way beyond the outlines. The design is then traced onto the velvet and the leather motifs are pasted to it.

DMC pearl cotton no. 8 in scarab green is used for the back stitch outlines, the working of which is shown in fig. 347.

The combination of velvet and leather in this work makes it particularly suitable for the seats of chairs and stools; if suede leather is used, it could be adapted to small sachets and blotters.

Cloth in Braid Appliqué (figs. 348 and 349). This design was copied from an eighteenth century saddlecloth. The motifs of the design are all

Fig. 348. Cloth in braid appliqué.

made with DMC superfine braid in four different widths, in ecru.

When the design has been traced onto pink linen, the wide braids are tacked over the whole cloth—the narrow braids need no tacking—then sewn down carefully with back stitching, which should be as invisible as possible, in DMC Alsatian sewing cotton no. 150. Where the design is rounded, the outer edge of the braid is sewn down first; then the inner edge

Fig. 349. Detail of the border in fig. 348.

is gathered to the required extent and sewn down in its turn; see also the chapter, "Embroidery on Linen," fig. 277.

At the corners, a fold is made in the braid at the spot indicated by the design, and secured with a few stitches, as has been explained in the description of embroidery with braid outlines, in the chapter, "Embroidery on Linen."

The large filled spaces in the border are divided into squares with narrow braid and each square is filled with a small chain stitch star. In the sprays in the center, the large leaves have veins in flat stitch, while the small leaves and the centers of the flowers are ornamented with French knots worked in DMC pearl cotton no. 3 in ecru.

So that the effect of this kind of embroidery may be better seen, we give, in addition to the small illustration of the whole cloth, a part of the border, from which the finished work can easily be judged.

Border of iris design in petit point.

CHAPTER IX
Tapestry

Tapestry is of very ancient origin and has been a favorite feminine occupation from the earliest times. Under the heading of tapestry are included nowadays all kinds of embroidery on counted threads in which the fabric of the foundation is entirely covered by the stitches. There is a great variety of such work, among them all kinds of embroidery on canvas in cross stitch, petit point, gobelin stitch, long or flat stitch; Florentine and Hungarian embroidery; as well as embroidery in knotted stitch, knitting stitch, etc.

We will begin this chapter with a few notes on the fabrics and threads to be used, after which we will review the various tapestry stitches, explaining how they are worked. At the end of the chapter, we will give a few simple designs for grounds, borders, and rugs.

Fabrics. The fabric on which tapestry is worked is called canvas. There are two different kinds: plan or congress canvas, which is woven with single threads; and Penelope canvas, in which the threads are laid two by two. These two kinds of canvas are manufactured in varying degrees of coarseness.

The choice of canvas will depend on the stitch to be worked; the majority of stitches, however, can be worked on either kind. For rugs made with knotted stitches, a linen foundation is to be preferred to canvas, as the soft threads of linen can be drawn together more easily than those of canvas, which are always stiff.

Preparatory Work. Tapestry can be worked either in a frame or in the hand; in the latter case, the canvas should be weighted down to prevent its pulling out of shape. Before the work is begun, a framework should be marked out on the canvas; the instructions for this will be found in the chapter ''Embroidery on Linen''; see fig. 166.

Needles. The needles used for tapestry are long, strong, and blunt-ended, with a long-shaped eye wide enough to allow them to be threaded easily. They can be obtained at all needlework shops, where they are sold under the name of tapestry or crewel needles.

Materials. For a long time, wool and silk were the only materials used in tapestry work, but with the great progress that has been made in the manufacture and dyeing of cotton threads, these latter have come to play a large part in this type of needlework. Silk, unrivalled for the production of rich embroidery, is hardly to be recommended for articles which are destined for frequent and long use; its delicate and fragile nature renders it too susceptible to the ravages of time and wear. Wool, though more durable than silk, has the great disadvantage of harboring destructive moths, to which cotton, as well as being cheaper than silk, is immune. Cotton, moreover, when faded by long use, can be restored to its first freshness by processes which are often very simple.

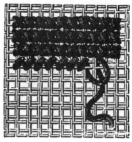

Fig. 350.
Plain cross stitch.

Among cotton threads which lend themselves to tapestry work, we particularly recommend DMC special stranded cotton and DMC pearl cotton. These are remarkable for their suppleness and brilliancy, and are also obtainable in shaded colors. DMC special stranded cotton is a loosely twisted thread which can be used with advantage to replace wool or silk where large, even surfaces are to be produced. With DMC pearl cotton nos. 1,3, 5, and 8, fine relief effects are obtained, and it is to be preferred when the stitch used is one in which several threads cross each other.

Fig. 351.
Half cross stitch.

In addition to these two varieties of cotton thread, which can in many cases replace wool and silk with advantage, we may mention for simpler pieces of work DMC embroidery twist, DMC floss flax or flourishing thread, and DMC special quality embroidery cotton. For rich embroideries worked entirely in silk, DMC embroidery rayon or DMC Persian silk can be used. Whatever the work, the threads must be carefully chosen so that the stitches made with them will entirely cover the canvas, the threads of which must never be visible between the rows of stitches.

Fig. 352.
Straight or upright
gobelin stitch.

Plain Cross Stitch (fig. 350). Plain cross stitch, also called marking stitch, is the basis of all tapestry stitches. It is worked in two journeys. In the first, the thread is carried diagonally over one double thread of the canvas, from left to right, then vertically under one transverse double thread. Returning, the same stitch is made from right to left. These crossed threads form the cross stitch.

Fig. 353.
Oblique gobelin stitch on congress canvas.

Half Cross Stitch (fig. 351). When the thread is too thick in proportion to the canvas to make the complete cross stitch, the thread is carried from right to left over the whole line to be covered by the stitches, and over this thread the half cross stitch is worked. This process of laying threads across the lines to be worked is called tramming, and is usually found in tapestry sold prepared for working.

Straight or Upright Gobelin Stitch (fig. 352). This stitch is always worked in horizontal rows. The thread is carried vertically over two threads of the canvas and one thread is left between the stitches.

Fig. 354.
Oblique gobelin stitch on Penelope canvas.

Oblique Gobelin Stitch (figs. 353 and 354). On congress canvas, oblique gobelin stitch is worked over one vertical and two horizontal threads. When the work is mounted in a frame, the stitch can be worked backward and forward, but when it is not mounted, the work must be turned upsidedown and the needle brought out behind the last stitch. On Penelope canvas, this stitch requires a rather thicker needle, which will separate the canvas threads well and prevent the embroidery thread from fraying.

Gobelin stitch, straight or oblique, is particularly suitable for the reproduction of old gobelin tapestries and enables copies to be made which very closely resemble the old originals.

Fig. 355.
Rep or Aubusson stitch on Penelope canvas.

Rep or Aubusson Stitch (fig. 355). This stitch produces a ribbed effect in imitation of rep. It is worked in vertical lines over one transverse thread and two vertical threads.

Petit Point or Tent Stitch (fig. 356). This stitch is simply the first half of cross stitch, worked over a single thread. The illustration shows the working of a return row from right to left. If the stitches are to be very even, the thread must be carried under two threads of the canvas on the wrong side.

Petit point is usually worked in combination with other stitches. Thus petit point will be used for flowers and delicate leaves or for flesh in figure compositions while the rest of the design is worked in cross stitch or other similar stitches.

Fig. 356.
Petit point or tent stitch.

Fig. 358.
Encroaching gobelin stitch.

Fig. 360.
Oblong cross stitch with back stitch.

Wide Gobelin Stitch (fig. 357). Two vertical and three horizontal threads are covered. The successive stitches advance one thread of the canvas.

Encroaching Gobelin Stitch (fig. 358). For filling fairly extensive spaces, we recommend this stitch, which consists of oblique stitches over five horizontal threads and one vertical thread, with one thread between the stitches.

The second row is begun only four threads below the first, so that the stitches overlap those of the first row by one thread and so form encroaching stitches.

Oblong Cross Stitch (fig. 359). For this stitch, cross stitches are worked over one and two double

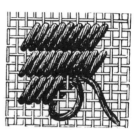

Fig. 357.
Wide gobelin stitch.

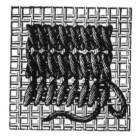

Fig. 359.
Oblong cross stitch.

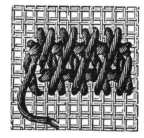

Fig. 361.
Double stitch.

threads or two and four single threads. It is to be recommended for filling large spaces, since, covering as it does double the number of threads of the canvas, it requires only half the time needed for ordinary cross stitch.

It can be successfully varied by alternating the stitches, that is to say setting the second stitch one thread higher and returning to the original level on the next and so on.

Oblong Cross Stitch with Back Stitch (fig. 360). After making a cross stitch according to the instructions for oblong cross stitch (fig. 359), that is to say over four threads in height and two in width, a back stitch is made horizontally across the center of the cross, over two threads of the canvas.

Fig. 362.
Rice stitch or crossed corners cross stitch.

Double Stitch (fig. 361). An ordinary cross stitch is made over every other intersection of the threads. Then a second row of stitches is made between the stitches of the first row but over one and three double threads, so that each stitch of this row extends beyond those of the first row at both top and bottom. In the succeeding rows, a normal stitch is placed below a long stitch and vice versa.

Rice Stitch or Crossed Corners Cross Stitch (fig. 362). The whole of the space to be filled is first covered with large cross stitches over four and four threads, and then only the crossing of the corners is done. This consists of stitches crossing the four arms of the cross stitch and meeting in the space between the stitches, forming another cross. The large crosses are worked in a fairly coarse thread and the second series of stitches in a finer thread of a different color.

Fig. 363.
Reversed cross stitch.

Reversed Cross Stitch (fig. 363). This consists of alternated diagonal and upright cross stitches. The first row is worked from left to right: the thread is carried down over four vertical threads and between two horizontal threads, as shown in the last row of stitches in the illustration. On the return journey the first threads are crosses and the thread is passed, in a straight line, under two threads of the canvas. In the third and fourth journeys, the stitches are set the opposite way from the first stitches. The second set of stitches is worked in gold thread. Instead of metal thread, DMC embroidery rayon in golden yellow can be used.

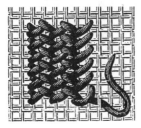

Fig. 364.
Plaited stitch on canvas.

Plaited Stitch on Canvas (fig. 364). A certain degree of care is required in the working of this stitch if it is to be worked backward and forward. Instead, it will be found easier to bring the thread back each time to the starting point. The thread is passed over four vertical threads and down over two horizontal threads, and under two threads from right to left, as can be seen in the illustration.

Fern Stitch (fig. 365). This stitch is worked in successive rows. The thread is passed over two double threads each way of the canvas, then from right to left, horizontally, under the middle pair of threads at the bottom. It is then passed obliquely up to the right over two double threads; see also the illustration.

Fig. 365.
Fern stitch.

Fig. 366.
Stem stitch on canvas.

Stem Stitch on Canvas (fig. 366). The thread is passed obliquely over two or four threads each way of the canvas, and brought back, under one or two threads, above the starting point of the first stitch. The second row is worked in the opposite direction. When all the rows are completed, a line of back stitching in a different color is added between the rows.

Fig. 367.
Fishbone stitch on canvas.

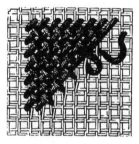

Fig. 368.
Web stitch.

Fishbone Stitch on Canvas (fig. 367). This stitch differs from the previous one in that the thread is passed

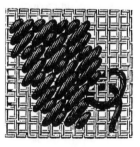

Fig. 369.
Cashmere stitch.

Fig. 370.
Florentine mosaic stitch.

over three and six threads and held by a back stitch over the last intersection of the canvas threads. The back stitches are worked according to the slope of the long stitches, sometimes from left to right and sometimes from right to left.

Web Stitch (fig. 368). A diagonal thread is first laid across the number of threads of canvas to be covered; these threads are then covered with overcast stitches. When this stitch is worked on Penelope canvas, the needle is passed in and out between the double threads. In the succeeding rows, the stitches are made to alternate with those of the preceding row, thus giving the embroidered surface the appearance of material laid diagonally.

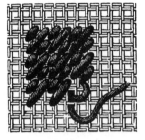

Fig. 371.
Hungarian mosaic stitch.

Cashmere Stitch (fig. 369). This fabric is imitated in tapestry by series of stitches, each consisting of one stitch over one intersection and two stitches over two intersections of the canvas, taken diagonally.

Florentine Mosaic Stitch (fig. 370). This stitch is worked in diagonal lines, passing alternately over one and two double threads of the canvas.

Hungarian Mosaic Stitch (fig. 371). The first row of this stitch consists of alternately one short and one long stitch, worked diagonally. In the second row, the design is completed by the addition of a second short stitch. These two rows are repeated until the space is filled.

Fig. 372.
Hungarian stitch.

Hungarian Stitch (fig. 372). To make the working of this stitch quite clear, we have illustrated it in two shades, but when it is used as a filling it should be worked in a single shade only. It is worked in horizontal rows, encroaching on each other so that the fabric is entirely covered.

The first stitch passes vertically over two threads; the next over four, extending one thread farther at the top and bottom than the first; the third passes over the same two threads as the first. A space of two threads is then left, and a second group of three stitches made, and so on. The illustration shows how, in the second row, the long stitch of each group is set exactly between two groups of the previous row, so that all the stitches touch each other.

Fig. 373.
Renaissance stitch.

Renaissance Stitch (fig. 373). This stitch is to be recommended for large pieces of work.

The work is begun with a horizontal stitch over two double threads, held at the left and in the middle by a vertical back stitch over one double thread.

The working thread is then carried down to the next double thread of the canvas below and a second horizontal stitch is made, held by two back stitches. This series of stitches corresponds to one square of a squared

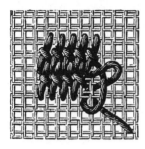

Fig. 374.
Knotted stitch on canvas.

design (tapestry type). To make each series of stitches stand out clearly, we have shown them in two different shades.

Knotted Stitch on Canvas (fig. 374). The thread is carried over two vertical and six horizontal threads; then the needle is passed vertically down and brought out four threads lower down. It is then inserted two threads higher up and behind the stitch just made, over the middle threads. It is then brought down to begin the next long stitch.

Each succeeding row is begun four threads below the previous one, upon which it encroaches by two threads.

Double or Smyrna Cross Stitch (fig. 375). A plain cross stitch is first made over four threads in width and height; an

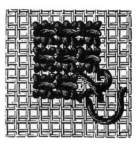

Fig. 375. Double or Smyrna cross stitch.

Fig. 377. French stitch.
First stitches to the left.

Fig. 379. French stitch.
Series of stitches completed.

Fig. 376.
Star stitch.

Fig. 378. French stitch.
Stitches to the right.

upright cross stitch is then made over it. The same stitch can also be worked over six or eight threads; when it is worked over more than four threads, the number of stitches is increased in proportion.

Star Stitch (fig. 376). Each little star is composed of eight stitches meeting in a single center. The star is begun with a stitch over one double thread slanting down from right to left; the needle is then passed straight up under the double thread and a vertical stitch is made on the right side of the work. The next stitch slants down from the left-hand corner, the next is horizontal, and so on until the star is complete. To make sure the stars are regular, they should be begun at the same point and worked in the same direction.

Fig. 380.
Parisian stitch.

Star stitch is also used singly as a powdering for backgrounds; see figs. 858, 861, 862, and 865 in the chapter, "Embroidered Laces."

French Stitch (figs. 377, 378, 379). The needle is brought through from the wrong to the right side and passed up over four single or two double threads. It is then passed to the left under one double thread (see fig. 377) and brought back to the space covered by the first stitch, where it is reinserted in the middle of the four threads and passed down to re-emerge alongside the first stitch. A stitch is then made to the right, similar to the one just made to the left.

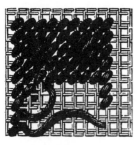

Fig. 381.
Greek stitch.

When a stitch has been completed, the needle is passed obliquely down under one thread (see fig. 378) for the next stitch. The whole design is worked in diagonal lines.

Parisian Stitch (fig. 380). This stitch, though usually worked on silk canvas, can also be used on various cotton and line materials. It lends itself admirably to filling all kinds of work and is particularly suitable where the material of the foundation is to be left visible between the stitches, as fig. 380 shows. The stitches are carried over one and three double threads, or two and six single threads.

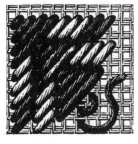

Fig. 382.
Scottish stitch.

Greek Stitch (fig. 381). The stitch called Greek differs from plain cross stitch in the slope of the stitches and the way in which they are begun. The first stitch is worked up from left to right over two double threads; the needle is brought back horizontally toward the left on the wrong side under two double threads; then a second oblique stitch is made down to complete the cross stitch, from left to right over four vertical and two horizontal double threads. The needle is then passed horizontally under two double threads to the left. The next stitch is worked like the first.

There are two ways of arranging the successive rows of this stitch. They can be set so that the short stitches of one row touch the long stitches of the row above, or so that the short stitches touch the short. The former style is usually found in Slavonic embroideries, whereas the latter is to be found in many Greek embroideries.

A coarse thread is preferable to a fine one for this stitch, as its effectiveness depends on the material being completely covered.

Scottish Stitch (fig. 382). This stitch is made up of squares composed of diagonal stitches over one, two, three, two, and one successive double threads, separated from each other by a row of half cross stitches.

Moorish Stitch (fig. 383). Instead of being surrounded on all four sides with a framing of small stitches, as in the previous stitch, the squares follow each other in an unbroken diagonal line, forming a succession of steps. Half cross stitches over one double thread separate the lines of squares.

Fig. 383.
Moorish stitch.

Oriental Stitch (fig. 384). Four stitches are made, the first of which passes over one intersection of the threads of the canvas, the second over two intersections, the third over three, and the fourth over four. These four stitches form triangles placed one above the other. The empty spaces at the edge of the rows are filled with slanting stitches.

Fig. 384.
Oriental stitch.

Shell Stitch (fig. 385). For this stitch the thread is passed four times vertically over six double threads of the canvas, leaving one double thread between the stitches. After the fourth stitch, the needle is brought out between the third and fourth horizontal double threads (that is to say, halfway up the long stitches) and between the second and third vertical threads. A back stitch is then made over one double thread and all four long stitches so as to draw the latter together, giving them the appearance of a sheaf of threads in drawn thread work.

Fig. 385.
Shell stitch.

A thread of a contrasting color is threaded spirally twice through the back stitches to form the shells over the stitches beneath. Horizontal back stitches over two double threads fill the space between the rows of long stitches that form the groundwork.

Jacquard Stitch (fig. 386). When large plain surfaces are to be covered, it is as well to choose a stitch which, while presenting an even surface, at the same time forms a pattern of itself. Jacquard stitch—and the stitches which follow—are charming stitches which give the embroidery the appearance of a brocaded material.

The first row consists of six oblique stitches down and six across, worked over two double threads. The second row consists of the same number of stitches arranged in the same way, but worked over one double thread only.

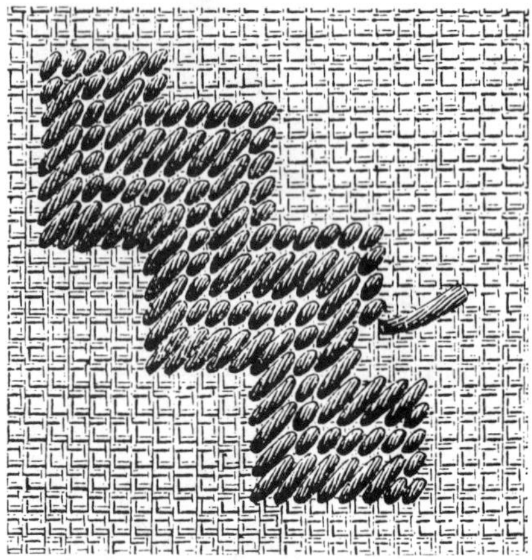

Byzantine Stitch (fig. 387). The rows in this stitch have the same number of stitches as in Jacquard stitch, arranged in the same way, the only difference being that the stitches of both rows are worked over two double or four single threads.

Milanese Stitch (fig. 388). This delightful ground is composed of little triangles consisting of four stitches and set opposite ways in alternate rows. The stitches are worked in diagonal rows. The first row is worked down and consists of alternate back stitches over one and four intersections of the canvas; the second row, worked up, consists of alternate back stitches over three and two intersections; the third, down, alternately over three and two intersections; the fourth, up, alternately over one and four intersections. In the next row the long stitch is placed next to the short stitch of the preceding row, and the short stitch next to the long.

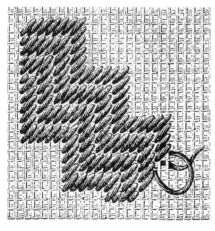

Fig. 386. Jacquard stitch.

Fig. 387. Byzantine stitch.

Velvet Stitch, With Loops Cut and Uncut (fig. 389). This stitch, which can be used to imitate oriental carpets, is composed of loops, each held in place by a cross stitch. The loops can be made more easily and more evenly if a gauge of bone or wood is used.

The method of working this simple stitch is clearly shown in the illustration. It can be varied, if preferred, by cutting the loops, which gives the embroidery the appearance of velvet. In the illustration only the central loops have been cut, for both styles can be used in the same piece of work. Thus the design shown in fig. 414 and 415 can be carried out in cut and uncut velvet stitch, the loops of the inner part being left intact and those of the border cut.

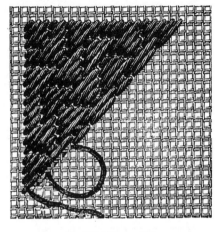

Fig. 388. Milanese stitch.

Tapestry Grounds. We will now give explanations of the stitches in a little series of grounds which can be used when large surfaces are to be filled. These grounds are usually worked in one color or in two shades of the same color, according to the design in which the ground is to be used.

As materials, a floss or lightly twisted thread can be used; the choice will depend on the stitch to be worked. We recommend once more DMC special stranded cotton, DMC floss flax or flourishing thread, DMC pearl cotton, DMC embroidery twist, DMC embroidery rayon, or DMC Persian silk.

Ground of Zigzag Lines Worked in Flat Stitch (fig. 390). This design is composed of zigzag lines. The wide bands are worked over six threads of the material, the narrow bands over two threads. Each line requires nine flat stitches, placed diagonally. When this ground is worked in two shades, the lighter should be used for the wide bands, the darker for the narrow bands.

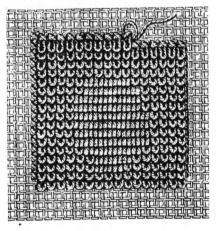

Fig. 389. Velvet stitch, with loops cut and uncut.

Ground of Vertical Bands Worked in Flat Stitch and Plait Stitch (fig. 391). The flat stitch bands require twelve threads of the material. Each

Fig. 390. Ground of zigzag lines worked in flat stitch.

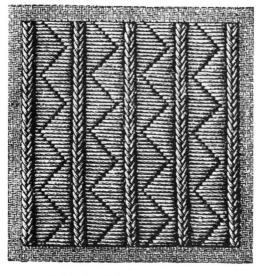

Fig. 391. Ground of vertical bands worked in
flat stitch and plait stitch.

band is composed of two rows of horizontal stitches, forming a zigzag line, the shortest stitch covering two threads of the material, the longest ten. The plait stitch requires three threads in width, but each stitch covers only two threads in height.

Ground of Vertical Bands Worked in Fishbone Stitch and Petit Point (Tent Stitch) (fig. 392). The light-colored bands consist of a half row of fishbone stitch worked over four threads in width and two in height. The dark bands which separate them are worked in petit point over one thread of the material.

Diagonal Ground Worked in Flat Stitch and Petit Point (Tent Stitch) (fig. 393). The work is begun with the dark zigzag lines in petit point over one thread of the material. When the dark lines are completed, the ground is filled in with diagonal flat stitches, the shortest of which is worked over two threads of the material and the longest over six.

Checkerboard Ground Worked in Flat Stitch (fig. 394). Each square in this design requires nine flat stitches, the shortest of which is worked over one thread, the longest—the middle one—over five threads of the material. The illustration shows clearly how the shades are arranged.

Ground of Vertical Bands Worked in Stem Stitch (Canvas) and Plait Stitch (fig. 395). The stem stitch is worked over eight threads in width and three in height; the plait stitch requires two threads in width and height. We advise the use of the lighter shade for the wide stem stitch bands and the dark for the plait stitch.

Ground Worked in Hungarian Mosaic Stitch (fig. 396). This simple little ground is particularly suitable for adorning small articles made by children. It is worked in Hungarian mosaic stitch (see fig. 371). The triangles are in bright green, the dark spots in deep red, and the ground in brown.

Ground in Hungarian Stitch (fig. 397). This

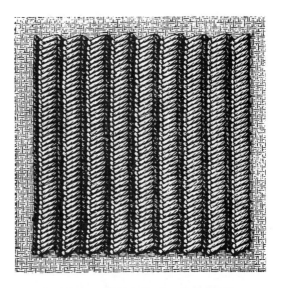

Fig. 392. Ground of vertical bands worked in fishbone stitch and petit point (tent stitch).

Fig. 393. Diagonal ground worked in flat stitch and petit point (tent stitch).

design is worked in Hungarian stitch, which has been shown in fig. 372. As for the arrangement of the colors, the interlacing figures are embroidered in green and pale yellow, the ground in red.

Fig. 394. Checkerboard ground worked in flat stitch.

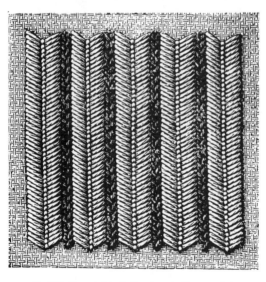

Fig. 395. Ground of vertical bands worked in stem stitch
(canvas) and plait stitch.

Florentine Stitch. This kind of embroidery, in which each motif of the design is worked in a single color in a whole range of shades, is known as Florentine work.

The four designs which follow—which are distinguished by the richness of their coloring—can be used for all kinds of cushions, for which they can take the place of colored fabrics. They should be worked with a very loosely twisted thread, such as DMC Persian silk, DMC embroidery rayon, DMC special stranded cotton, DMC embroidery twist, or DMC floss flax or flourishing thread.

Ground in Florentine stitch (fig. 398). The pointed figures are begun with the five black stitches, which pass up over four threads of the canvas. To these five stitches are then added five rows in color— one series of red and one series of brown— in which the number of stitches is always increased by two in each row. The figure is completed by three stitches in cream at the point.

Ground in Florentine stitch (fig. 399). The slanting lines which intersect the whole design and frame the black diamonds are worked in red; the triangles adjoining the diamonds are worked in three shades of green; the background is in cream. All the stitches pass vertically over four threads of the material.

Ground in Florentine stitch (fig. 400). The dark lines which outline the motifs are worked in black, with stitches

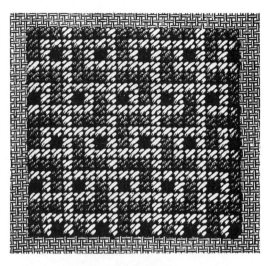

Fig. 396. Ground worked in Hungarian mosaic stitch.

Fig. 397. Ground in Hungarian stitch.

passing vertically over four threads of the material. The filling of the motifs is done alternately with four shades of brown and four shades of blue.

Fig. 398. Ground in Florentine stitch.

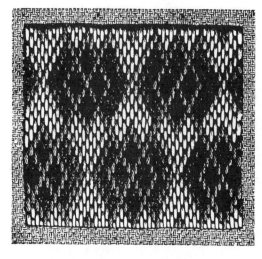

Fig. 399. Ground in Florentine stitch.

Ground in Florentine stitch (fig. 401). The horizontal line in black consists of alternately one stitch passing over eight threads and three stitches passing over two threads. Above this black line are worked four rows in successive shades of green, and below it three rows in successive shades of pink, so that the palest shades meet in the middle.

Allover Design in Medieval Embroidery Worked in Alternating Flat Stitch (figs. 402 and 403). The arrangement of this design, with its naive birds and little trees, is an indication of its age; it comes from a fourteenth century tapestry.

The embroidery is worked on congress canvas in floss silk, with vertical stitches over four threads of the material worked in horizontal rows, as is shown in the explanatory illustration, fig. 403.

The little tree between the birds is embroidered first, in bright green; then come the birds, in violet, and the small dark flowers, in indigo. The light-colored octogons are filled in with light brown; the rest of the background is worked in geranium red.

Modern Allover Tapestry Design Worked in Half Cross Stitch (fig. 404). The scope of this volume does not allow us to devote as much space to this chapter as we might have wished. We would have liked to present some interesting modern designs in the style of the one shown in fig. 404. Conventional flowers and leaves are the basis of this type of design and are particularly suited to tapestry work in half cross stitch and petit point.

Border in Petit Point (fig. 405). This border, composed of campion, open and in bud, is worked entirely in petit point (see fig. 356) with DMC pearl cotton; its execution therefore presents no difficulties.

The flowers are outlined in dark red and filled with pale pink; the calyx and stem are worked in green, while the background is a faded yellow shade.

This design is particularly well suited to the trimming of panels and portieres. It can also be used for trimming tablecloths, in which case it will be worked in

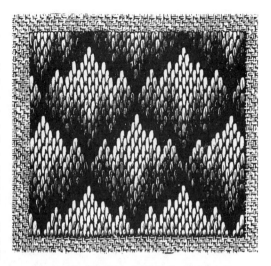

Fig. 400. Ground in Florentine stitch.

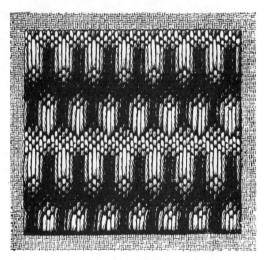

Fig. 401. Ground in Florentine stitch.

cross stitch on cream linen and the background will be left bare.

Embroideries Imitating Oriental Carpets. We give next several embroidery stitches by means of which it is possible to produce imitations of oriental carpets which can hardly be distinguished from the originals. Chain stitch and knitting stitch are used for the reproduction of Sumac carpets, while single knotted stitch and double knotted or Smyrna stitch serve for

Fig. 402. Allover design in medieval embroidery worked in alternating flat stitch.

Fig. 403. Detail of fig. 402.

copying carpets with a knotted pile.

Chain stitch on canvas (fig. 406). In certain museums, very interesting hangings, panels, figure compositions, etc., are to be found embroidered in chain stitch. This kind of stitch can be used to great advantage for designs in several colors, for it facilitates the blending of shades. The first stitch is always completed by the next, and the very form of the stitches helps to soften the contrast between different colors.

The explanation of the working of chain stitch given in fig. 256 has already made it clear that this stitch cannot be worked backward and forward like most other stitches. All the rows must be begun at the same end, and the thread must be fastened off as soon as the end of the row is reached. Nor can all the parts to be embroidered in one color be worked first, then another color, etc., as is done in cross stitch embroidery. Each line must be worked continuously to its end, a fresh thread being taken wherever there is a change of color.

Knitting stitch (fig. 407). This stitch is the embroidered counterpart

Fig. 404. Modern allover tapestry design worked in half cross stitch.

of Sumac rugs and is to be recommended for all designs requiring a large selection of colors. It has a great similarity to plaited Spanish stitch (figs. 190 and 191), and like the latter is worked in two rows. The stitches are set obliquely over two double threads in width and one-half double thread in height. The second row is set the opposite way to the first, which it completes. When a squared design is to be reproduced in this stitch, the left-

Fig. 405. Border in petit point.

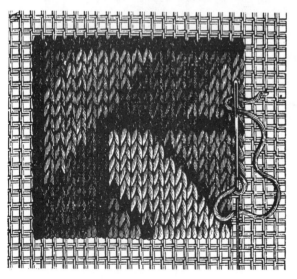

Fig. 406. Chain stitch on canvas.

hand point, where the two stitches meet, is to be considered the equivalent of one square.

For this stitch, it is advisable to provide oneself with a number of needles so that each color to be used in the design can be threaded separately. The same method should also be used for the chain stitch described above.

Single knotted stitch (figs. 408, 409, 410). Oriental carpets with a short knotted pile can be imitated by means of single knotted stitch, which is very similar to the single knotted stitch on linen, or candlewirk stitch, described in figs. 287 and 288. Here also each stitch consists of two short ends of thread, secured by a back stitch.

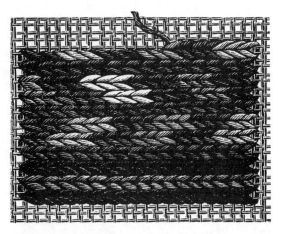

Fig. 407. Knitting stitch.

To economize thread and to facilitate the production of an even pile, a kind of gauge is used, which may terminate in a little blade at one end; the threads which are to form the loops to be cut are passed over this gauge. When a row of stitches has been completed, the gauge is withdrawn in such a way that the blade, if there is one, cuts the loops through the center as it passes. If the gauge is without a blade, the loops must be cut with the scissors.

Fig. 408.
Single knotted stitch, the knot open.

Fig. 409.
Single knotted stitch, the knot drawn tight.

In fig. 408 we show a single stitch, enlarged, not yet drawn tight; in fig. 409, a single stitch, drawn tight; while in fig. 410 we show several stitches worked over the gauge. As the illustrations show, each stitch requires a square of material

Fig. 410. Single knotted stitch.
A series of stitches worked over a gauge.

two threads in height and two in width.

Persian border worked in single knotted stitch (fig. 411). Our border, adapted from a seventeenth century Persian embroidery, has been worked in single knotted stitch. The depth of the pile is one-fifth of an inch.

The material used was DMC floss flax or flourishing thread no. 16, of which eight strands were used to make the stitches. The principal figures

Fig. 411. Persian border worked in single knotted stitch.

Fig. 412. Working of double knotted or Smyrna stitch.

are outlined alternately in red and cream, and filled with two shades of blue or red, with a yellow center; the indented leaves are worked in two shades of green and in light red. The dark green is also used for the connecting lines between the principal figures and the little flowers which form columns between them; the latter are outlined in blue and filled with red and yellow.

Fig. 413. Border in double knotted or Smyrna stitch.

The narrow borders at the top and bottom are outlined on the inner side with green and on the outer with yellow, and filled with red and cream; the background is deep purple.

Double knitted or Smyrna stitch (fig. 412). This stitch is used to imitate deep-piled oriental carpets. The method of working it is similar to that of double knotted stitch on linen (figs. 290 to 293). It is worked in horizontal rows, each stitch requiring four threads in width. Four horizontal threads are left between the rows. The method of working the stitch is clearly shown in fig. 412.

When a row of stitches has been completed, the loops must be carefully

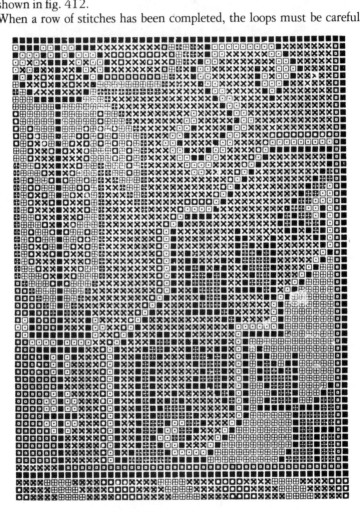

Fig. 414. Part of a design for a carpet.

cut to the required length. Any irregularities which may remain in the pile when the work is finished should be removed with the scissors.

Border in double knotted or Smyrna stitch (fig. 413). This border, which would lend itself particularly well to the edging of a bedside rug, is worked in double knotted stitch in six shades. The lightest shade is cream;

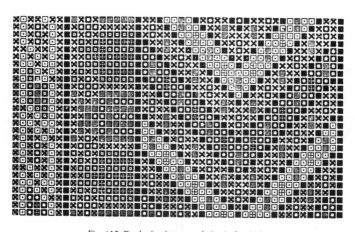

Fig. 415. Border for the carpet design in fig. 414.

the next lightest, hazelnut brown; the next, smoke grey; the medium shade, indigo; the dark shade, dark brown; and the darkest, black. The material to be used is DMC special stranded cotton no. 25, used five-fold, or ten strands of DMC Alsatia no. 30. The depth of the pile is in this case three-fifths of an inch.

Part of a design for a carpet (figs. 414 and 415). The limited space at our disposal prevents us from reproducing here more than a quarter of this carpet design. The colors should be chosen in the softest shades.

A black line separates the four quarters of the design. Of these four divisions, the upper right and lower left divisions are filled with blue, while the upper left section is to be worked according to the model in fig. 414. When the wide border shown in fig. 415 has been added, the narrow border is repeated, in shades of red, blue, and green. In this last part of the work, the background color of the various detached motifs can be very effectively varied.

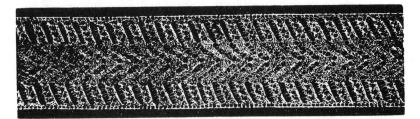

Insertion in openwork knitting.

CHAPTER X

Knitting

Of all the branches of needlework, knitting is one of the oldest and also one which has been carried to the highest degree of perfection; it is scarcely possible nowadays to invent new stitches or new patterns. Nevertheless there exist in some countries varieties of peasant work which offer very interesting and characteristic designs which are little known and can form the basis for new models.

Knitting has always been used principally for the making of stockings. However, there are countless other articles which can be knitted, such as vests, mufflers, scarves, rugs, blankets and coverlets, gloves, lace, etc.

Besides its usefulness, knitting is a pleasant pastime which can be picked up at odd moments and carried on while conversing and even while reading.

Knitting consists of loops or stitches made with a thread and two needles. Circular knitting is usually worked on four or five needles to ensure greater ease in handling the work. In recent times, circular needles or flexible metal, pointed at each end, have been introduced for this purpose and have the advantage of allowing the rows to be worked without a break. This kind of needle, which obviates all risk of dropping stitches at the ends of the needle, is also to be recommended for knitting wide strips. Since the loops which form the knitting are connected to each other in unbroken continuity, the finished work is very elastic and therefore particularly suitable for warm, close-fitting garments.

Needles. Knitting needles—or pins, as they are also called—whether they be made of steel, boxwood, or bone, should be of a thickness suited to the thread to be used.

Materials. Soft, silky threads, moderately twisted, are usually the best for knitted articles, but certain kinds of work require, on the contrary, a closely twisted thread.

For articles of clothing in which the knitting takes the place of a woven fabric, the most suitable threads are DMC Alsatian twist, DMC bell mark special quality knitting cotton, DMC Alsatia, DMC floss crochet, DMC knitting twist, DMC pearl cotton, and DMC special quality knitting cotton. We particularly recommend the last three articles.

Bedspreads and chair and sofa covers, as well as coarse lace edgings and insertions, can also be worked in DMC flax thread for knitting and crochet, DMC knitting twist, DMC crochet cotton, DMC shaded pearl cotton, and DMC knotting cotton. Fine lace work, on the other hand, requires a closely twisted thread, in which the openwork design will stand out well. For this purpose we cannot do better than recommend DMC Alsatian sewing cotton, DMC 6 cord cotton lace thread, DMC special quality crochet cotton, DMC 6 cord crochet cotton, DMC flax thread for knitting and crochet, DMC flax lace thread, and DMC Alsatia in fine numbers.

Position of the Hands in Knitting. The thread is passed over the little finger of the right hand, round which it is twisted, then brought under the two middle fingers and over the first finger, which should be held quite close to the work. The thumb and second finger hold the work. The role of the left hand is comparatively passive: it consists solely of pushing the stitches one by one forward toward the needle held in the right hand. The latter, by means of a small movement of the first finger, makes the stitches. In Germany the thread is laid over the left hand, which enables the movements of the hand to be made considerably more quickly.

In order to avoid making irregular stitches, the points of the needles should not be allowed to project more than a third to half an inch beyond the stitches. It is advisable to avoid all excessive movement of the arms when knitting, as the fatigue so caused makes it impossible to continue working for any length of time.

Casting On. The process of forming the series of loops on the needle which is to serve as the foundation for the work is called casting on.

There are four different ways of casting on:

(1) Crossed casting on, for which there are four different methods;

(2) Knitting on;

(3) Slipping on, which can be done in two different ways;

(4) Picot casting on.

(1) *Crossed casting on with a single thread* (fig. 416). This method, in which two ends of the thread are used, is also called double casting on.

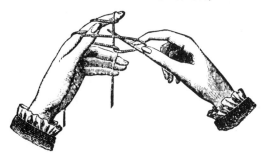

Fig. 416. Crossed casting on with a single thread.

thread is passed under the left hand and looped round the thumb so that the thread runs between the thumb and forefinger. A length of thread sufficient to make the required number of stitches is left hanging by the thumb. The needle is inserted up through the loop on the thumb and then passed, from right to left, under the part of the thread which lies between the thumb and forefinger; it is then brought back through the loop on the thumb, which is released and drawn tight against the needle. For the succeeding stitches the thread is placed so that the loose end is on the outside of the thumb. The needle is passed under the thread nearest to the point, and the stitch is completed in the same way as the first.

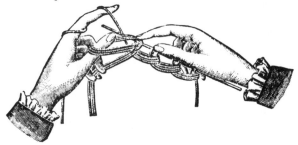

Fig. 417. Double crossed casting on with a triple thread.

This method of casting on is usually done on two needles held together in the right hand. One is withdrawn when all the stitches have been cast on, before the knitting off is begun, thus producing fairly loose stitches through which the needle passes easily when the first row is knitted.

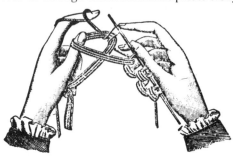

Fig. 418. Crossed casting on forming a chain.

Crossed casting on with a triple thread. The procedure in this case is the same as in the foregoing method, with this difference: a triple thread is prepared, which is passed through the loop formed by the returning thread. The single thread is then passed through the left hand and the triple thread over the thumb, as in fig. 416, and the stitches are made in the same way as before. The triple thread makes a chain at the bottom of the work.

Double crossed casting on with a triple thread (fig. 417). This method of casting on can be worked with a single or a triple thread. Our illustration shows the latter variation.

The first stitch is made as in the preceding methods, but the loop remains on the thumb and the needle is inserted into it a second time. The thread at the back is caught on the needle and brought through, and a second stitch is made on the needle. Only then is the loop allowed to slip off the thumb. By this method two stitches, very close together, are made in one operation.

Crossed casting on forming a chain (fig. 418). The first stitch is always made as shown in fig. 416. For the second stitch, and every second stitch following, the loose end of the thread is passed to the inside of the hand so that it lies between the thumb and forefinger; the other stitches are formed as explained in fig. 416.

(2) *Knitting on* (fig. 419). Begin by making a stitch as for crossed casting on, then transfer the needle to the left hand. Pass the thread round the little finger and over the first finger of the right hand, take a second needle in the right hand, and pass this needle through the front of the loop on the left-hand needle. Pass the thread over the right-hand needle and draw it back through the loop. Slip the loop thus made onto the left-hand needle,

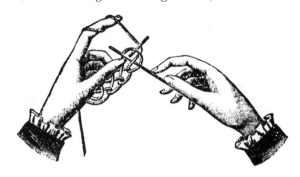

Fig. 419. Knitting on.

on which there will now be two loops. Pass the right-hand needle through this second loop, make another stitch in the same way, and continue thus until the required number of stitches has been cast on.

If the first row of stitches knitted after the casting on is worked into the front of the stitches, the edge will consist of a series of loose loops. This method will therefore

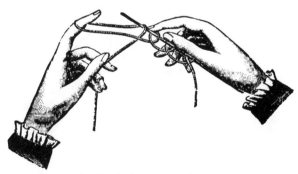

Fig. 420. Single casting on or slipping on.

be found suitable if the stitches of the edge are to be picked up later and knitted in the opposite direction. If, however, the cast-on edge is to form the outer edge of the article, the first row of stitches must be worked into the back of the cast-on stitches. In this way a close, firm edge will be formed.

(3) *Single casting on or slipping on* (fig. 420). Begin by making a single loop on the needle in the usual way. The thread is then held in the left hand, as in the German method of knitting, but passing only once round the first finger.

The needle is inserted up under the thread on the outside of the first finger; the finger is then withdrawn and the loop left on the needle. The thread is then placed on the finger again, the needle is once more passed under the thread, and so on.

Fig. 421. Single casting on or slipping on, with double loops.

Single casting on or slipping on, with double loops (fig. 421). Begin as usual by making a single loop. Pass the thread in the reverse direction over the first finger so that the crossing of the threads is between the hand and body, not on the far side of the finger. Pass the needle up under the inner thread and slip this thread onto the needle as a loop. Continue in this way, but passing the needle under the inner and outer thread alternately.

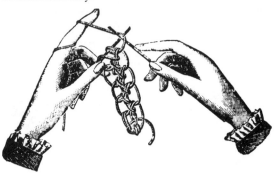

Fig. 422. Picot casting on.

This method of casting on is particularly suitable for lace patterns, in which it is often necessary to make several increases in succession.

(4) *Picot casting on* (fig. 422). Cast on two stitches according to the explanation accompanying fig. 416. Pass the thread over the right-hand needle, pass the latter from right to left through the first stitch, and slip the stitch off the left-hand needle onto the right-hand one; knit the second stitch, and pass the slipped stitch over the stitch just knitted. Turn the work, and continue repeating this process until the required length has been obtained. Then, along one side, pick up on a spare needle all the picots which have been formed and knit them like ordinary stitches.

This method can be varied in the following manner: after casting on two stitches, pass the thread over the needle and knit the two stitches together.

Stitches. By interlacing the threads in different ways, it is possible to produce different kinds of stitches. We shall describe those which are most commonly used.

Plain knitting (Stocking Stitch) (fig. 423). This stitch is the easiest to make and is the first taught to children. It is made as follows: the right-hand needle is passed down through the front part of the stitch on the left-

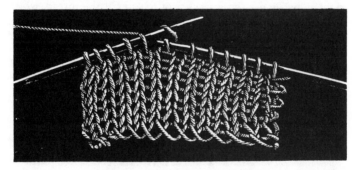

Fig. 423. Plain knitting (stocking stitch).

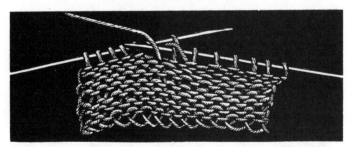

Fig. 424. Purling (stocking stitch, wrong side).

hand needle, the thread is passed from right to left round the right-hand needle, which is brought out again, bringing the thread with it, and the stitch on the left-hand needle is slipped off.

Plain knitting is used for making articles which are to have a smooth surface. The appearance of the wrong side is very different from that of the right side. The rows of knitting worked in this way produce vertical stripes resembling plaits.

Purling (fig. 424). Knitting can also be purposely worked wrong side out: this method is called purling. A purl stitch is made as follows: the thread is brought to the front of the work, the right-hand needle is inserted down behind the front thread of the first stitch on the left-hand needle, the thread is passed over and round the right-hand needle, which is withdrawn from the stitch on the left-hand needle, bringing a loop of thread with it, and the stitch through which the loop has been brought is slipped off the left-hand needle.

Purling is used in fancy knitting and to mark certain lines in plain knitting, such as, for instance, the seams of stockings. Purl stitches form horizontal stripes.

Knitting into the back of the stitches (fig. 425). The needle is inserted from right to left under the back part of the stitch; the thread, which lies

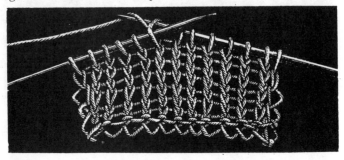

Fig. 425. Knitting into the back of the stitches.

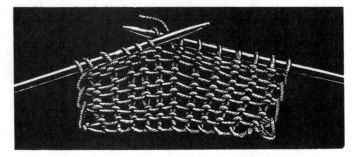

Fig. 426. Purling into the back of the stitches.

behind the needle, is passed from right to left over it and drawn out through the stitch. When stitches are knitted in this way, the threads are crossed instead of lying side by side as in plain knitting.

Purling into the back of the stitches (fig. 426). The needle is inserted up into the back part of the stitch, and the new stitch made in the same way as an ordinary purl stitch. This method is used only in certain openwork knitting designs.

Overs (fig. 427). These form openwork holes in plain knitting. They are used for making openwork designs, and also for increasing the number of stitches.

To make an over, the thread is passed over the needle; in the next round the loop thus made is knitted like an ordinary stitch. Each over increases by one the number of stitches on the needles. In pieces of work in which the number of stitches must remain the same throughout, one decrease must be made for every over. Overs can only be made in conjunction with other stitches.

Dot stitch (fig. 428). This stitch, which forms a raised spot in plain knitting, is made as follows: knit one stitch, but do not slip the left-hand stitch off the needle; place the stitch just made on the left-hand needle and knit it as a plain stitch.

Repeat this process four or five times, always knitting the new stitch into the same left-hand stitch. When there are five loops on the right-hand

Fig. 427. Overs.

Fig. 428. Dot stitch.

needle, slip the left-hand stitch off the needle and pass the first four loops on the right-hand needle over the last loop.

Chain edge. Bands and strips of knitting are usually worked with a chain or cable edge which, in addition to making the edge firmer and more even, provides a row of stitches that can be easily picked up.

There are two ways of doing this. In the first, the last stitch on the needle is knitted, the work is turned, and the needle inserted into the back of this same stitch, which is slipped onto the needle without being knitted; the thread lies behind the needle. The second method is as follows: all the stitches on the needle are knitted except the last; the thread is brought to the front of the work, as for a purl stitch; the last stitch is slipped onto the right-hand needle; the work is turned and the first stitch is knitted.

Names of stitches. The preceding stitches can be used to form many other varieties, which are usually described in instructions for knitted articles. We give here all the terms which will be used in the descriptions which follow, referring again to some of the stitches already described.

Single over (one openwork increase). This is shown in fig. 427, and consists of passing the thread once over the right-hand needle.

Double over (two openwork increases). The thread is passed twice over the right-hand needle.

Increase in plain knitting. The above method of increasing the number of stitches always makes an openwork hole in the work; it cannot, therefore, be used where the fabric of the knitting is to be close.

There are two methods of increasing without making a hole. The first is to knit two stitches into the same left-hand stitch: the first is knitted in the usual way into the front of the stitch, which is left on the needle until a second has been knitted into the back. The second method is to knit a stitch into the loop of thread between two stitches.

Single plain decrease. Insert the needle into two left-hand stitches at the same time, and knit them as one stitch. This method is used when the decreased stitch is to slope towards the right.

Single purl decrease. Purl two stitches together.

This method is used on the right side in plain knitting to emphasize the decrease, or on the wrong side when the knitting is worked backward and forward in a strip and the decrease is to slope to the right on the right side.

Double decrease on the right side. To give the effect of a neat point, this is worked as follows: slip the first stitch from the left-hand needle to the right, knit the next two stitches together, and pass the slipped stitch over the stitch just made.

Purl decrease with three or more stitches. It sometimes happens that more than two stitches are to be decreased at the same time. Instructions for purl decreases involving three or more stitches will be given as the occasion requires in the course of the instructions for each design.

Plain decrease worked into the back of the stitches. Insert the needle into the back of two stitches and knit them as one. This method is used when the decrease is to slope toward the left. A decrease sloping to the left can also be made by slipping one stitch onto the right-hand needle without knitting it, knitting the next stitch, and passing the slipped stitch over the stitch just knitted.

Purl decrease worked into the back of the stitches. Insert the needle into the back of two stitches and purl them as one. This method is used on the wrong side of knitting worked backward and forward in a strip, when the decrease is to slope to the left on the right side.

Crossing the stitches (cable stitch). This consists of knitting the stitches in the opposite order to that in which they are on the needle, beginning with those which are farthest to the left and ending with those which would normally have been knitted first. For this purpose a spare needle, pointed at both ends, is necessary. If four stitches are to be crossed, the first two are placed on the spare needle, which is then left hanging at the back of the work; the next two stitches are knitted, and then the two on the spare needle. The stitch thus produced is known as cable stitch.

Slipped stitches. Pass a stitch from the left-hand needle onto the right-hand needle without knitting it.

Passing the slipped stitch over. Slip one stitch, as described above; knit the next stitch; insert the left-hand needle into the slipped stitch and draw it over the stitch just knitted and off the needle. As already described, this process can be used for decreasing; two or three stitches can be passed over a knitted stitch in this way.

Casting off. To prevent stitches from coming undone, they are stopped, when the work is finished, in the following manner: Knit two stitches, pass the first over the second, knit the next stitch, pass the previous one over it, etc. This casting off should be neither too tight nor too loose: it should possess exactly the same degree of elasticity as the knitting that it finishes off. Sometimes, to form the toothed edge of lace, only a certain number of stitches will be cast off in this fashion.

Materials for Stockings. Stockings may be made of silk, wool, cotton, or flax thread. It is useless to dwell here on the respective merits of these various materials: the choice is a matter of individual taste. We can, however, recommend for this purpose, among cotton and flax threads, DMC bell mark knitting cotton, DMC flax thread for knitting and crochet, as well as brilliant threads such as DMC Alsatian twist, DMC special quality bell mark knitting cotton, and DMC Alsatia. To reinforce the heel and toe, DMC pearl cotton no. 12 should be used. An additional reason for recommending these articles is that they can be obtained in a great number of fast colors.

How to Make a Stocking. A stocking is composed of five parts: (1) the top, (2) the knee, (3) the leg, (4) the heel, and (5) the foot.

(1) The top may be ribbed, openwork, or double with a toothed edge, sometimes called ''dog-toothed''; see figs. 429 and 430.

(2) and (3) The knee and leg, that is to say, the part of the stocking between the top and the heel, are usually worked in plain knitting with a seam. Children's stockings and sports stockings, however, can be worked in fancy knitting or in ribbing.

(4) The heel is worked backward and forward in alternate rows of plain

and purl. It is shaped to the foot by means of decreases made at the end of the heel.

(5) The foot is worked in plain knitting. Starting from the heel, decreases are made to dispose of the superfluous stitches, then the required length to the toe is knitted, without a seam.

To ensure the correct proportions between the various parts of the stocking, the following rules should be borne in mind:

The top is never counted in measuring the length of the stocking. When the top is finished, a seam line is begun, consisting of one or two purl stitches at the beginning of the first needle of the round. Sometimes a narrow fancy design of purl stitches takes the place of a plain seam. This seam line marks the center of the back of the stocking.

For ordinary short socks, knit, after the last row of the top, a length equal to the width of the work.

For long stockings (above the knee), knit a length one and a half times the width of the folded stocking; then begin the decreases for the calf. After the seam, knit one stitch, slip the second, knit the third and pass the slipped stitch over. At the end of the same round, before the seam, knit together the second and third stitches from the end, knit the last stitch.

These decreases are at first repeated three or four times at intervals of twelve rows, then every eighth row until the length of the calf is one and a half times the width of the knee and its width only three-quarters that of the knee. For the lower part of the leg—the ankle—which is worked without decreasing, a length equal to half the width of the knee is knitted.

Before beginning the heel, the total number of stitches on all the needles, not counting the seam stitches, must be ascertained. On each of the two needles to the right and left of the seam, two stitches more than a quarter of the total number must be placed. For the heel to be a good fit, its length and width should be equal.

To strengthen the heels and toes of stockings, a thread of DMC pearl cotton no. 12 should be added to the thread used for the rest of the stocking.

For the instep, the part between heel and toe, the decreases should be continued until there are two stitches fewer on the needles than there were at the ankle. A piece is then knitted plain, of the same width as the ankle, until the toe is begun; the toe should be a quarter the total length of the foot.

This method of calculating the proportions of the stocking is the best way of arriving at a good shape; nevertheless we recommend counting the rows as well, to ensure perfect work.

The number of stitches to be cast on for a stocking will always depend on the thickness of the thread used.

The instructions which follow are based on the use of five needles; if only four are used, the distribution of the stitches on the needles will have to be rearranged accordingly. This will however, be found quite a simple matter.

Dog-toothed top (figs. 429 and 430). This is both the simplest and the strongest type of stocking top.

After casting on the stitches, knit, according to the thickness of the thread, from six to ten plain rounds; then knit one round consisting of alternately one over and one decrease. The same number of plain rounds as before is then knitted. Then take a spare needle, pick up the loops made by the casting on until there are on the spare needle the same number of loops as there are stitches on one of the needles in use; fold the work, wrong side in, so that the spare needle lies alongside the left-hand needle; and knit one stitch and one loop of the edge together. Continue thus until all the loops of the edge have been taken up.

It is important that each stitch should be knitted with the corresponding loop of the edge, otherwise the teeth will not be straight.

Usual or "Dutch" heel (fig. 431). The following manner of making and finishing the heel is both the simplest and the most generally used. It can be done with or without a seam at the edge.

After dividing the stitches and putting two more than a quarter of the total number on each of the heel needles, work, according to the thickness of the thread, from fifteen to twenty rows. To make a seam at the edge, knit, in the purl rows, the first three stitches on the right-hand needle and the last three on the left-hand needle.

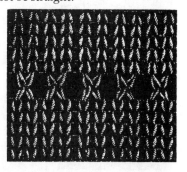

Fig. 429. Stocking top with dog-toothed edge. Open.

When the required number of rows has been knitted, knit all the stitches on the right-hand needle and one third of those on the left-hand needle. Suppose there are twenty four stitches on the needle: knit 8, slip the next, knit 1 stitch, pass the slipped stitch over, knit 2 more stitches, turn the work, slip the 1st stitch, and purl as far as the 8th stitch on the second needle; purl the 9th and 10th stitches together, purl 2 more stitches, turn the work, and slip the 1st stitch.

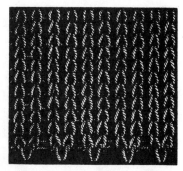

Fig. 430. Stocking top with dog-toothed edge. Folded.

These successive decreases after the eighth stitch form a kind of plait on each side of the heel. It is essential that the first decrease for this type of heel should be made on the right side and the last on the wrong side, so that the work can be continued on the right side once the heel is finished.

When only the original eight stitches, apart from the seam stitches, remain on each needle, the loops down the sides of the heel are picked up on a spare needle. These are then knitted onto the left-hand needle of the heel. Then knit the stitches left at the instep, pick up the loops left on the right-hand side of the heel, and place them on the fourth needle (the right-hand needle of the heel). In the next round, knit all the stitches on the first needle, except the last four; decrease one stitch, and knit the last two. At the beginning of the fourth needle (the right-hand needle of the heel), knit two stitches, slip one, knit one, and pass the slipped stitch over. The decreases are continued, with two plain rows between them, until the number of stitches is the same on all four needles.

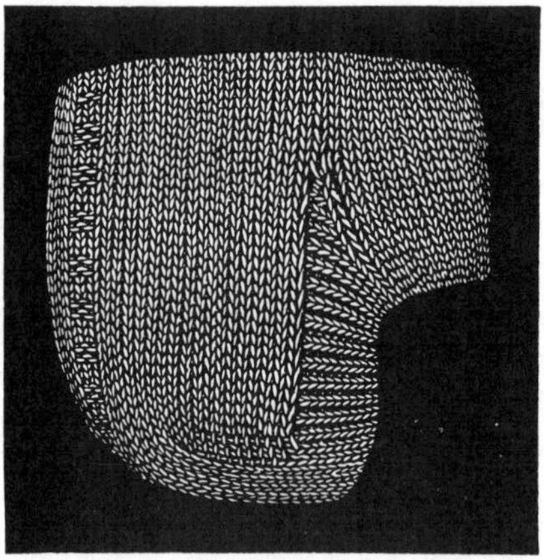

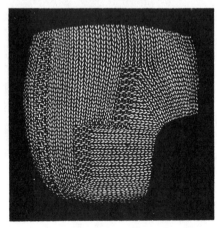

Fig. 431. Usual or "Dutch" heel.

Fig. 432. Stepped heel.

Stepped heel (fig. 432). After dividing the stitches as before, knit twelve to fourteen rows. Then, at the beginning of the second needle, knit the same number of stitches (twelve to fourteen, according to the number of rows just completed); turn the work, and begin the next row with seam stitches to match those at each end of the rows already worked. Knit the same number of stitches from the second needle as you have knitted from the first.

Knit the same number of rows as in the first part of the heel. When this has been done, pick up the loops on both edges; make one decrease by knitting together the last stitch of the narrow part and the first of the wide part; turn the work, slip the first stitch, purl to the second edge, and make another decrease like the first. When all the stitches have been decreased in this way, pick up the stitches along the edges of the first series of side seams and begin the decreases for the instep.

A heel made in this way requires no more work; it molds itself well to the foot and wears longer than any other type of heel.

Heel worked entirely in plain knitting (fig. 433). Those who do not like purling will find in the next two types methods of working heels entirely in plain knitting.

Knit the stitches on the needle which follows the seam, then take two extra needles and on each cast on eight stitches more than there are on each needle of the ankle, join the stitches of the third needle to those of the fourth, and knit the first round plain throughout.

2nd round: make 1 decrease with the 1st and 2nd stitches and 1 decrease with the 9th and 10th stitches of the first extra needle; 1 decrease with the 10th and 9th stitches from the end and 1 decrease with the last 2 stitches of the second extra needle.

3rd, 5th, 7th, 10th, 11th, 13th, 14th, 16th, 17th, 19th, and 20th rounds are knit throughout.

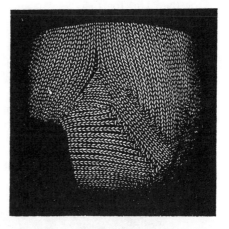

Fig. 433.
Heel worked entirely in plain knitting.

4th round: 1 decrease with the 1st and 2nd stitches and 1 decrease with the 7th and 8th stitches of the first extra needle; 1 decrease with the 8th and 7th stitches from the end and 1 decrease with the last 2 stitches of the second extra needle.

6th round: 1 decrease with the 1st and 2nd stitches, and 1 decrease with the 5th and 6th stitches of the first extra needle; 1 decrease with the 6th and 5th stitches from the end and 1 decrease with the last 2 stitches of the second extra needle.

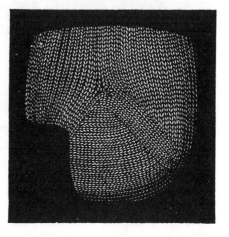

Fig. 434. Another heel worked in plain knitting.

8th round: 1 decrease with the 1st and 2nd stitches, and 1 decrease with the 3rd and 4th stitches of the first extra needle; 1 decrease with the 4th and 3rd stitches from the end and 1 decrease with the last 2 stitches of the second extra needle.

9th round: after the last 2 decreases, purl together the 4th and 3rd stitches from the end of the first and third needles, and the 3rd and 4th stitches at the beginning of the second and fourth needles.

12th, 15th and 18th rounds: decrease as in the 9th round.

21st round: at the beginning of each needle knit 2 stitches; purl the next 2 together; purl together the 4th and 3rd stitches from the end of each needle; knit the last 2.

Continue decreasing as in round 21 in every 3rd round, the 2 intervening rounds being knit throughout, until the purl decreases meet. Work 2 more plain rounds, then 1 round with 1 purl decrease above the former decreases; knit 4 more plain rounds, place the stitches for the sole on two needles, and cast off on the wrong side.

Now pick up the loops of the auxiliary stitches, and in the next rounds work as follows: make 1 decrease with the last stitch of the first needle and the 1st stitch of the second needle, 1 decrease with the last stitch of the third needle and the 1st stitch of the fourth needle. With the remaining extra stitches, purl decreases are made; 2 plain rounds are knitted after each round containing a decrease.

Another heel worked in plain knitting (fig. 434). The heel shown in

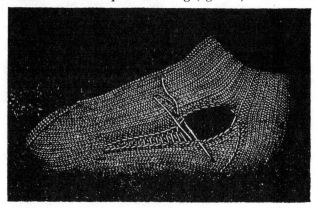

Fig. 435. Italian stocking.

fig. 434 is also knitted entirely in plain knitting with the help of additional stitches cast on extra needles.

Supposing there are 20 stitches on each needle: cast on 28 on each extra needle; make 1 decrease with the 4th and 3rd stitches from the end of the first and third needles, and 1 decrease with the 3rd and 4th stitches of the second and fourth needles, so that 4 plain stitches are left between 2 decreases. Continue decreasing in every 3rd round, until only 6 stitches remain on each needle. Then make 1 more decrease, with the last stitch of each needle and the 1st stitch of the next. Knit 1 more plain round, and end by casting off on the wrong side of the heel. Then pick up the auxiliary stitches and knit the instep.

Italian stocking (fig. 435). The heel, sole, and toe of a stocking are the parts subjected to the hardest wear, while the upper part and the instep almost always remain intact.

The Greeks and Italians have devised a means of saving, to some extent, time and material, and at the same time making the renewing of worn parts easier.

Fig. 436. Toe.

After the heel has been completed by any of the methods already described, the needles on which the heel has been knitted are left, and the work is continued backward and forward on the other two needles until the required length has been knitted. Chain edges must be made, as well as a narrow seam at each side.

When the upper part of the foot has been completed, the sole is worked, the decreases being made immediately after and before the seam stitches. When the sole contains the same number of rows as the upper part, the two are joined and the toe is begun. The opening on the two sides is closed by stitches made with a needle and thread, joining the loops of the chain edge. Care must be taken that each loop is sewn to the one exactly opposite. When one part of the stocking becomes worn, these stitches are unpicked, and it is an easy matter to replace the worn part with a new one.

Fig. 437. Toe.

Toe (fig. 436). Here again we give first the easiest and most commonly used method of working.

Before any type of toe is begun, the stitches must be divided equally on the four needles. Make 1 decrease with the 4th and 3rd stitches from the end of the first and third needles, and knit the last 2 stitches; on the second and fourth needles, knit the first 2 stitches, slip the 3rd, knit the 4th, and pass the slipped stitch over.

At first make these decreases in every 3rd round, later in every other round. When only 4 stitches remain on each needle, place them on two needles, parallel with the width of the stocking, and knit them together, 2 by 2, on the wrong side of the stocking.

Toe (fig. 437). Divide the stitches by 8, 10, or 12. Supposing them to be divisible by 10, knit 8, decrease 1, knit 8, decrease 1, and continue thus to the end of the round.

Then knit as many rounds as there are stitches between the decreases. In the next round, knit 7, decrease 1, and so on; this is followed by 7 plain rounds. In the next round there will be 6 stitches between the decreases; it is followed by 6 plain rounds. Continue thus until there are only 2 stitches between the decreases (the 7th decrease round). When only 4 stitches re-main on each needle, cast off on the wrong side of the stocking.

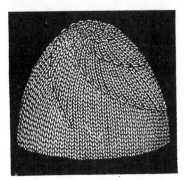

Fig. 438. Spiral toe.

Spiral toe (fig. 438). Begin by slipping the first stitch of each needle and passing it over the second.

Knit 1 round. Then decrease as follows, in alternate rounds, the in-tervening round being knit throughout: in the second decrease round, slip the 3rd stitch of each needle and pass it over the 4th; in the third, slip the 5th stitch of each needle and pass it over the 6th; in the fourth, slip the 7th stitch and pass it over the 8th, so that the decreases produce a spiral effect. Finish off in the usual way.

Toe (fig. 439). Here is yet another type of toe, no less pleasing in ap-pearance and just as easy to knit as the preceding ones.

1st round: purl the 1st two stitches of each needle together.

2nd and 3rd, 5th and 6th, 8th and 9th, 11th and 12th, 14th and 15th, 17th and 18th rounds: knit throughout.

Fig. 439. Toe.

4th round: in each needle, knit 1, decrease with the 2nd and 3rd, and again with the last 2 stitches.

7th round: knit 2, decrease with the 3rd and 4th, and again with the last 2 stitches.

In the successive decrease rounds, always knit one more at the beginning of the needle. When the decreases meet, slip the last stitch of each needle and pass it over the first stitch of the next; knit the stitches between. Con-tinue to decrease in this manner to the last stitches.

Reinforcing Knitting. Knitted articles are reinforced by reconstruct-ing the knitted stitches with needle and thread. When the threads are not actually broken, but are on the point of giving way, they can be strength-ened by means of auxiliary stitches.

Materials for reinforcing stockings. The thread used for this purpose should always be slightly finer than that used for the knitting itself. For this reason we recommend DMC special quality darning cotton, DMC superfine darning cotton, or DMC special stranded cotton, since, being composed of several untwisted strands, these threads can be divided or added to and the exact thickness required can thus be easily obtained.

Reinforcing the stitches. Swiss darning (figs. 440 and 441). Simple reinforcing can be done in two ways. In fig. 440, the needle is brought out between two horizontal threads, then, passing over one vertical thread it is carried up and reinserted, to re-emerge between the next two horizontal stitches. The second row of loops is made on the return journey; take up two threads on the left, pass down over one thread, pick up the thread on the needle, and so on.

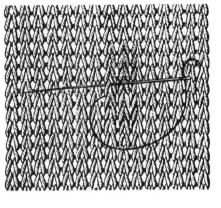

Fig. 440.
Reinforcing stitches in vertical rows.

Fig. 441 shows what is usually known as Swiss darning. The needle is brought out, and passed over one thread to the right and two threads up, then under two threads to the left, then down over two threads and to the right over one; it is then reinserted at the spot where it first emerged and passed under two threads to the left, then over two threads up and one to the right, and so on.

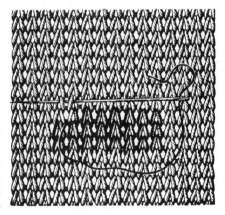

Fig. 441. Reinforcing stitches in horizontal rows. Swiss darning.

For the next row, the work is turned upside down; the needle is passed down over one horizontal thread and brought out between two opposed threads; then it is passed once more down over two horizontal threads, under two threads to the left, up over two threads and one thread to the right, under two threads to the left, etc.

Disengaging the Stitches (fig. 442). When the threads of the knitting are completely worn through, one must make new stitches and remove the old ones from all the worn part. The worn threads are cut, and the horizontal stitches freed; on the vertical sides the threads are cut in such a way that they form an even edge and a square hole is produced. In the corners, from two to four stitches are freed, and these are turned back behind the work, where they are caught down with a few stitches.

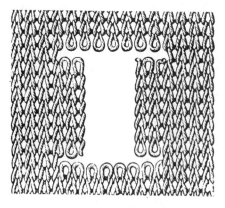

Fig. 442. Repairing.
Disengaging the stitches.

For the types of repair that are described further on, we recommend the use of a darning mold or egg; this lessens the danger of drawing the stitches too tight.

Repairing Plain Knitting Over Horizontal Threads (figs. 443 and 444). On the wrong side of the work, lay a thread horizontally for each row of stitches to be replaced, carrying each thread one or two stitches beyond the edge. When this foundation has been made, bring the needle out on the right side of the work, close to the nearest stitch of the sound part on the left. Then, working down, take up the nearest horizontal thread, from below up, in such a way that the working thread lies on the left of the needle; in this way cover all the threads of the foundation.

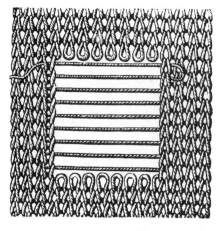

Fig. 443.
Repairing plain knitting over horizontal threads.
Laying the threads.

When the last thread has been taken up, the needle is passed down on the left of the nearest stitch and brought out again on the right of the same stitch.

The second half of the stitches is worked up, the thread still kepton the left of the needle (fig. 444). When the last thread has been reached, insert the needle into the stitch from which it originally emerged and carry the thread one stitch to the right to begin the third half-row.

Repairing Plain Knitting Over Oblique Threads (figs. 445 and 446). As can be seen from the illustration, all the freed stitches, as well as a few on each side of the open space, must be picked up. The number and length of the threads laid must correspond to those of the threads removed. Then, on the right side of the work, a thread—slightly finer than that used for the knitting itself—is fastened on; a few stitches are made over the existing stitches in the row which is to be replaced.

Pass the needle up through the first freed loop, pass it under two threads which emerge from the same loop, and reinsert it into the same stitch between the two slanting threads, to re-emerge up through the next stitch, and so on. The new loop should be of the same size as the knitted stitches. At the end of the row, as at the beginning, a few stitches should be made beyond the open space. The return row is worked in the same way as the first, with the sole difference that the work is turned the other way up.

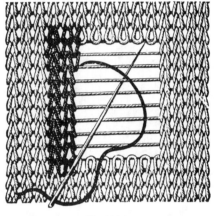

Fig. 444.
Repairing plain knitting over horizontal threads.
Covering the threads.

Repairing Purl Knitting Over Oblique Threads (fig. 447). The foundation threads are laid and covered with horizontal stitches, as for the repairing of plain knitting. The stitches which link two threads of the foundation are worked in double rows and alternate.

Repairing a Ribbed Pattern Over Oblique Threads (fig. 448). It frequently happens that articles knitted with a pattern have to be repaired; in such cases the repair is made as invisible as possible without interrupting the pattern. As an example, we have chosen a ribbed design,

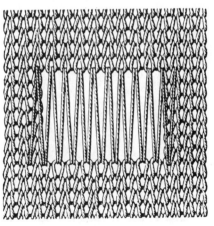

Fig. 445.
Repairing plain knitting over oblique threads.
Laying the threads.

consisting of two plain and two purl stitches, the most commonly used pattern for knitted garments. Here again the repairing is worked over oblique threads; the knit and purl stitches are made in the same order as in the knitting itself, according to the instructions for figs, 446 and 447. Our illustration, fig. 448, shows how to pass from purl to knit stitches.

Repairing an Openwork Design (figs. 449 and 450). In the more complicated case of an openwork design, it is essential that these stitches of the design and their arrangement should be reproduced as nearly as possi-

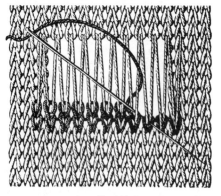

Fig. 446.
Repairing plain knitting over oblique threads.
Covering the threads.

ble. As an example we have chosen the allover design shown in fig. 469. The stitches are carefully disengaged, and on the wrong side the loose ends from these stitches are fastened off (fig. 449). Then, on the right side, the necessary oblique threads are laid and the already interlaced threads spread out to form the knitted bars of the openwork (fig. 450). The stitches are then made on these threads, copying the design and reproducing the exact number of stitches.

Grafting Plain Knitting (fig. 451). When it is necessary to replace part of a knitted article by a newly knitted piece, the new piece is joined to the old with the help of a sewing needle threaded with the thread used for the knitting.

For this purpose—called grafting—the stitches must be freed and picked up on knitting needles so they will not come undone. The two needles are placed side by side, with the stitches to be joined exactly opposite one another. Then the sewing needle is passed up into the first free stitch of the upper part; the stitch is slipped off the knitting needle, and the sewing needle is inserted down into the lower stitch exact-

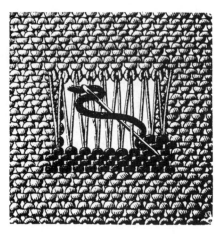

Fig. 447. Repairing purl knitting over oblique threads.

ly opposite the upper stitch, then up into the next stitch; the thread is drawn just tight enough to make the new stitch the same size as the knitted stitches. The needle is then passed down into the upper stitch through which is has already passed once and brought out through the next stitch, the thread is drawn tight, the needle is passed down to the lower row, the same process is repeated, and so on.

Grafting Purl Knitting (fig. 452). The illustration shows how this is done. The work is prepared as for grafting plain knitting; then the needle is brought to the upper row and passed up into the first stitch of this row, then down into the next stitch; the same process is repeated in the lower row, then in the upper, and so on.

In our two illustrations of the process of grafting, we have purposely exaggerated the space between the two pieces of knitting in order to make the course of the needle and the formation of the stitches clearer.

Fig. 448.
Repairing a ribbed pattern over oblique threads.

Ground in Piqué Knitting (Basket-weave pattern) (fig. 453). The designs which follow can be used for ornamenting bedspreads, pullovers, jumpers, and other articles. According to the purpose for which the work is intended, one of the following threads can be used, in the most suitable thickness: DMC special quality bell mark knitting cotton, DMC Alsatia, DMC knitting twist, DMC pearl cotton, DMC floss crochet, DMC special quality knitting cotton, or DMC flax thread for knitting and crochet.

The instructions for all the designs which follow are intended to be worked in strips (i.e., working backward and forward). The following abbreviations are used: k. = knit; p. = purl; st. = stitch; sts. = stitches.

The term ''piqué'' is used for those patterns which are made by varying arrangements of knit and purl stitches.

Cast on a number of stitches divisible by 6, with 5 extra stitches for the edges.

1st, 3rd, and 5th rows: slip 1 st., k. 1, * k. 1 into the back of the next st., p. 5; repeat from * to 3 sts. from the end, k. 1 into the back of the next st., p. 2.

2nd, 4th, and 6th rows: slip 1, k. 1, * p. 1 into the back of the next st., k. 5; repeat from * to 3 sts. from the end, p. 1 into the back of the next st., k. 2.

7th, 9th, and 11th rows: slip 1, k. 1, * p. 3, k. 1 into the back of the next st., p. 2; repeat from * to 3 from the end, p. 1, k. 2.

8th, 10th, and 12th rows: slip 1, k. 1, * k. 3, p. 1 into the back of the next st., k. 2; repeat from * to 3 from the end, k. 3.

Repeat from the 1st row.

Ground in Piqué Knitting (fig. 454). Cast on a number of stitches divisible by 14, with 5 extra stitches for the edges.

1st and 4th rows: slip 1, k. 1, * k. 1, p. 1, k. 1, p. 1, k. 7, p. 1, k. 1, p. 1; repeat from * to 3 from the end, k. 3.

2nd and 3rd rows: slip 1, k. 1, * p. 1, k. 1, p. 1, k. 1, p. 7, k. 1, p. 1, k. 1; repeat from * to 3 from the end, p. 1, k. 2.

Repeat from the 1st row.

Knitted Strip for Bedspreads in Piqué Knitting (fig. 455). These strips can be worked in a variety of ways using either one thread or two very different ones: for instance, DMC knitting twist—a matt thread which, though its surface is dull, can be obtained in the most vivid colors—and DMC special quality knitting cotton, a brilliant thread which gives great play of light and shade. These two threads harmonize excellently and their use in combination shows to the best advantage the difference in their appearance and their carefully studied qualities.

Cast on 28 stitches.

1st row: slip 1, k. 2, 1 over, k. 2, p. 1, k. 1, p. 2, k. 5, p. 2, k. 1, p. 1, k. 1, p. 1, k. 1, p. 1, k. 1, p. 1, k. 1, 1 over, k. 3.

2nd row: slip 1, p. 2, p. 2 together, p. 1, k. 1, p. 1, k. 1, p. 1, k. 1, p. 1, k. 2, p. 5, k. 2, p. 1, k. 1, p. 1, k. 1, p. 2 together, p. 3.

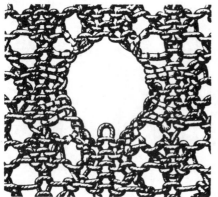

Fig. 449. Repairing an openwork design. Disengaging the stitches.

Fig. 450. Repairing an openwork design. Laying the foundation threads.

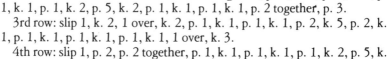

3rd row: slip 1, k. 2, 1 over, k. 2, p. 1, k. 1, p. 1, k. 1, p. 2, k. 5, p. 2, k. 1, p. 1, k. 1, p. 1, k. 1, 1 over, k. 3.

4th row: slip 1, p. 2, p. 2 together, p. 1, k. 1, p. 1, k. 1, p. 1, k. 2, p. 5, k.

2, p. 1, k. 1, p. 1, k. 1, p. 1, k. 1, p. 2 together, p. 3.

5th row: slip 1, k. 2, 1 over, k. 2, p. 1, k. 1, p. 1, k. 1, p. 1, k. 1, p. 2, k. 5, p. 2, k. 1, p. 1, k. 1, p. 1, k. 1, 1 over, k. 3.

6th row: slip 1, p. 2, p. 2 together, p. 1, k. 1, p. 1, k. 2, p. 5, k. 2, p. 1, k. 1, p. 1, k. 1, p. 1, k. 1, p. 2 together, p. 3.

7th row: same as the 5th row.

8th row: same as the 4th row.

9th row: same as the 3rd row.

10th row: same as the 2nd row.

Repeat from the 1st row.

The stripes are joined with crochet; several suitable stitches will be found among the examples explained in the next chapter.

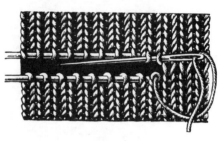

Fig. 451. Grafting plain knitting.

Square in Piqué Knitting (fig. 456). On each of four needles, cast on 2 sts. Each set of directions followed by an * is to be repeated three times.

1st round: 1 over, k. 1, 1 over, k. 1 *.

2nd round: 1 over, k. 3, 1 over, k. 1 *.

3rd round: 1 over, p. 1, k. 3, p. 1, 1 over, k. 1 *.

4th round: 1 over, p. 2, k. 3, p. 2, 1 over, k. 1 *.

5th round: 1 over, p. 3, k. 3, p. 3, 1 over, k. 1 *.

6th round: 1 over, p. 4, k. 3, p. 4, 1 over, k. 1 *.

7th round: 1 over, p. 5, k. 3, p. 5, 1 over, k. 1 *.

8th round: 1 over, k. 2, p. 4, k. 3, p. 4, k. 2, 1 over, k. 1 *.

9th round: 1 over, k. 4, p. 3, k. 3, p. 3, k. 4, 1 over, k. 1 *.

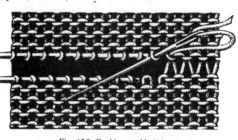

Fig. 452. Grafting purl knitting.

10th round: 1 over, k. 6, p. 2, k. 3, p. 2, k. 6, 1 over, k. 1 *.

11th round: 1 over, k. 8, p. 1, k. 3, p. 1, k. 8, 1 over, k. 1 *.

12th round: 1 over, k. 1, cross 2 sts. (i.e. knit the second stitch first and the first after the second), k. 5, p. 2, k. 3, p. 2, k. 5, cross 2 sts., k. 1, 1 over, k. 1 *.

13th round: 1 over, p. 1, k. 7, p. 3, k. 3, p. 3, k. 7, p. 1, 1 over, k. 1 *.

14th round: 1 over, p. 2, k. 1, cross 2 sts., k. 3, p. 4, k. 3, p. 4, k. 3, cross 2 sts., k. 1, p. 2, 1 over, k. 1 *.

Fig. 453. Ground in piqué knitting (basketweave pattern).

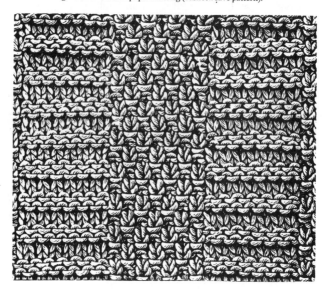

Fig. 454. Ground in piqué knitting.

15th round: 1 over, p. 3, k. 5, p. 5, k. 3, p. 5, k. 5, p. 3, 1 over, k. 1 *.
16th round: 1 over, p. 4, k. 1, cross 2 sts., k. 3, p. 4, k. 3, p. 4, k. 3, cross 2 sts., k. 1, p. 4, 1 over, k. 1 *.
17th round: 1 over, p. 5, k. 7, p. 3, k. 3, p. 3, k. 7, p. 5, 1 over, k. 1 *.

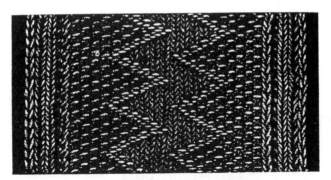

Fig. 445. Knitted strip for bedspreads in piqué knitting.

18th round: 1 over, k. 2, p. 4, k. 1, cross 2 sts., k. 5, p. 2, k. 3, p. 2, k. 5, cross 2 sts., k. 1, p. 4, k. 2, 1 over, k. 1 *.

19th round: 1 over, k. 4, p. 3, k. 9, p. 1, k. 3, p. 1, k. 9, p. 3, k. 4, 1 over, k. 1 *.

20th round: 1 over, k. 6, p. 2, k. 1, cross 2 sts., k. 5, p. 2, k. 3,

Fig. 456. Square in piqué knitting.

p. 2, k. 5, cross 2 sts., k. 1, p. 2, k. 6, 1 over, k. 1 *.

21st round: 1 over, k. 8, p. 1, k. 7, p. 3, k. 3, p. 3, k. 7, p. 1, k. 8, 1 over, k. 1 *.

22nd round: 1 over, k. 1, cross 2 sts., k. 5, p. 2, k. 1, cross 2 sts., k. 3, p. 4, k. 3, p. 4, k. 3, cross 2 sts., k. 1, p. 2, k. 5, cross 2 sts., k. 1, 1 over, k. 1 *.

Fig. 457. Brioche pattern.

23rd round: 1 over, p. 1, k. 7, p. 3, k. 5, p. 5, k. 3, p. 5, k. 5, p. 3, k. 7, p. 1, 1 over, k. 1 *.

24th round: 1 over, p. 2, k. 1, cross 2 sts., k. 3, p. 4, k. 1, cross 2 sts., k. 3, p. 4, k. 3, p. 4, k. 3, cross 2 sts., k. 1, p. 4, k. 3, cross 2 sts., k. 1, p. 2, 1 over, k. 1 *.

25th round: 1 over, p. 3, k. 5, p. 5, k. 7, p. 3, k. 3, p. 3, k. 7, p. 5, k. 5, p. 3, 1 over, k. 1 *.

26th round: 1 over, p. 4, k. 1, cross 2 sts., k. 3, p. 4, k. 1, cross 2 sts., k. 5, p. 2, k. 3, p. 2, k. 5, cross 2 sts., k. 1, p. 4, k. 3, cross 2sts., k. 1, p. 4, 1 over, k. 1 *.

27th round: 1 over, p.

Fig. 458. Double English knitting.

5, k. 7, p. 3, k. 9, p. 1, k. 3, p. 1, k. 9, p. 3, k. 7, p. 5, 1 over, k. 1 *.

Finish off the square with 3 rounds of purl, and cast off all the stitches.

Brioche Pattern (fig. 457). This is a very easy and very elastic stitch, suited to all kinds of garments, particularly to mufflers and scarves. It is worked on two needles.

Cast on a number of stitches divisible by 2.

1st row: 1 over, insert the needle purlwise into the next st., slip this st. onto the right-hand needle, k. 1, 1 over, slip 1 as before, and continue in this way to the end.

2nd row: 1 over, slip 1, k. the over and the slipped st. together. Continue repeating the 2nd row.

In circular knitting, the overs and slipped stitches must be knitted together and purled together in alternate rows.

Double English Knitting (fig. 458). This stitch is worked in 4 rows.
Cast on a number of stitches divisible by 2.
1st row: 1 over, slip 1 as in brioche pattern, k. 1.
2nd row: p. 1, slip the over from the left-hand to the right-hand needle,
p. 1,
3rd row: p. 2 together, slip 1, 1 over.
4th row: slip the over, p. 2.
5th row: slip 1, 1 over, p. 2 together.
Repeat from the 2nd row.

Tunisian Knitting. These stitches are particularly recommended for articles which are to be embroidered, since the stitches form very regular squares which serve as a foundation for the embroidery. Both stitches must be begun on the wrong side of the work.

Tunisian knitting with slanting stitches (fig. 459). 1st row: 1 over, slip 1.

2nd row: k. 2 together into the backs of the stitches.

Fig. 459. Tunisian knitting with slanting stitches.

Tunisian knitting with horizontal stitches (fig. 460). 1st row: slip 1, 1 over.

2nd row: k. 2, together into the backs of the stitches.

Ground of Piqué Knitting With Colored Spots (fig. 461). The foundation consists of knit and purl stitches; certain of the stitches are worked with a colored thread to form the spots.

Cast on a number of stitches divisi-

Fig. 460. Tunisian knitting with horizontal stitches.

ble by 4, with 5 extra stitches for the edges.
1st, 2nd, 4th, 5th, 6th, and 8th rows: with ecru thread slip 1, k. 1, * k.
1, p. 1, k. 1, p. 1; repeat from * to 3 from the end, k. 3.
3rd row: with ecru thread slip 1, k. 1, * k. 1; with colored thread: p. 1;
with ecru thread: k. 1, p. 1; repeat from * to 3 from the end, k. 3. At the
end of the row break off the colored thread.
7th row: with ecru thread: slip 1, k. 1, * k. 1, p. 1, k. 1; with colored
thread: p. 1; repeat from * to 3 from the end, k. 3. At the end of the row,
break off the colored thread.
Repeat from the 1st row.

Fig. 461. Ground of piqué knitting with colored spots.

Cable Stitch Design (fig. 462). Cable stitch is usually worked in conjunction with plain stitches, and is used to make bed and cot covers, etc. It is made by the crossing of stitches; that is to say, the second stitch on the left-hand needle is knitted before the first. When two or more stitches are crossed in a series of rows, the knitted stitches produce the effect of a plait or cable, as can be seen in fig. 462.

Cast on a number of stitches divisible by 6, with 6 extra stitches for the edges.

1st and 3rd rows: slip 1, k. 1, * p. 2, k. 4; repeat from * to 4 from the end, p. 2, k. 2.

Fig. 462. Cable stitch design.

2nd, 4th, and 6th rows: slip 1, k. 1, * k. 2, p. 4; repeat from * to 4 from the end, k. 4.

5th row: slip 1, k. 1, * p. 2, slip off 2 sts. on to a spare needle and leave this needle at the back of the work; k. 2, then k. the 2 sts. on the spare needle; repeat from * to 4 from the end, p. 2, k. 2.

Repeat from the 1st row.

A double cable can also be made with six stitches; in this case, the stitches are crossed alternately to the left and the right.

Knitted Ground in Turkish Stitch (fig. 463). This stitch is made in a single row: 1 over, slip 1, k. 1, pass the slipped st. over, 1 over, slip 1, k. 1, pass the slipped st. over, and so on.

Openwork Ground Knitted in Two Kinds of Thread (fig. 464). Stitches knitted with threads of different thicknesses can be used to produce the most charming designs for coverlets, shawls, curtains, etc.

To work this design and the next successfully, large needles must be used. Cast on a number of

Fig. 463. Knitted ground in Turkish stitch.

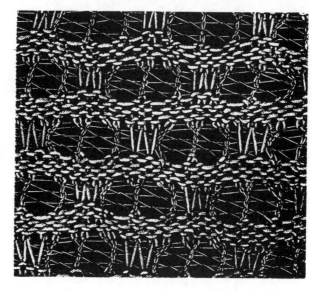

Fig. 464. Openwork ground knitted in two kinds of thread.

stitches divisible by 8, with 4 extra stitches for the edges.

1st and 11th rows: with coarse thread slip 1, k. 1, * p. 8; repeat from * to 2 from the end, k. 2.

2nd row: slip 1, k. 1, * k. 4, 2 overs, k. 4; repeat from * to 2 from the end; k. 2.

3rd row: with fine thread slip 1, * k. 2 together, 1 over, k. 2 together, 1 over, slip 1, drop the double over, slip 1, k. 2 together, 1 over; repeat from * to 3 from the end, k. 2 together, 1 over, k. 1.

4th, 6th, and 8th rows: slip 1, k. 1, * p. 3, slip 2, p. 3; repeat from * to 2 from the end, k. 2.

5th and 7th rows: slip 1, * k. 2 together, 1 over, k. 2 together, 1 over slip 2, k. 2 together, 1 over; repeat from * to 3 from the end, k. 2 together, 1 over, k. 1.

9th, 10th, 19th, and 20th rows: with coarse thread slip 1, k. to the end.

12th row: slip 1, k. 1, * 1 over, k. 8, 1 over; repeat from * to 2 from the end, in such a way as to have 2 overs between the groups of 8 k. sts., k. 2.

13th row: with fine thread slip 1, k. 1, * drop the over, slip 1, ** k. 2 together, 1 over, repeat from ** twice; slip 1, drop the over; repeat from * to 2 from the end, k. 2.

14th, 16th, and 18th rows: slip 1, k. 1, * slip 1, p. 6, slip 1; repeat from * to 2 from the end, k. 2.

15th and 17th rows: slip 1, k. 1, * slip 1, ** k. 2 together, 1 over, repeat from ** twice; slip 1, repeat from * to 2 from the end, k. 2.

Repeat from the 1st row.

Openwork Ground Knitted With Two Kinds of

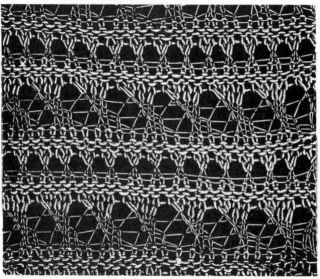

Fig. 465. Openwork ground knitted with two kinds of thread.

Thread (fig. 465). Cast on a number of stitches divisible by 4, with 4 extra stitches for the edges.

1st, 2nd, 11th and 12th rows: with coarse thread slip 1, k. 1, * p. 4; repeat from * to 2 from the end, k. 2.

3rd row: with fine thread slip 1, k. 1, * 1 over, slip 1, k. 1, pass the slipped st. over, k. 2; repeat from * to 2 from the end, k. 2.

4th, 6th, 8th, and 14th rows: slip 1, k. 1, * p. 4; repeat from * to 2 from the end, k. 2.

5th row: slip 1, k. 1, * k. 1, 1 over, slip 1, k. 1, pass the slipped st. over, k. 1; repeat from * to 2 from the end, k. 2.

7th row: slip 1, k. 1, * k. 2, 1 over, slip 1, k. 1, pass the slipped st. over; repeat from * to 2 from the end, k. 2.

9th, 10th, 15th, and 16th rows: with coarse thread slip 1, k. to the end.

13th row: with fine thread slip 1, k. 1, * k. 2 together, 1 over, k. 2 together, 1 over; repeat from * to 2 from the end, k. 2.

Repeat from the 1st row.

Ground in Openwork Knitting (fig. 466). Cast on a number of stitches divisible by 9, with 7 extra stitches for the edges.

1st row: slip 1, k. 1, * 1 over, slip 1, k. 2 together, pass the slipped st. over, 1 over, k. 1, 1 double over, k. 4, 1 double over, k. 1; repeat from * to 5 from the end, 1 over, slip 1, k. 2 together, pass the slipped st. over, k. 2.

2nd row: slip 1, k. 1, * p. 3 slip the next st., drop the double over, p. 4, turn the work, k. 4, turn, p. 4, drop the double over, slip the next st.; repeat from * to 5 from the end, p. 3, k. 2.

3rd row: slip 1, k. 1, * 1 over, slip 1, k. 2 together, pass the slipped st. over, 1 over, drop the slipped st., k. the st. which follows the second double over before and in front of the intervening sts., then k. the 4 other sts., lastly pick up the dropped st. and knit it across the front of the work; repeat from * to 5 from the end, 1 over, slip 1, k. 2 together, pass the slipped st. over, k. 2.

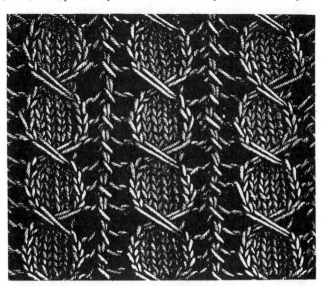

Fig. 466. Ground in openwork knitting.

4th and 6th rows: slip 1, k. 1, * p. 9; repeat from * to 5 from the end, p. 3, k. 2.

5th row: slip 1, k. 1, * 1 over, slip 1, k. 2 together, pass the slipped st. over, 1 over, k. 6; repeat from * to 5 from the end, 1 over, slip 1, k. 2 together, pass the slipped st. over, k. 2.

Repeat from the 1st row.

Ground in Openwork Knitting (fig. 467). Cast on a number of stitches divisible by 14, with 7 extra stitches for the edges.

1st and 3rd rows: slip 1, * slip 1, k. 1, pass the slipped st. over, 1 over, k.

1 into the back of the next st., 1 over, k. 2 together, k. 9; repeat from * to 6 from the end, slip 1, k. 1, pass the slipped st. over, 1 over, k. 1 into the back of the next st., 1 over, k. 2 together, k. 1.

2nd, 4th, 6th, 8th, 10th, 12th, and 14th rows: slip 1, k. 1, * p. 1, p. 1 into the back of the next st., p. 12; repeat from * to 5 from the end, p. 1, p. 1 into the back of the next st., p. 1, k. 2.

5th row: slip 1, * slip 1, k. 1, pass the slipped st. over, 1 over, k. 1 into the back of the next st., 1 over, k. 2 together, k. 2, k. 2 together, 1 over, k. 1, 1 over, slip 1, k. 1, pass the slipped st. over, k. 2; repeat from * to 6 from the end, slip 1, k. 1, pass the slipped st. over, 1 over, k. 1 into the back of the next st., 1 over, k. 2 together, k. 1.

Fig. 467. Ground in openwork knitting.

7th row: slip 1, * slip 1, k. 1, pass the slipped st. over, 1 over, k. 1 into the back of the next st., 1 over, k. 2 together, k. 1, k. 2 together, 1 over, k. 3, 1 over, slip 1, k. 1, pass the slipped st. over, k. 1; repeat from * to 6 from the end, slip 1, k. 1, pass the slipped st. over, 1 over, k. 1 into the back of the next st., 1 over, k. 2 together, k. 1.

9th row: slip 1, * slip 1, k. 1, pass the slipped st. over, 1 over, k. 1 into the back of the next st., 1 over, k. 2 together twice, 1 over, k. 5, 1 over, slip 1, k. 1, pass the slipped st. over; repeat from * to 6 from the end, k. 1, slip 1, pass the slipped st. over, 1 over, k. 1 into the back of the next st., 1 over, k. 2 together, k. 1.

11th row: slip 1, * slip 1, k. 1, pass the slipped st. over, 1 over, k. 1 into the back of the next st., 1 over, k. 2 together, k. 2, 1 over, slip 1, k. 1, pass the slipped st. over, k. 1, k. 2 together, 1 over, k. 2; repeat from * to 6 from the end, slip 1, k. 1, pass the slipped st. over, 1 over, k. 1 into the back of the next st., 1 over, k. 2 together, k. 1.

13th row: slip 1, * slip 1, k. 1, pass the slipped st. over, 1 over, k. 1 into the back of the next st., 1 over, k. 2 together, k. 3, 1 over, slip 1, k. 2 together, pass the slipped st. over, 1 over, k. 3; repeat from * to 6 from the end, slip 1, k. 1, pass the slipped st. over, 1 over, k. 1 into the back of the next st., 1 over, k. 2 together, k. 1.

Repeat from the 1st row.

Ground in Openwork Knitting (fig. 468). The patterns illustrated in figs. 468 and 469 are particularly suitable for scarves, shawls, and wraps. According to the thickness of the thread, steel or bone needles can be used; the former are best for fine threads.

Cast on a number of stitches divisible by 4, with 4 extra stitches for the edges.

1st row: slip 1, k. 1, * 1 over, slip 1, k. 1, pass the slipped st. over, k. 2; repeat from * to 2 from the end, k. 2.

2nd row: slip 1, k. 1, * p. 1, k. 2 together into the backs of the st., 1 over, p. 1; repeat from * to 2 from the end, k. 2.

Fig. 468. Ground in openwork knitting.

3rd row: slip 1, k. 1, * k. 2, 1 over, slip 1, k. 1, pass the slipped st. over; repeat from * to 2 from the end, k. 2.

4th row: slip 1, * p. 2 together into the backs of the sts., 1 over, p. 2; repeat from * to 3 from the end, p. 1, k. 2.

5th row: slip 1, k. 1, * k. 1, k. 2 together, 1 over, k. 1; repeat from * to 2 from the end, k. 2.

6th row: slip 1, k. 1, * p. 2, 1 over, p. 2 together; repeat from * to 2 from the end, k. 2.

7th row: slip 1, * k. 2 together, 1 over, k. 2; repeat from * to 3 from the end, k. 3.

8th row: slip 1, k. 1, * 1 over, p. 2 together, p. 2; repeat from * to 2 from the end, k. 2.

Repeat from the 1st row.

Ground in Openwork Knitting (fig. 469). Cast on a number of stitches divisible by 6, with 5 extra stitches for the edges.

1st row: slip 1, k. 1, * k. 1, 1 over, slip 1, k. 1, pass the slipped st. over, k. 1, k. 2 together, 1 over; repeat from * to 3 from the end, k. 3.

2nd, 4th, 6th, 8th, 10th, and 12th rows: slip 1, k. 1, p. to 2 from the end, k. 2.

3rd row: slip 1, k. 1, * k. 2, 1 over, k. 3, 1 over, k. 1; repeat from * to 3 from the end, k. 3.

5th row: slip 1, k. 1, k. 2 together, * 1 over, slip 1, k. 1, pass the slipped st. over, k. 1, k. 2 together, 1 over, slip 1, k. 2 together, pass the slipped st. over; repeat from * to 9 from the end, 1 over, slip 1, k. 1, pass the slipped st. over, k. 1, k. 2 together, 1 over, slip 1, k. 1, pass the slipped st. over, k. 2.

Fig. 469. Ground in openwork knitting.

7th row: slip 1, k. 1, * k. 1, k. 2 together, 1 over, k. 1, 1 over, slip 1, k. 1, pass the slipped st. over; repeat from * to 3 from the end, k. 3.

9th row: slip 1, k. 1, * k. 2, 1 over, k. 3, 1 over, k. 1; repeat from * to 3 from the end, k. 3.

11th row: slip 1, k. 1, * k. 1, k. 2 together, 1 over, slip 1, k. 2 together, pass the slipped st. over, 1 over, slip 1, k. 1, pass the slipped st. over; repeat from * to 3 from the end, k. 3.

Repeat from the 1st row.

Ground in Openwork Knitting (fig. 470). Cast on a number of stitches divisible by 14, with 5 extra stitches for the edges.

1st row: slip 1, k. 1, * k. 1, 1 over, k. 2, p. 3, p. 3 together, p. 3, k. 2, 1 over; repeat from * to 3 from the end, k. 3.

2nd row: slip 1, k. 1, * p. 4, k. 7, p. 3; repeat from * to 3 from the end, p. 1, k. 2.

3rd row: slip 1, k. 1, * k. 2, 1 over, k. 2, p. 2, p. 3 together, p. 2, k. 2, 1 over, k. 1; repeat from * to 3 from the end, k. 3.

4th row: slip 1, k. 1, * p. 5, k. 5, p. 4; repeat from * to 3 from the end, p. 1, k. 2.

5th row: slip 1, k. 1, * k. 3, 1 over, k. 2, p. 1, p. 3 together, p. 1, k. 2, 1 over, k. 2; repeat from * to 3 from the end, k. 3.

6th row: slip 1, k. 1, * p. 6, k. 3, p. 5; repeat from * to 3 from the end, p. 1, k. 2.

7th row: slip 1, k. 1, * k. 4, 1 over, k. 2, p. 3 together, k. 2, 1 over, k. 3; repeat from * to 3 from the end, k. 3.

8th row: slip 1, k. 1, * p. 7, k. 1, p. 6; repeat from * to 3 from the end, p. 1, k. 2.

9th row: slip 1, k. 1, p. 2 together, * p. 3, k. 2, 1 over, k. 1, 1 over, k. 2, p. 3 **, p. 3 together; repeat

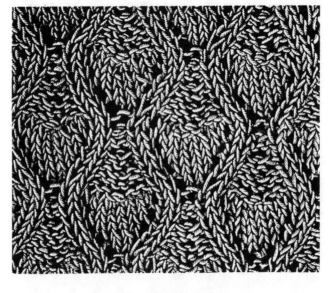

Fig. 470. Ground in openwork knitting.

from * to 4 from the end, but in the last repeat work only as far as **, p. 2 together, k. 2.

10th row: slip 1, k. 1, * k. 4, p. 7, k. 3; repeat from * to 3 from the end, k. 3.

11th row: slip 1, k. 1, p. 2 together, * p. 2, k. 2, 1 over, k. 3, 1 over, k. 2, p. 2 **, p. 3 together; repeat from * to 4 from the end, but in the last repeat work only as far as **, p. 2 together, k. 2.

12th row: slip 1, k. 1, * k. 3, p. 9, k. 2; repeat from * to 3 from the end, k. 3.

13th row: slip 1, k. 1, p. 2 together, * p. 1, k. 2, 1 over, k. 5, 1 over, k. 2, p. 1 **, p. 3 together; repeat from * to 4 from the end, but in the last repeat work only as far as * *, p. 2 together, k. 2.

14th row: slip 1, k. 1, * k. 2, p. 11, k. 1; repeat from * to 3 from the end, k. 3.

15th row: slip 1, k. 1, p. 2 together, * k. 2, 1 over, k. 7, 1 over, k. 2 * *, p. 3 together; repeat from * to 4 from the end, but in the last repeat work only as far as * *, p. 2 together, k. 2.

16th row: slip 1, k. 1, * k. 1, p. 13; repeat from * to 3 from the end, k. 3.

Repeat from the 1st row.

Knitted Lace (fig. 471). A smooth, well-twisted thread is usually chosen for knitted lace so that the pattern may stand out well against the ground. Small knitted articles can be very effectively finished off by the addition of a narrow edging of knitted lace in a similar style. We have chosen as our examples patterns which, though very easy to work, may be counted among the most charming of knitted lace designs.

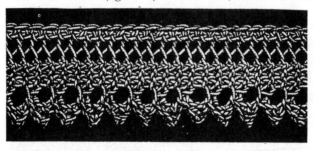

Fig. 471. Knitted lace.

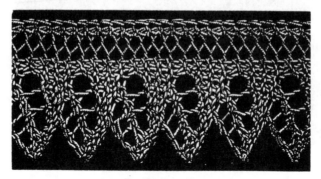

Fig. 472. Knitted lace.

Cast on 9 stitches.

1st row: slip 1, k. 2, 1 over, k. 2 together, k. 2, 1 double over, k. 2.

2nd row: slip 1, k. 2, p. 1, k. 4, 1 over, k. 2 together, k. 1.

3rd row: slip 1, k. 2, 1 over, k. 2 together, k. 6.

4th row: cast off 2, k. 5, 1 over, k. 2 together, k. 1.

Repeat from the 1st row.

Knitted Lace (fig. 472). Cast on 10 stitches.

1st row: slip 1, k. 2, 1 over, k. 2 together, k. 1, 2 overs, k. 2 together, 2 overs, k. 2 together.

2nd row: slip 1, k. 1, p. 1, k. 2, p. 1, k. 3, 1 over, k. 2 together, k. 1.

3rd row: slip 1, k. 2, 1 over, k. 2 together, k. 3, 2 overs, k. 2 together, 2 overs, k. 2 together.

4th row: slip 1, k. 1, p. 1, k. 2, p. 1, k. 5, 1 over, k. 2 together, k. 1.

5th row: slip 1, k. 2, 1 over, k. 2 together, k. 5, 2 overs, k. 2 together, 2 overs, k. 2 together.

6th row: slip 1, k. 1, p. 1, k. 2, p. 1, k. 7, 1 over, k. 2 together, k. 1.

7th row: slip 1, k. 2, 1 over, k. 2 together, k. 11.

8th row: cast off 6, k. 6, 1 over, k. 2 together, k. 1.

Repeat from the 1st row.

Knitted Lace (fig. 473).   Cast on 13 stitches.

1st row: slip 1, p. 1, p. 2 together, 1 over, k. 9.

2nd row: slip 1, k. 8, 1 over, k. 2, k. 1 into the back of the next st., k. 1.

3rd row: slip 1, p. 2, 1 over, p. 2 together, 1 over, k. 9.

4th row: slip 1, k. 8, 1 over, k. 2 together, 1 over, k. 2, k. 1 into the back of the next st., k. 1.

5th row: slip 1, p. 2, 1 over, p. 2 together, 1 over, p. 2 together, 1 over, k. 9.

6th row: slip 1, k. 8, 1 over, k. 2 together, 1 over, k. 2

Fig. 473. Knitted lace.

together, 1 over, k. 2, k. 1 into the back of the next st., k. 1.

7th row: slip 1, p. 2, 1 over, p. 2 together, 1 over, p. 2 together, 1 over, p. 2 together, 1 over, k. 9.

8th row: slip 1, k. 8, 1 over, k. 2 together, 1 over, k. 2 together, 1 over, k. 2 together, 1 over, k. 2, k. 1 into the back of the next st., k. 1.

9th row: slip 1, p. 2, 1 over, p. 2 together, 1 over, p. 2 together, 1 over, p.2 together, 1 over, p. 2 together, 1 over, k. 9.

10th row: cast off 8, k. 10, k. 1 into the back of the next st., k. 1.

Repeat from the 1st row.

Syrmia Lace (fig. 474).   The women of Syrmia, a district situated between Belgrade and Novi Sad, continue to the present day their ancient custom of trimming dresses and underlinen with knitted lace of a distinctive type, known as Syrmia openwork. The characteristic appearance of this openwork knitting is due to the large open spaces obtained by assembling together the overs made in several rows of the work, which form thick, irregularly overcast bars. These overs are double, and are preceded and followed by a purl decrease.

In the 1st row, the 1st of these decreases is made by purling together 2 ordinary stitches; this is followed by 2 overs, and then the next 2 stitches are purled together.

In the 2nd row, the 1st decrease is made with the stitch of the decrease below and the 1st over; the 2nd decrease is made with the 2nd over and the stitch of the other decrease below.

In the 3rd row, the 1st decrease is made with the stitch of the 1st decrease below and the needle is passed under the 2 superimposed overs below to form the purl decrease. The 2nd decrease is made like an ordinary purl decrease.

According to the design, 1 or 2 more rows can be worked in which the needle, to make the 1st decrease, is passed under 3 or 4 superimposed overs below. Fig. 474 shows the 1st decrease in the 3rd row, in which the needle

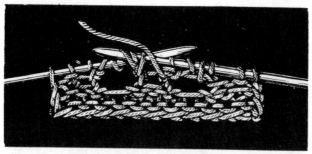

Fig. 474. Syrmia lace. Method of making the openwork spaces.

passes under the overs of 2 preceding rows.

We give an example of an edging and two insertions in this particular kind of work (see figs. 475, 476, 477), which will, we have no doubt, be much appreciated.

Knitted lace (fig. 475). Cast on 17 stitches.

1st and 3rd rows: * 1 over, p. 2 together; repeat once from *; k. 9, ** 1 over, p. 2 together; repeat once from **.

2nd and 4th rows: * 1 over, p. 2 together, repeat once from *; k. 11, 1 over, p. 2 together.

5th row: 1 over, k. 2 together, 1 over, k. 2, p. 2 together, 2 overs, p. 2 together, k. 5, * 1 over, p. 2 together, repeat once from *.

6th row: * 1 over, p. 2 together, repeat once from *; k. 5, p. 2 together, 2 overs, p. 2 together, k. 3, 1 over, p. 2 together.

7th row: 1 over, p. 2 together, 1 over, k. 3, 1 purl decrease for which the needle is passed under the 2 overs below, 2 overs, p. 2 together, k. 5, * 1 over, p. 2 together, repeat once from *.

8th row: * 1 over, p. 2 together, repeat once from *; k. 5, 1 purl decrease for which the needle is passed under the 3 overs below, 2 overs, p. 2 together, k. 4, 1 over, p. 2 together.

9th row: 1 over, p. 2 together, 1 over, k. 2, p. 2 together, 2 overs, 1 purl decrease for which the needle is passed under the 4 overs below, p. 2 together, 2 overs, p. 2 together, k. 3, * 1 over, p. 2 together, repeat once from *.

10th row: * 1 over, p. 2 together, repeat once from *; k. 3; ** p. 2 together, 2 overs, p. 2 together, repeat once from **; k. 3, 1 over, p. 2 together.

11th row: 1 over, p. 2 together, 1 over, k. 3, * 1 purl decrease for which the needle is passed under the 2 overs below, 2 overs, p. 2 together, repeat once from *; k. 3; ** 1 over, p. 2 together, repeat once from **.

12th row: * 1 over, p. 2 together, repeat once from *; k. 3, ** 1 purl decrease for which the needle is passed under the 3 overs below, 2 overs, p. 2 together, repeat once from **; k. 4, 1 over, p. 2 together.

Fig. 475. Knitted lace.

13th row: * 1 over, p. 2 together, repeat once from *; ** p. 2 together, 2 overs, 1 purl decrease for which the needle is passed under the 4 overs below, repeat once from **; p. 2 together, 2 overs, p. 2 together, k. 1, *** 1 over, p. 2 together, repeat once from ***

14th row: * 1 over, p. 2 together, repeat once from *; k. 1, ** p. 2 together, 2 overs, p. 2 together, repeat twice from **; k. 2, 1 over, p. 2 together.

15th row: * 1 over, p. 2 together, repeat once from *; ** 1 purl decrease for which the needle is passed under the 2 overs below, 2 overs, p. 2 together, repeat twice from **; k. 1, *** 1 over, p. 2 together, repeat once from ***.

16th row: * 1 over, p. 2 together, repeat once from *; k. 1, ** 1 purl decrease for which the needle passed under the 3 overs below, 2 overs, p. 2

together, repeat twice from * *; k. 2, 1 over, p. 2 together.

17th row: * 1 over, p. 2 together, repeat once from *; 1 purl decrease for which the needle is passed under the 4 overs below, * * p. 2 together, 2 overs, 1 purl decrease for which the needle is passed under the 4 overs below, repeat once from * *; k. 3, * * * 1 over, p. 2 together, repeat once from * * *.

18th row: * 1 over, p. 2 together, repeat once from *; k. 3, * * p. 2 together, 2 overs, p. 2 together, repeat once from * *; k. 3, 1 over, p. 2 together.

19th row: * 1 over, p. 2 together, repeat once from *; k. 1, * * 1 purl decrease for which the needle is passed under the 2 overs below, 2 overs, p. 2 together, repeat once from * *; k. 3, * * * 1 over, p. 2 together, repeat once from * * *.

Fig. 476. Knitted insertion.

20th row: * 1 over, p. 2 together, repeat once from *; k. 3, * * 1 purl decrease for which the needle is passed under the 3 overs below, 2 overs, p. 2 together, repeat once from * *; k. 3, 1 over, p. 2 together.

21st row: * 1 over, p. 2 together, repeat once from *; k. 1, 1 purl decrease for which the needle is passed under the 4 overs below, p. 2 together, 2 overs, 1 purl decrease for which the needle is passed under 4 overs below, k. 5, * * 1 over, p. 2 together, repeat once from * *.

22nd row: * 1 over, p. 2 together, repeat once from *; k. 5, p. 2 together, 2 overs, p. 2 together, k. 4, 1 over, p. 2 together.

23rd row: * 1 over, p. 2 together, repeat once from *; k. 2, 1 purl decrease for which the needle is passed under the 2 overs below, 2 overs, p. 2 together, k. 5, * * 1 over, p. 2 together, repeat once from * *.

24th row: * 1 over, p. 2 together, repeat once from *; k. 5, 1 purl decrease for which the needle is passed under the 3 overs below, 2 overs, p. 2 together, k. 4, 1 over, p. 2 together.

25th row: * 1 over, p. 2 together, repeat once from *; k. 2, 1 purl decrease for which the needle is passed under the 4 overs below, p. 2 together, k. 5, ** 1 over, p. 2 together, repeat once from **.

Repeat from the 2nd row.

Knitted insertion (fig. 476). Cast on 24 stitches.

1st row: slip 1, k. 2, 1 over, k. 2 together, k. 1, 1 dot st., k. 3, 1 over, slip 1, k. 1, pass the slipped st. over, k. 2 together, 1 over, k. 3, 1 dot st., k. 3, 1 over, k. 2 together, k. 1.

2nd, 4th, 8th, 12th, and 16th rows: slip 1, k. 2, 1 over, k. 2 together, p. 14, k. 2, 1 over, k. 2 together, k. 1.

3rd row: slip 1, k. 2, 1 over, k. 2 together, k. 3, k. 2 together, 1 over, k. 4, 1 over, slip 1, k. 1, pass the slipped st. over, k. 5, 1 over, k. 2 together, k. 1.

5th row: slip 1, k. 2, 1 over, k. 2 together, k. 2, k. 2 together, 1 over, k. 1, k. 2 together, 2 overs, slip 1, k. 1, pass the slipped st. over, k. 1, 1 over, slip 1, k. 1, pass the slipped st. over, k. 4, 1 over, k. 2 together, k. 1.

6th and 14th rows: slip 1, k. 2, 1 over, k. 2 together, p. 6, k. 1, p. 7, k. 2, 1 over, k. 2 together, k. 1.

7th row: slip 1, k. 2, 1 over, k. 2 together, k. 1, k. 2 together, 1 over, k. 8, 1 over, slip 1, k. 1, pass the slipped st. over, k. 3, 1 over, k. 2 together, k. 1.

9th row: slip 1, k. 2, 1 over, k. 2 together twice, 1 over, k. 1, k. 2 together, 2 overs, slip 1, k. 1, pass the slipped st. over, k. 2 together, 2 overs, slip 1, k. 1, pass the slipped st. over, k. 1, 1 over, slip 1, k. 1, pass the slipped st. over, k. 2, 1 over, k. 2 together, k. 1.

10th row: slip 1, k. 2, 1 over, k. 2 together, p. 4, k. 1, p. 3, k. 1, p. 5, k. 2, 1 over, k. 2 together, k. 1.

11th row: slip 1, k. 2, 1 over, k. 2 together, k. 2, 1 over, slip 1, k. 1, pass the slipped st. over, k. 6, k. 2 together, 1 over, k. 4, 1 over, k. 2 together, k. 1.

13th row: slip 1, k. 2, 1 over, k. 2 together, k. 3, 1 over, slip 1, k. 1, pass the slipped st. over, k. 2 together, 2 over, slip 1, k. 1, pass the slipped st. over, k. 2 together, 1 over, k. 5, 1 over, k. 2 together, k. 1.

15th row: slip 1, k. 2, 1 over, k. 2 together, k. 4, 1 over, slip 1, k. 1, pass the slipped st. over, k. 2, k. 2 together, 1 over, k. 6, 1 over, k. 2 together, k. 1.

Repeat from the 1st row.

Knitted insertion (fig. 477). Cast on 24 stitches.

1st row: * 1 over, p. 2 together, repeat once from *; ** p. 2 together, 2 overs, p. 2 together, repeat once from **; k. 8, *** 1 over. p. 2 together, repeat once from ***.

2nd row: * 1 over, p. 2 together, repeat once from *; k. 8, ** p. 2 together, 2 over, p. 2 together, repeat once from **; *** 1 over, p. 2 together, repeat once from ***.

3rd row: * 1 over, p. 2 together, repeat once from *; ** 1 purl decrease for which the needle is passed under the 2 overs below, 2 overs, p. 2 together, repeat once from **; k. 8, *** 1 over, p. 2 together, repeat once from ***.

4th row: * 1 over, p. 2 together, repeat once from *; k. 8, ** 1 purl decrease for which the needle is passed under the 3 overs below, 2 overs, p. 2 together, repeat once from **; *** 1 over, p. 2 together, repeat once from ***.

5th row: * 1 over, p. 2 together, repeat once from *; 1 over, ** 1 purl decrease for which the needle is passed under the 4 overs below, p. 2 together, 2 overs, repeat once from **; p. 2 together, k. 6, *** 1 over, p. 2 together, repeat once from ***.

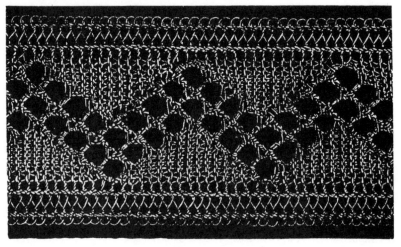

Fig. 477. Knitted insertion.

6th row: * 1 over, p. 2 together, repeat once from *; k. 6, ** p. 2 together, 2 overs, p. 2 together, repeat once from **; k. 1, k. 1 into the back of the next st., *** 1 over, p. 2 together, repeat once from ***.

7th and 31st rows: * 1 over, p. 2 together, repeat once from *; k. 2, ** 1 purl decrease for which the needle is passed under the 2 overs below, 2 overs, p. 2 together, repeat once from **; k. 6, *** 1 over, p. 2 together, repeat once from ***.

8th and 32nd rows: * 1 over, p. 2 together, repeat once from *; k. 6, ** 1 purl decrease for which the needle is passed under the 3 overs below, 2 overs, p. 2 together, repeat once from **; k. 2, *** 1 over, p. 2 together, repeat once from ***.

9th row: * 1 over, p. 2 together, repeat once from *; k. 2, 1 over, ** 1 purl decrease for which the needle is passed under the 4 overs below, p. 2

together, 2 overs, repeat once from * *; p. 2 together, k. 4, * * * 1 over, p. 2 together, repeat once from * * *.

10th row: * 1 over, p. 2 together, repeat once from *; k. 4, * * p. 2 together, 2 overs, p. 2 together, repeat once from * *; k. 1, k. 1 into the back of the next st., k. 2, * * * 1 over, p. 2 together, repeat once from * * *.

11th and 27th rows: * 1 over, p. 2 together, repeat once from *; k. 4, * * 1 purl decrease for which the needle is passed under the 2 overs below, 2 overs, p. 2 together, repeat once from * *; k. 4, * * * 1 over, p. 2 together, repeat once from * * *.

12th and 28th rows: * 1 over, p. 2 together, repeat once from *; k. 4, * * 1 purl decrease for which the needle is passed under the 3 overs below, 2 overs, p. 2 together, repeat once from * *; k. 4, * * * 1 over, p. 2 together, repeat once from * * *.

13th row: * 1 over, p. 2 together, repeat once from *; k. 4, 1 over, * * 1 purl decrease for which the needle is passed under the 4 over below, p. 2 together, 2 overs, repeat once from * *; p. 2 together, k. 2, * * * 1 over, p. 2 together, repeat once from * * *.

14th row: * 1 over, p. 2 together, repeat once from *; k. 2, * * p. 2 together, 2 overs, p. 2 together, repeat once from * *; k. 1, k. 1 into the back of the next st., k. 4, * * * 1 over, p. 2 together, repeat once from * * *.

15th and 23rd rows: * 1 over, p. 2 together, repeat once from *; k. 6, * * 1 purl decrease for which the needle is passed under the 2 overs below, 2 overs, p. 2 together, repeat once from * *; k. 2, * * * 1 over, p. 2 together, repeat once from * * *.

16th and 24th rows: * 1 over, p. 2 together, repeat once from *; k. 2, * * 1 purl decrease for which the needle is passed under the 3 overs below, 2 overs, p. 2 together, repeat once from * *; k. 6, * * * 1 over, p. 2 together, repeat once from * * *.

17th row: * 1 over, p. 2 together, repeat once from *; k. 6, 1 over, * * 1 purl decrease for which the needle is passed under the 4 overs below, p. 2 together, 2 overs, repeat once from * *; p. 2 together, * * * 1 over, p. 2 together, repeat once from * * *.

18th row: * 1 over, p. 2 together, repeat once from *; * * p. 2 together, 2 overs, p. 2 together, repeat once from * *; k. 1, k. 1 into the back of the next st., k. 6, * * * 1 over, p. 2 together, repeat once from * * *.

19th row: * 1 over, p. 2 together, repeat once from *; k. 8, * * 1 purl decrease for which the needle is passed under the 2 overs below, 2 overs, p. 2 together, repeat once from * *; * * * 1 over, p. 2 together, repeat once from * * *.

20th row: * 1 over, p. 2 together, repeat once from *; * * 1 purl decrease for which the needle is passed under the 3 overs below, 2 overs, p. 2 together, repeat once from * *; k. 8, * * * 1 over, p. 2 together, repeat once from * * *.

21st row: * 1 over, p. 2 together, repeat once from *; k. 6, * * p. 2

together, 2 overs, 1 purl decrease for which the needle is passed under the 4 overs below, repeat once from **; k. 2, *** 1 over, p. 2 together, repeat once from ***.

22nd row: * 1 over, p. 2 together, repeat once from *; k. 2, ** p. 2

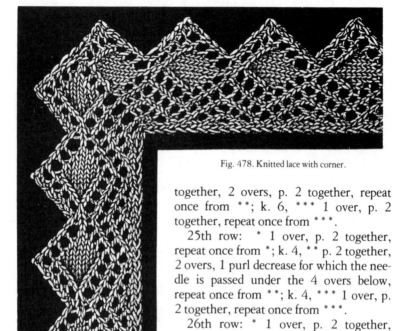

Fig. 478. Knitted lace with corner.

together, 2 overs, p. 2 together, repeat once from **; k. 6, *** 1 over, p. 2 together, repeat once from ***.

25th row: * 1 over, p. 2 together, repeat once from *; k. 4, ** p. 2 together, 2 overs, 1 purl decrease for which the needle is passed under the 4 overs below, repeat once from **; k. 4, *** 1 over, p. 2 together, repeat once from ***.

26th row: * 1 over, p. 2 together, repeat once from *; k. 4, ** p. 2 together, 2 overs, p. 2 together, repeat once from **; k. 4, *** 1 over, p. 2 together, repeat once from ***.

29th row: * 1 over, p. 2 together, repeat once from *; k. 2, ** p. 2 together, 2 overs, 1 purl decrease for which the needle is passed under the 4 overs below, repeat once from **; k. 6, *** 1 over, p. 2 together, repeat once from ***.

30th row: * 1 over, p. 2 together, repeat once from *; k. 6, ** p. 2 together, 2 overs, p. 2 together, repeat once from **; k. 2, *** 1 over, p. 2 together, repeat once from ***.

33rd row: * 1 over, p. 2 together, repeat once from *; ** p. 2 together, 2 overs, 1 purl decrease for which the needle is passed under the 4 overs below, repeat once from **; k. 8, *** 1 over, p. 2 together, repeat once from ***.

Repeat from the 2nd row.

Knitted Lace With Corner (fig. 478).   Cast on 11 stitches.

The straight part of the lace, without the corner, requires 16 rows to each pattern.

1st row: slip 1, k. 1 into the back of the next st., 1 over, k. 1, 1 over, slip 1, k. 1, pass the slipped st. over, 1 over, slip 1, k. 1, pass the slipped st. over, 1 over, slip 1, k. 1, pass the slipped st. over, k. 2.

2nd, 4th, 6th, 8th, 10th, 12th, 14th, and 16th rows: purl.

3rd row: slip 1, k. 1 into the back of the next st., 1 over, k. 3, 1 over, slip 1, k. 1, pass the slipped st. over, slip 1, k. 1, pass the slipped st. over, 1 over, slip 1, k. 1, pass the slipped st. over, k. 1.

5th row: slip 1, k. 1 into the back of the next st., 1 over, k. 5, 1 over, slip 1, k. 1, pass the slipped st. over, 1 over, slip 1, k. 1, pass the slipped st. over, k. 2.

7th row: slip 1, k. 1 into the back of the next st., 1 over, k. 7, 1 over, slip 1, k. 1, pass the slipped st. over, 1 over, slip 1, k. 1, pass the slipped st. over, k. 1.

9th row: slip 1, k. 1, pass the slipped st. over, k. 1, 1 over, slip 1, k. 1, pass the slipped st. over, k. 3, k. 2 together, 1 over, k. 2 together, 1 over, k. 3.

11th row: slip 1, k. 1, pass the slipped st. over, k. 1, 1 over, slip 1, k. 1, pass the slipped st. over, k. 1, k. 2 together, 1 over, k. 2 together, 1 over, k. 2 together, 1 over, k. 2.

13th row: slip 1, k. 1, pass the slipped st. over, k. 1, 1 over, slip 1, k. 2 together, pass the slipped st. over, 1 over, k. 2 together, 1 over, k. 2 together, 1 over, k. 3.

15th row: slip 1, k. 1, pass the slipped st. over, k. 2, k. 2 together, 1 over, k. 2 together, 1 over, k. 2 together, 1 over, k. 2.

Repeat from the 1st row.

When the required length has been knitted, the corner, which is worked in 36 rows, is begun after the 14th row.

1st row: slip 1, k. 1, pass the slipped st. over, k. 2, k. 2 together, 1 over, k. 2 together, 1 over, k. 2 together, 1 over, k. 1, slip the next st. onto a thread.

2nd, 4th, 6th, and 8th rows: slip 1, p. 9.

3rd row: slip 1, k. 1 into the back of the next st., 1 over, k. 1, 1 over, slip 1, k. 1, pass the slipped st. over, 1 over, slip 1, k. 1, pass the slipped st. over, 1 over, slip 1, k. 1, pass the slipped st. over, slip the next st. onto the spare thread.

5th row: slip 1, k. 1 into the back of the next st., 1 over, k. 3, 1 over, slip 1, k. 1, pass the slipped st. over, 1 over, slip 1, k. 1, pass the slipped st. over, slip the next st. onto the spare thread.

7th row: slip 1, k. 1 into the back of the next st., 1 over, k. 5, 1 over, slip 1, k. 1, pass the slipped st. over, slip the next st. onto the thread.

9th row: slip 1, k. 1 into the back of the next st., 1 over, k. 7, slip the next st. onto the thread.

10th row: 1 over, p. 10.

11th row: slip 1, k. 1, pass the slipped st. over, k. 1, 1 over, slip 1, k. 1, pass the slipped st. over, k. 3, k. 2 together slip the next st. (1 over) onto the thread.

12th row: 1 over, p. 8.

13th row: slip 1, k. 1, pass the slipped st. over, k. 1, 1 over, slip 1, k. 1, pass the slipped st. over, k. 1, k. 2 together, slip the next st. (1 over) onto the thread.

14th row: 1 over, p. 6.

15th row: slip 1, k. 1, pass the slipped st. over, k. 1, 1 over, slip 1, k. 2 together, pass the slipped st. over, slip the next st. (1 over) onto the thread.

16th row: 1 over, p. 4.

17th row: slip 1, k. 1, pass the slipped st. over, k. 2, slip the next st. (1 over) onto the thread.

18th row: slip 1, p. 2.

19th row: slip 1, k. 1 into the back of the next st. 1 over, slip 1, take up the last st. slipped onto the spare thread and k. 1 into the back of it, pass the slipped st. over.

20th row: slip 1, p. 3.

21st row: slip 1, k. 1 into the back of the next st., 1 over, k. 2, take up the next st. on the spare thread and k. 1 into the next back of it.

22nd row: slip 1, p. 5.

23rd row: slip 1, k. 1 into the back of the next st., 1 over, k. 4, take up the next st. on the spare thread and k. 1 into the back of it.

24th row: slip 1, p. 7.

25th row: slip 1, k. 1 into the back of the next st., 1 over, k. 6, take up the next st. on the spare thread and k. 1 into the back of it.

26th, 28th, 30th, 32nd, and 34th rows: slip 1, p. 9.

27th row: slip 1, k. 1, pass the slipped st. over, k. 1, 1 over, slip 1, k. 1, pass the slipped st. over, k. 3, k. 2 together, 1 over, take up the next st. on the spare thread and k. 1 into the back of it.

29th row: slip 1, k. 1, pass the slipped st. over, k. 1, 1 over, slip 1, k. 1, pass the slipped st. over, k. 1, k. 2 together, 1 over, k. 2 together, 1 over, take up the next st. on the spare thread and k. 1 into the back of it.

31st row: slip 1, k. 1, pass the slipped st. over, k. 1, 1 over, slip 1, k. 2 together, pass the slipped st. over, 1 over, k. 2 together, 1 over, k. 2 together, 1 over take up the next st. on the spare thread and k. 1 into the back of it.

33rd row: slip 1, k. 1, pass the slipped st. over, k. 2, k. 2 together, 1 over, k. 2 together, 1 over, k. 2 together, 1 over, take up the next st. on the spare thread and k. 1 into the back of it.

35th row: slip 1, k. 1 into the the back of the next st., 1 over, k. 1, 1 over, slip 1, k. 1, pass the slipped st. over, 1 over, slip 1, k. 1, pass the slipped st. over, 1 over, slip 1, k. 1, pass the slipped st. over, k. 1, take up the last st. on the spare thread and k. 1 into the back of it.

36th row: slip 1, p. 11.

Continue from the 3rd row of the instructions for the straight part of the lace.

Knitted Medallion (fig. 479).   Cast on 2 stitches on each of 4 needles. Each set of instructions followed by an * is to be repeated seven times.

1st round: 1 over, k. 1 *.

2nd and 3rd rounds: k. 2 *.

4th round: 1 over, k. 1, 1 over, k. 1 *.

5th round: k. 4 *.

Fig. 479. Knitted medallion.

6th round: 1 over, k. 3, 1 over, k. 1 *.

7th and 9th rounds: k. 6 *.

8th round: 1 over, k. 1, p. 3 together, k. 1, 1 over, k. 1 *.

10th round: 1 over, k. 5, 1 over, k. 1 *.

11th and 13th rounds: k. 8 *.

12th round: 1 over, k. 2, p. 3 together, k. 2, 1 over, k. 1 *.

14th round: 1 over, k. 7, 1 over, k. 1 *.

15th and 17th rounds: k. 10 *.

16th round: 1 over, k. 3, p. 3 together, k. 3, 1 over, k. 1 *.

18th round: 1 over, k. 9, 1 over, k. 1 *.

19th and 21st rounds: k. 12 *.

20th round: 1 over, k. 4, p. 3 together, k. 4, 1 over, k. 1 *.

22nd round: 1 over, k. 11, 1 over, k. 1 *.

23rd and 25th rounds: k. 14 *.

24th round: 1 over, k. 5, p. 3 together, k. 5, 1 over, k. 1 *.

26th round: k. 1, 1 over, k. 11, 1 over, k. 2 *.

27th and 29th rounds: k. 16 *.

28th round: 1 over, slip 1, k. 1, pass the slipped st. over, 1 over, k. 4, p. 3 together, k. 4, 1 over, k. 2 together, 1 over, k. 1 *.

30th round: k. 2 together, 1 over, k. 1, 1 over, k. 9, 1 over, k. 1, 1 over, slip 1, k. 1, pass the slipped st. over, k. 1 *.

31st and 33rd rounds: k. 18 *.

32nd round: ** 1 over, slip 1, k. 1, pass the slipped st. over, repeat once from **; 1 over, k. 3, p. 3 together, k. 3, *** 1 over, k. 2 together, repeat once from ***; 1 over, k. 1 *.

34th round: ** k. 2 together, 1 over, repeat once from **; k. 1, 1 over, k. 7, 1 over, k. 1, *** 1 over slip 1, k. 1, pass the slipped st. over, repeat once from ***; k. 1 *.

35th and 37th rounds: k. 20 *.

36th round: ** 1 over, slip 1, k. 1, pass the slipped st. over, repeat twice from **; 1 over, k. 2, p. 3 together, k. 2, *** 1 over, k. 2 together, repeat twice from ***; 1 over, k. 1 *.

38th round: ** k. 2 together, 1 over, repeat twice from **; k. 1, 1 over, k. 5, 1 over, k. 1, *** 1 over, slip 1, k. 1, pass the slipped st. over, repeat twice from ***; k. 1 *.

39th and 41st rounds: k. 22 *.

40th round: ** 1 over, slip 1, k. 1, pass the slipped st. over, repeat from ** three times; 1 over, k. 1, p. 3 together, k. 1, *** 1 over, k. 2 together, repeat from *** three times; 1 over, k. 1 *.

42nd round: ** k. 2 together, 1 over, repeat from ** three times, k. 1, 1 over, k. 3, 1 over, k. 1, *** 1 over, slip 1, k. 1, pass the slipped st. over, repeat from *** three times, k. 1 *.

43rd and 45th rounds: k. 24 *.

44th round: ** 1 over, slip 1, k. 1, pass the slipped st. over, repeat from ** four times; 1 over, p. 3 together, *** 1 over, k. 2 together, repeat from *** four times, 1 over, k. 1 *.

46th, 47th, 48th, and 49th rounds: p. 24 *.

In the remaining rows, each set of instructions followed by an * is to be repeated 15 times.

50th round: ** 1 over, slip 1, k. 1, pass the slipped stitch over, repeat once from **; 1 over, p. 3, *** 1 over, k. 2 together, repeat once from ***; 1 over, k. 1 *.

51st round: k. 5, p. 3, k. 6 *.

52nd round: 1 over, k. 1, ** 1 over, slip 1, k. 1, pass the slipped st. over, repeat once from * *; p. 3, * * * k. 2 together, 1 over, repeat once from * * *; k. 1, 1 over, k. 1 *.

53rd round: k. 6, p. 3, k. 7 *.

54th round: 1 over, k. 1, * * 1 over, slip 1, k. 1, pass the slipped st. over, repeat once from * *; k. 1, p. 3, k. 1, * * * k. 2 together, 1 over, repeat once from * * *; k. 1, 1 over, k. 1 *.

55th round: k. 7, p. 3, k. 8 *.

56th round: * * 1 over, k. 1, repeat twice from * *; * * * 1 over, slip 1, k. 1, pass the slipped st. over, repeat once from * * *; p. 3 together, * * * * k. 2 together, 1 over, repeat once from * * * *; k. 1, 1 over, k. 1, 1 over, k. 1, 1 over, k. 1 *.

57th round: k. 9, slip 1, k. 2 together, pass the slipped st. over, k. 10 *.

58th round: worked in crochet. Take the 1st st. on a crochet hook (in the repetitions, crochet this st. separately), * * make 9 chain and 1 double crochet joining the next 2 sts., repeat twice from * *; crochet the next 5 sts. separately, * * * join the next 2 sts., 9 chain, repeat from * * * three times; *. Join to the 1st st. and break off the thread.

Design for Bedspread With Knitted Medallions and Edging (fig. 480). The knitted medallions which form the ground are connected by small squares of linen ornamented with hem stitching; this ground is surrounded by a deep lace edging gathered at the corners. The medallions are made first.

Cast on 2 stitches on each of four needles; close the ring.

1st round: * 1 over, k. 1; repeat from * seven times.

2nd, 4th, 6th, 8th, 10th, 12th, 14th, 16th, 18th, 20th, 22nd, and 24th rounds: k. throughout.

Each set of instructions followed by an * is to be repeated three times:

3rd round: 1 over, k. 3, 1 over, k. 1 into the back of the next st. *.

5th round: 1 over, k. 5, 1 over, k. 1 into the back of the next st. *.

7th round: 1 over, k. 7, 1 over, k. 1 into the back of the next st. *.

Each set of instructions followed by an * is to be repeated seven times:

9th round: 1 over, slip 1, k. 1, pass the slipped st. over, k. 2 together, 1 over, k. 1 *.

11th round: k. 1, 1 over, k. 2 together, 1 over, k. 2 *.

13th round: k. 2, 1 over, k. 1 into the back of the next st., 1 over, k. 3 *.

15th round: k. 3, 1 over, k. 1 into the back of the next st., 1 over, k. 4 *.

17th round: k. 4, 1 over, k. 1 into the back of the next st., 1 over, k. 5 *.

19th round: k. 5, 1 over, k. 1 into the back of the next st., 1 over, k. 5 *.

21st round: k. 6, 1 over, k. 1 into the back of the next st., 1 over, k. 7 *.

23rd round: k. 7, 1 over, k. 1 into the back of the next st., 1 over, k. 8 *.

25th round: slip 1, k. 1, pass the slipped st. over, k. 5, 1 over, k. 3, 1 over, k. 5, k. 2 together, p. 1 *.

26th, 28th, 30th, 32nd, 34th, and 36th rounds: k. 17, p. 1 *.

27th round: slip 1, k. 1, pass the slipped st. over, k. 4, 1 over, k. 5, 1 over, k. 4, k. 2 together, p. 1 *.

29th round: slip 1, k. 1, pass the slipped st. over, k. 3, 1 over, k. 1, 1 over, slip 1, k. 1, pass the slipped st. over, k. 1, k. 2 together, 1 over, k. 1, 1 over, k. 3, k. 2 together, p. 1 *.

31st round: slip 1, k. 1, pass the slipped st. over, k. 2, 1 over, k. 3, 1 over, slip 1, k. 2 together, pass the slipped st. over, 1 over, k. 3, 1 over, k. 2, k. 2 together, p. 1 *.

33rd round: slip 1, k. 1, pass the slipped st. over, 1 over, k. 11, 1 over, k. 1, k. 2 together, p. 1 *.

Fig. 480. Design for bedspread with knitted medallions and edging.

35th round: slip 1, k. 1, pass the slipped st. over, 1 over, k. 1, 1 over, slip 1, k. 1, pass the slipped st. over, k. 1, k. 2 together, 1 over, k. 1, 1 over, slip 1, k. 1, pass the slipped st. over, k. 1, k. 2 together, 1 over, k. 1, 1 over, k. 2 together, p. 1 *.

37th round: slip 1, ** 1 over, k. 3, 1 over, slip 1, k. 2 together, pass the slipped st. over, 1 over, k. 3, 1 over, slip 1, k. 2 together, pass the slipped st. over, 1 over, k. 3, 1 over, k. 2 together, slip the next st. over this decrease, repeat seven times from **; after the seventh time, pass the first slipped st. of the round over the last decrease.

38th, 40th, and 42nd rounds: knit throughout.

39th round: 1 over, slip 1, k. 1, pass the slipped st. over, k. 1, k. 2 together, 1 over, k. 1, 1 over, slip 1, k. 1, pass the slipped st. over, k. 1, k. 2 together, 1 over, k. 1, 1 over, slip 1, k. 1, pass the slipped st. over, k. 1, k. 2 together, 1 over, k. 1 *.

41st round: k. 1, 1 over, slip 1, k. 2 together, pass the slipped st. over, 1 over, k. 3, 1 over, slip 1, k. 2 together, pass the slipped st. over, 1 over, k. 3, 1 over, slip 1, k. 2 together, pass the slipped st. over, 1 over, k. 2 *.

To finish off, work 3 more rounds, purled throughout, and cast off.

When the required number of medallions have been made, the squares of linen are hemstitched and joined to the knitted medallions with overcast seams.

For the edging, cast on 43 stitches.

1st row: cast off 2 sts., 1 over, k. 1 into the back of the next st., 1 over, k. 1 into the back of the next st., 1 over, k. 1, 1 over, slip 1, k. 1, pass the slipped st. over, k. 1, k. 2 together, 1 over, k. 1, 1 over, slip 1, k. 1, pass the slipped st. over, k. 1, k. 2 together, 1 over, k. 1, k. 1 into the back of the next st., p. 1, k. 1 into the back of the next st., 1 over, k. 1, k. 2 together, p. 1, slip 1, k. 1, pass the slipped st. over, k. 1, p. 1, k. 1, k. 2 together, p. 1, slip 1, k. 1, pass the slipped st. over, k. 1, 1 over, k. 1 into the back of the next st., p. 1, k. 1 into the back of the next st., 1 over, k. 2 together, k. 2.

2nd row: slip 1, k. 2, p. 1, p. 1 into the back of the next st., k. 1, p. 1 into the back of the next st., p. 3, k. 1, p. 2, k. 1, p. 2, k. 1, p. 3, p. 1 into the back of the next st., k. 1, p. 1 into the back of the next st., k. 14, p. 1 into the back of the next st., p. 4.

3rd row: cast off 2, 1 over, k. 1 into the back of the next st., 1 over, k. 1 into the back of the next st., 1 over, k. 3, 1 over, slip 1, k. 2 together, pass the slipped st. over, 1 over, k. 3, 1 over, slip 1, k. 2 together, pass the slipped st. over, 1 over, k. 2 together, 1 over, k. 1 into the back of the next st., p. 1, k. 1 into the back of the next st., 1 over, k. 1, 1 over, k. 2 together, p. 1, slip 1, p. 1, k. 2 together, p. 1, slip 1, 1 over, k. 1, 1 over, k. 1 into the back of the next st., p. 1, k. 1 into the back of the next st. 1 over, k. 2 together, k. 2.

4th and 20th rows: slip 1, k. 2, p. 1, p. 1 into the back of the next st., k. 1, p. 1 into the back of the next st., p. 4, k. 1, p. 1, k. 1, p. 1, k. 1, p. 4, p. 1 into the back of the next st., k. 1, p. 1 into the back of the next st., k. 1, p. 1 into the back of the next st., p. 15, p. 1 into the back of the next st., p. 4.

5th row: cast off 2, 1 over, k. 1 into the back of the next st., 1 over, k. 1 into the back of the next st., 1 over, k. 2, 1 over, slip 1, k. 1, pass the slipped st. over, k. 2 together, 1 over, k. 2, 1 over, slip 1, k. 1, pass the slipped st. over, k. 2 together, 1 over, k. 2, 1 over, k. 1, k. 1 into the back of the next st., p. 1, k. 1 into the back of the next st., 1 over, k. 3, 1 over, slip 1, k. 2 together, pass the slipped st. over, p. 1, slip 1, k. 2 together, pass the slipped st. over, 1 over, k. 3, 1 over, k. 1 into the back of the next st., p. 1, k. 1 into the back of the next st., 1 over, k. 2 together, k. 2.

6th row: slip 1, k. 2, p. 1, p. 1 into the back of the next st., k. 1, p. 1 into the back of the next st., p. 6, k. 1, p. 6, p. 1 into the back of the next st., k. 1, p. 1 into the back of the next st., p. 16, p. 1 into the back of the next st., p. 4.

7th row: cast off 2, 1 over, k. 1 into the back of the next st., 1 over, k. 1 into the back of the next st., 1 over, k. 1, 1 over, slip 1, k. 1, pass the slipped st. over, k. 1, k. 2 together, 1 over, k. 1, 1 over, slip 1, k. 1, pass the slipped st. over, k. 1, k. 2 together, 1 over, k. 2 together, 1 over, k. 2 together, 1 over, k. 1 into the back of the next st., p. 1, k. 1 into the back of the next st., 1 over, k. 5, 1 over, slip 1, k. 2 together, pass the slipped st. over, 1 over, k. 5, 1 over, k. 1 into the back of the next st., p. 1, k. 1 into the back of the next st., 1 over, k. 2 together, k. 2.

8th and 16th rows: slip 1, k. 2, p. 1, p. 1 into the back of the next st., k. 1, p. 1 into the back of the next st., p. 15, p. 1 into the back of the next st., k. 1, p. 1 into the back of the next st., p. 17, p. 1 into the back of the next st., p. 4.

9th row: cast off 2, 1 over, k. 1 into the back of the next st., 1 over, k. 1 into the back of the next st., 1 over, k. 3, 1 over, slip 1, k. 2 together, pass the slipped st. over, 1 over, k. 3, 1 over, slip 1, k. 2 together, pass the slipped st. over, 1 over, k. 2 together, 1 over, k. 2 together, 1 over, k. 1, k. 1 into the back of the next st., p. 1, k. 1 into the back of the next st., 1 over, k. 1, k. 2 together, p. 1, slip 1, k. 1, pass the slipped st. over, k. 1, p. 1, k. 1, k. 2 together, p. 1, slip 1, k. 1, pass the slipped st. over, k. 1, 1 over, k. 1 into the back of the next st., p. 1, k. 1 into the back of the next st., 1 over, k. 2 together, k. 2.

10th row: slip 1, k. 2, p. 1, p. 1 into the back of the next st., k. 1, p. 1 into the back of the next st., p. 3, k. 1, p. 2, k. 1, p. 2, k. 1, p. 3, p. 1 into the back of the next st., k. 1, p. 1 into the back of the next st., p. 18, p. 1 into the back of the next st., p. 4.

11th row: cast off 2, 1 over, k. 1 into the back of the next st., 1 over, k. 1 into the back of the next st. , 1 over, k. 2, 1 over, slip 1, k. 1, pass the slipped st. over, k. 2 together, 1 over, k. 2, 1 over, slip 1, k. 1, pass the slipped st. over, k. 2 together, 1 over, k. 2 together, 1 over, k. 2 together, 1 over, k. 1 into the back of the next st., p. 1, k. 1 into the back of the next st., 1 over, k. 1, 1 over, k. 2 together, p. 1, slip 1, k. 1, pass the slipped st. over, p. 1, k. 2 together, p. 1, slip 1, k. 1, pass the slipped st. over, 1 over, k. 1, 1 over, k. 1 into the back of the next st., p. 1, k. 1 into the back of the next st., 1 over, k. 2 together, k. 2.

12th row: slip 1, k. 2, p. 1, p. 1 into the back of the next st., k. 1, p. 1 into the back of the next st., p. 4, k. 1, p. 1, k. 1, p.1, k. 1, p. 4, p. 1 into the back of the next st., k. 1, p. 1 into the back of the next st., p. 19, p. 1 into the back of the next st., p. 4.

13th row: cast off 2, 1 over, k. 1 into the back of the next st., 1 over, slip 1, k. 1, pass the slipped st. over, 1 over, slip 1, k. 1, pass the slipped st. over, k. 1, k. 2 together, 1 over, k. 1, 1 over, slip 1, k. 1, pass the slipped st. over, k. 1, k. 2 together, 1 over, k. 1, 1 over, slip 1, k. 1, pass the slipped st. over, 1 over, slip 1, k. 1, pass the slipped st. over, 1 over, slip 1, k. 1, pass the slipped st. over, k. 1 into the back of the next st., p. 1, k. 1 into the back of the next st., 1 over, k. 3, 1 over, slip 1, k. 2 together, pass the slipped st. over, p. 1, slip 1, k. 2 together, pass the slipped st. over, 1 over, k. 3, 1 over, k. 1 into the back of the next st., p. 1, k. 1 into the back of the next st., 1 over, k. 2 together, k. 2.

14th row: slip 1, k. 2, p. 1, p. 1 into the back of the next st., k. 1, p. 1 into the back of the next st., p. 6, k. 1, p. 6, p. 1 into the back of the next st., k. 1, p. 1 into the back of the next st., p. 18, p. 1 into the back of the next st., p. 4.

15th row: cast off 2, 1 over, k. 1 into the back of the next st., 1 over, slip 1, k. 1, pass the slipped st. over, 1 over, slip 1, k. 2 together, pass the slipped st. over, 1 over, k. 3, 1 over, slip 1, k. 2 together, pass the slipped st. over, 1 over, k. 3, 1 over, slip 1, k. 1, pass the slipped st. over, 1 over, slip 1, k. 1, pass the slipped st. over, 1 over, k. 2 together, p. 1, k. 1 into the back of the next st., 1 over, k. 5, 1 over, slip 1, k. 2 together, pass the slipped st. over, 1 over, k. 5, 1 over, k. 1 into the back of the next st., p. 1, k. 1 into the back of the next st., 1 over, k. 2 together, k. 2.

17th row: cast off 2, 1 over, k. 1 into the back of the next st., 1 over, slip 1, k. 1, pass the slipped st. over, 1 over, slip 1, k. 1, pass the slipped st. over, k. 2 together, 1 over, k. 2, 1 over, slip 1, k. 1, pass the slipped st. over, k. 2 together, 1 over, k. 2, 1 over, slip 1, k. 1, pass the slipped st. over, 1 over, slip 1, k. 1, pass the slipped st. over, k. 1 into the back of the next st., p. 1, k. 1 into the back of the next st., 1 over, k. 1, k. 2 together, p. 1, slip 1, k. 1, pass the slipped st. over, k. 1, p. 1, k. 1, k. 2 together, p. 1, slip 1, k. 1, pass the slipped st. over, k. 1, 1 over, k. 1 into the back of the next st., p. 1, k. 1 into the back of the next st., 1 over, k. 2 together, k. 2.

18th row: slip 1, k. 2, p. 1, p. 1 into the back of the next st., k. 1, p. 1 into the back of the next st., p. 3, k. 1, p. 2, k. 1, p. 2, k. 1, p. 3, p. 1 into the back of the next st., k. 1, p. 1 into the back of the next st., p. 16, p. 1 into the back of the next st., p. 4.

19th row: cast off 2, 1 over, k. 1 into the back of the next st., 1 over, slip 1, k. 1, pass the slipped st. over, 1 over, slip 1, k. 1, pass the slipped st. over, k. 1, k. 2 together, 1 over, k. 1, 1 over, slip 1, k. 1, pass the slipped st. over, k. 1, k. 2 together, 1 over, k. 1, 1 over, slip 1, k. 1, pass the slipped st. over, 1 over, k. 2 together, p. 1, k. 1 into the back of the next st., 1 over, k. 1, 1 over, k. 2 together, p. 1, slip 1, k. 1, pass the slipped st. over, p. 1, k. 2 together, p. 1, slip 1, k. 1, pass the slipped st. over, 1 over, k. 1, 1 over, k. 1 into the back of the next st., p. 1, k. 1 into the back of the next st., 1 over, k. 2 together, k. 2.

21st row: cast off 2, 1 over, k. 1 into the back of the next st., 1 over, slip 1, k. 1, pass the slipped st. over, 1 over, slip 1, k. 2 together, pass the slipped st. over, 1 over, k. 3, 1 over, slip 1, k. 2 together, pass the slipped st. over, 1 over, k. 3, 1 over, slip 1, k. 1, pass the slipped st. over, k. 1 into the back of the next st., p. 1, k. 1 into the back of the next st., 1 over, k. 3, 1 over, slip 1, k. 2 together, pass the slipped st. over, p. 1, slip 1, k. 2 together, pass the slipped st. over, 1 over, k. 3, 1 over, k. 1 into the back of the next st., p. 1, k. 1 into the back of the next st., 1 over, k. 2 together, k. 2.

22nd row: slip 1, k. 2, p. 1, p. 1 into the back of the next st., k. 1, p. 1 into the back of the next st., p. 6, k. 1, p. 6, p. 1 into the back of the next st., k. 1, p. 1 into the back of the next st., p. 14, p. 1 into the back of the next st., p. 4.

23rd row: cast off 2, 1 over, k. 1 into the back of the next st., 1 over, slip 1, k. 1, pass the slipped st. over, 1 over, slip 1, k. 1, pass the slipped st. over, k. 2 together, 1 over, k. 2, 1 over, slip 1, k. 1, pass the slipped st. over, k. 2 together, 1 over, k. 2, 1 over, k. 2 together, p. 1, k. 1 into the back of the next st., 1 over, k. 5, 1 over, slip 1, k. 2 together, pass the slipped st. over, 1 over, k. 5, 1 over, k. 1 into the back of the next st., p. 1, k. 1 into the back of the next st., 1 over, k. 2 together, k. 2.

24th row: slip 1, k. 2, p. 1, p. 1 into the back of the next st., k. 1, p. 1 into the back of the next st., p. 15, p. 1 into the back of the next st., k. 1, p. 1 into the back of the next st., p. 13, p. 1 into the back of the next st., p. 4.

Repeat from the 1st row.

The finished lace is sewn onto the ground of knitted medallions and linen squares. See also, in the chapter ''Needlework Trimmings,'' the paragraph on lace trimmings.

Crochet lace with picot bars and small leaves.

CHAPTER XI

Crochet

This kind of work, which owes its name to the hook with which it is worked ("'crochet'' means hook in French), is not only easy and restful, but also produces quick results. It can be used equally well for articles of dress and for the trimming of underlinen and household furnishings.

In addition to a series of little edgings for underlinen, we present in this chapter designs for large bedspreads, for chair backs, and for a collar. We further explain two types of artistic crochet: coarse or gros crochet and Irish crochet. We give, however, only one example of each of these varieties, as the rather special work involved usually requires lengthy explanations and numerous explanatory illustrations, which would too greatly increase the bulk of this volume.

Hooks.   These vary according to the work for which they are intended. The largest, usually made of tortoiseshell, bone, or boxwood, are used for coarse work in cotton or flax thread; the smaller ones, for fine work, are usually of steel. For the type of crochet known as Tunisian crochet, long hooks, made all in one piece and of uniform thickness throughout their length, are always used.

It is essential that the working end of the hook should be of a high finish, well polished on the inner side and not too pointed; the back of the hook should be slightly rounded and the handle, whether it be made of bone, steel, or wood, should be light enough not to tire the hand.

Materials.   The great variety of uses to which crochet can be put demands a very wide choice of materials.

Small edgings and narrow insertions intended for the trimming of underlinen are worked in a fine, rounded thread, which can be chosen from among the fine numbers of DMC 6 cord crochet cotton and DMC special quality crochet cotton, DMC Alsatian sewing cotton, DMC 6 cord cotton lace thread, DMC pearl cotton, DMC Alsatia, DMC flax thread for knitting and crochet, and DMC flax lace thread in white or ecru, to which is frequently added a pale shade of blue, pink, mauve, or yellow, plain or shaded.

Trimmings for curtains, blinds, table covers, and bedspreads are worked in a fairly coarse thread: DMC 6 cord crochet cotton, and DMC special quality crochet cotton special quality nos. 1 to 20, DMC knotting cotton nos. 10 to 30, DMC Alsatia nos. 15 and 20, or DMC pearl cotton nos. 3 and 5 in white, cream, or ecru, according to the fabric of which the article itself is made.

For large bed and cot covers, which were at one time always made of wool, we recommend DMC knitting twist no. 4 and DMC pearl cotton no. 1. The same cotton in nos. 3, 5, 8, and 12, and DMC Alsatia in nos. 15 to 25, can be used with advantage to replace silk threads in many kinds of fancy crochet.

For mufflers, scarves, cardigans, etc., we particularly recommend DMC floss crochet and DMC special stranded cotton, which are very soft, silky threads, or DMC pearl cotton nos. 3, 5, and 8, and DMC special quality knitting cotton no. 4.

Explanation of the Signs. In crochet, as in knitting, it is often necessary to repeat the same series of stitches. These repetitions are indicated, as occasion requires, by the signs *, **, ***, etc.

Abbreviations. In the explanations which follow, we shall make use of the following abbreviations: ch. for chain, s. cr. for single crochet, d.c. for double crochet, tr. for treble crochet, st. for stitch, sts. for stitches.

Stitches. In reality, there is only one stitch in crochet, since the work consists solely of loops produced by means of the hook and variously joined to each other. Crochet can, nevertheless, be divided into two kinds, ordinary and Tunisian.

In ordinary crochet there are seven different kinds of stitches: (1) chain stitch, (2) single crochet, (3) double crochet, (4) treble crochet, usually called treble, (5) bullion stitch, (6) cluster stitch, and (7) Persian stitch.

The rows are worked, according to the stitch, either backward and forward or in one direction only. When they are worked backward and forward, the work is turned at the end of each row and, at the beginning of the new row, one or more chain stitches are made, according to the length of the stitch being used, so the outside edge shall not be shortened. If, on the other hand, the crochet is worked in one direction only, each row is begun afresh in the first stitch of the preceding row. The thread is drawn through and, as in any other new row, the necessary number of chain stitches is made.

At the end of a row the thread is cut and drawn through the last loop; every piece of work in crochet is finished off in this way. Sometimes a few stitches are worked over the ends of thread at the beginning and end of each row, or they are held down at the back of the work with a few sewing stitches, or they can be joined together in groups to make tassels or fringes, according to the style of trimming with which the work is to be completed.

(1) *Position of the hands and chain stitch* (fig. 481). The thread is held in the left hand in the same way that it is held in the right hand for knitting, so that it is secured over the first finger by the thumb.

The hook is held in the right hand in the same way that a pen is held in writing (that is to say, it is held

Fig. 481. Position of the hands and chain stitches.

between the thumb and first finger and rests on the middle finger); it is passed through the loop of thread held by the thumb and first finger of the left hand. The thread lying over the first finger is caught with the hook, and a first stitch is made as in knitting. This loop is drawn just tight enough to allow the hook to pass through it easily. The end of the thread is held by the thumb and first finger. The succeeding stitches are made by catching the thread with the hook and drawing it through the loop.

The process of passing the thread over the hook prior to drawing it through is called an over.

(2) *Single crochet* (fig. 482). The hook is passed on the right side of the work through the upper loop either of a chain stitch or of a stitch of the preceeding row. The thread is caught on the hook and drawn through both this loop and the loop on the hook produced by the previous stitch.

(3) *Double crochet* (fig. 483). The hook is passed, as for single crochet, from the front to the back of the work through the upper loop of a stitch of the previous row. The thread is caught on the hook and drawn through this loop. The thread is passed over the hook and drawn through both loops.

As can be seen from the illustrations and explanations which follow, the most varied stitches

Fig. 482. Single crochet.

can be produced by making the successive rows of double crochet in different ways.

Rose stitch (fig. 484). This stitch consists of rows of double crochet worked backward and forward. On each stitch the hook is passed through both horizontal loops of the stitch in the preceding row.

Rose stitch and ribbed stitch (fig. 486) are generally used for making cardigans, mufflers, shawls, etc.

Fig. 483. Double crochet.

Fig. 484. Rose stitch.

Fig. 485. Russian stitch.

Russian stitch (fig. 485). This stitch is worked like the preceding one, except that it is worked in one direction only, so that the thread must be cut at the end of each row.

Ribbed stitch (fig. 486). Here the rows are worked backward and forward, the hook being passed through only the back loops of the stitches of the preceding row.

Piqué stitch. This stitch, like Russian stitch, is worked on the right side only. The hook is passed under one of the vertical threads of a stitch, and the double crochet is completed.

This stitch has a charming wrong side in which the two threads which form a stitch meet. It is one of the best stitches for making warm articles which are not to be lined. We will merely mention that a comparatively large hook must be used to make this stitch successfully, especially when a fairly thick thread is used.

Bias stitch (fig. 487). Bias stitch is worked entirely on the right side of the work. The hook is passed through the back loop of a stitch of the preceding row, the thread is caught with the hook without being passed over it, and the loop is drawn through. The stitch is then completed like a double crochet.

Crossed stitch (fig. 488). This is the name given to the stitch made in the same way as the last, but passing the hook through both loops of the preceding row.

Russian crossed stitch (fig. 489). To make this stitch, which produces slanting lines, the hook is passed between the vertical threads and under the horizontal threads of the previous stitches.

Blanket stitch (fig. 490). Blankets can be made with rather less close stitches than those described above. To give the work greater softness and flexibility, the thread is passed over the hook, the latter is passed under both loops of the stitch, and the thread is caught and brought back under the two loops and the over. Another over is made and drawn through the two loops on the hook. This stitch is worked backward and forward.

Knotted stitch (fig. 491). This stitch is worked exactly like the preceding one, but in one direction only.

Looped stitch (fig. 492). Looped stitch is worked as follows: when the hook has been passed through the loop of the stitch below, the thread is passed down round a strip of cardboard or a flat wooden ruler; the stitch is then completed in the ordinary way as a single crochet or a Russian stitch.

Fig. 486. Ribbed stitch.

The worker who prefers to do without a gauge of this sort can also make long loops over the first finger, holding them with the thumb while working. We do not, however, recommend this method for the inex-

Fig. 487. Bias stitch.

perienced, as it is much more difficult to make regular loops in this way.

Each row of looped stitches is followed by a plain row of double crochet. The loops lie on the wrong side, which becomes the right side when the work is finished.

If this stitch is to be made even thicker and fuller, the thread can be passed two or three times round the gauge or forefinger and secured by a double crochet. If the loop is triple, it is followed by a double crochet.

The stitch we have just described is usually worked with very soft, fleecy threads, such as DMC floss crochet and DMC special stranded cotton.

Daisy stitch (fig. 493). This stitch is worked on the right side only. It is begun on a foundation chain consisting of an uneven number of stitches.

1st row: miss the 1st chain stitch, draw 1 loop through each of the next 4 stitches, pass the thread over the hook and draw it through all 5 loops; make 1 chain, draw 1 loop through the center of the group just made, 1 loop

Fig. 488. Crossed stitch.

Fig. 491. Knotted stitch.

Fig. 489. Russian crossed stitch.

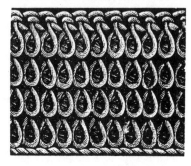

Fig. 492. Looped stitch.

Fig. 490. Blanket stitch.

Fig. 493. Daisy stitch.

through the vertical stitch, and 1 loop through each of the next 2 chain stitches, pass the thread over the hook and draw it through the 5 loops, and so on.

2nd row: begin by making 3 chain, miss the 1st of these, and draw 1 loop through each of the next 2 and 1 loop through each of the first 2 horizontal stitches of the previous row, pass the thread over the hook and draw it through the 5 loops, make 1 chain and continue as in the first row.

Double foundation chain (fig. 494). This is begun with two chain stitches, the hook is inserted between the threads composing the first chain stitch, the thread is passed over the hook, which is drawn through, bringing the loop of thread with it; the thread is again passed over the needle and drawn through both loops; the hook is then inserted into the left-hand loop of the stitch just made, the thread is passed over the hook and

Fig. 494.
Double foundation chain.

drawn through, then passed over it again and drawn through both loops, and so on.

This type of chain can often be used in place of narrow fancy braid, when the latter cannot be obtained in the required thickness or color.

(4) **Trebles.** This is the name given to little bars made with crochet stitches. Like all other crochet stitches, these can be worked either backward and forward or in one direction only.

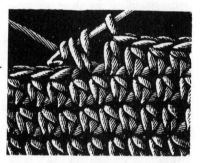

Fig. 495. Half trebles
worked through both loops of the stitch.

There are various kinds of treble: half (or short) treble; plain treble; double (or long) treble; triple, quadruple, or quintuple treble; joined trebles; crossed trebles.

When trebles are worked backward and forward, a few chain stitches are made at the beginning of each new row, and the first treble of the row beneath is missed, the chain stitches taking the place of the first treble.

Half trebles (fig. 495). Pass the thread from back to front round the hook, pass the hook between the

Fig. 496. Plain trebles
worked through one loop of the stitch.

stitches of the preceding row, make an over, draw the hook through to the front, bringing the thread with it, pass the thread round the hook again and draw it through all three loops.

Fig. 497. Double or long trebles
worked through one loop of the stitch.

Fig. 498. Triple trebles
worked through both loops of the stitch.

Fig. 499. Joined or tied trebles.

Plain trebles (fig. 496). To make a plain treble, the thread is first passed over the needle as for a half treble, the hook is then inserted into one loop of the preceding row, the thread is caught and drawn through to the right side, then passed over the hook and drawn through two loops, then passed over the hook again and drawn through the two remaining loops.

Double or long trebles (fig. 497). These are made like plain trebles, except that the thread is passed twice round the hook before the latter is inserted into the stitch below; successive overs are then made and drawn through the loops on the hook two by two until the treble is complete, that is to say, until only one loop remains.

Triple and quadruple trebles (fig. 498). For a triple treble, begin by passing the thread three times round the hook, for a quadruple treble four times; then proceed as for the others, always drawing the successive overs, after the thread has been drawn through the stitch below, through two loops at a time. When a series of gradually lengthening trebles is to be made, in every other treble the last over is drawn through the last three loops so that the lengths of the successive stitches will be equivalent to one treble, one and a half treble (one half long treble), one double treble, two and a half trebles (one half triple treble), before the triple treble is reached.

This variation in the length of trebles is often necessary for making flowers, leaves, indented edges, and scallops.

Joined or tied trebles (fig. 499). Joined or tied trebles can be worked backward and forward and can replace double crochet.

Having made a foundation of chain stitches, make a few more chain stitches or a treble of the required length; pick up on the hook as many loops as there are extra chain stitches or overs in the treble; pick up in addition the next stitch of the preceding row, pass the thread over the hook, draw it through, then draw successive overs through the loops two by two.

Fig. 500. Crossed trebles set one above the other.

Crossed trebles (figs. 500 and 501). This kind of treble produces an openwork effect and is often used for the heading of lace or for insertions for ladies' or children's underwear.

On a foundation of chain stitches, or of any kind of stitch forming a preceding row, work as follows: make 3 chain (these chain stitches take

Fig. 501. Crossed trebles set alternately.

the place of 1 plain treble), miss 1 stitch of the preceding row, work 1 plain treble into the 2nd stitch, 4 chain, 1 over, insert the hook between the loops at the junction of the treble and the chain stitches, and end with 1 plain treble and 1 chain.

Continue with 1 double over, insert the hook into the next stitch but 1 of the preceding row, make another over, pass the hook through the loop, make another over, and join the next 2 loops. There are now 3 loops on the hook; make 1 over, pass the hook through the next stitch but 1 of the preceding row, make 1 over and bring the hook out again on the right side; join the 5 loops on the hook 2 by 2, make 1 chain, 1 over, pass the hook through the upper part of the joined trebles, and end with 1 plain treble, 1 chain, and so on.

These crossed trebles can be made longer, but in that case their width must be increased in proportion to their length; they must also always be made with an even number of overs. Fig. 500 shows crossed trebles set one above the other, fig. 501 crossed trebles set alternately.

Fig. 502.
Treble foundation chain.

Treble foundation chain (fig. 502). To make a wide heading for a piece of crochet work more rapidly, trebles can be made in the following way: 4 chain, 2 overs, insert the hook into the 1st of the 4 chain, 1 over, bring the thread through the loop, * 1 over, draw the thread through the next 2 loops, repeat twice from *; ** 2 overs, insert the hook into lower left-hand part of the treble, complete the treble as before and repeat from **.

Fig. 503. Bullion stitch.

(5) *Bullion stitch and bullion stitch bars* (figs. 503 and 504). The hook used for bullion stitch should be rather thicker toward the handle and thinner toward the point than those used for other kinds of crochet.

To make ordinary bullion stitch, a very loose foundation chain is necessary. This made, the thread is wound very evenly several times

Fig. 504. Bullion stitch bars.

round the hook, which is then passed through one stitch of the chain, one over is made and drawn through the loop, then another over is made, which is drawn through all the loops on the hook.

Bullion stitch bars (fig. 504) are made in the same way, except that the thread is wound at least ten or twelve times round the hook, and the over is drawn through all the loops except the last two, which are joined by one fresh over. To make it easier to draw the hook through, the twists of the thread are held firm between the thumb and forefinger.

(6) *Cluster or pineapple stitch* (fig. 505). This stitch is usually used as an insertion between rows of double crochet.

Fig. 505. Cluster or pineapple stitch.

* Make 1 over, insert the hook under 1 stitch of the preceding row, make 1 over and draw it through as a loop, make another over, insert the hook a 2nd time under the same stitch and draw it through with another loop, make a 3rd over, insert the hook a 3rd time under the same stitch and draw 1 loop through, make a 4th over, insert the hook again and draw another loop through, make another over and draw the hook through the first 8 loops on the hook, make another over and draw it through the last 2 loops, 1 chain, miss 1 stitch of the preceding row, and repeat from *.

(7) *Persian stitch* (fig. 506). A fairly thick, firm thread, such as DMC 6 cord crochet cotton, and DMC special quality crochet cotton,

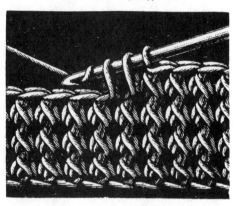

Fig. 506. Persian stitch.

Fig. 507. Raised trebles set alternately.

nos. 1 to 10, DMC knotting cotton nos. 10 to 30, or DMC flax thread for knitting and crochet nos. 3 to 12, will show up this stitch to better advantage than a loose, floss thread.

This stitch is worked on the right side of the work only.

Draw 1 loop through on each side of a stitch of the previous row so that there are 3 loops on the hook, including the one made by the last stitch, make 1 over and pass it through all 3 loops; draw another loop through beside the left-hand arm of the stitch just made, to form the right-hand arm of the new stitch, and another loop through the next stitch, make 1 over and draw it through all 3 loops.

Raised trebles set alternately (fig. 507).   All stitches of this type require several rows of plain crochet to serve as a foundation for the raised stitches. In the 4th row of double crochet in our example, it will be seen that the 4th stitch is 1 double treble worked into a loop of the corresponding stitch of the 1st row. The stitch of the preceding row which lies under the treble is missed, 3 double crochet are worked, and another double treble is worked, and so on. When the row is completed, the work is turned and 1 row of double crochet is worked.

The next row, that is to say, the sixth row, is begun with 1 double crochet, followed by 1 double treble into the 2nd stitch of the 3rd row, 3 double crochet, 1 double treble, and so on. In the 8th row of double crochet, the trebles are worked in the same order as in the 4th row.

Fig. 508. Raised trebles crossed.

Raised trebles crossed (fig. 508).   As for the stitch shown in fig. 507, three rows are worked in plain double crochet. The 4th row begins with 2 double crochet, followed by: * 1 double crochet worked into the upper part of the 1st stitch of the 1st row; the last 2 loops of this stitch are left on the hook; make a double over for the next double treble, pass the hook through the next stitch but 3 of the 1st row, pass the thread over the hook and draw it through, finish off the double treble to the last 3 loops, which are joined by a single over. Miss the stitch behind the treble, work 3 double crochet, and repeat from *, working the 1st of the next pair of double trebles into the same stitch as the preceding double treble, and missing 3 stitches at the bottom for the 2nd.

After this row, turn the work, work a row of plain double crochet, then turn the work with the right side out again. The 2nd row of double trebles begins with 1 double treble; the way in which the trebles are crossed is clearly shown in the illustration.

Raised pineapple stitch with clusters set alternately (fig.
509). Three rows are worked in plain double crochet; the 4th rows begins
with 3 double crochet, a loop is drawn through the next stitch, after which
the work proceeds as follows: * 6 trebles into the 4th double crochet of the
1st row, leaving the last loop of each stitch on the hook, so that there are 8
loops on the hook; make 1 over and draw it through all the loops; 1 chain;
miss the stitch beneath the cluster through which 1 loop was drawn, 3 double crochet, repeat from *.

This row is followed by 3 plain rows; in the 4th row the clusters are set
between those of the preceding row.

Raised clusters of trebles set alternately (fig. 510). After working
three rows of plain double crochet, turn the work, and begin the 4th row

Fig. 509. Raised pineapple stitch with clusters set alternately.

with 3 double crochet; then into the 4th stitch of the 1st row work as
follows: * 1 chain, 6 trebles, drop the last loop of the 6th treble, insert the
hook into the chain stitch between the last double crochet and the 1st treble, take up the dropped loop of the 6th treble and pass it through the loop
on the hook, miss the stitch beneath the cluster, work 5 double crochet and
repeat from *. In the succeeding rows the clusters are worked between
those of the previous row.

Raised pineapple stitch with clusters set in slanting lines (fig.
511). Begin as before with three rows of double crochet; in the 4th row,
instead of the 4th stitch, work a quadruple pineapple stitch (fig. 505), then
4 double crochet, 1 pineapple stitch, and so on. The next row is plain. In the
next row of pineapple stitches, work one more double crochet and work the

Fig. 510. Raised clusters of trebles set alternately.

Fig. 511. Raised pineapple stitch with clusters set in slanting rows.

pineapple stitches each time into the next stitch to the left in the second of the 3 rows covered by the first clusters. Each raised stitch in the successive rows is thus set one stitch further to the left, these stitches form slanting stripes on the surface.

Shell stitch (fig. 512). This stitch, which is worked in one direction only and in very loose thread, is used to make charming garments for children. It is very easy and quick to do, and can be ended at any row.

On a foundation of chain stitch, or any other stitch already worked, work the 1st row as follows: 1 ch., 7 tr. into the 1st st. of the preceding row, * 1 ch., 7 tr. into the 5th st., repeat from *

2nd row: * 7 tr. into the ch. of the preceding row which separates the two groups of 7 tr., 1 d.c. into the 4th of the 7 tr. of the preceding row, repeat from *.

In the succeeding rows, the 7 tr. are worked into the d.c. of the preceding row.

Picots. The last row of most crochet work is finished off with picots. This is the name given to various kinds of little points; they include close picots, chain picots, and lace (or purl) picots. Close picots can be subdivided in to small picots, large picots, pointed picots, rounded leaf picots, pointed leaf picots, etc.

Small round picots. These can be made either separately or along a crochet edge.

In the former case, make 3 ch.; then, returning, miss the 1st ch., 1 d.c. into each of the 2nd and 3rd ch.

In the second case, work 1 s. cr. into the edge, * 3 ch; then, returning, 1 d.c.

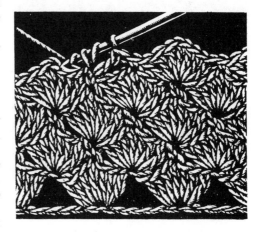

Fig. 512. Shell stitch.

into each of the 2nd and 3rd ch., miss 1 or 2 sts. of the row beneath, 1 s. cr.; repeat from *.

Large round picots. 5 ch., miss 3 ch., 1 tr. each into the 4th and 5th ch. When these picots are worked directly onto the edge of a piece of crochet, they are attached to it by 1 s. cr., and 3 or 4 sts. are missed instead of 1 or 2, as directed for the small picots.

Pointed picots. Make 6 ch., miss the 1st st., and into the remaining 5 work: 1 s. cr., 1 d.c., 1 half tr., 1 tr., and 1 double tr.

Leaf picots. * 4 ch., 3 tr. into the 1st ch., 1 s. cr. into the st. into which the tr. were worked, 2 or 3 ch., repeat from *. When these picots are worked into the plain edge of a finished piece of work, s. cr. are worked into this edge in place of the connecting ch.

Chain picots. Small chain picots require 5 ch., with 1 d.c. into the 1st ch. For large picots: 5 ch., and 1 tr. into the 1st ch.

Fig. 513. Downward picots.

Fig. 514. Lace or purl picots.

Fig. 515.
Lace or purl picots worked onto a crochet edge.

Fig. 516.
Picots with beading of trebles.

Bullion or post stitch picots. 5 ch., 1 bullion stitch bar drawn up to form a ring and attached to the 1st ch., 5 ch., and so on.

Downward picots (fig. 513). 5 ch., drop the loop and insert the hook into the 2nd of the 5 ch., pick up the dropped loop and draw it through the st.

Lace or purl picots (fig. 514 and 515). Fig. 514 shows picots worked in chain stitch as follows: 2 ch., pass the hook through the 1st ch., 1 over, draw the thread through, 2 ch., * remove the hook from the 2 loops and insert it into the 2nd loop and the 1st ch. at the same time, draw the thread through as a loop, 2 ch., repeat from *.

To make the loops firmer and more even, it is a good thing to work them over a thick knitting needle or a gauge.

Fig. 515 shows how to work these picots in double crochet along the edge of a finished piece of work, whether the last row of the work or a crochet chain: 1 d.c., draw out the loop produced by this st. to the length required for a picot and pass it over a gauge, insert the hook into the horizontal part of the last st., pass the thread over the hook and draw it through, 1 d.c. into the next st., and so on.

Picots with beading of trebles (fig. 516). Begin with 7 ch., 1 d.c. into the 4th ch., 1 triple tr. into the 1st of the 7 ch., * 1 picot consisting of 4 ch. closed by 1 d.c., 1 triple tr. into the 2nd of the 3 overs of the previous triple tr., catching the lower loop at the same time; repeat from *.

How to Copy Tapestry Designs in Crochet (figs. 517 and 518). Designs for cross stitch, tapestry, and filet lace, printed in the form of squared charts, can also serve as models for certain types of crochet, especially when they are meant to be worked in only two colors, or rather in one color on a plain background. All that is required to reproduce these designs in crochet is chain stitches and trebles, which, worked in rows one above the other, produce small squares. For every plain or background square on the chart, 1 tr. and 2 ch. are worked for the crochet background; every square of the design itself requires 3 tr.

The squares formed by the chain stitches must always begin and end with a treble. Each row is begun with 3 ch.—see also the instructions given for the working of trebles—and ended with a treble.

When a solid square comes between open squares, the complete square will consist of 4 tr., since the last tr. of the last open square touches the 3 tr. of the solid square. Thus two solid squares together will consist of 7 tr., and three together will consist of 10 tr.

Fig. 517.
Copy of a tapestry design in openwork crochet.

Fig. 518.
Copy of a tapestry design in close crochet.

Designs in several colors can be reproduced by means of rows of trebles worked in one direction only, or in double crochet worked backward and forward. If the first of these methods is used, the thread must be cut at the end of each row. If not more than three colors are used, two threads can be passed behind the stitches; if, however, more than this number of colors are used, the threads not in use are left for the time being on the wrong side of the work, to be taken up again when they are required. The thread no longer in use then takes the place on the wrong side of the one taken up again.

The threads not in use can only be passed behind the stitches when the article is one which can have a wrong side; if it is to be reversible, the threads must be passed under the stitches.

The arrangements of the colors should follow the chart; furthermore, the stitch which precedes a change of color cannot be finished in its own color: the fresh thread must be drawn through the last loops of this stitch, which must be united by it.

Bosnian Crochet. In Bosnia a special kind of crochet is found, resembling woven braid. Thanks to its elasticity and strength, it is particularly suitable for belts, collars, and cuffs, as well as fancy braids. The designs, which can be in one or several colors, are worked entirely in single crochet. Among the various articles bearing the DMC trademark, the most suitable for crochet in one color are: DMC 6 cord crochet cotton, DMC special quality crochet cotton, DMC knotting cotton, and DMC flax thread for knitting and crochet; for work in several colors we recommend DMC pearl cotton and DMC Alsatia.

Bosnian crochet braid in one color (fig. 519). Begin with a crochet

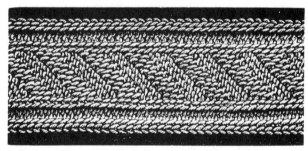

chain. By working the single crochet sometimes into the front loop and sometimes into the back loop of the stitch, a design is produced.

Fig. 519. Bosnian crochet braid in one color.

1st, 2nd, and 3rd rows: s. cr. worked into the back loops. s. cr. worked into the back loops.

4th and 5th rows: s. cr. worked into the front loops.

6th and 7th rows: s. cr. worked into the back loops.

8th to 15th rows: alternately 3 s. cr. worked into the back loops and 3 s. cr. worked into the front loops. In each successive row the design is worked 1 st. further to the left, so as to produce sloping stripes.

16th and 17th rows: s. cr. worked into the back loops.

18th and 19th rows: s. cr. worked into the front loops.

20th row: s. cr. worked into the back loops.

Bosnian crochet braid in several colors (fig. 520). In this case the design is produced by the alternation of colors. The whole design is worked

in single cro-
chet worked
into the back
loops of the
stitches. The
diamonds in
the central
band are in red
and blue, with
the centers in
brown; the

Fig. 520. Bosnian crochet braid in several colors.

dark sloping
bands in black and the background in cream. The outside borders are
worked in black and brown. The arrangement of the colors is shown in the
illustration; see also fig. 518.

How to Make a Crochet Square (fig. 521).   Begin with 4 ch., which
are joined into a ring by 1 s. cr. into the 1st ch.

1 ch., 2 d.c. into the
next ch., 3 d.c. into each
of the next 3 ch., 1 d.c.
into the ch. into which
the 1st 2 d.c. were
worked.

Slip the next st., that is
to say, insert the hook
between the horizontal
parts of the 1st d.c. of the
previous round and draw
the thread through with-
out making a stitch.
Then continue as follows:
1 ch., 2 d.c. into the
slipped st. Then work 1
d.c. into each d.c. of the
previous round, except at
the corners, where 3 d.c.

Fig. 521. Crochet square.

are worked into the 2nd of the 3 d.c. which form the corner.

The illustration shows a square worked in continuous rounds. When the
square is made in a stitch which must be worked backward and forward, the
work is turned on the completion of each round and the next round is
worked back over the stitches just made.

How to Make a Crochet Octagon (fig. 522).   Make 8 ch and join
them into a ring; into the 8 ch., work 16 d.c.; end the row with 1 s. cr. into
the 1st d.c.; turn; * 1 d.c. into the 1st st., 2 d.c. into the 2nd st. of the
preceding row; repeat from * 7 times; end the row with 1 s. cr.; turn; 2

Fig. 522. Crochet octagon.

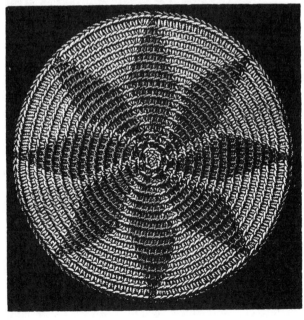

Fig. 523. Colored star on a plain ground.

d.c., 2 d.c. into the 2nd of the 2 sts. which were worked into the same st. in the previous row, 2 d.c., and so on. In the succeeding rows, always work 2 d.c. into the 2nd of the 2 sts. which were worked into 1 st. in the previous row.

These octagons can be made any size; they are generally joined to each other by means of trebles or loops of chain stitches.

How to Make a Colored Star on a Plain Ground (fig. 523). Begin with the light thread and make 4 ch., close the ring, 2 d.c. into each of the 4 ch.; then 1 d.c. with the dark thread and 1 d.c. with the light thread, which is to form the background, into each of the 8 d.c. For the method of changing from one color to another, consult fig. 518.

In the next row: 2 dark d.c. into each dark d.c., and 2 light d.c. into each light d.c. In the succeeding rows, always make 1 more dark st. to the left; the regular increases are worked into the light-colored st. by working 2 sts. into the last st. before the dark sts.

Continue thus until there are 8 dark stitches, then work one dark stitch fewer in each row on the right-hand side of the motifs, until there remains only one contrasting stitch against the light background; on the left-hand side of the motifs work 2 light d.c. into the 1st light stitch beneath.

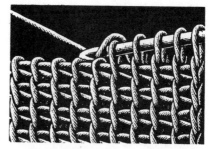

Fig. 524. Plain Tunisian crochet.

The circles can be used for making purses and bags, bonnets, caps, or small mats.

Tunisian Crochet. Tunisian crochet has more resemblance to knitting than any other kind of crochet, as all the stitches of a row are placed on the hook at the same time. As has been said at the beginning of this chapter, Tunisian crochet requires a special long hook with a handle of the same thickness throughout its length and provided with a knob at the end.

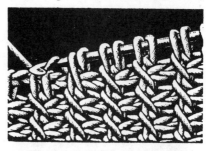

Fig. 525. Straight plaited Tunisian crochet.

Tunisian crochet stitches are all worked on the right side and produce a soft and elastic fabric. They are used for scarves, mufflers, wraps, baby booties, etc.

This kind of crochet can be worked solid or with openwork

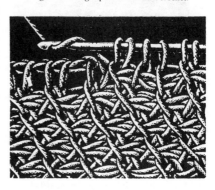

Fig. 526. Diagonal plaited Tunisian crochet.

spaces; the variety of stitches is, however, not so great as in ordinary crochet.

Tunisian crochet is begun on a foundation of crochet chain; it is ended with a row of single crochet.

Plain Tunisian crochet (fig. 524). Make a crochet chain of the length required for the width of the article. Work the first row, the loop row, as follows: insert the hook into the 2nd ch., draw a loop through; leaving this loop on the hook, insert the hook into the next ch., and draw another loop through; continue in this manner until a loop has been drawn through each st. of the foundation chain, all the loops thus made remaining on the hook.

After the last st. of this row, the 2nd row, which completes the stitch, is worked. Pass the thread over the hook and draw it through the 1st loop, then pass the thread over the hook again and draw it through 2 loops; continue in this way, drawing each over through 2 loops, until the last st. is reached. In the next row, a fresh series of loops is formed by drawing the thread through the vertical loops of the sts. in the preceding rows.

Straight plaited Tunisian crochet (fig. 525). The first double row is worked in the same way as for ordinary Tunisian crochet; in the 2nd double

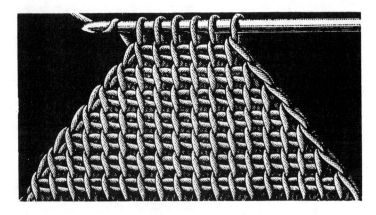

Fig. 527. Decreasing and increasing in Tunisian crochet.

row, the 1st loop is missed, the thread is drawn through the 2nd loop and then through the 1st, so that 2 loops are crossed. The second part of the row is then worked as for ordinary Tunisian crochet.

Diagonal plaited Tunisian crochet (fig. 526). For this stitch also a double row of plain Tunisian crochet is worked first; the 2nd double row is plaited, the 2nd loop being picked up before the 1st; in the 3rd double row, the 1st loop is picked up first and the 2nd and 3rd are crossed (that is to say, the 3rd is picked up before the 2nd), which produces diagonal lines over the surface of the work.

Openwork Tunisian crochet. Openwork stitches are very easy to make in Tunisian crochet. The first or loop row is made as for ordinary Tunisian crochet; in the return row, alternately 2 and 3, or 3 and 4 loops are joined, the extra loops thus disposed of being replaced by chain stitches.

In the succeeding loop row, loops are made by inserting the hook through these chain stitches and drawing loops through.

Decreasing and increasing in Tunisian crochet (fig. 527). Our illustration shows how to decrease at both ends of the work so that points can be formed. 1 st. is decreased at each end of every row. At the right, the 1st and 2nd loops are joined, then the row is continued normally as far as the last 2 loops at the left; these are joined by the 1st st. of the return row which is drawn through them both, and the return row is worked normally to the end.

Increases are made in the same order: first at the right-hand end, then at the left. To make 1 increase, a loop is made through 1 horizontal loop of the stitch in question.

Square with Raised Dots in a Contrasting Color (fig. 528). Fig. 528 shows a single square with a design of raised dots. These dots could be worked in a single color for each square, or in two alternating colors; the latter arrangement would make the assembled squares show up better, without spoiling in any way the harmony of shades.

Make 13 ch., close the ring.

Fig. 528.
Square with raised dots in a contrasting color.

1st round: 1 d.c. into the 1st of the 13 ch., 5 ch., 1 d.c. into the 4th ch., 5 ch., 1 d.c. into the 7th ch., 5 ch., 1 d.c. into the 10th ch., 5 ch., 1 d.c. into the 13th ch.

2nd round: * 1 d.c. into the 1st d.c. of the 1st round, 1 d.c. into the 1st of the 5 ch., 5 ch., 1 d.c. into the 5th of the 5 ch.; repeat from * three times. At the third repetition, end the round with the 5 ch.

3rd round: 1 d.c. into the ch. preceding the 3 d.c. in the previous round, 1 d.c. into each of the 3 d.c., 1 d.c. into the 1st of the next 5 ch., 5 ch., 5 d.c. arranged as before, and so on.

4th round: continue to increase as in the 3rd round, and in this round work the first raised dot as explained for fig. 509, after the 3rd d.c. in each quarter of the square. The number of dots is increased in the succeeding rounds until the square is of the required size; they are worked in every other round, with 3 d.c. between them. For their arrangement, see fig. 528.

The colored thread is not brought into use until the dots are to be worked, and must be broken off after the completion of each group of dots. The beginning and end of each colored thread must be folded back and worked in under the stitches of the next round.

The square can be made any size; it is edged with little picot points which could also serve to join the various square together.

Design for a Cot Cover Worked in Bands (fig. 529). This cot cover design is intended to be carried out in pale blue and white. The bands, as well as the lace edging, are worked in white cotton; the rounds which join the bands and frame the work are partly in blue and partly in white. The material used is DMC pearl cotton no. 1 in sky blue and white.

For the first band, make 29 ch. Miss 3 ch., insert the hook into the 4th and 5th ch. and draw an over through all 3 loops at once, 2 ch., insert the hook again into 2 ch. sts. and join the 3 loops, 2 ch., and so on. Each row is begun with 3 ch., which form the picots along the edge of the band. In the succeeding rows, draw the 1st loop through the loop of 3 ch. and the 2nd through the ch. which follows the joined loops of the previous row; 2 ch. over the joined loops of the previous row, insert the hook into each of the 2 ch. of the previous row and join the 3 loops, and so on to the end of the row.

When the band is finished, work with the colored thread into the picots along the edge, on the long sides which are to be joined to another band (but not along the side which is to form the outside bordered by the lace edging: the work along these edges is done only when the coverlet is completed), as follows: * 1 d.c. into the picot, 3 ch., repeat from *. This row is followed by a row of pineapple stitch (fig. 505) in white, with 2 ch. between the clusters; then another row in color, consisting of 2 ch. and 1 d.c. into the loop of 2 ch. of the previous row.

The second band, of the same width as the first, is worked in Tunisian crochet; it is edged with two rows in color, the first consisting of d.c., the second of 1 d.c., 3 ch.; these are followed by a row of pineapple stitch in white, then a row in color consisting of 2 ch., 1 d.c. into the loop of 2 ch. between the pineapple stitches of the previous row.

The final joining of the bands is effected by means of s. cr. worked in color on the wrong side, taking up 1 loop of the right-hand stitch and 1 loop of the left-hand stitch exactly opposite to it.

When the bands have been joined, the outer border is made. This consists of 7 straight rows and a scalloped edging.

1st row: using colored cotton: 1 d.c. into 1 picot, 3 ch., 1 d.c. into the next picot, 3 ch., and so on along the long sides of the bands; along the short sides (foundation chain or final row), 1 d.c., 3 ch., miss 2 sts., 1 d.c., etc. At the corners, 2 d.c., separated by 3 ch., into the corner st.

2nd row: using white cotton: 1 pineapple stitch (fig. 505) into each loop of 3 ch. in the previous row, with 2 ch. between; at the corners, work 3 pineapple stitches into the loop.

3rd, 4th, and 5th rows: using colored cotton: as 1st row. At the corners, in the 3rd and 4th rows 1 d.c., 3 ch., 1 d.c. into the 2nd pineapple stitch, 3

Fig. 529. Design for a cot cover worked in bands.

ch., 1 d.c.; in the 5th row, work 2 d.c., separated by 3 ch., into the corner loop.

6th row: using white cotton: as 2nd row.

7th row: using white cotton: 1 tr. into each st. of the preceding row; at the corner, 3 tr. into the same st.

Each scallop of the edging is worked over 13 tr. of the preceding row, with a space of 3 tr. between. For this reason it is preferable to do the corners first, then count the stitches along the sides and divide any extra stitches among the various scallops.

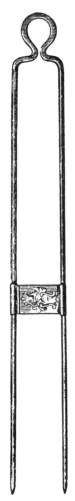

To make the corner scallop fasten on the thread on the wrong side to the st. which precedes the 3 corner sts., then work as follows: 6 ch., 1 s. cr. into the 4th tr. to the left, 1 s. cr. into the next tr.; turn; * 1 ch., 1 tr. into the loop of 6 ch., repeat from * 7 times; 1 ch., miss 1 tr., 1 s. cr. into each of the next 2 tr.; turn; 2 ch., 1 pineapple stitch into each loop of ch. between the tr. (9 pineapple sts. in all), 2 ch., miss 2 tr., 1 s. cr. into each of the next 2 tr.; turn; 2 ch., 1 pineapple st. into each of the first 4 loops of 2 ch., with 2 ch. between the pineapple sts.; 2 pineapple sts., separated by 2 ch., into each of the next 3 loops of 2 ch.; 1 pineapple st. into each of the remaining loops, with 2 ch. between the pineapple sts.; 2 ch., join to the next tr. but 1; break off.

For the scallops on the right-hand side, the sts. between the scallops at the corners are divided into equal parts. On the wrong side of the left-hand corner, count 11 tr. towards the right, fasten on the thread to the 11th st., 5 ch., miss 2 tr. of the preceding row, 1 s. cr. into the 3rd tr., 1 s. cr. into the next st.; turn; * 1 ch., 1 tr. into the loop of 5 ch., repeat from * 5 times; 1 ch., 1 s. cr. into the next tr. but 1, 1 s. cr. into the next tr.; turn; 2 ch., 1 pineapple st. into each of the first 2 loops of chain of the preceding row, 2 pineapple sts. between the 3rd and 4th tr., 1 each into the remaining loops between the tr. (always with 2 ch. between the pineapple sts.); after the 8th pineapple st., 2 ch., miss 1 tr., 1 s. cr. into each of the next 2 tr.; turn; 2 ch., into each of the first 3 loops of ch. work a pineapple st., into the 4th, 5th, and 6th loops work 2 pineapple sts., and into each of the last 3 work 1 pineapple st. (always with 2 ch. between the pineapple sts.); 2 ch., miss 1 tr., 1 s. cr. into each of the next 11 sts. Break off.

Fig. 530.
Steel fork for
hairpin crochet.

The final row consists of open picots, made with 5 ch. and 1 d.c. between the pineapple sts.; after the last pineapple st. and in the space between the scallops, make only 2 ch., followed by 1 d.c. into the 2nd of the tr. left between the scallops, 2 ch.; the 1st and 2nd picots of the next scallop are joined to the last and next to last picots of the previous scallop by the 3rd of the 5 ch.

Hairpin Crochet and Tools (fig. 530).   Hairpin crochet is worked on a very strong steel fork resembling a hairpin. With the help of these forks, lace, fringes, fancy trimm-ings, and a host of charm-ing little things can be made in a style quite dif-ferent from anything we have described so far.

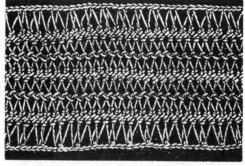

There are many different stitches in this kind of crochet, and a multitude of designs. Here we shall describe only those which will suffice to show our readers how the work is done and enable them to produce designs of their own in this type of work.

Fig. 531. Insertion in hairpin crochet.

Materials.   When hairpin crochet is in tended for the trimming of underlinen, we advise DMC special quality crochet cotton, DMC 6 cord crochet cotton, DMC 6 cord cotton lace thread, and DMC flax lace thread; fringes for articles of household furnishing wouldbe best made in DMC Alsatia or DMC pearl cotton; lastly, if the

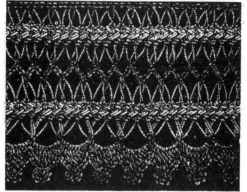

Fig. 532. Lace edging in hairpin crochet.

finished work is to have the appearance of soft floss silk, DMC special stranded cotton, DMC floss crochet, or DMC floss flax or flourishing thread should be used.

Stitches.   The work is begun, as always, with a single very loose chain stitch. The crochet hook is removed from the loop, into which the left prong of the fork is inserted; this prong is then held with the thumb and middle finger of the left hand. The thread with which the work is done is always turned toward the worker.

The thread is then passed round the front of the right prong to the back, the hook is inserted into the loop on the left prong, the thread is caught and drawn through the loop, the thread is passed over the hook and drawn through the loop which is on the hook; the thread is then passed round the back of the left prong to the front, the fork is turned to the right so that the thread is now round the right prong; the hook is inserted downward into the loop on the left prong; the thread is passed over the hook and drawn through, the loops are closed, and so on. When the fork is covered with loops, these are removed, and the hook is inserted into the last 4 or 5 loops, and the work proceeds as before.

Fig. 533. Lace edging in hairpin crochet.

These stitches can be doubled, or 1 d.c. and 2 tr. can be worked into each loop.

Insertion in hairpin crochet (fig. 531). First make three hairpin bands, covering each thread with 2 d.c. The bands are then joined by the loops, passing a left-hand loop over a right-hand loop, then a right-hand loop over the next left-hand one. When the end of the bands is reached, the last loops are stopped with a few stitches. To strengthen the edges, join 2 loops with 1 d.c., 2 ch., 1 d.c., and so on.

Lace edging in hairpin crochet (fig. 532). When two bands of hairpin crochet of the required length, with 2 half tr. in each loop, have been made, the loops are joined 2 by 2 with thread of a color contrasting strongly with that of the first part of the work.

The bands are joined as follows: 1 d.c. joining 2 loops on the right, 2 ch., 1 d.c. joining 2 loops on the left, 2 ch., 1 d.c. joining 2 loops on the right, and so on. This forms the zigzag line running through the center of the lace.

The scalloped edge of the lace is worked in 2 rows:
1st row: * join 3 loops with 1 d.c., 5 ch., repeat from *

2nd row: into each loop of 5 ch. work: 1 d.c., 1 half tr., 3 tr., 1 picot made with 5 ch., 3 tr., 1 half tr., 1 d.c.

The heading of the lace is made in the same way as the edge of the insertion in fig. 531.

Lace edging in hairpin crochet (fig. 533). This design, worked in DMC pearl cotton, is ideal for trimming small tablecloths, coverlets, and valances. It is begun with the two bands of hairpin crochet made with 1 d.c. in each loop. The loops are joined with a few rows of crochet in a different color, as follows: join 4 loops with 1 d.c., * 3 ch., join 2 loops with 1 d.c., 3 ch., join 2 loops with 1 d.c., ** 3 ch., 1 d.c. into the next loop, repeat from ** 4 times; 3 ch., join 2 loops, 3 ch., join 2 loops, 3 ch., join 8 loops; repeat from *.

The same process is repeated on the other edge of the band; it is begun, however, with 3 single loops; the 5 single loops will have to come exactly opposite the 8 loops joined by 1 d.c. on the other side.

The two bands are joined by the 2nd st. of each of the two little loops of 3 ch. at the top of the curve.

When the two bands have been joined, the open diamond-shaped spaces between them are filled with little medallions worked in 2 rounds with the light shade as follows:

1st round: * 1 tr. into the second loop of 3 ch. following the joined loops, 3 ch., 1 tr. into the next loop of ch., 3 ch., 1 tr. into each of the next 2 loops, join these 2 tr. by the last over; ** 3 ch., 1 tr. into the next loop of ch., repeat once from **; 3 ch., 1 tr. into the last loop of ch. in the first band, 1 tr. into the first loop of ch. in the second band, join these 2 tr. by the last over, 3 ch., repeat once from *; end the round with 1 s. cr. into the 1st tr., and 1 s. cr. into each of the next 2 ch.

2nd round: 3 ch., 1 tr. into each loop of ch. in the 1st round, 1 s. cr. into the 3rd ch.; break off.

Heading of the lace. 1st row: using light thread—1 quintuple tr. into the first loop of 3 ch., 1 quadruple tr. into the next loop, 1 triple tr. into the next loop, join the last overs of these 3 tr.; 5 ch., 1 tr. into the next loop of ch., ** 3 ch., 1 d.c., into the next loop, repeat once from **; 3 ch., 1 tr. into the next loop, 5 ch., into the next 6 loops work successively 1 triple tr., 1 quadruple tr., 2 quintuple tr., 1 quadruple tr., 1 triple tr., join the 6 tr by the last over; repeat from *.

2nd row: 1 d.c. into each st. of the previous row.

The edge of the lace, worked in the colored thread, consists of a row of little loops of 4 ch., 1 d.c. into each loop of the row beneath; in the indentation between the large scallops, the 4 ch. between the d.c. are omitted.

Lace Worked on a Foundation of Beading (fig. 534). Along one side of a braid or beading with looped edges, work a row of tr., separated from each other by 1 ch. On this row of tr. 2 more rows are worked to make the lace.

1st row: 1 tr. into the 1st tr. of the previous row, * 5 ch., 1 tr. into the same st. that the 1st tr. was worked into, 5 ch., miss 3 tr. of the previous row, 1 tr. into the 4th tr.; repeat from *.

2nd row: * 1 tr. into the 3rd ch. of the loop between the 3 tr. worked into the same st. in the 1st row, 3 ch., 1 tr. into the same st., 3 ch., 1 tr. into the same st., 3 ch., 1 d.c. into the 3rd st. in the next loop of 5 ch., 3 ch.; repeat from *.

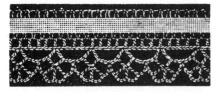

Fig. 534.
Lace worked on a foundation of beading.

Fig. 535.
Lace worked on a foundation of plain braid.

Fig. 536. Lace worked on a foundation of beading.

Fig. 537. Crochet guipure lace worked on a foundation of beading.

Lace Worked on a Foundation of Plain Braid (fig. 535). 1st row: 3 d.c. worked, very close together, into the braid, 14 ch., join them to the 3rd d.c. to the right (i.e. the 1st d.c. worked); * working back over these 14 ch., miss the 1st, 1 d.c. into each of the next 6 ch., into the 8th ch. work 3 d.c., then 1 d.c. into each of the last 6 ch., 7 d.c. into the braid, 14 ch., join to the 3rd d.c. on the right; repeat from *

2nd row: * miss 2 d.c. of the scallop, 1 d.c. into each of the next 5 d.c., 3 d.c. into the 2nd of the 3 d.c. at the point, 1 d.c. into each of the next 5 d.c.; repeat from *

To convert this design into an insertion, two bands are worked and joined by the stitch at the point; after the 2nd of the 3 stitches at the point, the loop on the hook is dropped, the hook is inserted into the stitch of the finished band, the dropped loop is picked up and drawn through the loop on the hook; the second side of the point is then worked like the first.

Lace Worked on a Foundation of Beading (fig. 536). The circles are worked as follows: 1 d.c. into the beading, 10 ch., join to the 7th ch. from the hook, and into this first circle work: 1 d.c., 1 half tr., 12 tr., 1 half tr., 1 d.c.; 1 s. cr. into the st. by which the ring was closed, 3 ch., 1 d.c. into the beading at a sufficient distance from the 1st d.c. to prevent the circles from overlapping each other; 10 ch., join to the 7th ch. from the hook, into the ring work: 1 d.c., 1 half tr., 2 tr., drop the loop, insert the hook into the 10th tr. of the 1st circle, pick up the dropped loop and draw it through to the right side, 10 tr., and so on.

For the heading: 1 tr., 1 ch., miss a few threads of the edge of the beading, 1 tr., and so on.

Crochet Guipure Lace Worked on a Foundation of Beading (fig. 537). This charming little edging can take the place of guipure as a finish for any article of fine underwear. It can

Fig. 538.
Lace worked on a foundation of medallion braid.

be worked with a row of trebles as a foundation instead of beading, or on a fancy braid along the edge of which picots have been made by means of double crochet and chain.

* 8 d.c., 8 ch., leave a space corresponding to 2 loops of the beading used in our example; into the beading work 7 d.c., 8 ch., join to the 3rd ch. to the right of the first loop of 8 ch., 11 ch., join to the 6th ch. of the same loop of 8 ch., join to the 7th d.c. to the right of the 1st group of 8 d.c.; repeat from *.

1st scallop: into the first loop of 8 ch. work 7 d.c., 5 ch., join to the 3rd d.c. to the right; into this loop of 5 ch. work 6 d.c.; into the loop of 8 ch. work 3 more d.c.

2nd scallop: into the loop of 11 ch. work as follows: ** 5 d.c., 5

Fig. 539. Lace with fancy braid.

ch., join to the 3rd d.c. to the right; into this loop of 5 ch. work to the right; into this loop of 5 ch. work 6 d.c.; work 2 more d.c. into the loop of 11 ch.; repeat twice from **

3rd scallop: into the loop of 8 ch. work 6 d.c., 5 ch., join to the 3rd d.c. to the right and into the loop of ch. work 6 d.c.; into the loop of 8 ch. work 4 more d.c.; repeat from *.

Lace Worked on a Foundation of Medallion Braid (fig. 538). For the vertical leaves, separate medallions must be prepared. Begin with 1 tr. over the bar that connects two medallions, 2 ch., 1 d.c. into the medallion, * 2 ch., 1 picot (composed of 4 ch. and 1 s. cr.), 2 ch., 1 d.c. into the medallion, repeat once from *; 2 ch., take a detached medallion and continue as follows: ** 1 d.c., 2 ch., 1 picot, 2 ch.; repeat from ** 6 times (the 4th picot must be at the point of the medallion), 1 more d.c., continue with 2 ch., 1 d.c. into the next medallion, *** 2 ch., 1 picot, 2 ch., 1 d.c., repeat once from ***; 2 ch., repeat from the beginning of the instructions.

Heading of the lace. 1st row: 1 double tr. close to the stem of the

medallion, * 4 ch., 1 tr. set at a distance of about one third the length of the medallion, 4 ch., 1 tr., 4 ch., 2 double tr., one into the right-hand medallion and the other into the left-hand medallion, join these 2 tr. by the last over; repeat from *.

2nd row: into each loop of 4 ch. in the previous row, 1 tr., 4 ch.

3rd row: 1 d.c. into each st. of the previous row.

Fig. 540. Crochet ground.

Lace with Fancy Braid (fig. 539). This lace forms a most useful and practical trimming for underwear of all kinds and for all ages.

Take three strips of fancy braid or beading and work along both sides of each, picking up all the loops, as follows: 1 d.c. into a loop of the braid, 1 ch.

The strips are then joined with crochet as follows: 1 tr. between 2 d.c., 3 ch., miss 2 loops of the braid, 1 tr. between the 2nd and 3rd loops, and so on. To join the bands, work in the same way along the edge of the next strip, but after the 2nd st. of each group of 3 ch. pass the thread, from the wrong side to the right, through the 2nd ch. of the first strip.

The edge, composed of strong, close scallops, is worked in 2 rows.

1st row: 1 tr. between 2 loops of the braid, 3 ch., miss 2 loops, 1 tr., 3 ch., and so on.

2nd row: 1 tr. into the 1st loop of 3 ch., * 3 ch., 1 tr. into the next loop, 3 ch., 3 tr. into the next loop, 7 ch., join to the 3rd of the 3 tr. to the right (i.e., to the 1st tr. worked in the group), 2 ch., join to the next tr. to the right, 12 tr. into the loop of 7 ch., leave the last loops of the last tr. on the hook and join them to the next tr. of the previous row; repeat from *.

Crochet Ground (fig. 540). This little allover design, as well as the next, worked cylindrically round and round, is intended for making handbags, tobacco pouches, etc.

It is begun on a foundation of ch. divisible by 8.

1st round: * 1 d.c. into each of the 1st 4 ch., 1 picot, 1 d.c. into each of the next 4 ch., 9 ch., join to the 1st d.c. to the right, into the loop of 9 ch. work 7 d.c., 3 picots joined by 1 s. cr., 7 d.c.; repeat from *.

2nd round: 1 d.c. into the middle picot of each group, with 8 ch. between the d.c. In the

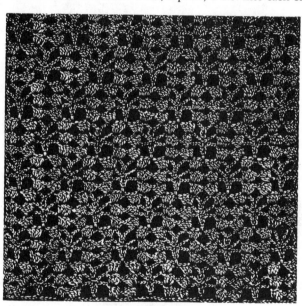

Fig. 541. Crochet ground.

succeeding rows, the scallops are arranged to alternate, the d.c. being missed.

Crochet Ground (fig. 541). The foundation chain for this ground requires a number of ch. divisible by 13.

1st round: 4 tr. into the 1st ch., * miss 4 ch., 4 tr. into the 5th ch., 5 ch., miss 3 ch., 1 d.c. into the next, 5 ch., miss 3 ch., 4 tr. into the next; repeat from *.

2nd round: 4 tr. into the 1st tr. of the previous round, * 4 tr. into the 8th tr., 3 ch., 1 s. cr. into the 3rd ch. of each of the 2 loops of 5 ch., 3 ch.,

4 tr. into the 1st tr. of the next group; repeat from *.

3rd round: 4 tr. into the 1st tr. of the 2nd round, * 4 tr. into the 8th tr., 5 ch., 1 s. cr. into the 2nd s. cr. of the previous round, 3 ch., join to the 3rd of the 5 ch. to the right, 3 ch., 4 tr. into the next tr.; repeat from *.

In the next 3 rounds, the motifs are arranged to alternate with those already worked, so that the groups of trebles are placed above the webs.

Ground Composed of Crochet Medallions (fig. 542).   Grounds composed of little medallions are most usually used to make cushion covers, chair backs, and place mats.

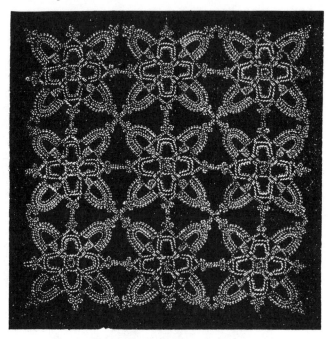

Fig. 542. Ground composed of crochet medallions.

Medallion.   1st round: 20 ch., 1 s. cr. into the 1st ch., 3 ch. (which count as the 1st tr.), 1 tr. into each of the next 4 ch., 2 tr. into each of the next 3 ch., 1 picot of 5 ch., 1 picot of 7 ch., 1 picot of 5 ch., 1 s. cr. into the 1st ch. of the 1st picot, 2 tr. into each of the next 3 ch., 1 tr. into each of the next 5 ch., 4 ch., 1 picot of 5 ch., 1 picot of 7 ch., 1 picot of 5 ch., 1 s. cr. into the 1st ch. of the 1st picot, * 27 ch., 1 s. cr. into the 7th ch., 1 s. cr. into each of the next 2 ch. towards the picots, complete the scallop like the preceding one, 4 ch., 3 picots, joined by 1 s. cr.; repeat twice from *; 4 ch., join to the first scallop.

2nd round: working towards the inside: * 5 ch., 1 d.c. into the ch. which precedes the scallop, 5 ch., 3 double tr., joined by the last overs, into the loop of ch. on the inside of the scallop, 5 ch., 1 d.c. into the ch. which follows the scallop; repeat from * 3 times.

3rd round: 1 d.c. into each ch. and 1 d.c. into the double tr., miss the d.c.; break off.

4th round: 1 tr. before and after the joined double tr. and into each of the d.c., 3 ch., 1 tr. before and after the next double tr., 3 ch., 2 tr., 3 ch., 2 tr., 3 ch., 1 s. cr. into the 1st tr.

5th round: 2 s. cr., 1 d.c. into the 2nd of the 3 ch., 1 ch., 1 d.c. into the 2nd ch., 1 ch., 1 d.c. into the 2nd ch., 1 ch., 1 d.c. into the 2nd ch., 1 ch., join to the 1st d.c.; break off.

The detached medallions are joined to each other by the middle and corner picots.

Crochet Lace. Diamond Design (fig. 543).   This model can always be relied upon to be successful and effective. We make no claim to originality for this design, which is probably familiar to many as a pillow lace design. It seemed to us, however, that those who do not like making pillow lace might appreciate a crochet version of this attractive trimming, which is equally suitable for household linen and furnishings and for personal wear.

For household decoration, the lace should be worked in a very strong ecru thread; if, on the other hand, it is intended for trimming blouses and jumpers of delicate material, or fine underwear, one of the threads especially meant for this purpose should be used.

The diamonds are begun in the center and worked round and round; begin with 5 ch. and close the ring.

1st round: * 5 ch., 1 d.c. into the ring, repeat from * three times.

2nd round: 1 ch., * into the first loop of ch. work 1 d.c., 5 ch., 1 d.c.; 2 ch., repeat from * three times.

3rd round: * into the first loop of 5 ch. work 1 d.c., 5 ch., 1 d.c.; 2 ch., 1 d.c. into the loop of 2 ch., 2 ch.; repeat from * three times.

4th to 11th rounds: continue increasing as in the 3rd round, until there are, along each side, 11 d.c. between the 5 ch. at the corners.

12th round: 1 d.c., * 5 ch., 1 d.c., ** 1 picot (composed of 4 ch. and 1 s. cr.), 1 d.c. between the 1st and 2nd d.c. of the previous round, 2 ch., 1 d.c. between the next 2 d.c.; repeat from ** until 6 picots have been made, then repeat from * three times; end the round with 1 s. cr. and break off.

The succeeding diamonds are joined to those already made as they are completed. After the last 12th d.c., 2 ch., drop the loop, insert the hook into the 3rd of the 5 ch. forming a corner of the finished square, draw the dropped loop through, 2 ch., end the square with 1 s. cr.

For the star composed of bars that fills the space between the diamonds, begin with 10 ch., close the ring.

Into this ring work: * 4 ch., 1 picot, 4 ch., 1 tr. into the picots on the right and left of the junction of two squares (1 picot at each side), 4 ch., 1 picot, 3 ch., 1 s. cr. into the 1st of the 4 ch., 2 d.c. into the ring, 8 ch., 1 tr. each into the 3rd and 4th picots of the diamond, 1 s. cr. into each of the 8 ch., 2 d.c. into the ring; repeat from * three times, break off.

For the half star which fills the space below the heading of the lace, make 9 ch., close the ring, 1 tr. into the 1st picot of the diamond, 4 ch., 1 picot, 3 ch., 1 s. cr. into the 1st of the 9 ch., 2 d.c. into the ring, 8 ch., join the 3rd and 4th picots of the diamonds with 1 tr. worked into each picot, 1 s. cr. in-

Fig. 543. Crochet lace. Diamond design.

to each of the 8 ch., 2 d.c. into the ring, 4 ch., 1 picot, 4 ch., 1 tr. into the 1st and last picots of the two opposite diamonds, 4 ch., 1 picot, 3 ch., 1 s. cr. into the 1st of the 4 ch., 2 d.c. into the ring, 8 ch., join the 3rd and 4th picots by 2 tr., 8 s. cr., 2 d.c. into the ring, 4 ch., 1 picot, 4 ch., 1 tr. in-to the last picot, 8 ch., 1 s. cr. into the 1st of the 4 ch.; break off.

The heading is made as follows: * 1 d.c. into the point of the diamond; 4 ch., 1 tr. into the 1st picot, 12 ch. reaching to the ring, 3 d.c. into the ring,

12 ch., 1 tr. into the last picot before the point of the next diamond, 4 ch., repeat from *. A row of d.c. or of tr. finishes the heading.

The outer edge of scallops is worked in two rows.

1st row: 1 tr. into the 1st picot; * 4 ch., 1 tr. into the next picot, repeat from * four times. Into the loop of 5 ch. at the point work: 4 ch., 1 double tr., 4 ch., 1 triple tr., 4 ch., 1 double tr.; then complete the second side of the diamond in the same way as the first; do not make any ch. at the inside angle where two diamonds meet.

2nd row: 2 d.c., 1 picot, and 2 d.c. into each loop of 4 ch.; at the point add 1 picot over the triple tr. At the inner angle, where two points meet, work only 4 d.c. into the last and first loops of 4 ch.

Crochet Lace. Star Design (fig. 544). Before passing to the instructions for working this lace, we would warn our readers that for the success of this design it is very necessary that the chain stitches which surround the stars and those which form the connecting bars should be worked with the greatest regularity. Since some people work more loosely and others more tightly, it will be advisable to work a trial medallion in order to

Fig. 544. Crochet lace. Star design.

ascertain whether the number of stitches that we give will prove correct for the individual worker's style; in this way it will be possible to tell whether it is necessary to increase or decrease their number.

Begin with the center stars, for which 18 ch. are made. Close the ring and mount it on a gauge or mold, wind a floss thread, such as DMC special stranded cotton no. 25, six to eight times round the mold, and cover this ring with 30 d.c., joining the last d.c. to the 1st with 1 s. cr.

1st round: * 13 ch.; working back over these 13 ch., miss the 1st (the st. next to the hook), and into the remaining 12 work: 1 s. cr., 2 d.c., 2 half tr., 2 tr., 2 double tr., 2 triple tr.; miss 4 sts. of the preceding round, 1 s. cr. into the 5th; repeat from * five times.

2nd round: 1 s. cr. into each of the 1st 5 sts. of the first pyramid, * 3 ch., pass these sts. round the back of the work, 1 s. cr. into the 5th st. of the left side of the same pyramid, 17 ch., 1 s. cr. into the 5th st. of the right-hand side of the next pyramid; repeat from * five times. After the 5th time, work 1 s. cr. into each st. up the side of the pyramid to the point.

3rd round: * 1 d.c. into the ch. at the point of the pyramid, 9 ch., 1 d.c. into the 9th of the 17 ch., 9 ch., repeat from * five times.

4th round: 1 d.c. into each st. of the previous round.

5th round: * 7 d.c., 3 ch., miss 2 sts. of the previous round; repeat from * 12 times. In the repetitions, miss 3 sts. instead of 2 sts.

6th round: 1 d.c. into each st. of the previous round, with 1 picot after every 7th d.c. Round the whole circumference there will be 19 picots, set 7 d.c. apart; to achieve this result, the d.c. following the 4th, 9th, and 14th picots will have to be worked into the same st. as the d.c. which precedes the picot. End the round with 1 s. cr., and break off.

When the circles are being joined, care must be taken to arrange each one so that 9 picots are turned toward the outer edge and 8 toward the heading. The 10th and 19th picots serve to join the medallions to each other.

Outer edge. 1st row: 1 tr. between the 19 and the 1st picots, * 7 ch., 1 tr. between the next 2 picots; repeat from * eight times. After the 10th tr., do not make any ch.; work another tr. between the 19th and the 1st picots of the next medallion.

2nd row: into the first 7 sts. of the previous row work: 2 s. cr., 2 d.c., 3 half tr.; into the succeeding sts., 3 tr., 1 picot, 3 tr., 1 picot, and so on, so that there will be 18 picots and 19 groups of 3 tr. in the half circle; into the last 7 sts. work: 3 half tr., 3 d.c., 2 s. cr.

The large scallops are joined by small ones, worked as follows, starting at the angle between the two scallops: 4 d.c., 3 half tr., join to the opposite half tr. of the preceding large scallop; then continue with 3 tr., 1 picot, 2 tr., 7 ch., join towards the right to the opposite tr.; into the loop of 7 ch. work: 1 d.c., 1 half tr., 3 tr., 1 picot, 3 tr., 1 half tr., 1 d.c.; continue the large scallop as explained above.

The ground and heading are composed of rings and bars.

Begin by making a ring like the one in the center of the star, with 16 ch. covered by 28 d.c., 3 d.c., 8 ch., miss 1 d.c., 3 d.c., 8 ch., miss 1 d.c., 3 d.c., 4 ch., join to the 12th picot of the first star, 4 ch., miss 1 d.c., 3 d.c., 4 ch., join to the 11th picot of the first star, 4 ch., miss 1 d.c., 4 ch., join to the 18th picot of the second star, 4 ch., miss 1 d.c., 3 d.c., 4 ch., join to the 17th picot of the second star, 4 ch., miss 1 d.c., 3 d.c., 8 ch., 1 s. cr. into the 1st d.c. of the round, break off.

Heading of the lace. 1st row: * 1 sevenfold tr. between the 12th and 13th picots, 6 ch., 1 sixfold tr. into the same st. as the sevenfold tr., 1 quintuple tr. between the 13th and 14th picots, 6 ch., 1 quadruple tr. into the same st. as the quintuple tr., 1 triple tr. between the 14th and 15th picots **; 6 ch.; repeat from ** to * (that is to say, in the reverse order) between the succeeding picots. Into the long loops of ch. round the top of the ring, work as follows: into the first long loop, 1 tr.; 6 ch., 1 d.c. into the middle loop, 6 ch., 1 tr. into the 3rd loop, 6 ch.

2nd row: 1 d.c. into each st.

Crochet Lace With Corner. Imitation of Reticella (fig. 545).   1st row: on a foundation of ch. work alternately 1 tr. and 1 ch.; at the corner work 1 tr., 2 ch., 1 double tr., 2 ch., 1 tr., all into the same st.

2nd row: 1 d.c. into each of the previous row; 3 d.c. into the middle tr. at the corner.

3rd row: counting toward the right from the 2nd of the 3 sts. at

Fig. 545.
Crochet lace with corner.
Imitation of Reticella.

the corner, but not counting this st. itself. work 1 d.c. each into the 56th, 55th, 54th, 53rd, and 52nd d.c., 8 ch., working back over these 8 ch., miss the 1st st., 1 d.c. into each of the remaining 7 ch., 1 d.c. on the second side into each of the 7 ch., 3 d.c. into the 8th ch. at the point, 1 d.c. into each of the first 7 d.c., 1 d.c. into each of the next 11 sts. of the 2nd row, 4 ch., miss 5 sts., into the next st. work 1 triple tr., 4 ch., 1 triple tr., 4 ch., 1 triple tr.; 4 ch., miss 5 sts., 1 d.c. into the 6th; turn; 7 d.c. into each loop of 4 ch. (28 d.c. in all), 1 s. cr. into the 2nd of the 11 d.c.; turn; miss the 1st of the 28 d.c., into the remaining 27 sts. work: 3 d.c., 1 picot, 3 d.c., 11 ch., working back over these 11 ch. miss the 1st st. (the st. next to the hook), and work 1 d.c. into each of the remaining 10 ch., on the other side of the ch. work 4 d.c., 8 ch., join toward the right to the 6th of the first 11 d.c., and into this loop of 8 ch. work: 5 d.c., 3 ch., join to the 5th d.c. of the first leaf, 3 d.c. into the loop of 3 ch., 6 d.c. into the 8 ch. below; along the leaf work: 3 d.c., 1 picot, 3 d.c.; into the ch. at the point, 3 d.c.; then, working down the second side,

3 d.c., 1 picot, 7 d.c.; into the remainder of the 28 d.c. work: 3 d.c., 1 picot, 4 d.c., * 11 ch., miss the 1st ch., 10 d.c.; on the second side of the chain work 4 d.c., 6 ch., join to the 4th of the last 7 d.c. of the preceding leaf; into the loop of 6 ch. work 9 d.c.; continue along this third leaf as follows: 3 d.c., 1 picot, 3 d.c., 3 d.c. into the ch. at the point, 1 d.c. into each of the next 3 sts., 1 picot, 7 d.c. **; into the 28 d.c. work 4 d.c., 1 picot, 3 d.c.; repeat once from * to **; 3 d.c., 1 picot, 3 d.c., miss the last of the 28 d.c.; on the row below work: 5 d.c., 8 ch., join to the 4th of the last 7 d.c. of the last leaf, 11 d.c. into the loop of 8 ch., on the row beneath work. * 5 d.c., 8 ch., miss the 1st ch., 7 d.c. into the next 7 ch.; on the second side of the ch., 4 d.c., 3 ch., join to the 6th of the last 11 d.c., 3 d.c. into the 3 ch., 3 d.c. into the leaf, 3 d.c. into the st. at the point, 7 d.c. into the leaf; repeat from *, and join the little horizontal bar to the leaf on the right.

Continue the work along the 2nd row and for the corner make: 9 d.c., 4 ch., into the corner st. work * 1 triple tr., 4 ch., repeat from * three times, 1 triple tr.; 4 ch., miss 4 sts. of the 2nd row, 1 d.c. into the 5th st.; turn; into each loop of 4 ch. work 6 d.c. (36 d.c. in all); 1 s. cr. into the 2nd of the 9 d.c.; turn; returning, into the first sts. of the 36 d.c. work 3 d.c., 1 picot, 3 d.c., 11 ch.; missing the 1st st. work 1 d.c. into each of the remaining 10 ch.; on the other side of the ch. work: 4 d.c., 8 ch., join to the 4th of the 9 d.c.; into the loop of 8 ch.: 5 d.c., 3 ch., join to the 4th d.c. of the last little leaf, 3 d.c. into the 3 ch.; into the loop of 8 ch. below: 6 d.c.; continue along the leaf: 3 d.c., 1 picot, 3 d.c., 3 d.c. into the st. at the point, 3 d.c., 1 picot, 7 d.c.

Continue into the 36 d.c.: * 3 d.c., 1 picot, 3 d.c., 11 ch., miss the 1st st., into the remaining 10 ch. work 10 d.c.; along the second side of the ch.: 4 d.c., 6 ch., join to the 4th of the last 7 d.c. of the last leaf, 9 d.c. into the loop of ch.; into the leaf: 3 d.c., 1 picot, 3 d.c., 3 d.c. into the st. at the point, 3 d.c., 1 picot, 7 d.c. **; repeat from * to ** three times; in the last sts. of the 36 d.c. add: 3 d.c., 1 picot, 3 d.c.

Continue the work along the 2nd row: 4 d.c., 8 ch., join to the 4th of the last 7 d.c.; into the loop of 8 ch.: 11 d.c.; along the 2nd row: 4 d.c., 8 ch., miss the 1st of these sts., 7 d.c. into the remaining 7 ch.; along the 2nd side of the ch.: 4 d.c., 3 ch., join to the 6th of the last 11 d.c.; into the loop of 3 ch.: 3 d.c.; into the leaf: 3 d.c., 3 d.c., into the st. at the point, 7 d.c.; begin again with 5 d.c., join the next leaf to the last leaf finished with 3 ch. and 3 d.c.

4th row: 1 d.c. into the point of the first little leaf, * 7 ch., 1 d.c. into the second leaf, 7 ch., 1 triple tr. into the 5th of the 9 d.c. between two leaves, 7 ch., 1 d.c. into the third leaf, 7 ch., 1 triple tr., 7 ch., 1 d.c. into the fourth leaf, 7 ch., 1 d.c. into the fifth leaf, 5 ch., 1 d.c. into the first leaf of the corner scallop; repeat from *, with this difference that 4 triple tr. are worked into the corner scallop.

5th row: into the first loop of 7 ch. of the 4th row: 12 d.c.; * into the next loop of ch., 12 d.c.; turn; work rows of d.c. backward and forward on these 12 sts., decreasing by 1 st. in every row, until only 1 st. remains; along the side of the pyramid work 10 s. cr.; repeat from * three times; 12 d.c. into the next loop of 7 ch., 6 d.c. into the loop of 5 ch., 12 d.c. into the first loop of 7 ch. of the corner.

Seven pyramids are worked in the corner scallop.

These seven pyramids are arranged as follows: * for the first pyramid 12 d.c. are worked into the first loop of 7 ch.; for the second, 10 d.c. are worked into the second loop of 7 ch. and 2 d.c. into the third loop; for the third pyramid, 7 d.c. into the third loop and 5 d.c. into the fourth loop **; for the fourth pyramid, 6 d.c. into the fourth loop and 6 d.c. into the fifth loop; repeat once from ** to * (i.e., in the reverse order); then 12 d.c. into the next loop of 7 ch., 6 d.c. into the loop of 5 ch.

6th row: * 1 d.c. into the first pyramid, 5 ch.; between the two pyramids: 1 crossed quadruple tr., separated at the top by 5 ch., 5 ch.; repeat twice from *; 1 d.c. into the fourth pyramid, 4 ch., 1 d.c. into the first pyramid of the corner scallop, 5 ch., 1 crossed quadruple tr. separated at the top by 5 ch., 5 ch., join to the next pyramid, 5 ch., and so on.

7th row: 6 d.c. into the first loop of 5 ch. of the 6th row, 6 d.c. into the next loop, 10 ch., join to the 6th d.c. to the right; into this loop of 10 ch. work: 5 d.c., 8 ch., join to the 6th d.c. to the right; 12 d.c. into this loop of 8 ch.; continue into the first loop: 3 d.c., 1 picot, 8 d.c.; into the next loop of 5 ch.: 6 d.c., 8 ch., join to the 5th d.c. to the right in the scallop; into this loop of 8 ch.: 3 d.c., 1 picot, 8 d.c.; * 6 d.c. into the next loop of 5 ch., repeat once from *, 10 ch., join to the 6th st. to the right of the last 12 d.c.; into this loop of 10 ch.: 5 d.c., 8 ch., join to the last of the 12 d.c. to the right; into this loop of 8 ch.: 5 d.c., 3 ch., join to the 5th d.c. to the right in the third scallop; into this loop of 3 ch.: 2 d.c., 1 picot, 2 d.c.; into the next scallop: 3 d.c., 1 picot, 3 d.c.; 6 d.c. into the next scallop, 10 ch., join to the 6th st. to the right of the last 6 d.c.; into this loop of 10 ch.: 5 d.c., 1 picot, 3 d.c., 1 picot, 3 d.c., 1 picot, 5 d.c.; 5 d.c. into the scallop below; into the loop of 5 ch. below: 6 d.c., 8 ch., join to the 5th of the last 5 d.c., to the right in the last scallop; into this loop of 8 ch.: 3 d.c., 1 picot, 8 d.c.; ** 6 d.c. into the next loop of 5 ch., repeat from ** once; 10 ch., join to the 6th of the 12 d.c. to the right; into this loop of 10 ch.: 5 d.c., 8 ch., join to the last of the 12 d.c. to the right; into this loop of 8 ch.: 5 d.c., 3 ch., join to the 5th of the 8 d.c. to the right in the last finished scallop; into this loop of 3 ch.: 2 d.c., 1 picot, 2 d.c.; into the next loop of ch.: 3 d.c., 1 picot, 3 d.c.; into the next loop of ch.: 3 d.c., 1 picot, 8 d.c.; into the loop of 5 ch. in the row below: 6 d.c., 8 ch., join to the 5th of the 8 d.c. to the right; into this loop of 8 ch.: 12 d.c.; 6 d.c. into the loop of ch. which connects the two points.

Continue the little scallops all round; the center scallop is repeated four times in the corner. To join two points, work as follows: after the 12 d.c. of the first scallop, 8 ch., join to the last d.c. of the last scallop of the preceding point to the right; into this loop of 8 ch.: 3 d.c., 1 picot, 3 d.c., 1 picot, 3 d.c., 1 picot, 3 d.c.

Crochet Lace. Imitation of Guipure Lace (fig. 546).   This kind of lace and insertion is generally used for curtains and blinds. The design is worked in squares and resembles the filet embroidery known as guipure lace or guipure net.

Begin with a foundation of 40 ch.

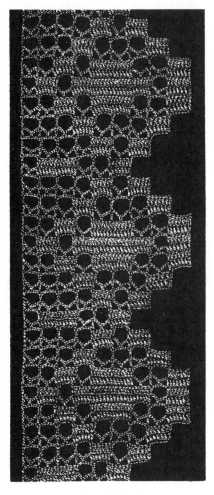

Fig. 546.
Crochet lace. Imitation of guipure lace.

1st row: miss 4 ch., 1 tr. into each of the next 6 sts., * 3 ch., miss 2 ch., 1 d.c. into the next st., 3 ch., miss 2 sts., 1 tr. into the next, repeat once from *; 1 tr. into each of the next 12 ch., 3 ch., miss 2 sts., 1 d.c. into the next, 3 ch., miss 2 sts., 1 tr.

2nd row: turn; 8 ch., 1 tr. into each of the 13 tr. below, 5 ch., 1 tr. into the next tr., 5 ch., 1 tr. into each of the last 7 sts.

3rd row: turn; 9 ch., miss 4 ch., 1 tr. into each of the next 6 sts., 3 ch., miss 2 tr., 1 d.c. into the next st., 3 ch., miss 2 tr., 1 tr. into each of the next 7 sts., * 3 ch., miss 2 sts., 1 d.c. into the next, 3 ch., miss 2 sts., 1 tr. into the next, repeat from * three times.

4th row: turn; 8 ch., 1 tr. into the next tr., * 5 ch., 1 tr. into the next tr., repeat twice from *; 1 tr. into each of the next 6 tr., 5 ch., 1 tr. into each of the last 7 sts.

5th row: turn; 9 ch., miss 4 sts., 1 tr. into each of the next 6 sts., * 3 ch., miss 2 sts., 1 d.c. into the next, 3 ch., miss 2 sts., 1 tr. into the next, repeat twice from *; 1 tr. into each of the next 6 sts., ** 3 ch., miss 2 sts., 1 d.c. into the next, 3 ch., miss 2 sts., 1 tr. into the next, repeat twice from **.

6th row: turn; 8 ch., 1 tr. into the next u, * 5 ch., 1 tr. into the next tr., repeat once from *; 1 tr. into each of the next 6 tr., ** 5 ch., 1 tr. into the next tr., repeat twice from **; 1 tr. into each of the last 6 sts.

7th row: turn; 9 ch., miss 4 sts., 1 tr. into each of the next 6 sts., * 3 ch., miss 2 sts., 1 d.c. into the next, 3 ch., miss 2 sts., 1 tr. into the next, repeat once from *; 1 tr. into each of the next 12 sts., 3 ch., miss 2 tr., 1 d.c. into the next, 3 ch., miss 2 tr., 1 tr. into each of the next 7 sts., ** 3 ch., miss 2 sts., 1 d.c., 3 ch., miss 2 sts., 1 tr. into the next, repeat once from **.

8th row: turn; 8 ch., 1 tr. into the next tr., 5 ch., 1 tr. into each of the next 7 tr., 5 ch., 1 tr. into each of the next 13 tr., 5 ch., 1 tr. into the next tr., 5 ch., 1 tr. into each of the last 7 sts.

9th row: turn; 3 ch., miss 1 tr., 1 tr. in each of the next 6 sts., 3 ch., miss 2 sts., 1 d.c. into the next, 3 ch., miss 2 sts., 1 tr. into each of the next 25 sts., 3 ch., miss 2 sts., 1 d.c. into the next, 3 ch., miss 2 sts., 1 tr. into each of the next 7 sts., 3 ch., miss 2 sts., 1 d.c. into the next, 3 ch., miss 2 sts., 1 tr. into the next.

10th row: turn; 8 ch., 1 tr. into each of the 7 tr., 5 ch., 1 tr. into each of the 25 tr., 5 ch., 1 tr. into each of the last 7 sts.

11th row: turn; 3 ch., miss 1 tr., 1 tr. into each of the next 6 tr., * 3 ch., miss 2 sts., 1 d.c. into the next, 3 ch., miss 2 sts., 1 tr. into the next, repeat once from *; 1 tr. into each of the next 12 sts., 3 ch., miss 2 sts., 1 d.c. into the next, 3 ch., miss 2 sts., 1 tr. into each of the next 7 sts., ** 3 ch., miss 2 sts., 1 d.c. into the next, 3 ch., miss 2 sts., 1 tr. into the next, repeat once from **.

12th row: turn; 8 ch., 1 tr. into the next tr., 5 ch., 1 tr. into each of the next 7 sts., 5 ch., 1 tr. into each of the next 13 sts., * 5 ch., 1 tr. into the next tr., repeat once from *; 1 tr. into each of the last 6 sts.

13th row: turn; 1 s. cr. into each of the first 7 sts., 3 ch., 1 tr. into each of the next 6 sts., * 3 ch., miss 2 sts., 1 d.c. into the next, 3 ch., miss 2 sts., 1 tr. into the next, repeat twice from *; 1 tr. into each of the next 6 sts., ** 3 ch., miss 2 sts., 1 d.c. into the next, 3 ch., miss 2 sts., 1 tr. into the next, repeat twice from **.

14th row: turn; 8 ch., 1 tr. into the next tr., * 5 ch., 1 tr. into the next tr., repeat once from *; 1 tr. into each of the next 6 sts., ** 5 ch., 1 tr. into the next tr., repeat twice from **; 1 tr. into each of the last 6 sts.

15th row: turn; 1 s. cr. into each of the first 7 sts., 3 ch., 1 tr. into each of the next 6 sts., 3 ch., miss 2 sts., 1 d.c. into the next, 3 ch., miss 2 sts., 1 tr. into each of the next 7 tr., * 3 ch., miss 2 sts., 1 d.c. into the next, 3 ch., miss 2 sts., 1 tr. into the next, repeat from * three times.

16th row: turn; 8 ch., 1 tr. into the next tr., * 5 ch., 1 tr. into the next tr., repeat twice from *; 1 tr. into each of the next 6 tr., 5 ch., 1 tr. into each of the last 7 tr.

17th row: turn; 1 s. cr. into each of the first 7 sts., 3 ch., 1 tr. into each of the next 6 tr., * 3 ch., miss 2 sts., 1 d.c. into the next, 3 ch., miss 2 sts., 1 tr. into the next, repeat once from *; 1 tr. into each of the next 12 sts., 3

ch., miss 2 sts., 1 d.c. into the next, 3 ch., miss 2 sts., 1 tr. into the next.
Repeat from the 2nd row.

Crochet Insertion. Imitation of Guipure Lace (fig. 547). Begin with 70 ch.

1st row: working back, miss 4 ch., 1 tr. into each of the next 12 sts., * 11 ch., miss 5 ch., 1 tr., ** 2 ch., miss 2 ch., 1 tr. into the next, repeat once from **; repeat twice from *; 11 ch., miss 5 ch., 1 tr. into each of the next 13 sts.

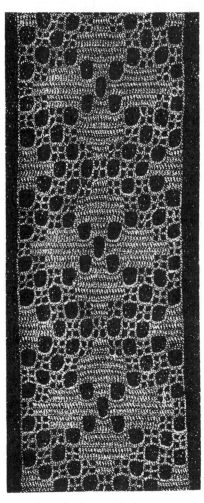

Fig. 547.
Crochet insertion. Imitation of guipure lace.

2nd row: turn; 3 ch., miss the 1st tr., 1 tr. into each of the next 11 sts., miss the next 3 sts. (the 13th tr. and the 1st and 2nd ch. of the row beneath), * 1 s. cr. into each of the next 7 ch., 2 ch., 1 tr. into the 2nd of the 3 tr., 2 ch., repeat twice from *; 1 s. cr. each into the 3rd to the 9th of the next 11 ch. beneath, miss the 1st tr., 1 tr. into each of the last 12 sts. of the preceding row.

3rd row: turn; 3 ch., miss the 1st tr., 1 tr. into each of the next 6 sts., * 11 ch., 1 tr. into the 1st s. cr., 2 ch., miss 2 sts., 1 tr. into the next 2 ch., miss 2 sts., 1 tr. into the next ** repeat once from * to **; 1 tr. into each of the next 6 sts., 2 ch., miss 2 sts., 1 tr. into the next, 2 ch., miss 2 sts., 1 tr. into the next; repeat once from * to **; 11 ch., miss 5 tr., 1 tr. into each of the last 7 sts.

4th row: turn; 3 ch., miss the 1st tr., 1 tr. into each of the next 5 sts., * 1 s. cr. each into the 3rd to the 9th ch., 2 ch., 1 tr. into the 2nd of the 3 tr., 2 ch., ** repeat once from * to **; 1 tr. into each of the next 7 tr., 2 ch., 1 tr. into the tr., 2 ch.; repeat once from * to **; 1 s. cr. each into the 3rd to the 9th of the 11 ch., miss 1 tr., 1 tr. into each of the next 6 sts.

5th row: turn; 3 ch., * 11 ch., 1

tr. into the 1st s. cr., 2 ch., miss 2 sts., 1 tr. into the next, 2 ch., miss 2 sts., 1 tr. into the next **; repeat once from * to **; 1 tr. into each of the next 18 sts., 2 ch., miss 2 sts., 1 tr. into the next, 2 ch., miss 2 sts., 1 tr. into the next; repeat once from * to **; 8 ch., 1 triple tr. into the last st.

6th row: turn; 1 s. cr. into the triple tr., 1 s. cr. into each of the next 6 sts., 2 ch., 1 tr. into the tr., 2 ch., * 1 s. cr. each into the 3rd to the 9th ch., 2 ch., 1 tr. into the 2nd of the 3 tr., 2 ch. **; 1 tr. into each of the next 19 tr., 2 ch., 1 tr. into the tr., 2 ch.; repeat once from * to **; 1 s. cr. each into the 3rd to the 9th ch.

7th row: turn; 5 ch., 1 tr. into the 4th s. cr., 2 ch., 1 tr. into the 7th s. cr.; * 11 ch., 1 tr. into the 1st s. cr., 2 ch., miss 2 sts., 1 tr. into the next, 2 ch., miss 2 sts., 1 tr. into the next **; 11 ch., 1 tr. into each of the 19 tr., repeat twice from * to **.

8th row: turn; 5 ch., 1 tr. into the 2nd tr., 2 ch., * 1 s. cr. each into the 3rd to the 9th ch., 2 ch., 1 tr. into the 2nd of the 3 tr., 2 ch. **; 1 s. cr. each into the 3rd to the 9th ch., miss 1 tr., 1 tr. into each of the next 17 tr.; repeat twice from * to **; 1 tr. into the 3rd of the 5 ch.

9th row: turn; 14 ch., 1 tr. into the 1st s. cr., 2 ch., miss 2 sts., 1 tr. into the next, 2 ch., miss 2 sts., 1 tr. into the next, 1 tr. into each of the next 12 sts., 11 ch., miss 5 tr., 1 tr. into each of the next 7 tr., 11 ch., miss 5 tr., 1 tr. into each of the next 13 sts., 2 ch., miss 2 sts., 1 tr. into the next, 2 ch., miss 2 sts., 1 tr. into the next, 8 ch., 1 triple tr. into the 3rd of the 5 ch.

10th row: turn; 1 s. cr. into the triple tr., 1 s. cr. into each of the next 6 ch., 2 ch., 1 tr. into the tr., 2 ch., 1 tr. into each of the next 12 sts., 1 s. cr. each into the 3rd to the 9th ch., miss 1 tr., 1 tr. into each of the next 5 sts., 1 s. cr. each into the 3rd to the 9th ch., miss 1 tr., 1 tr. into each of the next 12 sts., 2 ch., 1 tr. into the next tr., 2 ch., 1 s. cr. each into the 3rd to the 9th ch.

11th row: turn; 5 ch., 1 tr. into the 4th s. cr., 2 ch., 1 tr. into 7th s. cr., 1 tr. into each of the next 24 sts., 11 ch., miss 5 tr., 1 tr. into each of the next 25 sts., * 2 ch., miss 2 s. cr., 1 tr. into the next, repeat once from *.

12th row: turn; 5 ch., 1 tr. into the 2nd tr., 2 ch., 1 tr. into each of the next 24 sts. 1 s. cr. each into the 3rd to the 9th ch., miss 1 tr., 1 tr. into each of the next 24 sts., 2 ch., 1 tr. into the tr., 2 ch., 1 tr. into the 3rd of the 5 ch.

13th row: turn; 14 ch., 1 tr. into the 2nd tr., * 2 ch., miss 2 tr., 1 tr. into the next, repeat once from *; 1 tr. into each of the next 12 sts., 11 ch., 1 tr. into each of the 7 s. cr., 11 ch., miss 5 tr., 1 tr. into each of the next 13 sts., ** 2 ch., miss 2 tr., 1 tr. into the next, repeat once from **; 8 ch., 1 triple tr. into the 3rd of the 5 ch.

14th row: turn; 1 s. cr. into the triple tr., 1 s. cr. into each of the next 6 ch., 2 ch., 1 tr. into the tr., 2 ch., 1 tr. into each of the 12 tr., 1 s. cr. each into the 3rd to the 9th ch., miss 1 tr., 1 tr. into each of the next 5 sts., 1 s. cr. each into the 3rd to the 9th ch., miss 1 tr., 1 tr. into each of the next

12 sts., 2 ch., 1 tr. into the tr., 2 ch., 1 s. cr. each into the 3rd to the 9th ch.

15th row: turn; 5 ch., 1 tr. into the 4th s. cr., 2 ch., 1 tr. into the 7th s. cr., 11 ch., 1 tr. into the 2nd tr., * 2 ch., miss 2 tr., 1 tr. into the next, repeat once from *; 11 ch., miss 5 tr., 1 tr. into each of the next 19 sts., 11 ch., 1 tr. into the 6th tr., ** 2 ch., miss 2 sts., 1 tr. into the next, repeat once from **; 11 ch., 1 tr. into the 1st s. cr., *** 2 ch., miss 2 sts., 1 tr. into the next, repeat once from ***.

16th row: turn; 5 ch., 1 tr. into the 2nd tr., 2 ch., * 1 s. cr. each into the 3rd to the 9th ch., 2 ch., 1 tr. into the 2nd of the 3 tr., 2 ch. **; 1 s. cr. each into the 3rd to the 9th ch., miss 1 tr., 1 tr. into each of the next 17 sts.; repeat twice from * to **; 1 tr. into the 3rd of the 5 ch.

17th row: turn; 3 ch., * 11 ch., 1 tr. into the 1st s. cr., 2 ch., miss 2 sts., 1 tr. into the next, 2 ch., miss 2 sts., 1 tr. into the next **; 1 tr. into each of the next 18 sts., 2 ch., miss 2 sts., 1 tr. into the next, 2 ch., miss 2 sts., 1 tr. into the next, repeat once from * to **; 8 ch.; 1 triple tr. into the 3rd of the 5 ch.

18th row: turn; 1 s. cr. into the triple tr., 1 s. cr. into each of the next 6 ch., 2 ch., 1 tr. into the 2nd tr., 2 ch., * 1 s. cr. each into the 3rd to the 9th ch., 2 ch., 1 tr. into the 2nd of the 3 tr., 2 ch. **; 1 tr. into each of the 19 tr., 2 ch., 1 tr. into the tr., 2 ch.; repeat once from * to **; 1 s. cr. each into the 3rd to the 9th ch.

19th row: turn; 3 ch., miss the 1st s. cr., 1 tr. into each of the next 6 sts., ** 11 ch., 1 tr. into the 1st s. cr., 2 ch., miss 2 sts., 1 tr. into the next, 2 ch., miss 2 sts., 1 tr. into the next **; 11 ch., 1 tr. into the 2nd tr., *** 2 ch., miss 2 tr., 1 tr. into the next ****, repeat once from *** to ****; 1 tr. into each of the next 6 tr., repeat twice from *** to ****; repeat once from * to **; 11 ch., 1 tr. into each of the 7 s. cr.

20th row: turn; 3 ch., miss the 1st tr., 1 tr. into each of the next 5 sts., * 1 s. cr. each into the 3rd to the 9th ch., 2 ch., 1 tr. into the 2nd of the 3 tr., 2 ch. **; repeat once from * to **; 1 tr. into each of the 7 tr., 2 ch., 1 tr. into the tr., 2 ch.; repeat once from * to **; 1 s. cr. each into the 3rd to the 9th ch., miss 1 tr., 1 tr. into each of the next 6 sts.

21st row: turn; 3 ch., miss the 1st tr., 1 tr. into each of the next 12 sts., * 11 ch., 1 tr. into the 1st s. cr., 2 ch., miss 2 sts., 1 tr. into the next, 2 ch., miss 2 sts., 1 tr. into the next **; 11 ch., 1 tr. into the 2nd tr., 2 ch., miss 2 tr., 1 tr. into the next, 2 ch., miss 2 sts., 1 tr. into the next; repeat once from * to **; 11 ch., 1 tr. into each of the last 13 sts.

Repeat from the 2nd row.

Insertion in Gros Crochet (fig. 548). This type of crochet is of recent origin. It is more like the coarse kinds of lace trimming known as "passementerie," than ordinary lace, and is used principally for decorating household furnishings, such as cushions, bedspreads, curtains, valences, etc.

The method of working it somewhat resembles that of Irish crochet. The various motifs, worked separately in coarse thread, are afterward attached to a crochet net ground worked in a thread of moderate thickness.

Before the various parts of the work are assembled, it is essential to soak them in hot water and stretch them carefully on a board covered with molleton, fastening them all round the edges so that they will dry in the correct shape.

Baste the net foundation quite straight onto jap silk or paper of a dark shade, then attach the crochet motifs by means of invisible back-stitches in the stitches of the edges and, if necessary, in the center of the motifs.

When the work is completely finished, detach it from the paper or silk, soak it again, and pin it onto a board, wrong side up. Starch it slightly and do not detach it from the board until it is completely dry.

Large designs are worked only with fairly coarse thread.

Fig. 548. Insertion in ''Gros-Crochet.''

The best for this purpose are DMC 6 cord crochet cotton nos. 1 to 5, DMC special quality crochet cotton nos. 1 to 5, DMC knotting cotton nos. 20 and 30, or DMC flax thread for knitting and crochet nos. 4 to 12.

Network foundation: make 73 ch. Working back, miss the 1st ch., 1 d.c. in each of the remaining 72 sts. * 25 ch., join to the 9th d.c. to the right, miss the 1st ch., 1 d.c. into each of the next 8 ch., ** 17 ch., join to the 9th d.c. to the right, miss the 1st ch., 1 d.c. into each of the next 8 ch., repeat 6 times from **; 1 ch., *** 1 d.c. into the last d.c. beneath, 1 d.c. into each of the next 8 ch., repeat 7 times from ***; repeat from * until the required length has been worked. Then working down the left-hand side: 1 ch., **** 1 d.c. into the last d.c. beneath, 1 d.c. into each of the next 8 ch., repeat from ****; 1 d.c. into the last d.c. of the 1st row.

Outside edges of the long sides. 1st row: 1 d.c. into every st. of the network.

2nd row: 1 tr. into the 1st d.c., 1 ch., miss 1 st., 1 tr. into the next, 1 ch., miss 1 st., 1 tr., and so on.

The decorative motif consists of a spray with small leaves and a large flower.

Flower. Begin at the center with 26 ch. Working back, miss the 1st ch., 1 d.c. into the 2nd ch., 1 half tr. into the 3rd ch., 2 tr. into the 4th ch., 2 double tr. into the 5th ch., 1 half triple tr. each into the 6th, 7th, and 8th ch., 1 triple tr. each into the 9th, 10th, 12th, 14th, 16th, 18th, and 19th ch., 1 half triple tr. each into the 20th, 21st, and 22nd ch., 2 double tr. into the 23rd ch., 2 tr. into the 24th ch., 1 half tr. into the 25th ch., 1 d.c. into the 26th ch., 1 ch.

On the second side of the 26 ch. work: 1 d.c. into each of the 1st 3 ch., miss 1 ch., 1 d.c. into each of the next 17 ch., miss 1 ch., 1 d.c. into each of the next 3 ch., 3 d.c. into the ch. at the point; working upward, 1 d.c. into each of the 1st 12 sts., 6 ch; turn; 1 half double tr. into the 5th d.c. of the edge; turn; 13 ch., join to the 7th ch. to the right, 12 d.c. into the ring, 13 s. cr. into the stem, 7 ch.; turn; 1 half double tr. into the 6th s. cr. of the stem; turn; 12 ch., join to the 7th ch. to the right, 12 d.c. into the ring, 13 s. cr. into the stem, 6 ch.; turn; 1 half double tr. into the 7th s. cr. of the stem; turn; 13 ch., join to the 7th ch. to the right, 12 d.c. into the ring, 13 s. cr. into the stem, 1 more s. cr. into the ch. into which the last s. cr. of the 1st stem was worked, miss 1 st. of the flower, 5 d.c., turn; 1 half double tr. into the 6th s. cr. of the stem; turn; continue with 7 d.c. along the edge and 3 d.c. into the ch. at the point; break off.

Spray with leaves. Begin with 61 ch. Working back, miss the 1st ch., 1 d.c. into each of the next 7 ch., 7 ch., miss the 1st of these 7 ch., 1 d.c. into each of the next 5 ch., 1 d.c. joining the 7th ch. and the next st. of the 61 ch., 1 d.c. into each of the next 8 ch., 13 ch., join to the 9th of the 17 d.c. of the flower, miss the 1st of the 17 ch., 1 d.c. into each of the next 11 ch., 1 d.c. joining the 13th ch. and the next st. of the 61 ch., 1 d.c. into each of the next 14 ch., 8 ch., miss the 1st of these 8 ch., 1 d.c. into each of the next 6 ch., 1 d.c. joining the 8th ch. and the next of the 61 ch., 1 d.c. into each of the next 28 ch., 6 ch., * 18 ch., join to the 1st of the 18 ch. to the right, miss the 1st st., 1 d.c. into the 2nd st., 1 half tr. into the 3rd st., 1 tr. into each of the next 5 sts.; 1 tr. and 1 half tr. into the 8th ch., 3 d.c. into the 9th ch., 1 half tr. and 1 tr. into the 10th ch., 1 tr. into each of the next 5 ch., 1 half tr. into the next ch., 1 d.c. into the last ch., 1 ch.; 10 d.c. along the right-hand side of the leaf; into the st. at the point: 1 d.c., 1 picot (composed of 3 ch. and 1 s. cr.), 1 d.c.; 10 d.c. along the left-hand side of the leaf, ending with 1 s. cr. into the 1st ch. **; miss the 1st of the 6 ch., 1 d.c. into each of the next 5 ch., 1 s. cr. into the 1st of the 61 ch., 7 ch.; repeat once from * to **; miss the 1st of the 7 ch., 1 d.c. into each of the next 6 ch., 1 more s. cr. into the 1st of the 61 ch., 7 s. cr. into the stem, 8 ch.; repeat once from * to **; miss the 1st of the 8 ch., 1 d.c. into each of the next 7 ch., 11 s. cr. into the stem, 6 ch.; repeat once from * to **; miss the 1st of the 6 ch., 1 d.c. into each of the next 5 ch., 10 s. cr. into the stem, 6 ch.; repeat once from * to **; miss the 1st of the 6 ch., 1 d.c. into each of the next 5 ch., 8 s. cr. into the stem, 6 ch.; repeat once from * to **; miss the 1st of the 6 ch., 1 d.c. into each of the next 5 ch., 7 s. cr. into the stem, 7 ch., miss the 1st ch., 1 d.c. into each of the next 6 ch., 8 s. cr. into the stem, 7 ch.; repeat once from * to **; miss the 1st of the 7 ch., 1 d.c. into each of the next 5 ch., 1 d.c. joining the 7th ch. and the next ch. of the stem, continue along the stem with 2 d.c., 2 half tr., 3 tr.; break off.

Irish Crochet Lace (fig. 549, 550, 551). At the time of the great famine in Ireland towards the middle of the nineteenth century, an effort

Fig. 549. Irish crochet lace.

was made to imitate Venetian point lace in crochet in order to provide the impoverished population with a home industry. The first attempts were eminently successful, and the industry thus created has subsisted ever since in a more or less flourishing condition according to the fluctuations of fashion.

In this type of lace, rich floral motifs, flat or in relief, are connected by a background of crochet net and finished by a plain or scalloped outer edge. A characteristic of the working of the motifs is that the first crochet stitches are worked over a round padding cord instead of into a crochet chain, as in ordinary crochet. Further, the finished motifs are basted onto a tracing on jap silk; this tracing, in addition to the outlines of the motifs, comprises auxiliary lines which indicate the direction to be followed in the working of the net forming the background and of the outside edges.

Everything having been prepared, the ground is worked; this is attached on the inside to all sides of the motifs. When the ground has been worked along the whole length of the tracing, a crochet chain is made of the same length to obtain a straight edge over which a heading or scallops are later worked. This chain is joined to the ground with trebles, to make the edge even. The finished lace is detached from the tracing and all the tacking threads are removed.

Fig. 549 illustrates a lace design with large scallop. For our example we used, for the motifs and the outer edges, DMC special quality crochet cotton, no. 60, with DMC knotting cotton no. 10 as padding cord; the ground was worked with DMC special quality crochet cotton no. 120 in ecru.

The work is begun with the five-petalled flower.

Circle: 7 ch., * 1 tr. into the 1st of these 7 ch., 3 ch., repeat from * 4 times; 1 s. cr. into the 3rd of the 6 ch., 6 ch., ** 1 tr. into the loop of 3 ch. beneath, 3 ch., 1 tr. into the tr., 3 ch., repeat 4 times from **; 1 tr. into the last loop of 3 ch., 3 ch., 1 s. cr. into the 3rd of the 1st 6 ch.

Petals: * 1 ch.; turn; work 20 d.c. over a padding cord, 1 ch.; turn; working back, make 15 d.c. over the padding cord and into the d.c. below, the last 5 d.c. remaining free, 1 ch.; turn; working back, make 15 d.c. over the padding cord and into the previous d.c., 5 d.c. over the cord alone, 1 ch.; turn; working back, make 15 d.c. over the cord and into the previous d.c., the last 5 sts. remaining free, 1 ch.; turn; working back, make 10 d.c. over the cord and into the previous d.c., the last 5 sts. remaining free, 1 ch.; turn; working back, make 20 d.c. over the cord and into the previous d.c., as far as the beginning of the petal; repeat four times from *; after the first and third petals, work 4 d.c. over the cord and into the first loop of 3 ch. of the circle, 2 d.c. into the next loop of 3 ch.; after the second and fourth petals, work 2 d.c. over the cord and into the loop of 3 ch., and 4 d.c. into the next loop of 3 ch.; after the fifth petal: ** 4 d.c. over the cord and into the loop of 3 ch., repeat five times from **.

Outlining of the petals: Over the padding cord along the petal work: 5 d.c., 1 picot (composed of 5 ch. and 1 s. cr.), 5 d.c., 1 picot, 5 d.c., 1 picot, 5 d.c., 1 picot; * 1 d.c. over the cord into the first point of the petal, 8 d.c. over the cord alone; into the second point of the petal and over the cord: 2 d.c., 1 picot, 2 d.c.; 8 d.c. over the cord alone, 1 d.c. into the third point of the petal and over the cord; into the sts. beneath and over the cord: 5 d.c., 1 picot, 14 d.c.; miss the last d.c. of the petal and the 1st 2 sts. in the angle, 2 d.c. over the cord and into the next 2 d.c., miss the last 2 sts. in the angle and the 1st st. of the next petal, 14 d.c. over the cord and along the second petal, 3 ch., join to the picot of the finished petal on the right, 2 ch., 1 s. cr. into the 1st of the 3 ch., 5 more d.c. over the cord and into the d.c. beneath, 10 ch., join to the d.c. at the third point of the finished petal on the right; over these 10 ch. work: 5 d.c., 1 picot, 5 d.c., 1 picot, 5 d.c.; repeat three times from *; 1 d.c. over the cord and into the st. at the first point of the fifth petal, 8 d.c. over the cord alone; over the cord and into the st. at the second point: 2 d.c., 1 picot, 2 d.c.; 8 d.c. over the cord alone, 1 d.c. over the cord and into the 3rd point of the petal, 1 picot; over the cord and into the succeeding d.c.: 5 d.c., 1 picot, 5 d.c., 1 picot, 5 d.c., 1 picot, 5 d.c.

Row of rings: work 22 d.c. over the cord alone,

Fig. 550.
Net ground for the lace in fig. 549.

bend them into a ring, 1 d.c. into the 3rd of the 22 d.c. and over the cord; * 22 d.c. over the cord alone, bend into a ring, 1 d.c. into the 4th of the 22 d.c. and over the cord, repeat five times from *; join the 7 rings to the first petal by 1 d.c. and break off the threads.

Work a sufficient number of these flowers.

Leaves: Work 18 d.c. over a cord. * 1 ch.; turn; working back, make 12 d.c. over the cord and into the previous d.c., the last 6 sts. remaining free, 1 ch.; turn; working back, make 8 d.c. over the cord and into the previous d.c., the last 4 sts. remaining free, 10 d.c. over the cord alone; repeat once from *; 1 ch.; turn; working back, make 18 d.c. over the cord and into the previous d.c.; ** 1 ch.; turn; working back, make 8 d.c. over the cord and into the previous d.c., the last 10 sts. remaining free, 4 d.c. over the cord alone, 1 ch.; turn; working back, make 12 d.c. over the cord and into the previous d.c., 5 d.c. over the cord alone, 1 d.c. over the cord and into the 6th free st. below; repeat once from **; 16 d.c. over the cord alone, 1 ch.; turn; join to the d.c. to the right in the angle, working back, make 15 d.c. over the cord and into the previous d.c., the last st. remaining free, 3 d.c. over the two ends of the cord to finish the leaf; break off the threads.

Stem: Work 42 d.c. over a cord, 1 ch.; turn; working back, make 42 d.c. over the cord and into the previous d.c., then break off.

Detached ring. 1st round: 5 ch., * into the 1st of these 5 ch.: 1 tr., 1 ch., repeat from * eight times into the same st.; 1 s. cr. into the 4th of the 5 ch., 1 ch.

2nd round: * over a cord, work 2 d.c. into the loop of 1 ch. beneath, and 1 d.c. into the tr., repeat eight times from *; 1 d.c. into the last loop of 1 ch., 1 s. cr. into the 1st d.c., 1 ch.

3rd round: * over the cord and into the d.c. below: 4 d.c., 1 picot (composed of 5 ch. and 1 s. cr.), 1 d.c. into the same d.c. as the d.c. which precedes the picot, repeat six times from *; 1 d.c. into the 1st d.c.; break off.

Before the working of the ground is begun, it is advisable to work a small experimental piece, as shown in fig. 550.

Make 40 ch.

1st row: 1 tr. into the 4th ch.; * 9 ch., working back, make 1 d.c. over the 9 ch., 4 ch., turn the loop to the left, 1 d.c. into the loop below, com-

Fig. 551. How to work the ground between the motifs for the crochet lace in fig. 549.

plete the picot by drawing one loop very close to the other, 2 ch., 1 tr. into the 9th st. of the ch.; repeat from *; turn.

2nd row: 12 ch.; working back, make 1 d.c. over the 12 ch., 4 ch., 1 d.c. into the loop below, draw up the picot, 2 ch., 1 tr. over the ch. which follows the 1st picot, * 9 ch; working back, make 1 d.c. over the 9 ch., 4 ch., 1 d.c. into the loop below, draw up the picot, 2 ch., 1 tr. over the ch. which follows the next picot; repeat twice from *; 3 ch., 1 quadruple treble into the tr. below (in succeeding rows, work the quadruple tr. into the 3rd ch. from the bottom); turn.

3rd row: worked as the 2nd, but ending the row with 1 plain tr. into the last loop of ch. of the preceding row; turn.

Repeat from the 2nd row.

When this net ground has been sufficiently practised, the filling of the lace itself can be undertaken.

Scalloped edge. 1st row: work d.c. over a cord and over the crochet chain, as well as into the tr. of the first row which straightens the edge.

2nd row: 1 tr., 2 ch., miss 2 sts., 1 tr., 2 ch., miss 2 sts., 1 tr., and so on.

3rd row: following the tracing, work five little scallops on each large scallop.

Fig. 552. Crochet chair back.

Each small scallop requires 10 d.c. After the 8th d.c., make 7 ch., join to the 6th d.c. to the right, 12 d.c. into the loop of 7 ch., 1 s. cr., into the d.c. below, 2 more d.c. into the sts. of the little previous row, 14 ch., join to the 2nd d.c. to the right of the little scallop, into this loop of 14 ch. work: 4 d.c., 1 picot, 4 d.c., 1 picot, 4 d.c., 1 picot, 4 d.c., 1 picot, 4 d.c., 1 picot, 4 d.c.; 1 s. cr. into the d.c. below; continue with d.c. to the next small scallop.

Add 4 picots in the row of d.c. in the angle.

Heading: like the 1st and 2nd row of the scalloped edge.

Crochet Chair Back (fig. 552). If this design is to be used as a chair back, it should be worked in DMC 6 cord crochet cotton nos. 5 to 20, DMC knotting cotton no. 30, or DMC special quality crochet cotton nos. 5 to 20. In the finer numbers of 6 cord crochet cotton, it will work out much smaller, so that four squares will have to be joined to make a chair back. The eight sides that will then meet in the center of the square are joined by trebles.

In the same way, the squares can be used to composed bedspreads, cot covers, table runners, band to trim tablecloths, curtains, etc. The design can also, like the one in fig. 553, be used to make large or small doilies and mats.

Begin with 5 ch., close the ring with 1 s. cr.

1st round: 5 ch., * 1 tr. into the ring, 2 ch., repeat from * six times; 1 s. cr. into the 3rd of the 5 ch.

2nd round: * 4 d.c. into the loop of 2 ch., repeat from * seven times.

3rd and 4th rounds: 1 d.c. into each st. of the preceding round.

5th round: 9 ch., * miss 1 st. of the preceding round, 1 double tr. into the next st., 4 ch., repeat from * fourteen times; 1 s. cr. into the 5th of the 9 ch.

6th round: * 4 d.c. into the loop of 4 ch., 1 d.c. into the tr.; repeat from * 15 times.

7th round: 2 d.c., * 1 picot, 5 d.c., repeat from * fourteen times; 1 picot, 2 d.c., 1 s. cr.; the 3rd of the group of 5 d.c. should come above the double tr.

8th round: 12 ch., 1 tr. into the 3rd of the d.c. which follow the 1st picot, * 9 ch., 1 tr. into the 3rd of the next group of 5 d.c., repeat from * 13 times; 9 ch., 1 s. cr. into the 3rd of the 12 ch.

9th round: * 13 d.c. into the first loop of 9 ch., 6 d.c. into the next loop of 9 ch., 9 ch., join to the 7th of the 13 d.c. to the right that have just been worked, 15 d.c. into this new loop of 9 ch., 7 d.c. into the loop of ch. of the preceding row (into which 6 d.c. have already been worked), repeat from * seven times.

10th round: 12 s. cr. along the first scallop, 1 d.c. each into the 7th, 8th, and 9th of the 15 d.c. of the preceding round, * 5 ch., 1 downward picot, 5 ch., 1 downward picot, 5 ch., 1 d.c. each into the 7th, 8th, and 9th of the next 15 d.c., repeat from * six times; 5 ch., 1 downward picot, 5 ch., 1 downward picot, 5 ch.

11th round: 1 d.c. into each st. and each picot of the preceding round (160 d.c. in all).

12th round: 4 ch., miss 1 d.c. of the preceding round, 1 tr. into the next, * 1 ch., miss 1 st., 1 tr. into the next, repeat from * seventy-seven times; 1 ch., 1 s. cr. into the 3rd of the 4 ch.

13th round: 1 s. cr. into the next ch., * 5 ch., miss the 1st ch., 1 d.c., 1 tr., 1 double tr., miss 3 sts. of the preceding round, 1 s. cr. into the 4th, repeat from * thirty-nine times.

14th round: 4 s. cr. along the first pyramid, 1 d.c. into the st. at the point, * 5 ch., 1 d.c. into the point of the next pyramid, repeat from * thirty-eight times; 5 ch., 1 d.c. into the point of the first pyramid.

15th round: 4 ch., miss 1 st. of the preceding round, 1 tr. into the 2nd st., * 1 ch., miss 1 st., 1 tr. into the next, repeat from * one hundred and seventeen times; 1 ch., 1 s. cr. into the 3rd of the 4 ch.

16th round: 1 d.c. into each of the first 15 sts. of the preceding round, * 15 ch., join to the 9th ch. from the hook, 2 d.c. into the ring, 10 ch. join to the 4th d.c. to the right, miss the 1st ch., 1 s. cr. each into the 2nd, 3rd, and 4th ch., 6 ch., miss the 1st ch., 1 s. cr., 1 d.c., 1 tr., 3 ch., miss 2 ch., 1 tr. into the 3rd of the ch. which precede the 3 s. cr., 1 d.c., 1 s. cr., 1 ch., 2 d.c. into the loop ** 6 ch., join on the right to the 2nd of the last 3 ch., 7 ch., miss the 1st ch., 1 s. cr., 1 d.c., 2 tr., 3 ch., miss the 6th and 5th of the first 6 ch., 1 tr., 1 d.c., 1 s. cr., 1 ch., 2 d.c. into the loop ***; repeat four times from ** to ***; 6 ch., join to the 2nd of the last 3 ch., 6 ch., miss the 1st ch., 1 s. cr., 1 d.c., 1 tr., 3 ch., miss the 6th and 5th of the last 6 ch., 1 tr., 1 d.c., 1 s. cr., 1 ch., 2 d.c. into the ring, 1 s. cr. into each of the remaining 6 ch., 4 d.c. into the row below, 4 ch., join to the 2nd of the last 3 ch., miss the 1st ch., 3 s. cr., 11 d.c. into the sts. of the row below; repeat from * fifteen times; join the first and second points to the last and next to last points of the preceding leaf; when the sixth point of the sixteenth leaf is reached, join this to the second point of the first leaf, and join the seventh point to the first point of the first leaf, break off.

17th round: join on the thread to the second point on the right of the leaf which forms the corner; 13 s. cr., 1 picot of 3 ch. at the tip of the third point, 14 s. cr., * 1 picot at the tip of the fourth point, 14 s. cr., 1 picot at the tip of the fifth point, 27 s. cr., 1 ch. at the tip of the third point of the second leaf; turn; 1 triple tr. into the picot on the fifth point of the first leaf, 1 ch.; turn; 14 s. cr., 1 ch., turn; 1 quadruple tr. into the picot on the third point of the second leaf, 1 ch.; turn; 14 s. cr., 1 picot at the tip of the fifth point, 27 s. cr., 1 ch. at the tip of the third point of the third leaf; turn; 1 triple tr. into the picot on the fifth point of the second leaf, 1 ch.; turn; 14 s. cr., 1 picot at the tip of the fourth point, 14 s. cr., 1 picot at the tip of the fifth point, 27 s. cr., 1 ch. at the tip of the 3rd point of the fourth leaf; turn; 1 triple tr. into the picot on the fifth point of the third leaf, 1 ch.; turn; 14 s. cr., 1 picot at the tip of the fourth point of the fourth leaf, 14 s. cr., 1 ch.; turn; 1 quadruple tr. into the picot on the fourth point of the fourth leaf **, 1 ch.; turn; 27 s. cr., 1 ch.; turn; 1 triple tr. into the picot on the fifth point of the fourth leaf, 1 ch.; turn; 14 s. cr.. ***; repeat twice from * to *** and once from * to **; join the fifth point of the sixteenth leaf to the third point of the first leaf by 1 triple tr. and end with 13 s. cr.; break off.

For the small leaves in the corners, join on the thread to the fourth point of a corner leaf; 10 ch., join to the 9th ch. from the hook, 2 d.c. into the ring, 10 ch., join to the third point of the leaf below to the right, miss 1 ch.,

3 s. cr., 7 ch., miss the 1st ch., 1 s. cr., 1 d.c., 2 tr., 3 ch., miss the 6th and 5th of the 10 ch., 1 tr., 1 d.c. 1 s. cr., 1 ch., 2 d.c. into the ring, * 6 ch., join to the 2nd of the last 3 ch. to the right, 7 ch., miss the 1st ch., 1 s. cr., 1 d.c., 2 tr., 3 ch., miss the 6th and 5th of the last 6 ch., 1 tr., 1 d.c., 1 s. cr., 1 ch., 3 d.c. into the ring; repeat from * four times; 6 ch., join to the 2nd of the last 3 ch. to the right, 7 ch., miss the 1st ch., 1 s. cr., 1 d.c., 2 tr., 5 ch., join to the 5th point of the leaf below, miss the 1st ch., 3 s. cr., 1 ch., miss the 6th and 5th of the last 6 ch., 1 tr., 1 d.c., 1 s. cr., 1 ch., 2 d.c. into the ring; 2 s. cr. into the remainder of the 10 ch.; break off.

Fasten on the thread to the third point, into the st. into which was worked the s. cr. which precedes the first 10 ch., 10 s. cr., 1 ch.; turn; 1 triple tr. into the picot on the fifth point of the sixteenth leaf, 1 ch.; turn; 14 s. cr., 1 picot at the tip of the second point, 14 s. cr., 1 picot at the tip of the third point, 14 s. cr., 1 picot at the tip of the fourth point, 14 s. cr., 1 picot at the tip of the fifth point, 14 s. cr., 1 picot at the tip of the sixth point, 14 s. cr., 1 ch., 1 triple tr. into the picot on the third point of the second leaf, 1 ch., 10 s. cr.; break off.

Repeat the same figure in the other three corners.

18th round: * 1 d.c. into the picot on the fourth point of the third leaf, 4 ch., 1 triple tr. into the picot on the fifth point of the third leaf, 5 ch., 1 double tr. into the same picot, 3 ch., 1 triple tr. into the picot on the third point of the fourth leaf, 5 ch., 1 triple tr. into the picot on the fourth point of the fourth leaf, 8 ch., 1 double tr. into the same picot, 3 ch., 1 quadruple tr. into the picot on the first point of the isolated leaf in the corner, 6 ch., 1 triple tr. into the same picot, 1 ch., 1 double tr. into the picot on the second point of the corner leaf, 6 ch., 1 double tr. into the same picot, 5 ch., 1 d.c. into the picot on the third point of the corner leaf, 3 ch., 1 triple tr. into the picot on the fourth point of the corner leaf, 7 ch., 1 triple tr. into the same picot, 7 ch., 1 triple tr. into the same picot, 3 ch., 1 d.c. into the picot on the fifth point of the corner leaf, 5 ch., 1 double tr. into the picot on the sixth point of the corner leaf, 6 ch., 1 double tr. into the same picot, 1 ch., 1 triple tr. into the picot on the seventh point of the corner leaf, 6 ch., 1 quadruple tr. into the same picot, 3 ch., 1 double tr. into the picot on the fourth point of the sixth leaf, 8 ch., 1 triple tr. into the same picot, 5 ch., 1 triple tr. into the picot of the fifth point of the sixth leaf, 3 ch., 1 double tr. into the picot on the third point of the seventh leaf, 5 ch., 1 triple tr. into the same picot, 4 ch.; repeat from * three times.

19th round: 1 d.c. into each st. of the preceding round, with 3 d.c. into the corner st.

20th round: 1 s. cr. into each of the 1st 2 d.c. of the previous round, 4 ch., miss 1 st. of the previous round, 1 tr. into the next, 1 ch., miss 1 st., 1 tr. into the next, and so on; there should be 68 tr. along each side. Into the corner st. work: 1 tr., 2 ch., 1 double tr., 2 ch., 1 tr.; break off.

21st round: 1 d.c. into the loop of ch. preceding the double tr., * 6 ch., miss the 1st of these 6 ch. and into the remaining 5 work: 1 d.c., 2 tr., 2 double tr.; 1 d.c. into the loop of 2 ch. following the double tr., 6 ch., miss the 1st of these ch., 1 d.c., 2 tr., 2 double tr., miss 2 tr. of the previous round, 1 d.c. into the next loop of 1 ch.; * * 6 ch., miss the 1st ch., 1 d.c., 2 tr., 2 double tr., miss 3 tr. of the previous round, 1 d.c., repeat from * * twenty-one times; 6 ch., miss the 1st ch., 1 d.c., 2 tr., 2 double tr., miss 2 tr. of the previous row, 1 d.c.; repeat from * three times.

22nd round: 6 s. cr. along the pyramid, 1 picot of 3 ch. at the point, 6 s. cr. along the second side; surround all the other little pyramids in the same way.

Fig. 553. Crochet chair back composed of squares.

Crochet Chair Back Composed of Squares (fig. 553). This is an adaptation for crochet of one of the most charming designs for cut openwork, taken from an ancient collection of needlework. We have ourselves worked the design both in DMC special quality crochet cotton no. 15 and in DMC Alsatian sewing cotton no. 100.

1st round: 4 ch., close the ring with 1 s. cr..

2nd round: 2 d.c. into each ch. (8 d.c. in all); 1 s. cr. into the 1st d.c.

3rd round: 6 ch., * 1 tr., 3 ch., repeat from * six times, 1 s. cr. into the 3rd of the 6 ch. (8 tr. in all, including the first 3 ch.).

4th round: 5 d.c. into each loop of 3 ch., 1 d.c. into each tr.

5th round: 6 ch., 1 d.c. into the 3rd d.c. of the preceding row, * 3 ch., 1 tr. into the st. above the tr. of the 3rd round, 3 ch., 1 d.c. into the 3rd st. of the preceding row, repeat from * six times; 3 ch., 1 s. cr. into the 3rd of the 6 ch.

6th round: 8 ch., * 1 d.c. into the tr. of the preceding round, 7 ch., repeat from * six times; 1 s. cr. into the 1st of the 8 ch.

7th round: 3 ch., 1 tr. into the same st. below; 1 tr. into each ch., 2 tr. into each d.c. of the preceding round (72 tr. in all, including the 1st 3 ch.); 1 s. cr. into the 3rd ch.

8th round: * 8 ch., 1 d.c. between the 2 tr. of the increase, that is to say between the 9th and 10th tr.; turn; 12 d.c. into the loop of 8 ch.; turn; draw a loop through each of the 12 sts. for Tunisian crochet, which is worked for 10 rows, decreasing 1 st. in each row, alternately at the right-hand and left-hand sides, draw a single loop through the last three loops; 1 ch., then, working down the left-hand side of the pyramid, 1 s. cr. into each row of the Tunisian crochet, end with 1 s. cr. into the d.c. which follows the 8 ch.; repeat from * seven times.

9th round: working along the edge of the pyramid: 3 d.c., 1 picot, 3 d.c., 1 picot, 3 d.c., 1 picot, 1 d.c., 3 d.c. into the st. at the point. Repeat the same number of sts. along the second side and along all the other pyramids; at the end of the round, break off.

10th round: fasten on the thread to the 2nd of the 3 d.c. at the point of a pyramid, * 7 ch., 5 overs, draw a loop through the 2nd picot on the left side of the pyramid, draw a loop through the first 2 loops on the hook, draw another loop through the next 2 loops, make 2 more over, pass the hook through the corresponding picot opposite, draw a loop through the first 2 loops on the hook, draw another loop through the next 2 loops, draw a loop through the next 3 loops, draw loops through the remaining loops 2 by 2, 6 ch., 1 double tr. into the 3rd of the first 5 overs, 7 ch., 1 d.c. into the point of the next pyramid, 7 ch., 7 overs, draw a loop through the loop of the 2nd picot following, drawn a loop through the first 2 loops on the hook three times, 1 triple tr. into the corresponding picot opposite, draw successive loops through the loops on the hook 2 by 2 until the 4th over is reached, then draw a loop through 3 loops together, draw successive loops through the remaining loops 2 by 2, 7 ch., 1 quadruple tr. into the 4th of the first 7 overs, 7 ch., 1 triple tr. again into the 4th of the first 7 overs, 7 ch., 1 d.c. into the next pyramid; repeat from * three times.

11th round: 1 d.c. into each st. of the previous round, with 3 d.c. into the corner sts.

12th round: 1 s. cr. into the 1st d.c., 5 ch., 1 tr. into the 3rd d.c., * 2 ch., 1 tr. into the 3rd d.c., repeat from * ten times; 2 ch.; into the corner st. work: 1 tr., 2 ch., 1 tr., 2 ch., 1 tr.; 2 ch., continue as for the first side.

Between one corner and the next there should be 20 tr. and 21 groups of 2 ch.; end with 1 s. cr. into the 3rd of the 5 ch.

13th round: 1 d.c. into each st. of the preceding round, making 62 sts. along each side, without counting the 3 sts. that are worked into the corner st.

14th round: 1 d.c. into each of the first 13 sts., 1 ch., 24 d.c., leaving 4 sts. of the previous round, not counting the 3 sts. of the increase at the corner, unworked; turn; 1 ch., miss 2 sts., 22 d.c. worked through both loops of the sts. in the preceding round; turn; 1 ch., 21 d.c.; turn; 1 ch., 20 d.c.; continue thus until only 3 sts. are worked in the row; break off. For each decrease, miss the last st. but one in the return journey and the 1st st. in the alternate journey; begin each row with 1 ch

For the second half of these triangular sections, begun on the wrong side, fasten on the thread to the 28th st. after the 3 sts. at the corner, and work 23 d.c., leaving a space of 7 d.c. between the two triangular sections in d.c.; turn; 1 ch., miss 1 st., 22 d.c., 3 overs, insert the hook into the 4th of the 7 sts. between the two sections, draw a loop through the first 2 loops on the hook, draw another loop through the next 2 loops; make another over, insert the hook into the last st. of the 3rd row opposite, draw 4 successive loops each through 2 loops on the hook; turn; 21 d.c., 1 ch.; turn; 20 d.c., 2 overs, insert a hook into the tr. in the middle, draw a loop through the first 2 loops on the hook, 1 over, insert the hook into the opposite triangle, draw 4 successive loops through the loops on the hook 2 by 2, and so on until 10 connecting tr. have been worked; then break off, and work in the same way on the other three sides.

15th round: * 1 tr. into the corner st. of the right-hand triangle, 2 ch., 1 tr. into the same st., 2 ch., 1 tr. into the last d.c. of the first half of the triangular sections, 2 ch., 1 tr. into the middle of the 10th connecting tr., 2 ch., 1 tr. into the 1st d.c. of the 2nd triangular section, 2 ch., 1 tr. into the 3rd and last top st. of the triangular section, 2 ch., 1 tr. into the same st. as the preceding tr.

Working along the edge: 10 tr. separated from each other by 2 ch.; after the 10th tr.: 5 ch., 1 d.c. into the corner st. of the 13th round, 5 ch., 10 tr. separated from each other by 2 ch., 2 ch.; repeat from * three times.

16th round: 3 d.c. into each loop of 2 ch., 6 d.c. into each loop of 5 ch.

17th round: 7 ch., 1 d.c. into the 7th d.c. of the preceding round; make thirteen scallops along each side, the seventh scallop being exactly over the corner sts. of the 13th round; at the corner miss 4 sts. of the preceding row. and for the two scallops to the right and left of the corner miss 3 sts. only.

18th round: 7 d.c. into the loop of 7 ch., 5 ch., join to the 4th d.c. to the right, into the loop of 5 ch. work: 3 d.c., 1 picot, 3 d.c.; 3 d.c. into the loop of 7 ch. of the preceding row (into which 7 d.c. have already been worked), and so on.

When several of these squares are to be used for the same piece of work and have to be joined, 13 picots along the side are joined, the 14th—the corner picot—being left free. The 4 free picots are then joined by a small medallion.

The chair back design illustrated in fig. 533 can very well be used for doilies and mats.

Crochet Collar (fig. 554).   We have as far as possible avoided describing articles that are much affected by changes of fashion, and if we break our

Fig. 554. Crochet collar.

rule now by describing a collar composed of squares, medallions, diamonds, and lace, it is because it is classic in form and not likely to date. This delicate work can only be done in very fine cotton, and the best effects will be obtained with ecru threads. The soft shade and the brilliance of these threads impart to the new work an antique character which cannot be obtained with white thread.

The best threads to use for this collar are DMC special quality crochet cotton, DMC cotton lace thread, or DMC Alsatian sewing cotton in ecru, or DMC flax lace thread in white. The framed medallions of the inner half circles are worked first, then those of the outer half circle.

The four squares with interlaced figures, placed one at each end of the inner half circle and one on each side of the center square, are the same length on all four sides; where the same figure is used in the outer half circle, it is a little narrower at the outer edge.

Inner squares 1st round: 5 ch., close the ring; 5 ch., * 1 tr. into the ring, 2 ch., repeat from * six times; 1 s. cr. into the 3rd of the 5 ch.

2nd round: 3 d.c. into the loop of 2 ch., 1 d.c. into each tr.

3rd round: 9 ch., * 1 tr. into the d.c. over the tr. of the 1st round, 6 ch., repeat from * six times; 1 s. cr. into the 3rd of the 9 ch.

4th round: Small leaf: * 10 ch.; working back, miss the 1st ch., 1 d.c., 1 half tr., 4 tr., 1 half tr., 1 d.c., 1 s. cr.; into the loop of 6 ch. of the 3rd round: ** 1 d.c., 1 half tr., 1 tr., 3 double tr., 1 tr., 1 half tr., 1 d.c. ***; repeat once from ** to ***; repeat the whole series (from *) three times; 9 s. cr. along the first leaf.

5th round: * 1 d.c. into the st. at the point, 7 ch., 1 triple tr. into the 5th st. of the small scallop of the 4th round, 7 ch., 1 triple tr. into the next scallop, 7 ch.; repeat from * three times.

6th round: * 3 d.c. into the st. which forms the point, 1 d.c. into each ch. and each tr. of the preceding round as far as the 2nd tr. (15 d.c. in all); turn; 1 ch., 5 double tr., separated from each other by 1 ch., into the 4th d.c., 1 ch., 1 s. cr. into the 4th d.c.; turn; 2 d.c. into each loop of 1 ch., and 1 d.c. into each tr., with 1 picot above the 1st, 2nd, 3rd, 4th, and 5th double tr., 8 d.c.; repeat from * three times.

7th round: 2 s. cr., * 9 ch., 1 double tr. between the first 2 picots of the half circle made in the previous round, 8 ch., 1 triple tr. above the 3rd tr. of the half circle, 8 ch., 1 double tr. between the 3rd and 4th picots of the half circle, 9 ch., 1 d.c. into the corner st.; repeat from * three times.

8th round: 1 d.c. into each of the first 18 sts. of the 7th round, 3 d.c. into the corner st., 1 d.c. into each of the next 23 sts.; turn; 2 ch., 3 double tr., separated from each other by 2 ch., into the 5th d.c., 2 ch., 1 s. cr. into the 5th d.c.; turn; * 1 d.c., 1 picot, 1 d.c. into the loop of ch. below, 1 d.c. into the tr., repeat from * twice; 1 d.c., 1 picot, 1 d.c. into the last loop of 2 ch., 1 d.c. into each of the 4 ch. of the 7th round; turn; ** 5 ch., 1 double tr. above the next tr. of the little half circle, repeat from ** twice; 5 ch., 1 s. cr. into the 4th d.c., turn; 1 d.c. into the loop of 5 ch.; in this round the points are made as follows: 8 ch., miss the 1st ch., 1 s. cr., 1 d.c., 1 half tr., 1 tr., 1 half long tr., 2 double tr.; 1 d.c. into the loop of 5 ch. The next point is set half before and half beyond the tr.; seven points in all are made. After the seventh point: 8 d.c. into the ch. of the 7th round; turn; *** 7 ch., 1 d.c. into the ch. at the point, repeat from *** six times; 7 ch., 1 d.c. into the 9th d.c.; turn; pass the loop through the 1st d.c., 1 tr. into each of the next

8 sts., 1 picot above the point, 4 tr., 12 ch., join to the 4th tr. preceding the 1st picot to the right; into the loop of 12 ch.: 5 d.c., 1 picot, 4 d.c. 1 picot, 4 d.c., 1 picot, 5 d.c.; 4 tr. up to the next point, 1 picot, 4 tr., 12 ch., join to the 4th tr. on the right, and so on; make seven scallops in all. After the seventh scallop, add 4 tr. into the last ch., to the 4th tr. add 2 d.c., followed by the 3 d.c. of the corner; join the scallops in the angle by their last and 1st picots.

When all four sides of the figure described above have been completed, break off.

The framing of the upper squares is begun on the inner side, which will be a little narrower, and at the third little scallop: * 1 d.c. into the middle picot of the third scallop, 5 ch., 1 double tr. into the 1st picot of the fourth scallop, 5 ch., 1 triple tr. into the 2nd picot of the same scallop, 5 ch., 1 double tr. into the 3rd picot of the same scallop again, 5 ch., 1 d.c. into the middle picot of the fifth scallop, 10 ch., 1 d.c. in the middle picot of the sixth scallop, 9 ch. **, 1 double tr. into the middle picot of the seventh scallop, 1 double tr. into the middle picot of the next scallop, joining the last overs of these last 2 tr.; repeat once from ** to * (i.e., in the reverse order); continue as follows: *** 10 ch., 1 tr. into the sixth scallop, 11 ch., 2 quadruple tr., joined by their last overs, into the picots of the seventh and the first scallop, 11 ch., 1 tr. into the second scallop, 10 ch., 1 tr. into the third scallop, 8 ch., 1 half triple tr., 8 ch., 1 half quadruple tr., 8 ch., 1 double tr., 8 ch., 1 d.c., 12 ch., 1 tr., 14 ch. ****, 2 triple tr. joined by their last overs; repeat once from **** to *** (i.e., in the reverse order). End with a round of d.c., working 1 d.c. into each st. of the preceding round, with 3 d.c. into the st. which forms each corner. The narrow end will have 65 sts., the wide end 91 sts., and the two sides 75 sts. each, not counting the 3 sts. at the corners.

When the same figure is to be used in the large outer scallops, the work is the same as far as the 7th round; this round is worked half way exactly as already described. In the second half, however, make 1 ch. fewer in the spaces than in the first half.

8th round: work the first half of this round as already described; in the second half, each quarter of which is 4 ch. shorter, the little scallops also have 4 picots. The number of ch. and of tr. for the framing is also the same, but instead of seven scallops only five are made.

The outer edge round the top is made in the same way as for the wide part of the upper square, that is to say, as it was worked from the third scallop of the first half circle to the fifth scallop of the second half circle. From that point the work changes, so as to round the edge: * 10 ch., 1 tr. into the sixth scallop, 17 ch., 1 triple tr. into the seventh scallop and 1 triple tr. into the first scallop, joining these 2 tr. by their last overs, 17 ch., 1 tr. into the second of the five scallops, 17 ch., 1 tr. into the third scallop, 17 ch., 1 tr. into the fourth scallop, 18 ch. **, 1 triple tr. into the 5th scallop, 1 triple tr.

into the first scallop, joining the 2 tr. by their last overs; repeat once from ** to *. Add 1 round of d.c., working 1 d.c. into each st. of the previous round and 3 d.c. into the sts. at the upper corners. Three of these figures with outlines rounded on one side will be needed.

The second type of square is composed of eight leaves in the middle; begin with 5 ch. to form a ring.

1st round: 5 ch., * 1 tr. into the ring, 2 ch., repeat from * six times; 1 s. cr. into the 3rd of the 5 ch.

2nd round: 3 d.c. into each loop of 2 ch., 1 d.c. into each tr.

3rd round: 3 ch., * 7 ch.; working back, miss the 1st ch., 1 s. cr., 1 d.c., 1 half tr., 1 tr., 1 double tr., 1 triple tr., 1 tr. into the tr. of the 1st round, repeat from * seven times; at the last repetition, omit the last tr., but, when the eighth point is complete, work 1 s. cr. into the 3rd of the 3 ch., and 7 s. cr. up the side of the first point.

4th round: * 5 ch., 1 triple tr. into the tr. of the 3rd round, 5 ch., 1 d.c. into the ch. left at the point, repeat from * seven times.

5th round: 3 ch., 1 tr. into each st. of the preceding round, 1 s. cr. into the 3rd of the 3 ch. (making 96 tr. in all, counting the 3 ch. at the beginning).

6th round: * 10 ch., 1 d.c. into the tr. above the triple tr. of the 4th round, 10 ch., 1 d.c. into the tr. above the point, repeat from * seven times.

7th round: * 15 d.c. into the first loop of 10 ch., 7 d.c. into the next loop of 10 ch., 10 ch., join to the 8th d.c. to the right in the 1st scallop, 15 d.c. into this loop of 10 ch., 8 d.c. into the loop below (into which 7 d.c. have already been worked), repeat from * seven times; break off.

Fasten on the thread in the middle of one of the eight scallops.

8th round: * 19 ch., miss the 1st ch., 1 d.c., 1 half tr., 1 tr., 1 half long tr., 1 double tr., 1 half triple tr., 1 triple tr., 1 half quadruple tr., 1 quadruple tr., 1 quintuple tr., 1 sixfold tr.; after drawing the thread through the 3rd over, work 1 quadruple tr. between the two plain scallops, complete the sixfold tr., 7 ch., 1 d.c. into the next scallop; repeat from * seven times.

9th round: * 1 d.c. into each of the 7 ch., 1 d.c. into each st. of the pyramid, 3 d.c. into the st. at the point, 1 d.c. into each st. of the pyramid, 4 d.c. into the next loop of 7 ch.; turn; 1 ch., miss 3 d.c., 1 tr., 1 ch., miss 1 d.c., 1 tr.; after the 6th tr. do not miss 1 st. any more between the tr., set the 8th, 9th, and 10th tr. into the 2nd of the 3 sts. at the point; repeat the same process in the reverse order on the other side, making in all 17 tr., 1 s. cr. into the 4th d.c.; turn; 1 d.c. into each ch., 1 d.c. into each tr., with 1 picot above every 3rd d.c.; into the st. at the point work 2 d.c. separated by 1 picot, making 11 picots in all; 3 more d.c. into the loop of 7 ch.; repeat from * 7 times and break off.

The small medallion to the right, at the top of the square, is begun as follows: 9 ch., close the ring; 16 d.c. into the ring, 1 s. cr. into the 1st d.c., 4 ch., * 1 tr., 1 ch., repeat from * fourteen times; 1 s. cr. into the 3rd of the

4 ch., making in all 16 tr., including the 1st 3 ch.; 1 d.c. into each tr. and 1 d.c. into each ch., with 1 picot after every 3rd d.c.; join the 1st picot of the little medallion to the 3rd picot from the bottom of one of the points of the large medallion, ** 3 d.c., 1 picot, repeat once from **; 3 d.c., join the 4th picot to the 3rd picot of the second point, *** 3 d.c., 1 picot, repeat from *** six times, making 11 picots in all. The medallion on the right is made and joined on in the same way as the left-hand one.

The medallions at the bottom of the square require a ring of 13 ch., into which 21 d.c. are worked; 1 s. cr. into the 1st d.c., 4 ch., * 1 tr., 1 ch., repeat from * 19 times; 1 s. cr. into the 3rd of the 4 ch., making 21 tr. in all, including the 1st 3 ch.; ** 3 d.c., 1 picot, repeat twice from **; 3 d.c., join the 4th picot to the 4th picot of the eighth point, 3 d.c., 1 picot, 3 d.c., join the 6th picot to the 2nd picot of the eighth point, 3 d.c., 1 picot, 3 d.c., join the 8th picot to the 10th picot of the seventh point, 3 d.c., 1 picot, 3 d.c., join the 10th picot to the 8th picot of the seventh point; *** 3 d.c., 1 picot, repeat from *** three times, making in all 14 picots round the medallion.

Make a similar medallion on the second side.

The outlining of this second type of square is also a little different: for the motifs of the ground, fasten on the thread to the 6th picot of the first point before the small medallion, * 12 ch., 1 d.c. into the 2nd free picot of the medallion, 9 ch., 1 double tr. into the 4th picot of the medallion, 9 ch., 1 double tr. into the 6th picot of the medallion, 9 ch., 1 d.c. into the 6th picot of the second point, 12 ch. **, 1 quadruple tr. into the 9th picot of the second point, complete 2 overs, make 2 overs, join to the 3rd picot of the third point, complete the tr.; repeat once from ** to * (i.e., in the reverse order); 1 d.c. into the 6th picot of the fourth point, *** 14 ch., 1 sixfold tr. into the 9th picot of the fourth point, complete 4 overs, make 4 overs, join to the 3rd picot of the fifth point, complete the tr., 14 ch., 1 d.c. into the 6th picot of the fifth point, 12 ch., 1 double tr. into the 2nd picot of the large medallion, 9 ch., 1 triple tr. into the 4th picot of the medallion, 13 ch., 1 double tr. into the 6th picot of the medallion, 14 ch., 1 d.c. into the 6th picot of the sixth point, 16 ch. ****, 1 sevenfold tr. into the 9th picot of the sixth point, complete 4 overs, make 4 overs, join to the 3rd picot of the seventh point, complete the tr.; repeat once from **** to *** (i.e., in the reverse order), and end with 1 s. cr.

The square is completed by a round of d.c.; at each corner 3 d.c. are worked into the same st.; the short edge at the top will contain 65 sts., the two sides 75 sts. each, and the outer edge 91 sts., not counting the 3 sts. at the corners. Make three of these squares for the collar.

The same medallion with rounded edges: after completing the medallion according to the instructions already given, add two large wheels with 14 picots at the top edge.

The outline is begun between the two medallions: 1 d.c. into the 6th picot of the first point, 16 ch., 1 quintuple tr. each into the 9th picot of the first point and the 3rd picot of the second point, joining these 2 tr. by the last over only; 16 ch., 1 d.c. into the 6th picot of the second point, * 16 ch., 1 tr. into the 2nd picot of the medallion, 11 ch., 1 quadruple tr. into the 4th picot, 10 ch., 1 tr. into the 6th picot, 16 ch., 1 d.c. into the 6th picot of the third point, 17 ch., 2 joined sixfold tr., the 1st into the 10th picot of the third point and the 2nd into the 2nd picot of the fourth point, 17 ch., 1 d.c. into the 6th picot of the fourth point, 17 ch., 2 joined sixfold tr., the 1st into the 10th picot of the fourth point and the 2nd into the 2nd picot of the fifth point, 17 ch., 1 d.c. into the 6th picot of the fifth point, 19 ch. **, 2 joined sixfold tr., the 1st into the 10th picot of the fifth point and the 2nd into the 2nd picot of the sixth point; repeat once from ** to * (i.e., in the reverse order). Make four of these medallions with rounded edges.

The medallion is completed by a round of d.c.

When all the motifs for the ground are finished, they are joined to each other by bars of varying lengths. Draw the thread through the st. which forms the corner of the wide side of the eight-pointed square; 1 d.c., 5 ch., miss 1 st., 1 d.c. into each of the next 3 sts., 4 ch., miss 2 sts., 1 d.c. into each of the next 3 sts.; in this manner work eleven more groups of 4 ch. and 3 d.c., then two groups consisting of 3 ch. and 2 d.c.; then on the next square, at the edge of the collar, miss as many sts. as were left free on the first square, 2 d.c., passing the loop each time through the last 2 sts. of the opposite square, 1 ch., join to the ch. on the opposite side, 1 ch., miss 2 sts., 2 d.c. into the edge of the second square, 1 ch., join to the ch. of the opposite square, 1 ch., miss 2 sts. of the second square, 3 d.c., 1 ch., join to the ch. opposite, 1 ch., miss 2 sts., 3 d.c. From now on, each bar is joined to the loops produced by the same sts. on the second square. The first connecting bar is made of 5 ch., over which are worked 4 d.c., 1 ch., miss 2 sts., 3 d.c.; for the second bar: 7 ch., over which are worked 6 d.c., 1 ch., miss 2 sts., 3 d.c.; for the third bar: 9 ch., 8 d.c., 1 ch., miss 2 sts., 3 d.c.; fourth bar: 11 ch., 5 d.c., 1 picot, 5 d.c., 1 ch., miss 2 sts., 3 d.c.; fifth bar: 13 ch., 4 d.c., 1 picot, 4 d.c., 1 picot, 4 d.c., 1 ch., miss 2 sts., 3 d.c.; sixth bar: 16 ch., 5 d.c., 1 picot, 5 d.c., 1 picot, 5 d.c., 1 ch., miss 2 sts., 3 d.c.; seventh bar: 19 ch., 5 d.c., 1 picot, 4 d.c., 1 picot, 4 d.c., 1 picot, 5 d.c., 1 ch., miss 2 ch., 3 d.c.; eight bar: 21 ch., 5 d.c., 1 picot, 5 d.c., 1 picot, 5 d.c., 1 picot, 5 d.c., 1 ch., miss 2 sts., 3 d.c.; ninth bar: 24 ch., 5 d.c., 1 picot, 5 d.c., 1 picot, 5 d.c., 1 picot, 5 d.c., 1 picot, 5 d.c., 1 ch., miss 2 sts., 3 d.c.; tenth bar: 26 ch., 6 d.c., 1 picot, 5 d.c., 1 picot, 5 d.c., 1 picot, 5 d.c., 1 picot, 6 d.c., 1 ch., miss 2 sts., 3 d.c.; eleventh bar: 28 ch., 6 d.c., 1 picot, 6 d.c., 1 picot, 6 d.c., 1 picot, 6 d.c., 1 picot, 6 d.c., 1 ch., miss 2 sts., 3 d.c.; twelfth bar: 30 ch., 32 d.c., 2 ch., miss 1 st., 1 d.c.; break off.

When the seven upper motifs have been joined, the seven lower motifs are added, each separately, by means of a row of s. cr. worked on the wrong side.

Below the first square with semicircles, one with eight points is added; below the next, one with semicircles is added.

The outer edge of the large motifs consists of a narrow lace edging. Fasten on the thread to the corner st. of the first square, then work as follows: * 5 d.c., 1 picot, 5 d.c., 14 ch., join to the 1st of the first 5 d.c. to the right; into the loop of 14 ch.: 5 d.c., 1 picot, 11 d.c., 1 picot, 5 d.c.; into the sts. of the edge: 5 d.c., 1 picot, 5 d.c., 14 ch., join to the 1st of the 5 d.c. to the right, 5 d.c., 1 picot, 5 d.c., 14 ch., join to the 6th of the 11 d.c. of the first scallop to the right; into the loop of 14 ch.: ** 5 d.c., 1 picot, repeat twice from **; 5 d.c.; into the lower scallop: 5 d.c., 1 picot, 5 d.c. ***; into the d.c. of the edge: 4 d.c., 1 picot, 4 d.c.; 12 ch., join to the 1st of the first 4 d.c. to the right; into the loop of 12 ch.: 4 d.c., 1 picot, 4 d.c., 1 picot, 4 d.c., 1 picot, 4 d.c. ****; repeat once from * to ****, work the little scallop into 10 d.c., then repeat from * to ***.

The scallops vary slightly on the rounded sides.

On these sides there should be 122 sts., from the corner to the tr. at the center of the bottom. The single scallops of the edging will all be worked over 8 sts.; the triple scallops over 20 sts.; there will be no small scallop between the 4th, 5th, and 6th triple scallops. All round the first motif, there will be 9 triple scallops and 8 single scallops. After the 8th single scallop, work 3 d.c. into the connecting loop of 2 ch. Into the 32 d.c. of the last bar work: 8 d.c., 1 picot, 4 d.c., 12 ch., bring this chain back and join it to the 5th of the 8 d.c.; into the loop of 12 ch.: 5 d.c., 2 ch., pass the over through the middle picot of the last single scallop, 2 ch., close the picot, 9 d.c., 1 picot, 5 d.c.; into the bar: 4 d.c., 1 picot, 4 d.c., 12 ch., join to the 1st d.c., 5 d.c., 1 picot, 4 d.c., 12 ch., join to the 5th d.c. of the first scallop, 5 d.c., 1 picot, 9 d.c., 1 picot, 5 d.c.; into the scallop below: 5 d.c., 1 picot, 5 d.c.; into the bar: 4 d.c., 1 picot, 4 d.c., 12 ch., join to the 1st d.c., 5 d.c., 1 picot, 4 d.c., 12 ch., join close to the upper scallop, 5 d.c., 1 picot, 4 d.c., 12 ch., join to the 5th d.c. of the upper scallop, 5 d.c., 1 picot, 5 d.c., 1 picot, 5 d.c., 1 picot, 5 d.c.; into each of the two half-finished scallops: 5 d.c., 1 picot, 5 d.c.; end with 4 d.c., 3 d.c. into the loop of 2 ch., and repeat the same series of scallops round all the rounded parts.

The diamonds which fill the spaces left by the joining of the large motifs are worked in 7 rounds on a ring of 5 ch.

1st round: 5 ch., 1 tr. into the ring, 2 ch., 1 tr., and so on, making 8 tr. in all, including the initial ch.

2nd round: 3 d.c. into each loop of 2 ch., 1 d.c. into each tr.

3rd round: 8 ch., 1 tr. into the d.c. above the tr. of the first round, 5 ch., 1 tr. and so on; 8 tr. in all.

4th round: * into the loop of 5 ch: 1 d.c., 1 half tr., 1 tr., 3 double tr., 1 tr., 1 half tr., 1 d.c. **; 7 ch., miss the 1st ch., 1 d.c., 1 tr., 2 double tr., 1 tr., 1 d.c. repeat once from * to **; ***; repeat three times from * to ***; 5 s. cr. along the scallop.

5th round: 9 ch., * 1 d.c. into the point of the leaf, 6 ch., 1 tr. into the middle of the scallop, 7 ch., 1 tr. into the next scallop, 8 ch., 1 d.c. into the next leaf, 8 ch., 1 tr. into the scallop, 7 ch. **; 1 tr. into the scallop, 6 ch.; repeat once from * to **; 1 s. cr. into the 3rd ch.

6th round: 1 d.c. into each st. of the preceeding round, 3 d.c. at the point; break off.

7th round: begin in the 3rd of the 3 sts. at the corner; * 4 d.c., 1 picot, 4 d.c., 10 ch., join to the 1st of the first 4 d.c. to the right; into the loop of 10 ch.: 4 d.c., 1 picot, 3 d.c., 1 picot, 3 d.c., 1 picot, 4 d.c. **; repeat twice from * to **; 1 d.c., 3 d.c. at the point, 8 ch., join to the 1st of the 4 d.c. to the right; into the loop of 8 ch.: 4 d.c., 1 picot, 3 d.c., 1 picot, 3 d.c., 1 picot, 4 d.c.; repeat from * to ** three times; 4 d.c., 8 ch., join to the 1st of the 4 d.c.; into the loop of 8 ch.: 4 d.c., 1 picot, 3 d.c., join to the middle picot of the second triple scallop of the second square, 3 d.c., 1 picot, 4 d.c.; repeat from * to ** three times; then, starting from the 2nd picot of the third scallop of the diamond, work as follows: 7 ch., join to the middle picot of the first triple scallop; into the loop of 7 ch.: 5 d.c., 1 picot, 5 d.c.; end the scallop of the diamond, 4 d.c., 8 ch., join to the 1st of the 4 d.c. to the right; into the loop of 8 ch.: 4 d.c., 1 picot, 3 d.c., 2 ch., join to the middle picot of the scallop beneath the connecting bar, complete the picot, 3 d.c., 1 picot, 4 d.c.; repeat from * to ** three times; join the diamond by the first small scallop to the ninth triple scallop by means of a bar of 7 ch., as on the opposite side, 4 d.c., 8 ch., join to the 1st of the 4 d.c. to the right; into the loop of 8 ch.: 4 d.c., 1 picot, 3 d.c., 2 ch., join to the middle picot of the eighth triple scallop of the first square, 3 d.c., 1 picot, 4 d.c.; break off.

The lace which finishes the upper edge of the collar must stand up. To achieve this effect, 1 row of double tr. is worked into the d.c. Four decreases of 1 st. each are made in each square. When this row is finished, break off.

Fasten on the thread again to the right, at the base of the 1st tr., and work 4 d.c. along the length of this tr.; then work as follows: 24 d.c. into the row of tr., passing the hook through both horizontal loops of the tr.; turn; 2 ch., miss 4 d.c.; into the 5th st.: 1 double tr., 2 ch., 1 double tr., 2 ch., 1 double tr.; 2 ch., miss 4 d.c., 1 s. cr. into the 5th d.c.; turn; * 2 d.c., separated by 1 picot, into the loop of 2 ch., 1 d.c. into the tr., repeat twice from *; 2 d.c., separated by 1 picot, into the last loop of 2 ch.; 1 d.c. into each of the 4 tr. below; turn; ** 6 ch., 1 double tr. above the tr., repeat twice from **; 6 ch., 1 s. cr. into the 4th d.c.; turn; 1 d.c. into the loop of 6 ch., 8 ch., miss the 1st ch., 1 d.c., 1 half tr., 2 tr., 1 half long tr., 2 double tr., 1 d.c. into the loops of 6 ch. The next point is set above a tr.; seven points in all are worked. After the seventh point: 1 d.c. each into the next 8 tr.; turn; 1 d.c. into each point, with 7 ch. between. The eighth group of 7 ch. is joined to the 8th d.c. of the border; turn; then add: 2 ch., bring the loop out from the wrong side to the right through the 2nd d.c.; 8 tr., 1 picot, 4 tr., 12 ch., bring them back over the picot, join to the 4th tr., 5 d.c., 1 picot, 4 d.c., 1 picot, 4 d.c., 1 picot, 5 d.c.; 1 tr. into each of the next 4 sts.; 1 picot over each point, and over the picot a scallop as in the square. On the seventh point 1 picot only; after the last picot, 7 tr. into the last ch., miss 2 tr.; then continue the d.c. until 24 have been worked, and repeat from *

In the semicircles which follow, only 5 little scallops are made; the first and last of these scallops are joined by the first and last picots; in the last semicircle, as in the first, six little scallops are made.

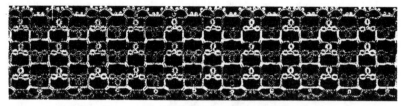

Tatted insertion composed of double stitches, plain picots, and Josephine knots.

CHAPTER XII

Tatting

The nature of tatting makes it an appropriate sequel to crochet, as well as a useful preparation for macrame, which we shall describe in the next chapter. Tatting is composed of knots or stitches, and picots, which form rings and semicircles; various types of designs are produced by the different arrangement of these motifs.

The French name for this kind of work—"frivolité"—has been adopted in almost every European country; the Italians, however, call it "occhi," while in oriental countries the ancient name "makouk," derived from the shuttles used to make it, has been retained.

The origin of the English term "tatting" is obscure, though various derivations have been suggested. It may perhaps have come from the word "tatter," and have been suggested by the nature of the earliest work of this kind, which was made entirely of single detached motifs which were afterward sewn together with needle and thread to make patterns.

Worked in a single color with a fairly fine brilliant thread, this kind of work is used for trimming clothing; worked in several colors in a coarser thread, it is used for edging furniture covers, curtains, portieres, cushion covers, etc. For children's garments, aprons, collars, and cuffs of all kinds, pale colors and thread of medium thickness are to be preferred. When tatting is to be used to trim underclothing or bed linen, a fairly fine white thread should always be chosen.

Shuttles. The tatting shuttle consists of two boat-shaped blades, pointed at the ends and joined in the middle. The shape of the shuttle is a matter of some importance, for a good shuttle contributes much to the ease and perfection of the work. In the eighteenth century, a period when tatting enjoyed great popularity, shuttles were longer than those in use today because tatting was worked with much thicker materials—frequently with silk cord.

The shuttle should not be more than three inches long and three-fourth of an inch wide. The ends of the two blades should be close enough together to prevent the thread from running out freely; this is particularly important

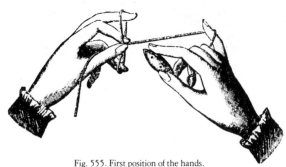

Fig. 555. First position of the hands.

when the work requires the simultaneous use of two shuttles.

The solid part which joins the two blades must be pierced by a hole large enough for the thread to be fastened through it before being wound onto the shuttle; the thread thus would must never project beyond the edges of the blades, for it would in that case lose something of its freshness by its constant passage through the worker's hands.

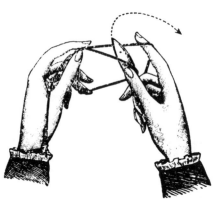

Fig. 556. Second position of the hands.

Materials. Owing to the great variety of articles that can be trimmed with tatting, the most varied materials can be used for working it, provided, however, that the thread chosen is sufficiently twisted.

This kind of work is suited, first and foremost, for the trimming of underlinen and children's clothing. For this purpose we recommend DMC Alsatian sewing cotton in balls, DMC 6 cord cotton lace thread, DMC 6 cord crochet cotton, DMC special quality crochet cotton and DMC knotting cotton. For bed linen, DMC flax thread for knitting and crochet and DMC flax lace thread are to be preferred. When tatting is to be used as ornamental braid or passementerie, whether for dresses or coats or for soft furnishings, tatting should be worked with DMC pearl cotton or DMC Alsatia.

A few rows of crochet are often used to finish off tatting or to join different parts of the work; in this case, the thread used for the crochet should be the same as that used for the tatting, but a few degrees finer.

Double Stitches or Knots. First Position of the Hands (fig. 555). The making of the stitches or knots appears at first sight to present many difficulties; these can, however, be easily surmounted if our instructions for the first steps are carefully followed. The most important thing to be kept in mind from the outset is that the right hand, as soon as it has passed the shuttle through the loop, must stop the thread and keep it drawn tight without making any movement until the left hand has closed the stitch.

When the required quantity of thread has been wound onto the shuttle, the end of the thread is taken between the thumb and first finger of the left

Fig. 557. Third position of the hands.

hand, the shuttle is held in the right hand, the thread is passed over the second and third fingers of the left hand and then brought back toward the thumb, and the two threads are crossed beneath the fingers, as shown in fig. 555.

The thread issuing from the shuttle is passed round the little finger of the right hand, and the shuttle is held in the manner shown in the illustration.

Second and Third Positions of the Hands (figs. 556 and 557). The free

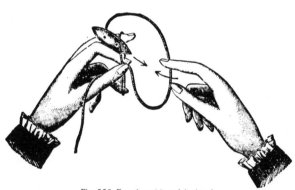

Fig. 558. Fourth position of the hands.

part of the shuttle thread is laid loosely over the left hand, the shuttle is slipped between the first and second fingers under the upper thread of the loop in the direction indicated in fig. 556, brought out behind the loop and back over it.

This is where beginners encounter the first difficulties, and we would advise them to practice this part of the work until they are sufficiently sure of the movements not to confuse those of the left hand with those of the right. In the first place, the length of free thread between the shuttle and the left hand should not be more than eight or ten inches long. As soon as the shuttle has been passed through the loop, the right hand should be placed on the table and the thread drawn very tight, the left hand, meanwhile, making no movement whatsoever.

When the right hand has taken up this passive position, the second and third fingers of the left hand are raised, lifting and closing the loop and at the

Fig. 559. Single or half stitches.

Fig. 560. Single or half stitches. Large Josephine picot.

same time spread wide enough apart to tighten the thread; see fig. 557. This movement forms a knot, which is the first half of a double stitch, the principal stitch used in tatting. It must be constantly borne in mind that the right-hand thread must not move until

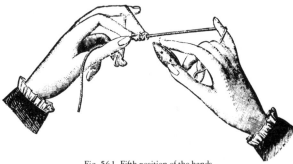

Fig. 561. Fifth position of the hands.

the left hand has completed these movements, and that the knot must be made only by the part of the thread which lies over the left hand.

The right hand or shuttle thread must always run free-

ly through the knots; if a knot were made with this thread, it would no longer be able to pass freely in order to lengthen or shorten the loop on the left hand.

Fourth Position of the Hands (fig. 558). The second part of a stitch or knot is made by the following movements: with the shuttle thread hanging in front of the left hand, the shuttle is passed from right to left over the stretched loop, then, as shown in fig. 558, from left to right between the first and second fingers under the stretched loop; the thread is drawn tight with the right hand; the left hand closes this second knot in the same way as the first. The two knots together make one double stitch.

Single or Half Stitches. Josephine Knots (figs. 559 and 560). A group of single or half stitches, consisting of the first knot only, is sometimes made; this group is called a Josephine knot or picot. This kind of picot can be made with only four or five stitches, as in fig. 559, or with ten or twelve, as in fig. 560.

Fifth Position of the Hands (fig. 561). When the second knot, completing the double stitch, has been made, the hands return to the position shown in fig. 555. Fig. 561 shows this position again, together with a few completed double stitches.

Position of the Hands for Making a Picot (fig. 562). As in crochet and macrame, picots can be introduced into tatting designs. The picots are also used to join the different parts of the work, and with their help it is possible to make the most charming and varied designs. Fig. 562 shows how picots are made.

Picot, Open and Closed (figs. 563 and 564). These picots are made by means of a single stitch, making a loop over the stretch-

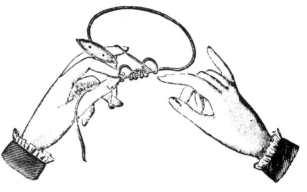

Fig. 562. Position of the hands for making a picot.

ed thread as in fig. 563, and leaving a little distance between the last knot and the next. The double stitch is completed and drawn up close to the previous knots. The picot, as shown in fig. 564, is then formed of itself.

In all instructions for tatting, the knot which follows the picot is independent of the loop. Thus if the instructions indicate 2 stitches or knots, 1 picot, 3 stitches, 1 picot, 2 stitches, etc., the knot by which the picot has been made will always be counted as forming one of the next group of stitches; the first picot will be followed by a total of 3 stitches (not 4) and so on.

How to Join by the Picots. To join the various rings, scallops, etc., by means of picots, the thread running over the left hand is caught with a hook inserted down through the picot and drawn through the picot; the shuttle is passed through the loop thus brought through, which is drawn tight like an ordinary knot.

How to Arrange the Threads of Two Shuttles on the Hands (fig. 565). Tatting is worked with two shuttles when the little rings or scallops are not to be connected at the base by a thread, when the passage of the thread from one group of stitches to another is to be concealed, or when threads of different colors are used.

Fig. 563. Picot, open.

Fig. 564. Picot, closed.

Fig. 565. How to arrange the threads of two shuttles on the hands.

When two shuttles are used, the ends of the two threads are tied together. One of the threads is passed over the second finger of the left hand and wound twice round the third finger, and the shuttle is left hanging loose. The second shuttle is then held in the right hand, which makes the same movements as when one shuttle is used.

Note on Abbreviations. From here on, we shall often use the abbreviation d. for double, st. for stitch, and sts. for stitches.

Detached Scallops (fig. 566). Working with one shuttle, make 12 d. sts., then draw up the thread so that the stitches form a semicircle; the

Fig. 566. Detached scallops.

first stitch of the next scallop must be made so close to the last stitch of the preceding scallop as to touch it.

Joined Scallops (fig. 567). With one shuttle, make 4 d. sts., 1 picot, * 8 d. sts., 1 picot, 4 d.sts., close the scallop, 4 d.sts., draw the thread through the 2nd picot of the previous scallop and repeat from *.

Fig. 567. Joined scallops.

Rings With Picots (fig. 568). With one shuttle, make 4 d. sts., 1 picot, * 3 d. sts., 1 picot, 2 d. sts., 1 picot, 2 d. sts., 1 picot, 3 d. sts., 1 picot, 4 d. sts.; close the ring. Before

Fig. 568. Rings with picots.

beginning the next ring, leave a length of thread sufficiently long to prevent the rings from overlapping: make 4 d. sts., draw the left-hand thread through the 5th picot of the preceding ring, and repeat from *.

Tatted Braid (fig. 569). With one shuttle, make a ring like the ones shown in fig. 568. Turn the work. Then, leaving one fourth to three eighths of an inch of thread free, make a second ring. Turn. Leaving the same length of thread free, begin a third ring, which is joined after the 4th

d. st. to the 5th picot of the first ring. After each complete ring, turn the work so that all the upper rings are right side out and all the lower rings wrong side out.

When this braid is to be used as an insertion for underlinen, the picots are strengthened with a narrow crochet heading, such as those shown in several of the following figures.

Tatted Braid (fig. 570). Worked with two shuttles. Knot the ends of the two threads together. Then, beginning with one thread and one shuttle, make a first ring like the one in figs. 568 and 569. Turn. With the second shuttle make a second ring, like the first and quite close to it. When this second ring has been completed, pass the thread which has just been in use over the left hand, take the free shuttle in the right hand and make 6 d. sts. over the second thread. Turn. Then once more make a ring above and one below with one shuttle, joining these rings to the first ones by the picots, as shown in figs. 568 and 569.

Edging in Tatting and Crochet (fig. 571). With one shuttle, make 1 d. st., 1 picot, 2 d. sts., 1 picot, 2 d. sts., 1 picot, 2 d. sts., 1 picot twice as long as the others, 2 d. sts., 1 picot, 2 d. sts., 1 picot, 2 d. sts., 1 picot,

Fig. 569. Tatted braid.

Fig. 570. Tatted braid.

Fig. 571. Edging in tatting and crochet.

Fig. 572. Tatted edging.

2 d. sts., 1 long picot, 1 d. st., close the ring. Fasten off the two ends of thread on the wrong side with a few stitches made with a needle.

Continue as described above, but before making the last d. st join the unfinished ring to the preceding one by the long picot, then make the last d. st. and fasten off the threads.

When the required length has thus been made, the crochet is begun. Into each picot work 1 treble, with 3 chain between. Along this 1st row, a 2nd row is worked, consisting of 1 double crochet into the treble of the previous row, 2 chain, 1 picot, 2 chain, 1 double crochet into the next treble, 2 chain, etc.

For the heading, work as follows: 1 double crochet into the 1st picot, 3 chain, 1 double crochet into the 2nd picot, 3 chain, 1 double crochet into the 3rd picot, 3 chain, 1 double crochet into the 1st picot of the second ring, and so on. The heading is completed by a row of double crochet worked into this row.

Tatted Edging (fig. 572).   Worked with two shuttles.

The 1st row is worked with one shuttle, as for fig. 567. The 2nd and 3rd rows are worked with two shuttles.

The thread of the right-hand shuttle is passed through the 1st picot and fastened to it; then, over this thread and with the left-hand thread, the same number of d. sts. and picots as in the 1st row is made, each half circle being joined to the picot of the preceding row. In the 3rd row, 3 picots are made between the 8 d. sts. at the top.

Edging in Tatting and Crochet (fig. 573).   Worked in two colors with two shuttles. After completing, with the light thread, a row of rings

Fig. 573. Edging in tatting and crochet.

like those in fig. 571, the ends of the threads from the two shuttles, one wound with light thread and the other with dark, are fastened to the 1st picot following the long picot. With the light thread in the right hand and the dark thread passing over the left hand, make: * 3 d. sts., 1 picot, 3 d. sts.—draw the right-hand thread through the next picot—3 d. sts., 1 picot, 3 d. sts.— draw the right-hand thread separately through the 2 picots of the two adjoining rings; repeat from *.

The next row is also worked with two shuttles. Fasten the dark thread, which lies over the left hand, to the 1st dark picot, the light thread being in the right hand; then work as follows: * 4 d. sts., 1 picot, 2 d. sts., 1 picot, 2 d. sts. Turn. With the right-hand shuttle make: 6 d. sts., draw the thread through the small picot formed above the central picot of the rings, 6 d. sts., close the ring. Turn. With two shuttles: 2 d. sts., 1 picot, 2 d. sts., 1 picot, 4 d. sts., draw the light thread through the 2 dark picots; repeat from *.

The heading consists of two rows.

1st row: * 1 treble into the 1st picot, 3 chain, 1 double crochet into the 2nd picot, 3 chain, 1 treble into the last picot of the ring, 1 chain; repeat from *.

2nd row: 1 treble, 1 chain, miss 1 st., 1 treble into the next, 1 chain, and so on.

Edging in Tatting and Crochet (fig. 574). Worked in two colors with two shuttles. With one shuttle, wound with light thread: 2 d. sts., 1 short picot, 2 d. sts., 1 long picot, * 2 d. sts., 1 picot of normal size, 2 d. sts., 1 picot, 2 d. sts., 1 picot, 2 d. sts., 1 picot, 2 d. sts., 1 picot, 2 d. sts., 1 picot, 2 d. sts., 1 long picot, 2 d. sts., 1 short picot, 2 d. sts., close the ring. Turn. With two shuttles, the dark thread over the left hand and the light thread in the right hand: 3 d. sts., 1 short picot, 3 d. sts., 1 long picot, 2 d. sts. Turn. With the shuttle wound with light thread: 4 d. sts., draw the thread through the 9th picot of the first ring, 4 d. sts., 1 short picot, 4 d. sts., close

Fig. 574. Edging in tatting and crochet.

the ring. Turn. With two shuttles, the dark thread over the left hand and the light thread in the right hand: 2 d. sts., 1 long picot, 3 d. sts., 1 short picot, 3 d. sts. Turn. With the shuttle wound with light thread: 2 d. sts., draw the thread through the free picot of the small ring, 2 d. sts., draw the thread through the long picot of the large ring; repeat from *. The dark scallops are joined by the small picot.

The crochet edge of the lace requires 2 rows.

1st row: * 1 double crochet into the 1st of the 5 picots of the large ring, 4 chain, 1 double crochet into the 2nd picot, 4 chain, 1 double crochet into the 3rd picot, 4 chain, 1 double crochet into the 4th picot, 4 chain, 1 double crochet into the 5th picot, 4 chain; repeat from *.

2nd row: * 2 double crochet into the first loop of 4 chain; ** into the next loop of 4 chain: 1 double crochet, 1 half treble, 2 treble, 1 half treble, 1 double crochet; repeat once from **; 2 double crochet into the last loop of 4 chain; repeat from *.

For the heading, work as follows: 1st row: * 1 double crochet into the long picot, 5 chain, 1 double crochet into the next picot, 3 chain, 1 double treble into the small picot, leave the last 2 overs of the double treble on the hook—2 trebles into the first loop of the double treble, keeping the last overs of these trebles also on the hook, after the last treble pass the hook through all these loops, 3 chain; repeat from *.

2nd row: * 1 treble into the loop of 5 chain, 3 chain, 1 treble into the first loop of 3 chain, 1 chain, 1 treble into the second loop of 3 chain, 3 chain; repeat from *.

Edging in Tatting and Crochet (fig. 575). 1st row: with one shuttle: * 4 d. sts., 1 picot, 3 d. sts., 1 picot, 3 d. sts., 1 picot, 4 d. sts., close the ring. Turn. With two shuttles: 3 d. sts., 1 picot, 2 d. sts., 1 picot, 3 d. sts. Turn. With one shuttle: 4 d. sts., join to the last picot of the preceding ring, 2 d. sts., 1 picot, 2 d. sts., 1 picot, 4 d. sts., close the ring. Turn. With two shuttles: 4 d. sts. With the left-hand shuttle: 4 d. sts., close the ring—With two

Fig. 575. Edging in tatting and crochet.

shuttles: 2 d. sts.—with the left-hand shuttle: 4 d. sts., close the ring— with two shuttles: 2 d. sts.—with the left-hand shuttle: 4 d. sts., close the ring— with two shuttles: 4 d. sts., join the right-hand thread to the ring below, 3 d. sts., 1 picot, 2 d. sts., 1 picot, 3 d. sts. Turn. With one shuttle: 4 d. sts., join to the last picot of the preceding ring, 3 d. sts., 1 picot, 3 d. sts., 1 picot, 4 d. sts., close the ring; repeat from *.

2nd row: with one shuttle: * 2 d. sts., join to the middle picot of the first ring, 2 d. sts., join to the middle picot of the second ring, 2 d. sts., join to the middle picot of the third ring, 2 d. sts., close the ring; leave free a length of thread equal to one repeat of the pattern, and repeat from *.

The crochet heading is made in two rows. 1st row: 1 double crochet into the free picot of the first ring and over the free thread issuing from the first small ring, * 4 double crochet over the free thread, 1 treble into the ring and over the free thread, 4 double crochet over the free thread, 1 double crochet into the next picot and over the free thread, 5 double crochet over the free thread, 1 double crochet into the next

Fig. 576. Edging in tatting and crochet.

picot and over the free thread; repeat from *.

2nd row: 1 treble into the 2nd st., 1 chain, miss 1 st., 1 treble into the next, 1 chain, miss 1 st., 1 treble, and so on.

Edging in Tatting and Crochet (fig. 576). 1st row: with one shuttle: * 2 d. sts., 1 picot, 2 d. sts., close the scallop; 4 d. sts., 1 picot, 4 d. sts., 1 picot, 4 d. sts., close the scallop; 4 d. sts., join to the last picot of the preceding scallop; * * 2 d. sts., 1 picot, repeat from * * seven times; 4 d. sts., close the ring; 4 d. sts., join to the last picot of the preceding ring, 4 d. sts., 1 picot, 4 d. sts., close the scallop; repeat from *.

2nd row: with two shuttles: join the threads to the picot of the first small scallop, * 2 d. sts., 1 picot, 2 d. sts., 1 picot, 2 d. sts., join the right-hand thread to the free picot of the first large scallop, 3 d. sts., join to the 1st free picot of the ring, * * 2 d. sts., 1 picot, 2 d. sts., 1 picot, 2 d. sts., 1 picot, 2 d. sts., join to the 2nd free picot of the ring; repeat twice from * *; 3 d. sts., join to the free picot of the second scallop, 2 d. sts., 1 picot, 2 d. sts., 1 picot, 2 d. sts., join to the picot of the next small scallop; repeat from *.

The crochet heading is worked in 2 rows. 1st row: 3 double crochet over the free thread of the first small scallop, * 9 double crochet over the free thread of the first large scallop, 1 chain, 1 treble into the ring, 1 chain, 9 double crochet over the free thread of the second large scallop, 3 double crochet over the free thread of the next small scallop; repeat from *.

2nd row: 1 treble into the 2nd st., 1 chain, miss 1 st., 1 treble into the next, 1 chain, miss 1 st., 1 treble, and so on.

Edging in Tatting and Crochet (fig. 577). Worked in two colors, with two shuttles. Begin with the shuttle wound with light thread: 6 d. sts., 1 picot, 6 d. sts., close the ring. Turn. Make a second ring like the first. Turn. With two shuttles, the dark thread over the left hand and the light thread in the right: 6 d. sts., 1 picot, 6 d. sts., Turn. With

Fig. 577. Edging in tatting and crochet.

the shuttle wound with light thread: 6 d. sts., join the thread to the picot of the opposite ring, 6 d. sts., close the ring. Turn. Make a second ring like the first. Turn. With two shuttles: 6 d. sts., 1 picot, 6 d. sts., and so on.

Make 3 rows of scallops connected by rings. In the 2nd and 3rd rows, the thread of the ring is passed through the picot to which the second ring was joined in the 1st row, and the scallops are likewise joined by the picots.

For the outer scallops, work as follows with one shuttle through the picot which joins two rings, 5 d. sts., close the ring. Turn. With two shuttles, the dark thread over the left hand and the light thread in the right: 4 d. sts. Turn. With the shuttle wound with light thread: 2 d. sts., 1 picot, 2 d. sts., 1 picot, 2 d. sts., pass the thread through the picot of the scallop in the 3rd row, 2 d. sts., ** 1 picot, 2 d. sts., repeat from ** seven times; close the ring. Turn. With the two shuttles, the dark thread over the left hand and the light thread in the right: 4 d. sts., 1 long picot, 2 d. sts., 1 picot, 2 d. sts., 1 picot, 2 d. sts. Turn. With the shuttle wound with light thread: 4 d. sts., pass the thread through the 3rd picot of the large ring, 4 d. sts., close the ring. Turn. With two shuttles, the dark thread over the left hand and the light thread in the right: 2 d. sts., *** 1 picot, 2 d. sts., repeat from *** five times. Turn. With the shuttle wound with light thread: 4 d. sts., pass the thread through the 3rd picot of the large ring, 4 d. sts., close the ring. Turn. With two shuttles, the dark thread over the left hand and the light thread in the right: 2 d. sts., 1 picot, 2 d. sts., 1 picot, 2 d. sts., 1 long picot, 4 d. sts., pass the thread through the 6th picot of the large ring, 4 d. sts. Turn. Repeat from *.

The detached points are joined by the long picots as the work proceeds.

The edging is finished off with a crochet heading.

1st row: 1 treble into the picot which joins two small rings, 9 chain, 1 double crochet into the picot of the scallop, 9 chain, and so on.

2nd row: 1 treble into each st.

An insertion can be made to go with this edging, by working two rows of scallops, edged top and bottom with the crochet heading.

Braid in Tatting and Crochet (fig. 578). Wind two shuttles, one with light and the other with dark thread. Beginning with the shuttle wound with dark thread, make: * 4 d. sts., 1 picot, 8 d. sts., 1 picot, 4 d. sts., close the ring. Turn. With the two shuttles, the light thread over the left hand and the dark thread in the right: 4 d. sts., 1 picot, 2 d. sts., 1 picot, 2

Fig. 578. Braid in tatting and crochet.

d. sts., 1 picot, 4 d. sts., pass the right-hand thread through the picot of the first ring; then add: 4 d. sts., 1 picot, 2 d. sts., 1 picot, 2 d. sts., 1 picot, 4 d. sts. Turn. With the shuttle wound with dark thread: 4 d. sts., pass the thread through the picot of the first ring, 8 d. sts., 1 picot, 4 d. sts., close the ring. Then leaving a short length of thread, make 6 d. sts., pass the thread through the picot of the preceding ring, 8 d. sts., 1 picot, 6 d. sts., close the ring; repeat from *, joining the first ring to the middle ring as the work proceeds.

When two equal lengths have been worked, they are joined with crochet worked in the finer thread, as indicated, as follows: 1st row: 1 double crochet into the 1st picot, 5 chain, * 1 double crochet into the middle picot, 5 chain, 1 double crochet into the 3rd picot of the same ring and the 1st of the next ring, 5 chain; repeat from *.

2nd row: into each loop of 5 chain work 1 sixfold pineapple stitch (see fig. 505), followed by 5 chain.

When the second row of crochet is being worked along the second tatted band, the hook is withdrawn from the 3rd chain stitch and inserted up from below through the 3rd chain stitch on the opposite band, thus joining the two bands and completing the design.

Braid in Tatting and Crochet (figs. 579 and 580).   Worked with one shuttle. Two strips are worked first, consisting of scallops made as follows: 2

Fig. 579. Braid in tatting and crochet.

d. sts., 1 short picot, 2 d. sts., 1 long picot, 2 d. sts., 1 short picot, 2 d. sts., 1 long picot, 2 d. sts., 1 short picot, 2 d. sts., 1 long picot, 2 d. sts., 1 short picot, 2 d. sts. Between the scallops leave a length of thread equal to the diameter of the scallop. When these two strips are completed, work the crochet in the finer thread, as follows: 1st row: 6 double crochet over each length of thread between and across the base of the scallops.

2nd row: 1 double crochet into the 1st double crochet of the 1st row, 5 chain, 1 double crochet into the 3rd double crochet, and so on.

In the row which joins the two strips of tatting, pass the 3rd chain stitch through the corresponding stitch of the opposite band.

Fig. 580. Detail of fig. 579.

The outer edge is made as follows: 1st row: 1 double crochet into the 1st short picot, 8 chain, * 1 treble into the 2nd short picot, 7 chain, 1 treble into the 3rd short picot, 8 chain, 1 double crochet into the 4th short picot, 1 double crochet into the 1st short picot of the next scallop, 3 chain, pass the thread through the 4th of the last 8 chain, 4 chain; repeat from *.

2nd row: 1 double crochet each into the last 3 sts. of the 8 chain, * 1 picot of 5 chain over the treble, 1 double crochet into each of the next 4 chain, 1 picot, 1 double crochet into the st. into which the 4th double crochet before the picot was worked, 3 double crochet, 1 picot, 3 double crochet, miss the 1st and last sts., 3 double crochet along the next point; repeat from *.

Tatted Medallion (fig. 581). Take thread of two colors and wind two shuttles with light thread and two with dark.

Fig. 581. Tatted medallion.

With one shuttle wound with light thread: 1 d. sts., * 1 very short picot, 2 d. sts., 1 long picot, repeat from * five times: 1 d. sts.; close the ring and fasten off the thread on the wrong side with a few stitches made with a sewing needle.

The next 4 rounds are worked with two shuttles.

1st round: with the two shuttles wound with light thread: fasten the threads to one of the short picots, 3 d. sts., 1 short picot, 2 d. sts., 1 long picot, 2 d. sts., 1 long picot, 2 d. sts., 1 short picot, 3 d. sts.; pass the right-hand thread through a short picot of the first ring; repeat from * five times and join the scallops by the short picot. In the sixth scallop, instead of making the 2nd short picot, pass the left-hand thread through the small picot of the first scallop, then complete the 3 last d. sts., cut off the threads, pass them through the picot of the ring and fasten them off on the wrong side.

2nd round: with the shuttles wound with light thread: fasten the threads to one of the large picots, * 4 d. sts., 1 short picot, 4 d. sts., pass the right-hand thread through the picot of the 1st round; repeat from * seventeen times.

3rd round: with the shuttles wound with dark thread: fasten the threads to one of the picots of the previous round, 4 d. sts., pass the right-hand thread through the picot of the 2nd round, 1 large picot, 4 d. sts., and continue in the same way all round the medallion so that there will be in all eighteen scallops.

4th round: with the shuttles wound with dark thread: fasten the threads to one of the picots of the 2nd row, * 2 d. sts., 1 picot, 2 d. sts., 1 picot, 2 d. sts., 1 picot, 2 d. sts., pass the right-hand thread to the wrong side through the light colored picot of the 2nd round; repeat from *

These little medallions, joined together to form an allover pattern, can be used to make chair backs, pincushions, etc.; see also the allover design in fig. 583. The open spaces which occur here and there between the

Fig. 582. Tatted medallion.

medallions can be filled with crochet motifs.

Tatted Medallion (fig. 582).   This charming medallion could be used as a place mat, a pincushion cover, or an ornament on a sachet. It is worked in two colors, with two shuttles.

1st round: with one shuttle wound with light thread: 1 d. st., * 1 picot, 2 d. sts., repeat from * five times; 1 d. st., close the ring.

2nd round: with two shuttles, the dark thread over the left hand and the light thread in the right: fasten one thread to one of the picots of the 1st round, 2 d. sts., 1 long picot, 2 d. sts., pass the right-hand thread through a picot of the ring, 1 long picot, 2 d. sts., 1 long picot; continue in the same way, making in all 12 long picots; fasten off the threads.

3rd round: with one shuttle wound with light thread: * 3 d. sts., pass the thread through one of the picots of the 2nd round, 3 d. sts., close the ring. Turn. Leave 5 millimeters (not quite a quarter of an inch) of thread free—4 d. sts., 1 picot, 4 d. sts., close the ring. Turn. Leave the same length of thread as before; repeat from * eleven times.

4th round: with two shuttles, the dark thread over the left hand and the light thread in the right: fasten one end of thread to the picot of one of the twelve rings of the 3rd round, * 3 d. sts., 1 picot, 3 d. sts.,—with the shuttle wound with dark thread: 2 d. sts., pass the thread through the dark picot, 2 d. sts., 1 picot, 2 d. sts., 1 picot, 2 d. sts., close the ring—3 d. sts., join the thread to the 2nd picot of the first ring, 3 d. sts., 1 picot, 3 d. sts., close the ring—2 d. sts., join the thread to the picot of the second ring, 2 d. sts., 1 picot, 2 d. sts., 1 picot, 2 d. sts., close the ring—continue with two shuttles: 3 d. sts., pass the thread through the 2nd picot of the third round, 3 d. sts., fasten the right-hand thread to the picot of the ring in

Fig. 583. Tatted ground.

the third round; repeat from * eleven times, joining the rings by the free picots.

5th round: with two shuttles, the light thread over the left hand and the dark thread in the right: fasten one thread to a picot between two motifs, above each lower ring make 2 d. sts., 1 picot, 2 d. sts., 1 picot, 2 d. sts.; above each upper ring, 2 d. sts., 1 picot, 2 d. sts., 1 picot, 2 d. sts., 1 picot, 2 d. sts., 1 picot, 2 d. sts.

Tatted Ground (fig. 583). This ground is made up of medallions with six scallops joined to each other by the middle picot, as can be seen in the illustration.

1st round: begin with one shuttle: 3 d. sts., 1 picot, 2 d. sts., 1 picot, 2 d. sts., 1 picot, 3 d. sts., close the ring. Turn the work so that the ring points down. Continue with two shuttles: 8 d. sts. Turn. * with one shuttle: 3 d. sts., join to the last picot of the finished ring, 2 d. sts., 1 picot, 2 d. sts., 1 picot, 3 d. sts., close the ring. Turn. With two shuttles: 8 d. sts. Turn. Repeat from * four times, joining the sixth ring to the 1st picot of the first ring; fasten off the threads.

2nd round: with two shuttles: fasten the threads into the angle between two scallops, * 3 d. sts., 1 picot, 2 d. sts., 1 picot, 2 d. sts., 1 long picot, 2 d. sts., 1 picot, 2 d. sts., 1 picot, 3 d. sts., fasten the right-hand thread into the angle between the next scallops; repeat from * five times; fasten off the threads.

Design for Bedspread in Tatting and Crochet (fig. 584). This handsome bedspread design, which is reminiscent of old lace, is made up of large tatted medallions with raised centers joined to each other by small crochet stars.

The lace border is joined to the ground by a band of crochet trimmed with two rows of small tatted rings forming raised edges.

Star-shaped medallion. Small tatted rings, made with one shuttle, with coarse thread: 1 d. st., 1 picot, 2 d. sts., 1 picot, 2 d. sts., 1 picot, 2 d. sts., 1 picot, 2 d. sts., 1 picot, 2 d. sts., 1 picot, 2 d. sts., 1 picot, 2 d. sts., 1 picot, 1 d. st., close the ring and fasten off the threads.

The sixteen small rings of which the inner edge is composed are made first, then eight groups of three rings are added outside these to form the points of the star. For the order in which these rings are joined, see the illustration.

For the raised center of the medallion, eleven small rings are made as follows: with one shuttle: * 3 d. sts., 1 picot, 3 d. sts., 1 picot, 3 d. sts., 1 picot, 3 d. sts., close the ring; repeat from * ten times, leaving 2 millimeters (about a sixteenth of an inch) of thread between the rings.

Connecting bars of crochet, worked in coarse thread: over the free thread which precedes the first ring work 1 double crochet, 1 double crochet over the thread between the first and second rings, 1 double crochet between the second and third rings, 1 double crochet between the third and fourth rings,

1 double crochet between the fourth and fifth rings, 1 double crochet between the fifth and sixth rings, these last two double crochet to be worked into the double crochet which precedes the first ring; 1 double crochet between the sixth and seventh rings, 1 double crochet between the seventh

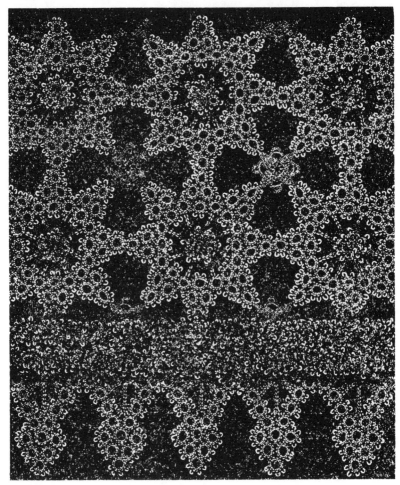

Fig. 584. Design for bedspread in tatting and crochet.

and eighth rings, these two double crochet to be worked into the double crochet between the first and second rings; 1 double crochet between the eighth and ninth rings, 1 double crochet between the ninth and tenth rings, these two double crochet to be worked into the double crochet between the second and third rings; 1 double crochet between the tenth and eleventh rings, 1 double crochet over the thread which follows the eleventh ring, these two double crochet to be worked into the double crochet between the third and fourth rings; 1 single crochet into the next stitch, 10 chain, join the chain to the free picot of a small ring between two points of the star, miss the 1st of the 10 chain, 1 single crochet into each of the remaining 9 chain, 1 double crochet into the next double crochet, * 10 chain, join to the free picot of the next ring but one, miss the 1st chain, 9 single crochet along the chain, 1 double crochet into the next double crochet; repeat from * six times; end with 1 single crochet. Fasten off the thread. The separate medallions are joined by the picots, as shown in the illustration.

Small crochet medallions worked in fine thread: 5 chain, close the ring.

1st round: 5 chain, * 1 treble into the ring, 2 chain; repeat from * six times; 1 single crochet into the 3rd of the 5 chain.

2nd round: 1 chain, 2 double crochet into the stitch into which the single crochet was worked, 3 double crochet into the loop of 2 chain, 1 double crochet into the treble, 3 double crochet into the loop of 2 chain, * 3 double crochet into the treble, 3 double crochet into the loop of 2 chain, 1 double crochet into the treble, 3 double crochet into the loop of 2 chain; repeat twice from *; 1 single crochet into the chain and 1 single crochet into the 1st double crochet.

3rd round: 9 double crochet. Turn. Miss 1 st., 8 double crochet. Turn. Miss 1 st., 7 double crochet. Turn. Miss 1 st., 6 double crochet. Turn. Miss 1 st., 5 double crochet. Turn. Miss 1 st., 4 double crochet. Turn. Miss 1 st., 3 double crochet. Turn. Miss 1 st., 2 double crochet. Turn. Miss 1 st., 1 double crochet, join the little pyramid thus made to a free point of the large medallion, between two picots, and break off the thread.

Work the three other little pyramids in the same way, beginning the bars which connect them after the 2nd row of double crochet, that is to say after the 8 double crochet; 7 chain, join to the finished pyramid; work 8 double crochet over the 7 chain, 6 chain, join toward the right to the 4th double crochet; over the 6 chain work 8 double crochet, 4 double crochet over the 7 chain, then complete the pyramid like the first.

The lace border is also made up of small tatted rings, fourteen to each point; they are joined by the picots in the order shown in the illustration.

The connecting bars of crochet, worked in coarse thread, are begun on the wrong side of the work: * 1 double crochet into the 3rd free picot of the first ring of the point, counting from left to right, 3 chain, 1 double crochet into the next picot, 20 chain. Turn. Join the chain to the 1st picot of the next ring, 1 single crochet into the 2nd chain, 2 chain, join to the next picot, 1 single crochet into the 2nd chain, 5 single crochet, 13 chain, join to the free picot of the next ring but one, 1 single crochet into the 2nd chain, 2 chain, join to the free picot of the next ring, 1 single crochet into the 2nd chain, 11 single crochet, 7 chain, join to the 1st free picot of the next ring but one, 1 single crochet into the 2nd chain, 2 chain, join to the next picot, 1 single crochet into the 2nd chain, 5 single crochet, then 4 more single crochet, 9 chain. Turn. 1 double crochet into the 2nd free picot of the next ring, 3 chain, 1 double crochet into the next picot; 2 chain; repeat from *.

The band which joins the lace to the ground is worked separately in coarse thread.

It is begun with 8 rows of double crochet, to which the raised edges are afterward added. These edges are composed of small tatted rings like those described for the inside of the large medallions; they are added to the 8 rows of double crochet by means of two more rows in which one tatted ring is caught into every stitch. A row of trebles, separated from each other by 2 chain, completes each edge of the band. The ground and the edging are seamed to the band.

We advise those who would prefer a simpler piece of work to turn to fig. 480, which shows a design for a bedspread in which the medallions are connected by squares of linen. These could, in the present case, replace the crochet stars.

Macrame strip with a design composed of bars, flat knots, and shell knots.

CHAPTER XIII

Macrame

"Macrame" is an Arabic word for ornamental fringes and braids; its use has been extended to include certain types of work made by means of knots and plaited threads, sometimes also known as knotted fringes. However, the Arabic term also has a wider meaning, and includes strips, braids, grids, squares, and medallions as well as fringes and scallops.

For many years, macrame fell into disuse and almost became a lost art, its tradition barely surviving in a few convents and among certain Slavonic peoples. For this reason it seemed like a new invention when it was reintroduced in the last century. Macrame is most interesting and varied work since it can be used for trimming and ornamenting a host of articles; it is, moreover, remarkably strong and durable, a circumstance which has greatly helped to increase its popularity.

It follows that a knowledge of macrame is well worth acquiring. The work is much easier than it appears, and if our instructions are carefully followed it will soon be possible to produce charming pieces of work, some of which recall the carved wooden lattices adorning the windows of oriental houses.

Cushion and Accessories for Macrame (fig. 585). Macrame requires only one basic accessory—a simple cushion, padded and mounted on a wooden frame. It is an advantage to be able to screw this cushion to the edge of a table, like the Swiss embroidery frame.

There are other types of frames for macrame, but these are not, in our opinion, very practical. With some, it is impossible to avoid constantly rubbing the fingers against the board which takes the place of the cushion, and this rubbing is both tiring and irritating to the worker. Others are not heavy enough to resist the rapid movements which must be made when a certain degree of skill has been attained.

The cushion illustrated in fig. 585 is suitable for every kind of macrame work; moreover, it is essential for those pieces of work which are begun with a heading of picots, as well as for those which are edged with picots. The round-headed nails which can be seen on the narrow sides of the cushion serve to hold in place both the mounting threads and the knot-bearing threads.

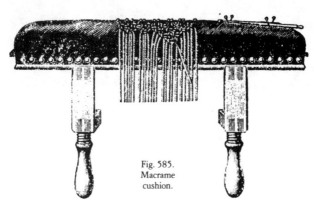

Fig. 585.
Macrame
cushion.

In addition to the cushion, very strong, round-headed pins are required, specially made for holding loops and picots in place; also a crochet hook for mounting the threads and passing them through the material; scissors; and finally a ruler or tape measure for gauging the length of the threads.

To the various accessories we would add a metal comb for straightening the fringes and a steel ruler, which serves both to press the fringes when they have been combed and line up the protruding ends of thread to be cut with the scissors.

The length of the threads will depend on the kind of thread used: if the thread is thick and stiff, the making of a knot will take up more of it and it will have to be longer than if a fine, soft thread is used.

For this reason, we give, accompanying each design, the total length, the kind, and the thickness of the threads to be used. If a design is worked in thicknesses of thread other than those we suggest, it must be borne in mind that the threads will have to be longer or shorter, according to whether the thread is coarser or finer. This will make it possible to embark on the work itself without making any preliminary experiments, which are almost always wasted.

Materials. Macrame, consisting as it does entirely of knots, requires very strong threads which will not break in the working. These threads must therefore be very tightly twisted and consequently well rounded; this enables knots to be made which stand out like a row of beads, greatly enhancing the beauty of the work and the distinctness of the design. A lightly twisted thread, being looser and softer, would become frayed in working, and the finished appearance of the work would be untidy and fluffy.

For fringes and braids in several colors, used when trimming furniture and household articles, the best cotton thread is DMC knotting cotton nos. 10 to 30. Silk can be replaced by DMC pearl cotton, which is manufactured in more than three hundred shades in nos. 1, 3, 5, 8, and 12, or DMC

Alsatia. Household linen is always trimmed with the color of the article itself; if the latter is embroidered in colors, a few threads of the same colors can be used for the macrame. We advise, however, always using as few shades as possible. For this kind of work, we recommend DMC knotting cotton, DMC flax thread for knitting and crochet, DMC 6 cord crochet cotton, and DMC special quality crochet cotton.

Formation of the Knots. Those who attempt macrame for the first time will find it necessary, as in tatting, to take particular care to keep the thread which is to carry the knots quite still. This thread is called the knot-bearer, while the thread with which the knots themselves are made is called the working thread.

These two threads frequently change places. Sometimes the one with which the knots have been made becomes the knot-bearer, while sometimes the knot-bearer becomes the working thread. The knot itself is a kind of loop which is drawn very tight over a thread.

Explanation of the Designs. Since macrame is composed of a more or less regular sequence of knots, there is some difficulty in providing clear instructions for working designs. We trust, however, that the method we have chosen for explaining the crossing of the threads and the interchanging of the colors as the work proceeds will prove satisfactory. This method proceeds by groups or series of knots rather than by rows or rounds as in knitting and crochet.

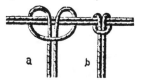

Mounting Threads Onto a Knot-Bearer (fig. 586). Except when the work is done with the unravelled threads of a fabric, the lengths of thread must be mounted on a foundation knot-bearer. The lengths are prepared by cutting them to double the required length and folding

Fig. 586.
Mounting threads onto a knot-bearer.

them in half; the loop thus produced serves to fasten them to the knot-bearer, which acts as a foundation for the fringe.

The loop

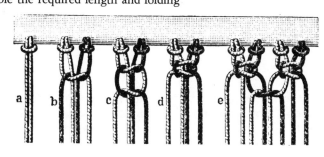

Fig. 587.
Mounting threads onto material and formation of a flat knot.

is passed in front of the knot-bearer, then down be-hind it. The ends of the thread are passed through the loop, and the loop is drawntight. In fig. 586, the first detail, *a,* shows the loop open, and the second detail, *b,* shows it drawn up.

Mounting Threads Onto Material and Formation of a Flat Knot (fig. 587). Insert a crochet hook from back to front through the edge of the material, catch the thread by the loop made by folding it, draw it through to the wrong side and pass the ends through the loop as at *a.* Mount two folded threads in this way side by side, and make the first interlacing of the threads for the flat knot. For this purpose, take the two outside threads of the four and pass the right-hand thread under and the left-hand thread over the two middle threads. While making the movement which crosses the outer threads, hold the middle threads in place by pulling them with the second and third fingers of the left hand; see *b.* The return of the crossed threads is shown in the third detail, *c;* the thread is then drawn tight, and the flat knot is complete, as shown in the fourth detail, *d.* The fifth detail, *e,* shows two flat knots finished, with the method of passing to a third knot in which two of the right-hand and two of the left-hand threads are joined.

Mounting With Plain Picots (fig. 588). Pin the series of loops on the cushion, a quarter or at most three-eighths of an inch apart. Fasten the

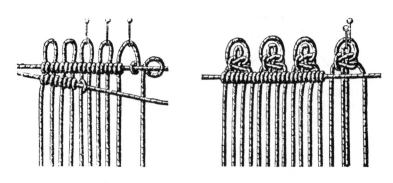

Fig. 588.
Mounting with plain picots.

Fig. 589.
Mounting with picots and flat knot.

knot-bearer, on the left, to one of the nails, and stretch it very tight, with the right hand, in a strictly horizontal line. Make the knots with the left hand. Take separately each end of the threads held by the pins and pass it twice up over the knot-bearer.

The first time, the thread remains on the left; the second time, it passes also from right to left so that when it has passed the second time it is caught between two loops or knots, which form the ''double knot''; this double twisting of the thread round the knot-bearer is shown in fig. 588.

A series of knots forms a bar. The second bar is made in the same way as the first. Hold the knot-bearer as close as possible to the first bar so that the passage of the threads from one bar to the next shall not be visible. Bars can be made horizontally, vertically, and diagonally, as will be seen in the illustration and instructions that follow.

Mounting With Picots and Flat Knot (fig. 589). Take two lengths of thread, pin them very close together, make a flat knot (fig. 587) with the outer threads over the inner threads, and loop the ends over the knot-bearer to make a bar of knots.

Mounting With Picots and Two Flat Knots (figs. 590 and 591). Fix two lengths of thread as for the preceding, and make first one flat knot and then a second. See fig. 590: detail *a* shows the beginning of the knot, detail *b* the picot completed with two knots. Fig. 591 shows the picots secured by a horizontal bar of knots.

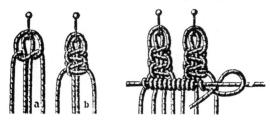

Fig. 590.   Fig. 591.
Mounting with picots and two flat knots.

Mounting With Round Scallops of Single Buttonhole Knots (fig. 592). The threads with which the scallops are to be made must be cut longer than those which will be placed in the middle of the scallops.

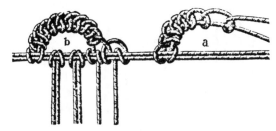

Fig. 592.
Mounting with round scallops of single buttonhole knots.

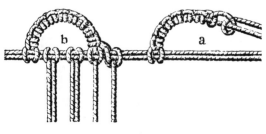

Fig. 593.
Mounting with round scallops of double buttonhole knots.

The knots are turned to the outside of the scallop, and ten knots are made with the left- hand thread over the right-hand thread (seedetail *a*); then two double threads are mounted under the scallop, after which knots are finally made with the two threads of the scallop (detail *b*).

Mounting With Round Scallops of Double Buttonhole Knots (fig. 593). In fig. 593 we show a method of mounting the threads with scallops made of double buttonhole knots. With the first thread on the left, and over

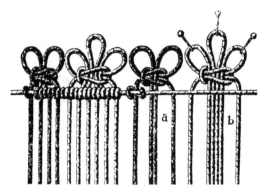

Fig. 594. Mounting with loops.

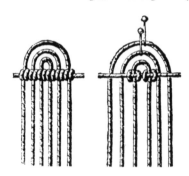

Fig. 595. Mounting with triple picots.

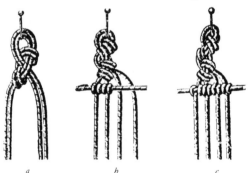

Fig. 596. Mounting with picots and double chain.

the second thread, make knots alternately down and up; this produces knots exactly similar to the double stitch in tatting.

Mounting With Loops (fig. 594). Pin two folded lengths of thread at a little distance from each other (detail *a*) and join them with a flat knot.

Pin three more lengths quite close to the first two (detail *b*) and join them with a large collecting knot (fig. 601) made over four threads. A flat knot made over more than two threads is known as a large collecting knot.

The rest of themounting is done in the usual way.

Mounting With Triple Picots (fig. 595). The threads are knotted on singly, one after the other: first the middle one, then the second knotted to right and left of the first and with the loop pinned at the distance required to make the picot, then the third in the same way.

Mounting With Picots and Double Chain (fig. 596). Take a double thread and make a bar of knots as in detail *a* of fig. 596, then finish and secure the picots with a horizontal bar, as shown in details *b* and *c*.

Mounting to Form a Braid (fig. 597). This mounting, which forms a wide braid, is made up entirely of vertical bars worked over a single knot-bearer.

Along one edge of the braid, this knot- bearer makes picots, which are secured with pins. When the braid is finished, groups of threads are knotted into these picots to serve either as the foundation of macrame work or as a simple fringe.

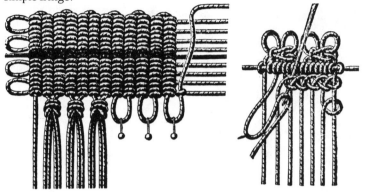

Fig. 597. Mounting to form a braid.   Fig. 598. Plaited knot.

Plaited Knot (fig. 598). This knot is most frequently found in work of Italian and Slavonic origin, in which it takes the place of horizontal knots.

As can be seen in fig. 598, the row of knots is begun with the second thread on the right, with which a loop is made over the first thread. Passing the third thread in front of the second, draw it out with a crochet hook behind the first loop, which has been drawn tight.

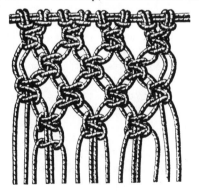
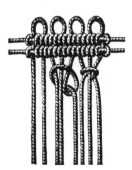

Fig. 599. Triple knot.   Fig. 600. Small collecting knot.

Triple Knot (fig. 599). This is the name given to a flat knot followed by another half knot, that is to say the first half of a flat knot.

Small Collecting Knot (fig. 600). A collecting knot is one which is used to unite several threads. For the small collecting knot, fig. 600, after the double bar which forms the heading has been worked, a knot is made with the first thread on the right over the next two threads. For this purpose, a loop is made with the right-hand thread, which is passed over the two threads, then under the same threads and into the loop, which is drawn

Fig. 601. Large collecting knot.

tight with the knot at the back so that only a single thread shows in the front.

L a r g e Collecting Knot (fig. 601). As has been mentioned in the description of fig. 594, this is the name given to a flat knot joining more two threads. The first detail of the illustration shows the flat knot over two threads, finished, and the first crossing of the threads for

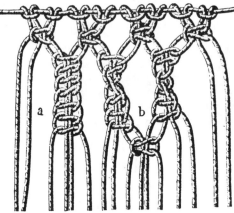

Fig. 602. Braided knot and wave knot.

the collecting knot; the second detail shows the second crossing of the threads; the third shows how the making of collecting knots over four threads can be continued as desired; while the fourth detail shows the usual method of finishing the large collecting knot with a flat knot.

Braided Knot and Wave Knot (fig. 602). Braided knots are produced by the uninterrupted repetition of the crossing of the threads which forms the first half of a flat knot (detail *a*); wave knots by a slight twisting of the threads from left to right (detail *b*). The plait formed by the wave knot is secured by joining the threads of opposite groups together, two by two, with a flat knot.

Single and Double Crossed Knots (figs. 603 and 604). The first knot, which is shown completed in detail *b,* is formed by two single cross-

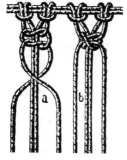

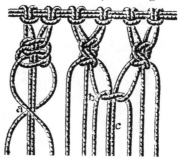

Fig. 603. Single crossed knot.

Fig. 604. Double crossed knot.

ings of the threads (detail *a*), after which the knot is quickly turned to the wrong side of the work and at the same time drawn up very tight.

The second knot, fig. 604, is made with three single crossings (detail *a*), after which the threads are quickly changed over to form the knot shown in detail *b.* When a series of these knots is made, the order of the threads is always reversed so that the knots shall be alternating, as in detail *c.*

Looped Picot (fig. 605). Looped picots are formed along the edges of a braid of flat knots by leaving a sufficient space between the successive knots

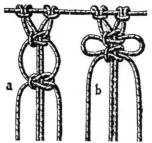

Fig. 605. Looped picot.

Fig. 606. Knotted picot.

so that the thread left between them forms a picot when the knots are drawn close to each other. In fig. 605, detail *a* shows the picot begun, detail *b* the finished picot.

Knotted Picot (fig. 606). Knotted picots are made after one or more flat knots. The picot is produced by a knot made with the outer thread; this knot is placed as close as possible to the flat knot. To achieve this, a large pin is inserted into the loop; with this pin the loop is brought to the spot it is to occupy, and the pin is not removed until the knot has been made. These picots are almost always made on both sides and can be repeated several times in the course of a series of knots.

Detail *a* shows how to interlace the threads to make the picots, while at *b* the completed picots are seen followed by a flat knot.

Bead Knots or Sm ! Shell Knots Composed of Flat Knots (fig.

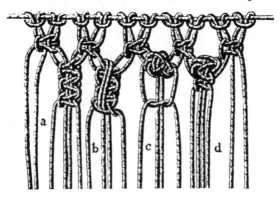

607). This bead or small shell knot is obtained by passing the threads back over a series of completed flat knots. Detail *a* shows three flat knots finished, while detail *b* shows how the inner threads are passed back over the knots and between the threads; in detail *c* the threads with which the knots have been made are

Fig. 607. Bead knots or small shell knots composed of flat knots.

passed between the two threads coming from left and right, and make the first crossing for a flat knot; detail *d* shows the shell knot finished and followed by a flat knot.

Bead Knot or Small Shell Knot Composed of a Small Chain of Knots (fig. 608). In this case the bead knot is made with a little chain of four single buttonhole knots (see fig. 617), preceded and followed by a flat knot. Detail *a* shows the upper flat knot followed by the four single buttonhole knots; detail *b* the rounded bead knot, and the first interlacing for the lower flat knot; detail *c* the finished bead knot.

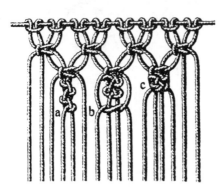

Fig. 608. Bead knot or small shell knot composed of a small chain of knots.

Bars of Knots to the Right and Left (figs. 609, 610, 611, 612, 613, 614, 615, 616).

After mounting a sufficient number of threads on a double knot-bearer, make two single buttonhole knots with the right-hand thread over the left-hand thread (fig. 609). It is advisable to complete one type or series of knots along the whole length of the work before going on to the next; the work becomes more regular as the hand becomes more accustomed to the movement required to make the knot, and the movement itself can be made much more rapidly through continued practice.

A second horizontal bar is then made by knotting each thread twice over the knot-bearer (fig. 610); these knots should be drawn as tight as possible. When this bar is finished, the diagonal bars are begun, going from left to right, with four threads (fig. 611).

The first thread to the left, numbered 1 in fig. 612, serves as knot-bearer

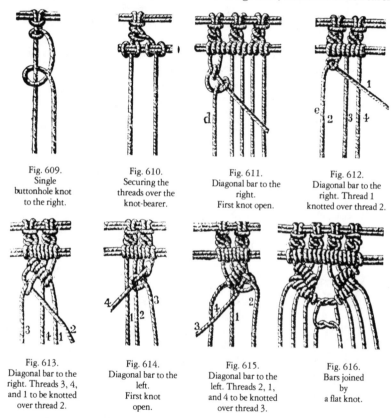

Fig. 609.
Single
buttonhole knot
to the right.

Fig. 610.
Securing the
threads over the
knot-bearer.

Fig. 611.
Diagonal bar to the
right.
First knot open.

Fig. 612.
Diagonal bar to the
right. Thread 1
knotted over thread 2.

Fig. 613.
Diagonal bar to the
right. Threads 3, 4,
and 1 to be knotted
over thread 2.

Fig. 614.
Diagonal bar to the
left.
First knot
open.

Fig. 615.
Diagonal bar to the
left. Threads 2, 1,
and 4 to be knotted
over thread 3.

Fig. 616.
Bars joined
by
a flat knot.

to threads 2, 3, and 4, which are successively looped over thread 1.

Fig. 613 shows threads 2, 3, and 4 knotted over thread 1, and in addition how, in the second row of the bar, thread 2 becomes the knot-bearer, replacing thread 1, and threads 3, 4, and 1 are looped and knotted twice over thread 2, which must be kept tightly stretched by the right hand. The knots are made with the left hand.

In fig. 614, which illustrates a bar going from right to left, the knots are made with threads 3, 2, and 1 over thread 4; in the second row (fig. 615), the knots are made with threads 2, 1, and 4 over thread 3. Here it is the left hand which keeps the thread taut from right to left, while the right hand makes the knots.

Fig. 616 shows how the double bars are joined by a flat knot.

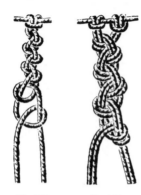

Single Chain (fig. 617). The single chain in macrame is made with single threads and is produced by the constant interchanging of the threads and the direction imparted to them while the knots are being made. Thus, a single buttonhole knot is made over the left-hand thread, then the right- hand thread is drawn taut and the same movements executed over it with the left-hand thread.

Double Chain (fig. 618). The double chain is made in the same way as the single chain, except that a double or even triple thread is used.

Fig. 617.
Single chain.

Fig. 618.
Double chain.

These two kinds of chain are used principally along macrame braids and are a means of passing from one color to another, or of changing threads which could not be carried by any other method to the required place to continue a given design.

Narrow Braid With Bars (fig. 619). Unlike the process used for the bars of knots described in figs. 611 to 616, in this braid the same thread serves as knot-bearer throughout and passes backward and forward under

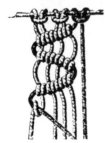

the four threads to be knotted. To make it easy to distinguish between the working threads and the knot-bearer, we have shown the latter in a darker shade than the former.

Macrame Fringe (figs. 620, 621, 622). Total length of the threads for DMC pearl cotton no. 3: 32 inches. Design worked in three colors.

1st series: mount the threads as shown in fig. 586 in the following order: 1 blue thread, 1 white thread, 1 red thread, and so on.

Fig. 619.
Narrow braid with bars.

2nd series: make a horizontal bar of knots (figs. 588 and 589) over a second knot-bearer.

3rd series: 3 buttonhole knots (fig. 609), worked with pairs of threads.

4th series: same as the 2nd.

5th series: bars made with two rows of double knots, slanting to the right and left, counting 6 threads for each bar, that is to say, 12 threads for the two bars. The 1st and 12th threads are covered with knots made with the

10 threads which separate them. In the second series of knots which makes the double bar, 1 more double knot is made over the knot-bearer with the thread which served as knot-bearer in the previous series.

When these bars are finished, they are brought as close together as possible, the last left-hand

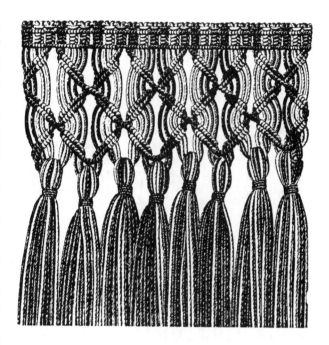

Fig. 620. Macrame fringe.

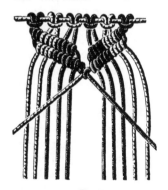

Fig. 621.
Method of joining the bars.
Detail of fig. 620.

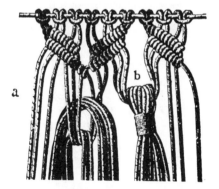

Fig. 622. Method of making the tassels.
Detail of fig. 620.

thread is held taut, and another double knot is made with the right-hand thread (fig. 621). Then the bars are continued in the opposite direction so that the left-hand knot-bearer is stretched across the right-hand group of threads and the right-hand knot-bearer across the left- hand group.

Three rows of double bars are made, after which 3 threads are taken from a left-hand group and 3 threads from a right-hand group; they are tied loose-ly together with a single knot; a bunch of 9 threads, 6 inches long, is passed between the threads above the knot (fig. 622, *a*), which is then drawn up close to the bars and a thread is wound several times round the tassel (fig. 622, *b*). The intermediate tassels are attached at the same level, in the space between two bars.

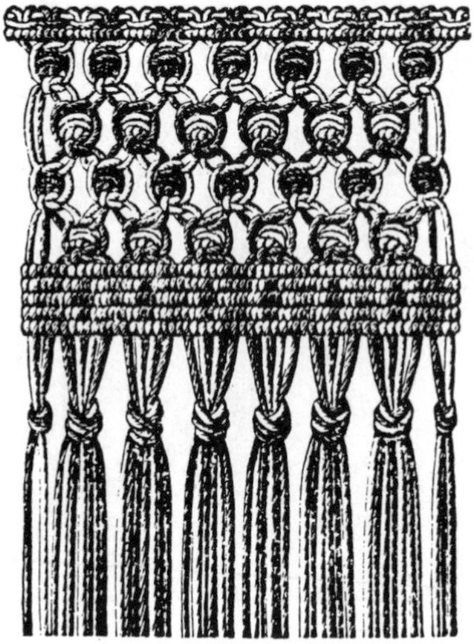

Fringe With Bead Knots and Mosaic Band (figs. 623, 624, 625). Total length of the threads for DMC pearl cotton no. 3: 40 inches. Design worked in three colors.

1st series: mount the threads as shown in fig. 586, with alternately 1 ecru and 1 dark grey thread, beginning and ending with a single ecru thread, and make a single bar of double knots in which the knots are not placed too close together.

2nd, 3rd, 4th, and 5th series: four rows of bead knots, the making of which is shown in fig. 624, in which the knot is half made, and fig. 625, in which it can be seen closed and followed by a complete flat knot.

The colors alternate in the knots; in the 2nd and 4th series, the light thread frames the bead knot, while in the 3rd and 5th series the dark thread frames it.

6th series: a horizontal bar of dou-ble knots, over a fresh knot-bearer.

7th series: add a 2nd knot-bearer and make another horizontal bar in which, between 2 light colored knots, 1 red thread is added; the loop by which the thread is mounted takes the place of the knot.

Fig. 623.
Fringe with bead knots and mosaic band.

Fig. 624.
Bead knot open.
Detail of fig. 623.

Fig. 625.
Bead knot closed.
Detail of fig. 623.

8th series: add a 3rd knot-bearer; with the red threads make 2 double knots between the knots made with the ecru thread.

9th series: add a 4th knot-bearer; make a half knot with each red thread.

10th series: add a 5th knot-bearer; make a horizontal bar as for the 6th series. Pass the red threads at the back of the work without knotting them.

The ends of the threads are grouped in sixes and joined with a plain knot half an inch from the last bar.

The same design can be used as a ground; in this case the red threads will have to be fastened off on the wrong side, and the series of bead knots is repeated after the mosaic band.

Macrame Fringe (fig. 626). Total length of the threads for DMC knotting cotton no. 10: 48 inches. Design worked in one color.

1st series: mount the threads as shown in fig. 596; make a double horizontal bar.

2nd series: wave knots with 4 knots (fig. 602).

3rd series: double horizontal bar.

4th series: 1 double diagonal bar from left to right, 1 bar from right to left; join these bars by the last threads.

5th series: with the 4 threads issuing from the bar, make a single chain (fig. 617), with 4 crossings of the threads, close to the point where the bars meet, and a small chain, with 7 crossings with the 2 outer threads.

Fig. 626. Macrame fringe.

6th series: groups of bars as in the 4th series, but in the reverse direction, ended by a single horizontal bar.

To make the tassels, add a thick bunch of threads to each group of 6 threads issuing from the work.

Fringe With Ground Design Worked on the Wrong Side (figs. 627, 628, 629, 630). Total length of the threads for DMC pearl cotton no. 3: 44 inches. Design worked in two colors.

Begin by mounting the threads in the ordinary way (fig. 588), with 5 yellow threads and 5 blue threads alternately; after the horizontal bar, make, from left to right over the 1st thread, 1 double knot with the 2nd thread and 1 double knot with the 3rd thread. Then, over the 2nd thread, which has now become the 1st, make double knots with the next 4 threads; then leave 2 threads on the left and over the 3rd thread make 2 double knots with the next 2 threads.

Make a similar group down from right to left, except that at the 3rd change of thread, 5 double knots are made in the middle of the figure instead of 2, the last of these knots counting toward the new reversed group of bars below; see fig. 628.

Between two groups of reversed bars, make 1 flat knot with 2 threads from the left and 2 from the right.

The second horizontal bar having been made, turn the work wrong side out and continue the work on the wrong side, making ordinary double knots inclined alternately from right to left in one row and from left to right in the next.

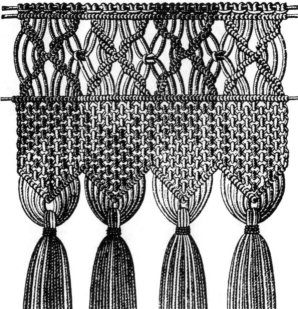

When ten rows have been worked in this way, the threads are divided into groups and one knot fewer is made on each side of each group, so as to form the points; then the work is

Fig. 627. Fringe with ground design worked on the wrong side.

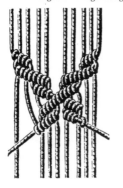

Fig. 628.
Reversed bars.
Detail of fig. 627.

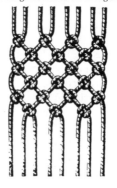

Fig. 629. Formation of the
knots on the wrong side.
Detail of fig. 627.

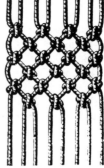

Fig. 630. Appearance of the
knots on the right side.
Detail of fig. 627.

turned right side out again; the knots worked on the wrong side (fig. 629) present on the right side the appearance shown in fig. 630. Finally, the bottom edge is finished with a single bar, and tassels are made with the ends of thread issuing from each point.

Macrame Fringe (figs. 631 and 632). Length of the double threads for

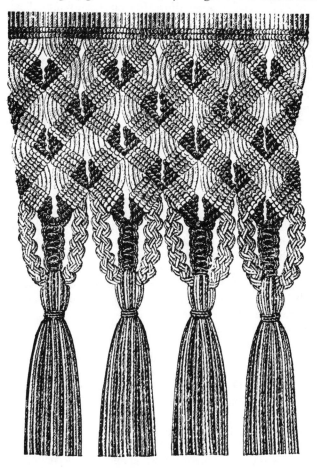

Fig. 631. Macrame fringe.

DMC pearl cotton no. 3: 56 inches; length of the single threads: 32 inches. Design worked in three colors.

1st series: mount the threads as shown in fig. 588 in the following order: 2 double threads of blue, 3 single threads of dark yellow, 1 double thread of light yellow, 3 single threads of dark yellow, then 4 double threads of blue, and so on; end with 2 double threads of blue. When the work is finished, cut the loops and cut all the threads to the same length.

2nd series: divide the threads into groups, leaving the yellow threads in the middle and 4 blue threads on each side. Begin on the left—cover the 4th blue thread (the one nearest the yellow threads) with double knots made with the 1st, 2nd, and 3rd dark yellow threads and the 1st light yellow thread—cover the 3rd blue thread with the 4 yellow threads and the 4th blue thread (the one which served as knot-bearer in the 1st row of knots)—cover the 2nd blue thread with the 4 yellow threads and the 4th and 3rd blue threads—cover the 1st blue thread with the 4 yellow threads and the 4th, 3rd, and 2nd blue threads. In the detail shown in fig. 632, the blue threads are shown dark, the yellow threads medium and light.

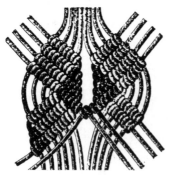

Fig. 632. Detail of fig. 631.

When the fourfold bar sloping from left to right has been completed, a similar bar is made from right to left, then both are joined by 1 double knot, and the 1st blue thread on the left is passed under the right-hand group and the 1st blue thread on the right is passed under the left-hand group.

3rd series: the same groups are made in the opposite directions so that the yellow knots will lie alongside the last blue knots and the blue knots will again end the groups of bars; the yellow threads are laid between the preceding group and the next one.

4th and 6th series: same as the 1st.

5th series: same as the 2nd.

After the 5th series of groups, join the 4 yellow threads on the two sides of the blue knots and with them make a double chain (fig. 618) consisting of 12 knots. With the blue threads make 4 flat knots. Finally, join all the threads from each group of bars and, with the addition of extra threads, make a fairly full tassel.

Macrame Fringe (figs. 633 and 634). Total length of threads for DMC knotting cotton no. 20: 90 inches. Design worked in two colors.

1st series: mount the threads as shown in fig. 586, alternating 8 light colored threads and 6 dark, and beginning and ending with 3 dark threads; make a double horizontal bar.

2nd series: with 4 threads each, make a row of little crosses with a single bar from left to right; begin and end this row with 2 double knots, one above the other.

3rd series: double horizontal bar.

4th series: with the first 4 and the last 4 of the 12 dark threads make little crosses; then, beginning with the 4 center threads, make a diagonal double bar to the left and one to the right, completed in the middle by a little cross. At the sides make only half motifs.

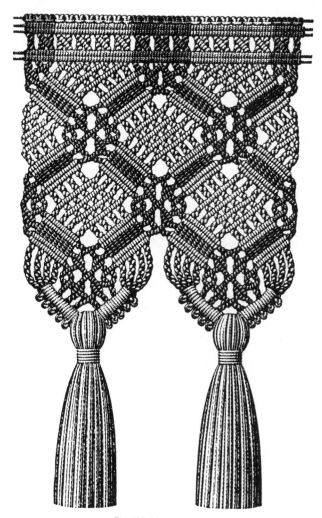

Fig. 633. Macrame fringe.

5th series: with the 16 light threads make a grid as shown in fig. 634, but finish at the bottom with 2 double knots one above the other.

6th, 9th, and 12th series: take 6 dark and 8 light threads; with the 8 light threads make two diagonal bars to the right over the 6th and 5th dark

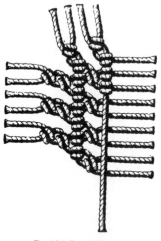

Fig. 634. Detail of fig. 633.

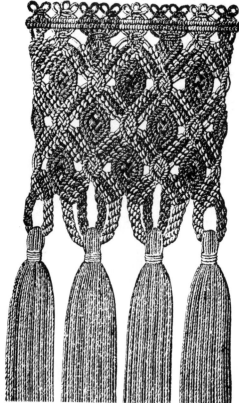

Fig. 635. Macrame fringe.

threads; with the 4th and 3rd dark threads make 2 double knots over each of the 8 light threads; with the 8 light threads make two diagonal bars to the right over the 2nd and 1st dark threads. Work the next group in the opposite direction, with 8 light and 6 dark threads.

7th, 10th, and 13th series: with the 12 dark threads, make motifs composed of four leaves and little crosses.

8th and 11th series: with the 16 light threads, make grids begun and ended with 2 double knots one above the other; see fig. 634.

14th series: tassels: with the left-hand 8 light threads, make four bars of respectively 6, 5, 4, and 3 double knots one above the other; with the 1st thread make, over the remaining 7 threads: 3 single buttonhole knots, 1 picot, 3 buttonhole knots, 1 picot, add 2 dark threads, 3 buttonhole knots, 1 picot, add 2 dark threads, 3 buttonhole knots, 1 picot, add 2 dark threads, 3 buttonhole knots, 1 picot, 3 buttonhole knots; repeat the same group to the right, reversed. Finally join all the threads and make them into a fairly full tassel by adding 16 light and 12 dark threads.

Macrame Fringe (figs. 635 and 636). Total length of the threads for DMC pearl cotton no. 3: 52 inches. Although this design worked in two colors may appear rather complicated, it will soon be found that it is extremely easy to copy; we shall not, therefore, give detailed instructions for the work. The method of mounting the threads shown in fig. 594, single bars (figs. 611 to 616), and collecting knots (figs. 601), must be sufficiently familiar to those who have followed the instructions we have given in the course of this chapter.

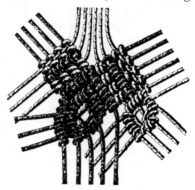

Fig. 636. Detail of fig. 635.

The only point which may present some difficulty is the checkered design formed by the threads inside the bars; a careful study of the course of the knots, clearly shown in fig. 636, will make the solution of this problem easy.

The bottom of the work is finished with tassels made of threads of the two shades.

Macrame Fringe (fig. 637). Total length of the threads for DMC special quality crochet cotton no. 3: 70 inches. Design worked in one color.

1st series: mount the threads as shown in fig. 586; make a double horizontal bar.

2nd series: double chains with 4 knots; see fig. 618.

3rd series: double horizontal bar.

4th series: with the 1st thread, make 4 double buttonhole knots over the 2nd and 3rd threads; with the 4th thread, 2 double buttonhole knots over the 5th and 6th threads; repeat in the opposite direction with the 11th to the 16th threads. Make 1 flat knot with the 7th and 10th threads. Between the motifs leave 4 threads which will later be fastened off on the wrong side; see fig. 637.

5th series: beginning over the 8th thread, make a triple bar diagonally to the left, and over the 9th thread a triple bar diagonally to the right.

6th series: as filling between the diagonal bars, make 9 inverted flat knots, and to connect the motifs add to the bars 2 more double knots turned out, 1 flat knot to join, then 2 more double knots turned in.

7th series: triple diagonal bars, turned in.

8th series: make scallops with 12 and 9 double buttonhole knots, and a vertical bar with 4 flat knots.

Repeat series 5, 6, 7, and 8 once, but making the vertical bar with only 1 flat knot.

To make the tassels, add a bunch of 16 threads, 12 inches long, and cut the tassels to a length of 5 inches.

Macrame Fringe (fig. 638). Total length of the threads for DMC pearl cotton no. 3: 32 inches. Design worked in two colors.

1st series: mount the threads as shown in fig. 586, but in the reverse direction, with double threads, which will count in the instructions as one thread: * 1 dark blue thread, 3 ecru threads, 1 dark blue thread, 1 light blue

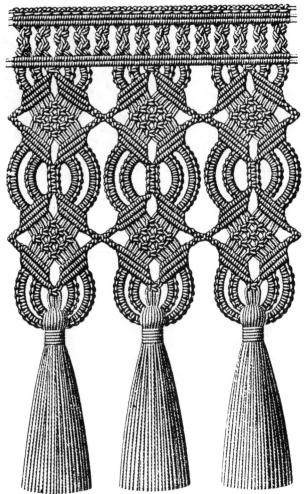

Fig. 637. Macrame fringe.

thread, 3 ecru threads, 1 light blue thread, repeat from *. Make a single horizontal bar.

2nd series: make a double chain, with 5 interchanges of the threads.

3rd series: single horizontal bar.

4th series: make large collecting knots (fig. 601) with the ecru threads over the 4 light blue and dark blue threads, and flat knots over the ecru threads.

5th series: make flat knots over the ecru threads with 2 light or dark blue threads and with 1 ecru thread.

Fig. 638. Macrame fringe.

6th series: make flat knots with and over the ecru threads in the middle of the group of knots.

7th series: same as the 5th. Then take once more the light and dark blue threads from the right and left, roll them from left to right between the thumb and forefinger, each group separately, as for making a cord. When they have been twisted several times, let them run together, twisting them now from right to left. The two twistings are done simultaneously, and the cord produced in this way is secured with a knot, beneath which the ends form a little tassel.

The ecru threads are joined with a flat knot and additional threads are added to them to make a full tassel.

Knotted Fringe (fig. 639). Total length of the threads for DMC Alsatian twist no. 12: 40 inches. Design worked in one color. Prepare bunches of 6 threads, thread them into a coarse crewel needle, and draw them through the edge of a piece of material in groups of four, with a quarter of an inch between the bunches in each group and five-eighths of an inch between the groups.

Each repeat of the design requires 4 bunches, which must be drawn

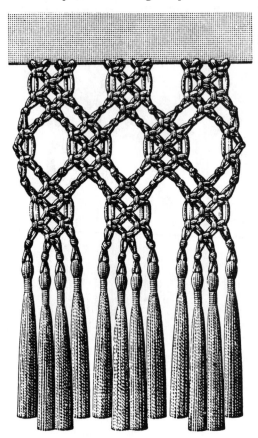

through the material to half their length, so that they form 8 bunches of equal length ready for the work.

1st series: with the 1st and 4th bunches, make a flat knot close to the material over the 2nd and 3rd bunches; with the 5th and 8th bunches, make a flat knot over the 6th and 7th bunches; continue down with 4 alternated flat knots, as shown in the illustration.

2nd, 4th, and 6th series: make a single knot with the 1st and 2nd, the 3rd and 4th, the 5th and 6th, and the 7th and 8th bunches, at a distance of a quarter of an inch from the motifs of the preceding series.

3rd and 5th series: make motifs consisting of 7 alternated flat knots, a quarter of an inch from the single knots.

Fig. 639. Knotted fringe.

The half motifs at the sides are composed of 2 flat knots and 1 buttonhole knot.

To give fullness to the tassels, add an additional bunch of 24 threads, 10 inches long, and cut the tassels to a length of 4 inches.

Fringe With Three Rows of Tassels (fig. 640). This kind of fringe is best suited for trimming rugs, curtains, etc. Therefore, the coarsest grades of thread are recommended. Length of the dark threads for DMC pearl cotton no. 1: 80 inches; length of the light threads: 56 inches.

For the braid heading allow 40 inches of DMC pearl cotton no. 1 for 6 inches of braid.

The interlacings and crossings of the threads are so simple that we need only refer the reader to fig. 597 for the mounting of the braid, and to fig. 602 for the waved plait.

The small tassels between the knots are made separately with DMC

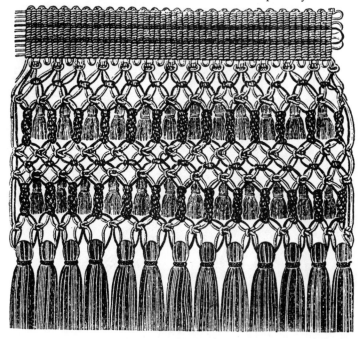

Fig. 640. Fringe with three rows of tassels.

special stranded cotton no. 25, and are attached to the knots by means of the thread by which they are tied.

Macrame Fringe With Corner (figs. 641, 642, 643). Length of the threads for DMC knotting cotton no. 10: 40 inches. Design worked in two colors, cream and red.

Owing to the way in which they are made, macrame fringes cannot be gathered to turn a corner, as can net, crochet, or filet lace. The close knots of the mounting make it impossible to draw the inner thread tight enough to give the necessary extra length round the outside edge. It is therefore necessary, according to the design, to increase the number of threads by a given quantity in order to make a corner that will lie flat round the article which is to be trimmed.

The detail in fig. 642 shows the addition of 5 extra threads to the 4th series of knots.

One group of intersecting bars requires 16 threads, corresponding to four groups of small squares set between the diamonds. Then, the bars having been prepared in advance, as can be seen in fig. 643, an extra thread, thread 6, is placed in the middle and just below the intersecting bars. (The extra threads are shown in a darker shade in the illustration). The bar which extends to the right and left is worked over thread 6.

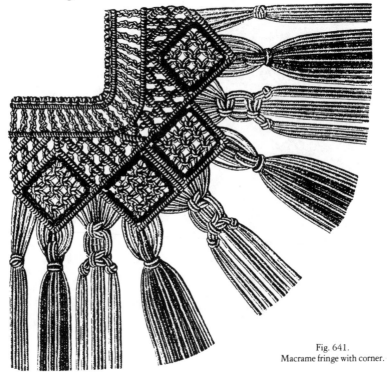

Fig. 641.
Macrame fringe with corner.

A further 7 threads are then mounted onto the threads between which the extra thread passes. Thread 7 is mounted single; threads 8 and 9 are mounted double; threads 10, 11, 12, and 13 single. In this way, threads 7, 10, 11, 12, and 13 connect the knot-bearers, while threads 8 and 9 alone are mounted separately at each side.

The bars formed by the knots of the extra threads must be made close together, as in any other double bar. We have purposely shown the knot-bearers a little distance apart, to enable the added threads to be clearly distinguished from the original threads.

At the point where the bars meet, a very long thread of red is fastened on, with which knots are made over the 14 threads inside the diamond.

The 7th thread on the right and the 1st on the left are folded and a double knot is made over each with the red thread.

The center of the diamond is filled with 9 flat knots; when these have been made, the knotting of the red thread is continued along the sides; a single bar in cream thread forms the outer edge of the diamond.

Knotted tassels and tassels ornamented with fancy knots, each requiring 10 threads, complete the fringe.

Macrame Ground (figs. 644, 645, 646). The threads, the length of which depends on the size of the ground, are wound on macrame bobbins; see fig. 653. For DMC pearl cotton no. 3, allow 14 inches for each repeat of the design. Design worked in two colors.

1st series: mount the threads as shown in fig. 586. Begin with 2 blue threads, then mount alternately 4 cream and 4 blue threads, end with 2 blue threads, and make a double horizontal bar.

2nd series: begin in the middle, making 2 flat knots with the 8 blue threads; with the 4 left-hand blue threads

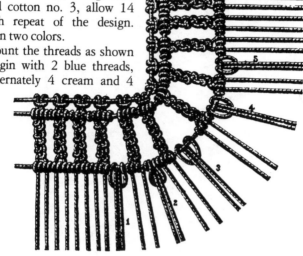

Fig. 642. Adding the first extra threads.
Details of fig. 641.

make a quadruple bar over the 4 right-hand blue threads. These quadruple bars, which make a kind of shell knot, are shown in detail in fig. 645.

Join the blue threads at the bottom with 2 flat knots.

The method of beginning and continuing the openwork motifs is clearly shown in fig. 646.

The threads which issue from the last group of knots serve to make the bars of knots, of which the two inner rows are light and the two outer rows dark.

When the bars in two colors are completed, all the cream threads are again collected to make the next openwork motifs, so that all the shell knots are blue and all the openwork motifs cream.

Macrame Ground With Openwork Heading (fig. 647). The threads, the length of which depends on the size of the ground, are wound on macrame bobbins; see fig. 653. For DMC special quality crochet cotton no. 1, allow 10 inches for the heading and 40 inches for each repeat of the ground design. Design worked in two colors.

Mount the threads as shown in fig. 586. Begin with 3 double threads of red, then mount alternately 6 double threads of grey and 6 double threads of red; end with 3 double threads of red.

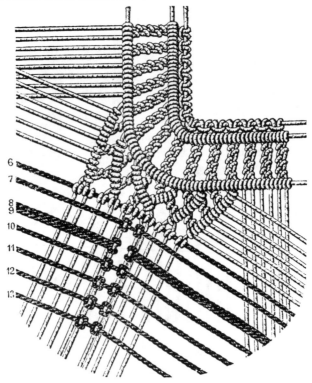

Fig. 643. Adding the second extra threads. Detail of fig. 641.

1st series: heading: make a double horizontal bar.

2nd series: vertical bars composed of 3 double knots, one above the other.

3rd series: make a double horizontal bar.

4th series: ground: begin the left-hand part of the leaf with 1 double knot with the 1st thread over the 2nd thread and 1 double knot with the 2nd thread over the 1st thread, 1 double knot with the 4th thread over the 3rd thread; then, over the 6th thread make a quadruple bar diagonally to the left. With the next 12 red threads, make a quadruple bar to the right and one to the left, and so on.

5th series: with the 12 light threads make a grid as shown in fig. 634; complete it at the bottom with 2 double knots one above the other.

6th series: connecting motif: over the first 6 dark threads make 2 double knots with the 1st and 2nd grey threads, over the 3rd and 4th grey threads

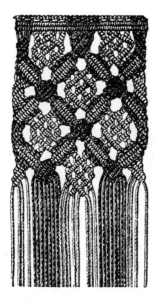

Fig. 644. Macrame ground.

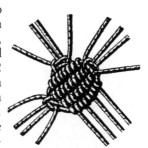

Fig. 645. Shell knot.
Detail of fig. 644.

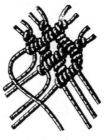

Fig. 646.
Openwork motif.
Detail of fig. 644.

make two diagonal bars with the 6 red threads, over the 6 red threads make 2 double knots with the 5th and 6th grey threads. Repeat the same motif in the opposite direction with the next 6 grey threads and 6 red threads.

7th series: with the first 6 red threads, make a quadruple bar toward the left, and with the next 6 red threads a quadruple bar toward the right; with the 4th red thread, 1 double knot over the 3rd thread; and with the 3rd thread, 1 double knot over the 4th thread; repeat the same motif to the right, in the opposite order.

In the middle, with the 5th, 6th, 7th, and 8th threads make two little crosses one above the other, then add on the left a quadruple bar toward the right, and on the right a quadruple bar toward the left.

8th series: with the 12 grey threads: begin with 2 double knots one above the other, then make the grid ground and end with 2 double knots one above the other.

Continue from the 6th series until the required depth has been worked and end, if required, with a repetition of the heading.

Macrame Insertions (figs. 648, 649, 650, 651). These two insertions or borders are worked across from edge to edge. The threads, for DMC pearl cotton no. 3, should be 30 inches long. Designs worked in one color.

Both designs are begun by mounting the threads as shown in fig. 586, followed by a single horizontal bar. For fig. 648, triple bars of knots are made, with 4 threads, slanting alternately from right to left and from left to right; these are followed by another single bar, after which another series of triple bars is made, sloping in the opposite direction; the work is finished with a single horizontal bar. The work is then turned wrong side up and another knot-bearer is placed in position and another horizontal bar worked over it. To end, the threads are knotted together 2 by 2, as shown in fig. 650, *a;* the ends are cut *(b)*; and the knots are firmly pressed on the wrong side of the work *(c).*

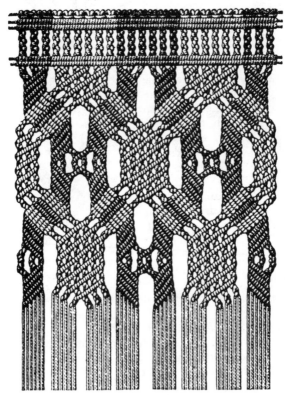

Fig. 647. Macrame ground with openwork heading.

For fig. 649, 8 single threads must be allowed for each repeat of the design.

All the diagonal double bars slanting down from right to left are made first (fig. 651); then, counting from left to right, take the 5th thread as the 1st knot-bearer (fig. 651), and begin the second series of bars, the bars in this series slanting down from left to right. Fasten off the threads after this series of knots, as shown in fig. 650.

Braid Made with Macrame Bobbins (figs. 652, 653, 654). In order to avoid the inconvenience of having, on the one hand, to join on additional lengths of thread in the course of the work or, on the other hand, to work with very long hanging threads which would hamper the work, we advise the use of macrame bobbins, which resemble those used in making lace.

The threads are wound onto these bobbins and secured by a knot. For the method of securing them, see the chapter "Pillow Laces," fig. 1036.

Prepare 8 double threads of a length corresponding to that of the braid which is required. For DMC pearl cotton no. 3, allow 10 inches of thread for each repeat of the design. Design worked in two colors, blue and brown.

Mount the threads as shown in fig. 586, with 3 blue threads, 2 brown, and 3 blue. Make a single bar of knots, then leave 2 threads on the left and 2 threads on the right; with the 12 threads remaining in the middle, grouped in sets of 4, make 3 flat knots.

Make double knots over the 16th thread to the right, with the 15th,

Fig. 648. Macrame insertion.

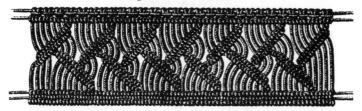

Fig. 649. Macrame insertion.

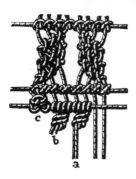

Fig. 650. Method
of fastening off the threads.
Detail of figs. 648 and 649.

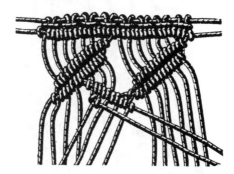

Fig. 651.
Method of alternating the bars.
Detail of fig. 649.

14th, 13th, 12th, 11th, 10th, and 9th threads; then with the same threads make knots over the 15th thread.

Work a similar bar on the left over the 1st thread with the 2nd, 3rd, 4th, 5th, 6th, 7th, and 8th threads and over the 2nd thread with the same threads. Join the two bars by making double knots with the knot-bearer of the left-hand bar over the knot-bearer of the right-hand bar.

At each side, with the 4 outer threads of blue, make 4 flat knots (fig. 587, d); make two more bars, one at each side, but sloping in the opposite direc-

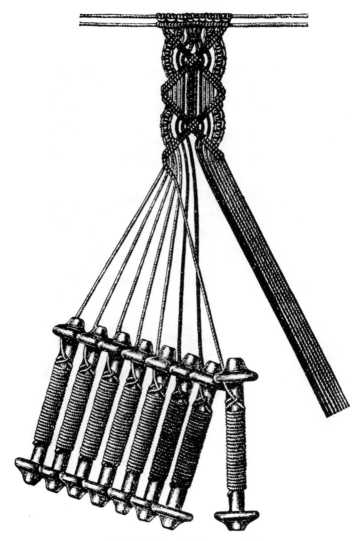

Fig. 652. Braid made with macrame bobbins.

tion, knotting all the threads including the last one (fig. 654). Take 4 brown threads in the center and make 6 flat knots, then work the bars of knots in to the center again. The return of the thread is also shown in fig. 654.

Braid With Large Shell Knots (figs. 655, 656, 657, 658). The length of the threads depends on the length of braid to be made. For DMC pearl cotton no. 3, allow 16 inches for each repeat of the design, which is

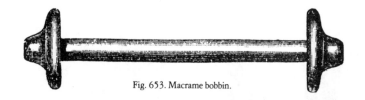

Fig. 653. Macrame bobbin.

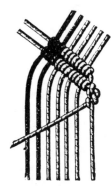

Fig. 654.
Diagonal bar, with the
knot-bearer returning.
Detail of fig. 652.

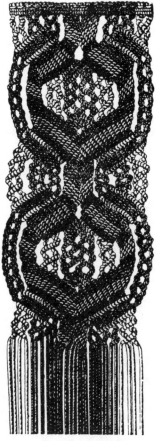

Fig. 655. Braid with large shell knots.

worked in two colors. Wind the threads onto macrame bobbins.

Mount the threads as shown in fig. 588, with the loops cut, in the following order: 1 red thread, 6 green, 2 red, 6 green, 1 red. Make a single bar.

From left to right over the 1st red thread: 1 double knot with the 2nd thread; over the 1st green thread: 1 double knot with the 2nd; from right to left over the 4th green thread: double knots with the 3rd, 2nd, and 1st green threads. From left to right: 1 double knot with the 6th green thread over the 5th and with the 4th over the 3rd thread. From right to left: 5 double knots over the 8th green thread. From left to right: 1 double knot over the 9th thread, 1 double knot over the 7th thread, 1 double knot over the 5th thread. From right to left: 7 double knots over the 12th thread. From left to right: 3 detached double knots. From right to left: 1 double knot with the 3rd dark thread over the 4th dark thread.

Then, first from left to right, then from right to left, with 6 green threads: two diagonal double bars over the 2 red threads (see also top of fig. 658);

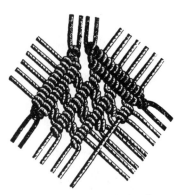

Fig. 656.
Large shell knot,
begun.
Detail of fig. 655.

Fig. 657.
Large shell knot,
finished.
Detail of fig. 655.

Fig. 658. Interchanging the threads.
Detail of fig. 655.

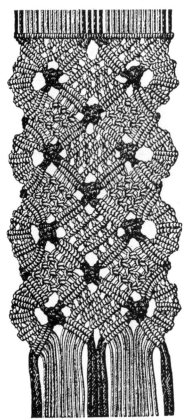

Fig. 659.
Macrame braid with crossed bars.

join the 4 red threads in the middle and make a large shell knot, (fig. 657), consisting of 6 flat knots (fig. 656), take 2 threads on the right and 2 threads on the left, turn these threads back on the left and right, then bring them from the wrong side to the right side over the threads issuing from the bars and draw them tight with 1 flat knot.

At the sides, make a scallop of three double bars, and between each bar and the next, a single chain with two interchanges of the threads.

Fill the space beneath the outer shell knots with 9 flat knots; beneath the center shell knot make bars of crossed knots, the method of working which is clearly shown in fig. 658.

Macrame Braid With Crossed Bars (figs. 659, 660, 661). Wind the threads onto macrame bobbins, allowing, for DMC pearl cotton no. 3, 20 inches of blue and green threads and 24 inches of brown and black threads for each repeat of the design. Mount the threads as shown in fig. 586, in the following order: 2 double threads of light blue, 2 double threads of light green, 2 double threads of dark green, 1 double thread of dark brown, 1 single thread of black, 2 double threads of light brown, 1 single thread of black, 1 double thread of dark brown, 2 double threads of dark green, 2 double threads of light green, 2 double threads of light blue.

Make a double horizontal bar.

Begin at each side with the openwork groups of crossed bars (figs. 660 and 661), using 4 blue threads and making 4 interchanges out and 3 in— bars with 4 light green threads and 3 interchanges out and 2 in—crossed bars with 4 dark green threads with 2 interchanges out and 3 in. Over the 1st dark green thread, 1 double knot with the 4 light green and 4 blue threads.

The other dark green threads are knotted, from right to left, then from left to right, over the 4 light green threads and the 4 blue threads, which together form 8 bars across the first bar—knot these 8 threads again over the last dark green thread—add a crossed bar with 14 interchanges out and 12 in.

Fig. 660.
Bar crossed from
left to right.
Detail of fig. 659.

Middle group, left side: 1 double knot with the 1st dark brown thread over the 2nd thread; for the first bar, 3 double knots with the black thread and the 2 dark brown threads over the 1st light brown thread—for the second bar: 4 double knots with 1 black thread, with the 2 dark brown threads, and with the 1st light brown thread, over the 2nd light brown thread—for the third bar: 4 double knots with the 2 dark brown threads and the 2 light brown threads, over the black thread.

On the right: a similar group, slanting from left to right.

On the left: over the 1st dark brown thread on the right, 1 double knot with 2 dark brown threads, 2 light brown threads, and 1 black thread, all coming from the left.

Fig. 661.
Bar crossed from
right to left.
Detail of fig. 659.

On the right: over the 1st dark brown thread coming from the left, 1 double knot with 1 dark brown thread, 2 light brown threads, and 1 black thread.

On the left: over the dark brown thread coming from the right, 1 double knot with 1 dark brown thread, 2 light brown threads, and 1 black thread.

On the right: over the dark brown thread, 1 double knot with 2 light brown threads and 1 black thread.

On the left: a similar group to the one on the right.

On the right: over the 1st light brown thread, 1 double knot with 1 light brown thread and 1 black thread.

On the left: a similar group to the one on the right.

On the right: over the last light brown thread, 1 double knot with the black thread.

On the left: 1 double knot with the 2 black threads.

On the left: over the 4 light green threads, then over the 4 blue threads: 1 double knot with each of the 2 dark brown threads and 2 light brown threads and with the black thread, that is to say, 8 cross bars—1 double

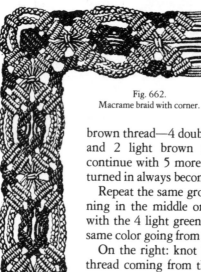

Fig. 662.
Macrame braid with corner.

knot with the 1st dark brown thread over the 2nd thread of the same color—2 double knots with the 2 dark brown threads over the 1st light brown thread—3 double knots with 2 dark brown threads and 1 light brown thread over the 2nd light brown thread—4 double knots with 2 dark brown threads and 2 light brown threads over the black thread—continue with 5 more bars in which the thread which is turned in always becomes the knot-bearer.

Repeat the same groups from right to left; then, beginning in the middle on the left, make the double knots with the 4 light green threads over the 1st thread of the same color going from right to left.

On the right: knot 3 light green threads over the 1st thread coming from the left and repeat the same group twice more.

The third bar forms at the same time the first scallop of a triple crossed bar, which is also made to the right.

The two crossed bars end in a triple group of bars; the last bar on the right consists of only one double knot. There remain to be worked on each side crossed bars in light blue, consisting of 3 complete scallops on the inner side and one complete scallop on the outer side, with a half scallop at the top and bottom.

Knot all the other threads over the 4 blue and 4 light green threads—in the middle, knot the right-hand and left-hand threads alternately, until the black threads meet at the bottom.

The group of green and blue bars is again worked in from the outside and completed with a crossed bar with three scallops on the inner side.

Fig. 663.
Group of leaves.
Detail
of fig. 662.

Macrame Braid With Corner (fig. 662 and 663). When braid is to be made to frame a rectangular article, each length of thread is fastened in the middle to the macrame cushion, and the two ends are wound separately onto bobbins. The braid is worked in two directions, and at the point where the two ends meet the threads are fastened off invisibly on the wrong side. For DMC pearl cotton no. 3, allow 11 inches for each repeat of the design. The braid illustrated in fig. 662 requires 8 green and 8 violet threads; they are arranged so that the 8 green threads are in the middle, with 4 violet threads on each side, and the work is begun with the diagonal bars made with the light threads over the dark. The two bars turned toward the outside of the corner and one toward the inside are made; this done, 6 dark threads in the middle are taken and with them the dark quadruple bar turned toward the corner is made. With the 4 outer light threads, single chains are knotted, forming a scallop round the corner, after which three light-colored diagonal bars are made, and the corner is finished. There are now 8 light threads in the middle and 4 dark threads on each side; the dark threads serve to make the little dark outer leaves; the light threads are joined in the middle by a wave knot (fig. 602, *b*), with two interchanges of the threads. The light-colored diagonal bars are made next; the working of the dark- colored motif with four little leaves is clearly shown in fig. 663.

Macrame Medallion (figs. 664 and 665). Total length for DMC pearl cotton no. 3: cream threads, 56 inches and 30 inches; colored threads, 60 inches and 120 inches. Design worked in cream, dark brown, light brown, and light blue.

Beginning in the center, take 8 cream threads, 56 inches long, and with them knot the square of bars set opposite ways, as shown in fig. 665; there will be 4 threads of equal length hanging from each corner. These threads serve as knot-bearers for the double bars, ending in 1 double knot, for each of which 4 more cream threads are added. The 4 threads hanging at each side of the bars are joined by 1 flat knot.

Then take 6 colored threads, 60 inches long, to make the sixfold bars which surround the center figure. The cream threads serve as knot-bearers. The dark brown threads turned toward the middle are knotted first, then the light brown, and finally the light blue. The three single chains, which are made between the groups of bars, consist of 5, 6, and 7 knots. When the eight bars, with the three intermediate chains, have been made, the ends of the colored threads are knotted on the wrong side of the work, secured with a few overcast stitches, and cut off close.

For the row of light-colored double bars, 32 cream threads, 56 inches long, are added. They are grouped 4 by 4, and knotted in the middle of their length with 1 flat knot. The flat knot is placed on the macrame cushion, close to the colored band, and double bars are made to right and left, working in also the 3 existing cream threads on each side. Leave a space of a quarter of an inch and make a second series of bars, each ended on the outside by 1 flat knot. The second colored band is made like the first, except that in this case the bars are sevenfold instead of sixfold, and the colored threads are 120 inches long.

To make the scallops which complete the medallion, 48 more cream

Fig. 664. Macrame medallion.

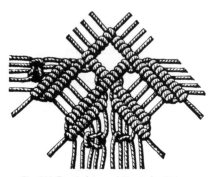

Fig. 665. Detail of the medallion in fig. 664.

threads, 30 inches long, are added. They are joined in the middle, 3 by 3, with 1 flat knot, which is fastened to the cushion close to the colored band, and the double bars are made. In every other group, 1 more cream thread is added, so that each group of knots contains 8 threads. Leave a space of a quarter of an inch and make the second row of bars; in the third row, the bars are placed so as to form points; in the center of the diamond-shaped spaces thus formed, the threads are collected with 1 flat knot.

When the work is finished, all the threads are fastened off, making 6 plain picots round each point.

This kind of medallion, which is very strong and lasting, can be used as a place mat, pincushion cover, etc.

Macrame Edging With Deep Scallops (fig. 666). Total length of the threads for DMC knotting cotton no. 10: 88 inches. Design worked in one color.

The threads are mounted with plain round picots, as shown in fig. 588, with a double horizontal bar followed by a row of small collecting knots (fig. 600), and a second double horizontal bar.

In the border itself, the design consists of two different motifs, the smaller of which requires 12 threads in width, the larger 22 threads; 10 threads at each side are to be used for the knotting, while the 2 center threads are fastened off on the wrong side of the work. Two threads are missed each

Fig. 666. Macrame edging with deep scallops.

time between two motifs, and fastened off on the wrong side; when the border is finished, the design is completed with two double bars and a row of small collecting knots in which fresh threads are added to replace those which were fastened off at the top. This assures that the number of threads is the same at the top and bottom.

Beginning with the small motif, make 1 flat knot with the 3rd, 4th, 5th, and 6th threads and 1 flat knot with the 7th, 8th, 9th, and 10th threads; then the triple bars are knotted over the 1st thread on the left and the 12th on the right, 6 threads being taken for each bar.

The scallops which edge the motifs are made with 12 buttonhole knots and 2 knotted picots (fig. 606) over 2 knot-bearers; the vertical bar, worked with 6 threads, requires 4 flat knots and 1 picot on each side in the middle. The triple bars are repeated in the opposite direction at the bottom and ended with 2 flat knots.

The large motif of the border is begun with the first scallop on the left, with the 1st thread, making 3 buttonhole knots over the 2nd and 3rd threads, 1 knotted picot, and 4 buttonhole knots; with the 4th thread over

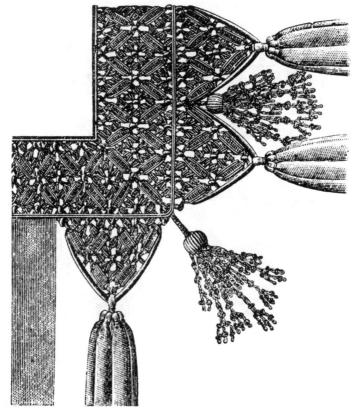

Fig. 667. Fringe with pointed scallops and large tassels.

the next 3 threads make 6 buttonhole knots ornamented with 1 picot; with the 10th thread make, over the 8th and 9th threads, 3 buttonhole knots, 1 picot, 3 buttonhole knots; then continue toward the left with the threads issuing from the second scallop, making 4 double knots over the 2 knot-bearers, to which are further added 1 picot and 2 buttonhole knots, after which these threads are joined to the threads issuing from the first scallop by 1 flat knot. Divide the 6 threads thus joined into two groups of 3 and make, toward the left, a scallop consisting of 12 buttonhole knots and 2 picots, and, toward the right, a scallop with 9 knots and 2 picots; these two scallops are joined again at the bottom by 1 flat knot.

Repeat the same series of knots on the right-hand side of the motif, but reversing them.

There will be 8 threads in the middle which serve to make the central motif consisting of four triple bars, completed at the bottom toward the right and left by scallops like those at the top.

Scallops: each scallop requires 39 threads. Between the scallops 1 small picot is made with 2 threads and 2 double knots, the threads being then fastened off on the wrong side. The 39 threads for each scallop are divided into nine groups: the 1st, 5th, and 9th consist of 5 threads each, the others of 4 threads each.

Fig. 668. Adding the first extra thread. Detail of fig. 667.

The work is begun with the first group on the left, making 2 flat knots over 3 threads, followed by 2 single chains, 1 to the right and 1 to the left, made with the 1st and 2nd threads and the 4th and 5th threads and consisting of 8 single knots; these are joined at the bottom by 2 flat knots. With the next two groups of threads make a shell knot (fig. 645); with the threads hanging on the left make 4 flat knots; take the 5 threads of the first group on the left and make 1 flat knot over 7 threads,

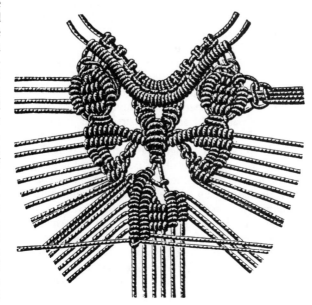

Fig. 669. Adding further extra threads. Detail of fig. 667.

take out 2 threads on the wrong side of the work, make 1 flat knot over 5 threads, take out 2 threads, make 1 flat knot over 3 threads, followed by a motif of small chains as described above. With the 4 threads issuing on the right of the shell knot, make a scallop, and with the 1st thread on the left make, over the next 3 threads, 9 buttonhole knots, 1 picot, 9 buttonhole knots. With the fourth group of threads make another scallop composed of 7 knots, 1 picot, 7 knots; with the fifth group of threads repeat the motif made with the first group, but ending with only 1 flat knot.

The right-hand half of the scallop is made in the same way, but reversed; then make 3 flat knots over the three middle groups of threads, that is to say over 11 threads, take out 3 threads, bring in the large scallops from each side and make 3 flat knots over 16 threads; divide the threads into three groups so that there are 5 threads on each side and 8 in the middle.

To the right and left, repeat the motifs of single chains and join them to the outer motifs with 3 flat knots; take out 5 threads, and repeat the same motif once more.

With the 8 threads in the middle, make a bar consisting of 14 wave knots; then divide the 8 threads into two groups of 4 to make, toward each side, a bar of 4 flat knots ornamented with picots; join these bars to the outer motifs with 1 flat knot, take out 4 threads, then make a scallop with 5 knots, 1 picot, 5 knots. The 5 threads issuing from the left-hand scallop are knotted over the 5 issuing from the right-hand scallop; then on each side a knotted picot is made with 5 threads, which are then fastened off invisibly on the wrong side of the work.

Fringe With Pointed Scallops and Large Tassels (figs. 667, 668, 669, 670, 671, 672, 673, 674). Total length of the threads for DMC knotting cotton no. 10: 140 inches.

The macrame design worked in one color with which we end this chapter is not only one of the most charming, but also one of those which require the greatest accuracy and care, particularly as to the direction of the knot-bearers. The groups of double knots and the bars must be drawn as close as possible so that the design shall stand out well all over the work and the various motifs be clearly defined. Each repeat requires 16 double threads.

The half stars on either side of a diamond are begun with the 15th and 16th double threads of the first repeat, and 3 buttonhole knots are made with the 4th thread over the other 3 (fig. 668).

Over 2 knot-bearers on the right and 1 on the left, that is to say over 3 threads, make 5 buttonhole knots with the 4th thread, and with the free threads make 1 flat knot over the 4 threads. This makes a small shell knot, on each side of which 3 buttonhole knots are made over 3 threads.

For the groups of bars, take the 11th, 12th, 13th, and 14th double threads on the left and the 3rd, 4th, 5th, and 6th double threads on the right. These groups are joined by buttonhole knots.

Over the 1st knot-bearer on the right, knot the 4 threads of the left-hand group; over these last threads, knot the next 2 threads on the right; over the 4th thread on the right, knot the 4 left-hand threads; over the 3 threads at the bottom and to the side, make 2 buttonhole knots with the 4th thread.

Over the 4 threads issuing on the left and right, work two quadruple bars, cross the upper threads after the second row of bars, with the next thread make 2 buttonhole knots over the 4th thread, then complete the third and fourth bars of knots.

Make another motif at the bottom with the 4 left-hand threads over the 4 right-hand threads.

To make the olive-shaped groups of knots on either side, the threads issuing from the large shell knot are taken as knot-bearers.

Fig. 668 shows the addition of the 1st extra thread, and fig. 669 the addition of 13 more threads which, mounted on the 1st thread, form with the latter the group of bars on the diagonal line of the corner.

For the next large shell knot, 2 more extra double threads are mounted, to which is added 1 thread from the preceding motif.

Two more extra threads are added to the free threads on either side. These 4 threads again serve as knot-bearers for the groups of bars on each side.

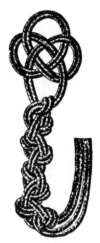

Fig. 670.
Chinese knot and double chain ready to make a bell knot.

The fourth group of bars, which is the one which forms the corner of the fringe, is mounted on the 4 threads issuing from the large shell knot, over which the 4th set of 12 extra threads is mounted; the shell knot at the bottom requires 4 more extra threads. A half star completes the ground and a double bar separates the ground from the large pointed scallops, which are also begun with two half stars and five large shell knots. Below the half stars come four groups of bars, then a complete star, two large shell knots on either side, and finally two more groups of bars joined by a large shell knot, which comes at the point of the scallop.

The threads which issue from the various groups are joined successively from the top of the scallop onward and are covered with very close overcasting so that they form a kind of round cord along the edge of the scallop, thin at the top and getting gradually thicker as it nears the point, where the threads are arranged to make a full tassel. This is further enriched by the addition of from six to eight tassels made separately and fastened by their tie-threads to the twisted part of the main tassel.

Fig. 671.
Bell knot made with a single chain.

Between the points there are also rich pendants, for which a large bell knot, or berry, is first made with 21 knot-bearers, in the manner shown in fig. 672.

The 21 threads are knotted together at the beginning and the ends passed

Fig. 672.
Macrame
berry.

Fig. 673.
Small pendant
of the tassel in
fig. 667.

Fig. 674. Large
pendant of the tassel
in fig. 667.

inside the bell; then 2 rounds of knots are made over 12 threads, 1 round over 15 threads, 3 rounds over 21 threads, 1 round over 15 threads, and 2 rounds over 12 threads. The ends are again passed inside the bell, which is stuffed with cotton wool to make it firmer and then closed with a few stitches.

Five large and six small pendants are attached to the bottom of the bell. The small pendants (fig. 673) are begun with a Chinese knot (fig. 670), which is followed by a chain with which a bell knot is made.

When the chain is double, cut 3 threads; when it is single, cut 1 thread. The ends are concealed inside the bell knot and secured with a few stitches; see the top of fig. 673.

The remaining thread is made into a loop from which are hung three bell knots made with a single chain (fig. 671), the 2 threads of which are fastened off inside the bell knot after a loop has been made at the top and bottom.

The large pendant (fig. 674) is begun with a single chain, transformed into a bell knot ending in a loop. Below this are suspended successively two Chinese knots, each followed by a bell knot with a loop; from the last of these loops are suspended three small pendants composed of bell knots and loops made with a single chain, as shown in fig. 671.

The large bell, or berry, is completed at the top with a crochet or knotted braid, for which instructions will be found in the chapter "Needlework Trimmings," figs. 1112 to 1116, 1118, and 1119, and by means of which the tassel is attached between the points of the fringe.

Insertion in embroidered filet with various fillings and outlines in darning stitch.

CHAPTER XIV

Filet Lace

The foundation of filet lace is netting, a handicraft so ancient that it would be exceedingly difficult to determine its origin. It is found among all primitive peoples, who use it to make fishing nets and snares for game.

Consisting originally of simple meshes joined by knots, netting has undergone successive modifications which have converted it into a most fascinating occupation. It has been so greatly perfected that it has become a means of producing veritable works of art, thanks to the practice of ornamenting the network with embroidery worked in the most varied materials. This kind of work is usually known as filet lace.

Among the many types of filet lace, we find, in Persia, for instance, silk net embroidered in gold and silver; in Italy, cut filet lace; in France, "filet Richelieu''; but the German filet lace of the eighteenth century, with its large conventional flower designs, is unquestionably the richest.

Modern filet lace, embroidered with simple stitches, is characterized by the use of different kinds and thicknesses of thread, which produce interesting effects of transparency. Netting or filet work can be divided into two very distinct categories: netting proper or plain filet, and embroidered netting or filet lace. Instead of net made by hand or by machine, a fabric imitating the latter and known as fishnet is often used.

Like all kinds of hand embroidery, filet embroidery can also be worked with the sewing machine. Large designs in cloth, or toile, stitch and darning, or reprise, stitch lend themselves particularly well to this method. Work executed in this way is much more rapid, and large articles can be made in a short time. Fillings in interlocking lace stitch or fancy stitches can also be embroidered. For small surfaces, the net ground itself can be made in a framework of woven fabric.

Implements for Plain Filet (figs. 675, 676, 677). Filet consists of loops of thread called meshes, secured by knots. To make these meshes, shuttles and gauges are necessary.

The shuttles are made of steel, wood, or bone. The first are used for fine work; they have at each end two curved prongs resembling tongs, beneath which is an eye to hold the thread (fig. 675); the middle of the shuttle is like a knitting needle. Wood and bone shuttles are used only for coarse work; the prongs are larger (fig. 676), and the shaft is not pierced. The thread is

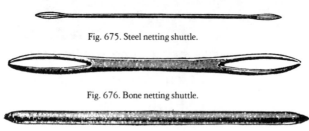

Fig. 675. Steel netting shuttle.

Fig. 676. Bone netting shuttle.

Fig. 677. Netting gauge.

wound onto the shuttle, the quantity being limited by the size of the mesh, through which the shuttle must be able to pass easily.

The gauges (fig. 677) are made of wood, steel, or bone. They should be well rounded and of uniform thickness throughout their length so that they may slip easily through the meshes and the latter may be quite equal in size. For making fringes, a flat gauge is used instead of the round one. Both shuttle and gauge must always be proportionate to the size of the meshes and the thickness of the thread used.

In addition to these implements, a heavy cushion is required, to which is fastened the loop of coarse thread which holds the net in place while it is being made.

Materials.   The choice of thread depends entirely on the use for which the work is intended. Filet can be made with cotton, flax, or silk thread; work in one color is usually done with cotton or flax thread, work in several colors with silk or a thread imitating silk.

Among the articles bearing the DMC trademark, we recommend DMC flax thread for knitting and crochet, DMC flax lace thread, as well as DMC Alsatia, DMC 6 cord crochet cotton, DMC special quality crochet cotton, DMC 6 cord cotton lace thread, DMC Alsatian sewing cotton, and DMC pearl cotton. All these threads are very evenly twisted and do not become knotted in working.

Filet Meshes.   In reality, all filet meshes are of the same shape: square or diamond. The patterns produced in plain filet result from the use of gauges of different sizes and the more or less elaborate way of interlacing the loops. Several different kinds of mesh can thus be produced, the chief of which are: (1) single or plain mesh, (2) double mesh, (3) oblong mesh, and (4) slipped mesh.

(1) *Single or plain mesh. First position of the hands* (fig. 678).   The work is begun by making a loop of very strong thread, four to eight inches

Fig. 678. Single or plain mesh. First position of the hands.

long; this is pinned to a weighted cushion. The thread from the shuttle is fastened to this loop. The gauge is then taken between the thumb and first finger of the left hand, and the fingers are held stiff. The thread is passed over the gauge and over the first, second, and third fingers; it is then passed up behind these three fingers and carried to the left, where it is held by the thumb.

Second and third positions of the hands (figs. 679 and 680).   The thread is brought down again behind all four fingers and the shuttle is

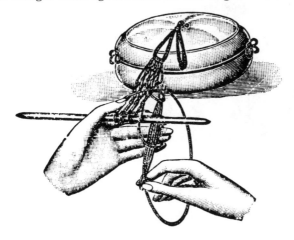

Fig. 679. Second position of the hands.

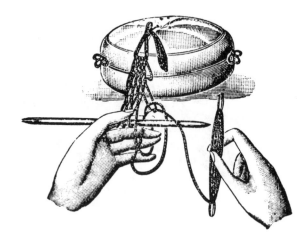

Fig. 680. Third position of the hands.

passed up through the loop on the fingers and through the loop behind the gauge, or through the loop to which the thread is fastened; a second loop is thus made over the left hand and is held by the little finger.

The thread is gradually drawn tight, the fingers are slipped out of the loop held by the thumb, then the loop round the three fingers is drawn tight. The last loop is kept on the little finger until the first is quite closed. Then only, the little finger is withdrawn from the loop, the knot is drawn tight, and a mesh is completed. The succeeding meshes are made in the same way, whether they are to form the edge of the work or the ground.

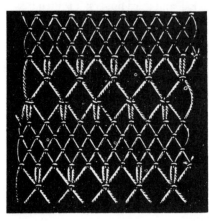

Fig. 681.
Fancy filet produced by increasing and decreasing.

When a sufficient number of loops for the edge have been made, the gauge is withdrawn, and the work is turned. To begin a new row, the gauge is laid along the edge of the finished row of meshes. The shuttle now passes through the last mesh of the preceding row, and as many knots are made as there are loops. These loops form plain or diagonal filet, for which the work is turned after each row, since it is worked backward and forward.

(2) *Double mesh.* To make a double mesh, the thread is wound two or

three times round the gauge. The mesh made in this way will be longer than the plain mesh.

(3) *Oblong mesh.* To make oblong meshes, the knot is made at a little distance from the gauge.

(4) *Slipped mesh.* Bring the thread over the gauge and fingers as for plain mesh, pass the shuttle as for any other type of mesh, but withdraw the gauge before tightening the knot.

Fancy Filet Produced by the Use of Gauges of Different Sizes.
Plain filet can be varied by the use of gauges of different sizes. In this case, one or two rows are made over a fine gauge, and the same number of rows over a coarser gauge. The two gauges are alternated at regular intervals.

Fancy Filet Produced by Increasing and Decreasing (fig. 681). The most charming and varied designs can be produced by joining several loops with a single knot in a first row, and then making in the second row as many new loops as were decreased in

Fig. 682.
Fancy filet with looped tufts.

he first. The increases and decreases can be made in the same row, or at fixed intervals.

It will be noticed that in fig. 681 two threads of different thickness have been used. Three rows of plain mesh are made with the finer thread; one plain row with the thicker thread and a proportionately larger gauge; one row in which decreases are made by joining two loops with one knot with the coarse thread and large gauge; and one row with the coarse thread and large gauge in which increases are made by working two knots into each loop. This is followed by three rows of plain mesh with the fine thread.

Fancy Filet With Looped Tufts (figs. 682 and 683). The loops which form the tufts are made in the filet as follows:

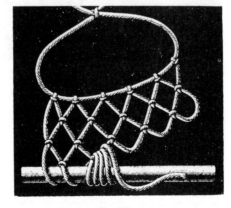

Fig. 683.
Fancy filet with looped tufts.

1st row: begin with one mesh, knotted at a little distance from the gauge; pass the thread over the gauge and the shuttle through the mesh into which the knot is made; repeat this process several times, taking care to make all the loops the same length. Then make one knot over all the loops by passing the shuttle from right to left, round the loops, instead of passing it through the mesh of the preceding row.

2nd row: make one mesh in each mesh of the preceding row, but not into the loops forming the tuft.

Fancy Filet With Plain Mesh, Double Mesh, and Oblong Mesh (fig. 684). Filet composed of large and small meshes is usually used as a foundation for embroidered filet (filet lace). Further on, we give two delightful grounds embroidered on fancy filet; see figs. 742 and 743. In fig. 684 the filet is made with straight meshes, but it can also be made as a diagonal foundation.

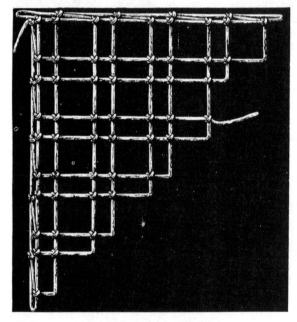

Fig. 684. Fancy filet with plain mesh, double mesh, and oblong mesh.

1st row: one double mesh and one plain mesh.

2nd row: consists entirely of oblong meshes, for which the thread is passed only once round the gauge.

The knot which secures the double mesh should be drawn as close as possible to the gauge; the one which secures the plain mesh should be made at the head of this mesh so that when the row is finished all the loops lie in an even line.

The third row is like the first, care being taken that the plain meshes lie in the small spaces and the double meshes in the large spaces.

Further varieties of fancy filet can be made by alternating four, nine, or sixteen small meshes with one large mesh and the corresponding number of oblong meshes.

Filet Medallion With Long and Short Meshes (fig. 685). Over a fairly large gauge and with very coarse thread used double, make thirty or thirty-one loops, then draw up the thread on which the meshes are strung. Make the opening in the center as small as possible and fasten off the thread in it.

For the next round, which is also worked with the coarse double thread, fasten the thread to one of the long loops, and make a mesh into each mesh of the first round, using a small gauge. Keep the same gauge for the succeeding rounds, which are worked in a finer thread used single. The necessity for fastening on the thread afresh for each new round can be avoided by making a slipped mesh.

Fig. 685.
Filet medallion with long and short meshes.

Filet Medallion Made by Increasing (fig. 686). Make twelve meshes into the loop and close the loop. In the next round, make one knot in the first mesh and two knots in the second mesh, and continue thus to the end of the round. In the succeeding rounds, continue the increases by making two knots into each increase of the preceding round.

Filet Square (figs. 687 and 688). To make a perfectly-

Fig. 686.
Filet medallion made by increasing.

regular square in filet, begin by making two meshes and three knots. In each succeeding row make two knots in the last loop, so that each row is increased by one mesh. Continue to increase until there is one mesh more than the finished square is to measure. After this row, work a row with the extra mesh without increasing or decreasing; then, in the next row, begin the decreasing by joining the last two loops of each row with a single knot. Slip the last two meshes.

Band of Straight Filet (fig. 689). To make a band of filet, begin by making the number of meshes required for the width; then, as the work pro-

Fig. 687. Filet square begun.

Fig. 688.
Filet square completed.

ceeds, increase at one side by making two knots in one mesh and decrease at the other side by joining two meshes with one knot.

Care must be taken always to make the increases and decreases on the correct side, otherwise the line of the edge will be broken and it will be impossible to embroider the band, unless the latter is wider than the design of the embroidery, in which case the extra meshes can be cut away and the edges straightened when the embroidery has been completed. Care is also necessary to ensure that the meshes at the edge on which the increases are made do not become too short; this is a common fault, due to the fact that the two knots of the increase take more space than the decrease, in which two meshes are joined by one knot.

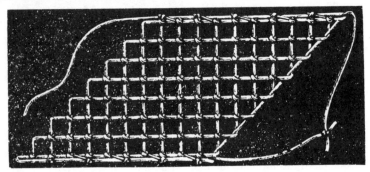

Fig. 689. Band of straight filet.

Edging of Straight Filet With Closed Heading and Scalloped Edge of Open Loops (fig. 690). Begin as for a filet square. After making two meshes, continue with rows in which an increase is made at the end of the row until there are twelve meshes. From now on, the increases are continued at the left-hand edge, while the points are made at the other side: the last three meshes are left open, then four rows are worked without increasing or decreasing on this side, in the next row the last four meshes are left open, and so on.

Filet Frame (fig. 691). Filet borders for handkerchiefs, bedspreads, chair backs, etc. can be made in one piece, leaving the center open.

Begin as for ordinary filet (as shown at *a* in the illustration) and increase until there are 8 meshes (*c* to *c*); make 4 meshes, omit the last 4 meshes of the preceding row. Turn. Make 5 meshes, increase in the last mesh. Turn. Make 4 meshes, decrease in

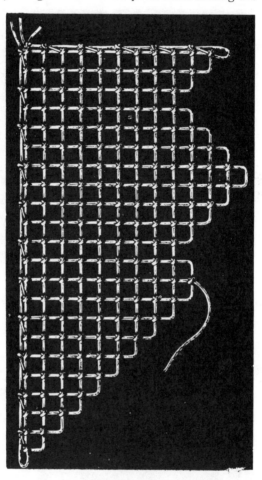

Fig. 690.
Edging of straight filet with closed heading and
scalloped edge of open loops.

the last mesh. Turn. Make 5 meshes, increase in the last mesh. Turn. Make 4 meshes, decrease in the last mesh, then increase in the same mesh. Turn. Make 4 meshes and decrease in the last mesh. Turn. Make 5 meshes, increase in the last mesh. Turn. Make 4 meshes, decrease in the last mesh. Turn. Make 5 meshes, increase in the last mesh, cut the thread.

Fasten on the thread to the outer edge of the 4 meshes left unworked at *c*, make 4 meshes. Turn. Make 5 meshes, increase in the last mesh. Turn. Make 4 meshes, decrease in the last mesh. Turn. Make 5 meshes, increase

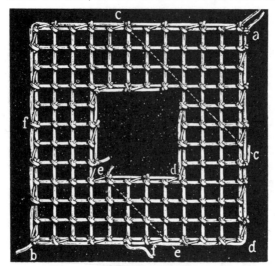

Fig. 691. Filet frame.

in the last mesh. Turn. Make 4 meshes, decrease in the last mesh and increase in the same mesh. Turn. Make 4 meshes, decrease in the last mesh. Turn. Make 5 meshes, increase in the last mesh. Turn. Make 4 meshes, decrease in the last mesh. Turn. Make 5 meshes, increase in the last mesh, then cut the thread and fasten it on again at the outer edge.

Slip the 1st mesh, make 6 meshes and join the two separate bands with 1 knot between the 3rd and 4th meshes, the last mesh of the left-hand band and the 1st mesh of the right-hand band; decrease in the last of the 6 meshes. Turn. Make 6 meshes. Turn. Make 5 meshes and from now on diminish in the last mesh of each row. Turn. Make 4 meshes. Turn. Make 3 meshes. Turn. Make 2 meshes. Turn. Slip the last 2 meshes.

Fig. 692.
Metal frame for filet lace.

Embroidered Filet (Filet Lace). Embroidered filet or filet lace is also known as guipure net, "filet Richelieu," Cluny guipure, etc. It consists of a foundation of plain filet on which delightful designs are reproduced.

Implements. The only implements required for embroidering filet lace are a light steel frame, scissors, and needles. It is in consequence a very popular form of needlework.

Metal frame for filet lace (fig. 692). The metal frame in which the filet foundation is mounted must be made of steel wire strong enough not to bend when the net is stretched tight. It can be square or rectangular, according to the shape of the work.

The wire is covered with cotton wool (fig. 692), round which a narrow ribbon or tape is then wound. This latter must be wound very tightly, especially at the corners of the frame, so that it will remain quite firm when the filet is secured to it. The end of the ribbon is fastened with a few stitches.

Mounting the filet in the frame without tape (fig. 693). When the filet foundation is of exactly the same size as the inside of the frame, it is merely secured with stitches drawn especially tight at the corners.

Mounting the filet in the frame with tape (fig. 694). If, on the other hand, the filet foundation is smaller than the frame, the former is edged all round with tape, which is eased on so that it is slightly gathered all round the filet. This makes it possible to stretch the filet very tightly without danger of breaking the threads of the outside meshes. Fig. 694 shows how the tape is sewn on, folded at the corners, and fixed in the frame.

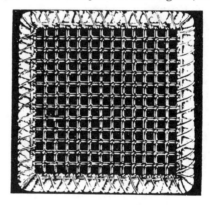

Fig. 693.
Mounting the filet in the frame without tape.

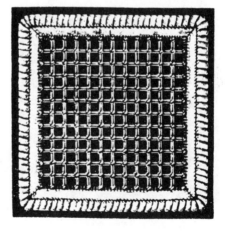

Fig. 694.
Mounting the filet in the frame with tape.

Needles. This work requires special long needles without points called filet darning needles.

Materials. Embroidery on filet should be worked in the same kind of material as the foundation. Twisted threads are used for the various lace stitches and for cloth or toile stitch. Floss threads are used for darning or reprise stitch and for outlining.

The best twisted threads for this kind of work are DMC flax lace thread, DMC flax thread for knitting and crochet, DMC 6 cord cotton lace thread, DMC Alsatia, or DMC pearl cotton. When the work calls for floss threads, we recommend DMC special stranded cotton, DMC floss flax or flourishing thread, DMC embroidery rayon, or DMC Persian silk.

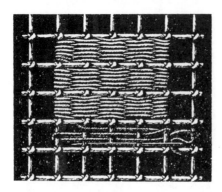

Fig. 695.
Darning or reprise stitch.

Stitches. The little squares of the filet serve as a foundation for a number of different stitches, and these stitches lend themselves to an infinite variety of combinations.

Darning or reprise stitch (fig. 695). This is the simplest of all the stitches used for embroidering filet lace. It is worked over a given number of squares, through which the thread is passed backward and forward as often as is necessary to fill them. This stitch is usually used when a design for counted stitches—a cross stitch design, for instance—is to be reproduced on a foundation of filet.

We particularly recommend this stitch, which is quickly worked and shows up the design to advantage, for large pieces of work, such as curtains and bedspreads.

Fig. 696. Cloth or toile stitch.
Laying the first threads.

Cloth or toile stitch (figs. 696, 697, 698). This is the stitch most frequently found in ancient embroideries; the solid parts of flowers, leaves, and borders are usually worked in it.

The thread is first fastened onto one of the knots of the foundation; it is then passed twice over and twice under the threads of the foundation so that every other thread passes, at the end of the row, under the thread of the foundation and over it when it is brought back. This forms the skeleton of the cloth stitch.

It is completed by the second series of stitches. This is worked like darning in linen (fig. 59), that is to say, the needle passes alternately under and over successive threads.

When the cloth stitch is to form a corner, the threads are first laid over a given number of squares.

The first series of threads must be left very loose. To ensure their all being exactly the same length, a fine gauge or coarse knitting needle is laid over the last square, and the threads are laid over this gauge. When a few squares have been worked in cloth stitch, the gauge is removed. The threads of the first series become gradually shorter as those of the second series pass alternately under and over them and draw them up or press them down, until they end by being just the right length to prevent the working of the last squares from being too tight.

When the corner is reached, the threads of the previous row are crossed, as shown in fig. 698. The first threads of the second side complete the cloth stitch in the corner square; from the second corner square the work is continued to the third and from the third to the fourth, always passing alternately under and over the threads of the first series.

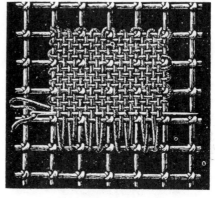

Fig. 697. Cloth or toile stitch.
Laying the second threads.

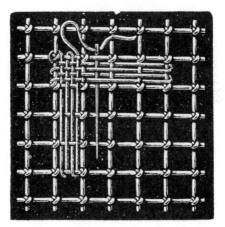

Fig. 698. Cloth or toile stitch.
Making a corner.

Lace filling stitch or interlocking lace stitch (figs. 699 and 700). This stitch is generally used to make a ground that is rather less transparent than the plain filet.

The thread is fastened onto the middle of a vertical bar of the filet, then a loop is made to the middle of the next horizontal bar; see fig. 699. These loops are always made from left to right; the thread is placed on the right, and the needle passes down under the bar and in front of the size of the loop must correspond to half the length of a bar of the filet.

In the second row, the work is turned, a stitch is made over the vertical bar of the foundation, and the thread is passed under the bar of the filet as in the first row. Then it is passed over the loop and under the bar which lies under the loop.

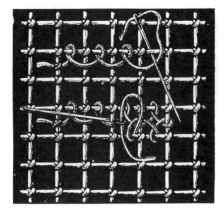

Fig. 699.
Lace filling stitch or interlocking lace stitch.
First and second rows.

In fig. 700 we show how the rows of interlocking lace stitch are linked together and how the needle is passed under the existing stitches.

Lace filling stitch or interlocking lace stitch, worked diagonally (fig. 701). To work this stitch diagonally (see fig. 701), the loops are made round the knots instead of the bars so that the stitches naturally follow each other in a diagonal line. The thread is passed round the knots, not over them, and the threads must be interwoven with perfect regularity.

As fig. 701 shows, only every other mesh of the filet can be filled; this ground is consequently much more transparent than the previous one. This stitch bears a close resemblance to Maltese cross stitch; see figs. 311 and 312.

Star composed of laid threads (figs. 702, 703, 704). To make this star, sixteen squares of the foundation must be allowed. The thread is fastened to the central knot of the sixteen squares, then it is passed diagonally from left to right under a knot of the

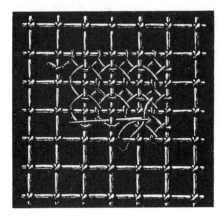

Fig. 700.
Lace filling stitch or interlocking lace stitch.
Series of completed rows.

filet, then back to the opposite corner of the square formed by the sixteen meshes and under the knot. Then three more threads are laid in the same direction. The lower rays of the star are formed in this way; see fig. 702.

The stitches which complete the figure are also begun in the center;

following the direction of the arrow, the filet is covered with three threads laid vertically and three more laid horizontally (see fig. 703).

When all these threads have been laid, the needle is passed four or five times under the laid threads—never under the foundation—then the thread is fastened off on the wrong side.

Fig. 704 shows a completed star.

Darned leaves (figs. 705 and 706). This is a type of stitch used principally for the fine, delicate leaves with which filet lace is often ornamented.

Fig. 701. Lace filling stitch or interlocking lace stitch, worked diagonally.

The needle is passed from the center, now to the right, now to the left, under the laid threads which form the foundation. Each stitch is pushed close to the preceding one by means of the needle. These stitches can easily be made perfect if it is remembered that the work should always be turned so the finished stitches are toward the worker. Three or four threads are laid first, as seen in the illustration; then the leaf is made, with one or often even with several veins.

When the leaf is to have only one vein, as in the left-hand part of fig. 706, the prepared threads are divided by the needle into two parts. When the leaves are of a certain width and require, for artistic effect, two or three veins, the threads are divided into three or four groups, as required.

Care must be taken in the working of these leaves that the stitches at the beginning and end

Fig. 702. Star composed of laid threads. Laying the lower threads.

be drawn tighter than those in the middle in order to give the latter more play. Fig. 706 shows two finished leaves, one with one vein, the other with two.

Darned points or pyramids (fig. 707). Besides stitches which fill the spaces of the foundation and leaves which cover them, little triangles can

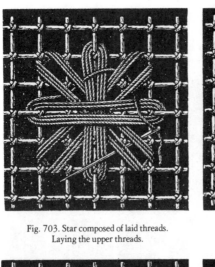

Fig. 703. Star composed of laid threads.
Laying the upper threads.

Fig. 704.
Star composed of laid threads, completed.

Fig. 705.
Darned leaves, begun.

Fig. 706.
Darned leaves, completed.

also be worked. The simplest form of these is worked as follows: the thread is carried from the corner knot to the middle of the bar and down again to the opposite knot, then up again to the middle of the bar. This makes a kind of scaffolding for the darning stitch, which is always begun at the top of the point.

Buttonhole points or pyramids (fig. 708). Another method, no less effective and no less easy, consists of making two buttonhole stitches on one side of the scaffolding and then passing to the other side, where the same process is repeated.

Veined points or pyramids (fig. 709). A third way of making points is begun by stretching a thread once up and down across the middle of the square. This done, the needle is passed from left to right under the center thread, then from above down under the left-hand bar, after which it is passed from right to left over the laid thread and under the right-hand bar, and so on.

Draw the thread fairly tight over the thread that it enlaces so that the stitches produce a round, very even vein on the wrong side. As many stitches are made as may be necessary to cover the thread well and fill the bottom of the square.

Points in Venetian stitch (open buttonhole filling stitch) (fig. 710). The daintiest points and those most in keeping with the general character of filet lace are those worked in Venetian stitch, commonly known as open buttonhole filling stitch. Seven or eight buttonhole stitches are first made over the bar of the foundation; then the same stitch is continued, backward and forward, decreasing by one stitch in every row, until only one stitch remains to be made, by which the point is attached to the upper bar. The thread is brought back on the wrong side for the next figure.

Darned and woven wheels (figs. 711 and 712). To make a wheel, the thread

Fig. 707. Darned points or pyramids.

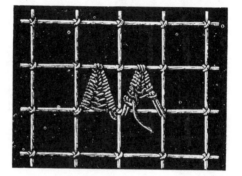

Fig. 708. Buttonhole points or pyramids.

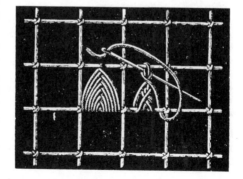

Fig. 709. Veined points or pyramids.

is fastened on at the junction of four squares; it is passed diagonally (see fig. 711, right-hand detail) over one space, then it is brought back to its starting

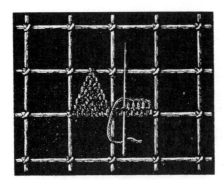

Fig. 710.
Points in Venetian stitch (open buttonhole
filling stitch).

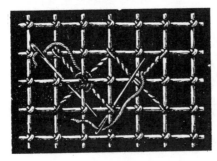

Fig. 711.
Laying the flat threads or spokes of a wheel,
and the wheel begun.

Fig. 712.
Darned and woven sheels.

point and at the same time wound round the first stitch a sufficient number of times to give the appearance of a closely twisted cord. This process is repeated across each of the four squares.

When the thread has returned to the center after making the fourth diagonal bar, it is passed spirally over the diagonal bars and under the bars of the filet as many times as may be necessary for the wheel to cover half the length of the bars of the filet; see fig. 711, left-hand detail.

In fig. 712, on the right, can be seen a wheel completed in this manner; this is known as a darned wheel. The left-hand drawing in the same illustration shows a woven wheel, in the making of which alternate threads are picked up and left as in darning. This illustration also shows how, when the thread that forms the skeleton of the wheel starts from the corner of the square formed by the four meshes, the first diagonal thread remains single until the wheel has been worked. When the latter is of the required size, the thread is secured by passing it in front of the double thread which forms the continuation of the single one, and then passed through the wheel to emerge at the opposite side and complete the first (single) thread.

Ribbed or back stitch wheels (fig. 713). The skeleton is prepared as for the preceding wheels. Then a back stitch is made over a bar of the filet; the needle is passed under the next bar, over which another back stitch is made; and so on until the threads of the filet are covered.

Ribbed or back stitch diamonds (fig. 714). No skeleton is made for diamonds; the back stitches are worked over the bars of the filet alone. Both sides of wheels and diamonds can be used in the same piece of work: in fig. 714 the wrong and right sides are seen side by side.

Wheels framed with interlocking lace stitch (fig. 715). A wheel may often be used in a large square which it cannot adequately fill; in this case it is surrounded with loops or lace filling stitches which fill the empty space around it. The left-hand side of the illustration shows very clearly how the thread, passing beneath the wheel and once round the thread of the foundation, is carried round the square to form eight loops. These loops are then picked up and the first circle round the wheel is completed. The second detail in the same illustration shows how a second thread is run through the loops to form a second circle, which is completed by overcasting. The third detail shows a completely finished wheel.

Buttonhole star (fig. 716). Few motifs in filet lace are so quickly

Fig. 713. Ribbed or back stitch wheels.

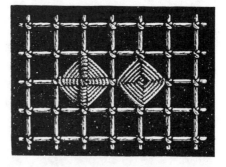

Fig. 714. Ribbed or back stitch diamonds.

Fig. 715. Wheels framed with interlocking lace stitch.

Fig. 716. Buttonhole star.

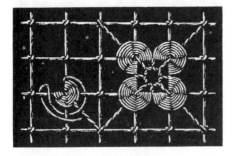

Fig. 717. Darned corners.

Fig. 718.
Cloth or toile stitch surrounded with darning stitch.

worked as the one illustrated in fig. 716. Two buttonhole stitches at the outer side and a simple crossing of the threads at the base form the little triangles which compose this charming star. The center square is ornamented with a little wheel.

Darned corners (fig. 717). Here we have a delightful little motif made with darning stitch worked over and under one diagonal bar and four bars of the foundation. The detail on the left shows a corner begun.

Cloth or toile stitch surrounded with darning stitch (fig. 718). It would be almost impossible to reproduce certain designs in filet lace if the outlines could not be softened by means of darning stitch as described in the preceding paragraph.

When cloth stitch is to be surrounded with darning stitch, there should be fewer rows of the latter than appear in fig. 717; also, instead of being ended at each corner, they can be carried all the way around a square, as in the left-hand detail of fig. 718.

Cloth or toile stitch surrounded with bars and overcast stitch (fig. 719). Overcast bars and overcast stitch are often used to edge motifs in cloth stitch. This can be done either in the thread used for the cloth stitch or in a coarser thread, which will make the framing stand out better.

Flower in bullion stitch on a foundation of cloth stitch (fig. 720). Bullion or post stitch, described in the chapter ''Embroidery on White Materials'' and illustrated in fig. 90, can be used to make varied details and additional ornaments on a foundation of cloth stitch.

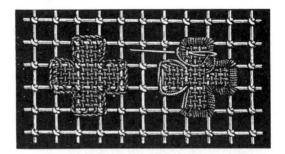

Fig. 719. Cloth or toile stitch surrounded with bars and overcast stitch.

Buttonhole edging (fig. 721). Scalloped edges in filet lace are surrounded with buttonhole stitch, always worked from right to left. An outline consisting of several threads is first made, over which the buttonholing is worked, and the bars of the filet are not cut until the whole of the edge has been finished.

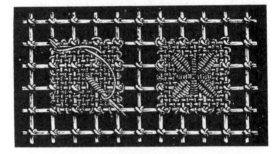

Fig. 720.
Flower in bullion stitch on a foundation of cloth stitch.

Cutwork in Filet Lace (fig.

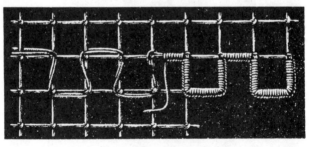

Fig. 721. Buttonhole edging.

722). Cutwork in filet lace consists of covering half the length of the bars of the filet with buttonhole stitches and cutting away the other half. The inner bars are often covered with a double row of buttonholing (see fig. 722) and knotted picots. The stitches of the first row of buttonholing are made not quite touching each other so that those of the second row can be worked between them; see the chapter ''Needlemade Laces,'' figs. 921 and 924.

Grounds Worked With Thread of One Thickness. In ancient filet

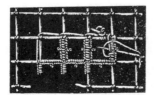

Fig. 722. Cutwork in filet lace.

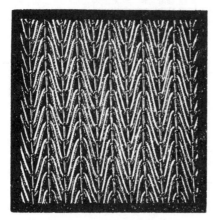

Fig. 723. Wave stitch ground.

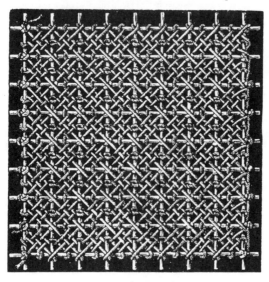

Fig. 724.
Ground in crossed lace filling stitch.

lace in which the motifs are filled with various grounds, these latter are worked sometimes with threads of two thicknesses, sometimes with only one. We will give first some simple grounds worked with thread of one thickness.

Wave stitch ground (fig. 723). This stitch is formed by passing the thread along each row of the foundation over two squares and under one knot.

Ground in crossed lace filling stitch (fig. 724). The whole surface to be embroidered with this ground is first covered with lace filling stitch (see fig. 700). When this is done, threads are laid diagonally. The first threads pass over the lace filling and under the knots of the filet; the second threads pass in the opposite direction, under the lace filling stitch and over the knots and the first threads. The crossing of these threads must be done very regularly and methodically.

Ground of darned squares and over-casting (fig. 725). Grounds in which darning stitch predominates or is used in equal proportion to other stitches are always heavier in appearance than the ones we have just described. They should therefore be used only for those parts of the design that are to give an effect of shadow or are to be very closely filled.

Fill the squares in diagonal rows with darning stitch (fig. 695). Make the stitches as close together as possible but the same number in each square; then lay a thread between the squares and on the return journey cover it with overcasting.

Ground of darned squares and small wheels (fig. 726). For the ground in fig. 726 squares are filled with darning stitch exactly as for the previous example, but instead of the long overcast bars a small wheel is worked in each open space.

Ground of darned squares and large wheels (fig. 727). In this ground, both darning stitches and wheels cover four meshes of the filet.

Ground of large wheels (fig. 728). Ground which are to cover a considerable extent can be ornamented with large wheels executed as shown in figs. 711 to 713.

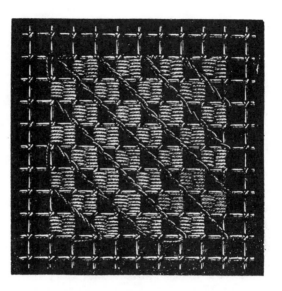

Fig. 725.
Ground of darned squares and overcasting.

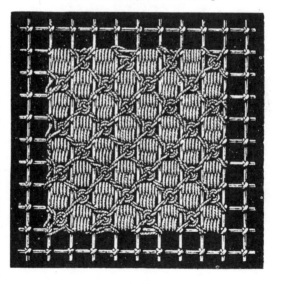

Fig. 726.
Ground of darned squares and small wheels.

Ground of darning stitch and cross stitch (fig. 729). After having, as always, worked the darning stitch first, proceed with the cross stitch. To ensure that the stitches are correctly formed, all the rows in one direction are worked first; in the succeeding rows, which cross these, the thread is passed between the stitches which were crossed in the first place.

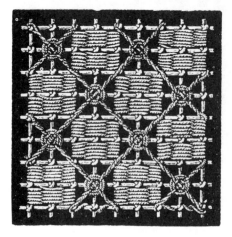

Fig. 727.
Ground of darned squares and large wheels.

Ground of geometrical figures (fig. 730). This stitch, which has no resemblance to the previous ones, consists of simple geometrical lines.

The thread is fastened onto a knot of the foundation and then passed, always in a diagonal line, under three other bars of the foundation. This process is repeated three more times, then the thread is secured by being wound once round the fourth bar. It is brought back to the knot already surrounded to begin another series of four encircling stitches like the ones just made. As the thread is always brought back to the point where the first square ended, there will be five threads on two sides of the square and four on the other two sides.

Grounds Worked in Thread of Two Thicknesses. We begin at this point the series of stitches, mentioned at the beginning of this chapter, which we have copied from

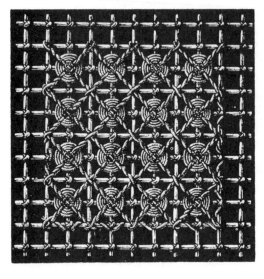

Fig. 728. Ground of large wheels.

one of the most curious and ancient examples of old filet lace in existence. Another piece of work of the same style served as a model for the insertion shown in fig. 751.

In all grounds worked in two kinds of thread, all the stitches which are to be worked in the coarser thread must be completed first.

Ground of darning stitch and lace filling stitch (fig. 731). The coarse thread is used for the oblong figures in darning stitch, with which the work is begun, and for the ovals which connect them; the lace filling stitch is worked in the fine thread.

Ground of small wheels and lace filling stitch (fig. 732). The wheels are worked first, in the coarse thread, over the bars of the filet only, covering all the surface to be worked. Then, with a finer thread, these are surrounded with lace filling stitch, worked in rows as shown in fig. 700.

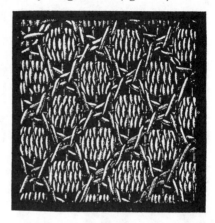

Fig. 729. Ground of darning stitch and cross stitch.

Ground of darned squares and lace filling stitch (fig. 733). Darning stitch, worked horizontally with coarse thread over squares consisting of four meshes, alternates with lace filling stitch in fine thread, covering the same number of meshes.

Diagonal ground with framed stitches (fig. 734). Pass the needle, threaded with coarse thread, from right to left under the first knot, then from left to right under the next. Repeat these

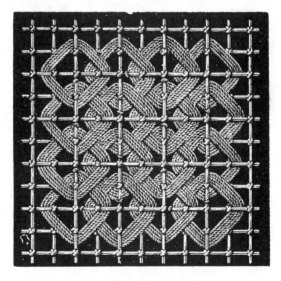

Fig. 730. Ground of darning stitch and lace filling stitch.

stitches twice in each direction so that the meshes of the filet have a double frame.

When the whole surface has been covered with these stitches, take the

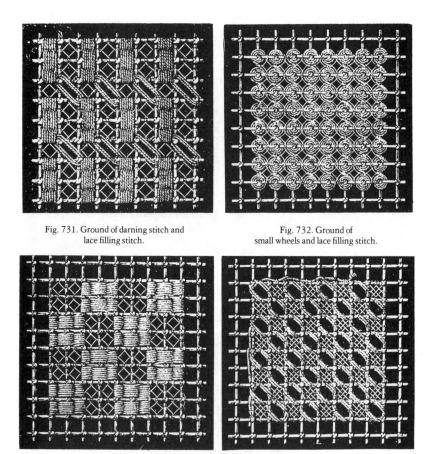

Fig. 731. Ground of darning stitch and
lace filling stitch.

Fig. 732. Ground of
small wheels and lace filling stitch.

Fig. 733. Ground of
darned squares and lace filling stitch.

Fig. 734. Diagonal ground
with framed stitches.

fine thread and work lace filling stitch into the squares between the rows of
stitches, always passing the needle over the double threads. Finally run
diagonal threads intersecting the lace filling stitch, passing the needle each
time through the knot of the filet.

Diagonal ground with cross stitch (fig. 735). For this stitch, which
is not unlike the preceding one, the meshes of the foundation are framed
with three threads in each direction; then a fourth and fifth row of stitches
are worked in finer thread, making cross stitches over those already made.

Darned Filet Lace Insertion (fig. 736). The insertion illustrated here
offers, to those who lack the patience necessary for minute and time-
consuming work, the means to produce a most delightful trimming for any
article, whether underlinen, curtains, or table linen.

The method of making the straight filet is shown in figs. 687 to 689; the darning stitch in fig. 695. For those who prefer not to make the filet by hand, we recommend the use of machinemade filet, an attractive, strong material which is an exact imitation of the handmade article.

The main design of the insertion is worked all in one direction; the small motifs of the edges, however, are worked in the opposite direction.

Square in Richelieu Filet Lace (figs. 737 and 738). Richelieu filet lace is distinguished from other types of filet lace by the simplicity of the work and the originality of the designs. It is worked on very fine filet and consists of flower and leaf motifs, forming little sprays, sometimes grouped round an elegantly shaped vase. The chief figures are worked in cloth toile stitch; their outlines, in coarse thread, stand out sharply against the filet. The same coarse thread is also used for the stems, twigs, and small sprays.

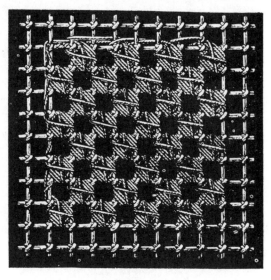

Fig. 735. Diagonal ground with cross stitch.

For the filet and the cloth stitch, a coarse grade of DMC flax lace thread or DMC Alsatia is used. The outlines are worked in a coarse grade of DMC flax lace thread or DMC pearl cotton.

The cloth stitch is worked in two rows, instead of the four shown in figs. 696 to 698. The thread is fastened onto a knot of the filet and the needle is passed over and under the bars of the filet, picking up every other bar; on the return journey, the threads left on the first journey are picked up. The second series of stitches, which completes the cloth stitch, is worked in the same way as the first, that is to say, one thread is picked up by the needle and the next is left, exactly as in darning on linen.

The outlining in coarse thread and the working of the small sprays and stems are clearly shown in the illustration and require no further explanation.

Filet Lace Square Embroidered in Various Stitches (fig. 739). We have already, in the preceding explanations, had occasion to point out the great advantage of using threads of different thicknesses and kinds together in making filet lace, but it is only in a fairly large motif that it is possible to really judge the happy effect produced by combining several threads noticeably different from each other in thickness and twist.

Fig. 736. Darned filet lace insertion.

The filet foundation of this square is made in DMC flax lace thread no. 30 in ecru. The cloth stitch parts are worked in DMC flax lace thread no. 45 in ecru; the darning stitch parts in DMC floss flax or flourishing thread no. 16 in corn yellow; while the lace filling stitch is worked in DMC flax lace

Fig. 737. Square in Richelieu filet lace.

thread no. 30 in ecru.

Many-colored Filet Lace Ground (fig. 740). This unpretentious design has a charm all its own, due chiefly to the variety of the materials and colors which appear in it.

The filet foundation, made with DMC pearl cotton no. 8 in dark brown, is covered first with scattered lace filling stitches worked in a pale shade of grey, connected by darning stitch in DMC pearl cotton no. 8 in moss green. DMC special stranded cotton no. 25 in geranium red is used for the little central squares, and the same material, in golden yellow, for the stitches which surround the red stitches.

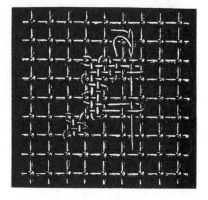

Fig. 738.
Method of working a small flower in cloth stitch. Detail of fig. 737.

Border and Allover Design in Filet Lace, Persian Style (fig.

741). The plain filet is made with DMC Alsatia no. 30 in red. The embroidery is worked in DMC embroidery rayon no. 60 in saffron and ash grey, used three strands at a time, which makes the work quicker to do and also makes the stitches stand out better. The zigzag lines which edge the narrow border are worked in yellow silk for the outer line and grey for the inner; each requires two rows, one in each direction.

In the first row, the thread is passed horizontally under two vertical bars, then diagonally up over the knot of the filet and under two vertical bars

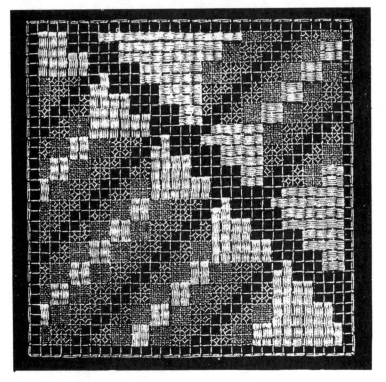

Fig. 739. Filet lace square embroidered in various stitches.

again, then down over a knot, under the next two vertical bars, and so on, until the whole row has been worked. The second row, which completes the zigzag line, is worked in the opposite direction, the thread passing over all the bars picked up on the first journey, and under the knots over which it passed before.

The border itself, worked in yellow, is also completed in two rows. In the first, the motifs in darning stitch are worked and the first threads laid for the bars which connect them. These are completed on the return journey, when the outlining of the darned figures is also done.

The detached figures in the upper part of the border are embroidered in yellow and grey. The yellow silk is used for the parts worked in darning stitch, and the grey for the lace filling stitch, which is worked diagonally; see fig. 701.

The ring which ends the vein at the bottom of the leaf is worked at the same time as the lace filling stitch; the mesh of the filet is first surrounded with a ring of stitches which serve as padding, and then covered with overcast stitches so as to form an overcast eyelet; finally a ring of running stitches is added.

Fig. 740. Many-colored filet lace ground.

The simple diamond pattern which forms the ground seen in the upper part of the illustration is worked in yellow, the thread run horizontally in zigzag lines over four meshes of the foundation.

Ground Worked on Filet With Meshes of Different Sizes (fig. 742). The fancy filet with plain mesh, oblong mesh, and double mesh, previously described and illustrated in fig. 684, reappears here richly embroidered.

For the single lace filling stitches the thread must be brought to the middle of the bar, then the loops forming the stitch are made and the thread is brought back to the starting point. There, the first spoke of the central wheel is laid, then the darning stitch is worked, three stitches of the latter crossing each other between only two bars of the filet, while the remainder

Fig. 741. Border and allover design in filet lace, Persian style.

are extended over four bars. Then the thread laid diagonally is covered halfway with overcast stitches and the thread is carried to the next corner to make the darned semicircle, and so on.

Ground Worked on Filet With Meshes of Different Sizes (fig.

Fig. 742. Ground worked on filet with meshes of different sizes.

Fig. 743. Ground worked on filet with meshes of different sizes.

743). Here the foundation consists of a large mesh and a square of nine small meshes, connected by oblong meshes. On this foundation, two kinds of stars are worked, as shown in the illustration. The larger figures are worked in darning stitch, in the shape of small pyramids surrounding a little star composed of threads laid and overcast. The smaller figures are made up

Fig. 744. Guipure net square.

of darned triangles, worked round a thread laid diagonally and forming a small wheel in the center.

Two Guipure Net Squares (figs. 744 and 745). These two squares, worked on a foundation of plain filet, lend themselves well to making chair backs or place mats, for which purposes they will look well alternating with squares of plain linen. They can also be made into an insertion by placing them side by side.

The outer edge could be trimmed with one of the filet lace edgings which follow. All these examples should be worked in DMC flax lace thread in a single thickness for both filet and embroidery.

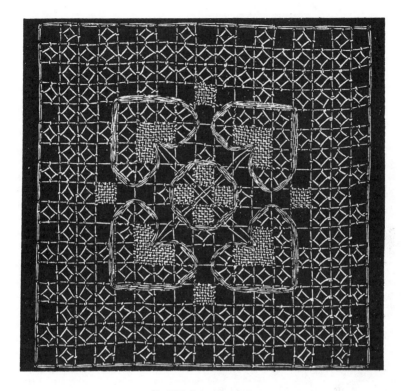

Fig. 745. Guipure net square.

When the filet has been mounted in the frame, the cloth stitch parts are embroidered first (see figs. 696 to 698), then the outer parts in lace filling

Fig. 746. Guipure net edging.

stitch (figs. 699 and 700). When these have been done, the small leaves in relief are worked in darning stitch with two veins (figs. 705 and 706); then the stems, the central wheel, and the circle in cloth stitch and darning

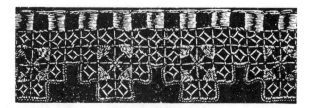

Fig. 747. Guipure net edging.

Fig. 748. Guipure net insertion.

stitch, which passes over the stems; and finally the lace filling stitch in the center of the circle.

The second square is worked in the same manner. When the lace filling stitch and the cloth‑ stitch parts have been worked, the outlines of the leaves are embroidered in six rounds of darning stitch, then the stems, and finally the middle circle, which also requires six rounds of darning stitch.

Two \ Guipure Net Edgings (figs. 746 and 747). The filet for these two edgings can be made either in a straight band or with a scalloped edge of open meshes, according to the instructions given at the beginning of this chapter. When the embroidery has been completed, the edge is buttonholed; then, if it has been worked on a straight band, the superfluous meshes are cut away.

In the edging in fig. 746, the ground is filled with lace filling stitch and the stars are worked in buttonhole stitch, as shown in fig. 716; they are ornamented in the center with a small wheel and surrounded with a circle consisting of four rounds of darning stitch, which makes the motif stand out better.

In the edging in fig. 747, the ground is also filled with lace filling

Fig. 749. Square in cut filet lace.

stitch; the heading consists of detached squares of darning stitch, while the principal figure is a square with a small ribbed wheel in the center and buttonhole triangles in the four corners.

Guipure Net Insertion (fig. 748).　This insertion is composed of two different motifs separated by cloth stitch bands. Each motif is surrounded by lace filling stitch and buttonhole triangles. The motifs themselves are made

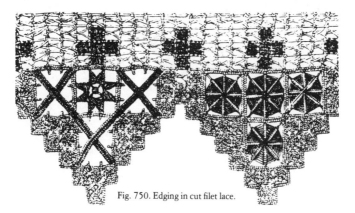

Fig. 750. Edging in cut filet lace.

up of buttonhole triangles variously arranged; a diamond in darning stitch surrounds the wheel worked in the center.

Fig. 751.

Design for insertion in German filet lace.

Square in Cut Filet Lace (fig. 749). There are few designs in which all the stitches so far described can be used to such advantage as in this square. The foundation is very fine filet. The embroidery, in a coarser thread, is worked in the following order: first the cloth stitch, then the lace ground and the ribbed wheels (fig. 713), the cut bars (fig. 722), the wheels set close together in the middle (fig. 728), and the darned bars (fig. 706).

Edging in Cut Filet Lace (fig. 750). In this edging, several colors are again used; thus the filet itself is made in white and the lace stitches are worked in cream; the wheels along the edge, which almost entirely fill the squares, are in the same color; for the ribbed wheels and the star, violet was used; and, for the long darned bars, golden green; the cloth stitch crosses are in mauve and green alternately.

Design for Insertion in German Filet Lace (figs. 751 and 752). This design is an example of eighteenth century German filet lace. Rich floral ornament stands out against a background of fine filet, whose meshes measure three millimeters. The flowers and leaves are filled with various stitches chosen from among those shown in figs. 723 to 735, except the small leaves, which are simply filled with lace filling stitch. The outlines are made with several rows of darning stitch worked so close together as to touch. For the veins, these darning stitch rows of ray out like a fan.

This kind of filet lace requires a tracing on jap silk which is fixed under the filet in the frame. All the outlines are run in with a fine thread using small stitches to follow the lines of the design; then the tracing is removed.

The actual embroidery is begun with the filling of the motifs; we recommend beginning with the stitches that require the most work and then working the simpler ones, which are more quickly done. Some of the filling stitches require thread of only one thickness, some require two. It goes without saying that the thread used for the embroidery must be suited to that which has been used to

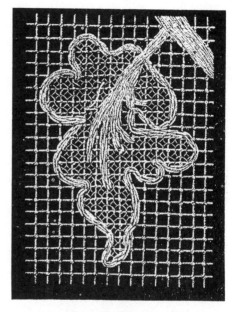

Fig. 752.
Detail of the insertion in fig. 751.

make the filet foundation. When all the filling stitches have been worked, the outlines are embroidered. Several rows of darning stitch are worked close to the tracing thread. All the outlines are of the same width and are composed of four rows of stitches, while the stems require ten rows. Finally, the veins are added, following the illustration; see also the explanatory detail in fig. 752.

DMC flax lace thread no. 40 was used for the foundation, outlines, and veins; nos. 16, 40, 50, and 70 was used for the filling stitches. This design could also be worked on filet with larger meshes, in which case coarser threads would have to be used.

The lace could be used to trim cushions or small panels; with a slight modification in the design it could be made into a border for curtains or blinds.

Embroidery on Fishnet. Since filet net is slow and laborious to make by hand, manufacturers have long had the idea of producing a machinemade material to replace it—in particular to replace fine- meshed filet. This material, generally known as fishnet, can be obtained today in various sizes of mesh in ecru, white, and in colors, and work executed on it can compare with the finest work on handknotted filet.

The most interesting of all types of embroidery on fishnet is that which is worked in flat stitch with colored silk on fine-meshed net. The earliest embroideries of this type, known as Sicilian embroidery, came from Italy and Spain, where this kind of work has always been particularly popular. Large designs are worked withfillings in darning stitch and embroidered outlines.

Fabrics. Modern fabrics are manufactured with various sizes of mesh in white, cream, and in colors.

Materials. Since fishnet is a very soft material, the embroidery should be worked in a floss thread, such as DMC special stranded cotton, DMC floss flax or flourishing thread, DMC embroidery rayon, or DMC Persian silk. Occasionally, the outlines are embroidered in a more tightly twisted thread, such as DMC flax lace thread, DMC knotting cotton, DMC pearl cotton, or even a metal thread.

Insertion embroidered on fishnet. Imitation of Richelieu filet lace (fig. 753). The foundation of this insertion is cream fishnet with large meshes, woven with fine thread; the working of the embroidery is the same as for the square shown in fig. 737.

DMC pearl cotton no. 8 in ecru is used for the cloth stitch, and DMC pearl cotton no. 3 in golden yellow for the outlining.

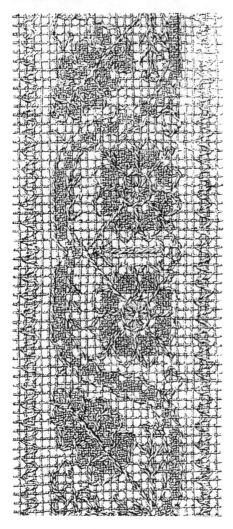

Fig. 753. Insertion embroidered on fishnet. Imitation of Richelieu filet lace.

Border embroidered on fishnet, Sicilian style (fig. 754). This border, worked in very rich colorings on a foundation of bronze net, is one

Fig. 754. Border embroidered on fishnet, Sicilian style.

of the most delightful designs in our volume, not only because of the simplicity of the flat stitch and Holbein stitch embroidery, but also because of the ease with which the number of colors used may be increased. Many cross stitch designs can be reproduced in this way, and almost all conventional flower designs can, with little modification, be translated into flat stitch embroidery on fishnet.

The embroidery itself is worked with counted stitches, without a tracing. This method of working has the additional advantage of making the passage from one shade to another very easy: all that is necessary is that the ends of the two colored threads be tied together with a reef knot.

Since most embroidery on fishnet is used unlined, it is essential to knot the threads together when passing from one color to another. This eliminates long, irregular stitches in all directions on the wrong side, which, owing to the transparency of the work, would be most disfiguring.

The reef knot is made in such a way that when it is drawn tight it comes at about the middle of the stitch. When several colors are used, it naturally follows that as many needles will have to be threaded as there are shades in use.

Fig. 755.
Border embroidered on fishnet in darning stitch with braided outlines.

Our border is worked entirely in DMC Persian silk. In the center of the large motifs are two small diamonds in yellow and two in green in a red frame, itself surrounded by four detached figures embroidered in dark blue. The carnations are worked in pale mauve or pale pink, with stems and

Fig. 756. Detail of the border in fig. 755.

calices in ivy green; the small figures in the corners of the blue figures are rust brown on the outside, with ivory inside.

The central design is completed at the four corners by rectangular figures worked in wallflower yellow and old rose; the diamond-shaped frame is embroidered in dark green, dark rose, dark mauve, and dark blue.

The repeats of the principal motif are worked in the same shades, except that they are so arranged that four pale mauve carnations are turned toward the inside of the border and one whole carnation and

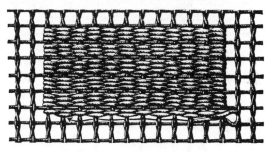

Fig. 757.
Darning stitch worked in fine thread.

two half carnations in pale pink toward the outside edge. The zigzag line in Holbein stitch is worked in dark rose and wallflower yellow; in the little flowers which end the border toward the outside edge, all the colors used for the border itself are used in succession.

Border embroidered on fishnet in darning stitch with braided outlines (figs. 755 and 756). Like embroidery on linen, embroidery on fishnet can be worked from a tracing. In this case, the motifs are covered with darning stitch and afterward outlined.

Fig. 755 shows a design of this type, part of which is shown in fig. 756.

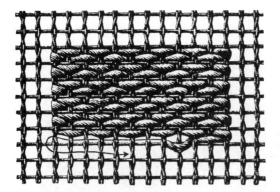

Fig. 758. Darning stitch worked in coarse thread.

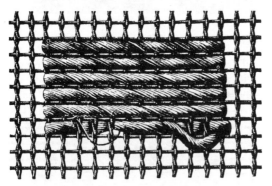

Fig. 759. Crossed darning stitch.

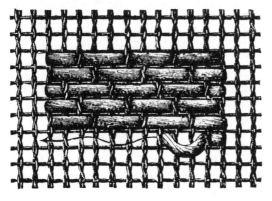

Fig. 760. Single darning stitch forming diagonal stripes.

As can be seen, the darning stitch is worked in one row, once backward and forward through the series of meshes, picking up every other thread of the foundation.

The outlining is done with two complementary rows of running stitches, that is to say, the second picks up those threads which were passed over in the first. Worked close to the darning stitch, these two rows form an outline resembling braid. The foundation is of dark blue fishnet; the darning stitch requires a floss thread, such as DMC Persian silk, in light brown; the outlines are worked in DMC pearl cotton no. 5 or DMC floss flax or flourishing thread no. 8 in geranium red. The DMC Persian silk can, if preferred, be replaced by DMC embroidery rayon or DMC special stranded cotton in light brown.

Various kinds of darning stitches (figs. 757, 758, 759, 760). We add here a few varieties of darning stitch which could equally well be used as fillings for the band shown in fig. 755. In fig. 757 we illustrate darning stitch worked in a fine thread, which necessitates passing five or six times through each row of meshes of the foundation. If, on the other hand, a thick thread is used, it will only be necessary to pass twice through each row of meshes; see fig. 758. Instead of regularly picking up every other thread, the stitches can be made over several threads, passing over the same number between; on the return journey, the meshes passed over are covered and the new stitches at the same time cross the previous ones; see fig. 759.

Finally, fig. 760 shows a stitch worked

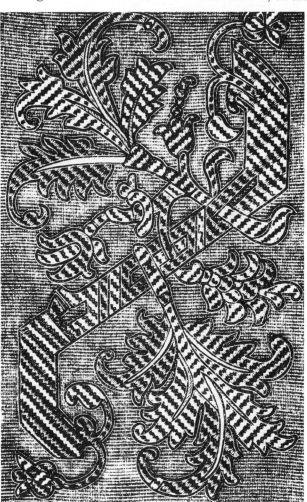

Fig. 761. Cushion embroidered on fishnet with filling stitches and braided outlines.

in a single row. The stitches are carried over two threads and the third is picked up. The diagonally striped effect is obtained by picking up a thread one mesh further to the left (or right) in each successive row.

Cushion embroidered on fishnet with filling stitches and braided outlines (figs. 761 and 762). There is more variety in the working of this design than the preceding one. There are different filling stitches, worked in

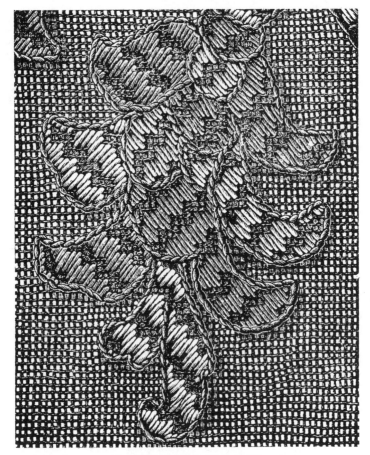

Fig. 762. Detail of the cushion in fig. 761.

two colors. The outline again consists of two complementary rows of running stitch forming a braid; see fig. 762. The veins of the leaves and the stems are worked in oblique flat stitch, the direction of which is changed according to the motif.

The foundation is dark red fishnet; two tones of yellow are used for the fillings and bright blue for the outlines. The finished work would be improved by being lined with material of the same shade of blue. This lining, showing through the meshes of the net, will soften the effect of the embroidery.

Insertion with rows of openwork and embroidered stars.

CHAPTER XV

Openwork on Linen

Openwork is the name given to those kinds of needlework in which some of the warp or weft threads, or both, are withdrawn from the material, and the isolated threads left by this process are drawn together in groups by means of various stitches to form open patterns. The different ways of grouping the threads and oversewing them with numerous stitches produce varied combinations and rich designs which can be used as the sole ornament of a piece of work. They can also be combined with any other type of embroidery, such as cross stitch.

There are two kinds of openwork on linen. One is produced by removing either the warp or the weft threads, and is known as drawn thread work or single openwork (the Italian "punto tirato"). For the second, both warp and weft threads are removed; this type is called cut-and-drawn work or cut openwork (the Italian "punto tagliato").

Openwork with drawn threads, as well as cut-and-drawn work, can be worked with the sewing machine. The machine, being quicker than the hand, is often preferred for large articles of household linen. Narrow, simple openwork strips can be worked without being mounted in a frame; but the frame is indispensable for rich designs with darned motifs and for cut-and-drawn work.

Materials. Fabrics woven with coarse threads, used to imitate medieval embroideries, require a thread of similar thickness to those of the fabric. This can be chosen from among the following: DMC flax lace thread nos. 6 and 12; DMC flax thread for knitting and crochet nos. 3, 4, 6, 8, 10, and 12; DMC 6 cord crochet cotton, DMC special quality crochet cotton nos. 5, 10, 15, and 20; DMC Alsatia nos. 15, 20, 25, 30, and 40; and DMC knotting cotton no. 20 or 30.

For finer materials, we recommend DMC flax lace thread or DMC flax thread for knitting and crochet in nos. 12, 16, 20, and 25; DMC floss flax or flourishing thread nos. 16 to 100; DMC 6 cord cotton lace thread nos. 30 to 90; DMC 6 cord crochet cotton and DMC special quality crochet cotton in nos. 30 to 100; as well as DMC Alsatian sewing cotton nos. 30 to 100.

If the embroidery is worked in colors, colored threads can also be used for the openwork; in such cases, DMC 6 cord cotton lace thread, DMC special quality embroidery cotton, DMC pearl cotton, DMC Alsatia, DMC special stranded cotton, DMC floss flax or flourishing thread, and DMC embroidery rayon are recommended.

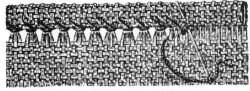

Fig. 763. Simple hem stitch.

Fig. 764. Another hem stitch.

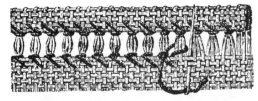

Fig. 765. Ladder hem stitch.

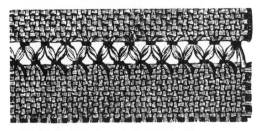

Fig. 766. Serpentine or trellis hem stitch.

Drawn Thread Work or Single Openwork (Punto Tirato). The openwork strips are produced, as has already been said, by withdrawing threads of the material in one direction only. Openwork hems are the starting point for this kind of work. These hems often take the place of the ordinary hem (fig. 8), when the latter is not considered decorative enough for the article being made.

To simplify the copying of the examples, we indicate in each case the number of threads to be withdrawn.

Simple hem stitch (fig. 763). According to the nature of the fabric, draw out from two to four threads below the edge of the turning, then tack down the hem two threads above the isolated strands. Fasten on the thread at the left, then pass the needle from right to left under three or four isolated threads, draw it out, and pass it from below up under one or two threads of the turning.

The same stitch is also used for securing the fringes of cloths and napkins (see the chapter "Needlework Trimmings," figs. 1121 and 1124).

Another hem stitch (fig. 764). This is prepared in the same way as the preceding and, like it, worked from left to right. But after the needle has been passed from right to left under three threads, it is inserted into the hem from above down over two threads so that it comes out exactly at the sharp edge of the fold. These stitches, which can also be worked on the right side of the article, form a kind of cord at the base of the hem.

Ladder hem stitch (fig. 765). After the first row of the hem stitching has been worked as in fig. 763, a few more threads of the material are drawn out, making from five to seven threads in all. The work is then turned the other way round, and a second row of stitches, like the first, is made. The same threads as in the first row must be taken up in each stitch in order to form vertical bars like the rungs of a ladder.

Serpentine or trellis hem stitch (fig. 766). Here again the first row is worked as in fig. 763, the number of threads taken up in each stitch being even. In the second row, the groups of threads are divided, each stitch taking up half of each of two groups, thus forming a zigzag line.

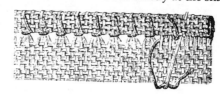

Fig. 767. Antique hem stitch.
Wrong side.

Fig. 768. Antique hem stitch.
Right side.

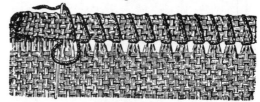

Fig. 769. Another antique hem stitch.
Wrong side.

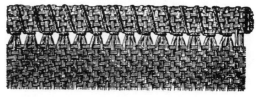

Fig. 770. Another antique hem stitch.
Right side.

Antique hem stitch (figs. 767 and 768). In the handsome linen embroideries of the Renaissance period, two ways of making a hem are often seen. These are, however, rarely explained in modern manuals of needlework. Figs. 767 to 770 show these two openwork hems on an enlarged scale.

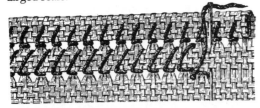

Fig. 771. Double-rowed openwork or Italian hem stitch.
Wrong side.

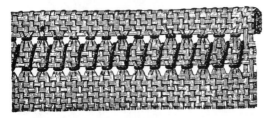

Fig. 772. Double-rowed openwork or Italian hem stitch.
Right side.

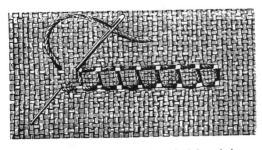

Fig. 773. Four-sided or square openwork stitch, worked
in horizontal rows. Right side.

Fig. 774. Four-sided or square openwork stitch, worked
in horizontal rows. Wrong side.

A single thread is drawn out at a sufficient distance from the edge to allow for a narrow hem (in transparent or very fine materials no thread is drawn out). This edge is then rolled (not folded). The thread is fastened on at the left and the stitches worked from left to right, as follows: pass the needle, from right to left, under four vertical threads of the rolled edge, draw it out, reinsert it and bring it out again in the middle of the threads which are to form the next group. That is to say, if the groups are to consist of four threads, the needle is brought out on the middle of these four threads and one thread below the upper edge of the rolled hem. Fig. 768 shows the right side of this hem.

Another antique hem stitch (figs. 769 and 770). The edge is rolled as for the hem just described. However, the stitches are worked from right to left. Instead of inserting the needle into the material, it is passed round the roll, thus making the stitch visible on both sides of the work.

Double-rowed openwork or Italian hem stitch (figs. 771 and 772). When one of the hems just described has been completed, another thread of the material is drawn out, leaving between the first and second drawn threads one thread more than the number of threads composing a group in the completed row. The same threads as before are then grouped together by the next row of stitches. The working of these stitches is shown in fig. 771; the right side, with the vertical stitches, can be seen in fig. 772.

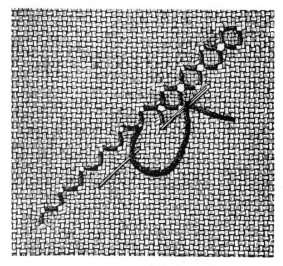

Fig. 775. Four-sided or square openwork stitch, worked in diagonal rows (single faggot stitch).

Four-sided or square openwork stitch. Before proceeding to openwork strips, we shall describe the manner of working four-sided openwork stitch, which is found in many types of embroidery on linen. Though this stitch is usually worked without withdrawing any threads from the material, it is nevertheless included in the category of openwork stitches because it presents an open appearance and is used in the same kinds of work and for the same purpose as true openwork.

This stitch is never used for working an entire design; it is only used for embroidering insertions or strips, or for dividing a large design in flat stitch into squares or diamonds.

Four-sided openwork stitch is found in ancient embroideries on linen of Italian and German origin, as well as in Hungarian and Slavonic work. It can be worked in straight or diagonal lines; in the first case it is worked in one row, in the second in two rows. The stitches are made over three or four threads of the fabric; by drawing the working thread very tight, the threads of the material are brought close together and the openwork pattern is thus produced.

Four-sided or square openwork stitch worked in horizontal rows (figs. 773 and 774). The stitch is worked in rows from right to left. Begin with a vertical stitch up over four threads. Then the needle is passed, at the back of the work, down and four threads to the left, and a horizontal stitch is made at the bottom, from left to right, the needle being reinserted at the exact spot where the vertical stitch begins. The needle is then passed, at the back of the work, up and four threads to the left, and another horizontal

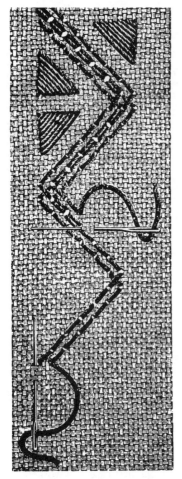

stitch is made to the right, the needle entering the material at the top of the vertical stitch. The needle is then brought out again at the left-hand end of the lower horizontal stitch, another vertical stitch is made from this point to the left-hand end of the upper horizontal stitch, and so on.

Four-sided or square openwork stitch, worked in diagonal rows, and reversed faggot stitch (figs. 775 and 776). Four-sided openwork stitch, worked in diagonal rows, is also known as single faggot stitch. The working is begun on the right, with a horizontal stitch over four threads, then the needle is brought down diagonally under four threads to the left and a vertical stitch is made up on the right side, the needle reentering the material at the left-hand end of the horizontal stitch. Another oblique stitch is now made on the wrong side, slanting toward the left to enable another horizontal stitch to be made to the right, and so on. The row should end with a vertical stitch.

The second row, which completes the stitch, is made in the same way, but is begun with a vertical stitch, so as to complete the squares. On the wrong side of the work, this stitch produces two single lines and one double line of diagonal stitches.

Fig. 776. Reversed faggot stitch worked in zigzag lines.

The wrong side of this stitch is often used for the right side of the work. In this case, the oblique stitches are made on the right side and the squares on the wrong side. Worked in this way, it is known as reversed faggot stitch.

In fig. 776, we show this stitch used in zigzag lines to form a narrow insertion. Where the direction of the lines changes, the oblique stitches form cross stitches.

Various Ways of Working Drawn Thread Work or Single Open-work. Openwork patterns can be produced in various ways: (1) by crossing the groups of threads, (2) by knotting the groups, (3) by embroidering over the groups, and (4) by connecting the groups with small decorative motifs.

Various ways of crossing the groups of threads (figs. 777, 778, 779, 780, 781, 782). The groups are crossed with the help of a needle, thread-

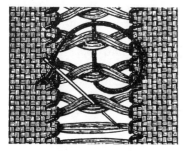

Fig. 777
Whole groups crossed once.

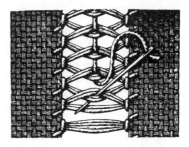

Fig. 778.
Groups divided and crossed once.

ed with coarse thread, which is passed under a group; this group is at the same time slipped over a preceding group. To maintain the groups in their new positions, the thread is drawn through between them.

The groups can be crossed in a single row or in several parallel rows; the groups may be taken whole, or divided, or several at a time, as will be seen in the examples that follow.

We begin with narrow strips worked in a single row; fig. 777 shows the simplest form: two complete groups crossed once. To work it, the second group, as we have just said, is slipped over the first, and the coarse thread is passed over the second and under the first group.

For the strip in fig. 778, the groups are divided before being crossed, which produces a less open effect. In the strip in fig. 779, each complete motif is composed of two whole groups and four half groups. In fig. 780, the motif consists of four groups crossed in one operation. The third and fourth

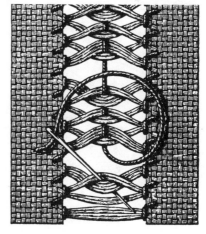

Fig. 779.
Two whole groups crossed once with
four half groups.

groups are slipped over the first and second, thus producing a single crossing in the motif.

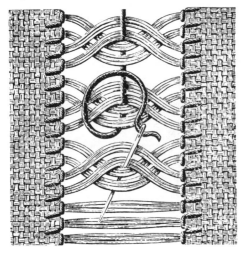

Fig. 780.
Four groups crossed once in pairs.

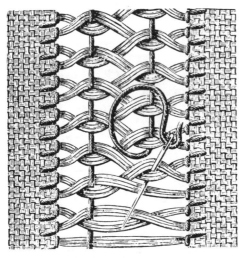

Fig. 781.
Two groups crossed once, in two rows.

We add two more designs in which the groups are crossed in two parallel rows. Fig. 781 shows a double row of the pattern in fig. 777, and fig. 782 a double row crossed twice, in which the first group is interlaced with the third and the second with the fourth. The position of the needle shows how the second row is worked.

Various ways of knotting the groups of threads (figs. 783, 784, 785, 786, 787). Strips with knotted groups constitute a second variety of openwork on linen. Knotted groups can be worked in one row or several parallel rows, and the auxiliary thread which is used to make the knots may either be visible and form part of the design itself, or it may be used for the knots only and pass more or less invisibly from one group of threads to another.

For simple openwork patterns, the threads are knotted together with a knot consisting of a coral stitch; in richer designs, overcasting and buttonhole stitch are used in addition.

We begin our series of examples with strips worked in one row and in which the auxiliary thread remains visible. Fig. 783 shows the working of a reversed chain stitch knot in a strip consisting of triple groups, knotted once. The thread with which the knotting is done passes vertically down and connects the groups. For the pattern in fig. 784, the groups are knotted together in fours, which are divided for the second row, producing a trellis effect.

In the examples which follow, the thread which is used to make the knots passes over the groups, without showing in the open spaces of the design.

For the strip in fig. 785, the groups are knotted together in fours; the zigzag bars in the middle are lightly overcast. The strip in fig. 786 is worked in two rows, the groups being knotted together in sheaves of six; the bars in the middle, arranged in diamonds, are covered with buttonhole stitch. Fig. 787 shows the use of knot stitch to join two groups in a wider strip. In this way, small isolated crosses are made, unlike those in fig. 783, where the motifs are visibly connected by the thread with which the knots have been made.

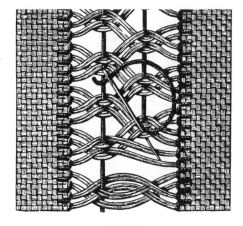

Fig. 782.
Four groups crossed twice, in two rows.

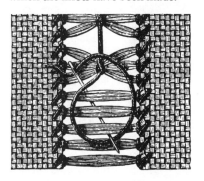

Fig. 783. Triple groups knotted once, with a vertical thread.

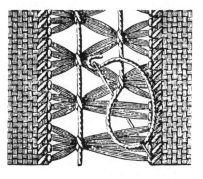

Fig. 784. Quadruple groups, divided and knotted twice, with two vertical threads.

Various ways of embroidering over the groups of threads (figs. 788, 789, 790, 791). The third category of drawn thread work comprises openwork strips with embroidered groups. The stitch most often used for this type of openwork is darning stitch (also known as ''needle weaving''), sometimes accompanied by overcasting and buttonhole stitch.

Fig. 788 shows how to make the overcast bars that are used to ornamena narrow hem or make openwork grills in large pieces of work. As fig. 788

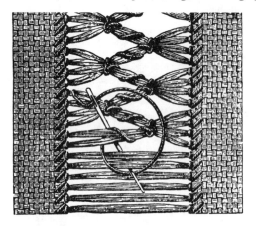

Fig. 785. Groups knotted together once in fours, with a zigzag overcast design.

shows, the thread is carried down through the group to be overcast; then, beginning at the bottom, the group—composed in this case of four threads of the material—is entirely covered with overcast stitches.

Fig. 789 shows zigzag overcast bars. In this case the bars are worked alternately up and down over groups of only three threads. The bars are joined at the top and bottom by two overcast stitches over the six threads together; in this way the zigzag effect is obtained.

Darned bars (fig. 790) always require groups containing an even number of threads. The bars are worked from right to left, backward and forward, the needle always entering the middle of the group. When the bar is finished, thework is turned so that the next bar can be worked in the same direction, that is to say, with the finished part on the right of the needle.

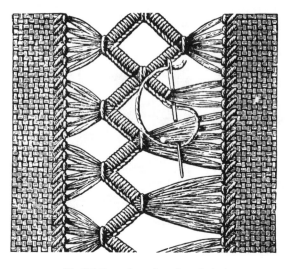

Fig. 786. Groups knotted together twice in sixes, with a diamond design in buttonhole stitch.

To illustrate how large motifs can be worked in needle weaving, we give in fig. 791 a strip composed of pyramids, shown in the course of work so that the method can be followed. The needle passes backward and forward under and over a given number of groups until all the threads of the material are entirely covered.

Drawn Thread Strip in Three Rows (fig. 792). The examples of openwork strips which follow can be used equally well as ornaments to a hem, as insertions, or to divide bands of embroidery or material; they can even on many occasions take the place of lace.

The simple strip in three rows, shown in fig. 792, is so easy to work that it can always be used with advantage when a rich effect is desired but little time is available. The stitch shown in fig. 763 is repeated six times: the first and sixth times for the outside edges of the strip; the second and fifth times for the inner edges of the outer rows, for each of which six threads of the material are withdrawn; and the third and fourth times for the two edges of the center row, for which eight threads are withdrawn. All the groups must consist of an even number of threads. The first and third rows are worked as in fig. 766, the middle row as in fig. 765. The threads in the vertical groups in the middle row are divided equally; then the needle is inserted from right to left under half the threads of the second group and, with another movement, the eye of the needle is brought back from right to left, and the second half of the first group is picked up and passed under and in front of the first group. Care should be taken not to draw the thread too tight.

Openwork Strip With Threads Crossed Three Times (fig. 793). Draw

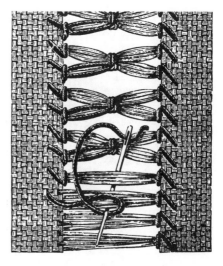

Fig. 787. Double groups knotted together with knot stitch.

Fig. 788. Isolated overcast bars.

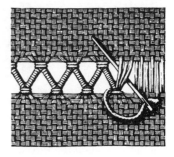

Fig. 789. Zigzag overcast bars.

out twenty-five threads of the material; keep the threads of the edges from pulling out by means of slanting overcast stitches over six threads.

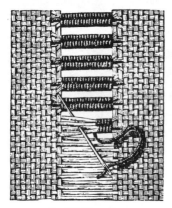

Fig. 790. Darned bars.

The threads are divided into groups, then crossed in the middle as shown in fig. 792, after which another thread is run in on each side of the first, following the groups made by the first thread. This done, these two threads and the groups of threads of the material are overcast. The groups are, as it were, held between two threads.

Openwork Strip With Two Rows of Clusters (fig. 794). Remove two sets of twelve threads, leaving four threads between, and work the edges as in fig. 763 over two threads. The working thread is fastened on and passed three times round three groups. At the third turn, the needle is passed under the first two turns to secure the thread. The thread, in its passage from one cluster to the next, should always be allowed a little play. Groups thus tied together in clusters are sometimes known as "faggots."

Openwork Strip in Needle Weaving (fig. 795). Draw out fourteen threads. The working thread is passed from one bar to the next in such a way that it is concealed under the darning stitches, which are worked backward and forward over ten threads until these threads are covered halfway up. The needle is always passed between the threads eye first, the point turned toward the thimble.

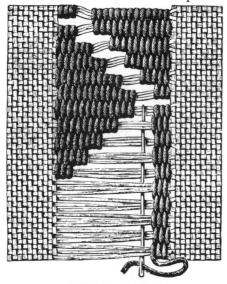

Fig. 791. Darned pyramids.

To pass to the second group of threads, the needle is inserted under the last darning stitches and under the isolated threads; the second group is then begun by dividing the threads as shown in the illustration. The working of darning stitch is also explained in the chapter "Filet Lace"; see figs. 695 and 705.

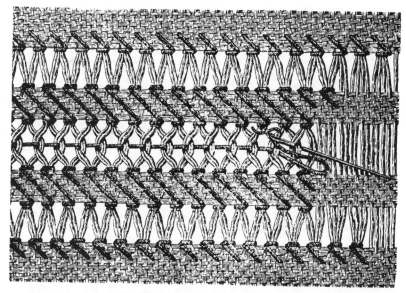

Fig. 792. Drawn thread strip in three rows.

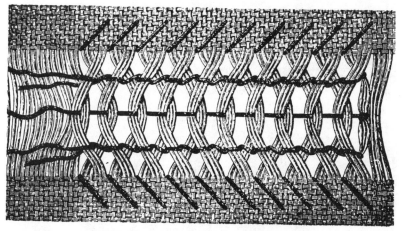

Fig. 793. Openwork strip with threads crossed three times.

Openwork Strip in Needle Weaving Worked in Three Colors (fig. 796). Eighteen threads of the material having been withdrawn, the groups of threads are assembled in the same way as for fig. 795, and the same stitch is worked. The groups or bars, worked also over ten threads, can be done in different colors. Our example is worked in three colors, the same shade being used for three bars arranged diagonally.

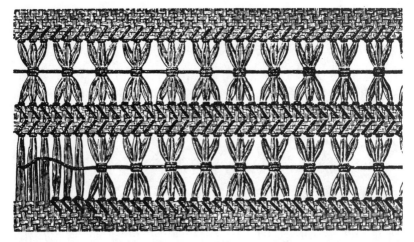

Fig. 794. Openwork strip with two rows of clusters.

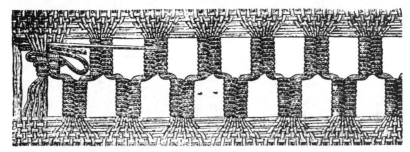

Fig. 795. Openwork strip in needle weaving.

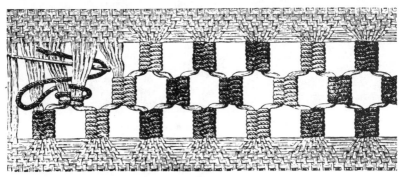

Fig. 796. Openwork strip in needle weaving worked in three colors.

Openwork Strip With Detached Clusters (fig. 797). For this strip twenty threads are withdrawn. The stitches which edge it are worked over four threads, according to the instructions for fig. 773. The groups, secured and assembled at the edges, are covered in the middle with from ten to twelve darning stitches. The thread is fastened off after the completion of each bar.

Openwork Strip With Alternated Groups (fig. 798). Before remov-

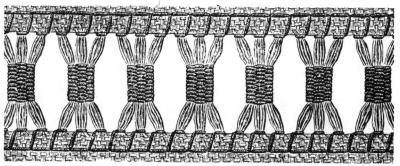

Fig. 797. Openwork strip with detached clusters.

ing the fifteen threads which have to be drawn out for the openwork, work the four-sided stitch on both sides. The thread is carried up over four threads, then horizontally under three threads to the right; a back stitch is made to the left, and the needle passes diagonally on the wrong side to emerge three threads to the right of the starting point of the vertical stitch;

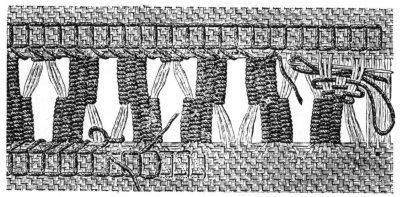

Fig. 798. Openwork strip with alternated groups.

another back stitch is made to the left; and the next square is begun with another vertical stitch. The course of the stitches on the wrong side is shown by a dotted line, that of the stitches on the right side by black lines.

The darning stitch is then worked over nine threads, that is to say, three groups, as far as the center of the openwork. At that point, one group, on the left and right alternately, is dropped and another group taken up to compensate. This produces a design in which groups of uncovered threads and darned bars are arranged in alternating pairs. The strip is completed by oblique overcast stitches over the threads left between the border of four-sided stitch and the openwork.

Openwork Strip in Needle Weaving and Overcast Stitch (fig. 799). Draw out twenty threads. The openwork is edged with overcast stitches over three vertical and three horizontal threads. This row of overcast stitches is followed by another, in which the stitches are made in the same direction over three, six, and nine threads.

The working thread is wound six times round the first group of three

Fig. 799. Openwork strip in needle weaving and overcast stitch.

threads of the material, then brought back to the edge, where it passes to the second and third groups. Six darning stitches are made over these two groups, followed by twelve darning stitches over the first and second groups, leaving just the length necessary for the six overcast stitches over the first group. The second part is worked to match, in the opposite direction.

Openwork Strip in Needle Weaving Worked in Four Colors (fig. 800). Remove twenty-eight threads. The pyramids are worked over six groups of three threads each in a medium and a dark shade of the same color. The center figure, worked in a third shade, lighter than the two others, takes up three groups from the left and three from the right. The small dark square or kernel in the middle is worked in a contrasting color, dark red or black.

Persian Openwork Strip With Single and Double Bars (fig. 801). For this design, thirty threads are drawn out, and each repeat of the design requires twenty groups of three threads. The whole of the work is done in needle weaving, in three colors.

Persian Openwork Strip, Check Design (fig. 802). This design, for which thirty-two threads are drawn out, can also be worked in three dif-

Fig. 800. Openwork strip in needle weaving worked in four colors.

Fig. 801. Persian openwork strip with single and double bars.

ferent colors or shades. One repeat of the design requires twenty-two groups of three threads each.

Openwork Strip With Darned Wheels (fig. 803). Draw out sixteen threads. The threads of the edge are held with herringbone stitch (fig. 83). Each wheel takes in four groups of threads. The thread is fastened on in the middle of the strip and passes alternately over and under one group. Several spiral turns are made, as in darning. Then, when the needle is at the point where the thread entered to form the wheel, it is passed under the wheel to

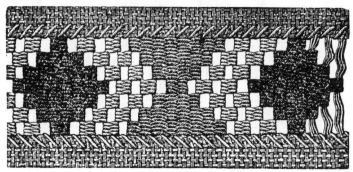

Fig. 802. Persian openwork strip, check design.

reach the next four groups. For the working of the wheels, see also the chapter "Filet Lace," figs. 711 and 712.

Openwork Strip in Three Rows With Darned Wheels (fig. 804). In this case, five threads are drawn out for each of the narrow rows, and twenty-two threads for the wide row; the threads are assembled in

Fig. 803. Openwork strip with darned wheels.

groups of four. The rows are edged with herringbone stitch, which can be worked on the right or the wrong side; see figs. 82 and 83. The groups in the middle row are held together on both sides by knotted back stitches, as shown in the illustration; they are then bunched together in the middle with three overcast stitches, after which the thread is carried to the intersection of the two threads used to make the first two lines of stitches, and a wheel is worked over five threads before passing on to the next cluster.

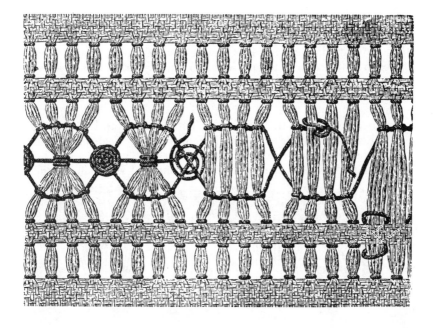

Fig. 804. Openwork strip in three rows with darned wheels.

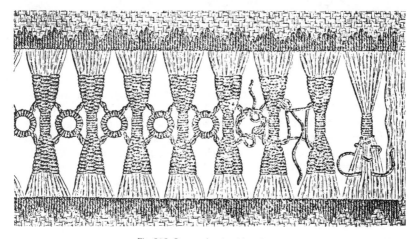

Fig. 805. Openwork strip with eyelets.

Openwork Strip With Eyelets (fig. 805). Remove twenty-eight threads. The edges are ornamented with reversible stitches over from two to five threads from the edge. The design itself is begun in the middle, over nine threads, with eight or nine overcast stitches. These nine threads are then divided into three equal parts, and from twelve to fourteen darning stitches are added on either side of the overcasting, leaving at most only a fifth of an inch of the threads uncovered. When two darned bars have been completed, they are joined with four buttonhole stitches, the single thread is interlaced several times, and the ring thus made is covered with close overcasting.

Openwork Strip With Bullion Stitch Rosettes and Picots (fig. 806). Remove twenty-four threads. The edges are ornamented with reversible stitches over two, three, four, and five threads. The overcast bars require four threads each; the darned bars ornamented with bullion stitch

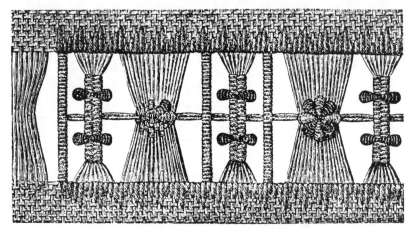

Fig. 806. Openwork strip with bullion stitch rosettes and picots.

picots require eight threads (for the method of working bullion stitch, see the chapter "Embroidery on White Materials," fig. 90); and the foundation of the rosettes require sixteen threads. These sixteen threads are drawn together by means of a darned wheel which is afterwards entirely covered with bullion stitches. The loops which connect the bars are made in the course of working the bars and wheels themselves. When the required point is reached, the thread is carried across to the previous bar and then back to the bar that is being worked in order to complete the latter. As can be seen in the illustration, the model is worked in two shades.

Making Corners in Openwork Strips (figs. 807, 808, 809, 810). When the openwork is used to edge a square piece of work, the threads are cut half an inch from the edge of the hem or from the edge of the openwork itself and detached, as can be seen in fig. 807. The detached threads are turned back into the fold of the hem and secured there by means of buttonhole stitches (fig. 808), or, if the stitch used for the hem is such that it cannot be interrupted, they are turned onto the wrong side of the work and secured there by a few stitches (fig. 809). Fig. 810 shows an openwork strip in which the empty space at the corner has been filled with a darned wheel.

The thread with which the openwork design has been worked is carried across the open space to the opposite side, where it is inserted into the hem, and brought back to the center of the open space where the wheel is to be made; the other spokes of the wheel are made, the wheel is worked over seven spokes, and the thread is stopped on the side opposite to the second strip; it is then passed through the wheel, and the eighth spoke is made by passing the thread to the second strip.

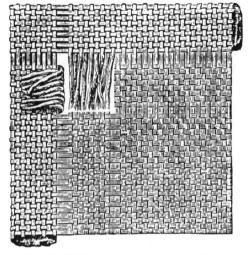

Fig. 807. How to cut and detach the threads at the corners.

Making Corners in Openwork Strips Consisting of Several Rows (figs. 811 and 812). This can be done in two different ways: either the band of solid material can be maintained between the rows at the corner, the threads of the inner rows being cut at the required distance inside the outer rows, or all the threads can be drawn out to the hem. We give here an example of each method.

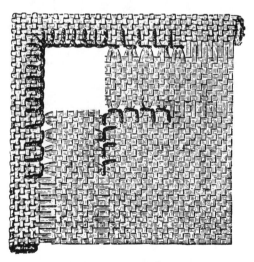

Fig. 808. Securing the threads at the corner with buttonhole stitches.

Fig. 811 shows the corner of the openwork strip in fig. 804, in which the material has been left between the rows. The small open spaces in the corners have been filled with plain four-spoked wheels, while the large space has been filled with a double twelve-spoked wheel. For the working of the wheels, see the chapter "Filet Lace," figs. 711 and 712.

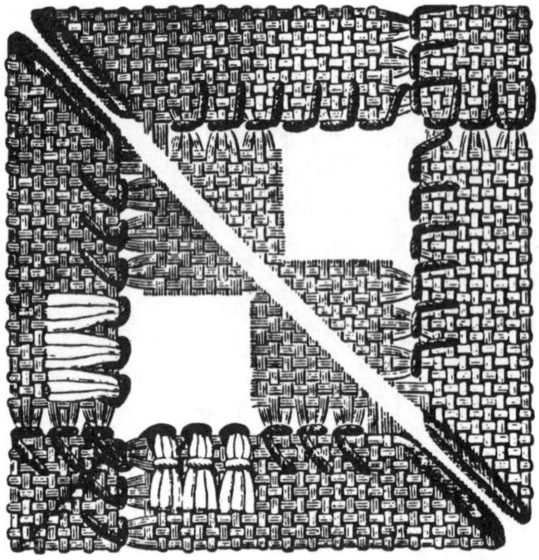

The corner in fig. 812, for the openwork strip in fig. 794, requires more work. Here all the threads have been cut close to the hem; the free threads left by the removal of the threads from the dividing bands of material are converted into bars with darning stitch (see figs. 705 and 790), and the four open spaces are filled with eight-spoked wheels.

Yugoslav Openwork Strip (fig, 813). For the working of openwork strips of a certain width, the women of Yugoslavia have discovered a very practical method. The design, which is fairly large, is worked in several steps, that is to say, it is divided into several strips separated by narrow bands of material. For the example we illustrate, three sets of nine threads are withdrawn, separated by three threads of the material. It is advisable to begin by drawing out the first and last threads of each row, and then to embroider the edges of the

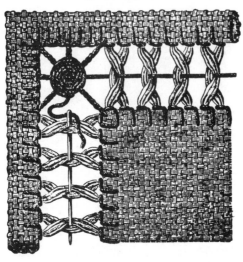

Fig. 809. Turning in and securing threads.
Right and wrong sides.

Fig. 810. Filling up a corner with a darned wheel.

material and the intermediate bands. Then the remaining threads of the first row are removed, and the first part of the design is worked. The greater part of the work is done in needle weaving, the rest consists of overcast bars.

When the first row is finished, the second is drawn out and worked, then finally the third.

Ukrainian Myreschka and Prutik Drawn Thread Work. The Ukrainians have long practiced a type of openwork characterized by its particular method of working. The threads are cut horizontally only, and the free vertical threads are overcast at the same time as the horizontal bands of material.

This Ukrainian work is divided into two groups known as Myreschka and Prutik. In the former, the design is formed solely by darning stitch; in the latter, darning stitch alternates with overcast bars. We recommend cutting the threads by degrees as the work progresses, that is to say, one row at a time and not all the rows required for the whole border at once.

Ukrainian Myreschka drawn thread work (fig. 814). The stitch which edges the border at the top and bottom is the same as the one described in fig. 813; it requires the drawing of two threads

Fig. 811. Formation of the corner for the openwork strip in fig. 804.

Fig. 812. Formation of the corner for the openwork strip in fig. 794.

and is worked over five threads in width. For the design of the border itself, five threads are drawn out for each row, with a space of four threads between the rows. All the rows are worked from right to left, except the upper edge, which is worked from left to right.

The band of material, four threads in width, is covered with vertical stitches—5 threads apart, like those of the first row at the edge—which at the same time lead from one group of darning stitches to another. Beginning at the right, sufficient vertical stitches are made, according to the design, to reach the left-hand end of the first darned figure. From this point,

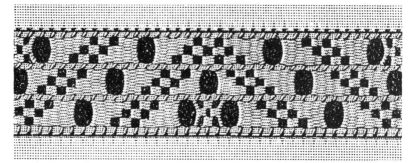

Fig. 813. Yugoslav openwork strip.

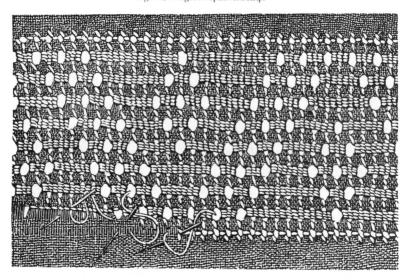

Fig. 814. Ukrainian Myreschka drawn thread work.

the thread is laid from left to right over all the groups of threads to be covered by the darning stitch. Then, returning, the thread is passed under each group, and between each group and the next a vertical overcast stitch is made over the thread laid over the groups. The method of laying and overcasting the thread is shown in the illustration.

In each row this process of laying and overcasting threads is repeated three times, after which vertical stitches are made over the band of the

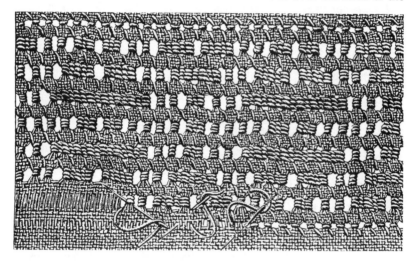

Fig. 815. Ukrainian Prutik drawn thread work.

Fig. 816. Spanish openwork.

material, to reach the next figure. The succeeding rows are worked in the same way, following a sketch or embroidered model. The final row, consisting of the same stitch as the first, is worked from right to left, like the other rows of the design.

Ukrainian Prutik drawn thread work (fig. 815). This type of work is very similar to Myreschka work. However, it produces a more open effect, due to the overcast bars forming the ground, against which the darned figures stand out clearly. These bars, which distinguish Prutik from Myreschka work, are composed of three overcast stitches over a group of threads; see fig. 815.

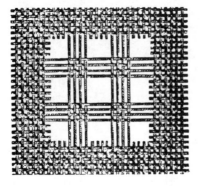

Spanish Openwork (fig. 816). This Spanish openwork strip is begun by edging the strip at the top and bottom with a row of four-sided stitch worked over four threads of the material, leaving a space of fifty threads between for the openwork. The same stitch is repeated above and below at a distance of eight threads from the first row. The thread which crosses the groups unites them in clusters of eight and six. On either side of this central thread, three threads are laid in undulating lines which intersect in the center of the large rosettes and, in the intermediate figures, join and cross the groups; see fig. 816, at one end of which these threads are shown uncovered.

Fig. 817. Cutting threads in the interior of the fabric.

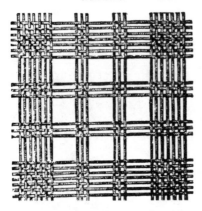

Fig. 818. Drawing out threads over the whole surface of the material.

When the groups have thus been arranged and secured in clusters, they are embroidered upon. This work is begun with the large, ten-petalled rosette; the little pyramids which compose this are worked in darning stitch, beginning at the center. The whole is then surrounded with coral stitches. The second row of coral stitches is made at the same time as the small oval figure which connects the rosettes. It must therefore be worked in two rows. In the second row, add the little wheels at the points where the ovals join the outer ring of knot stitches. Finally, work the remaining parts in darning stitch, and add two double buttonhole stitches to the middle groups of threads of the large rosettes.

Cut Openwork (Cut-And-Drawn Work, Punto Tagliato). For cut openwork, threads of the material are drawn out in both directions. The number of threads to be drawn out depends not only on the design to be worked, but also on the nature of the fabric on which it is to be carried out. The threads which remain between the open spaces serve as a foundation for various stitches.

Preference should be given to materials in which the warp and weft threads are of the same thickness, so that the open spaces formed by the removal of the threads will always be exactly square.

Cutting threads in the interior of the fabric (fig. 817). Cut openwork is often worked in a framework of embroidery of a different type. In such cases, the threads should be cut a fraction of an inch in from the edge of the work and then detached, so as to have a perfectly smooth edge to the material. The same number of threads must be drawn out in each direction. For most designs, the number of threads which must be left intact is the same as the number removed. Fig. 817 shows four threads removed and four left intact.

Drawing out threads over the whole surface of the material (fig. 818).

—Fig. 819. Buttonholed edge for cut openwork.

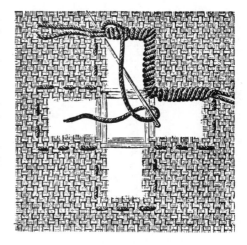

Fig. 820. Overcast edge for cut openwork.

In fig. 818, in which the threads of the material are removed from edge to edge, it will be seen that four threads have been removed and three left intact. This variation is permissible when the work is to be more transparent than it would be if the number of threads removed

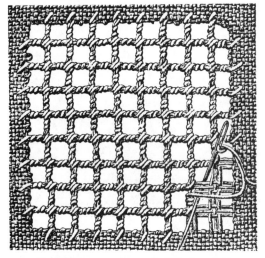

Fig. 821. First openwork ground, with horizontal and vertical bars (Russian overcast filling).

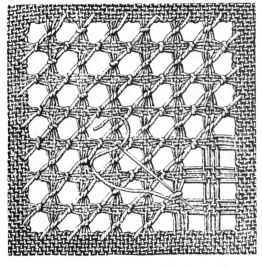

Fig. 822. Second openwork ground, with groups of threads tied in diagonal rows.

and left intact were the same.

Buttonholed edge for cut openwork (fig. 819). In certain very closely woven linens the threads can be cut without the finish of the work suffering. If, however, the material is somewhat coarser, and if the ends of the openwork are arranged in steps, the cut edge is surrounded with buttonhole or blanket stitch (figs. 40, 41, and 77).

Overcast edge for cut openwork (fig. 820). An overcast or narrow corded edge is just as satisfactory as buttonholing to strengthen the edges of fine designs. Before the material is cut, the number of threads that will have to be removed or cut is calculated, and the design which is to be worked is outlined with a tacking thread. This done, the threads which have to be removed are cut at a distance of two threads inside the tacking thread; the cut edge is then overcast immediately over one or two padding threads.

Openwork Grounds. In the eight illustrations which follow, we present to our readers a series of grounds which can be used independently to ornament various small articles; they can also be arranged as strips or used as filling stitches for large designs.

First openwork ground, with horizontal and vertical bars (fig. 821). In both directions, alternately cut and leave three threads. By the withdrawal of the threads, an openwork foundation resembling net is produced. The free threads are overcast in diagonal rows, so as to make rounded bars. The points of intersection of the threads are covered at each passage with an oblique stitch; the bars, according to their direction, are covered with two or three vertical or horizontal stitches, as shown in the illustration. This ground is usually known as Russian overcast filling.

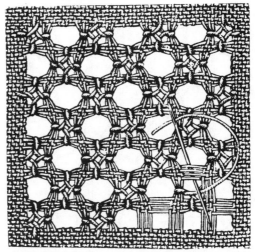

Fig. 823. Third openwork ground, with interlocking lace stitches set alternately.

Second openwork ground, with groups of threads tied in diagonal rows (fig. 822). In both directions, alternately cut and leave four threads. Here again the ground is worked in diagonal rows; the design is formed by a coarse thread which ties the groups of threads by means of a simple knot, the formation of which is explained by the illustration.

Third openwork ground, with interlocking lace stitches set alternately (fig. 823). In both directions, alternately cut and leave four threads. In this ground, the design is produced by interlocking lace stitches or lace fill-

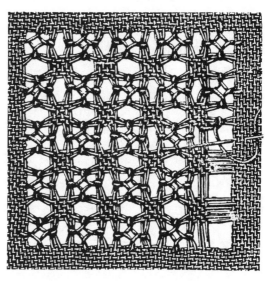

Fig. 824. Fourth openwork ground, with interlocking lace stitches set in straight lines.

ing stitches (see fig. 699 in the chapter "Filet Lace"), worked in every other space and taking up all four free threads of the foundation in each direction. As can be seen in the illustration, these stitches are worked in diagonal rows, and the passage of the thread from one stitch to another is hidden under the little square of material.

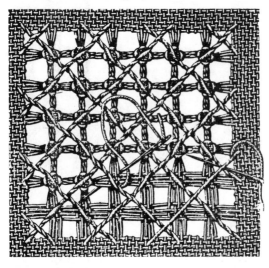

Fig. 825.
Fifth openwork ground, with diagonal network.

Fourth openwork ground, with interlocking lace stitches set in straight lines (fig. 824). In both directions, alternately cut and leave six threads. This ground has a less open appearance than the preceding one, since every open space is filled by an interlocking lace stitch; these stitches are worked in vertical rows and over only three of the free threads. In this way, small oval eyelets are produced between the squares of material by the division of the threads into groups.

Fifth openwork ground, with diagonal network (fig. 825.) In both directions, alternately cut and leave four threads. The work is begun by making the diagonal network, for which

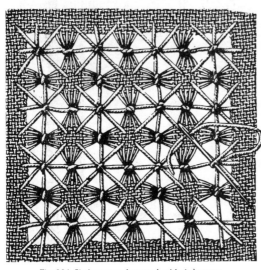

Fig. 826. Sixth openwork ground, with tied groups of threads and plain wheels.

threads are laid across the work and afterward covered with widely spaced overcast stitches. The illustration shows all the threads which lie from right to left laid and overcast, as well as some of those which lie from left to right and cross the others; the method of laying and overcasting the threads can also be seen.

When the network is completely finished, each little square of material— which appears covered by a diagonal thread—is framed in a four-sided stitch; these last stitches are worked in horizontal lines.

Sixth openwork ground, with tied groups of threads and plain wheels (fig. 826). In both directions, alternately cut and remove nine threads. The free threads are formed into groups tied in horizontal and vertical rows by means of the knot shown in fig. 822.

When all the groups have been tied, the diagonal threads which complete the wheels are laid. Here the thread passes — always diagonally—over the first, second, and third; under the fourth, fifth, and sixth; and over the seventh, eighth and ninth threads of the

Fig. 827. Seventh openwork ground, with crossed groups of threads, plain wheel, and darned circles.

Fig. 828. Eighth openwork ground, with tied groups of threads, wheels in interlocking lace stitch, and diamonds in flat stitch.

squares of material, a method which gives greater strength to the openwork. The threads from left to right are laid first. Then, when all these have been laid, a second set is laid in the opposite direction. Where the threads cross in the middle of the open spaces, they are joined with a knot, thus making a wheel with eight spokes in each open space.

Seventh openwork ground, with crossed groups of threads, plain wheels, and darned circles (fig. 827). In both directions, alternately cut and leave twelve threads. The free threads are divided into three equal groups, which are again divided and crossed in horizontal and vertical rows. When all the groups have been crossed, the diagonal threads are laid, passing over the first to the fourth, under the fifth to the eighth, and over the ninth to the twelfth threads of the squares of the material. Where the threads cross in the center of the open spaces, they are joined by a plain knot, thus forming wheels. Finally, the squares of material are ornamented with little circles worked in darning stitch, for which the thread is passed four times under the diagonally laid threads.

Eighth openwork ground, with tied groups of threads, wheels in interlocking lace stitch, and diamonds in flat stitch (fig. 828). In both directions, alternately cut and leave twelve threads. The free threads are divided into two equal groups, which are tied with a plain knot, horizontally and vertically. Each space is filled with an interlocking lace stitch worked into the corners of the squares of material and knotted, with a plain knot, to the stretched threads wherever it crosses them. Finally, the squares of material are ornamented with diamonds in flat stitch, set alternately horizontally and vertically.

Fig. 829. Band in cut-and-drawn work and flat stitch.

Band in Cut-And-Drawn Work and Flat Stitch (fig. 829). To join laces, pillow lace insertions, or bands of colored embroidery, a simple, narrow band with motifs in cut-and-drawn work and flat stitch, such as the one shown in fig. 829, is often used. The design is finished off at the top and bot-

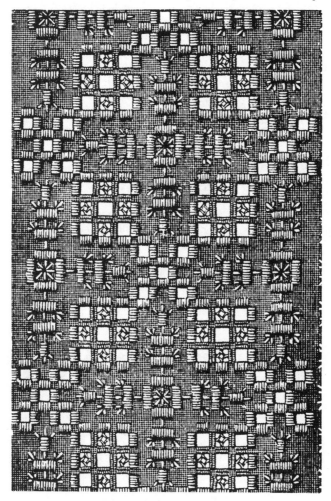

Fig. 830. Border in Norwegian Hardanger work.

tom with a row of four-sided openwork stitch (figs. 773 and 774), worked over three threads of the material; by means of the same stitch worked diagonally (simple faggot stitch, fig. 775), the interior of the band is divided into squares and triangles. The triangles are filled first, with a design in horizontal flat stitch; then the threads are cut inside the squares to make the openwork figure, and the edges are overcast; see fig. 820.

The groups of threads are overcast to form bars, and the center squares are ornamented with a darned wheel, surrounded by eight small crosses, composed of two intersecting overcast bars.

As materials, a moderately twisted thread like DMC flax lace thread should be used for the cut-and-drawn work; a floss thread, DMC special stranded cotton or DMC embroidery rayon, for the flat stitch. For this design we specially recommend the use of white thread and ecru or cream material.

Border in Norwegian Hardanger Work (figs. 830 and 831). This

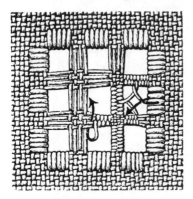

Fig. 831. Overcasting of the edges, and working of the darned bars and interlocking lace stitches. Detail of the border in fig. 830.

border is an example of a type of Norwegian openwork known as Hardanger. Ecru linen, woven with coarse threads, is used for the foundation, and on this the flat stitch parts are embroidered with DMC pearl cotton no. 5 in white; for the darned bars and the lace filling stitches, DMC flax lace thread no. 25 is used.

The embroidery is begun by overcasting all the outlines with flat stitch, accompanied by ornamental stitches, worked over four threads of the material; when all the embroidered outlines have been completed, the threads of the openwork parts are very carefully removed with a sharp pair of

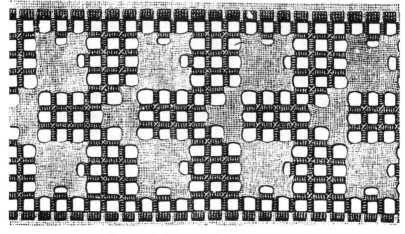

Fig. 832. Band in cut-and-drawn work with solid design worked in cloth or toile stitch.

scissors. Fig. 831 shows how the darned bars and the lace filling stitches are worked.

When used as a trimming for towels, sideboard cloths, etc., this border should be finished off with an openwork hem, a short fringe, or a narrow edging of pillow lace; in no case should this finishing be important enough in itself to detract from the effect of the border.

Band in Cut-And-Drawn Work With Solid Design Worked in Cloth or Toile Stitch (figs. 832 and 833).   There are a great number of designs in cut-and-drawn embroidery in which the design is solid, or "reserved," that is to say, in which the background is hidden or covered

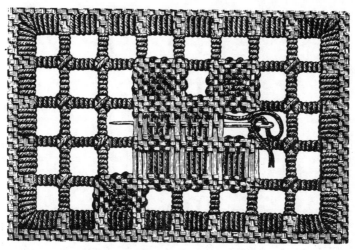

Fig. 833. Method of working cloth or toile stitch to form a solid design in cut-and-drawn work. Detail of fig. 832.

with stitches while the design is formed by the material which is left un-covered. It is, however, very difficult, especially if the design is composed of fine detail, to cut the threads without spoiling the uniformity of the back-ground. The threads are therefore drawn out over the whole of the surface to be occupied by the design, all the bars are worked, then the threads which have been drawn are reconstructed with the needle to form the solid design. The method of doing this is shown in fig. 833, in which, to show the work-ing more clearly, the threads of the material are in a lighter shade, and the stitches made with the needle are darker.

This border can be worked on most materials in which the threads can be counted, and is suitable for trimming tablecloths, napkins, towels, aprons, and many other articles. If it is used in conjunction with cross stitch em-broidery, the bars should be worked in the color of the embroidery. The design itself, worked in cloth stitch, can be done in white or ecru, according to the material used as the foundation.

Band in Cut-And-Drawn Work With Solid Design Worked in Darning Stitch (figs. 834 and 835). The stitch illustrated in fig. 835 is easier and pleasanter to work than the preceding one. It is worked like darning stitch in net guipure (fig. 695), that is to say, by taking up and passing over the same number of bars of the material.

A floss thread is used for this filling, while a more tightly twisted thread is

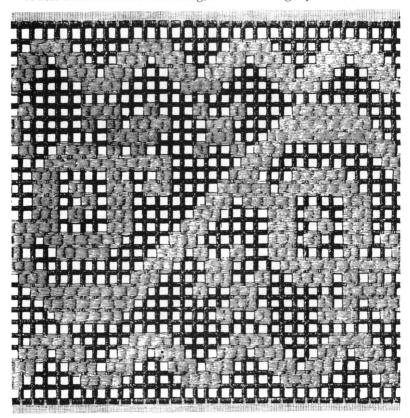

Fig. 834. Band in cut-and-drawn work with solid design worked in darning stitch.

required for the bars. The method of making the stitches is clearly shown in the illustration. In this case also, the bars are worked first, and the solid design filled in when these have been completed. The details shown in fig. 835 render fuller explanation superfluous.

This border can be used for the trimming of curtains, table cloths, napkins, and other decorative articles, the material on which it is worked being chosen to suit the article.

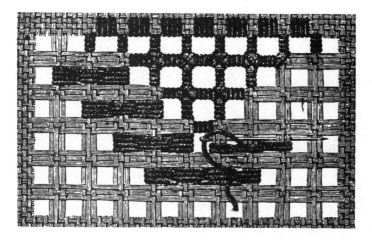

Fig. 835. Method of working darning stitch to form a solid design in cut-and-drawn work.
Detail of fig. 834.

If the border is worked on a white ground and is to be added to a piece of white embroidery or white material, a most charming and distinguished effect will be obtained by using cream thread for the bars and white for the filling of the design, which should stand out very clearly against the background.

Band in Cut-And-Drawn Work, Italian Style (figs. 836 and

Fig. 836. Band in cut-and-drawn work, Italian style.

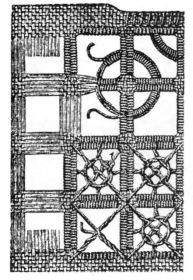

Fig. 837. Working detail of the band in fig. 836.

837). The variety of stitches used in this work is somewhat reminiscent of Reticella lace. This border can be worked in different widths at will, and makes an extremely rich trimming, eminently suitable for ecclesiastical linen.

The course of the work is explained in fig. 837. In both directions, ten threads are drawn out, and six threads left to serve as a basis for the bars. The threads of the cut edges are covered with close overcasting; the hem which finishes the band on either side is worked according to figs. 769 and 770.

The buttonholed circles are worked over three threads, which are stretched from one bar to the other when the bars have been worked half way. The wheels are begun in the corner of a square and ended, as the arrow in-

Fig. 838. Band in cut-and-drawn work. Greek style.

dicates, at the same point.

Band in Cut-And-Drawn Work, Greek Style (fig. 838). After the various instructions that have been given, the copying of this classic design should present no difficulty. In the original, which is worked on very fine linen, we have drawn out forty-eight threads for the large squares and left six for the bars. For the narrow border, we have drawn out twenty-one threads in each direction. The cut edges are bound with the stitches shown in figs. 769 and 770. Between the two rows of edging stitches, four threads of material are left, forming a narrow margin. The long bars which cross in the second square are made with double buttonhole stitch, ornamented with picots, for which instructions will be found in the chapter "Needlemade Laces," figs. 921 and 924.

Small Mat or Tray Cloth in Mexican Openwork (figs. 839 and 840). Our illustration, fig. 839, shows a type of openwork on linen which is very popular in South and Central America, particularly in those countries whose population is of predominantly Spanish origin. It is commonly called Mexican openwork. We append the necessary explanations for working this example.

Fig. 839. Small mat or tray cloth in Mexican openwork.

After binding the inner edges with buttonhole stitch (see fig. 819), seven sets of twenty threads are drawn out in each direction, leaving six intermediate groups of twelve threads, so that a foundation network with large open spaces is produced.

The embroidery is then begun in the lower left-hand corner, where a long diagonal stitch is made to the center of the first square of material, returning to the starting point with a second diagonal stitch; at the third diagonal

Fig. 840. Working of the openwork ground of the small mat in fig. 839.

stitch, the two threads already laid are tied together at each end with a buttonhole stitch. All the open spaces are crossed successively in this way with three long diagonal stitches from left to right.

The second row is begun at the bottom right-hand corner. The working is almost the same as for the first row: the only difference is that wherever the stitches of the second row cross those of the first they are knotted together; see the explanatory detail, fig. 840.

When the whole of the ground has been covered with diagonal threads, the little leaves are worked in darning stitch (see also figs. 705 and 706) and the thread is hidden on the wrong side, behind the squares of material. Finally the circles, consisting of laid threads and plain knots, are added. Those which touch the small darned leaves are made in one round; the others, which surround the unadorned squares of material, require two rounds.

For the outside trimming a band of material about two inches wide is left and ornamented with an openwork strip; then, the outer edge of the band having been surrounded with the stitch shown in fig. 763, the threads parallel to the band are withdrawn to a depth of one and a half to two inches all round to from the fringe.

Afternoon Tea Cloth in Danish Hedebo Openwork (figs. 841 and 842). Our readers are already acquainted with the term "Hedebo," since

Fig. 841. Afternoon tea cloth in Danish Hedebo openwork.

we gave an example of this Danish work in the embroidered insertion in the chapter "Embroidery on White Materials," fig. 164. We give here an example of openwork on linen of the same type—an afternoon tea cloth with richly worked triangular corners, finished at the edge with needlemade lace.

To reproduce the triangular corners, twelve sets of twenty-eight threads

Fig. 842. One quarter of the afternoon tea cloth in fig. 841.

are cut, leaving twelve threads between. Then the edges are buttonholed.

The network of free threads is converted into bars with darning stitch, and the design is worked bit by bit as the bars are completed. The model shows three large stars; the two stars at the sides are composed of eight darned triangles, worked over a thread laid diagonally, surrounding a center consisting of four wheels; the corner star is composed of four little pyramids and half circles in buttonhole stitch trimmed with picots. The remaining open spaces are filled with small rosettes, pyramids, and circles worked in buttonhole stitch, as well as various wheels formed by overcast bars.

For the narrow openwork edging, fifteen threads are withdrawn; the free threads are joined with overcast stitches, as shown in fig. 842.

The method of making lace is clearly explained in the chapter "Needlemade Laces"; see fig. 1005 and 1006. Instructions for the various stitches used in the openwork triangles will also be found in the same chapter.

Strip of embroidery on net. Imitation of Brussels lace.

CHAPTER XVI

Embroidered Laces

As a sequel to openwork on linen, we have collected in the present chapter, under the title of "Embroidered Laces," various forms of embroidery which, though they are often worked on a fabric foundation, resemble true lace by reason of their open, transparent effect.

We shall first present to our readers some examples worked in the style of Dresden lace, which were originally worked exclusively on a foundation of cambric. This kind of embroidery, adapted to modern taste and worked on loosely woven linen or washed (soft) congress canvas, is known as Colbert embroidery.

In the second part of this chapter we shall discuss embroideries on net, with a few simple examples in running and darning stitches, followed by richer designs with various filling stitches and examples of appliqué work on net.

The last part of the chapter will deal with the type of embroidery known as Spanish lace, worked in colored and metal threads, with or without a linen foundation.

All kinds of embroidered lace with a fabric foundation can be worked with the sewing machine, a method to be recommended for large articles in which the openwork stitches or the designs on net occupy large surfaces. This method of working is as pleasant as it is rapid. It goes without saying that Spanish lace, on a cambric ground, can equally well be worked with the machine.

Dresden Lace. In Germany, in the eighteenth century, shawls, collars, and even headdresses were made of fine cambric, trimmed with openwork embroidery of a very rich type, which was called Dresden lace. The designs of this embroidery were always composed of conventional flowers, accompanied by ornaments in the rococo style.

According to the method of working, Dresden lace can be divided into various types. In the first, the motifs of the designs are outlined with stem stitch or overcast stitch, the ground is entirely covered with openwork stitches, and a few isolated parts of the design are filled with damask stitches.

In the second type, the outlines of the large figures—which must be set fairly wide apart—and the small, narrow motifs are embroidered on the wrong side with herringbone stitch, drawn very tight to impart a certain degree of relief to them; the background is left plain, and the insides of the figures are filled with various stitches. If the herringbone is too much trouble, it can be replaced by buttonhole stitch or Cretan stitch.

In the richest types of lace, the background is entirely worked in openwork, and the motifs of the design in various stitches. Fairly large damask stitches are chosen for the outer parts, smaller ones for the inner parts, and for the openwork background a small, simple pattern.

Fabrics. This kind of work is simplified to a remarkable extent by the use of materials which imitate an openwork ground. When a fairly coarse material is used, the design can be reproduced on a larger scale, but the proportions should be carefully preserved, so as not to spoil the beauty of the work.

Worked on materials of medium coarseness, these laces can be used to trim curtains and blinds; they will also be found suitable for chair backs, pincushion covers, etc. Worked on finer materials, they can serve as trimming for dresses, underlinen, etc. They can further be used for ecclesiastical linen—albs, rochets, and altar cloths. For the latter, the embroidery will be worked directly onto the cloth.

In Colbert embroidery, for which coarse washed congress canvas or stiff linen is used, the character of the embroidery is slightly modified. For the outlines, stem stitch is replaced by braid; the embroidery, instead of being white or cream, is worked in several colors with, in some cases, gold or silver threads in addition. The motifs of the design are covered with damask stitches and the background is in openwork. This kind of embroidery is used for articles of furnishing: cushions, panels, chair backs, etc.

Materials. For embroidery on cambric we advise the fine numbers of DMC flax lace thread, DMC floss flax or flourishing thread, DMC 6 cord cotton lace thread, DMC Alsatian twist, and DMC Alsatian cordonnet in white; for work on soft congress canvas, DMC pearl cotton, DMC 6 cord crochet cotton, and DMC special quality crochet cotton, and for certain flat stitches DMC special stranded cotton in white and ecru.

For Colbert embroidery, we recommend, for those parts of the work that require a twisted thread, DMC pearl cotton and DMC embroidery twist; for the parts worked in a floss thread, DMC special stranded cotton, DMC embroidery rayon, or DMC Persian silk; for the outlines, braid is used, or DMC pearl cotton, DMC floss flax or flourishing thread, or fairly thick metal threads; to enhance the effect of certain damask stitches worked in floss thread, fine metal threads are used.

Filling Stitches. The effectiveness and beauty of the embroidery depend largely on the choice of filling stitches. These can be classed in three main groups: (1) filling stitches composed of flat stitches called damask stitches, (2) openwork filling stitches produced by drawing together the threads of the fabric, called drawn fabric stitches, and (3) filling stitches consisting of drawn fabric grounds and embroidered motifs.

To facilitate the reproduction of the various stitches which we are about to describe, we indicate in each case the number of threads required for one repeat.

(1) *Filling stitches composed of flat stitches called damask stitches.* The designs of these fillings are composed of vertical, horizontal, or diagonal flat stitches; they sometimes imitate damask materials. In this case, they almost entirely cover the foundation, on which they form small patterns between which the fabric is barely visible. The use of these stitches for various parts of flowers and leaves has already been mentioned in connection with piqué embroidery, fig. 165, in the chapter "Embroidery on White Materials."

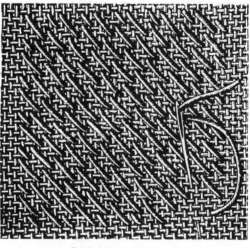

Fig. 843. First damask stitch.

First damask stitch (fig. 843). Each repeat requires four threads each way of the material.

The close design consists of encroaching diagonal flat stitches worked in diagonal rows. After the thread has been brought out to the right side of the work, the needle is passed up from right to left over four threads of the material and brought back to the right side under six horizontal and two vertical threads. Then another diagonal stitch is made from right to left over four threads, and so on. The second row of stitches is worked in the same way; the stitches are set between those of the preceding row, on which they encroach by two threads of the material.

Second damask stitch (fig. 844). Each repeat requires eight threads in height and six in width.

Our example is composed of superimposed rows of small points worked in vertical flat stitch. It is begun with a straight stitch up over two threads of

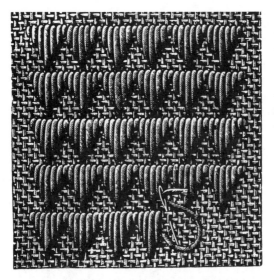

Fig. 844. Second damask stitch.

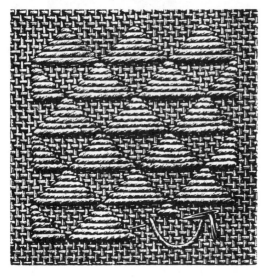

Fig. 845. Third damask stitch.

the material, then the needle passes down under four horizontal threads and one vertical thread to make the second vertical stitch over four threads; in the same way a third stitch is made over six and a fourth over eight horizontal threads, after which the length of the stitches is gradually diminished. The last stitch—which can also be considered as the first stitch of the next point—is two threads in height. In this way the whole of the row of points is worked. The straight edge of the next row touches the points of the preceding row.

Third damask stitch (fig. 845). Each repeat requires six threads in height and twelve in width.

The design is formed of inverted triangles, worked with horizontal flat stitches in diagonal rows. The embroidery is begun at the top with the shortest stitch, which is worked from left to right over two threads of the material; this stitch is followed by five more horizontal stitches becoming gradually wider by one thread of the material at each side, so that the longest stitch will be worked over twelve threads. The next triangle is then begun, to the left; worked in this way, the triangles will of themselves be set alternately, the point of one being always just under the junction of two bases in the row above.

Fourth damask stitch (fig. 846). Each repeat requires twelve threads each way of the material.

In this filling, the foundation is almost entirely covered with diamonds, each composed of ten horizontal flat stitches. These diamonds are worked in diagonal rows, as follows: after the thread has been brought out at the required point, a horizontal stitch is made from left to right over two threads; this stitch is repeated one thread lower; then, again one thread lower for each stitch, two stitches are made over six threads, extending two threads at each end beyond the first stitches; then two horizontal stitches over ten threads for the middle of the diamond. The remaining stitches are made in the same manner, but two threads shorter at each end, so that the last two will be worked over two threads, like the first two.

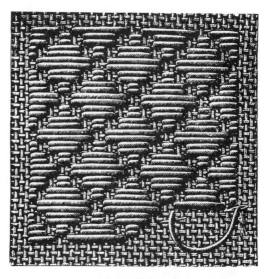

Fig. 846. Fourth damask stitch.

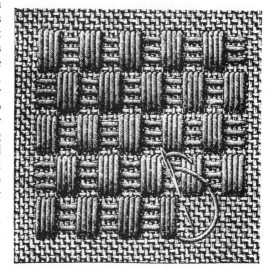

Fig. 847. Fifth damask stitch.

Fifth damask stitch (fig. 847). Each repeat requires eight threads each way of the material.

The work is begun with four vertical stitches over eight threads; then the

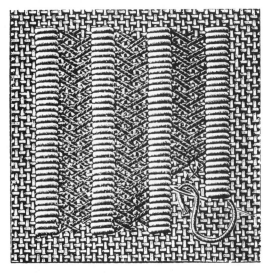

Fig. 848. Sixth damask stitch.

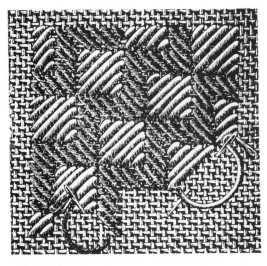

Fig. 849. Seventh damask stitch.

needle is passed down under two horizontal threads and one vertical thread (see fig. 847), and the three horizontal stitches are worked from left to right, leaving two threads between the stitches. When the third horizontal stitch has been made, the needle once more passes down to the right under two horizontal threads and one vertical thread to continue the work with the next group of four vertical stitches. The second row of the pattern is worked like the first, except that the stitches are arranged so that the horizontal stitches of the second row come under the vertical stitches of the first and vice versa.

Sixth damask stitch (fig. 848). Each repeat requires two threads in height and ten in width.

Here vertical stripes of horizontal flat stitches alternate with stripes in crossed back stitch. The flat stitch stripes, four threads in width, are worked first, leaving six threads between the stripes. The double or crossed back stitch (fig. 83) is worked over these threads. The needle is brought out between the fourth and fifth threads of the space, and a slanting stitch is made down from right to left over four vertical and two horizontal threads; the needle is brought out again two threads higher to make a second slanting stitch down to the right over six vertical and three horizontal threads, crossing the first stitch; the needle passes vertically up under two threads, a sloping stitch is made to the left, and so on.

This filling gains greatly in effectiveness if it is worked in two kinds of thread; a coarse thread should be chosen for the flat stitch and a fine thread for the double back stitch.

Seventh damask stitch (fig. 849). Each repeat requires twelve threads each way of the material.

Squares of diagonal flat stitch, separated by zigzag stripes, entirely cover the foundation. The zigzag stripes are worked first, and consist of five diagonal stitches in each direction, worked over four threads of the material, with two

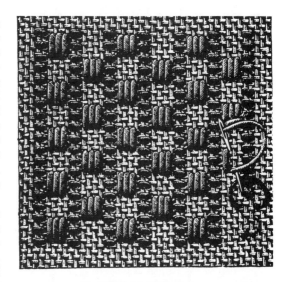

Fig. 850. Eighth damask stitch.

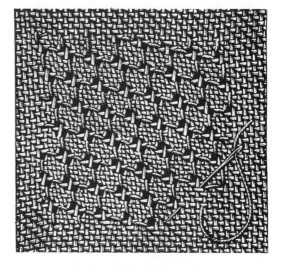

Fig. 851. First drawn fabric ground
(diagonal drawn filling).

threads between them. The stripes are so arranged as to form square spaces, eight threads in height and width. These squares are then filled with diagonal flat stitches set in the opposite direction from the stitches in the stripes.

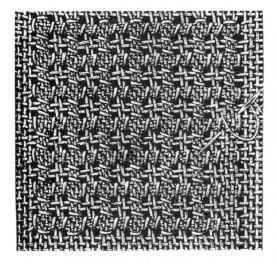

Fig. 852. Second drawn fabric ground
(cobbler filling stitch).

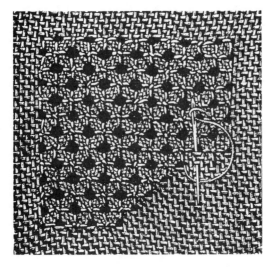

Fig. 853. Third drawn fabric ground
(lace filling stitch).

The first and seventh stitches of the squares are worked over two threads of the material, the second and sixth over four threads, the third and fifth over six threads, and the fourth over eight threads.

Eighth damask stitch (fig. 850). Each repeat requires eight threads in height and six in width.

The vertical lines of the pattern are made as follows: after the needle has been brought out, a horizontal stitch is made from right to left over two threads; then, passing down to the right, under two horizontal and two vertical threads, a second horizontal stitch is made, and so on. A space of four threads is left between the stripes; in it the little squares are worked, each consisting of three vertical flat stitches over four threads, with spaces of four threads between the squares.

In the next plain stripe, the squares are set alternately with those in the preceding stripes, that is to say, between them.

(2) *Drawn fabric grounds.* By means of stitches which draw certain groups of threads of the fabric close together, openwork grounds can be produced which resemble to a great extent the openwork grounds on linen described in the previous chapter. These, from the way in which they are made, are known as drawn fabric grounds, and must not be confused with the drawn thread grounds previously described.

Drawn fabric stitches are made without withdrawing any threads from the material; they can only be worked on rather loosely woven materials, unlike drawn thread work, which always requires a close-

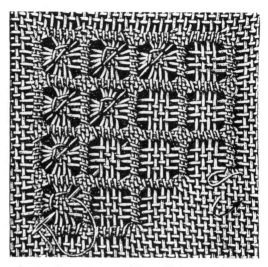

Fig. 854. Fourth drawn fabric ground (mosaic filling stitch).
Working of the 1st and 2nd row.

ly woven fabric. Drawn fabric stitches are used as fillings; they can be divided into two kinds:

(a) Stitches worked with a very fine thread, in which the design is formed entirely by the drawing together of the threads of the material into groups; see figs. 851 to 855.

(b) Stitches worked with a coarse thread which forms a design in relief against the background of material, the threads of which no longer form the whole of the design; see figs. 856 to 860.

First drawn fabric ground (diagonal drawn filling) (fig. 851). Each repeat requires five threads each way of the material. This ground is worked in diagonal rows.

The working is begun with a vertical stitch up over four threads; then the needle is passed down from right to left under four threads; a horizontal stitch is made from left to right over four threads; the needle passes down from right to left under four threads; and the next stitch is begun with a vertical stitch up to the starting point of the horizontal stitch already made. The row is continued in the same way. The second row is begun one thread lower down, and one to the right, and the stitches are made in the same way as in the first row. In this way, the drawing of the fabric held by the tight stitches produces small crosses, formed by the threads left between the rows of stitches. To produce the openwork design, the stitches must be drawn very tight.

Second drawn fabric ground (cobbler filling stitch) (fig. 852). Each repeat requires six threads each way of the material. This filling is worked in two directions, in horizontal and vertical rows; all the rows in one direction are completed first, then those in the other direction, crossing the first.

The horizontal rows are worked first, the needle passing vertically up over four threads to return diagonally under four threads each way of the material and make a second vertical stitch up. Only two vertical threads are left between the second and third stitches, the third being another vertical stitch like the first two. In this way the vertical stitches are separated by alternately four and two threads. The vertical rows, which cross the horizontal rows, consist of horizontal stitches worked in the same way.

The completed stitch shows little squares surrounded by four-sided stitches, between which appear little openwork crosses formed by the two threads of the material left between the squares.

Third drawn fabric ground (lace filling stitch) (fig. 853). Each repeat requires six threads each way of the material.

In this case, interlocking lace stitch has been used to draw the threads of the material together; see the chapter "Filet Lace," figs. 699 and 700. As the illustration shows, the stitch is worked in diagonal rows.

After the needle has been brought out on the right side, it is carried up toward the right over three threads, and a buttonhole stitch is made over three horizontal threads; a second buttonhole stitch is made over three threads to the right, and a third over three threads down; to complete the fourth stitch the needle is passed over the first stitch and, passing down to the left under three horizontal and six vertical threads, begins the second interlocking lace stitch.

Fig. 855. Fourth drawn fabric ground (mosaic filling stitch). Working of the 3rd row.

Fourth drawn fabric ground (mosaic filling stitch) (figs. 854 and 855). Each repeat requires eight threads each way of the material.

This stitch is more complicated than the preceding ones, and is worked in three rows. The stitches which form the checkered effect are worked first, in zigzag rows. These rows consist of five horizontal stitches, worked from left to right over four threads, with one thread between; then the needle is passed down from right to left under four threads to work five vertical stitches up over four threads, after which it is again passed diagonally down under four threads, to continue with the five horizontal stitches.

The working of successive zigzag rows produces small squares of material composed of four threads each way. These are afterward covered by a cross stitch, framed in a four-sided stitch, worked in two rows. This part of the work is begun at the top right-hand corner; the thread is passed diagonally under the four free threads, a vertical stitch is made up, the needle is passed horizontally from left to right under four threads and returns to make a horizontal stitch over these four threads; it then passes vertically back under the first vertical stitch to make a diagonal stitch up from left to right over four threads. To reach the next stitch, a long sloping stitch is made on the wrong side, the needle emerging at the lower left-hand corner of the next little square.

This square is filled in the same way as the preceding one, beginning with the vertical stitch up. When these rows have been completed over the whole surface to be embroidered, the third row, which completes the ground, is begun. These last stitches are worked in the same way as the second set, but in the opposite direction.

The finished filling shows a checkered ground filled with small framed crosses, and if it is held against the light the long slanting stitches on the wrong side will also be seen, forming, with the framed crosses, little stars.

Fifth drawn fabric ground (wave stitch filling) (fig. 856). Each repeat requires four threads each way of the material. This ground, rather like coarse net in effect, is worked in horizontal rows; it requires the threads of the material to be very tightly drawn together.

It is begun with a slanting stitch up over two vertical and four horizontal threads; the needle is then brought horizontally under four threads to the left to make a slanting stitch down to the right over two vertical and four horizontal threads; the

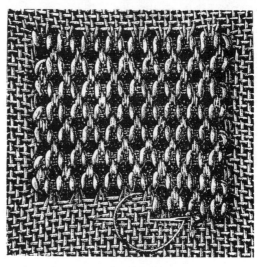

Fig. 856. Fifth drawn fabric ground (wave stitch filling).

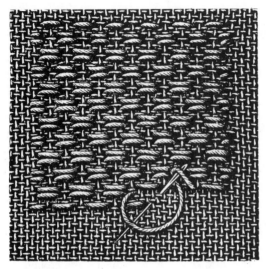

Fig. 857. Sixth drawn fabric ground (double stitch filling).

Fig. 858. Seventh drawn fabric ground
(Algerian eye stitch filling).

needle is passed horizontally to the left under four threads and another slanting stitch like the first is made, and so on.

The succeeding rows are alternated in such a way that four slanting stitches always meet in the same openwork hole in the material.

Sixth drawn fabric ground (double stitch filling) (fig. 857). Each repeat requires six threads each way of the material.

This very simple filling is worked in two rows of horizontal stitches. The first horizontal stitch is made from left to right over five threads; the needle is then passed diagonally down from right to left under two threads to make a second horizontal stitch to the right over five threads; the needle is passed diagonally up to the left under two threads, and the first stitch is repeated. The succeeding rows are worked in the same way, with one thread between them, and the stitches set so that they lie in alternating pairs. In this way a little openwork cross is produced between the embroidered stitches, formed by the threads of material left between the horizontal stitches.

Seventh drawn fabric ground (Algerian eye stitch filling) (fig. 858).

Each repeat requires eight threads each way of the material.

This ground consists of star stitches set alternately, dividing the material into diamonds. Algerian eye stitch is worked in the same way as star stitch, which is described in the chapter "Tapestry," fig. 376, but the stitches are drawn very tight in the working, thus producing small openwork spaces in the center of the star. This stitch will be found again used as a detached motif to fill squares or diamonds in the grounds which are described further on.

Eighth drawn fabric ground (checker filling stitch) (figs. 859 and 860). Each repeat requires eight threads each way of the material.

This filling, consisting of two diagonal rows of oblong cross stitch, produces a charming effect when it is worked with a fairly coarse thread.

Fig. 859 shows the first rows of cross stitches, worked up from left to right. It is

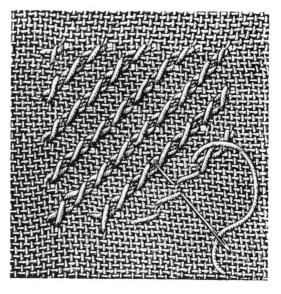

Fig. 859.
Eighth drawn fabric ground (checker filling stitch).
First rows of cross stitches.

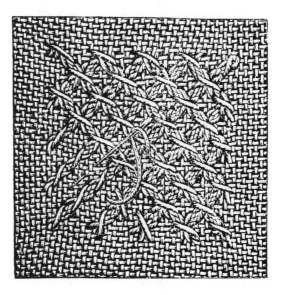

Fig. 860. Eighth drawn fabric ground (checker filling stitch).
Second rows of cross stitches.

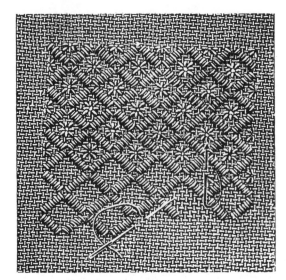

Fig. 861.
First drawn fabric ground, with overcast bars
(diagonal overcast ground).

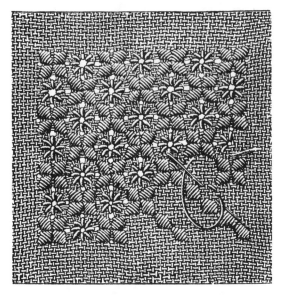

Fig. 862. Second drawn fabric ground,
with diamonds in flat stitch and Algerian eye stitch.

begun with a slanting stitch over six vertical and two horizontal threads, then the needle passes, on the wrong side, diagonally up and to the left, under two threads, to make another long oblique stitch on the right side; on the return journey, the row of cross stitches is completed. Fig. 860 shows how the second set of cross stitches is worked in diagonal rows over and crossing the first. Between the crosses in relief, the drawing together of the threads forms small openwork crosses.

(3) *Drawn fabric grounds with embroidered motifs.* These grounds, composed of drawn fabric stitches combined with motifs in flat stitch or fancy stitches, are the richest type of these fillings. We give eight examples in this chapter, but our readers will find it easy to add to this number, since there is no limit to the possible combinations.

By way of materials, a well-twisted thread

should be used for the drawn fabric stitches, and a floss thread for the flat or fancy stitches. See the paragraph on materials at the beginning of the chapter.

First drawn fabric ground, with overcast bars (diagonal overcast ground) (fig. 861). Each repeat requires twelve threads each way of the material. Diagonal bars, worked in horizontal rows, divide the ground into diamonds.

The bars are begun with a diagonal stitch down from right to left over two threads, then the needle passes up under two vertical threads and one horizontal thread to make a diagonal stitch down over one thread; it is then carried up again under two vertical threads and one horizontal thread to make a second diagonal stitch down over two threads, and so on. Each bar consists of nine diagonal stitches, five long and four short. After the fifth long stitch, the needle is brought out through the hole by which it emerged to

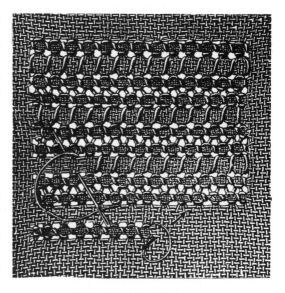

Fig. 863. Third drawn fabric ground, with flat stitch stripes and four-sided openwork stitch (four-sided border stitch).

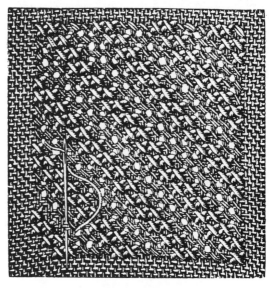

Fig. 864. Fourth drawn fabric ground, with reversed faggot stitch and stripes in cross stitch.

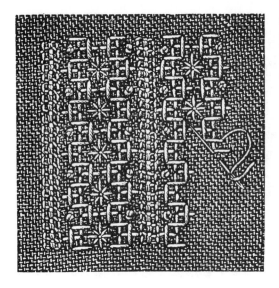

Fig. 865. Fifth drawn fabric ground,
with four-sided openwork stitch, cross stitch, and
Algerian eye stitch.

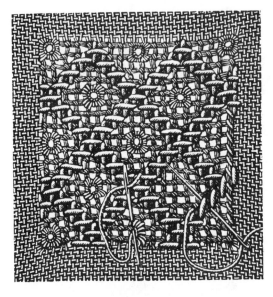

Fig. 866. Sixth drawn fabric ground,
with reversed faggot stitch, buttonhole eyelets, and
square in cross stitch.

make the last stitch, and another bar is made, like the first bar, but in the opposite direction. The succeeding rows of bars are made to alternate so as to form diamond-shaped spaces, which are finally filled with Algerian eye stitch.

To work this latter stitch, the needle is brought out in the center of the lower right-hand bar and a diagonal stitch is made up from right to left over two threads of the material; this is followed by a two-sided horizontal stitch to the right, then a diagonal stitch down to the left, a vertical stitch up, and so on, until eight stitches have been made, meeting in the center of the diamond, where they form an open eyelet.

Second drawn fabric ground, with diamonds in flat stitch and Algerian eye stitch (fig. 862). Each repeat requires sixteen threads each way of the material.

This design is made up of little motifs composed of four diamonds in diagonal flat stitch, alternating with

Algerian eye stitches. The small diamonds each contain seven stitches, the first and seventh worked diagonally over one thread, the second and sixth over two threads, the third and fifth over three threads, and the fourth over four threads. As the illustration shows, these diamonds are worked in diagonal rows in two directions. The Algerian eye stitches which fill the empty squares consist of eight stitches, meeting in the center; the diagonal stitches are worked over three threads of the material, the horizontal and vertical stitches over four threads.

Third drawn fabric ground with flat stitch stripes and four-sided openwork stitch (four-sided border stitch) (fig. 863). Each repeat requires thirteen horizontal and four vertical threads.

Two rows of four-sided openwork stitch, set alternately, form the serpentine openwork line; see also the chapter "Openwork on Linen," figs. 773 and 774. Between these double rows of four-

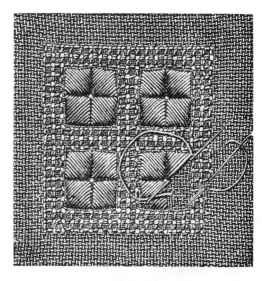

Fig. 867.
Seventh drawn fabric ground, with four-sided openwork stitch and squares in flat stitch.

Fig. 868. Eighth drawn fabric ground, with Algerian filling stitch, double back stitch, and diamonds in flat stitch.

sided stitches, which are worked over four threads of the material, five threads are left. Over these are worked vertical flat stitches set immediately below the vertical stitches of the four-sided stitch.

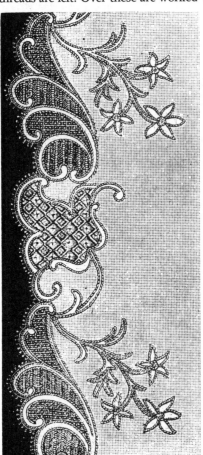

Fig. 869. Dresden lace worked on a foundation of cambric.

Fourth drawn fabric ground, with reversed faggot stitch and stripes in cross stitch (fig. 864). Each repeat requires fifteen horizontal and three vertical threads.

This filling, with its diagonal stripes, is composed of double rows of cross stitch and rows of reversed faggot stitch, which has been described in the chapter "Openwork on Linen," fig. 776.

The rows of cross stitch are worked first; the stitches are worked backward and forward in horizontal rows. Between the double rows of cross stitch, nine threads of the material are left, and the reversed faggot stitch is worked over these threads when the cross stitch has been completed. The first stitch is worked up, from right to left, over three threads; the needle is brought vertically down under three threads to make a second diagonal stitch up to the left; next it is passed horizontally to the right under three threads to make another diagonal stitch up to the left, and so on. The second row, which completes the drawn fabric stitch, is worked in the same way, but down. The holes in which two diagonal stitches meet form openwork spaces.

Fifth drawn fabric ground, with four-sided openwork stitch, cross stitch, and Algerian eye stitch (fig. 865). Each repeat requires twelve horizontal and thirty vertical stitches.

This rather large ground is used to cover fairly important surfaces. It is divided into stripes by two rows of four-sided openwork stitch, worked over three threads of the material. The strips of material between these double rows are filled with serpentine lines composed of straight cross stitches worked over six threads each way of the material; the open spaces between the two rows of cross stitch are filled with Algerian eye stitches, and in the outer spaces of the serpentine lines single French knots are worked.

Sixth drawn fabric ground, with reversed faggot stitch, buttonhole eyelets, and squares in cross stitch (fig. 866). Each repeat requires twenty- four threads each way of the material.

Like the preceding one, this ground is chiefly used in large pieces of work. Before the design itself is worked, the whole surface of the material to be covered is embroidered with the drawn fabric stitch illustrated in fig. 776 (reversed faggot stitch). This ground is worked in diagonal rows as follows: a diagonal stitch is made to the

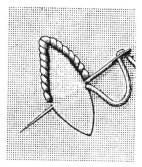

Fig. 870.
Method of working a leaf
in double back stitch.
Right side.

left over three threads, the needle passes down under three threads, a second diagonal stitch is made up to the left, after which the needle passes horizontally to the right under three threads, to continue with a third diagonal stitch to the left. The next row is worked in the opposite direction, that is to say, down. If the thread is drawn very tight in the working, a very open groundwork is obtained, and on this the design itself is embroidered. The diagonal lines which divide the surface into diamonds are composed of straight cross stitches, worked over two groups of threads of the material. The work is begun at the top, with a stitch passing vertically down over two groups; the needle passes diagonally up from right to left under one group,

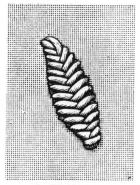

Fig. 871.
Method of working a leaf
in double back stitch.
Wrong side.

and another stitch is made vertically down. On the return journey, horizontal stitches are made to complete the crosses. When all the cross stitches have been worked, the center openwork space of each diamond is surrounded with buttonhole stitches. This produces an eyelet hole with a raised edge.

Seventh drawn fabric ground, with four-sided openwork stitch and squares in flat stitch (fig. 867). Each repeat requires twenty-four threads each way of the material.

The foundation is divided into squares with double rows of four- sided openwork stitch (see fig. 773); the plain squares of material are filled with little squares embroidered in diagonal flat stitch. The four-sided stitch, which should be completed first, is worked over three threads each way of the material. The plain squares measure eighteen threads each way, and the large squares of flat stitch which fill them are each composed of four smaller squares. Each of these smaller squares contains fifteen diagonal stitches, of which the shortest is worked over one thread and the longest over eight threads; these longest stitches should all meet in the same hole in the center.

Eighth drawn fabric ground, with Algerian filling stitch, double back stitch, and diamonds in flat stitch (fig. 868).

Note: each repeat requires twenty-eight horizontal and twenty-six vertical threads. In this ground, diamonds with wide borders on flat stitch and openwork centers alternate with quadruple squares in double back stitch.

The framing of the diamonds is begun at the left-hand point with a ver-

Fig. 872. Imitation of Dresden lace worked on soft congress canvas with openwork ground.

tical stitch down over two threads, then the needle passes up to the right under three horizontal threads and one vertical thread and a second vertical stitch is made down over four threads. Continuing in the same way, vertical stitches are made over six, eight, and ten threads, and the needle is brought

Fig. 873. Cushion in Colbert embroidery.

out once more at the top, one thread above the last stitch; nine more vertical stitches are made over six threads, each being set one thread higher than the last. The ninth forms the point of the diamond, and is followed by eight stitches down to the right, each one thread lower than the preceding one.

The next stitch is made over ten threads, and is followed by four more, each one thread shorter at each end than the preceding one, so that the last stitch—which forms the right-hand corner of the diamond—covers

Fig. 874. Part of the cushion in fig. 873.

only two threads. The bottom of the diamond is completed by seventeen vertical stitches over six threads. In the center a little openwork figure is embroidered, consisting of four groups of three horizontal stitches over four threads; this drawn fabric stitch is known as Algerian filling stitch (not to be confused with Algerian eye stitch); it is surrounded with a serpentine line composed of double overcast stitches over two threads. The squares in double back stitch are worked in diagonal rows.

Dresden Lace Worked on a Foundation of Cambric (figs. 869, 870, 871). This fine, delicate design is comparatively easy to work; nevertheless, when embroidered on fine cambric it requires a great deal of patience.

After the design has been traced and the material mounted in a frame, the insides of the figures are filled with the stitches shown in figs. 854, 855, 863, and 868; then the outlines and the delicate small figures of the design are embroidered in double back stitch, which gives a certain relief to these parts and helps to make them stand out against the transparent background. The method of working double (or crossed) back stitch has been explained in the chapter ''Embroidery on White Materials,'' figs. 82 and 83; we show it again, however, in figs. 870 and 871. Fig. 870 shows the right side of the work; it shows how a back stitch is made on the right and left sides of the leaf alternately; fig. 871 shows the wrong side, where the back stitches cross very evenly.

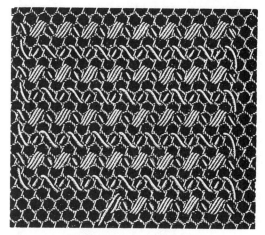

Fig. 875. First openwork filling on net.

Fig. 876. Second openwork filling on net.

After the fillings and outlines have been completed, the work is removed from the frame for the working of the buttonholed outer edge, in which a buttonhole (or Venetian) picot is made after every fourth stitch; see the chapter "Needlemade Laces," fig. 921.

As materials we recommend DMC floss flax or flourishing thread no. 30 for all the parts worked in double back stitch, and nos. 60 and 100 for the filling stitches and the buttonholing.

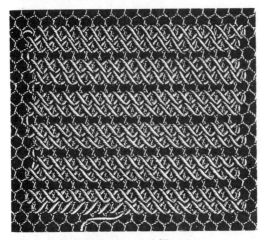

Fig. 877. Third openwork filling on net.

Imitation of Dresden Lace Worked on Soft Congress Canvas With Openwork Ground (fig. 872). For those who prefer work that is less fine, we give here an example of lace embroidered on soft congress canvas, which produces a coarse imitation of Dresden lace. After the design has been traced, the background is first covered with the drawn fabric stitch illustrated in fig. 851; this stitch can be replaced, if preferred, by the one shown in fig. 852, or that in fig. 853. The interior of the flowers filled with the stitch in fig. 861, the leaves with the one in fig. 862; these stitches can also be replaced by one of the others explained in this chapter.

Fig. 878. Fourth openwork filling on net.

When all the background and filling stitches have been worked, the outlines are embroidered in stem stitch, so that they stand out in relief against the background and the parts of the canvas that are not embroidered will show up well.

The outer edge of the lace is finished off with a row of plain buttonhole stitching worked over two rows of running stitch. As materials, we advise DMC floss flax or flourishing thread no. 25 for the filling stitches and no. 16 for the stem stitch outlines.

Cushion in Colbert Embroidery (figs. 873 and 874). Large designs worked on coarse, transparent material with various filling stitches and braid outlines are known as Colbert embroidery. We give an example in the cushion shown in fig. 873.

The explanatory illustration, fig. 874, is large enough to permit the filling stitches to be copied; these stitches have, in any case, already been explained in this chapter; we need only point out that Hungarian stitch (see the chapter "Tapestry," fig. 372) has been used to partially fill the scrolls.

The foundation is soft (washed) congress canvas; the filling stitches are worked in DMC Persian silk (in two shades of pale yellow, or in DMC embroidery rayon no. 30 in cream and tangerine, with the addition here and there of DMC pearl cotton no. 8 or DMC embroidery rayon no. 60 in red- brown.

Fig. 879. Fifth openwork filling on net.

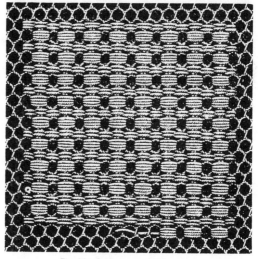

Fig. 880. Sixth openwork filling on net.

The small leaves, the calyx of the flowers, and the stems are worked in encroaching satin stitch in two shades. When all the parts of the design have been filled, the ground is embroidered with the drawn fabric stitch shown in fig. 857. The thread used for this should be DMC special quality crochet cotton, no. 20, in cream.

Fig. 881. Seventh openwork filling on net.

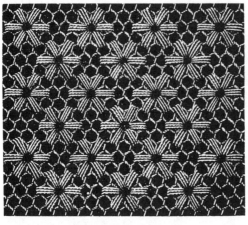

Fig. 882. Eighth openwork filling on net.

The background completed, the motifs are outlined with a thread of DMC pearl cotton in ecru, no. 3 for the larger figures and no. 5 for the smaller, stitched down all round. A row of stem stitch in dark brown silk, outside the ecru pearl cotton, completes the work.

Net Embroidery. In embroidery on net, darning stitch is most generally used either to cover whole motifs or merely to outline them. In the latter case, the motifs are filled with other stitches. Appliqué work can also be done on net; the motif, usually in cambric, is then surrounded with buttonhole stitch, and the net takes the place of an openwork ground. The simplest designs are worked in one color in darning stitch, either on counted threads or following a tracing. Where filling stitches are used, these are worked on counted threads; the outlines are always worked from a tracing; they are first traced with a single thread, then covered with some kind of fancy stitch or with a braid. The latter method constitutes an imitation of Brussels or Brabant lace; the net ground replaces the made ground, and the filling stitches take the place of the various fancy fillings made with bobbins, and are finished off with a thick outline, like real lace.

Materials. For embroidery on net, one or more strands of a silky floss thread are used; on fine net, in white or cream, we recommend using DMC pearl cotton nos. 8 and 12; DMC special stranded cotton no. 25, divided if necessary; DMC embroidery rayon no. 60; or DMC Persian silk. On black net, nothing but silk is ever used. Coarse net, which is often used for modern work, requires a thicker thread, such as DMC pearl cotton nos. 3 and 5, DMC shaded pearl cotton nos. 3 and 5, DMC special stranded cotton no. 25, DMC embroidery twist no. 4, DMC floss flax or flourishing thread nos. 8 and 16, or DMC embroidery rayon no. 30. Appliqué on net requires two kinds of thread: a supple, moderately twisted thread, DMC special quality embroidery cotton, for the button holing; a very round thread, tightly twisted, DMC Alsatian sewing cotton or DMC 6 cord cotton lace thread, for the bars and wheels in the cut parts.

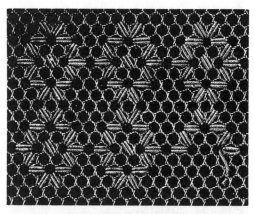

Fig. 883. Ninth openwork filling on net.

Fig. 884. Tenth openwork filling on net.

Preparatory work. The first step before beginning to embroider a design on net is to trace the design onto linen paper or architect's linen; then the net is stretched very evenly over the tracing to prevent it from becoming pulled out of shape or puckered during the working, which would spoil the finished effect of the work. When the design includes filling stitches, the outlines are first run in, following the lines of the tracing beneath, in running stitch with a fine thread; then the true embroidery is begun.

Openwork fillings on net. We give first a series of little fillings, powderings, and insertions, very easy to work, which will be used later in the lace designs which will follow.

First openwork filling on net (fig. 875). This filling is worked in two journeys. The first consists of simple overcast stitches from left to right; returning, three stitches are worked into one mesh, sloping in the opposite direction from the stitches of the preceding row.

Fig. 885. Eleventh openwork filling on net.

Second openwork filling on net (fig. 876). A double row of stitches forming eyelets is worked first. This is followed by a row of cross stitches worked under one bar and over one mesh on the first journey and covered, to complete the crosses, on the return journey.

Third openwork filling on net (fig. 877). First a row of cross stitches, like those in the preceding ground, is worked; then another row is added, in which the thread passes under the bar between the first two stitches, so that the two rows of stitches cover only three threads of the net.

Fourth openwork filling on net (fig. 878). In this stitch, the thread passes horizontally under two bars and under one mesh of the net; then, passing obliquely down over two bars and one mesh, it is again passed horizontally under two bars, then obliquely up, and so on. In the next row the same stitches are made, so that four stitches meet in one mesh and two threads pass under one mesh.

Fifth openwork filling on net (fig. 879). This is worked like the stitch in fig. 878, except that on one side three horizontal stitches are made over the meshes of the net and a single oblique stitch under the meshes.

Sixth openwork filling on net (fig. 880). The thread is run twice backward and forward through one row of meshes, as in darning. In the next row, dots are made by covering two bars and one mesh with four stitches. After the last stitch, the thread passes under the net to the next dot.

Seventh openwork filling on net (fig. 881). Three stitches are worked obliquely over three bars and two meshes, then, returning to the mesh from which the first stitches began, three more are made in the opposite direc-

Fig. 886. Twelfth openwork design on net.

tion. In the second row, the stitches meet in a mesh through which those of the first row have been made.

Eighth openwork filling on net (fig. 882). The rays of the little stars, composed of three stitches over one mesh of the net, are made so as to produce a powdering which may be closely or widely spaced. To make them more conspicuous, it suffices to increase the number of stitches worked into one mesh.

Ninth openwork filling on net (fig. 883). The little rosettes, like the stars in the previous example, can be made closer together or farther apart. In making the center dot, the thread should be passed as invisibly as possible

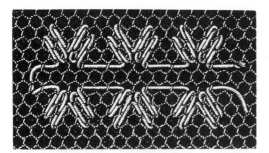

Fig. 887. Thirteenth openwork design on net.

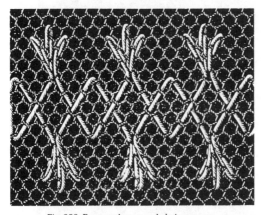

Fig. 888. Fourteenth openwork design on net.

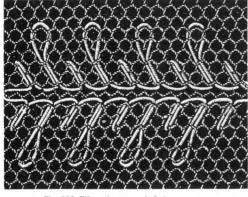

Fig. 889. Fifteenth openwork design on net.

to the center and back. The effect of these rosettes is particularly delightful when several rows are placed one above the other. In addition, they can be used as fillings for other designs and, when they are skillfully arranged, contribute greatly to the charm of the simplest grounds.

Tenth openwork filling on net (fig. 884). The long straight stitches are worked over three bars and two meshes; the other are worked up and down following the line of the meshes.

Eleventh openwork filling on net (fig. 885). Darning stitch is again used for this ground. The threads pass through every other diagonal row of meshes, over all the surface to be covered, and are crossed in the same way in the second row. By setting the lines farther apart, a different design can be produced, and the spaces left between the lines can be ornamented with little flowers.

Twelfth openwork design on net (fig. 886). These diamonds, worked singly or in rows, are very effective, though simple and easy to work. A flat thread is preferable to a twisted one. The central star can be embroidered in DMC embroidery rayon in golden yellow.

Thirteenth, fourteenth, and fifteenth openwork designs on net (fig. 887, 888, 889). These three designs worked, like the following ones, in darning stitch, can take the place of crochet insertions or pillow lace and even of embroidered insertions for the trimming of all kinds of underlinen.

The designs, which are very simple to copy, need no further explanation. We recommend, however, the use of a thread which will show up well: DMC pearl cotton, DMC special stranded cotton, DMC embroidery twist, or DMC floss flax or flourishing thread, for instance; DMC superfine braid could also be used.

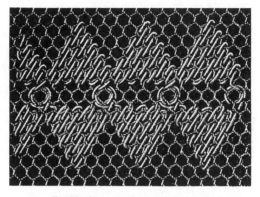

Fig. 890. Sixteenth openwork design on net.

Sixteenth openwork design on net (fig. 890). The thread encircles one mesh of the net each time before beginning the triangle, which is worked in darning stitches over successively five, four, three, two, and one mesh of the net. In the second row, opposite the first, the thread again encircles the same mesh before beginning the second triangle.

Fig. 891. Seventeenth openwork design on net.

Seventeenth openwork design on net (fig. 891). This design is worked in darning stitch and flat stitch. The thread passes backward and forward over four, three, two, and one mesh of the net; the stitch shown in fig. 878 has been used for the insertion. When this design is repeated, the points across from those in the first row should slope in the opposite direction. Small stars, such as those shown in fig. 882, could take the place of the insertion used here.

Fig. 892. Braid insertion on net.

Braid Insertion on Net (fig. 892). To make the design and colors stand out better on coarse net, cotton thread can be replaced by DMC superfine braid.

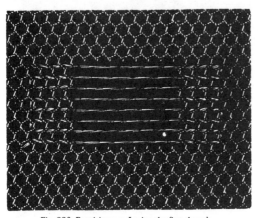

Fig. 893. Repairing net. Laying the first threads.

Work done with braid requires more care than work done with thread because the braid must not become twisted; to do this, a large needle is passed under the last stitch to straighten out any twists that may have formed.

Repairing Net (figs. 893, 894, 895). The art of reconstructing damaged meshes in net is one which may be of great help in preserving valuable or interesting articles. The method is the same for coarse and fine net. It is only necessary to choose a thread of a thickness proportionate to that of the damaged fabric. The torn piece is tacked, a little way beyond the tear, to colored paper or American cloth; the edges are then cut straight by the thread.

Net is darned in three operations. The first consists of laying horizontal threads from one side to the other, continuing, as in all other forms of darning, several stitches beyond the hole on each side. The second set of stitches is begun at the left-hand corner of the tear, and the threads already stretched across are enlaced one by one in a diagonal line. These overcast stitches should be carried a little way beyond the edge of the tear, so as to join the new stitches firmly to the original fabric. The third set of stitches is also set diagonally, but in the opposite direction. They are carried beyond the edge of the tear to the same distance as those of the preceding set, and the threads laid in the first operation are overcast, any slackness remaining being thus taken up.

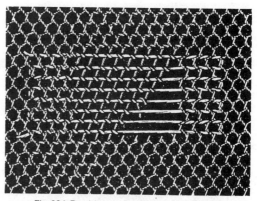

Fig. 894. Repairing net. Laying the second threads.

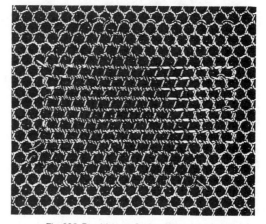

Fig. 895. Repairing net. Laying the third threads.

To strengthen the cut edges, every straight bar is overcast with a stitch worked up. Then, to make the crossed bar of the material, the thread is passed, with a second stitch, under the single horizontal thread, then brought to the surface and carried to the next thread. In the same way, always following the direction of the thread, worn parts of the net that are not actually torn can be reinforced.

Lace Embroidered in Darning Stitch on Net With Buttonholed Edge (fig. 896). After the design has been traced on linen paper, the net is secured over the paper and all the outlines are followed in darning stitch with DMC floss flax or flourishing thread no. 25.

The little flowers and leaves are entirely filled by a second row of darning stitch, worked inside the outlines. The scalloped edge is worked in buttonhole stitch over two rows of running stitch.

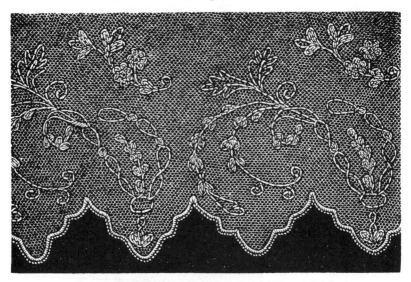

Fig. 896. Lace embroidered in darning stitch on net with buttonholed edge.

Corner for a Handkerchief. Lace Embroidered in Darning Stitch on Net With Outlining and Buttonholed Edge (fig. 897). Floral designs resembling those of real lace are particularly suitable for this kind of work.

The net is first secured over linen paper on which the design has been traced, then all the outlines are followed with a very fine thread, DMC floss flax or flourishing thread no. 70. All the motifs are then filled with darning stitch, picking up every other bar of the net. The materials used are DMC floss flax or flourishing thread no. 50 for the filling, and no. 25 of the same thread for the thick outlines in running stitch. The outer edge, composed of rose scallops, is finished off with buttonholing worked over a double row of running stitch.

Limerick Lace (fig. 898). Limerick lace, so called from its place of origin, is a type of lace embroidered on net in imitation of the bobbin lace of Brussels. It is rich work with floral designs embroidered on net. The small solid parts are worked in darning stitch or chain stitch, and the large, ornamented parts are embroidered with openwork fillings. The outside edge is strengthened with a woven braid with picots, held in place by a row of buttonhole stitching.

This kind of work requires a tracing, over which the net is carefully secured. The outlining is done with a coarse thread—DMC special quality embroidery cotton no. 20 was used for our example—in running stitch with little eyelets here and there. The solid parts are worked in darning stitch with DMC special quality embroidery cotton no. 30; no. 50 of the same thread is used for the open overcast eyelet holes and for the openwork fill-

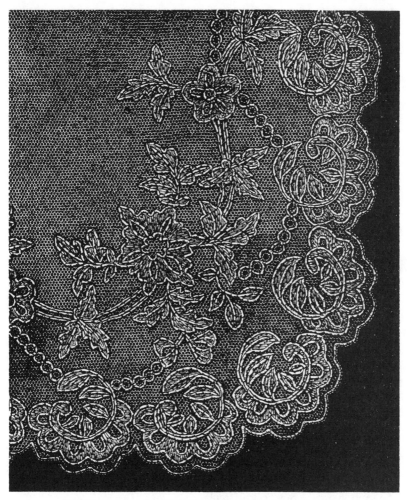

Fig. 897. Corner for a handkerchief. Lace embroidered in darning stitch on net with outlining and buttonholed edge.

ings, which are copied from figs. 878, 882, and 885, except for the large leaves, which are ornamented with diagonal stripes in darning stitch.

Wide Lace Embroidered on Net With Various Fillings and

Outlines in Crochet Braid (figs. 899 and 900). This wide lace edging, worked on coarse-meshed net, is intended for trimming curtains, blinds, and altar cloths. Lack of space forces us to illustrate this example in two parts; the letters A and B show where the two sections join.

Fig. 898. Limerick lace.

The work is begun by tracing the outlines with two strands of DMC special stranded cotton no. 25, after which the filling stitches are worked with nine strands of the same thread. The fillings used are those with small designs, figs. 875 to 881, for the stems and leaves; those with large designs, figs. 883, 884, or 886, for the large spaces inside the other motifs. When all the stitches have been finished, the leaves and flowers are surrounded with a crochet chain, and the circles with treble crochet, worked in DMC special stranded cotton no. 25. At the center of the flowers and leaves, a wheel is made in darning stitch. The heading of the lace is finished off with a row of herringbone stitch, edged with crochet chain, and followed by a row of open treble and a row of close treble.

The edge of the lace is finished with a row of crochet picots. The crochet braids are worked separately and then sewn to the net with DMC Alsatian sewing cotton no. 50.

Lace Embroidered on Net. Imitation of Needlepoint (figs. 901 and 902). Our illustration shows an imitation of needlepoint worked on a foundation of net with buttonholed outlines. When all the outlines have been traced, the closely filled figures are embroidered with the lace stitch

Fig. 899. Wide lace embroidered on net with various filling stitches and outlines in crochet braid. First part.

that is explained later in the chapter ''Needlemade Laces,'' fig. 960. Every stitch takes up not only the little loop of thread but also one mesh of the net;

see the explanatory illustration, fig. 902. The more transparent parts are filled with simpler stitches, which can be chosen from among those shown in figs. 875 to 885. When all the fillings are completed, the outlines are

Fig. 900. Wide lace embroidered on net with various filling stitches
and outlines in crochet braid. Second part.

worked in buttonhole stitch over a fourfold padding thread; then the net is cut away from the centers of the circles and flowers, which are filled with a

Fig. 901. Lace embroidered on net. Imitation of needlepoint.

Fig. 902. Detail of the lace in fig. 901.

small wheel. A little rosette in bullion stitch is next worked in the middle of the large scallops.

If the lace is to be added to cambric or linen, the two are joined by the last row of buttonholing; the edges of the material are afterward carefully cut away with scissors.

The materials to be used are DMC floss flax or flourishing thread no. 60 for the buttonholed outlines, and no. 100 of the same thread for the lace stitches.

Handkerchief Corner in Appliqué on Net (fig. 903). The handkerchief corner shown in our illustration is completely different from the ex-

Fig. 903. Handkerchief corner in appliqué on net.

amples of lace embroidered on net that we have given up to now. Here the motifs of the design consist of cambric appliqués sewn to the net foundation. The design is traced onto the cambric itself; the latter is laid, straight by the threads, over fine net, and secured all round the edges with running stitches. This double layer of material is mounted on American cloth, then all the outlines are followed with short stitches, which are then covered with buttonholing. Care must be taken that every stitch penetrate both cambric and net. When all the outlines have been buttonholed, the cambric is cut away outside the figures of the design so that the net alone forms the background. The completely open parts, for which both layers of material are cut away, are ornamented with overcast bars and wheels.

As materials, a supple thread, DMC special quality embroidery cotton no. 50, should be used for the buttonholing, and a twisted thread, DMC 6 cord cotton lace thread no. 50, for the bars and wheels.

Carrickmacross Lace (figs. 904 and 905).   Carrickmacross lace, like Limerick lace, is made in Ireland, but it is of more recent origin. It is a kind

Fig. 904. Carrickmacross lace.

of appliqué work in which all the motifs are in cambric appliqué on fine net. They rest in part on the net, and elsewhere are joined to it or to each other by buttonholed bars. Embroidery stitches or openwork fillings are sometimes worked on the net inside the motifs, when the size of these permits this treatment.

The design is traced on cambric, which is mounted in a frame and backed with a layer of Brussels net; the outlines are followed with a line of very small running stitches which join the two layers of material.

The outlines are embroidered, and the buttonholed bars which join the different parts of the design are worked at the same time. The edges of this lace are very characteristic: they are not buttonholed in the usual way; instead a round cord is simply sewn on all round the edge with moderately

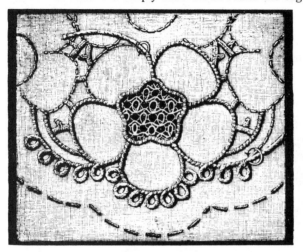

tight overcast stitch in fine thread, DMC 6 cord cotton lace thread no. 50, for instance. This cord forms eyelets round the outside of the lace; see fig. 905. The working of the buttonhole bars and picots is explained in the chapter ''Needlemade Laces,'' fig. 921. When the outlines and the connecting bars

Fig. 905.
Method of working the outlines for the lace in fig. 904.

are finished, the cambric and net are cut away from the inside as indicated by the illustration, fig. 904.

The openwork filling on the net consists of eyelets. In the middle of the leaves, the openwork filling surrounded by buttonholing is worked in herringbone stitch or in plain overcast bars. Some of the flower centers are filled with wheels within a circle of buttonhole stitches; for all these stitches, DMC 6 cord cotton lace thread no. 70 is used. When all the work is completely finished, the cambric is cut away round the outside.

Spanish Laces. Embroideries in Metal Threads and Colored Luster Threads.   The richest embroidered laces are those that come from Spain and Italy, worked in metal threads and colored luster threads, with or without a foundation of linen. We give three characteristic examples of this kind of work. The first is an insertion embroidered on ecru cambric with gold thread and green thread, and easy to work; the second is a Moorish square, rich in color, with outlines and ornamental stitches in gold; finally, we give a specimen of filigree lace in gold and silver threads superembroidered in colored threads.

Materials.   For the working of our examples, we recommend the use of well twisted metal threads. For the outlines, gold and silver threads are worked over in buttonhole stitch with a moderately twisted luster thread such as DMC Alsa. For the fillings in encroaching satin stitch in the Moorish embroidery, we advise the use of DMC Persian silk. When gold and silver thread or spangles are to be secured invisibly, this should be

Fig. 906. Insertion in Spanish embroidery.

done with DMC Alsa in golden yellow or ash grey.

Insertion in Spanish embroidery (figs. 906 and 907).   This type of embroidery consists of sur-
rounding every
part of a design
traced on linen
or cambric with
a double thread
of metal held
down with
buttonhole
stitches worked
in a colored
thread. The in-
sides of the
figures are filled
with ornamental
stitches in gold
or silver
threads. The
material lying
between the or-
naments is cut
away when the

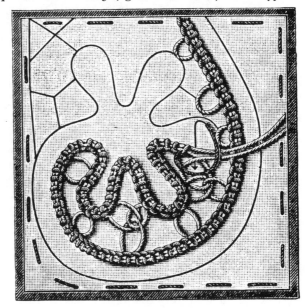

Fig. 907. Method of making the picoted outlines
in the insertion in fig. 906.

embroidery is finished; picots formed by the metal threads of the outline connect the various parts of the design. The outlines are worked first: two metal threads are laid side by side and held down with buttonhole stitches. Where required by the design a small loop is made—a picot—which is also secured by a buttonhole stitch. Fig. 907 shows how the picots are interlaced to join the motifs across the open spaces of the design. To fill the figures themselves, wheels with six spokes are embroidered in darning stitch in the center of the leaves; two threads of gold form little eyelets which fill all the other parts of the design.

Ecru cambric is used for the foundation; the buttonhole stitches are worked in DMC Alsa in golden green; the gold thread which forms the eyelets is secured with DMC Alsa in golden yellow.

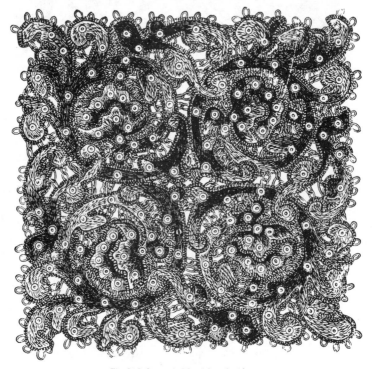

Fig. 908. Square in Moorish embroidery.

When the embroidery is completely finished, the cambric foundation is cut away from beneath the picots, close to the buttonholing.

Square in Moorish embroidery (figs. 908 and 909). The preparatory work is the same for this kind of embroidered lace as for Spanish embroidery, that is to say, the design is first outlined in a double thread of metal. In the interior of the figures the ornamental stitches in gold and

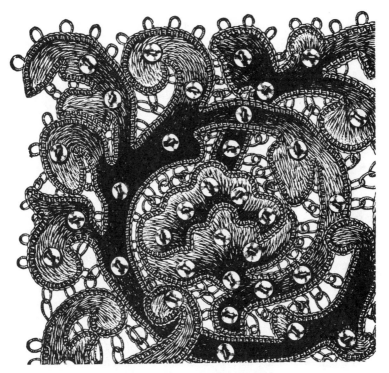

Fig. 909. One quarter of the square in fig. 908.

silver are replaced by a filling of encroaching satin stitch worked with colored silk and further enriched by the addition of gold or silver spangles. Fig. 909 show one quarter of this design. This beautiful work

Fig. 910. Filigree lace.

could be used to trim a small cushion or sachet.

The materials used are: fine gold thread and DMC Alsa in golden yellow for the outlines; for the satin stitch, DMC Persian silk in indigo and old rose for the large flowers and the foliage proceeding from those flowers, yellow-green and golden green are used for the other ornaments of the square.

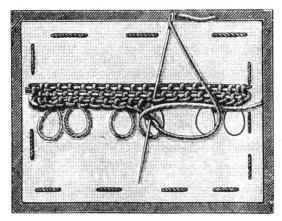

Fig. 911. How to make the plain picots.

The materials used are: fine gold thread and DMC Alsa in golden yellow for the outlines; for the satin stitch, DMC Persian silk in indigo and old rose for the large flowers and the foliage proceeding from those flowers, yellow- green and golden green are used for the other ornaments of the square.

Filigree lace (figs. 910, 911, 912, 913). Of all Spanish laces, filigree lace is the most delicate; we give an example of it in fig. 910. The original trims a silk tablecloth of the seventeenth century, of Spanish origin.

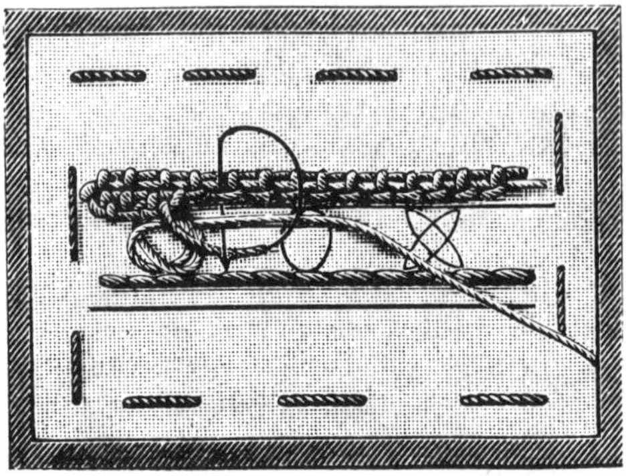

The working of this kind of embroidery is more difficult than the preceding ones, and requires a very sure hand. The various parts of the design are made of metal thread united by buttonhole stitches in brilliant cotton, worked from a tracing on linen paper, without a foundation of material.

Fig. 912. How to make the interlacing picots.

After the design has been traced onto the unglazed side of the linen paper, the latter is tacked down to dark American cloth, glazed side up. The preparatory work consists of embroidering a line in stem stitch (fig. 80) along the top of each part of the design, on which the first line of buttonhole stitch will later be worked. The line of stem stitch should penetrate both the linen paper and the American cloth. When this preparatory work has been done, the making of the lace itself can be begun.

As we have already said, the lace is composed of metal threads joined by buttonhole stitching in colored thread. The first row of buttonholing is worked over a metal thread and into the line of stem stitch; when the end of the motif is reached, the metal thread is doubled back and a second row of buttonhole stitches is worked in the opposite direction, the stitches being set

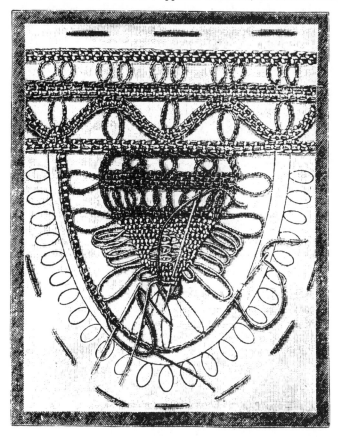

Fig. 913. Method of working a scallop of the lace in fig. 910.

into the loops formed by the previous row. In this way successive rows of stitches are added until the figure is completely filled. In the last row of buttonholing, picots are formed with the metal thread, serving either to connect the motifs or to finish off the outside edge. Where the picots are to connect parts of the design, they must be joined by a buttonhole stitch to the next part to be embroidered. When a fresh thread has to be joined in, a few buttonhole stitches are worked over the beginning of the new thread and the end of the old one, after which the protruding ends are cut off.

For the working of our example, fig. 910, we advise beginning the work at the top, with the upper edge of the heading which borders the wavy line. The first row of buttonholing is worked up with gold thread and green Alsa. Plain picots are made here. The second row of stitches, buttonholed down, is worked in red; the third in blue. In this row the large picots which join the heading to the wavy line are made. The latter is also worked in blue. In the first row the large picots hanging down from the previous row are joined in, and the large lower picots are made in the second row. A straight line is then worked with a row of blue followed by a row of red, the lower picots of the serpentine line being joined into the first of these rows. At the top of the heading two rows of red are added, joining in the plain picots.

The scallops are begun with the inner horizontal bars, with picots interlaced as shown in fig. 912; the course of the work is shown in fig. 913. The coloring of the scallops is varied in groups of three; blue, green, and cream are used for the buttonholing over the gold thread, grey and red over the silver thread. The first scallop of the group is begun at the top with blue; this is followed by two little pyramids in grey and one in red; the outer semicircle is in green.

The second scallop is begun with cream, followed by two pyramids in green and one in blue, and completed with a semicircle in red. In the third scallop, green bars, two red pyramids, and one cream are followed by a semicircle in blue.

When the embroidery is finished, the rows of stem stitch are cut at the back, stitch by stitch, and the lace comes away of itself from the foundation. Any little ends of thread remaining in the lace must be carefully removed.

Needlemade lace. Sixteenth century Venetian point.

CHAPTER XVII

Needlemade Laces

The kind of work known as needlemade lace may be considered a derivative of openwork on linen. As their name suggests, needlemade laces are made without the help of any implement except a needle; they consist of buttonhole stitches and knot stitches variously combined and worked with a single thread.

The most ancient of these laces is Reticella, the designs of which closely resemble those of openwork on linen. Lace with designs in relief and irregular bars, known as Venetian point and "point de France," came into being in the seventeenth century.

The eighteenth century gave preference to lace worked on a foundation of loops or net, such as "point d'Alencon," "point d'Argentan," etc. Nowadays the very fine needlemade laces produced in Belgium, Saxony, and Bohemia are much appreciated and, even though they require a great deal of time and patience to work, their production is not confined to commerce but ranks also among the branches of needlework practised at home as a pastime.

The type of lace most popular among amateurs is Renaissance lace. This is made with plain or fancy braids which are arranged according to the lines of a given design and connected either by bars alone, by lace stitches alone, or by both bars and lace stitches. Next to Renaissance lace, Reticella lace, worked with fairly coarse thread, is greatly appreciated.

Beside classic laces of Italian origin, we shall introduce our readers to several types of oriental lace worked in knot stitches, most frequently in silk; then to the coarse lace made with flax thread known as Hedebo, which comes to us from Norway and Sweden; and finally the fine Spanish and Brazilian laces known as Sol and Teneriffe lace.

We begin our explanations with a description of Renaissance lace, which will give us an occasion to show the way of working the various bars and lace stitches which reappear in most other types of lace. Thus Renaissance lace may be considered as a kind of training ground for the most elaborate work.

Braids. The braids used for Renaissance lace are usually to be had in white, ecru, straw color, and black, and in the most varied shapes and sizes; they may be narrow or wide, coarse or fine, with or without openwork edges or picots, or again in the form of medallions of various sizes. Fig. 914 shows the most generally used braids, as well as a specimen of picot edging which can be obtained ready made, unless, of course, one prefers to make the picots by hand.

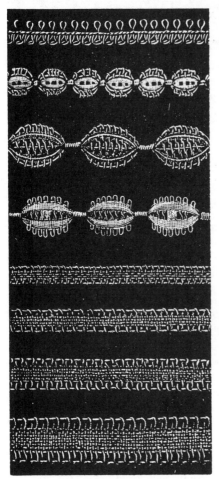

Fig. 914. Various fancy braids and beadings for Renaissance lace.

Materials. For making bars and working lace stitches in all kinds of lace, the best threads are DMC 6 cord cotton lace thread, DMC Alsatian sewing cotton, DMC special quality crochet cotton, DMC 6 cord crochet cotton, DMC flax lace thread, DMC flax thread for knitting and crochet, or DMC Alsatia, all of which have the necessary qualities—brilliance and suppleness—for this kind of work. They are, furthermore, very pleasant to use and can be obtained in the same shades as the braid.

For oriental knot stitch laces, which are sometimes made in several colors, we recommend DMC pearl cotton or DMC Alsatia.

Copying Designs for Renaissance Lace. The design to be copied is usually traced onto transparent architect's linen (tracing linen), on which the design is drawn with a special ink; the linen should be carefully placed with the shiny side next to the original so that the tracing can be done on the matt side, which takes the ink better than the shiny surface. With this linen, it is possible to trace the design directly, without having recourse to any of the more elaborate methods of tracing. Before the work is begun, the linen can be backed with colored paper or material to avoid eye strain.

Designs for Renaissance lace consist of double lines, between which the braid is tacked with small running stitches.

How to Tack On and Gather the Braid (fig. 915). The running stitches must be very regular and slightly longer on the surface of the work

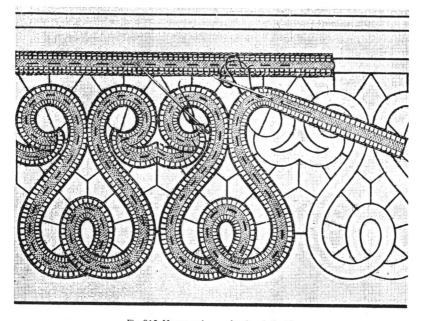

Fig. 915. How to tack on and gather the braid.

than on the wrong side. When the lines of the design are curved, the braid is sewn to the outer line so that it is slightly gathered on the inner side.

When the braid has been tacked on all over the design, the fullness on the inner side of all the curves is drawn up, using a very fine thread and making overcast stitches over the edge of the braid, so that the excess length disappears and the edge just fits the design.

The stitches made for connecting bars and openwork stitches which fill the spaces must be drawn to exactly the degree of tightness which will avoid either pulling the edges of the braid out of shape or allowing the bars or fillings to sag. Further, the stitches must never penetrate the tracing linen, but only rest on it.

When the work is finished, it is turned wrong side up and every second or third stitch of the tacking is cut. Then all the little ends of thread are pulled out, and the lace comes away of itself from the foundation.

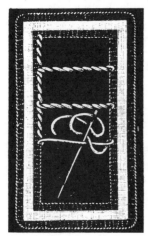

Fig. 916.
Overcast bars.

It does not matter which are worked first, the bars or the openwork stitches; we would, nevertheless, advise finishing the bars first, particularly if they are buttonholed, for once the bars have been done, there is less danger of the work being pulled out of shape during the embroidering of the openwork stitches. When the lace is finished, it is ironed and starched. Directions for this will be found in the chapter "Miscellaneous Directions."

Needles. No special needles are made for lacemaking; we advise the use of long sewing needles, of a thickness proportionate to the thread used.

Fig. 917.
Double overcast bars.

Fig. 918.
Plain buttonhole bars.

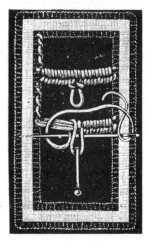

Fig. 919.
Bars with pinned or loop picots.

Stitches. We are now about to give a series of charming stitches of various kinds which will, at the same time, serve as practice for the fine laces, Venetian point and needlepoint, which we shall describe later. We cannot claim to give all the lace stitches in existence, but we have collected a large enough number of examples to enable every worker to find some that will suit her personal taste and ability.

As for the names of these stitches, it happens so often that the same stitch has been given many different names that we have thought it better, except in the case of stitches which are generally known by one particular name, to distinguish them only by numbers.

Fig. 920. Bars with pinned or loop picots.

Fig. 921. Bars with buttonhole or Venetian picots.

Overcast bars (fig. 916). The thread is fastened on and stretched across the empty space from one selvedge to the other. The needle is then passed down and the first thread is overcast as many times as may be necessary to give the two threads the appearance of a twisted cord. If there are insufficient overcast stitches, the bars will have a loose, untidy appearance which will detract from the beauty of the work.

When the bar is finished, the overcasting is continued along the edge of the braid as far as the spot marked for the next bar.

Fig. 922. Bars with bullion picots.

Fig. 923. Bars with ring picots.

Double overcast bars (fig. 917). For these bars, three threads are stretched across the space and then covered with overcast stitches set rather farther apart than for the bars shown in fig. 916.

Plain buttonhole bars (fig. 918). Three threads are first laid, then covered from right to left, with buttonhole stitches. It will be noticed in the illustration that the needle is passed eye first under the threads; strange as this may appear, it will be found helpful, as there is less danger in this way of splitting or separating the threads.

Fig. 924.
Bars with double buttonholing.

The thread with which the buttonhole stitches are worked should be brought out from the edge of the braid one or two threads distant from the threads laid for the bar; this will keep the bars from being uneven in width or twisting at the beginning.

Bars with pinned or loop picots (figs. 919 and 920). When the buttonhole stitches have been worked along one-third or half the length of the bar, the thread is passed, without making a loop, under the laid threads; the loop is held by a pin passed under the work; the needle is passed from right to left under the three threads (see fig. 919); and the stitch is drawn tight in such a way as to bring it as close as possible to the buttonhole stitch of the bar.

In fig. 920 we show a picot made in the same way, but with two buttonhole stitches between the loop and the bar.

Bars with buttonhole or Venetian picots (fig. 921). After the bar has been prepared and buttonholed to the required distance, a loop is made as for the type of picot shown in figs. 919 and 920. The thread is then

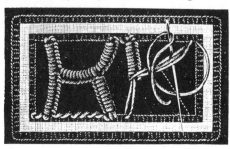

Fig. 925. Branched bars.

brought back to the middle of the loop, the pin is inserted, the threads are drawn tight, the needle is passed behind the pin, and the buttonhole stitches are begun quite close to the pin and below it, thus covering the threads behind which it is set.

The pin should be set at a distance from the bar equivalent to the width of six stitches, so that the threads may be completely hidden by these stitches.

Bars with bullion picots (fig. 922). The needle is inserted into the last buttonhole stitch and half its length brought through; it is twisted ten to twelve times round the thread, from left to right, and then drawn through the twists of thread thus made round it; the thread is then drawn up so that the twists form a semicircle and the bar is continued; see also figs. 991 and 993.

Bars with ring picots (fig. 923). The buttonholing of the bar is continued to a little distance beyond the middle of the bar; then the thread is brought back and three threads are laid, secured in the seventh or eighth buttonhole stitch; and buttonhole stitches are worked over these threads until they are covered; the bar is then completed in the usual way. This type of picot is used for the outside edge of lace edgings.

Bars with double buttonholing (fig. 924). Two threads are laid and over them double buttonhole stitches are worked, with sufficient space between the groups for the stitches which will be worked on the second side of the bar. These double buttonhole stitches consist of an ordinary buttonhole stitch, followed by a reversed stitch; that is to say, the needle is passed under the laid threads, then up under the loop, so that the thread lies behind the stitch and not in front of it as in ordinary buttonholing.

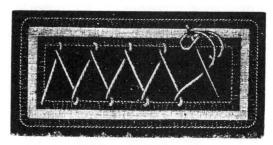

Fig. 926. Plain herringbone stitch.

Fig. 927. Twisted insertion stitch.

Fig. 928. Column stitch.

Branched bars (fig. 925). When a fairly large surface is to be covered with bars it is usually necessary to make the bars branched. For the example shown in our illustration, the threads are laid as for any other type of bar and then covered with buttonhole stitches to half their length; from that point, threads are laid for another bar branching from the first; these threads are then covered as far as the dotted line, and further threads are laid from this point and buttonholed; then the uncovered part of the second bar is worked, and finally the first bar is finished.

Plain herringbone stitch (fig. 926). In addition to bars, all kinds of stitches are used to join the braids and fill the spaces which frequently remain between them. These stitches, which form a kind of insertion, are sometimes quite elementary, while others require considerable skill and patience.

Fig. 929. Single loop insertion stitch.

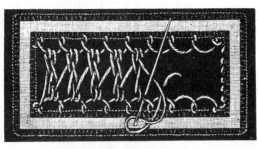

Fig. 930. Double loop insertion stitch (plaited insertion stitch).

Fig. 931. Bead stitch insertion.

The simplest of all these stitches is herringbone stitch, which, as used in lace, is essentially the same as herringbone stitch in plain sewing (fig. 49), and double back stitch (fig. 83). The needle is passed down under the selvedge of the braid, then up under the opposite selvedge, keeping the thread always in front of the needle. The same number of loops of the edge of the braid should always be left between the stitches, and the lower stitches should be placed exactly halfway between those of the upper row.

Twisted insertion stitch (fig. 927). This is in reality a variation of herringbone stitch. Instead of passing the needle behind the thread, it is passed in front of and around the thread, so that the needle always emerges beneath the thread, which is twisted twice.

Column stitch (fig. 928). This is yet another variation of herringbone stitch. A plain herringbone stitch is made at the bottom, and the stitch shown in fig. 927 at the top, passing the second thread three times round the first.

Fig. 932.
Cluster insertion.

Loop inser-tion stitch (figs. 929 and 930). Along two edges of braid very loose buttonhole stitches are made, all the same size and the same distance apart. When this is done, the two sets of loops are joined by the stitches shown in figs. 926 and 927.

In fig. 930, two herringbone stitches are work-ed into each buttonhole loop; three or four stitches can be worked in this way into each loop, according to the degree of transparency desired. When two or more stitches are work-ed into each loop, the stitch is often known as plaited insertion stitch.

Bead stitch in-sertion (fig. 931). The loops at opposite sides are joined with

Fig. 933.
Plain branch insertion.

Fig. 934.
Branch insertion with wheels.

Fig. 935.
Insertion with darned leaves.

four stitches. The threads forming these stitches must lie flat, side by side; they must never overlap each other. After the fourth stitch, the thread is wound round the lower loop and then carried to the next loop, where the four stitches are repeated.

Cluster insertion (fig. 932). Two bars are made as in fig. 916, a short distance apart, then a third, which is, however, covered only halfway with the second thread. When the middle of this bar is reached, the three are joined by five or six buttonhole stitches, then the rest of the third bar is overcast. For the next cluster the needle is brought out quite close to the third bar of the preceding cluster.

Fig. 936. Insertion with small wheels.

Fig. 937. Insertion with large wheels.

Branch insertions (figs. 933 and 934). The thread is laid lengthwise along the middle of the space between two selvedges, from one to the other of the selvedges at the ends of the space; the thread is passed under two or three threads of the braid across the end of the space, according to the thickness of the braid; it is then brought back along the first thread and inserted into the selvedges on the long sides, first up on the left, then down on the right, forming three loops which are secured by a knot, as is clearly shown in fig. 933. After the first time, the stitch up to the edge of the braid at the end is naturally omitted.

The insertion shown in fig. 934 is begun in the same way and the branch loops are also the same, but each intersection of the threads is adorned with a large wheel which is added when the knot has been made.

Insertion with darned leaves (fig. 935). The thread is fastened on at the point where the first leaf, according to the design, is to be made. It is then carried to the opposite side, passed through the edge of the braid and brought back again to the starting point; the threads at either side are laid as in figs. 933 and 934 and secured by a knot as in fig. 933; the thread is carried up along the middle leaf, brought up from below through the braid, and a small leaf is worked in darning stitch as explained in the chapter "Filet Lace," figs. 705 and 706.

Insertion with small wheels (fig. 936). For this stitch, two rows of herringbone stitch are worked, crossing each other; then the thread is brought to the level of the intersections of the stitches, a wheel is made over five threads, and the needle is passed under the finished wheel and carried to the next intersection. If larger wheels are desired, the herringbone stitches must be set farther apart.

Insertion with large wheels (fig. 937). The thread is fastened on at the middle of one of the short sides of the insertion and laid across the space; it is secured at the opposite side and then brought by means of overcast stitches to the corner. From there, a loose loop is made to the opposite corner, the needle is passed under six or eight threads of the selvedge, then passed under the first thread and behind the loop, and the stitch is secured in the opposite selvedge.

The thread is again laid across the space and over the first thread, the needle is brought back to the middle and a large wheel is worked over four threads, always

Fig. 938. Insertion with darned pyramids.

Fig. 939. Insertion with darned pyramids.

Fig. 940. Insertion with buttonholed squares.

picking up the same threads, then the single thread is overcast, the needle is brought back to the selvedge and the second loop is made by bringing out the thread at the point at which it emerged for the other two stitches.

Insertion with darned pyramids (figs. 938 and 939). Herringbone stitches, set very far apart, are worked between two edges of braid; the thread is then brought to the point of one of these stitches, that is to say, to the edge of the braid, and darning stitches are worked over half the height of the herringbone stitch. In this way little pyramid-shaped points are made;

see also fig. 707. To pass to the next point, a few overcast stitches are made over the thread of the herringbone stitch.

If two rows of herringbone stitch are worked, as in fig. 939, the darning can be done in such a way that the points of the pyramids touch, their bases resting on the edge of the braid.

Insertion with buttonholed squares (fig. 940). When rows of loops have been made along the edges of the braid, as in figs. 929, 930, and 931, a thread is run through these loops; this thread serves as a foundation for the herringbone stitch which connects the two edges. The empty squares between the herringbone stitches are filled with buttonhole stitches, worked as shown in fig. 710 in the chapter "Filet Lace."

Insertion with half bars (fig. 941). The thread is fastened on at one corner of the braid and brought to the middle of the width of the insertion, it is then inserted into the edge of the braid on the right-hand side and covered with buttonhole stitches to halfway across the space. It is then carried to the left-hand edge and inserted a little below the half bar on the right and covered with the same number of buttonhole stitches as the first half.

Fig. 941. Insertion with half bars.

This insertion can also be varied by making more buttonhole stitches on one side than on the other.

Lace stitches. When working lace stitches, care must be taken that the number of loops in each row remains the same when a regular space is being filled; further, if one row begins or ends with a whole loop, there must be a half loop in the next row, and a whole loop again in the succeeding row.

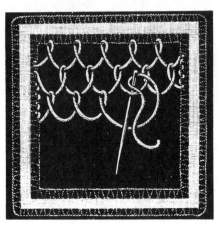

Fig. 942. First lace stitch. Tulle stitch.

When the space to be filled becomes narrower or wider, the number of loops must be decreased or increased in proportion to the changes in the design. The depth allowed for each loop should be the same number of threads of the braid as was passed over for each loop in the first row.

First lace stitch. Tulle stitch (fig. 942). Buttonhole stitches are worked in rows backward and forward, loosely enough to form loops into which the next row is worked. This stitch is also commonly known as open buttonhole filling.

Second lace stitch (fig. 943). The same distances are allowed for these stitches as for those in fig. 942, but two buttonhole stitches are made close together. It is advisable to make the loops a little less rounded than for tulle stitch.

Fig. 943. Second lace stitch.

Third lace stitch (fig. 944). Here three buttonhole stitches are made close together, connected by a loop of thread. This loop should be only just long enough to take the three buttonhole stitches of the next row.

Fourth lace stitch (fig. 945). The work is begun from left to right, with two buttonhole stitches fairly close together followed by one of twice the length.

In the second row, worked from right to left, one stitch is worked into the loop between the two stitches set close together, and three stitches are worked into the long loop. Fig. 945 shows how the next row is worked.

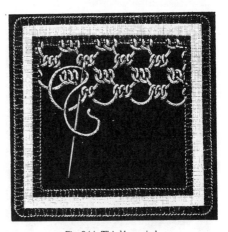

Fig. 944. Third lace stitch.

Fifth lace stitch (fig. 946). As in fig. 945, this stitch is begun from left to right, but in this case three stitches are made close together, followed by a loop equal in length to the three stitches.

In the next row, one buttonhole stitch is worked into each of the loops between the three stitches, and nine into the long loop.

Sixth lace stitch (fig. 947). The first row, worked from left to right, consists of tulle stitches set at least six to eight threads of the braid apart and drawn rather tight; in the second row as many buttonhole stitches are worked into each loop as may be necessary to cover the thread completely.

In the third row, the needle is inserted into the little loop between two groups of buttonhole stitches, so that these groups of close stitches are arranged in vertical lines over the surface they cover.

Fig. 945. Fourth lace stitch.

Seventh lace stitch (fig. 948). The first row, from left to right, is made up of groups of two buttonhole stitches, the two stitches in the group being separated by a slightly shorter space than that between the groups. In the next row the long loops are missed, and a single stitch is worked into each short loop of the first row. In the third row, two stitches are worked into each loop.

Eighth lace stitch (fig. 949). This stitch, with its round openings produced by the arrangement of the stitches, is frequently called perforated net stitch.

The first row consists of stitches placed fairly close together and all the same distance apart. In the second row, one buttonhole stitch is worked into the last stitch of the first row, then three stitches and two loops are missed, one buttonhole stitch is worked into each of the next two loops, etc.

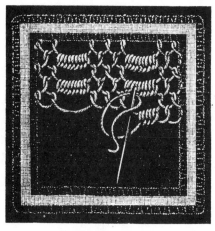

Fig. 946. Fifth lace stitch.

In the third row, three stitches are worked into the long loop and one into the loop between the two stitches of the previous row, etc. In the fourth row, the openings, or perforations, are placed between those of the preceding row.

Ninth and tenth lace stitches (figs. 950 and 951). The stitches shown in these two illustrations are variants of Venetian or tulle pyramid stitch.

Both are begun with a row of buttonhole stitches set very close together. The stitch in fig. 950 is worked in three rows; in the second, two stitches are missed and one stitch worked into each of the next two loops; in the third, the loops below the missed stitches are again missed, and only one stitch is made. In the next row, the same number of stitches as in the first row is again worked.

The stitch in fig. 951 requires five rows. The first is very close; in the second, the stitches are made in groups of four, missing two of the previous row between the groups; in the third, the stitches are made in groups of three; in the fourth in groups of two; and in the fifth, single stitches.

The threads which separate the groups of stitches must be drawn very evenly and fairly tightly, particularly those between the single stitches of the fifth row, so that the stitches of the next row, which form the first row of the next series of pyramids, may cover them well.

This last stitch is frequently called V filling stitch.

Eleventh lace stitch (fig. 952). The first row consists of plain tulle stitch; the second row is the same, except that a group of three buttonhole stitches is worked into the middle loop; in the third row three stitches are worked into the

Fig. 947. Sixth lace stitch.

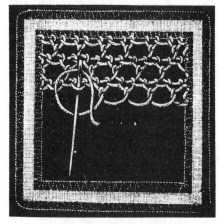

Fig. 948. Seventh lace stitch.

complete loops to the right and left of the group of three stitches of the second row, and one stitch into each half loop on either side of the central group; the fourth row is like the second.

In the fifth row, the position of the groups of close stitches is reversed: they are worked into the fourth loop, counting the half bar before and after the group of three stitches of the fourth row, so that there will be, between

Fig. 949. Eighth lace stitch.

Fig. 950. Ninth lace stitch.

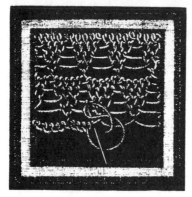

Fig. 951. Tenth lace stitch.

two groups of three stitches, six single buttonhole stitches and seven loops.

Twelfth lace stitch (fig. 953). The thread is fastened on at the left, a quarter of an inch down the edge of the braid, then carried up to the top edge, where three very close buttonhole stitches are made; a loop of thread is left, long enough to reach to the level of the first stitch, and three more stitches are made in the top edge.

In the second row, three stitches are worked into each loop, but the thread is drawn tight between the groups. The third row is like the first, except that the needle is inserted between the threads of the buttonhole stitches and not into the loops.

Thirteenth lace stitch (fig. 954). For this stitch, two buttonhole stitches are made very close together in the edge of the braid, then a third is made completing these at the bottom and drawn as close to them as possible; the threads which connect the groups of stitches should be drawn very tight, so that the rows of stitches form straight lines and not scallops.

Fourteenth lace stitch (fig. 955). This is begun by a row of buttonhole stitches set well apart; in the next row, two buttonhole stitches are worked into each loop and at the bottom of these not one stitch, as in fig. 954, but two are worked, producing a ground of vertical bars.

Fifteenth lace stitch (fig. 956). This is another stitch resembling the first two: groups of three stitches are made into the edge of the braid, or into the loops between the groups; these stitches are then united by a transverse stitch at the bottom.

Sixteenth lace stitch (fig. 957). The first row, worked once more from left to right, consists of short sloping seed-shaped bars, worked like the picot in fig. 921. The first stitch is made through the loop of the previous row, the second over the two threads at a distance corresponding to the space which will be occupied by the three stitches which are made over the second stitch.

The first stitch of the next group of four buttonhole stitches must always be quite close to the last stitch of the preceding group.

Seventeenth lace stitch (fig. 958). This stitch is a variant of the preceding one, and both are frequently known under the name of "point de grains." In this version, the stitches are worked backward and forward, without the intermediate row of plain tulle stitch; the illustration shows the direction of the needle for the stitches which are made from right to left.

Eighteenth lace stitch (fig. 959). This figure and those that follow represent a series of stitches frequently found in old Venetian lace; it is therefore reasonable that they should be generally known as Venetian lace stitches. The stitch shown in fig. 959 is also frequently known as Hollie or Holy point, from its use in the once popular lace of that name, and as "point d'entoilage."

The arrangement and sequence of the rows produce less transparent effects than the grounds we have so far described. In these grounds a row of tulle stitch is first worked, then a thread is laid across level with the bottom of the loops; in the next row, the needle passes through each loop and at

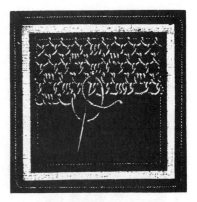

Fig. 952. Eleventh lace stitch.

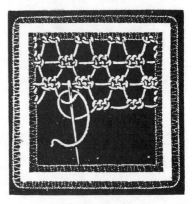

Fig. 953. Twelfth lace stitch.

Fig. 954. Thirteenth lace stitch.

the same time over the laid thread. Fig. 959 shows how the thread is laid.

Nineteenth lace stitch (fig. 960). In old examples of lace these stitches are often to be found worked as in fig. 959, but very close together, giving the appearance of a braided fabric, as can be seen in fig. 960.

Twentieth lace stitch (fig. 961). Openings can be made in the rows of close stitches by missing a few loops on the return journey. In the next

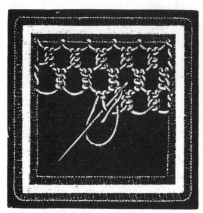

Fig. 955. Fourteenth lace stitch.

Fig. 956. Fifteenth lace stitch.

Fig. 957. Sixteenth lace stitch.

Fig. 958. Seventeenth lace stitch.

journey, the bar, composed now of three threads, is covered with the same number of stitches as were missed before. These openings can be arranged according to a regular pattern, traced beforehand, or according to individual fancy.

Twenty-first lace stitch (fig. 962). There are still other ways of varying Venetian lace stitches. They consist of embroidering the needlemade ground in various manners.

Fig. 962 shows a ground of close stitches embroidered with raised spots, for which a more loosely twisted thread is used than that used for the ground. Lace grounds can further be trimmed with little buttonholed rosettes, bullion stitch stars, or other fancy stitches.

Twenty-second lace stitch (fig. 963). This is the stitch commonly known as double tulle stitch. The thread is fastened onto the left-hand braid

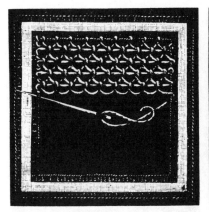

Fig. 959. Eighteenth lace stitch.

Fig. 960. Nineteenth lace stitch.

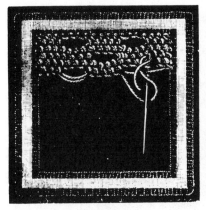

Fig. 961. Twentieth lace stitch.

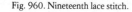

Fig. 962. Twenty-first lace stitch.

edge and held with the left thumb, the needle is inserted into the braid at the top and at the same time into the loop of thread, as shown in the illustration. When the thread has thus been twisted round the needle, the latter is drawn through the loop and the thread drawn out to the length necessary to make bars of uniform length.

In the next row the bars are made in the opposite direction, that is to say, the needle passes up through the loops of the row above and down to the right into the newly formed loop.

Twenty-third lace stitch (fig. 964). This stitch is begun in the same way as the one in fig. 963, from left to right. Then an overcast stitch is made over each loop between the vertical bars. Each stitch must be drawn up to the required degree of tightness as it is made, for several stitches cannot be drawn up at the same time: this would disarrange the position of the bars, which must always remain vertical.

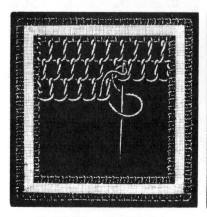

Fig. 963. Twenty-second lace stitch.

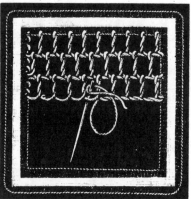

Fig. 964. Twenty-third lace stitch.

Fig. 965. Twenty-fourth lace stitch.

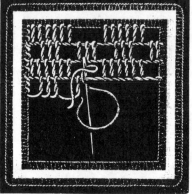

Fig. 966. Twenty-fifth lace stitch.

Twenty-fourth lace stitch (fig. 965). This stitch consists of double tulle bars arranged in groups of three, separated by loops twice the length of the loops which separate the single bars in each group. The thread is carried back after each row of bars, making overcast stitches as in fig. 964, with one overcast stitch into each short loop and two into each long loop.

In each succeeding row, the first bar is worked into the loop between the first and second bars of the preceding row, and the third into the long loop, so that the design forms slanting lines of steps.

Twenty-fifth and twenty-sixth lace stitches (figs. 966 and 967). These illustrations show how this type of lace stitch can be varied by arranging the bars in different combinations and groupings. The bars are all made as in fig. 964. The thread which connects the groups of bars must be drawn tight so that the lines of the pattern shall all be straight.

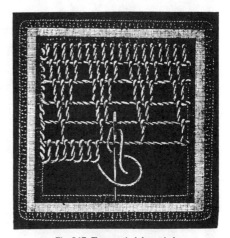

Twenty-seventh lace stitch (fig. 968). Here bars are worked in groups of three, very close together, the groups separated by a space equal to that occupied by the group; then the thread is stretched across just below the bars. In the second row three bars are worked into the space between two groups of the previous row, two bars between the bars of the group, and three more bars into the next space, making eight bars in all. The third row is worked like the first.

Fig. 967. Twenty-sixth lace stitch.

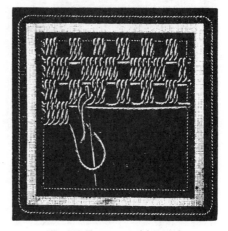

Twenty-eighth lace stitch (fig. 969). This is begun with two rows of plain tulle stitch (fig. 942), followed by two rows of close stitches as shown in fig. 960 and one row of the stitch in fig. 964. The bars can be made longer, if preferred, by twisting the thread once or twice more round the needle.

Twenty-ninth lace stitch (fig. 970). This stitch, which imitates large-meshed net, is often called Greek stitch or

Fig. 968. Twenty-seventh lace stitch.

mesh stitch. It is to be recommended for the background of lace designs rather than for filling motifs; it can also be used as a substitute for the Venetian bar grounds in figs. 980 and 981.

Double tulle bars, as shown in fig. 963, are worked from left to right, a little distance apart and not too tight, so that the loops, overcast with two stitches each on the return journey, will make a series of slightly rounded scallops.

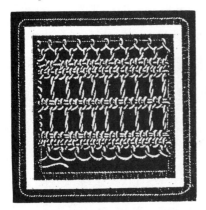

Fig. 969. Twenty-eighth lace stitch.

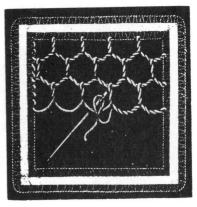

Fig. 970. Twenty-ninth lace stitch.

Fig. 971. Thirtieth lace stitch.

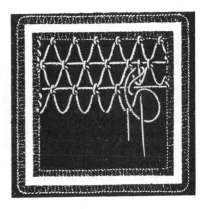

Fig. 972. Thirty-first lace stitch.

In the next row the bar is worked into the middle of the loop and drawn up with the needle sufficiently for the loops to form hexagonal meshes like those of net.

Thirtieth lace stitch (fig. 971). An initial row is worked consisting of double buttonhole stitches separated by loops as long as the space between the pairs of stitches; then the thread is brought down to the level of the bottom of the loops, laid across the space, and fastened to the braid on the other side; another row of double buttonhole stitches and loops is made in the same way as the first.

It is essential that the loops should be perfectly uniform; this can be more easily achieved if lines are drawn on the tracing to divide the surface which is to be covered. A pin is then inserted on the line and the thread passed round it, as can be seen in the illustration.

Thirty-first lace stitch (fig. 972). At first glance, this stitch appears identical to the preceding one; the manner of knotting the threads, however, is completely different.

The needle is passed under the loop and the laid thread; then the pin is inserted at the required distance; the thread is passed behind the pin and a loop is made round the point of the needle, as shown in the illustration; then the knot is drawn tight.

Thirty-second lace stitch (fig. 973). This stitch, which offers another means of varying lace stitches, is an imitation of filet and is known as filet stitch. It is begun in the corner of a square and worked in diagonal lines. The knots are made as in fig. 972, and a pin is inserted at the appropriate spot to ensure that the loops are uniform.

The little squares must be made with the greatest care; if they are well made, the majority of the stitches described in the chapter ''Filet Lace'' can be used to ornament them, and it will be found possible to fill the smallest spaces with delightful openwork stitches which nowadays are seldom used except in guipure net.

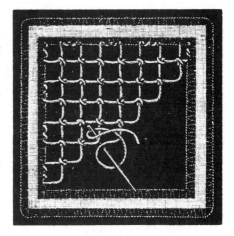

Fig. 973. Thirty-second lace stitch.

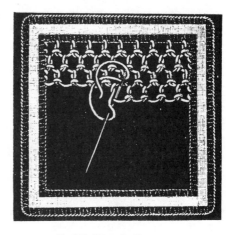

Fig. 974. Thirty-third lace stitch.

Thirty-third lace stitch (fig. 974). This is a stitch seen in ancient Renaissance lace, only a few specimens of which have been preserved. This ground, which resembles very close tulle stitch, appears at first sight almost uniform, so closely are the stitches set. On examining it more closely, however, we discovered that it was quite a new stitch. The loop, formed by a plain tulle stitch, is fastened at a little distance from the top by a buttonhole stitch. The stitches should be set as close together as possible, so that there is scarcely any space between them.

Thirty-fourth lace stitch (fig. 975). To make this filling of wheels, the space is first covered with threads stretched diagonally backward and forward, at equal distances apart. These double threads lie flat so that they do not overlap each other. When the whole surface has thus been covered with double threads, they are crossed with a second series of threads. The wheels are made during the laying of this second series of threads: one thread is laid straight, then on the return journey the thread is passed two or three times under the double threads of the first series and over the single thread just laid, thus producing little wheels like those described in the chapter ''Filet Lace,'' figs. 711 and 712.

Fig. 975. Thirty-fourth lace stitch.

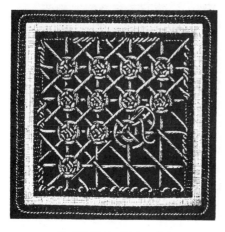

Fig. 976. Thirty-fifth lace stitch.

Thirty-fifth lace stitch (fig. 976). A foundation is first made of very regular filet stitch, but without knots at the intersections of the threads. A third series of threads is laid diagonally over the first two so that they cross them at their point of intersection. There will thus be six rays or spokes meeting in a common center. Finally, a fourth series is laid, making a seventh spoke for the wheel which is worked over these seven threads; the needle is then passed under the wheel that has just been made and brought out on the other side to form the eighth spoke and at the same time pass to the point where the next wheel is to be made.

Thirty-sixth lace stitch (fig. 977). The whole space to be filled is first covered with threads laid horizontally, and these are then covered with loops passing from one thread to the other in a zigzag line and passing through the loops in the preceding row; that is to say, the needle will have to pass under two threads. When this foundation has been prepared, it is covered with pyramids worked in very close darning stitch, begun at the point, as shown in figs. 938 and 939.

Thirty-seventh lace stitch (fig. 978). The foundation of this stitch consists of an imitation of the Penelope canvas used for tapestry. This is made by covering the whole of the space with threads laid two by two and interlacing at their points of intersection, like those of the canvas. The intersections are then surrounded several times with thread; this should be done as many times as possible, for the fuller the padding, the greater will be the relief of the buttonholing and the richer the effect of the embroidery.

Fig. 977. Thirty-sixth lace stitch.

Each of the little buttonholed eyelets or rosettes is begun and ended independently of the others.

Thirty-eighth lace stitch (fig. 979). Plain tulle stitch is the easiest and quickest to do and there is therefore a temptation to use it more often than any other. It is, however, inclined to be rather monotonous in appearance, and it is as well therefore to relieve it with various additional stitches. A favorite and particularly effective method of doing this is to

Fig. 978. Thirty-seventh lace stitch.

work a regular powdering of buttonholed eyelets or rosettes, as shown in our illustration. Here, as in the preceding stitch, each eyelet is worked independently of the others.

Thirty-ninth lace stitch (fig. 980). Spaces can also be filled with branched bars, worked in overcast stitch. Five or six threads are laid, as required by the direction of the bars and each branch is overcast to the point where it joins the principal line; from there more threads are laid for a fresh branch, so that, when a given point has been reached and the threads left bare on the first journey are covered, there will be six to eight sections thus remaining to be covered.

The overcasting is always worked from right to left; it will consequently be necessary to turn the work frequently.

Fig. 979. Thirty-eighth lace stitch.

Fig. 980. Thirty-ninth lace stitch.

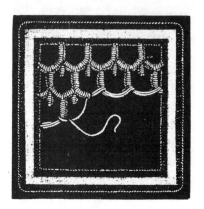

Fig. 981. Fortieth lace stitch.

Fig. 982. Wheel composed of buttonholed bars.
Making and picking up the loops.

Fortieth lace stitch (fig. 981). Among all the stitches we have described, we consider this one, which ends the series, as the one which requires the greatest patience. It is copied from an ancient Brabantine lace, all the openwork parts of which were filled with this stitch. Grounds composed of bars, buttonholed as in the present example, or overcast as in the previous one, are commonly known as Venetian bar grounds.

In the first row, after the three foundation threads have been laid, eight or ten buttonhole stitches are worked down over them from right to left, to the point where the next bar starts, for which three more foundation threads are laid.

When the end of the row is reached, the thread is fastened into the braid on the right and, working back, the second part of each bar is buttonholed from right to left. Then a fresh set of foundation threads is laid, and each bar is partially buttonholed, as in the first row, the bars of the preceding row being completed at the same time. A picot, worked as in fig. 921, marks the point where two bars join.

Wheels Composed of Buttonholed Bars (figs. 982, 983, 984, 985). As we have already had occasion several times to describe the methods of making wheels, both in this chapter and in the chapter on filet lace, we will confine ourselves here to the instructions necessary for working a buttonholed wheel in a square opening.

Fig. 982 shows how to make the first eight loops which form the skeleton for the bars. In fig. 983 it will be seen that the loops have been drawn up by means of a thread run through them; further, the buttonholing has been begun over a foundation of two threads added to the loop. The buttonholing is always begun at the end nearest

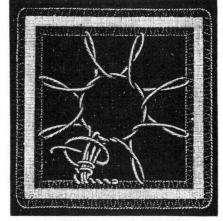

Fig. 983. Wheel composed of buttonholed bars.
Loops picked up and a bar begun.

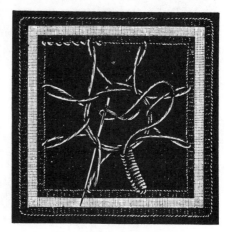

Fig. 984. Wheel composed of buttonholed bars.
First bar completed,
and method of passing to the next bar.

to the braid. Fig. 984 shows, finished, the bar begun in fig. 983, and the passage of the thread to the next bar. In fig. 985 can be seen the buttonholed ring which is worked after all the bars have been completed.

How to Fill Round Openings (figs. 986, 987, 988). The stitches which lend themselves best to the filling of the round spaces which sometimes occur in lace designs are those whose shape allows them to be made smaller in successive rows as the circumference of the circle decreases, and those which, thanks to their arrangement, make it possible to miss at regular intervals a few stitches of the outer rows.

Braid tacked onto a round design must, as we pointed out at the beginning of the chapter, be gathered round the inner edge before the lace stitches are worked.

In fig. 986 we show how a round opening can be filled with three rows of tulle stitch. It will be noticed that at the end of the round the thread is wound round the first loop to reach the point at which the second round is begun. The third round is reached in the same way. When it is completed, a thread is run through all the loops, after which it is brought back to the edge of the braid in the way indicated by the dotted line and fastened off.

Fig. 985. Wheel composed of buttonholed bars. Completed.

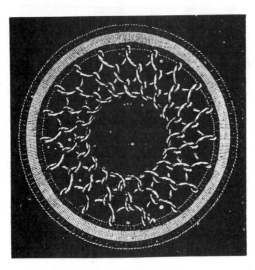

Fig. 986. Circular opening filled with three rows of tulle stitch.

Fig. 987 shows a row of loops completed with wheels worked over only three threads. In the first round, a wheel is worked over every bar; in the second over every other bar. The filling of the circle is completed by another round of bars, through which a thread is run; the thread is then brought back by means of overcast stitches along the bars (see fig. 988) to the edge of the braid, where it is fastened off.

Needlemade Picots (figs. 989, 990, 991). The outer edges of Renaissance lace are often finished with picots which can be bought ready- made; see fig. 914. These picots, however, are not very strong, and we cannot recommend them for work on which care and patience have been lavished.

In fig. 989 we show how to make connected or looped picots. A knot, as shown in fig. 973, is first made, over which the thread is twisted in the way explained by the illustration. Needless to say, all the loops must be knotted at the same level, and all must be of the same size and set apart.

Fig. 990 illustrates the kind of needlemade picot which most nearly resembles the machinemade variety, while fig. 991 shows an edging of small buttonhole scallops (ring or rose point picots) surmounted by bullion picots.

Further, as a substitute for picots, one or two rows of the lace stitch in fig. 958 could be used, or the scallops in fig. 923, or even the first rows of

Fig. 987. Circular opening filled with bars and wheels. First ring of wheels.

Fig. 988. Circular opening filled with bars and wheels. Two rings of wheels completed.

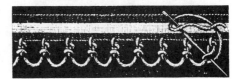

Fig. 989. Connected or looped picots.

Fig. 990. Detached needlemade picots.

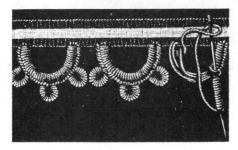

Fig. 991.
Ring or rose point picots with small
bullion picots.

the stitches in figs. 971, 972, and 973.

Renaissance Lace With Ground of Bars (fig. 992). The simplest type of Renaissance lace is that in which the motifs, formed of braid of various kinds, are joined by overcast bars, with wheels and fillings of herringbone stitch. We give an example of this type in fig. 992, in which a plain braid and a medallion braid have been used. The overcast bars are worked according to the explanations which accompany fig. 916; the herringboning will be found in fig. 926, and for the darned wheels we refer the reader to the chapter "Filet Lace," figs. 711 and 712. The lower edge of the lace is finished off with a picot-edged braid overcast to it.

Renaissance Lace With Net Ground (fig. 993). The working of this lace requires more time and patience than the previous one. When the braids have been tacked onto the design, the background is filled with the stitch in fig. 970. To make it easier to work this filling uniformly, we advise drawing a few additional lines on the tracing, which can then be followed for the working of the filling stitch.

When all the background has been filled, the motifs themselves are filled;

Fig. 992. Renaissance lace with ground of bars.

for this purpose the stitches shown in figs. 944, 957, and 959 are used. The edge of the lace is finished with scallops ornamented with bullion picots (fig. 991). A fine flax thread is used for the gathering of the braids, and a rather coarser thread for the lace stitches.

Motif in Venetian Point (figs. 994, 995, 996, 997, 998, 999, 1000). The term ''Venetian point'' usually covers needlemade laces whose outlines are edged with rich scalloping in high relief. The professional lacemaker calls these ''broiders'' or ''raised cordonnets.''

For this, as for most other kinds of work, the design must first be prepared. The design, traced on paper, is lined with matt-surfaced black paper (a special paper exists for this purpose), then holes are pricked through the tracing at regular intervals, the tracing is removed, and the black

Fig. 993. Renaissance lace with net ground.

paper mounted on fairly coarse linen, used double. This done, from three to five strands of the thread with which the lace is to be made are laid along the lines marked by the holes and held down at each hole by a stitch made over them.

Fig. 994 shows the actual distance apart that the holes should be, as well as the beginning of the tracing, while fig. 995 shows the tracing finished, even to the eyelets which will later be worked into the fillings.

Only when the tracing is completed can the actual fillings be begun. This part of the work must be done with the greatest care, in order that the

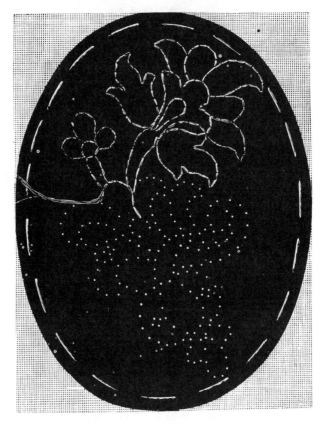

Fig. 994. How to make the tracing.

thread shall remain perfectly clean. To this end, all the parts of the tracing that are not to be worked immediately are covered with a sheet of blue paper; the parts to be worked at once are left uncovered. In addition, a piece of paper a little larger than the uncovered portion is taken, and an opening about half an inch in diameter is cut in it; this is placed with the opening over the spot where the work is to be begun. The fillings are worked only through this opening. The paper, being loose, can be moved backward and forward as the rows are worked, so that the opening is always just over the part being worked; see fig. 996.

All the fillings are worked thus, in close or transparent stitches according to the design, until all the spaces have been filled; see figs. 997 and 998.

The finished fillings are immediately protected with a paper tacked down over them. This is not removed until the bars and outlines are to be worked. The stitches, of whatever kind, must all be fastened off in the tracing,

Fig. 995. The tracing completed.

without, however, making the latter too heavy.

We would once more remind our readers that fine lace stitches are always worked with the eye of the needle turned toward the worker and the point out. Work done in this way will be more regular and more accurate.

When all the fillings have been worked, the outlines are very closely buttonholed. These outlines are sometimes in relief, of varying width and very heavy; see fig. 1000; they are thickly padded with thread, as explained in fig. 162 for Venetian embroidery; sometimes, on the other hand, they are flat and of uniform width, as in fig. 999. In the latter case, a round thread is used as a padding cord.

Needlepoint Lace Edging (fig. 1001). In detached motifs, such as the one in figs. 999 and 1000, the outlines are buttonholed as soon as all the fillings are completed, but in lace in which the various parts are connected by bars or network, the buttonholed outlines are worked last. Thus, in the

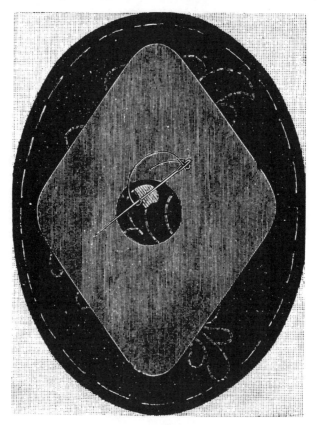

Fig. 996. How to protect the work.

lace shown in fig. 1001, all the fillings inside the flowers and foliage are completed first; then the net ground, which can also be replaced by bars with picots, is worked; and last of all the raised outlines and outer scallops.

This kind of lace requires the same preparatory work as Venetian point, but there is less variety in the stitches; those that are most frequently met with are the ones illustrated in figs. 942 and 960.

Square in Reticella Lace (figs. 1002 and 1003). Reticella lace, like Venetian point, requires a pattern traced on special black paper. This must reproduce the outlines, the veinings of the motifs, and the connecting bars.

The tracing is pricked, lined with a double layer of stout white material, and completely outlined. The tracing for the square in fig. 1002 was worked in DMC crochet special quality cotton no. 60, held down with overcast stitches in DMC Alsatian sewing cotton no. 300.

Fig. 997. How to work the fillings.

The principal lines are traced with a double thread, and those of the small secondary figures with a single thread. In the latter case, the thread is carried backward and forward from end to end of the branch, and joined, at its starting point, to the second thread, so that the tracing of the principal lines can be continued with the double thread. When a part that has already been traced is reached, the needle is passed between the two threads already in place, so that the tracing may be quite even and uninterrupted.

The work itself is begun with the little ovals, worked in DMC special quality crochet cotton no. 50. Two rows of buttonhole stitch are made over the center line, then the two halves are worked separately. When this is finished, they are joined to the outside line with overcasting, making the picots at the same time.

The little pyramids are composed of ten rows of buttonhole stitch; each

Fig. 998. Filling stitches completed.

row is fastened to the traced outline. A picot is made after the third and fourth rows. The method of working these filled motifs is shown on the right at the bottom of fig. 1003. The overcast bars which connect the motifs are worked at the same time as the motifs themselves.

The rows of detached bars in the large circle and in the ovals are worked with DMC special quality crochet cotton no. 100. An overcast stitch is made over the outer thread of the tracing, then the needle is passed under the thread of the inner tracing line; returning, a stitch is made over the thread laid for the bar, and the needle finally passes once more over the outer thread. Finally the outlines are embroidered. The small inner circle is worked at the same time as the overcast bars, then the little scallops which surround the large circle are buttonholed, and last of all the outlines of the ovals and of the large circle are buttonholed, these stitches being always

Fig. 999. Venetian motif with even outlines.

turned toward the outside of the row of detached bars.

Reticella motifs, rarely used alone, are usually inset in material. In this case, the outside lines of tracing are covered only with spaced overcast stitches.

Reticella Lace Insertion (fig. 1004). This insertion in Reticella lace, fig. 1004, is worked in the same manner and with the same materials as the square in fig. 1002.

When the tracing is finished, the work is begun in the center, and the little ovals with overcast bars are worked first. Only one row of buttonhole stitches over the tracing thread is required, with a buttonholed outline.

Then, returning to the center, the vertical and horizontal bars are worked with a double row of buttonhole stitches ornamented with picots.

When the large circle is finished, the connecting bars are overcast, as well

Fig. 1000. Venetian motif with outlines in relief.

as the vertical bars which separate the squares; finally the scallops, ornamented with picots, are worked.

Danish Hedebo Lace Edging (figs. 1005 and 1006). This lace—already known to our readers from fig. 841, in which it appears as the trimming of the little openwork cloth—is shown here attached to a linen edge, but it can also be worked free and finished with a row of buttonhole stitches worked over a few tracing threads. The working of the medallions is clearly shown in fig. 1006.

The design is traced onto tracing linen and fixed onto American cloth; the circles are then outlined with two strands of thread held in place with overcast stitches. Returning to the starting point, the circle is covered with buttonhole stitches, under which the two threads used for the tracing are laid again. Before the circle is completely finished, the little buttonholed pyramids are worked over the buttonhole stitches of the circle, passing the thread, after each row, back over the stitches just made, so that each row is worked in the same direction. The thread thus laid is covered by the buttonholing of the next row. The pyramid is shaped to a point by decreasing the number of stitches by one in each row. From the point, the thread is brought back to the circle by overcasting down the side of the pyramid.

Then a second pyramid is made opposite the first, the circle is ended, and the thread fastened off. Where the rows touch, they are joined by a few stitches. The inner circle, which connects the eight pyramids, is completed with a row of overcast bars, set apart to make an openwork row.

The medallions are connected at the top by a band of linen trimmed with a row of drawn thread work; the spaces between the medallions and the band are filled with a little pyramid.

Insertion in Brazilian Sol Lace (figs. 1007, 1008, 1009). We give here an example of the Brazilian lace known as Sol lace; this work is distinguished above all by the delicacy of the work and the designs composed of

Fig. 1001. Needlepoint lace edging.

medallions of laid threads. In spite of the simplicity of the designs, a certain degree of skill is necessary before work of this kind is undertaken, since the lace is worked with free thread—that is, threads unattached to a foundation—and it is very difficult to undo a finished part.

The preparatory work consists of tracing the design—made up of circles

Fig. 1002. Square in Reticella lace.

and arcs—on tracing linen. Each circle is divided into as many parts as there are rays in the medallion—in our example it is divided into forty-eight equal parts—which are marked by lines meeting in the center. For the arcs between the medallions, nine divisions and eight equal rays are drawn. When the tracing is finished, it is fixed onto a piece of strong linen and

Fig. 1003. How to work the square of Reticella lace in fig. 1002.

Fig. 1004. Reticella lace insertion.

Fig. 1005. Danish Hedebo lace edging.

Fig. 1006. Detail of the Danish Hedebo lace in fig. 1005.

the outlines are traced with running stitches, one stitch to every division of the outer edge, missing every other division. These running stitches are the only foundation for the whole of the work. The thread is wound onto a small netting shuttle and fastened onto one of the running stitches with a knot; the thread is passed across the circle and the shuttle inserted under the opposite stitch, then brought back under the next stitch and across the circle to the opposite outline stitch, and so on; see the explanatory illustration,

Fig. 1007. Insertion in Brazilian Sol lace.

fig. 1008. The thread is passed twice through each running stitch, and in this way the circle is filled with rays. When the last ray has been laid, all the rays are knotted together in the center, and the thread does not return again to the outside edge. It is advisable not to draw the threads too tight. Forty-seven rays have been made in this way; the forty-eighth is made as the work proceeds out from the center, by the passage of the thread from one row of stitches to another.

The design itself is worked in two different stitches: a knotted stitch, like the one used in drawn thread work on linen to join groups of threads (see fig. 783), and darning, or reprise, stitch, which we have explained in the chapter "Filet Lace," for the leaves; see figs. 705 and 706, and in the present chapter, figs. 935, 938, and 939.

A wheel is made in the center of the medallion with a few rounds of darning stitch. Then, in the next round, the laid threads are knotted together in sixes. In the following round, the groups of six threads are divided, and three threads of one group joined to three of the next group. Up to this point the working of both types of medallion is the same.

For one medallion, this is followed by eight little darned pyramids with their points toward the center; they must always be begun at this point (see fig. 1009).

At the beginning of each round the thread is left free; it is then knotted to the nearest ray. At the end of the round, the thread is knotted to the first loop of the same round, so that there is no interruption in the design, and in this way the forty-eighth ray is made.

At the outside, the pyramids are connected by threads laid to form scallops, and two circles of laid threads which complete the medallion. The thread is then carried to the edge, where it is fastened off, after which the next medallion is worked; for this, the darned wheel and the two rounds of alternately grouped threads are worked as before, then the forty-eighth ray is completed.

The motif is also made in darning stitch, with laid threads, beginning always at the center.

When the medallions are finished, the intermediate figures are filled in, according to fig. 1007 and with the stitches we have just described.

When all this work is finished, three or four threads are laid close to the outline and buttonhole stitches are worked over this padding and the tracing stitches; then the finished lace is detached from the foundation by cutting all the tracing stitches on the wrong side.

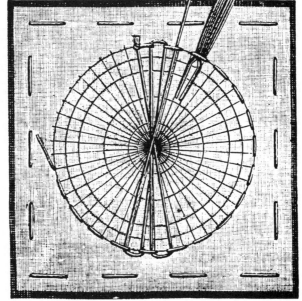

Fig. 1008.
How to lay the threads for the lace in fig. 1007.

Medallion in Spanish Sol Lace (fig. 1010). The medallion in fig. 1010 is an example, both rich and delicate, of the ancient Sol lace, closely allied to the more modern Teneriffe lace, which is developed from it. The diameter of this medallion is 106 millimeters—about four and a half inches.

It consists of motifs repeated eight times in each round and divided into ten regularly knotted concentric circles.

A piece of strong, closely woven linen is mounted in a frame; the eleven circles are traced onto it. The diameters of these circles are respectively 8, 17, 25, 29, 34, 42, 58, 64, 72, 98, and 106 millimeters, all, of course, measured through the same center.

Round the outer circumference make 80 stitches at equal distances apart, for the 80 rays of the medallion; the method of laying the threads for the rays is shown in fig. 1008. The last thread is laid only as far as the center, for the working of the central wheel. As the work proceeds, the thread is carried toward the outer circumference and is thus laid right across the circle, from one edge to the other.

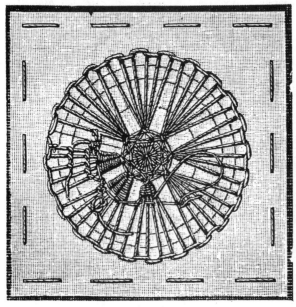

Fig. 1009.
How to fill the circles for the lace in fig. 1007.

The central wheel is darned over groups of four threads. It should touch the first circle, the knots of which are also made over four threads. The second and third circles are made with knots joining two threads; the thread which makes the third circle is further covered with overcasting, and isolated interlocking lace stitches are made at the same time. In the fourth circle, a knot is made over each thread separately. Then follows a circular band in darning stitch; after this, the fifth circle, in which the threads are again knotted together two by two.

In the sixth circle, the threads are again knotted singly. This circle is overcast, to enable the scrolls to be worked. These latter are composed of two rows of darning stitch surrounded by two rows of knots. The thread is carried to the seventh circle, and three overcast stitches are made over each single thread; the pull of the connecting threads makes these little bars form a zigzag line. Then the eighth and ninth circles are worked, with detached interlocking lace stitches filling the space between them, exactly as in the center.

The tenth circle of knots is made before the wide border is worked. Then the motifs of squares are darned. It is sometimes necessary to bring the thread back under the squares to the middle of the border and fasten it on there with a knot.

To work the wheels within the ovals, a knot is made over each of the five successive rays. Then, working back, each intersection of the threads is or-

Fig. 1010. Medallion in Spanish Sol lace.

namented with a darned wheel. The whole is surrounded with a row of knots, then two rows of darning stitch, and finally another row of knots. The thread is brought back through the wheels to work the next group of darned squares.

The eleventh circle completes the medallion. It is joined to the tenth by interlaced loops.

Square in Teneriffe Lace (figs. 1011, 1012, 1013).   Teneriffe lace motifs are worked over molds of metal, wood, or rubber. This does away

Fig. 1011. Square in Teneriffe lace.

with the necessity for tracings on linen, which are indispenpensable for Sol lace. It is, further, pleasant and simple to work on an object that is easy to handle and can be turned about and held in whatever way is most convenient. Molds can be obtained in all sizes and shapes: round, square, rectangular; with scalloped outlines; with metal teeth or notches to hold the threads.

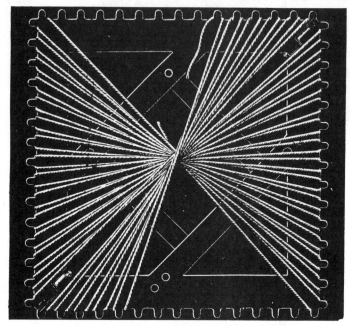

Fig. 1012. Square in Teneriffe lace. How to lay the threads.

Our example is worked in DMC special quality crochet cotton no. 15 on afolding square metal mold with sides 85 millimeters (3⅜ inches) long. The laying of the threads which form the rays is begun and ended at the center. Care must be taken not to stretch the threads too tight. Fig. 1012 shows how they should be laid; the metal mold can be seen in the parts that are still uncovered. The embroidery is begun at the center of the wheel. Eight threads are alternately picked up and left, advancing two threads in each

Fig. 1013. Square in Teneriffe lace. How to work the embroidered motifs.

row to form the spiral. The needle is then passed through the mold and brought out on the other side. The first round of knots is made, beginning at the inner angle between the arches, each knot uniting two threads. The filling between the arches is worked in darning stitch, edged with a row of knots at the top and bottom. Then the last row of knots is worked, at the outside of the square, in the same way as those of the first row. Finally, the long scallops are knotted, the groups of threads being divided and alternated. These scallops are completed in the corners with darning stitch, edged top and bottom with a short row of knots. Six darned points are worked above the knots of this last short row. To work them, the threads

Fig. 1014. Single knot worked from right to left.

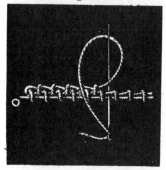

Fig. 1015. Single knot worked from left to right.

Fig. 1016. Double knot.

must be brought to the top of the square, fastened onto the outside thread, and the darning worked down with stitches becoming gradually wider.

Fig. 1013 shows in detail the working of the various rows of knots and the fillings in darning stitch. To remove the lace from the mold, the two arms are pushed in and the square is folded. The lace then comes away of itself from the metal teeth.

Knot Stitch Laces. Knot stitch laces are found only on the shores of the Mediterranean. According to the method of working them, they can be divided into single knot stitch laces and double knot stitch laces. The former are known in Italy as ''punto avorio''; they have been made for centuries by the peasants for their personal use, but have lately become much sought after as articles of commerce. In Albania narrow insertions made with single knots are used to join strips of material that are insufficiently wide by themselves. Finally, the charming laces of Algeria and Tunisia are also made with single knots. All these laces are made without picots.

Turkish laces, worked directly onto an edge of fabric, and Albanian laces, with geometrical designs, are made with double knots. These latter are richly adorned with picots.

Wide punto avorio lace is worked over a simple tracing which gives the principal lines of the design. The outer edges of Arab lace are prepared by means of a line of machine stitching on dark-colored jap silk or matt black paper. Albanian and Turkish lace are worked freely in the hand without tracing of any kind.

Single knot (figs. 1014 and 1015). To work the single knot from right to left, the needle is inserted from below up under the thread or edge of material which serves as a foundation for the lace, and to which the thread has first been fastened. Pass the thread from right to left over the needle and bring it back toward the right under the needle. Draw the latter up and out, tightening the loop to form the knot; see fig. 1014.

Fig. 1015 shows how to work a row of knots from left to right. The needle is inserted under one of the horizontal threads which connect the knots of the previous row; the thread is passed from left to right over the needle, then back toward the left under the needle; the latter is drawn out and the loop tightened.

Double knots (figs. 1016 and 1017). A single thread, to serve as padding, is laid alongside the foundation thread; then the needle is inserted from below up, the thread remaining to the left over the needle; this thread is held and twisted once from right to left round the needle. The latter is drawn out through the double loop and the knot is drawn tight. This double knot is always made in rows from right to left.

If several short rows are to be worked one above the other, the thread is simply laid back from left to right along the row to serve as padding thread for the next row. See fig. 1017, which also shows how to work a pyramid in double knots by decreasing one knot in each row.

Bar stitch (fig. 1018). Albanian lace very often has a heading of little bars made with the simple stitch which we have named bar stitch. A double thread is used as a foundation, and over this is worked a single knot accompanied by two more single knots worked horizontally at the top of the first knot. This stitch can be worked in both directions, and the spaces between the stitches are longer than in the ordinary stitch. This bar stitch is also found in punto avorio, in which it is sometimes used to form whole motifs.

Long bullion picots (fig. 1019). The

Fig. 1017. Double knot.

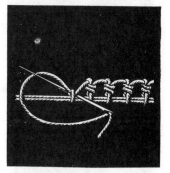

Fig. 1018. Bar stitch.

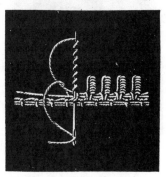

Fig. 1019. Long bullion picots.

frequent use of long bullion picots is characteristic of Albanian lace. The method of making these picots is very different from that of the round picots seen in fig. 922. A single knot is first made into the stitches of the preceding row; then the needle is inserted into the next loop, as for a single knot, and drawn through, making a large loop of thread; the needle is held in the right hand and with the left hand the thread is wound several times round the needle; see fig. 1019. The needle and thread are then drawn slowly and carefully through the loops; these are drawn tight; and the picot is made. The thread emerging from the point of the picot is carried down to the left and fastened to the loop of the previous row with a single knot.

Insertion in Italian punto avorio lace (figs. 1020 and 1021).   These narrow insertions were once used to join widths of material, and were

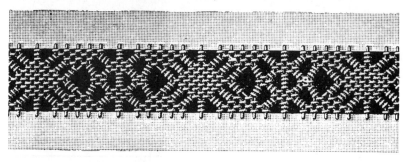

Fig. 1020. Insertion in Italian punto avorio lace.

worked almost exclusively in single knots. Our example, fig. 1020, made in DMC special quality crochet cotton no. 20, is begun at the bottom and worked up. The thread is fastened onto the left-hand edge of material and inserted into the right-hand edge opposite; then, working back, it is covered with twelve single knots; see fig. 1021. It is then brought out again a little higher up on the left, leaving the intermediate thread rather short; a knot is made over the thread between the third and fourth knots and another between the fourth and fifth knots of the horizontal bar already made, leaving the intermediate thread rather long to form a loop; a knot is

Fig. 1021. Method of working the insertion in punto avorio in fig. 1020.

made over the thread between the eighth and ninth knots and another between the ninth and tenth knots of the bar, the thread is left short and fastened to the right-hand edge. The knots of the first row are slightly separated by those of this second row, so that there will be three knots close together at each side, followed by one isolated knot, with four knots close together in the middle. Working back, four knots are made over the first thread, one knot between the two knots of the previous row, five knots over the center loop of thread, one knot between the two knots of the previous row, and four knots over the last free thread.

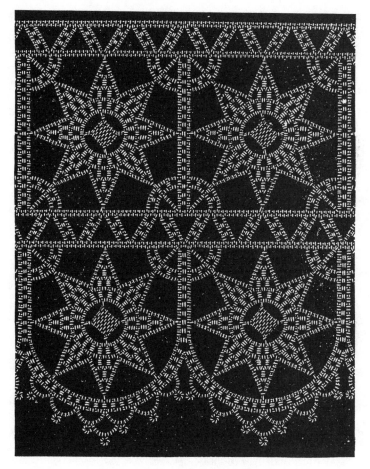

Fig. 1022. Edging in Italian punto avorio lace.

The thread is now fastened to the left-hand edge, one knot is made between the first and second knots of the first little scallop, a small intermediate loop of thread is left, then a knot is made between the second and third knots and another between the third and fourth knots of the middle scallop, a loop of thread is left, a knot is made between the third and fourth knots of the next scallop, the thread is fastened to the right-hand edge, one knot close to the edge, four knots over the loop of thread, one knot between the two middle knots, four knots over the loop of thread, one knot close to the left-hand edge, fasten the thread to the left-hand edge, one knot between the first and second knots and one knot between the second and third knots

Fig. 1023. Method of working the edging in Italian punto avorio in fig. 1022.

of the little loop, leave a loop of thread, one knot between the third and fourth knots and one knot between the fourth and fifth knots of the little loop, fasten the thread to the right-hand edge, one knot close to the edge, one knot between the first and second knots, six knots over the loop of thread, one knot between the last two knots, one knot close to the edge; fasten the thread to the left hand edge, etc. The course of the work can easily be followed in the illustration.

*Edging in Italian **punto avorio** lace* (figs. 1022 and 1023). Punto avorio lace, as it is called, made of single knots, is worked from a tracing made on lacemaking paper. The tracings for this type of lace require less minute care than those for Venetian and Reticella lace; only the main lines of the design need be traced.

The tracing is covered with transverse stitches corresponding to the design, which will later serve to hold the tracing threads. For our model, the horizontal line across the top of the band of squares is made first, then the lower horizontal line. The vertical bars are worked at the same time: the thread is laid vertically up, then a row of single knots is worked down over it, followed by a row of bar stitches up and another row of single knots down; the thread is then laid along the line of the design to the

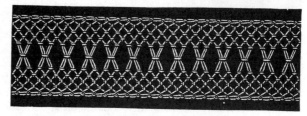

Fig. 1024. Narrow insertion in Arab lace.

next bar. The working of the bar stitch with two transverse knots is shown in fig. 1018; this stitch is, in this design, sometimes made with three transverse knots instead of two.

The working of the lace itself is begun with the little diamonds in the center of the stars. The circle is first outlined, then a square, made like an interlocking lace stitch, is made inside this outline; see fig. 699. One side is covered with single knots, then the square is filled with rows of knots worked backward and forward. The square is completed, then the close inner circle is worked, followed by the openwork round of bar stitch and, over this last, the close outer circle. Then follow the eight points made of bar stitches. The middle points touch the outside line of the square; the corner points are lengthened by a bar worked into the corner. The little scallops of bar stitch which fill the spaces are worked at the same time.

The working of the narrow bands is begun with two rows of single knots, close together, into the edges of the squares; then come the little slanting openwork bars: the thread is fastened onto the outer tracing thread, the first thread is laid obliquely and passed through the second close row of knots; working back over this thread, six knots are made. The outline is continued; then, working back, two bar stitches are made; the thread is fastened to the second close row; working back, six knots are made. The outline is continued, the thread laid for the second slanting bar, etc. Finally, over the outline thread two rows of close knots are worked. A similar band is worked on the opposite side.

The inner curved edge of the first scallop is first outlined with tracing thread; then over this thread the row of close knots and the row of bar stitches are worked, then the filling of the first scallop. The small scallops, ornamented with round bullion picots, as shown in fig. 922, are worked at the same time as the outer row of close knots.

The work can easily be carried out with the help of the explanatory figure, fig. 1023. The thread chosen should be well twisted and of medium thickness; our model was worked in DMC special quality crochet cotton no. 15.

Fig. 1025. How to reinforce the machine-stitched edge.

Arab lace. Chebka. Whereas the designs of Italian, Turkish, Albanian, and Armenian laces are formed of knots set various distances apart, Arab lace, the designs of which resemble fancy net, are made up of loops of thread of varying lengths, secured by single knots.

The net grounds of these laces, being very elastic, require very strong edges. These consist of two rows of machine stitching, strengthened by hand, on dark paper, or rows of braid or beading mounted on a foundation of paper. We recommend the first of these two methods because, though it entails a little more work, it ensures greater durability in the finished lace. Before the actual work is begun, the paper must be backed with a piece of linen.

Fig. 1026. Method of working the insertion in fig. 1024.

The work itself is done backward and forward between the two edges, whichever way these have been prepared. It is begun at the top, on the left, and worked down. The making of single knots, worked in rows from left to right and right to left, is explained in figs. 1014 and 1015, but in those figures the method of making the knots when working from the bottom up is shown; therefore, in the explanatory fig. 1026, which shows how the insertion in fig. 1024 is worked, we give the method of making the knots when working down.

The linen backing is removed when the lace is finished. When the edges consist of machine stitching, the paper can simply be ripped away along the stitching, and the lace is free. If braid has been used for the edges, the tacking threads must be removed.

Narrow insertion in Arab lace (figs. 1024, 1025, 1026). For the insertion in fig. 1024, two parallel lines of machine stitching must be prepared, on black paper, two centimeters apart and with stitches three millimeters long. Over these stitches, small loops of thread are made with the needle, the loops are turned in, and little stitches hold them toward the outside, as can be seen in fig. 1026, which gives a working detail of the insertion, and fig. 1025, which shows the working of one of these rows of loops.

So that the design shall be the same at both edges, a vertical row of knots must be worked into one of these rows of loops; this is essential if the work is to proceed uninterrupted. For the insertion in fig. 1024, this row of knots is worked along the right-hand edge. The lace itself is begun at the left. The thread is fastened onto the first loop with a single knot, laid across to the right and

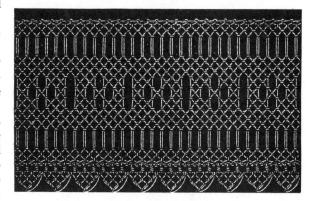

Fig. 1027. Scalloped edging in Arab lace.

fastened there with a knot into the first loop of the vertical row. Working back, three loops are made—the first four millimeters, the second eight millimeters, and the third four millimeters long—each secured by a single knot; a short loop is left and the thread is fastened into the second loop at the left-hand edge.

Working toward the right, a loop four millimeters long is made, followed by one twelve millimeters long, knotted into the loops of the previous row, then a short loop, and the thread is fastened to the second loop on the right. Returning toward the left, a loop four millimeters long is made and a knot set in the long (twelve millimeters) loop above, the three threads above are joined by one knot in the center, another knot is made into the long loop at the same distance from the center as the first, one loop four millimeters long, one short loop, fasten the thread to the third loop at the left-hand edge. Working toward the right: one loop four millimeters long, one loop twelve millimeters long, one short loop, fasten the thread to the third loop at the right-hand edge, etc.

The material used for this insertion was DMC 6 cord crochet cotton no. 40 in white; other varieties of thread bearing the DMC trademark could also be used, to suit individual taste, as well as finer or coarser grades; in this case the length of the stitches and loops and the space between the two edges will naturally have to be altered proportionately.

Scalloped edging in Arab lace (figs. 1027 and 1028). The preparatory work is the same as for the insertion in fig. 1024. The machine stitches should again measure three millimeters, but the space between two rows is forty-two millimeters. The vertical row is worked along the left-hand edge.

The designs of Arab lace are made up of loops of varying lengths, which are always made in the row worked from left to right, the pattern row. In

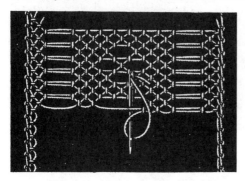

the return row, from right to left, only short loops, all of the same length, are made. In the next row, from left to right, one or more of these short loops are missed, according to the size of the openwork spaces; in the following row, as many knots are made into the long loops as there were loops missed in the preceding row.

Fig. 1028. Method of working the scalloped edging in fig. 1027.

For the lace edging in fig. 1027, the thread is fastened into the first loop of the left-hand vertical row, laid across to the right-hand edge to which it is fastened—a loop three millimeters long is made and knotted to the laid thread, then a loop six millimeters long, seven loops three millimeters long,

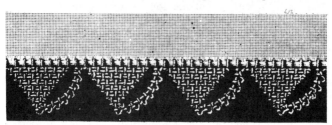

another loop six milli-meters long; fasten the thread to the second loop of the row of knots on

Fig. 1029. Turkish lace edging.

the left—toward the right make a loop eight millimeters long, knot it into the first little loop above, make six loops each three millimeters long, knotted into the next six loops above, one loop eight millimeters long, knotted to the last loop above, one short loop and fasten to the second loop of the right-hand edge—returning toward the left, one loop three millimeters long, one loop six millimeters long, seven loops each three millimeters long, one loop six millimeters long, fasten the thread, leaving a small loop, to the next loop of the left-hand edge—one loop eight millimeters long, two loops each three millimeters long, one loop six millimeters long, missing one loop of the preceding row, two loops each three millimeters long, one loop eight millimeters long, knotted into the last loop above, one short loop fastened to the right-hand edge, etc.

The course of the work can easily be followed from the explanatory illustration, fig. 1028. The large openwork spaces in the middle are made by means of a loop twelve millimeters long. When the main strip is finished, the left-hand edge is completed with a row of spaced bars which serves as a foundation for the little scallops.

The scallops have four knots, with three loops three millimeters long at the base; two loops are made in the second row, then one loop, and finally a single knot into the topmost loop; the thread is then carried down to the base of the point, fastened by a knot, and the three loops for the base of the next scallop are made.

Fig. 1030. Method of working the Turkish lace edging in fig. 1029.

Turkish lace edging (figs. 1029 and 1030). Turkish lace, made of double knots, is worked into the edge of the material which it is to trim. The double knots are always worked from right to left; the thread must therefore always be laid from

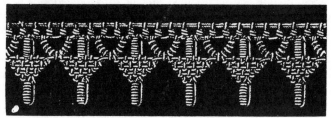

Fig. 1031. Narrow edging in Albanian lace.

left to right at the end of each row for the beginning of the next, as we have explained in fig. 1017.

Our example, fig. 1029, consists of a narrow edging worked in DMC cotton lace thread no. 50 in white.

The work is begun on the right. The edge of the cambric is rolled and eight double knots are made over the roll; the thread is brought back to the right and fastened on between the first and second knots, seven double knots are made between the eight knots of the previous row and over the laid thread. Continue in this way, but decreasing, until there are only two double knots in the last row. Carry the thread down to the left, to the base of the pyramid, insert it through the material close to the pyramid, carry it up again to the top between the last two double knots; working down, make seven double knots over the double thread, leaving a sufficient length of thread between them to make little loops resembling picots. Each successive motif is made in the same way, always beginning with eight double knots.

Narrow edging in Albanian lace (fig. 1031). Albanian lace is made with single and double knots and openwork bars, trimmed with long bullion picots. Albanian and Turkish women, sitting cross-legged on a cushion on the ground, fasten the double thread which serves as the foundation for the lace to their right knee. This method of working will hardly appeal to our readers, and we recommend that they fasten the double thread to lacemaking paper or tracing linen.

The thread used is DMC special quality crochet cotton no. 15 in white.

The lace edging in fig. 1031 is begun with a row of bar stitch (see fig. 1018). The scalloped design itself is worked in a single row.

Fasten on the thread between the first and second bars, miss two bars, lay the thread to the left and return to the starting point. Make nine single knots over this double thread, pass the thread between the next two knots, make a long bullion picot, winding the thread eight times round the needle (see fig. 1019), pass the thread between the next two bars, miss two bars, bring the thread out again and carry it back to the right. Make four single knots over the double thread, pass to the right, make a single knot into the top of the picot, lay the thread toward the right, make a double knot between the fifth and sixth knots of the first scallop, working back make four double knots, lay the thread toward the right, one double knot over the thread before the first double knot of the preceding row, three double knots between the succeeding knots, lay the thread toward the right, one double knot before the first of the three double knots of the preceding row, two double knots to the left, lay the thread to the right, one double knot before the first of the two double knots, one bullion picot, return to the base of the motif by means of overcast stitches, complete the lower scallop with five single knots, bring out the thread between the next two bars, one picot, etc.

Wide edging in Albanian lace (fig. 1032). The heading consists of two rows of spaced bar stitches. The motif itself is begun with eighteen double knots set between the bar stitches. Lay the thread to the right, insert it between the ninth and tenth knots and secure it there with a double knot; working back, make eight double knots, set between the knots below and over the laid thread. Lay the thread to the right and continue in the same way, decreasing by one knot in each row. In the sixth row, lay the thread to the right, secure it with a double knot between the fifth and sixth knots, make one double knot, one long bullion picot with the thread wound eight times round the needle (see fig. 1019), two double knots; lay the thread to the right, one single knot into the picot, lay the thread to the right and fasten it to the end of the last row of the pyramid, lay the thread to the left, then to the right; make ten knots into the triple loop thus formed, fasten the thread to the pyramid, lay it to the right, fasten it to the pyramid; * one picot, one double knot into the loop, repeat from * three times; one picot;

Fig. 1032. Wide edging in Albanian lace.

descend to the base of the pyramid with overcast stitches, fasten the thread on the row of bars, lay the thread to the right, making a single knot into each picot, and fasten the thread to the right of the pyramid, lay the thread to the left and back again to the right; make five double knots into each division, over the triple thread. Fasten the thread, lay it to the right, fasten it to the right of the pyramid, and into the semicircle work: two double knots, one picot, ** one double knot, one picot, repeat eleven times from **, two double knots; three double knots into the row of bars; returning toward the right, make one single knot into each picot, fasten the thread between the second and third knots of the horizontal row, lay the thread to the left and back again to the right; three double knots over the triple thread in each divison, fasten the thread, lay it to the right and fasten it, make four double knots to the left, lay the thread to the right, fasten it between the third and fourth double knots and make four single knots over this thread, lay the thread to the right, fasten it between the third and fourth double knots of the horizontal row, make four single knots and continue in the scallop already begun with four single knots; four double knots into the semicircle; lay the thread to the right, fasten it at the base of the last small scallop, make four single knots, lay the thread to the right, fasten it to the middle of the finished scallop, make nine single knots, complete the scallop already begun with four single knots, four double knots into the semicircle, and so on. Complete the row of small scallops as shown in the illustration.

Join the two triple scallops between the semicircles, and make in addition a connecting bar with ten single knots. Finally, add to this bar a little tassel consisting of twenty strands of DMC special stranded cotton no. 25.

Pillow lace, seventeenth century Flemish style.

CHAPTER XVIII

Pillow Laces

Pillow lace may be considered an invention of the sixteenth century. First made in Genoa, it spread rapidly throughout Italy and then to Spain, the Netherlands, Germany, and Sweden. Later, it was introduced among the Slavonic countries and in South America; more recently, it has also been taught in the East.

Unlike needlemade lace, in which the various parts of the design are made with a single thread and a needle, pillow laces—or bobbin laces, as they are also called—are made with an unlimited number of threads wound on bobbins. Since it would be impossible in a volume of this kind to describe every variety of pillow lace, we have been obliged to confine ourselves to those which present the least difficulty.

Implements. The making of pillow lace requires several implements and accessories: first a "pillow" or cushion, then bobbins, a bobbin winder, patterns, pins, and a pricker.

Lacemaker's pillow (fig. 1033). The cushion

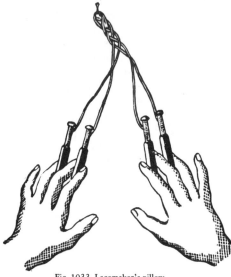

Fig. 1033. Lacemaker's pillow.

used for lacemaking is known in different countries by different names—pillow, cushion, or frame. Its shape and arrangement vary also according to the country and type of lace to be made.

Fig. 1033 shows a pillow of the type used in Saxony, where pillow lace has always been one of the chief occupations of the inhabitants of certain districts. It consists of a roll, shaped like a muff, which can easily be made at home with a piece of material half a yard in width and twenty-four inches long. The two long sides are very firmly sewn together, and a hem is made along the other two sides, through which a tape is run. One end is then drawn up tight over a disc of very strong cardboard. The bag thus made is tightly stuffed with sawdust, bran, or horsehair, then the other end is drawn up over a second cardboard disc. Finally, the pillow is covered with dark cloth or flannel.

The pillow is laid in a basket or cardboard box with sides high enough to keep it from moving, and the basket or box is weighted with lead weights placed in the bottom. This primitive type of pillow can be made by the worker without help.

There are also more elaborate pillows, which can be stood on a table or mounted on a stand. In the latter case, the pillow itself is movable; the work can therefore be continued without interruption. The frame, sometimes called a ''maid,'' consists of a board twenty inches long and sixteen inches wide, resting on two transverse bars one and a half inches high at the back and half an inch high at the front. This board is covered with very thick molleton or is slightly padded, and then covered with dark cloth.

At the outside edge of the board are two small uprights supporting the cylinder, composed of two discs which revolve upon a rod about nine inches long. This rod is covered with a thick layer of tow and then with cloth or flannel. To the left of the cylinder is a ratchet wheel with a spring or pawl fixed onto the board. This engages the teeth of the ratchet so that the cylinder can turn in only one direction.

The frame used in the Vosges district and in Normandy consists of a square box, padded and covered on the outside. The top of the box slopes slightly, and is about one and a quarter inches higher at the back than at the front; it has a deep groove in which a thickly padded cylinder revolves on an axle. This

Fig. 1034.
Lace
bobbin.

cylinder, instead of being above the board, projects only slightly above the edges of the groove. A second opening at the back of the frame gives access to the part of the box in which the finished lace is put as it comes off the cylinder. For Valenciennes lace the pillow used is rather differently constructed.

Lace bobbin (fig. 1034). The bobbin is a kind of wooden spool with a handle; it exists in infinite variety, but we illustrate here only the type which we consider most suitable for beginners. It should always be borne in mind that the size of the bobbins must be suited to the thread to be used and the particular type of lace to be made.

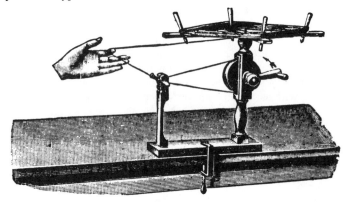

Fig. 1035. Bobbin winder.

The bobbin winder (fig. 1035). We advise those who wish to take up lacemaking to provide themselves with a bobbin winder such as the one shown in fig. 1035. For use, the winder is screwed firmly to a table, then the leather belt is passed round the bobbin between the spool and the thick part of the handle, and the bobbin is placed in the notch in the upright sup-

Fig. 1036. Looping the bobbin.

port. The extended skein of thread is placed round the pegs of the winder, and the thread is wound from left to right onto the bobbin by turning the handle attached to the wooden disc from right to left.

Stopping the thread on the bobbin (looping the bobbin) (fig. 1036). When the thread has been cut, it is stopped at the top of the bobbin by means of the loops shown in fig. 1036, known as a half hitch; this prevents the thread from unwinding but is, at the same time, loose enough to enable the thread issuing from the bobbin to be lengthened or shortened as required. This process is known as looping the bobbin.

The pattern. The pattern, one of the most important accessories of lacemaking, consists of a design transferred onto a card and with certain parts pricked. The lines and arrangement of the design must be absolutely correct; only in this way is it possible to make perfect lace. To render the making of the patterns easier, we give several repeats for each example, and the complete design can be traced from the illustration. The design must then be reproduced on strong paper or cardboard, lined with some very thin material such as muslin.

The repeats of the design must be worked out in such a way that when the pattern is laid round the cylinder they meet exactly, the design continuing in an uninterrupted line. If the circumference of the cylinder is too small, it can be increased by adding the requisite number of layers of cloth.

When the design has been worked out to the required length, the pricking is done as follows: the drawing is laid on a pad of cloth and each numbered dot of the pattern is perforated. When a corner is to be made, a piece of felt is first placed on the ordinary pattern; then the pattern of the corner itself is laid on this felt, taking into account the exact width of one repeat of the design. When the corner has been worked, the felt, complete with pattern and lace, is lifted—without removing the pins—turned, and replaced on the ordinary pattern, so that the work can be continued.

When an unbroken frame of lace is to be made, we recommend winding the bobbins in pairs at opposite ends of the same thread so that they can be fastened onto the mounting lines by means of loops of thread instead of knots. To finish off the work, the threads from the last motif of the lace are passed through these loops, then firmly knotted and overcast.

Pricker (fig. 1037). The type of holder required for the process of pricking can be had at any stationer's; with a coarse sewing needle screwed into the holder, the pricker is complete.

The little holes pricked in the card show the points where pins are to be stuck to stop the threads as the work advances, to

Fig. 1037.
Pricker.

form picots (by the twisting of the thread round them), and to hold the stitches in position.

Pins. The pins used in lacemaking should be of white metal and not of steel, for fear of rust; they should have round heads and be fairly long; and they should be coarse or fine according to the nature of the thread used.

Materials. For pillow lace likely to be subjected to frequent washing, a moderately twisted flax or cotton thread is used, such as DMC flax lace thread, DMC flax thread for knitting and crochet, DMC 6 cord cotton lace thread, DMC Alsatia, and DMC pearl cotton in white or ecru. Multicolored laces are usually made with silk thread. Silk can also be replaced by DMC floss flax or flourishing thread, DMC Alsatian twist, DMC pearl cotton, or DMC embroidery rayon, which can be obtained in a wide range of colors. Very effective lace can be made with DMC shaded pearl cotton. Metal lace is made with gold and silver threads of various thicknesses.

Position and Movements of the Hands (fig. 1038). The actual work in pillow lace is almost always done with four bobbins simultaneously: two bobbins are held in the right hand and two in the left, and the various stitches are made by the different ways in which the threads are twisted and crossed.

The number of pairs of bobbins used varies with the type of lace. As, however, it often happens that one part of the design is worked before another, or that some of the bobbins are momentarily idle, those which are not in use at the moment are held at the side of the cushion with pins, as shown in fig. 1038. The thread unwound from the bobbins should never be more than five inches long, to prevent the bobbins from becoming entangled.

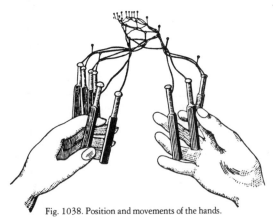

Fig. 1038. Position and movements of the hands.

Twisting (fig. 1039). Twisting is the process of passing the right-hand bobbin of each pair over the left-hand bobbin of the same pair. This movement is always done with one hand.

Crossing (fig. 1040). Crossing consists of passing the inner bobbin of the left-hand pair over the inner bobbin of the right-hand pair; the outer bobbins remain motionless; this movement therefore always requires both hands and two pairs of bobbins.

Stitches or "Passées." When two pairs of bobbins have been twisted and crossed, a half stitch or ''demipassée'' has been made, and two half stitches make a whole stitch or ''passée double.''

The first half stitch varies in form, but the second is always the same; it is made by twisting the two pairs once and crossing the inner bobbins. In order to shorten the text, in the instructions that follow we shall call the second half stitch a passée since this continental name has often been used in

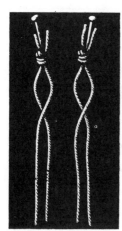

Fig. 1039. Two pairs
of bobbins twisted once.

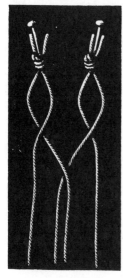

Fig. 1040. Two pairs
of bobbins twisted and
crossed once.

England and has the advantage of avoiding confusion with the ground known as half stitch (fig. 1042).

During the course of the work, the threads are held by pins at certain points of the pattern. These pins are usually stuck just between the pairs in use. When it happens that the pins must be stuck to the right or left of the pairs of bobbins, this will be mentioned in the instructions.

Grounds. In pillow lace, the principal parts of the design are worked in close stitches, such as lattice ground or half stitch, shown in fig. 1042, or linen or cloth stitch, also called whole stitch, illustrated in fig. 1044, which is sometimes ornamented with little motifs in leaf or spot stitch (figs. 1059 and 1061). As a background and to connect the motifs, openwork stitches are preferred (see figs. 1046, 1048, 1049, 1050, 1051, 1053) or dots like those in fig. 1057.

We give here a little series of plaits, or braids, and grounds which are often found in the best known laces and which will serve as useful practice for those who are new to this kind of work. Beside each example will be found the pattern and detailed instructions.

The pairs of bobbins are numbered from left to right; the first pair fastened onto the left on the pattern therefore counts also as the first in the instructions, and the first pair on the right counts as the highest number in the instructions.

Fig. 1041.
Single plait.

Single plait (fig. 1041). This plait is made with two pairs of bobbins; each pair is twisted once, then the inner threads are crossed. By repeating this process, the little plait shown in fig. 1041 is produced.

Lattice ground or half stitch (figs. 1042 and 1043). One pair of bobbins is hung onto the pattern in fig. 1043 at each of the points marked *a, b, c, d, e*.

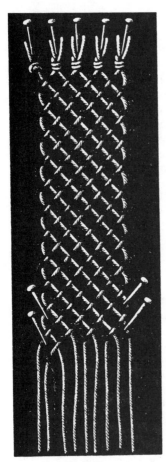

Fig. 1042.
Lattice ground or half stitch.

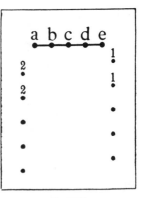

Fig. 1043.
Pattern for the lattice ground
or half stitch in fig. 1042.

Twist the 1st and 2nd pairs once, cross—* twist the 2nd and 3rd pairs once, cross—twist the 3rd and 4th pairs once, cross—twist the 4th and 5th pairs once, cross, stick a pin at point 1, twist the 4th pair once, twist the 5th pair twice, cross—twist the 3rd and 4th pairs once, cross—twist the 2nd and 3rd pairs once, cross—twist the 1st and 2nd pairs once, cross, stick a pin at point 2, twist the 1st pair twice, twist the 2nd pair once, cross; repeat from *.

Linen or whole stitch (figs. 1044 and 1045). Two pairs of bobbins are hung on each of the points *a, b, c* on the pattern in fig. 1045.

Cross the 1st and 2nd pairs, one passée— * cross the 2nd and 3rd pairs, one passée — cross the 3rd and 4th pairs, one passée— cross the 4th and 5th pairs, one passée— cross the 5th and 6th pairs, one passée, stick a pin at point 1, do not twist the 5th pair, twist the 6th pair once, cross, one passée—cross the 4th and 5th pairs, one passée—cross the 3rd and 4th pairs, one passée—cross the 2nd and 3rd pairs, one passée—cross the 1st and 2nd pairs, one passée, stick a pin at point 2, twist the 1st pair once, do not twist the 2nd pair, cross, one passée; repeat from *.

Torchon net ground (figs. 1046 and 1047). Two pairs of bobbins are hung on at each of the points *a, b, c, d, e* on the pattern in fig. 1047.

Twist the 2nd and 3rd pairs once, cross, stick a pin at 1, one passée— twist the 1st and 2nd pairs once, cross, stick a pin at 2, one passée—twist the 4th and 5th pairs once, cross, stick a pin at 3, one passée—twist the 3rd and 4th pairs once, cross, stick a pin at 4, one passée—twist the 2nd and 3rd pairs once, cross, stick a pin at 5, one passée—twist the 1st and 2nd

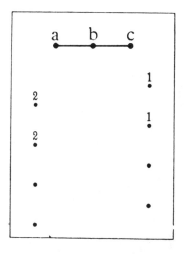

Fig. 1045. Pattern for the linen
or whole stitch in fig. 1044

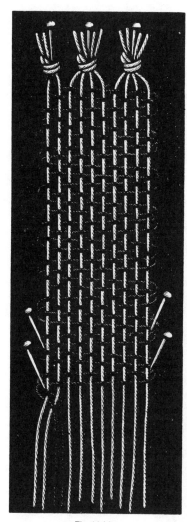

Fig. 1044.
Linen or whole stitch.

pairs once, cross, stick a pin at **6**, one
passée—twist the 6th and 7th pairs
once, cross, stick a pin at **7**, one
passée—twist the 5th and 6th pairs
once, cross, stick a pin at **8**, one
passée—twist the 4th and 5th pairs
once, cross, stick a pin at **9**, one
passée—twist the 3rd and 4th pairs
once, cross, stick a pin at **10**, one
passée—twist the 2nd and 3rd pairs
once, cross, stick a pin at **11**, one
passée—twist the 1st and 2nd pairs
once, cross, stick a pin at **12**, one
passée—twist the 8th and 9th pairs
once, cross, stick a pin at **13**, one
passée—twist the 7th and 8th pairs
once, cross, stick a pin at **14**, one
passée—twist the 6th and 7th pairs

once, cross, stick a pin at **15**, one passée—twist the 5th and 6th pairs once,
cross, stick a pin at **16**, one passée—twist the 4th and 5th pairs once, cross,
stick a pin at **17**, one passée—twist the 3rd and 4th pairs once, cross, stick a
pin at **18**, one passée—twist the 2nd and 3rd pairs once, cross, stick a pin at
19, one passée—twist the 1st and 2nd pairs once, cross, stick a pin at **20**,
one passée—* twist the 9th and 10th pairs once, cross, stick a pin at **21**,
one passée—twist the 8th and 9th pairs once, cross, stick a pin at **22**, one

passée—twist the 7th and 8th pairs once, cross, stick a pin at **23**, one
passée—twist the 6th and 7th pairs once, cross, stick a pin at **24**, one
passée—twist the 5th and 6th pairs once, cross, stick a pin at **25**, one
passée—twist the 4th and 5th pairs once, cross, stick a pin at **26**, one passée—twist the 3rd and 4th pairs once, cross, stick a pin at **27**, one passée—twist the 2nd and 3rd pairs once, cross, stick a pin at **28**, one passée—twist the 1st and 2nd pairs once, cross, stick a pin at **29**, one passée; repeat from *.

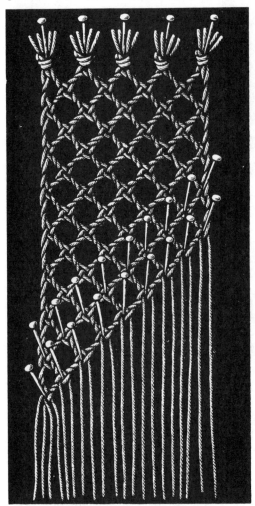

Fig. 1046. Torchon net ground.

Dieppe net ground (figs. 1048 and 1047). Two pairs of bobbins are hung on at each of the points *a, b, c, d, e* on the pattern in fig. 1047.

Twist the 2nd and 3rd pairs twice, cross, stick a pin at **1**, one passée—twist the 1st and 2nd pairs twice, cross, stick a pin at **2**, one passée—twist the 4th and 5th pairs twice, cross, stick a pin at **3**, one passée—twist the 3rd and 4th pairs twice, cross, stick a pin at **4**, one passée—twist the 2nd and 3rd pairs twice, cross, stick a pin at **5**, one passée—twist the 1st and 2nd pairs twice, cross, stick a pin at **6**, one passée—twist the 6th and 7th pairs twice, cross, stick a pin at **7**, one passée—twist the 5th and 6th pairs twice, cross, stick a pin at **8**, one passée—twist the 4th and 5th pairs twice, cross, stick a pin at **9**, one passée—twist the 3rd and 4th pairs twice, cross, stick a pin at **10**, one passée—twist the 2nd and 3rd pairs twice, cross, stick a pin at 11, one passée—twist the 1st and 2nd pairs twice, cross, stick a pin at 12, one passée—twist the 8th and 9th pairs twice, cross, stick a pin at 13, one passée—twist the 7th and 8th pairs twice, cross, stick a pin at 14, one passée—twist the 6th and 7th pairs twice, cross, stick a pin at 15, one passée—twist the 5th and 6th pairs twice, cross, stick a pin at 16, one passée—twist the 4th and 5th pairs twice, cross, stick a pin at 17, one passée—twist the 3rd and 4th pairs twice, cross, stick a pin at 18, one passée—twist the 2nd and 3rd pairs twice, cross, stick a pin at 19, one passée—twist the 1st and 2nd pairs twice, cross, stick a pin at 20, one passée—* twist the 9th and 10th pairs twice, cross, stick a pin at 21, one passée—twist the 8th and 9th pairs twice, cross, stick a pin at 22, one passée—twist the 7th and 8th pairs twice, cross, stick a pin at 23, one passée—twist the 6th and 7th pairs twice, cross, stick a pin at 24, one passée—

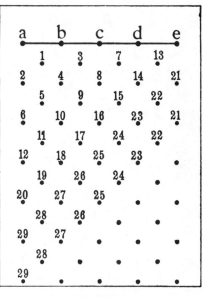

Fig. 1047.
Pattern for Torchon net ground, fig. 1046; Dieppe net ground, fig. 1048; Tulle net ground, fig. 1049; and Brussels net ground, fig. 1050.

twist the 5th and 6th pairs twice, cross, stick a pin at 25, one passée—twist the 4th and 5th pairs twice, cross, stick a pin at 26, one passée—twist the 3rd and 4th pairs twice, cross, stick a pin at 27, one passée—twist the 2nd and 3rd pairs twice, cross, stick a pin at 28, one passée—twist the 1st and 2nd pairs twice, cross, stick a pin at 29, one passée; repeat from *.

Tulle net ground (figs. 1049 and 1047). Two pairs of bobbins are hung on at each of the points *a, b, c, d, e* on the pattern in fig. 1047.

Twist the 2nd and 3rd pairs three times, cross, stick a pin at 1, twist the 1st and 2nd pairs three times, cross, stick a pin at 2, twist the 4th and 5th pairs three times, cross, stick a pin at 3—twist the 3rd and 4th pairs three times, cross, stick a pin at 4—twist the 2nd and 3rd pairs three times, cross, stick a pin at 5—twist the 1st and 2nd pairs three times, cross, stick a pin at 6—twist the 6th and 7th pairs three times, cross, stick a pin at 7—twist the 5th and 6th pairs three times, cross, stick a pin at 8—twist the 4th and 5th pairs three times, cross, stick a pin at 9—twist the 3rd and 4th pairs three times, cross, stick a pin at 10—twist the 2nd and 3rd pairs three times, cross, stick a pin at **11**—twist the 1st and 2nd pairs three times, cross, stick a pin at **12**—twist the 8th and 9th pairs three times, cross, stick a pin at **13**—twist the 7th and 8th pairs three times, cross, stick a pin at **14**—twist the 6th and 7th pairs three times, cross, stick a pin at **15**—twist the 5th and 6th pairs three times, cross, stick a pin at **16**—twist the 4th and 5th pairs three times, cross, stick a pin at **17**—twist the 3rd and 4th pairs three times, cross, stick a pin at **18**—twist the 2nd and 3rd pairs three times, cross, stick a pin at **19**—twist the 1st and 2nd pairs three times, cross, stick a pin at **20**—* twist the 9th and 10th pairs three times, cross, stick a pin at **21**—twist the 8th and 9th pairs three times, cross, stick a pin at **22**—twist the 7th and 8th pairs three times, cross, stick a pin at **23**—twist the 6th and 7th pairs three times, cross, stick a pin at **24**—twist the 5th and 6th pairs three times, cross, stick a pin at **25**—twist the 4th and 5th pairs three times, cross, stick a pin at **26**—twist the 3rd and 4th pairs three times, cross, stick a pin at **27**—twist the 2nd and 3rd pairs three times, cross, stick a pin at **28**—twist the 1st and 2nd pairs three times, cross, stick a pin at **29**; repeat from *.

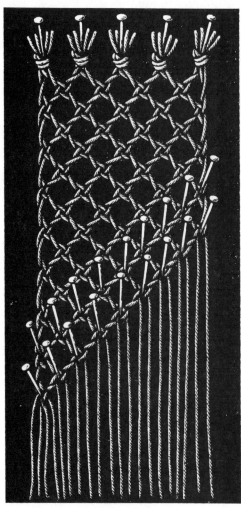

Fig. 1048. Dieppe net ground.

Brussels net ground (figs. 1050 and 1047). Two pairs of bobbins are hung on at each of the points *a, b, c, d, e* on the pattern in fig. 1047.

Twist the 2nd and 3rd pairs twice, cross, one passée, stick a pin at **1**, two passées—twist the 1st and 2nd pairs twice, cross, one passée, stick a pin at 2, two passées—twist the 4th and 5th pairs twice, cross, one passée, stick a pin at 3, two passées—twist the 3rd and 4th pairs twice, cross, one passée, stick a pin at 4, two passées— twist the 2nd and 3rd pairs twice, cross, one passée, stick a pin at 5, two passées—twist the 1st and 2nd pairs twice, cross, one passée, stick a pin at 6, two passées—twist the 6th and 7th pairs twice, cross, one passée, stick a pin at 7, two passées— twist the 5th and 6th pairs twice, cross, one passée, stick a pin at 8, two passées—twist the 4th and 5th pairs twice, cross, one passée, stick a pin at 9, two passées—twist the 3rd and 4th pairs twice, cross, one passée, stick a pin at 10, two passées— twist the 2nd and 3rd pairs twice, cross, one passée, stick a pin at 11, two passées—twist the 1st and 2nd pairs twice, cross, one passée, stick a pin at 12, two passées—twist the 8th and 9th pairs twice, cross, one passée, stick a pin at 13, two passées—twist the 7th and 8th pairs twice, cross, one passée, stick a pin at 14, two passées— twist the 6th and 7th pairs twice, cross, one passée, stick a pin at 15, two passées—twist the 5th and 6th pairs twice, cross, one passée, stick a pin at 16, two passées—twist the 4th and 5th pairs twice, cross, one

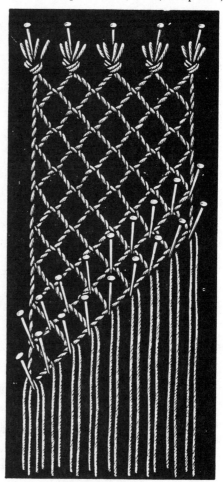

Fig. 1049. Tulle net ground.

passée, stick a pin at 17, two passées— twist the 3rd and 4th pairs twice, cross, one passée, stick a pin at 18, two passées—twist the 2nd and 3rd pairs twice, cross, one passée, stick a pin at 19, two passées—twist the 1st and 2nd pairs twice, cross, one passée, stick a pin at 20, two passées—* twist the 9th and 10th pairs twice, cross, one passée, stick a pin at 21, two passées—twist the 8th and 9th pairs twice, cross, one passée, stick a pin at

22, two passées—twist the 7th and 8th pairs twice, cross, one passée, stick a pin at 23, two passées—twist the 6th and 7th pairs twice, cross, one passée, stick a pin at 24, two passées—twist the 5th and 6th pairs twice, cross, one

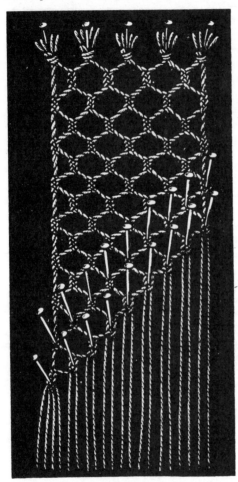

Fig. 1050. Brussels net ground.

passée, stick a pin at 25, two passées— twist the 4th and 5th pairs twice, cross, one passée, stick a pin at 26, two passées—twist the 3rd and 4th pairs twice, cross, one passée, stick a pin at 27, two passées—twist the 2nd and 3rd pairs twice, cross, one passée, stick a pin at 28, two passées—twist the 1st and 2nd pairs twice, cross, one passée, stick a pin at 29, two passées; repeat from *.

Point de la Vierge or maiden's net ground (figs. 1051 and 1052). Hang on two pairs of bobbins at each of the points *a, b, c, d, e, f* on the pattern in fig. 1052.

Twist the 2nd and 3rd pairs once, cross, stick a pin at 1, one passée— twist the 1st and 2nd pairs once, cross, stick a pin at 2, one passée—twist the 3rd and 4th pairs once, cross, stick a pin at 3, one passée—twist the 2nd and 3rd pairs once, cross, stick a pin at 4, one passée—twist the 1st and 2nd pairs once, cross, stick a pin at 5, one passée—twist the 6th and 7th pairs once, cross, stick a pin at 6, one passée—twist the 5th and 6th pairs once, cross, stick a pin at 7, one passée—twist the 7th and 8th pairs once, cross, stick a pin at 8, one passée—twist the 6th and 7th pairs once, cross, stick a pin at 9, one passée—twist the 5th and 6th pairs once, cross—twist the 3rd and 4th pairs once, cross—twist the 4th and 5th pairs once, cross, stick a pin at 10, one passée—twist the 3rd and 4th pairs once, cross, stick a pin at 11, one passée—twist the 5th and 6th pairs once, cross, stick a pin at **12**, one passée—twist the 4th and 5th pairs once, cross, stick a pin at **13**, one passée—twist the 3rd and 4th pairs once, cross—twist the 2nd and 3rd and 4th pairs once, cross—twist the 2nd and 3rd pairs once, cross, stick a pin at **14**, one passée—twist the 1st and 2nd pairs once, cross, stick a pin at **15**, one passée— twist the 3rd and 4th pairs once, cross, stick a pin at **16**, one passée—twist the 2nd and 3rd pairs once, cross, stick a pin at **17**, one passée—twist the 1st and 2nd pairs once, cross, stick a pin at **18**, one passée—* twist the 10th and 11th pairs once, cross, stick a pin at **19**, one passée— twist the 9th and 10th pairs once, cross, stick a pin at **20**, one passée— twist the 11th and 12th pairs once, cross, stick a pin at **21**, one passée— twist the 10th and 11th pairs once, cross, stick a pin at **22**, one passée—

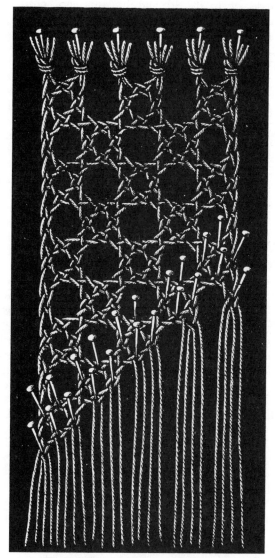

Fig. 1051. Point de la Vierge or maiden's net ground.

twist the 9th and 10th pairs once, cross—twist the 7th and 8th pairs once, cross—twist the 8th and 9th pairs once, cross, stick a pin at **23**, one passée— twist the 7th and 8th pairs once, cross, stick a pin at **24**, one passée—twist the 9th and 10th pairs once, cross, stick a pin at **25**, one passée—twist the 8th and 9th pairs once, cross, stick a pin at **26**, one passée—twist the 7th and 8th pairs once, cross—twist the 5th and 6th pairs once, cross— twist the 6th and 7th pairs once, cross, stick a pin at **27**, one passée—twist the 5th and 6th pairs once, cross, stick a pin at **28**, one passée—twist the 7th and 8th pairs once, cross, stick a pin at **29**, one passée—twist the 6th and 7th pairs once, cross, stick a pin at **30**, one passée—twist the 5th and 6th pairs once, cross— twist the 3rd and 4th pairs once, cross—twist the 4th and 5th pairs once, cross, stick a pin at **31**, one passée—twist the 3rd and 4th pairs once, cross, stick a pin at **32**, one passée—twist the 5th and 6th pairs once, cross, stick a pin at **33**, one passée—twist the 4th and 5th pairs once, cross, stick a pin at **34**, one passée—twist the 3rd and 4th pairs once, cross— twist the 2nd and 3rd pairs once, cross, stick a pin at **35**, one passée—

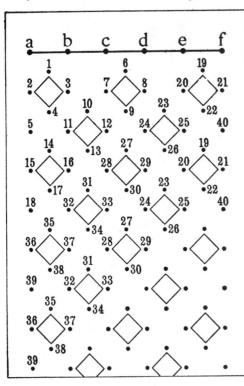

Fig. 1052. Pattern for point de la Vierge or maiden's net ground, fig. 1051.

twist the 1st and 2nd pairs once, cross, stick a pin at **36**, one passée— twist the 3rd and 4th pairs once, cross, stick a pin at **37**, one passée— twist the 2nd and 3rd pairs once, cross, stick a pin at **38**, one passée— twist the 1st and 2nd pairs once, cross, stick a pin at **39**, one passée— twist the 11th and 12th pairs once, cross, stick a pin at **40**, one passée—twist the 9th and 10th pairs once, cross; repeat from *.

Point de mariage or rose net ground(figs. 1053 and 1054). Two pairs of bobbins are hung on at each of the points, *a, c, d, f,* and one pair of bobbins each at the points *b* and *e*, on the pattern in fig. 1054.

Twist the 2nd and 3rd pairs twice, cross, stick a pin at **1**, twist twice, cross—twist the 5th and 6th pairs twice, cross, stick a pin at 2, twist twice, cross—twist the 4th and 5th pairs twice, cross, stick a pin at 3, twist twice, cross—twist the 3rd and 4th pairs twice, cross, stick a pin at 4, twist twice, cross—twist the 2nd and 3rd pairs twice, cross, stick a pin at 5, twist twice, cross—twist the 1st and 2nd pairs twice, cross, stick a pin at 6, twist twice, cross—twist the 2nd and 3rd pairs twice, cross, stick a pin at 7, twist twice, cross—twist the 4th and 5th pairs twice, cross, stick a pin at 8, twist twice, cross—twist the 6th and 7th pairs twice, cross, stick a pin at 9, twist twice, cross—* twist the 8th and 9th pairs twice, cross, stick a pin at 10, twist twice, cross—twist the 7th and 8th pairs twice, cross, stick a pin at 11, twist twice, cross—twist the 6th and 7th pairs twice, cross, stick a pin at 12, twist twice, cross—twist the 5th and 6th pairs twice, cross, stick a pin at 13, twist twice, cross—twist the 4th and 5th pairs twice, cross, stick a pin at 14, twist twice, cross—twist the 3rd and 4th pairs twice, cross, stick a pin at 15, twist twice, cross—twist the 2nd and 3rd pairs twice, cross, stick a pin at 16, twist twice, cross—twist the 1st and

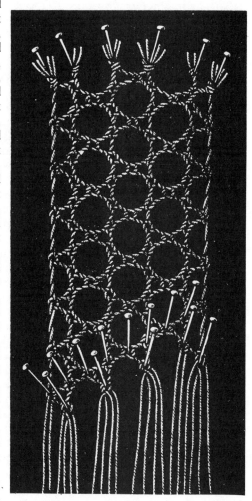

Fig. 1053. Point de mariage or rose net ground.

2nd pairs twice, cross, stick a pin at 17, twist twice, cross—twist the 2nd and 3rd pairs twice, cross, stick a pin at 18, twist twice, cross—twist the 4th and 5th pairs twice, cross, stick a pin at 19, twist twice, cross—twice the 6th and 7th pair twice, cross, stick a pin at 20, twist twice, cross—twist the 8th and 9th pairs twice, cross, stick a pin at **21**, twist twice, cross—twist the 9th and 10th pairs twice, cross, stick a pin at **22**, twist twice, cross; repeat from *.

Valenciennes net ground (figs. 1055 and 1056). Valenciennes net is composed of little plaits which require the use of two pairs of bobbins each. Two pairs of bobbins are hung on at the point *a*, and four pairs of bobbins each at points *b* and *c*, on the pattern in fig. 1056.

Twist the 1st and 2nd pairs once, cross, five passées—twist the 3rd and 4th pairs once, cross, five passées—twist the 2nd and 3rd pairs once, cross, stick a pin at **1**, one passée—twist the 1st and 2nd pairs once, cross, five passée, stick a pin at **2**, twist once, cross, five passées—twist the 3rd and 4th pairs once, cross, five passées—twist the 5th and 6th pairs once, cross, five passées—twist the 7th and 8th pairs once, cross, five passées—twist the 6th and 7th pairs once, cross, stick a pin at **3**, one passée—twist the 5th and 6th pairs once, cross, five passées—twist the 4th and 5th pairs once, cross, stick a pin at **4**, one passée—twist the 3rd and 4th pairs once, cross, five passées—twist the 2nd and 3rd pairs once, cross, stick a pin at **5**, one passée—twist the 1st and 2nd pairs once, cross, five passées, stick a pin at **6**, twist once, cross, five passées—twist the 3rd and 4th pairs once, cross, five passées— twist the 5th and 6th pairs once, cross, five passées—twist the 7th and 8th

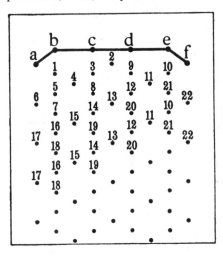

Fig. 1054. Pattern for point de mariage or rose net ground, fig. 1053.

pairs once, cross, five passées—* twist the 9th and 10th pairs once, cross, five passées, stick a pin at **7**, twist once, cross, five passées—twist the 8th and 9th pairs once, cross, stick a pin at **8**, one passée—twist the 7th and 8th pairs once, cross, five passée—twist the 6th and 7th pairs once, stick a pin at **9**, one passée—twist the 5th and 6th pairs once, cross five passées— twist the 4th and 5th pairs once, cross, stick a pin at **10**, one passée—twist the 3rd and 4th pairs once, cross, five passées—twist the 2nd the 3rd pairs once, cross, stick a pin at **11**, one passée—twist the 1st and 2nd pairs once, cross, five passées, stick a pin at **12**, twist once, five passées—twist the 3rd and 4th pairs once, cross, five passées—twist the 5th and 6th pairs once, cross, five passées—twist the 7th and 8th pairs once, cross, five passées; repeat from *.

Dieppe net ground with dots (figs. 1057 and 1058). Two pairs of bobbins are hung on at each of the points *a, b, c, d, e* on the pattern in fig. 1058.

Twist the 2nd and 3rd pairs twice, cross, stick a pin at 1, one passée— twist the 1st and 2nd pairs twice, cross, stick a pin at 2, one passée—twist

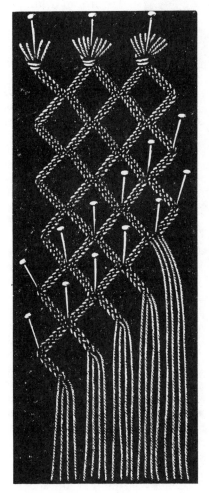

Fig. 1055. Valenciennes net ground.

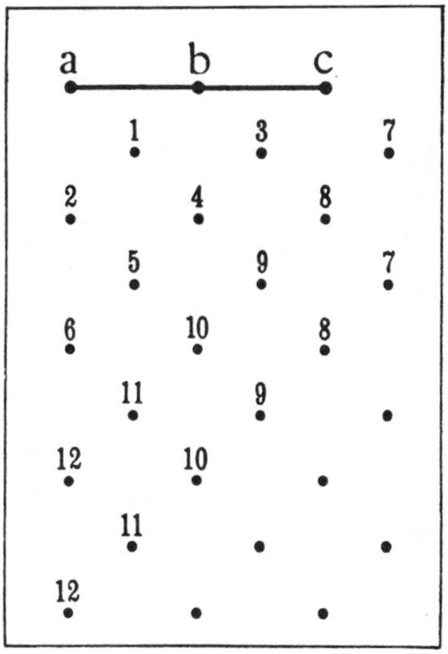

Fig. 1056. Pattern for Valenciennes net ground, fig. 1055.

the 4th and 5th pairs twice, cross, stick a pin at 3, one passée—twist the 3rd and 4th pairs twice, cross, stick a pin at 4, one passée—twist the 2nd and 3rd pairs twice, cross, stick a pin at 5, one passée—twist the 1st and 2nd pairs twice, cross, stick a pin at 6, one passée—twist the 8th and 9th pairs twice, cross, stick a pin at 7, one passée— twist the 9th and 10th pairs twice, cross, stick a pin at 8, one passée—twist the 6th and 7th pairs twice, cross, stick a pin at 9, one passée—twist the 7th and 8th pairs twice, cross, stick at pin at 10, one passée—twist the 8th and 9th pairs twice, cross, stick a pin at 11, one passée—twist the 9th and 10th pairs twice, cross, stick a pin at 12, one passée—* twist the 5th and 6th pairs

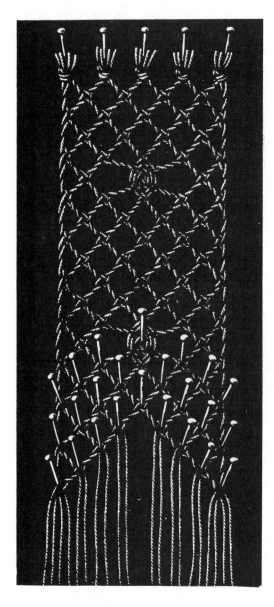

Fig. 1057. Dieppe net ground with dots.

twice, cross, stick a pin at **13**, one passée—twist the 4th and 5th pairs twice, cross, stick a pin at **14**, one passée—twist the 3rd and 4th pair twice, cross, stick a pin at **15**, one passée—twist the 2nd and 3rd pairs twice, cross, stick a pin at **16**, one passée—twist the 1st and 2nd pairs twice, cross, stick a pin at **17**, one passée—twist the 6th and 7th pairs twice, cross, stick a pin at **18**, one passée—twist the 7th and 8th pairs twice, cross, stick a pin at **19**, one passée—twist the 8th and 9th pairs twice, cross, stick a pin at **20**, one passée—twist the 9th and 10th pairs twice, cross, stick a pin at **21**, one passée—twist the 5th and 6th pairs three times, cross, one passée—twist the 4th pair three times, do not twist the 5th pair, cross, one passée—do not twist the 6th pair, twist the 7th pair three times, cross, one passée—cross the 5th and 6th pairs, one passée, stick a pin at **22**, cross, one passée—cross the 4th and 5th pairs, one passée—twist the 3rd pair twice, twist the 4th pair three times, cross, stick a pin at **23**, one passée—twist the 2nd and 3rd pairs twice, cross, stick a pin at **24**, one passée—twist the 1st and 2nd pairs twice, cross, stick a pin at **25**, one passée—cross the 6th and 7th pairs, one passée—twist the 7th pair three times, twist the 8th pair twice, cross, stick a pin at **26**, one passée—twist the 8th and 9th pairs twice, cross, stick a pin at **27**, one passée—twist the 9th and 10th pairs twice, cross, stick a pin at **28**, one passée—cross the 5th and 6th pairs, one passée—twist the 4th pair twice,

twist the 5th pair three times, cross, stick a pin at **29**, one passée— twist the 3rd and 4th pairs twice, cross, stick a pin at **30**, one passée—twist the 2nd and 3rd pairs twice, cross, stick a pin at **31**, one passee—twist the 1st and 2nd pairs twice, cross, stick a pin at **32**, one passée—twist the 6th pair three times, twist the 7th pair twice, cross, stick a pin at **33**, one passée—twist the 7th and 8th pairs twice, cross, stick a pin at **34**, one passée—twist the 8th and 9th pairs twice, cross, stick a pin at **35**, one passée—twist the 9th and 10th pairs twice, cross, stick a pin at **36**, one passée—twist the 5th and 6th pairs twice, cross, stick a pin at **37**, one passée—twist the 4th and 5th pairs twice, cross, stick a pin at **38**, one passée— twist the 3rd and 4th pairs twice, cross, stick a pin at **39**, one passée—twist the 2nd and 3rd pairs twice, cross, stick a pin at **40**, one passée—twist the 1st and 2nd pairs twice, cross, stick a pin at **41**, one passée—twist the 6th and 7th pairs twice, cross, stick a pin

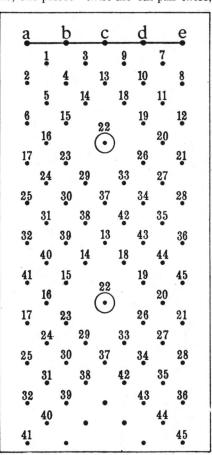

Fig. 1058. Pattern for Dieppe net ground with dots, fig. 1057.

at **42**, one passée—twist the 7th and 8th pairs twice, cross, stick a pin at **43**, one passée—twist the 8th and 9th pairs twice, cross, stick a pin at **44**, one passée—twist the 9th and 10th pairs twice, cross, stick a pin at **45**, one passée; repeat from *.

Torchon net ground with squares in leaf stitch (figs. 1059 and

1060.) Two pairs of bobbins are hung on at each of the points *a, b, c, d* on the pattern in fig. 1060.

Twist the 2nd and 3rd pairs once, cross, stick a pin at 1, one passée—twist the 1st and 2nd pairs once, cross, stick a pin at 2, one passée—twist

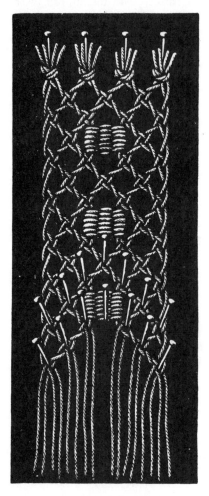

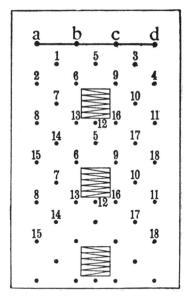

Fig. 1060. Pattern for Torchon net ground with squares in leaf stitch, fig. 1059.

Fig. 1059. Torchon net ground with squares in leaf stitch.

the 6th and 7th pairs once, cross, stick a pin at 3, one passée—twist the 7th and 8th pairs once, cross, stick a pin at 4, one passée—* twist the 4th and 5th pairs once, cross, stick a pin at 5, one passée—twist the 3rd and 4th pairs once, cross, stick a pin at 6, one passée—twist the 2nd and 3rd pairs once, cross, stick a pin at 7, one passée—twist the 1st and 2nd pairs once, cross, stick a pin at 8, one passée—twist the 5th and 6th pairs once, cross,

stick a pin at 9, one passée—twist the 6th and 7th pairs once, cross, stick a pin at 10, one passée—twist the 7th and 8th pairs once, cross, stick a pin at 11, one passée—twist the 4th and 5th pairs twice, cross, work the square in leaf stitch as follow: ** twist the 4th pair twice, do not twist the 5th pair, cross, do not twist the 4th pair, twist the fifth pair twice, cross; repeat from ** five times, (draw all the passées equally tight, so as to give the square a good shape); stick a pin at 12—twist the 3rd pair once, twist the 4th pair twice, cross, stick a pin at 13, one passée—twist the 2nd and 3rd pairs once, cross, stick a pin at 14, one passée—twist the 1st and 2nd pairs once, cross, stick a pin at 15, one passée—twist the 5th pair twice, twist the 6th pair once, cross, stick a pin at 16, one passée—twist the 6th and 7th pairs once, cross, stick a pin at 17, one passée—twist the 7th and 8th pairs once, cross, stick a pin at 18, one passée; repeat from *.

Torchon net ground with leaves in leaf stitch (figs. 1061 and 1062). Two pairs of bobbins are hung on at each of the points *a, b, c, d* on the pattern in fig. 1062.

Twist the 2nd and 3rd pairs once, cross, stick a pin at 1, one passée—twist the 1st and 2nd pairs once, cross, stick a pin at 2, one passée—twist the 6th and 7th pairs once, cross, stick a pin at 3, one passée—twist the 7th and 8th pairs once, cross, stick a pin at 4, one passée—* twist the 4th and 5th pairs once, cross, stick a pin at 5, one passée—twist the 3rd and 4th pairs once, cross, stick a pin at 6, one passée—twist the 2nd and 3rd pairs once, cross, stick a pin at 7, one passée—twist the 1st and 2nd pairs once, cross, stick a pin at 8, one passée—twist the 2nd and 3rd pairs once, cross, stick a pin at 9, one passée—twist the 1st and 2nd pairs once,

Fig. 1061. Torchon net ground with leaves in leaf stitch.

cross, stick a pin at 10, one passée—twist the 5th and 6th pairs once, cross, stick a pin at 11, one passée—twist the 6th and 7th pairs once, cross, stick a pin at 12, one passée—twist the 7th and 8th pairs once, cross, stick a pin at 13, one passée—twist the 6th and 7th pairs once, cross, stick a pin at 14, one passée—twist the 7th and 8th pairs once, cross, stick a pin at 15, one passée—twist the 4th and 5th pairs twice, cross, stick a pin at 16, work the leaf stitch as follows: * * twist the 4th pair twice, do not twist the 5th pair, cross, do not twist the 4th pair, twist the 5th pair twice, cross, repeat from * * nine times (draw the 1st and 10th passées very tight and leave those between looser, to give the leaf a good shape); stick a pin at 17—twist the 3rd pair once, twist the 4th pair twice, stick a pin at 18, one passée—twist the 2nd and 3rd pairs once, cross, stick a pin at 19, one passée—twist the 1st and 2nd pairs once, cross, stick a pin at 20, one passée—twist the 5th pair twice, twist the 6th pair once, cross, stick a pin at 21, one passée—twist the 6th and 7th pairs once, cross, stick a pin at 22, one passée—twist the 7th and 8th pairs once, cross, stick a pin at 23, one passée; repeat from *.

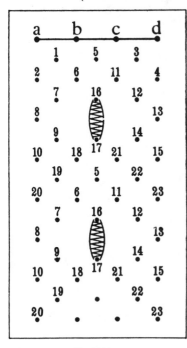

Fig. 1062.
Pattern for Torchon net ground with leaves in leaf stitch, fig. 1061.

Everlasting Lace in Two Rows (figs. 1063 and 1064). This is the name given to lace with no definite pattern. Both insertions and scalloped edgings can be made in this type of lace, the width depending on the number of rows.

For an edging consisting of a single row of open holes, five pairs of bobbins are needed; for two rows of holes, seven pairs of bobbins; for three rows, nine pairs of bobbins. Thus two more pairs of bobbins must be added for each extra row of holes. Insertions require an extra pair of bobbins for the working of the second straight edge.

Three pairs of bobbins are hung on at point a, and two pairs each at points b and c, on the pattern in fig. 1064.

* Twist the 2nd and 3rd pairs once, cross, one passée—twist the 3rd and 4th pairs once, cross, stick a pin at 1, one passée—twist the 4th and 5th pairs once, cross, one passée—twist, the 5th and 6th pairs once, cross, stick a pin at 2, one passée—twist the 6th and 7th pairs once, cross, stick a pin at 3, twist the 6th and 7th pairs once, cross, one passée—twist the 4th and 5th pairs once, cross, one passée—twist the 2nd and 3rd pairs once, cross, one

passée—twist the 1st pair three times, twist the 2nd pair once, cross, one passée, stick a pin at 4 to the right of the 2nd pair; repeat from *.

Torchon Lace Edging (figs. 1065 and 1066). Three pairs of bobbins are hung on at each of the points *a* and *b*, and two pairs of bobbins at each of the points *c* and *d*, on the pattern in fig. 1066.

Twist the 3rd and 4th pairs once, cross, stick a pin at 1, one passée—twist the 4th and 5th pairs once, cross—twist the 5th and 6th pairs once, cross—twist the 6th and 7th pairs once, cross—twist the 7th and 8th pairs once, cross—twist the 8th and 9th pairs once, cross—twist the 9th and 10th pairs once, cross, stick a pin at 2, one passée—twist the 8th

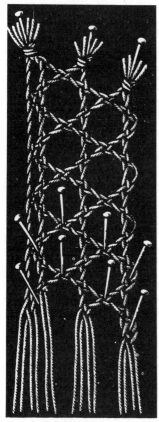

Fig. 1063.
Everlasting lace in two rows.

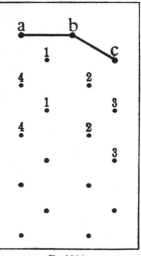

Fig. 1064.
Pattern for everlasting lace
in two rows, fig. 1063.

and 9th pairs once, cross—twist the 7th and 8th pairs once, cross—twist the 6th and 7th pairs once, cross—twist the 5th and 6th pairs once, cross—twist the 4th and 5th pairs once, cross, stick a pin at 3, one passée— twist the 5th and 6th pairs once, cross—twist the 6th and 7th pairs once, cross—twist the 7th and 8th pairs once, cross—twist the 8th and 9th pairs once, cross— twist the 9th and 10th pairs once, cross, stick a pin at 4, one passée—twist the 8th and 9th pairs once, cross—twist the 7th and 8th pairs once, cross— twist the 6th and 7th pairs once, cross—twist the 5th and 6th pairs once, cross, stick a pin at 5, one passée—twist the 6th and 7th pairs once, cross— twist the 7th and 8th pairs once, cross—twist the 8th and 9th pairs once, cross—twist the 9th and 10th pairs once, cross, stick a pin at 6, one passée—twist the 8th and 9th pairs once, cross—twist the 7th and 8th pairs once, cross—twist the

6th and 7th pairs once, cross, stick a pin at **7**, one passée—twist the 7th and 8th pairs once, cross—twist the 8th and 9th pairs once, cross—twist the 9th and 10th pairs once, cross, stick a pin at **8**, one passée—twist the 8th and 9th pairs once, cross—twist the 7th and 8th pairs once, cross—twist

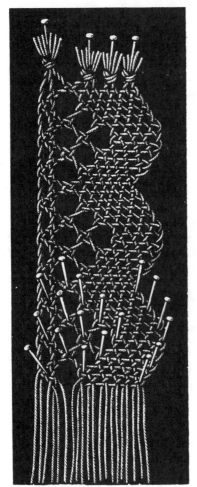

Fig. 1065. Torchon lace edging.

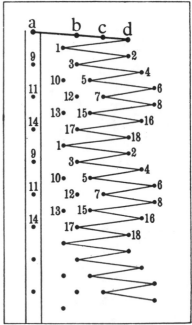

Fig. 1066. Pattern for the Torchon lace edging in fig. 1065.

the 6th and 7th pairs once, cross— twist the 2nd and 3rd pairs once, cross, one passée—twist the 1st pair twice, twist the 2nd pair once, cross, one passée, stick a pin at **9** to the right of the 2nd pair—twist the 3rd and 4th pairs once, cross, stick a pin at **10**, one passée—twist the 2nd and 3rd pairs once, cross, one passée— twist the 1st pair twice, twist the 2nd

pair once, cross, one passée, stick a pin at **11** to the right of the 2nd pair— twist the 2nd and 3rd pairs once, cross, one passée—twist the 4th and 5th pairs once, cross, stick a pin at **12**, one passée—twist the 3rd and 4th pairs once, cross, stick a pin at **13**, one passée—twist the 2nd and 3rd pairs once, cross, one passée—twist the 1st pair twice, twist the 2nd pair once, cross, one passée, stick a pin at **14** to the right of the 2nd pair—twist the 2nd and 3rd pairs once, cross, one passée—twist the 5th and 6th pairs once, cross, stick a pin at **15**, one passée—twist the 6th and 7th pairs once, cross—twist the 7th and 8th pairs once, cross—twist the 8th and 9th pairs once, cross—twist the 9th and 10th pairs once, cross, stick a pin at **16**, one passée—twist the 8th and 9th pairs once, cross—twist the 7th and 8th pairs once, cross— twist the 6th and 7th pairs once, cross—twist the 5th and 6th pairs once, cross—twist the 4th and 5th pairs once, cross, stick a pin at **17**, one passée—twist the 5th and 6th pairs once, cross—twist the 6th and 7th pairs once, cross—twist the 7th and 8th pairs once, cross—twist the 8th and 9th pairs once, cross— twist the 9th and 10th pairs once, cross, stick a pin at **18**, one passée—twist the 8th and 9th pairs once, cross— twist the 7th and 8th pairs once, cross—twist the 6th and 7th pairs once, cross— twist the 5th and 6th pairs once, cross—twist the 4th and 5th pairs once, cross. Repeat from the beginning.

Plaited Braid With Picots (fig. 1067). To ornament the plain edges of lace, picots are often made with one of the outside threads, with the help of a pin set in the pattern at a given spot. These picots are often found in plaited braids, as shown in fig. 1067; see also the laces in figs. 1070, 1076, and 1078.

Crossing With Three and Four Pairs of Bobbins (figs. 1068 and 1069). There is a type of lace in which the design is made up principally of plaited and twisted braids. A peculiarity of the working of this kind of lace is that where the braids intersect the passées are made with three or four pairs of bobbins. The pairs are then counted as if they were single threads and are twisted and crossed in the same way. The pins which hold these crossings are set exactly in the center of the crossed threads, as can be seen in the illustrations.

Fig. 1067.
Plaited braid
with picots.

Fig. 1068 shows a crossing with three pairs of bobbins, while in fig. 1069 the crossing is made with four pairs. These crossings are used in making the lace edgings in figs. 1070, 1076, and 1078.

Plaited Lace (figs. 1070 and 1071). Four pairs of bobbins are hung on at the point *a,* and one pair of bobbins at the point *b,* on the pattern in fig. 1071.

Twist the 1st and 2nd pairs once, cross, six passées—twist the 3rd and 4th pairs once, cross, three passées—do not twist the 3rd and 4th pairs, twist the 5th pair three times, cross as shown in fig. 1068, stick a pin at

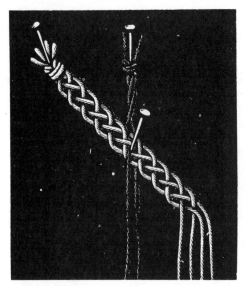

Fig. 1068.
Crossing with three pairs of bobbins.

Fig. 1069.
Crossing with four pairs of bobbins.

1—twist the 4th and 5th pairs once, cross, three passées, one picot to the right at 2, three passées, one picot to the right at 3, three passées, one picot to the right at 4, three passées— twist the 3rd pair three times, do not twist the 4th and 5th pairs, cross as shown in fig. 1068, stick a pin at 5—twist the 3rd and 4th pairs once, cross, three passées—cross as shown in fig. 1069 with the 1st, 2nd, 3rd, and 4th pairs, stick a pin at 6. Repeat from the beginning.

Torchon Lace Insertion (figs. 1072 and 1073). One bobbin is hung on at each of the points *a, c, d, e, f, g, h, j,* and three bobbins each at the points *b* and *i,* on the pattern in fig. 1073.

Twist the 9th and 10th pairs twice, cross, stick a pin at 1, one passée— twist the 8th pair twice, twist the 9th pair once, cross, stick a pin at 2, one passée—twist the 9th and 10th pairs once, cross—twist the 10th and 11th pairs once, cross, stick a pin at 3, one passée—twist the 9th and 10th pairs once, cross—twist the 8th and 9th pairs once, cross—twist the 7th pair twice, twist the 8th pair once, cross, stick a pin at 4, one passée—twist the 8th and 9th pairs once, cross—twist the 9th and 10th pairs once, cross, stick a pin at 5, one passée—twist the 8th and 9th pairs once, cross—twist, the 7th and 8th pairs once, cross—twist the 6th pair twice, twist the 7th pair once, cross, stick a pin at 6, one passée—twist the 7th and 8th pairs once, cross—twist the 8th and 9th pairs once, cross—twist the 9th and

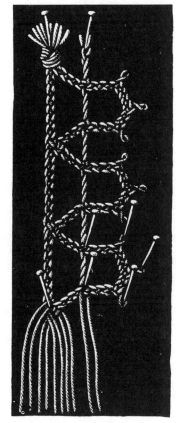

Fig. 1070. Plaited lace.

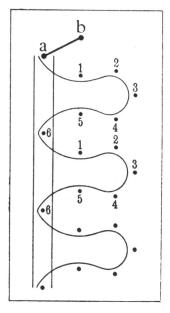

Fig. 1071.
Pattern for the plaited lace in fig. 1070.

10th pairs once, cross—twist the 11th pair once, do not twist the 12th pair, cross, one passée—cross the 12th and 13th pairs, one passée—twist the 13th pair once, twist the 14th pair twice, cross, one passée, stick a pin at 7, two passées—do not twist the 12th pair, twist the 13th pair once, cross, one passée—cross the 11th and 12th pairs, one passée—twist the 10th and 11th pairs once, cross, stick a pin at 8, one passée—twist the 9th and 10th pairs once, cross—twist the 8th and 9th pairs once, cross—twist the 7th and 8th pairs once, cross—twist the 6th and 7th pairs once, cross—twist the 5th pair twice, twist the 6th pair once, cross, stick a pin at 9, one passée—twist the 6th and 7th pairs once, cross—twist the 7th and 8th pairs once, cross—twist the 8th and 9th pairs once, cross—twist the 9th and 10th pairs once, cross, stick a pin at 10, one passée—twist the 8th and 9th pairs once, cross—twist the 7th and 8th pairs once, cross—twist the 6th and 7th pairs once, cross—twist the 5th and 6th pairs once, cross—twist the 4th and 5th pairs once, cross, stick a pin at **11,** one passée—do not twist the 3rd pair, twist the 4th pair once, cross, one passée—cross the 2nd and 3rd pairs, one passée—twist the 1st pair twice, twist the 2nd pair once, cross, one passée, stick a pin at **12,** two passées— twist the 2nd pair once, do not twist the 3rd pair, cross, one passée—cross the 3rd and 4th pairs, one passée—twist the 5th and 6th pairs once, cross— twist the 6th and 7th pairs once, cross—twist the 7th and 8th pairs once, cross—twist the 8th and 9th pairs once, cross—stick a pin at **13,** one passée—twist the 7th and 8th pairs once, cross—twist the 6th and 7th pairs once, cross—twist the 5th and 6th pairs once, cross, stick a pin at **14,** one passée—twist the 6th and 7th pairs once, cross—twist the 7th and 8th pairs once, cross, stick a pin at **15,** one passée—twist the 6th and 7th pairs once, cross—twist the 5th and 6th pairs once, cross—twist the 4th and 5th pairs

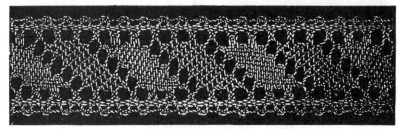

Fig. 1072. Torchon lace insertion.

once, cross, stick a pin at **16,** one passée—do not twist the 3rd pair, twist the 4th pair once, cross, one passée—cross the 2nd and 3rd pairs, one passée—twist the 1st pair twice, twist the 2nd pair once, cross, one passée, stick a pin at **17,** two passées— twist the 2nd pair once, do not twist the 3rd pair, cross, one passée—cross the 3rd and 4th pairs, one passée—twist the 5th and 6th pairs once, cross— twist the 6th and 7th pairs once, cross, stick a pin at **18,** one passée—twist the 5th and 6th pairs once, cross, stick a pin at **19,** one passée—twist the 4th pair once, twist the 5th pair twice, cross, stick a pin at **20,** one passée— do not twist the 3rd pair, twist the 4th pair once, cross, one passée—cross the 2nd and 3rd pairs, one passée—twist the 1st pair twice, twist the 2nd pair once, cross, one passée, stick a pin at **21,** two passées—twist the 2nd pair once, do not twist the 3rd pair, cross, one passée—cross the 3rd and 4th pairs, one passée—twist the 11th pair once, do not twist the 12th pair, cross, one passée—cross the 12th and 13th pairs, one passée—twist the 13th pair once, twist the 14th pair twice, cross, one passée, stick a pin at **22,** two passées—do not twist the 12th pair, twist the 13th pair once, cross, one passée—cross the 11th and 12th pairs, one passée—twist the 10th pair twice, twist the 11th pair once, cross, stick a pin at **23,** one passée—twist the 11th pair once, do not twist the 12th pair, cross, one passée—cross the 12th and 13th pairs, one passée—twist the

13th pair once, twist the 14th pair twice, cross, one passée, stick a pin at 24, two passées—do not twist the 12th pair, twist the 13th pair once, cross, one passée—cross the 11th and 12th pairs, one passée—twist the 9th and 10th pairs twice, cross, one passée, stick a pin at 25, do not twist the 9th pair, twist the 10th pair once, cross, one passée, twist the 8th pair twice, do not twist the 9th pair, cross, one passée, stick a pin at 26, twist the 8th pair once, do not twist the 9th pair, cross, one passée—cross the 9th and 10th pairs, one passée—do not twist the 10th pair, twist the 11th pair once, cross, one passée, stick a pin at 27, do not twist the 10th pair, twist the 11th pair once, cross, one passée— cross the 9th and 10th pairs, one passée—cross the 8th and 9th pairs, one passée—twist the 7th pair twice, do not twist the 8th pair, cross, one passée, stick a pin at 28, twist the 7th pair once, do not twist the 8th pair, cross, one passée—cross the 8th and 9th pairs, one passée—cross the 9th and 10th pairs, one passée, stick a pin at 29, do not twist the 9th pair, twist the 10th pair once, cross, one passée—cross the 8th and 9th pairs, one passée— cross the 7th and 8th pairs, one passée—twist the 6th pair twice, do not twist the 7th pair, cross, one passée, stick a pin at 30, twist the 6th pair once, do not twist the 7th pair, cross, one passée—cross the 7th and 8th pairs, one passée—cross the 8th and 9th pairs, one passée—cross the 9th and 10th pairs, one passée—twist the 11th pair once, do not twist the 12th pair, cross, one passée—cross the 12th and 13th pairs, one passée—twist the 13th pair once, twist the 14th pair twice, cross, one passée, stick a pin at 31, two passées—do not twist the 12th

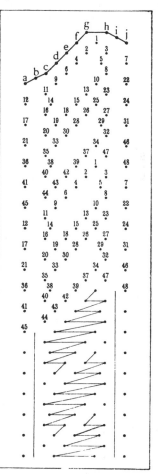

Fig. 1073.
Pattern for the Torchon lace insertion in fig. 1072.

pair, twist the 13th pair once, cross, one passee—cross the 11th and 12th pairs, one passée—do not twist the 10th pair, twist the 11th pair once, cross, one passée, stick a pin at 32, do not twist the 10th pair, twist the 11th pair once, cross, one passée—cross the 9th and 10th pairs, one passée—cross the 8th and 9th pairs, one passée—cross the 7th and 8th pairs, one passée—cross the 6th and 7th pairs, one passée—twist the 5th pair twice, do not twist the 6th pair, cross, one passée, stick a pin at 33, twist the 5th pair once, do not twist the 6th pair, cross, one passée—cross the 6th and 7th pairs, one passée—cross the 7th and 8th pairs, one passée—cross the 8th and 9th pairs, one passée— cross the 9th and 10th pairs, one passée, stick a pin at 34, do not twist the 9th pair, twist the 10th pair once, cross, one passée—cross the 8th and 9th pairs, one passée—cross the 7th and 8th pairs, one passée—cross the 6th and 7th pairs, one passée—cross the 5th and 6th pairs, one passée—twist the 4th pair once, do not twist the 5th pair, cross, one passée, stick a pin at 35, twist the 4th pair once, do not twist the 5th pair, cross, one passée—do not twist the 3rd pair, twist the 4th pair once, cross, one passée—cross the 2nd and 3rd pairs, one passée—twist the 1st pair twice, twist the 2nd pair once, cross, one passée, stick a pin at 36, two passées—twist the 2nd pair once, do not twist the 3rd pair, cross, one passée—cross the 3rd and 4th pairs, one passée—cross the 5th and 6th pairs, one passée—cross the 6th and 7th pairs, one passée—cross the 7th and 8th pairs, one passée—cross the 8th and 9th pairs, one passée, stick a pin at 37, do not twist the 8th pair, twist the 9th pair once, cross, one passée—cross the 7th and 8th pairs, one passée—cross the 6th and 7th pairs, one passée—cross the 5th and 6th pairs, one passée, stick a pin at 38, twist the fifth pair once, do not twist the 6th pair, cross, one passée—cross the 6th and 7th pairs, one passée—cross the 7th and 8th pairs, one passée, stick a pin at 39, do not twist the 7th pair, twist the 8th pair once, cross, one passée—cross the 6th and 7th pairs, one passée—cross the 5th and 6th pairs, one passée—twist the 4th pair once, do not twist the 5th pair, cross, one passée, stick a pin at 40, twist the 4th pair once, do not twist the 5th pair, cross, one passée—do not twist, the 3rd pair, twist the 4th pair once, cross, one passée—cross the 2nd and 3rd pairs, one passée—twist the 1st pair twice, twist the 2nd pair once, cross, one passée, stick a pin at 41, two passée—twist the 2nd pair once, do not twist the 3rd pair, cross, one passée—cross the 3rd and 4th pairs, one passée— cross the 5th and 6th pairs, one passée—cross the 6th and 7th pairs, one passée, stick a pin at 42, do not twist the 6th pair, twist the 7th pair once, cross, one passée—cross the 5th and 6th pairs, one passée, stick a pin at 43, twist the 5th pair once, do not twist the 6th pair, cross, one passée—twist the 4th pair once, twist the 5th pair twice, cross, stick a pin at 44, one passée—do not twist the 3rd pair, twist the 4th pair once, cross, one passée—cross the 2nd and 3rd pairs, one passée—twist the 1st pair twice, twist the 2nd pair once, cross, one passée, stick a pin at 45, two passées— twist the 2nd pair once, do not twist the 3rd pair, cross, one passée—cross the 3rd and 4th pairs, one passée— twist the 11th pair once, do not twist the 12th pair, cross, one passée— cross the 12th and 13th pairs, one passée— twist the 13th pair once, twist the 14th pair twice, cross, one passée, stick a pin at 46, two passées—do not twist the 12th pair, twist the 13th pair once, cross, one passée—cross the 11th and 12th pairs, one passée—twist the 10th pair twice, twist the 11th pair once, cross, stick a pin at **47**, one passée—twist the 11th pair once, do not twist the 12th pair, cross, one passée—cross the 12th and 13th pairs, one passée— twist the 13th pair once, twist the 14th pair twice, cross, one passée, stick a pin at **48**, two passées—do not twist the 12th pair, twist the 13th pair once, cross, one passée—cross the 11th and 12th pairs, one passée.

Repeat from the beginning.

Torchon Lace Edging (figs. 1074 and 1075). One pair of bobbins is hung on at each of the points *a, c, d, e, f, g, h,* two pairs of bobbins at the point *b,* and three pairs of bobbins at the point *i* on the pattern in fig. 1075.

Fig. 1074. Torchon lace edging.

Twist the 6th and 7th pairs twice, cross, stick a pin at **1,** one passée— twist the 5th and 6th pairs twice, cross, stick a pin at **2,** one passée—twist the 4th and 5th pairs twice, cross, stick a pin at **3,** one passée—twist the 3rd pair once, twist the 4th pair twice, cross, stick a pin at **4,** one passée—twist the 2nd and 3rd pairs once, cross, one passée—twist the 1st pair twice, twist the 2nd pair once, cross, one passée, stick a pin at **5,** two passées—twist the 2nd and 3rd pairs once, cross, one passée—twist the 7th and 8th pairs twice, cross, stick a pin at **6,** one passée—twist the 8th and 9th pairs twice, cross, stick a pin at **7,** one passée—twist the 6th and 7th pairs once, cross, make the leaf stitch square as follows: * twist the 6th pair twice, do not twist the 7th pair, cross, do not twist the 6th pair, twist the 7th pair twice, cross, repeat from *eight times (draw all the passées equally tight, to give the square a good shape); stick a pin at **8**—twist the 5th pair twice, twist the 6th pair once, cross, stick a pin at **9,** one passée—twist the 4th and 5th pairs twice, cross, stick a pin at **10,** one passée—twist the 3rd pair once, twist the 4th pair twice, cross, stick a pin at **11,** one passée—twist the 2nd and 3rd pairs once, cross, one passée—twist the 1st pair twice, twist the 2nd pair once, cross, one passée, stick a pin at **12,** two passées—twist the 2nd and 3rd pairs once, cross, one pasée—twist the 7th pair once, twist the 8th pair twice, cross, stick a pin at **13**, one passée—twist the 6th and 7th pairs twice, cross, stick a pin at **14**, one passée—twist the 5th and 6th pairs twice, cross, stick a pin at **15**, one passée—twist the 4th and 5th pairs twice, cross, stick

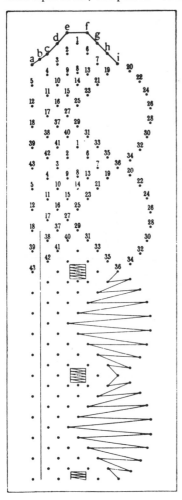

a pin at **16**, one passée—twist the 3rd pair once, twist the 4th pair twice, cross, stick a pin at **17**, one passée— twist the 2nd and 3rd pairs once, cross, one passée—twist the 1st pair twice, twist the 2nd pair once, cross, one passée, stick a pin at **18**, two passées—twist the 2nd and 3rd pairs once, cross, one passée—twist the 11th and 12th pairs once, cross— twist the 10th and 11th pairs once, cross—twist the 9th pair twice, twist the 10th pair once, cross, stick a pin at **19**, twist the 9th pair twice, twist the 10th pair once, cross—twist the 10th and 11th pairs once, cross— twist the 11th and 12th pairs once, cross, stick a pin at **20**, twist the 11th pair once, twist the 12th pair twice, cross—twist the 10th and 11th pairs once, cross—twist the 9th and 10th pairs once, cross— twist the 8th pair twice, twist the 9th pair once, cross, stick a pin at **21**, twist the 8th pair twice, twist the 9th pair once, cross— twist the 9th and 10th pairs once, cross—twist the 10th and 11th pairs once, cross—twist the 11th and 12th pairs once, cross, stick a pin at **22**, twist the 11th pair once, twist the 12th pair twice, cross—twist the 10th and 11th pairs once, cross— twist the 9th and 10th pairs once, cross—twist the 8th and 9th pairs once, cross—twist the 7th pair twice, twist the 8th pair once, cross, stick a pin at **23**, twist the 7th pair twice,

Fig. 1075. Pattern for the Torchon lace edging in fig. 1074.

twist the 8th pair once, cross—twist the 8th and 9th pairs once, cross— twist the 9th and 10th pairs once, cross— twist the 10th and 11th pairs once, cross—twist the 11th and 12th pairs once, cross, stick a pin at **24**, twist the 11th pair once, twist the 12th pair twice, cross—twist the 10th and 11th pairs once, cross—twist the 9th and 10th pairs once, cross—twist the 8th and 9th pairs once, cross—twist the 7th and 8th pairs once,cross—twist the 6th pair twice, twist the 7th pair once, cross, stick a pin at 25, twist the 6th pair twice, twist the 7th pair once, cross—twist the 7th and 8th pairs once, cross—twist the 8th and 9th pairs once, cross—twist the 9th and 10th pairs once, cross—twist the 10th and 11th pairs once, cross—twist the 11th and 12th pairs once, cross, stick a pin at 26, twist the 11th pair once, twist the 12th pair twice, cross—twist the 10th and 11th pairs once, cross—twist the 9th and 10th pairs once, cross—twist the 8th and 9th pairs once, cross—twist the 7th and 8th pairs once, cross—twist the 6th and 7th pairs once, cross—twist the 5th pair twice, twist the 6th pair once, cross, stick a pin at 27, two passées—do not twist the 6th pair, twist the 7th pair once,cross, one passée—do not twist the 7th pair, twist the 8th pair once, cross, one passée—do not twist the 8th pair, twist the 9th pair once, cross, one passée—do not twist the 9th pair, twist the 10th pair once, cross, one passée—do not twist the 10th pair, twist the 11th pair once, cross, one passée—do not twist the 11th pair, twist the 12th pair once, cross, one passée, stick a pin at 28, do not twist the 11th pair, twist the 12th pair twice, cross, one passée—cross the 10th and 11th pairs, one passée—cross the 9th and 10th pairs, one passée—cross the 8th and 9th pairs, one passée—cross the 7th and 8th pairs, one passée—cross the 6th and 7th pairs, one passée, stick a pin at 29, twist the 6th pair once, do not twist the 7th pair, cross, one passée—cross the 7th and 8th pairs, one passée—cross the 8th and 9th pairs, one passée—cross the 9th and 10th pairs, one passée—cross the 10th and 11th pairs, one passée—cross the 11th and 12th pairs, one passée, stick a pin at 30, do not twist the 11th pair, twist the 12th pair twice, cross, one passée—cross the 10th and 11th pairs, one passée—cross the 9th and 10th pairs, one passée—cross the 8th and 9th pairs, one passée—cross the 7th and 8th pairs, one passée, stick a pin at 31, twist the 7th pair once, do not twist the 8th pair, cross, one passée—cross the 8th and 9th pairs, one passée—cross the 9th and 10th pairs, one passée—cross the 10th and 11th pairs, one passée—cross the 11th and 12th pairs, one passée, stick a pin at 32, do not twist the 11th pair, twist the 12th pair twice, cross, one passée—cross the 10th and 11th pairs, one passée—cross the 9th and 10th pairs, one passée—cross the 8th and 9th pairs, one passée, stick a pin at 33, twist the 8th pair once, do not twist the 9th pair, cross, one passée—cross the 9th and 10th pairs, one passée—cross the 10th and 11th pairs, one passée—cross the 11th and 12th pairs, one passée, stick a pin at 34, do not twist the 11th pair, twist the 12th pair twice, cross, one passée—cross the 10th and 11th pairs, one passée—cross the 9th and 10th pairs, one passée, stick a pin at 35, twist the 9th pair once, do not twist the 10th pair, cross, one passée—cross the 10th and 11th pairs, one passée—cross the 11th and 12th pairs, one passée, stick a pin at 36—twist the 4th and 5th pairs twice, cross, stick a pin at 37, one passée— twist the 3rd pair once, twist the 4th pair twice, stick a pin at **38,** one passée—twist the 2nd and 3rd pairs once, cross, one passée, twist the 1st pair twice, twist the 2nd pair once, cross, one passée, stick a pin at **39,** two passées—twist the 2nd and 3rd pairs once, cross, one passée—twist the 5th and 6th pairs twice, cross, stick a pin at **40,** one passée—twist the 4th and 5th pairs twice, cross, stick a pin at **41,** one passée—twist the 3rd pair once, twist the 4th pair twice, cross, stick a pin at **42,** one passée—twist the 2nd and 3rd pairs once, cross, one passée—twist the 1st pair twice, twist the 2nd pair once, cross, one passée, stick a pin at **43,** two passées—twist the 2nd and 3rd pairs once, cross, one passée.

Repeat from the beginning.

Braided Lace (figs. 1076 and 1077). Four pairs of bobbins are hung on at each of the points *a* and *b,* and two pairs of bobbins at the point *c,* on the pattern in fig. 1077.

Fig. 1076. Braided lace.

Cross the 1st, 2nd, 3rd, and 4th pairs (see fig. 1069), stick a pin at 1—with the 1st and 2nd pairs four passées, stick a pin at 2, four passées— with the 3rd and 4th pairs four passées—cross the 5th, 6th, 7th, and 8th pairs, stick a pin at 3—with the 5th and 6th pairs four passées—cross the 3rd, 4th, 5th, and 6th pairs, stick a pin at 4—with the 3rd and 4th pairs four passées—cross the 1st, 2nd, 3rd, and 4th pairs, stick a pin at 5 —with the 1st and 2nd pairs five passées—with the 3rd and 4th pairs four passées—with the 5th and 6th pairs four passées, with the 7th and 8th pairs four passées—cross the 7th, 8th, 9th, and 10th pairs, stick a pin at 6—with the 7th and 8th pairs four passées—cross the 5th, 6th, 7th, and 8th pairs, stick a pin at 7—with the 7th and 8th pairs four passées—with the 9th and 10th pairs five passées—cross the 7th, 8th, 9th, and 10th pairs, stick a pin at 8—with the 5th and 6th pairs four passées—cross the 3rd, 4th, 5th, and 6th pairs, stick a pin at 9—with the 3rd and 4th pairs four passées—cross the 1st, 2nd, 3rd, and 4th pairs, stick a pin at 10—with the 1st and 2nd pairs four passées, stick a pin at 11, four passées—with the 3rd and 4th pairs five passées—cross the 1st, 2nd, 3rd, and 4th pairs, stick a pin at **12**—with the 1st and 2nd pairs five passées—with the 3rd and 4th pairs five passées—with the 5th and 6th pairs four passées—with the 7th and 8th pairs four passées—cross the 5th, 6th, 7th, and 8th pairs, stick a pin at **13**—with the 5th and 6th pairs five passées—cross the 3rd, 4th, 5th, and 6th pairs, stick a pin at **14**—with the 5th and 6th pairs five passées—with the 7th and 8th pairs seven passées— cross the 5th, 6th, 7th, and 8th pairs, stick a pin at **15**—with the 7th and 8th pairs four passées— with the 9th and 10th pairs five passées—cross the 7th, 8th, 9th, and 10th pairs, stick a pin at **16**—with the 9th and 10th pairs four passées, one picot to the right at **17**, four passées, one picot to the right at **18**, four passées, one picot to the right at **19**, four passées—with the 7th and 8th pairs three passées— cross the 7th, 8th, 9th, and 10th pairs, stick a pin at **20**—with the 7th and 8th pairs, four passées— with the 5th and 6th pairs two passées—cross the 5th, 6th, 7th, and 8th pairs, stick a pin at **21**—with the 7th and 8th pairs four passées—with the 9th and 10th pairs two passées—cross the 7th, 8th, 9th, and 10th pairs, stick a pin at **22**—with the 9th and 10th pairs four passées, one

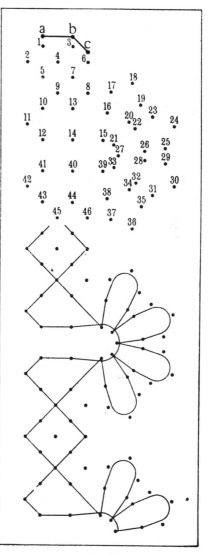

Fig. 1077.
Pattern for the braided lace in fig. 1076.

picot to the right at **23**, four passées, one picot to the right at **24**, four passées, one picot to the right at **25**, four passées—with the 7th and 8th pairs three passées—cross the 7th, 8th, 9th, and 10th pairs, stick a pin at **26**—with the 7th and 8th pairs four passées—with the 5th and 6th pairs

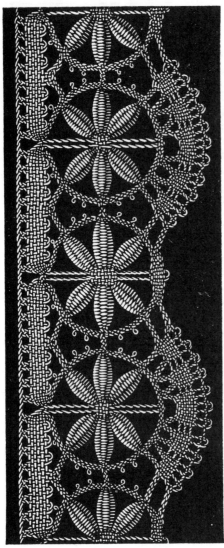

Fig. 1078.
Lace edging with leaves in leaf stitch.

two passées—cross the 5th, 6th, 7th, and 8th pairs, stick a pin at **27**—with the 7th and 8th pairs four passées—with the 9th and 10th pairs two passées—cross the 7th, 8th, 9th, and 10th pairs, stick a pin at **28**—with the 9th and 10th pairs four passées, one picot to the right at **29**, four passées, one picot to the right at **30**, four passées, one picot to the right at **31**, four passées—with the 7th and 8th pairs three passées—cross the 7th, 8th, 9th, and 10th pairs, stick a pin at **32**—with the 7th and 8th pairs four passées— with the 6th and 7th pairs two passées—cross the 5th, 6th, 7th, and 8th pairs, stick a pin at **33**—with the 7th and 8th pairs four passées—with the 9th and 10th pairs two passées—cross the 7th, 8th, 9th, and 10th pairs, stick a pin at **34**—with the 9th and 10th pairs four passées, one picot to the right at **35**, four passées, one picot to the right at **36**, four passées, one picot to the right at **37**, four passées—with the 7th and 8th pairs three passées— cross the 7th, 8th, 9th, and 10th pairs, stick a pin at **38**—with the 7th and 8th pairs four passées—with the 5th and 6th pairs two passées—cross the 5th, 6th, 7th, and 8th pairs, stick a pin at **39**—with the 5th and 6th pairs five passées—with the 3rd and 4th pairs five passées—cross the 3rd, 4th, 5th, and 6th pairs, stick a pin at **40**—with the 3rd and 4th pairs five passées— cross the 1st, 2nd, 3rd, and 4th pairs, stick a pin at **41**—with the 1st and

2nd pairs four passées, stick a pin at **42**, four passées—with the 3rd and 4th pairs five passées—cross the 1st, 2nd, 3rd, and 4th pairs, stick a pin at **43**—with the 1st and 2nd pairs five passées—with the 3rd and 4th pairs four passées—with the 5th and 6th pairs five passées—with the 7th and 8th pairs seven passées—cross the 5th, 6th, 7th, and 8th pairs, stick a pin at **44**—with the 5th and 6th pairs four passées—cross the 3rd, 4th, 5th, and 6th pairs, stick a pin at **45**—with the 3rd and 4th pairs four passées—with the 5th and 6th pairs four passées—with the 7th and 8th pairs four passées—with the 9th and 10th pairs five passées—cross the 7th, 8th, 9th, and 10th pairs, stick a pin at **46**—with the 7th and 8th pairs four passées— with the 9th and 10th pairs five passées.

Repeat from the beginning.

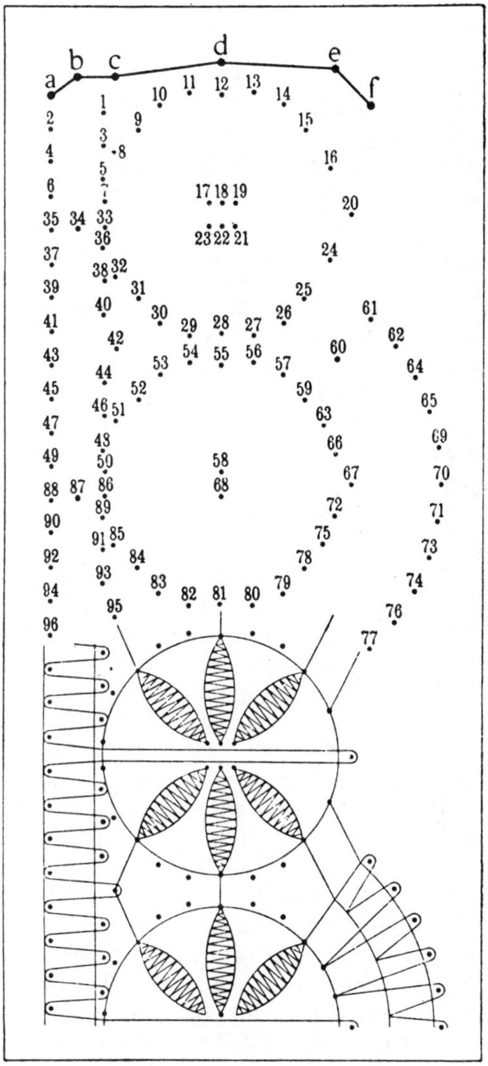

Lace Edging With Leaves in Leaf Stitch

Fig. 1079. Pattern for the lace edging with leaves in leaf stitch in fig. 1078.

(figs. 1078 and 1079). Two pairs of bobbins are hung on at each of the points *a, c, d, e, f,* and three pairs of bobbins at the point *b,* on the pattern in fig. 1079.

Twist the 2nd pair once, do not twist the 3rd pair, cross, one passée—cross the 3rd and 4th pairs, one passée—cross the 4th and 5th pairs, one passée, stick a pin at 1, do not twist the 4th pair, twist the 5th pair once, cross, one passée—cross the 3rd and 4th pairs, one passée—cross the 2nd and 3rd pairs, one passée—twist the 1st pair twice, twist the 2nd pair once, cross, one passée, stick a pin at 2 on the right of the two pairs—twist the 2nd pair once, do not twist the 3rd pair, cross, one passée—cross the 3rd and 4th pairs, one passée—cross the 4th and 5th pairs, one passée, stick a pin at 3, do not twist the 4th pair, twist the 5th pair once, cross, one passée—cross the 3rd and 4th pairs, one passée—cross the 2nd and 3rd pairs, one passée—twist the 1st pair twice, twist the 2nd pair once, cross, one passée, stick a pin at 4 on the right of the two pairs—twist the 2nd pair once, do not twist the 3rd pair, cross, one passée—cross the 3rd and 4th pairs, one passée—cross the 4th and 5th pairs, one passée, stick a pin at 5, do not twist the 4th pair, twist the 5th pair once, cross, one passée—cross the 3rd and 4th pairs, one passée—cross the 2nd and 3rd pairs, one passée—twist the 1st pair twice, twist the 2nd pair once, cross, one passée, stick a pin at 6 on the right of the two pairs—twist the 2nd pair once, do not twist the 3rd pair, cross, one passée—cross the 3rd and 4th pairs, one passée—cross the 4th and 5th pairs, one passée—cross the 2nd and 3rd pairs, one passée—cross the 3rd and 4th pairs, one passée—cross the 4th and 5th pairs, one passée, stick a pin at 7, five passées, one picot to the right at 8, three passées—cross the 6th and 7th pairs, four passées—cross the 4th, 5th, 6th, and 7th pairs at 9 (see fig. 1069)—twist the 6th and 7th pairs once, cross, two passées, one picot to the right at 10, three passées, one picot to the right at 11, three passées—twist the 8th and 9th pairs once, cross, two passées—cross the 6th, 7th, 8th, and 9th pairs at 12—twist the 8th and 9th pairs once, cross, two passées, one picot to the right at 13, three passées, one picot to the right at 14, three passées—twist the 10th and 11th pairs once, cross, three passées—cross the 8th, 9th, 10th, and 11th pairs at 15—twist the 10th and 11th pairs once, cross, three passées—twist the 12th and 13th pairs once, cross, three passées—cross the 10th, 11th, 12th, and 13th pairs at 16—cross the 12th and 13th pairs, one passée—cross the 11th and 12th pairs, one passée—cross the 10th and 11th pairs, one passée—cross the 11th and 12th pairs, one passée—cross the 12th and 13th pairs, one passée—cross the 11th and 12th pairs, one passée—cross the 10th and 11th pairs, one passée—twist the 4th and 5th pairs once, cross, make the leaf as follows: * twist the 4th pair twice, do not twist the 5th pair, cross, do not twist the 4th pair, twist the 5th pair twice, cross, repeat from * fifteen times (draw the first and last passées very tight, to give the leaf a good shape)—twist the 6th and 7th pairs once, cross, work another leaf—twist the 8th and 9th pairs once, cross, work another leaf—twist the 3rd pair six times, cross the 3rd, 4th, and 5th pairs at 17 (see fig. 1068)—cross the 7th, 8th, and 9th pairs at 19—twist the 9th pair six times, do not twist the 10th pair, cross, one passée—cross the 10th and 11th pairs, one passée—cross the 11th and 12th pairs, one passée—cross the 12th and 13th pairs, one passée, stick a pin at **20**, do not twist the 12th pair, twist the 13th pair twice, cross, one passée—cross the 11th and 12th pairs, one passée—cross the 10th and 11th pairs, one passée—cross the 9th and 10th pairs, one passée—twist the 9th pair six times, cross the 7th, 8th, and 9th pairs at **21**—cross the 5th, 6th, and 7th pairs at **22**—cross the 3rd, 4th, and 5th pairs at **23**—twist the 4th and 5th pairs once, cross, work a leaf—twist the 6th and 7th pairs once, cross, work a leaf—twist the 8th and 9th pairs once, cross, work a leaf—cross the 10th and 11th pairs, one passée—cross the 11th and 12th pairs, one passée— cross the 12th and 13th pairs, one passée—cross the 11th and 12th pairs, one passée—cross the 10th and 11th pairs, one passée—cross the 11th and 12th pairs, one passée—cross the 12th and 13th pairs, one passée, stick a pin at **24**, four passées—twist the 10th and 11th pairs once, cross, three passées—cross the 8th, 9th, 10th, and 11th pairs at **25**—twist the 10th and 11th pairs once, cross, three passées—twist the 8th and 9th pairs once, cross, two passées, one picot to the right at **26**, three passées, one picot to the right at **27**, three passées—cross the 6th, 7th, 8th, and 9th pairs at **28**—twist the 8th and 9th pairs once, cross, two passées—twist the 6th and 7th pairs once, cross, two passées, one picot to the right at **29**, three passées, one picot to the right at **30**, three passées—cross the 4th, 5th, 6th, and 7th pairs at **31**—twist the 4th and 5th pairs once, cross, two passées, one picot to the right at **32**, four passées, stick a pin at **33**, one passée— twist the 3rd pair six times, do not twist the 4th pair, cross, one passée— cross the 2nd and 3rd pairs, one passée, stick a pin at **34**—cross the 4th and 5th pairs, one passée—cross the 3rd and 4th pairs, one passée—cross the 2nd and 3rd pairs, one passée— twist the 1st pair twice, twist the 2nd pair once, cross, one passée, stick a pin at **35** on the right of the two pairs— continue the left-hand edge to **41**—twist the 2nd pair once, do not twist the 3rd pair, cross, one passée— cross the 3rd and 4th pairs, one passée—cross the 4th and 5th pairs, one passée—twist the 6th and 7th pairs once, cross, three passées—cross the 5th and 6th pairs, one passée—cross the 6th and 7th pairs, one passée, stick a pin at **42** on the left of the two pairs—cross the 5th and 6th pairs, one passée—cross the 4th and 5th pairs, one passée— cross the 3rd and 4th pairs, one passée—cross the 2nd and 3rd pairs, one passée—twist the 1st pair twice, twist the 2nd pair once, cross, one passée, stick a pin at **43** on the right of the two pairs—continue the left-hand edge over points **44** to **49**—twist the 2nd pair once, do not twist the 3rd pair, cross, one passée— cross the 3rd and 4th pairs, one passée—cross the 4th and 5th pairs, one passée—cross the 2nd and 3rd pairs, one passée—cross the 3rd and 4th pairs, one passée—cross the 4th and 5th pairs, one passée, stick a pin at **50**, five passées, one picot to the right at **51**, three passées—cross the 6th and 7th pairs, four passées—cross the 4th, 5th, 6th, and 7th pairs at **52**—twist the 6th and 7th pairs once, cross, two passées, one picot to the right at **53**, three passées, one picot to the right at **54**, three passées—cross the 6th,

7th, 8th, and 9th pairs at 55—twist the 8th and 9th pairs once, cross, two passées, one picot to the right at 56, three passées, one picot to the right at 57, three passées—twist the 4th and 5th pairs once, cross, work a leaf—twist the 6th and 7th pairs once, cross, work a leaf—cross the 4th, 5th, 6th, and 7th pairs at 58—twist the 6th and 7th pairs once, cross, work a leaf—cross the 6th, 7th, 8th, and 9th pairs at 59—twist the 8th and 9th pairs once, cross, three passées—cross the 8th, 9th, 10th, and 11th pairs at 60—cross the 9th and 10th pairs, one passée— cross the 10th and 11th pairs, one passée—do not twist the 11th pair, twist the 12th pair once, cross, one passée—twist the 12th pair twice, twist the 13th pair once, cross, one passée, stick a pin at 61, twist the 12th pair once, twist the 13th pair twice, cross, one passée—do not twist the 11th pair, twist the 12th pair twice, cross, one passée—cross the 10th and 11th pairs, one passée—cross the 9th and 10th pairs, one passée—cross the 8th and 9th pairs, one passée—cross the 9th and 10th pairs, one passée—cross the 10th and 11th pairs, one passée—cross the 11th and 12th pairs, one passée—twist the 12th and 13th pairs twice, cross, one passée, stick a pin at 62, twist the 12th pair once, twist the 13th pair twice, cross, one passée— do not twist the 11th pair, twist the 12th pair twice, cross, one passée— cross the 10th and 11th pairs, one passée—cross the 9th and 10th pairs, one passée—cross the 8th and 9th pairs,four passées—twist the 6th and 7th pairs, one, cross, two passées—cross the 6th, 7th, 8th, and 9th pairs at 63—twist the 6th and 7th pairs once, cross, two passées—cross the 8th and 9th pairs, four passées—do not twist the 9th pair, twist the 10th pair twice, cross, one passée—do not twist the 10th pair, twist the 11th pair twice, cross, one passée—do not twist the 11th pair, twist the 12th pair twice, cross, one passée—twist the 12th and 13th pairs twice, cross, one passée, stick a pin at 64, twist the 12th pair once, twist the 13th pair twice, cross, one passée— do not twist the 11th pair, twist the 12th pair twice, cross, one passée— cross the 10th and 11th pairs, one passée—cross the 9th and 10th pairs, one passée—cross the 8th and 9th pairs, one passée—cross the 9th and 10th pairs, one passée—cross the 10th and 11th pairs, one passée— cross the 11th and 12th pairs, one passée—twist the 12th and 13th pairs twice, cross, one passée, stick a pin at 65, twist the 12th pair once, twist the 13th pair twice, cross, one passée—do not twist the 11th pair, twist the 12th pair twice, cross, one passée—cross the 10th and 11th pairs, one passée—cross the 9th and 10th pairs, one passée—cross the 8th and 9th pairs, four passées—cross the 6th, 7th, 8th, and 9th pairs at 66—twist the 6th and 7th pairs once, cross, one passée—twist the 8th and 9th pairs once, cross, three passées—twist the 3rd pair six times, cross the 3rd, 4th, and 5th pairs— twist the 5th pair six times, do not twist the 6th pair, cross, one passée— cross the 6th and 7th pairs, one passée, stick a pin at 67, two passées—cross the 5th and 6th pairs, one passée—twist the 5th pair six times, cross the 3rd, 4th, and 5th pairs at 68—do not twist the 9th pair, twist the 10th pair twice, cross, one passée—do not twist the 10th pair, twist the 11th pair twice, cross, one passée—do not twist the 11th pair, twist the 12th pair twice, cross, one passée—twist the 12th and 13th pairs twice, cross, one passée, stick a pin at 69, twist the 12th pair once, twist the 13th pair twice, cross, one passée— do not twist the 11th pair, twist the 12th pair twice, cross, one passée— cross the 10th and 11th pairs, one passée—cross the 9th and 10th pairs, one passée—cross the 8th and 9th pairs, one passée—cross the 9th and 10th pairs, one passée—cross the 10th and 11th pairs, one passée—cross the 11th and 12th pairs, one passée—twist the 12th and 13th pairs twice, cross, one passée, stick a pin at 70, twist the 12th pair once, twist the 13th pair twice, cross, one passée—do not twist the 11th pair, twist the 12th pair twice, cross, one passée—cross the 10th and 11th pairs, one passée—cross the 9th and 10th pairs, one passée—cross the 8th and 9th pairs, one passée—cross the 9th and 10th pairs, one passée—cross the 10th and 11th pairs, one passée—cross the 11th and 12th pairs, one passée—twist the 12th and 13th pairs twice, cross, one passée, stick a pin at 71, twist the 12th pair once, twist the 13th pair twice, cross, one passée— do not twist the 11th pair, twist the 12th pair twice, cross, one passée— cross the 10th and 11th pairs, one passée—cross the 9th and 10th pairs, one passée—cross the 8th and 9th pairs, four passées—twist the 6th and 7th pairs once, cross, one passée—cross the 6th, 7th, 8th, and 9th pairs at 72—beginning with the 8th and 9th pairs, work two more little points at the right-hand edge over points 73 to 78—cross the 6th, 7th, 8th, and 9th pairs at 78—twist the 6th and 7th pairs once, cross, work a leaf—cross the 4th, 5th, 6th, and 7th pairs, remove the pin from 68 and reset it below the crossed threads— twist the 8th and 9th pairs once, two passées, one picot to the right at 79, three passées, one picot to the right at 80, three passées— twist the 6th and 7th pairs once, cross, work a leaf—cross the 6th, 7th, 8th, and 9th pairs at 81—twist the 6th and 7th pairs once, cross, two passées, one picot to the right at 82, three passées, one picot to the right at 83, three passées—twist the 4th and 5th pairs once, cross, work a leaf—cross the 4th, 5th, 6th, and 7th pairs at 84—twist the 4th and 5th pairs once, cross, two passées, one picot to the right at 85, four passées, stick a pin at 86, one passée—twist the 3rd pair six times, do not twist the 4th pair, cross, one passée—cross the 2nd and 3rd pairs, one passée, stick a pin at 87—cross the 4th and 5th pairs, one passée—cross the 3rd and 4th pairs, one passée— cross the 2nd and 3rd pairs, one passée—twist the 1st pair twice, twist the 2nd pair once, cross, one passée, stick a pin at 88 on the right of the two pairs—continue the left-hand edge over points 89 to 94—twist the 2nd pair once, do not twist the 3rd pair, cross, one passée—cross the 3rd and 4th pairs, one passée—cross the 4th and 5th pairs, one passée—twist the 6th and 7th pairs once, cross, three passées—cross the 6th and 7th pairs, one passée, stick a pin at 95 on the left of the two pairs—cross the 5th and 6th pairs, one passée—cross the 4th and 5th pairs, one passée—cross the 3rd and 4th pairs, one passée—cross the 2nd and 3rd pai the 1st pair twice, twist the 2nd pair once, cross, one passée, stick a pin at 96 on the right of the two pairs.

Repeat from the beginning.

Gold Braid With Motifs in Leaf Stitch and Outlining or Gimp (figs. 1080 and 1081). One pair of bobbins is hung on at each of the points *a* and *g,* two pairs of bobbins at each of the points *b, c, e, f,* and four outlining threads or gimps at point *d* on the pattern in fig. 1081.

Twist the 3rd pair once, twist the 4th pair twice, cross, one passée, stick a pin at **1,** two passées—twist the 2nd and 3rd pairs once, cross, stick a pin

Fig. 1080. Gold braid with motifs in leaf stitch and outlining or gimp.

at **2,** one passée—twist the 1st and 2nd pairs once, cross, one passée, stick a pin at **3,** two passées—twist the 2nd and 3rd pairs once, cross, stick a pin at **4,** one passée—slip gimps I and II through the 5th, 4th and 3rd pairs twisted once—twist the 7th pair twice, twist the 8th pair once, cross, one passée, stick a pin at **5,** two passées—twist the 8th and 9th pairs once, cross, stick a pin at **6,** one passée—twist the 9th and 10th pairs once, cross, one passée, stick a pin at **7,** two passées—twist the 8th and 9th pairs once, cross, stick a pin at **8,** one passée—slip gimps IV and III through the 6th, 7th, and

8th pairs twisted once—twist the 5th and 6th pairs once, cross, one passée, stick a pin at **9**, one passée—twist the 4th pair once, twist the 5th pair twice, cross, one passée, stick a pin at **10**, one passée—twist the 6th pair

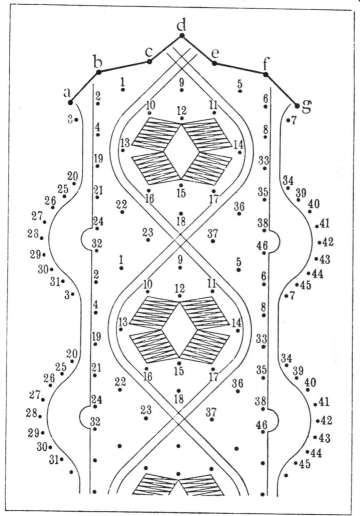

Fig. 1081. Pattern for the gold braid with motifs in leaf stitch and outlining or gimp, fig. 1080.

twice, twist the 7th pair once, cross, one passée, stick a pin at **11**, on passée—twist the 5th and 6th pairs twice, cross, one passée, stick a pin at **12**, one passée—eight leaf stitches (see fig. 1059) with the 4th and 5th pairs—twist the 3rd and 4th pairs once, cross, one passée, stick a pin at **13**, two passées—twist the 4th pair once, twist the 5th pair twice, cross, eight leaf stitches—eight leaf stitches with the 6th and 7th pairs—twist the 7th and 8th pairs once, cross, one passée, stick a pin at **14**, two passées—twist the 6th pair twice, twist the 7th pair once, eight leaf stitches—twist the 5th and 6th pairs once, cross, one passée, stick a pin at **15**, one passée—twist the 4th pair once, twist the 5th pair twice, cross, stick a pin at **16**, two passées—twist the 6th pair twice, twist the 7th pair once, cross, stick a pin at **17**, two passées—twist the 5th and 6th pairs twice, cross, stick a pin at **18**, two passées—slip gimps II and I through the 3rd, 4th, and 5th pairs

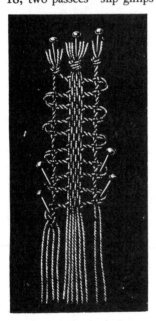

Fig. 1082. Straight braid in linen or whole stitch.

twisted once—twist the 2nd and 3rd pairs once, cross, stick a pin at **19**, one passée—twist the 1st pair twice, twist the 2nd pair once, cross, one passée, stick a pin at **20**, two passées—twist the 2nd and 3rd pairs once, cross, stick a pin at **21**, one passée—twist the 3rd pair twice, twist the 4th pair once, cross, one passée, stick a pin at **22**, two passées—twist the 4th pair twice, twist the 5th pair once, cross, one passée, stick a pin at **23**, two passées— twist the 2nd and 3rd pairs once, cross, stick a pin at **24**, one passée—twist the 1st and 2nd pairs once, cross, stick a pin at **25**, twist the 1st pair twice, do not twist the 2nd pair, cross, twist the 1st pair once, twist the 2nd pair twice, cross, stick a pin at **26**, twist the 1st pair twice, do not twist the 2nd pair, cross, twist the 1st pair once, twist the 2nd pair twice, cross, stick a pin at **27**, twist the 1st pair twice, do not twist the 2nd pair, cross, twist the 1st pair once, twist the 2nd pair twice, cross, stick a pin at **28**, twist the 1st pair twice, do not twist the 2nd pair, cross, twist the 1st pair once, twist the 2nd

pair twice, cross, stick a pin at **29**, twist the 1st pair twice, do not twist the 2nd pair, cross, twist the 1st pair once, twist the 2nd pair twice, cross, stick a pin at **30**, twist the 1st pair twice, do not twist the 2nd pair, cross, twist the 1st pair once, twist the 2nd pair twice, cross, stick a pin at **31**, twist the 1st pair twice, do not twist the 2nd pair, cross—twist the 2nd and 3rd pairs once, cross, stick a pin at **32**, one passée—slip gimps III and IV through the 8th, 7th, and 6th pairs twisted once—twist the 8th and 9th pairs once, cross, stick a pin at **33**, one passée—twist the 9th pair once, twist the 10th pair twice, cross, one passée, stick a pin at **34**, two passées—twist the 8th and 9th pairs once, cross, stick a pin at **35**, one passée—twist the 7th pair once—twist the 8th pair twice, cross, one passée, stick a pin at 36, two passées—twist the 6th pair once, twist the 7th pair twice, cross, one passée, stick a pin at 37, two passées—twist the 8th and 9th pairs once, cross, stick a pin at 38, one passée—twist the 9th and 10th pairs once, cross, stick a pin at 39, do not twist the 9th pair, twist the 10th pair twice, cross, twist the 9th pair twice, twist the 10th pair once, cross, stick a pin at 40, do not twist the 9th pair, twist the 10th pair twice, cross, twist the 9th pair twice, twist the 10th pair once, cross, stick a pin at 41, do not twist the 9th pair, twist the 10th pair twice, cross, twist the 9th pair twice, twist the 10th pair once, cross, stick a pin at 42, do not twist the 9th pair, twist the 10th pair twice, cross, twist the 9th pair twice, twist the 10th pair once, cross, stick a pin at 43, do not twist the 9th pair, twist the 10th pair twice, cross, twist the 9th pair twice, twist the 10th pair once, cross, stick a pin at 44, do not twist the 9th pair, twist the 10th pair twice, cross, twist the 9th pair twice, twist the 10th pair once, cross, stick a pin at 45, do not twist the 9th pair, twist the 10th pair twice, cross—twist the 8th and 9th pairs once, cross, stick a pin at 46, one passée—cross gimps I and II with gimps III and IV, and repeat from the beginning.

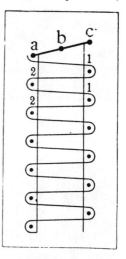

Fig. 1083. Pattern for the straight braids in figs. 1082 and 1086.

Pillow Laces With Braid Designs. As the name suggests these laces consist of braids made after the manner of pillow lace with bobbins and arranged in straight or curved lines. The braids are made with only a few bobbins in plain linen or whole stitch with openwork or ornamental stitches. We give next, accompanied by all the necessary instructions, one lace made of plain linen stitch braid and one made of braid worked in plain and fancy linen stitch (sometimes known as chain linen stitch).

Before any lace of this type is made, it is absolutely essential to know how to work straight and curved braids. We therefore advise our readers, in order to attain ease and proficiency, to work first the introductory examples given here.

Straight braid in linen or whole stitch (figs. 1082 and 1083). Two pairs of bobbins are hung on at point *a,* three pairs of bobbins at point *b,* and one pair of bobbins at point *c,* on the pattern in fig. 1083.

* Twist the 2nd pair twice, do not twist the 3rd pair, cross, one passée—cross the 3rd and 4th pairs, one passée—cross the 4th and 5th pairs, one passée—twist the 5th and 6th pairs twice, cross, one passée, stick a pin at 1, twist the 5th pair once, twist the 6th pair twice, cross, one passée—do not twist the 4th pair, twist the 5th pair twice, cross, one passée—cross the 3rd

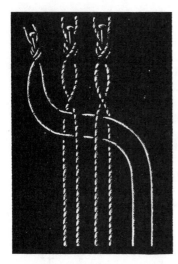

Fig. 1084.
How to slip a pair of bobbins from left
to right through four coarse threads.

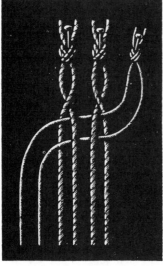

Fig. 1085.
How to slip a pair of bobbins from
right to left through four coarse threads.

and 4th pairs, one passée—cross the 2nd and 3rd pairs, one passée—twist the 1st and 2nd pairs twice, cross, one passée, stick a pin at 2, twist the 1st pair twice, twist the 2nd pair once, cross, one passée; repeat from *.

Fancy linen stitch (chain linen stitch) (figs. 1084 and 1085). For this stitch, two pairs of bobbins

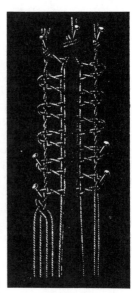

Fig. 1086. Straight braid
in plain and fancy linen stitch
(chain linen stitch).

wound with coarse thread are used. The first pair is twisted once from right to left, the second from left to right. When working from left to the right, the left-hand pair of bobbins is slipped over the first and fourth coarse threads and under the second and third coarse threads (see fig. 1084); when working from right to left, the right-hand pair is similarly slipped over the fourth and first coarse threads and under the third and second coarse threads, as shown in fig. 1085.

Straight braid in plain and fancy linen stitch (chain linen stitch) (figs. 1086 and 1083). Two pairs of bobbins wound with fine thread are hung on at point *a*, two pairs of bobbins wound with fine thread and two pairs wound with coarse thread at *b* (the two pairs of bobbins wound with coarse thread must be in the middle, between the two pairs wound with fine thread), and one pair of bobbins wound with fine thread at *c*, on the pattern in fig. 1083.

* Twist the 2nd pair once, do not twist the 3rd pair, cross, one passée— twist the 1st and 2nd coarse threads once from right to left and slip the 3rd pair through—twist the 3rd and 4th coarse threads once from left to right and slip the 3rd pair through (see fig. 1084)—cross the 3rd and 4th pairs, one passée—twist the 4th pair once, twist the 5th pair twice, cross, one passée, stick a pin at 1, two passées—do not twist the 3rd pair, twist the 4th pair once, cross, one passée—twist the 3rd and 4th coarse threads once from left to right and slip the 3rd pair through—twist the 1st and 2nd coarse threads once from right to left and slip the 3rd pair through (see fig. 1085)—cross the 2nd and 3rd pairs, one passée—twist the 1st pair twice, twist the 2nd pair once, cross, one passée, stick a pin at 2, two passées; repeat from *.

Curved braid in linen or whole stitch (figs. 1087 and 1088). One pair of bobbins is hung on at *a*, three pairs of bobbins at *b*, and two pairs of bobbins at *c*, on the pattern in fig. 1088.

Do not twist the 4th pair, twist the 5th pair twice, cross, one passée— cross the 3rd and 4th pairs, one passée—cross the 2nd and 3rd pairs, one passée—twist the 1st and 2nd pairs twice, cross, one passée, stick a pin at 1, twist the 1st pair twice, twist the 2nd pair once, cross, one passée—twist the 2nd pair twice, do not twist the 3rd pair, cross, one passée— cross the 3rd and 4th pairs, one passée— cross the 4th and 5th pairs, one passée— cross the 3rd and 4th pairs, one passée— cross the 2nd and 3rd pairs, one passée—

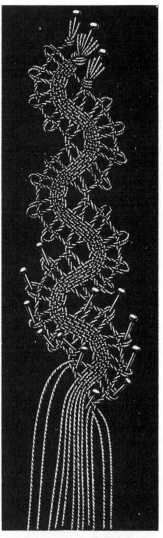

Fig. 1087. Curved braid in linen or whole stitch.

twist the 1st and 2nd pairs twice, cross, one passée, stick a pin at 2, twist the 1st pair twice, twist the 2nd pair once, cross, one passée—twist the 2nd pair twice, do not twist the 3rd pair, cross, one passée—cross the 3rd and 4th pairs, one passée—cross the 4th and 5th pairs, one passée— cross the 3rd and 4th pairs, one passée—cross the 2nd and 3rd pairs, one passee— twist the 1st and 2nd pairs twice, cross, one passée, stick a pin at 3, twist

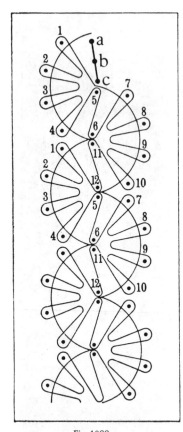

Fig. 1088.
Pattern for the curved braid in fig. 1087.

the 1st pair twice, twist the 2nd pair once, cross, one passée—twist the 2nd pair twice, do not twist the 3rd pair, cross, one passée—cross the 3rd and 4th pairs, one passée—cross the 4th and 5th pairs, one passée— cross the 3rd and 4th pairs, one passée—cross the 2nd and 3rd pairs, one passée— twist the 1st and 2nd pairs twice, cross, one passée, stick a pin at 4, twist the 1st pair twice, twist the 2nd pair once, cross, one passée—twist the 2nd pair twice, do not twist the 3rd pair, cross, one passée—cross the 3rd and 4th pairs, one passée—cross the 4th and 5th pairs, one passée— twist the 5th pair twice, do not twist the 6th pair, cross, one passée, stick a pin at 5 on the

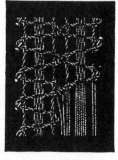

Fig. 1089. Sewing.
How to join braids by
short points.

left of the 5th pair—do not twist the 4th pair, twist the 5th pair twice, cross, one passée—cross the 3rd and 4th pairs, one passée—cross the 2nd and 3rd pairs, one passée—twist the 1st and 2nd pairs twice, cross, one passée, stick a pin at 6 on the right of the 2nd pair—twist the 2nd pair twice, do not twist the 3rd pair, cross, one passée— cross the 3rd and 4th pairs, one passée—cross the 4th and 5th pairs, one passée—twist the 5th and 6th pairs twice, cross, one passée, stick a pin at 7, twist the 5th pair once, twist the 6th pair twice, cross, one passée—do

Fig. 1090. Sewing.
How to join braids by long points.

not twist the 4th pair, twist the 5th pair twice, cross, one passée—cross the 3rd and 4th pairs, one passée—cross the 2nd and 3rd pairs, one passée—

cross the 3rd and 4th pairs, one passée—cross the 4th and 5th pairs, one passée—twist the 5th and 6th pairs twice, cross, one passée, stick a pin at 8, twist the 5th pair once, twist the 6th pair twice, cross, one passée—do not twist the 4th pair, twist the 5th pair twice, cross, one passée—cross the 3rd and 4th pairs, one passée—cross the 2nd and 3rd pairs, one passée—cross the 3rd and 4th pairs, one passée—cross the 4th and 5th pairs, one passée—twist the 5th and 6th pairs twice, cross, one passée, stick a pin at 9, twist the 5th pair once, twist the 6th pair twice, cross, one passée—do not twist the 4th pair, twist the 5th pair twice, cross, one passée—cross the 3rd and 4th pairs, one passée—cross

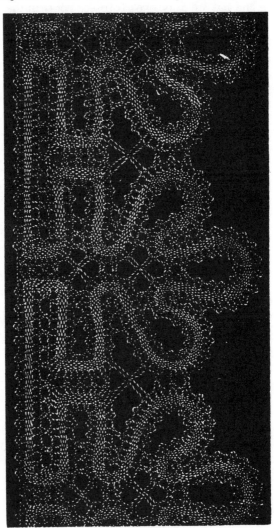

Fig. 1091.
Lace edging with plain linen or whole stitch braid.

the 2nd and 3rd pairs, one passée—cross the 3rd and 4th pairs, one passée—cross the 4th and 5th pairs, one passée—twist the 5th and 6th pairs twice, cross, one passée, stick a pin at 10, twist the 5th pair once, twist the

6th pair twice, cross, one passée—do not twist the 4th pair, twist the 5th pair twice, cross, one passée—cross the 3rd and 4th pairs, one passée—cross the 2nd and 3rd pairs, one passée—do not twist the 1st pair, twist the 2nd pair twice, cross, one passée, stick a pin at 11 on the right of the 2nd pair—twist the 2nd pair twice, do not twist the 3rd pair, cross, one passée—cross the 3rd and 4th pairs, one passée—cross the 4th and 5th pairs, one passée—twist the 5th and 6th pairs twice, cross, one passée, stick a pin at 12 on the left of the 5th pair.

Repeat from the beginning.

Sewing. How to join braids by short and long points (figs. 1089 and 1090). When two braids meet, the points or picots of the edges are joined by a loop of thread. This process is known as a sewing.

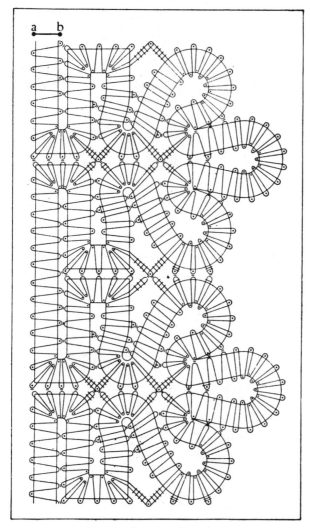

Fig. 1092. Pattern for the lace edging in fig. 1091.

The spots where the work is to be joined to a braid are marked on the pattern by a small curved line; this indicates that the unfinished braid on the right of the curved line is to be joined to the point of the finished braid which is on the left of the line. This is done by taking the bobbin of the pair nearest to the finished work, catching the thread with a hook and drawing a loop through the finished picot; the second bobbin of the pair is then passed through this loop and the threads are drawn tight.

Fig. 1089 shows the process clearly. However, it does not very often happen that the short points meet, and it is therefore often necessary to fill a more or less extensive space by lengthening the points, which are shown correctly on the pattern. To make these of various lengths, the pair of bobbins at the edge must be twisted several times. On the patterns, little straight lines can be seen at the spots where picots are to be made: these indicate the number of times the pair must be twisted when making the picot. Where the picot is to be made in the manner we have already described in our instructions for straight and curved braids, no special sign has been used.

These long points can be joined two, three, or four together. When three points happen to touch, the first is finished and the second and third joined to it as the work proceeds.

Fig. 1093. Lace edging with design of braid in plain and fancy (chain) linen stitch.

When four points converge towards one center, the first and second are made over the same pin; then the third is joined to the first and the fourth to the second. Fig. 1090 shows

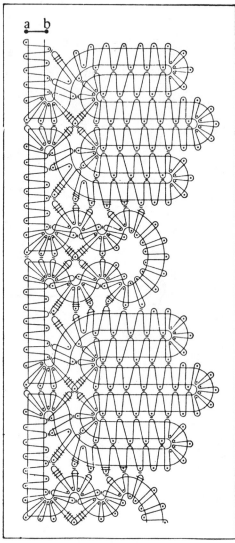

Fig. 1094.
Pattern for the lace edging in fig. 1093.

a motif in which four points are to be joined, in course of working.

Lace edging with design in plain linen or whole stitch braid (figs. 1091 and 1092). The reader who is familiar with the making of straight braid (fig. 1082) and curved braid (fig. 1087) will be able to undertake the lace shown in fig. 1091. The transition from straight to curved braid can be followed on the pattern. As the lace is made with a single braid and the braid is worked with only six pairs of bobbins, it is very simple to make and particularly suitable for beginners.

Lace edging with design of braid in plain and fancy (chain) linen stitch (figs. 1093 and 1094). This lace is also made with a single braid, but the linen stitch is enriched with chain stitch in a colored thread. Fig. 1086 shows how to make straight braid with plain linen stitch and chain stitch; the curves of the braid are worked in the same way as in fig. 1087 and do not require any special instructions.

Tasseled fringe with crochet heading.

CHAPTER XIX

Needlework Trimmings

In the preceding chapters we have described the working of various types of embroidery and lace. To complete this encyclopedia we will give our readers a few instructions for finishing off and trimming needlework.

Embroideries that do not need to be lined are edged with a hem or a small fringe; those which are lined are finished off with a cord or a narrow braid. For richer embroideries, heavy fringes are usually chosen as trimming, and tassels can be added at the corners; fine embroideries look best edged with lace.

Whatever the style of the work, the trimming must be carefully chosen to harmonize with it. Too important or too rich a trimming will detract from the effectiveness of the embroidery. It should, on the contrary, enhance the embroidery by its simplicity and good taste.

Hems. Articles which will require frequent laundering should be finished with only a hem. These hems can be quite plain, or decorated in various ways. They can be divided into (1) openwork or hem-stitched hems; (2) hems with ornamental stitches; and (3) hems with picots, points, or scallops.

For openwork hems, a few threads must be drawn out across the width of the material; see the chapter "Openwork on Linen."

Very happy effects can be obtained by ornamenting hems with embroidery stitches worked in thread of the same shade as the material or in some other shade; these stitches can be varied indefinitely, according to the taste and the patience of the worker. We suggest here edgings in satin or flat stitch and buttonhole stitch, as well as plait stitch and herringbone or double back stitch. Beside these, almost all the stitches we have described in the chapters "Embroidery on White Materials" and "Linen Embroidery" could be used.

We recommend trimming narrow hems with picots made in crochet, tatting, pillow lace, or with the needle. All the necessary instructions for making these different kinds of picots will be found in the appropriate chapters.

How to make the corners of hems (figs. 1095 and 1096). The beauty of a hem depends largely on the neatness of the corners. After drawing out the threads—or marking the position of the hem with a colored tacking thread—the corner of the material is folded diagonally, with the right side in. Then, leaving a space corresponding to the width of the hem, a back stitch seam is made down at right angles to the fold; see fig. 1095.

Fig. 1095. Back stitch seam to form the corner of a hem. Inside.

As can be seen in the illustration, the back stitching is ended at about a quarter of an inch from the edge of the material to allow for the fold. The corner is then turned over, folded, and tacked, and the hemming is begun. Fig. 1096 shows the corner of a hem finished.

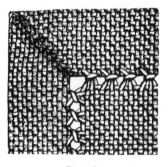

Fig. 1096.
Corner of finished hem. Outside.

Hem with picots (figs. 1097, 1098, 1099, 1100, 1101). The edge of the hem must be covered with very close overcasting, as shown in fig. 1097.

In fig. 1098 the thread can be seen passing from left to right, forming a little loop, which can if necessary be secured with a pin. It then returns to the middle, where it is twisted round the first loop to form a small picot, which can also be secured for the time being with a second pin. The thread is then drawn tight and the space between the threads held by the pins is filled with from three to five herringbone stitches (fig. 1099), worked with this difference from ordinary herringbone stitch—instead of merely crossing the threads, the needle picks up the intermediate thread before passing to the next stitch.

The picots can be made several stitches apart, as in fig. 1100 and 1101, or close together, according to individual taste.

A moderately twisted thread is the most suitable for this work; for instance, DMC pearl cotton or DMC special quality embroidery cotton in scarlet.

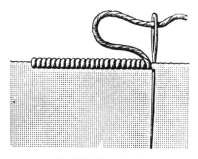

Fig. 1097. Hem with picots.
Overcasting a selvedge or hem.

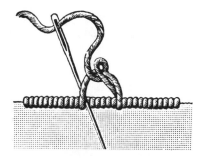

Fig. 1098. Hem with picots.
Making the small picot at the top.

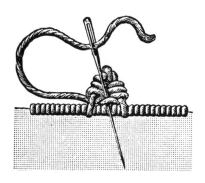

Fig. 1099. Hem with picots.
Method of working the herringbone stitch
to fill the picots.

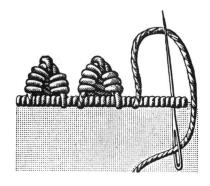

Fig. 1100. Hem with picots.
Two picots finished, and passage of the
needle to the next picot.

Hem with triple buttonholed scallops (fig. 1102). Copying this charming example of triple scalloping will be an easy matter for anyone who can work buttonhole stitch. We advise working from right to left, as we have already explained in the chapter "Needlemade Laces." These scallops can be worked in several shades, that is to say, each triple scallop can be made in a different shade. A moderately twisted thread should be used, such as DMC special quality embroidery cotton, DMC pearl cotton, or DMC Alsatia.

Hem with crochet picots and cross stitch (fig. 1103). Before the hem is folded, the row of single cross stitches is worked. Then the hem is sewn down with overcast stitches. The edge of crochet picots is made as follows: 1 double crochet into the edge of the hem, 5 chain, 1 treble into the 1st chain; repeat frostitch and crochet are worked in DMC pearl cotton no. 5 in garnet red.

Hem with crochet picots and openwork strip (fig. 1104). The openwork strip is worked in DMC pearl cotton no. 8 in saffron, the alter-

Fig. 1101. Hem with picots.
Series of picots finished.

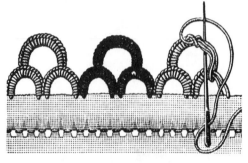

Fig. 1102. Hem with triple buttonholed scallops.

Fig. 1103. Hem with crochet picots and cross stitch.

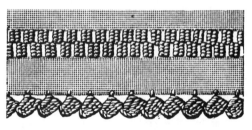

Fig. 1104. Hem with crochet picots and
openwork strip.

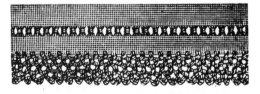

Fig. 1105. Openwork hem with narrow crochet edging.

nated bars are made in needle weaving; see fig. 795. The crochet picots, worked with the same thread, are made as follows: 1 treble into the edge of the hem, 3 chain, 3 treble over the treble below; 1 treble into the edge of the hem, and so on.

Openwork hem with narrow crochet edging (fig. 1105). After working a plain hem-stitched hem, according to the instructions accompanying figs. 763 and 764, the narrow crochet lace is worked in four rows.

1st row: 1 double crochet into the edge, 2 chain, 1 double crochet into the edge, 2 chain, and so on.

2nd row: 1 double crochet into the loop of 2 chain below, 3 chain, 1 double crochet into the next loop, 3 chain, and so on.

3rd row: 1 double crochet into the loop of 3 chain below, 4 chain, 1 double crochet into the next loop, and so on.

4th row: 1 double crochet into the loop of 4 chain, 1 chain, 1 picot, 1 chain, 1 double crochet into the next loop, and so on.

According to the nature of the fabric, one of the following threads will be found suitable: DMC Alsatian sewing cotton nos. 30 to 50, DMC 6 cord cotton lace thread nos. 30 to 50, or DMC flax lace thread nos. 20 to 40, in white or ecru.

Mounting Embroidery. The mounting of embroidery on wood or metal is work which requires a great deal of skill and experience; we therefore advise our readers to entrust it to an upholsterer, or to have it done by a firm which specializes in this kind of work, since imperfect mounting will spoil the appearance of the embroidery.

Lining Embroidery. When the embroidery is merely to be lined with material, this can be done at home without great difficulty. The laying of the lining must be done with the greatest care. The material used for this purpose should always be very soft and should be, if possible, of the same color as the material of which the article is made, or of a color that goes well with it. It should be cut straight by the thread of the material and folded in at the edges. When it has been prepared in this way, it is tacked to the embroidery, which has also been folded in at the edges. The two layers of material are then joined with a hemmed seam, which will afterward be concealed beneath a thick cord, a fringe, or braid, which completes the article on the outside.

Cords. The art of making all kinds of cords is a very useful one; it enables cords to be made with the threads that have been used for the embroidery itself, thus ensuring the most perfect match in shade and texture. The easiest kinds of cord to make are those for which the cord wheel, which we are about to describe, is used; next come crochet, macrame, and hand-knotted cords.

Cord wheel. This little implement is a most useful possession; with its help all kinds of cords can be made.

The apparatus consists of a large wheel mounted on an upright support with a base which, by means of a belt, turns three small wheels mounted on the same support. The large wheel is provided with a handle and a diagram showing how to mount the cord on the wheels. To ensure the even working of the apparatus, the thread which passes over the wheels must be drawn very tight.

Each small wheel is armed with a metal hook, to which the threads with

Fig. 1106. Cord wheel in action.

which the cord is to be made are attached. If a cord is to be made by one person without help, a small piece of wood, also provided with metal hooks, will be necessary; this piece of wood is screwed to a table and holds the other ends of the threads. Fig. 1106 shows how the wheel is worked when the threads have been mounted and stretched tight.

How to make cords (fig. 1106). The simplest cord that can be made with the cord wheel consists of two threads. At the end of each thread a loop is made, which is hooked onto the small wheels of the apparatus. The opposite ends are fastened to the hooks of the little board screwed to the table, then the cord wheel is drawn back until the threads are stretched quite tight. Then the handle is turned from left to right, or from right to left, according to the twist of the thread used, until the threads begin to twist. Then one thread is detached from the small wheel and fastened to the one to which the second thread is hooked, and the wheel is turned in the opposite direction until the cord is complete.

Cords composed of three strands are made in the same way, using all three small wheels.

With two cord wheels, cords composed of four, five, or six strands can be made. To make thicker cords, several threads are fastened to each small wheel together.

Upholstery cords made with cotton threads (figs. 1107 and 1108). To finish off heavy embroideries intended for furniture and cushions, thick cords made of cotton threads are used, such as those illustrated in figs. 1107 and 1108.

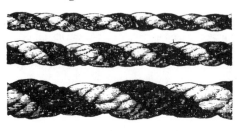

Fig. 1107. Twofold cords made with cotton thread.

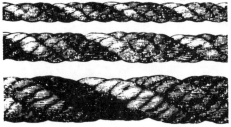

Fig. 1108. Threefold cords made with cotton thread.

Fig. 1107 shows three twofold cords made with DMC pearl cotton no. 1 in two shades. They are twisted first from left to right, then from right to left. The threads were used single for the thin cord, double for the medium cord, and quadruple for the thick cord. The threefold cords shown in figs. 1108 are made in the same way, with three strands and three shades.

Brilliant, firm cords can be made with DMC pearl cotton. Soft, matt cords can be made with DMC embroidery twist no. 4 or DMC knitting twist no. 4.

Embroidery cords made

with cotton, flax, or rayon threads, and with metal threads (figs. 1109, 1110, 1111). Certain kinds of colored embroidery and particularly appliqué work require fine cords of brilliant thread or metal thread, which can easily be made at home from the instructions which we have just given.

Fig. 1109 shows two twofold cords and fig. 1110 two threefold cords. In each case, the finer cord is made with single and the thicker with double threads of DMC pearl cotton no. 8, twisted in the same way as those already described, that is to say, first from left to right and then from right to left.

Fig. 1111 shows two cords, one made with single threads of gold and silver, the other made with double threads of each metal, and twisted first from right to left and then from left to right, or inversely.

Hand-knotted cord (figs. 1112, 1113, 1114, 1115, 1116). This is a purely fancy kind of cord in which the hands do the work of a crochet hook. This cord, composed entirely of loops passed through each other and drawn very tight, is extremely simple and easy to make.

Two ends of thread are knotted together; one end is held in the left hand (fig. 1112), a loop is made by passing the thread over the right hand and raising the first finger, and the thread is drawn tight with the left hand. Then, the thread still held taut with the left hand, the first finger of the left hand is inserted into the loop on the first finger of the right hand, and the thread issuing from the left hand

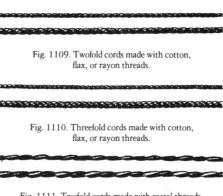

Fig. 1109. Twofold cords made with cotton, flax, or rayon threads.

Fig. 1110. Threefold cords made with cotton, flax, or rayon threads.

Fig. 1111. Twofold cords made with metal threads.

and behind the loop is drawn through the latter; see fig. 1113.

At the moment when the first finger of the left hand brings the fresh loop through, the loop on the first finger of the right hand is dropped, and the knotted end passes between the thumb and second finger of the left hand, while the right hand draws the knot tight; see fig. 1114.

Fig. 1115, illustrating the fourth position of the hands, shows how the first finger of the right hand raises the thread and passes through the loop on the left hand; the end will therefore pass immediately into the right hand, while the left hand tightens the knot.

It is, therefore, by tightening now the left-hand and now the right-hand knot that this charming cord is produced; the process is so easy that it is a recreation rather than a task.

Macrame cord (fig. 1117). Our example is made with DMC knotting cotton no. 10. The length of the threads will depend on the length of cord to be made; in any case, the threads will have to be wound onto macrame bobbins; see fig. 653.

At the top, ends of thread four inches long are left. These are later joined with a knot and fastened to the macrame cushion. Over the knot-bearer *a,* knot three light threads from left to right, then knot three dark threads over knot-bearer *b* and the same threads also over knot-bearer *a,* to the right of the light knots. Take a third knot-bearer, *c,* add three more light and three more dark threads, and knot these threads also over threads *a* and *b,*

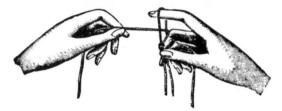

Fig. 1112. Hand-knotted cord. First position of the hands.

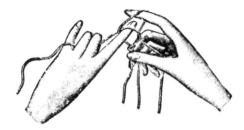

Fig. 1113. Hand-knotted cord. Second position of the hands.

Fig. 1114. Hand-knotted cord. Third position of the hands.

The ring is closed by knotting these twelve threads over thread *c*; then the work is continued by knotting the threads over threads *a* and *b,* and so on. In this way a round, hollow cord is produced, with a design of stripes sloping spirally from right to left.

Crochet cord (figs. 1118 and 1119). This crochet cord is specially to be recommended because of the ease with which it is made; the method is shown clearly in fig. 1119.

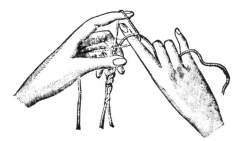

Fig. 1115. Hand-knotted cord. Fourth position of the hands.

Begin with four chain, close the ring and work one single crochet into each chain, then one single crochet into each single crochet, working into the back loop of each stitch. The work is not done from the outside toward the inside but, contrary to the usual method in crochet, from the inside out.

Braids. Pieces of embroidery used to cover furniture, screens, etc., require very simple trimming. For such articles a thick cord, or better still a flat braid, is used. The braid should not be too elaborate either in design or in coloring; simple designs and quiet colors are to be preferred.

Fig. 1116.
Hand-knotted cord.

The methods of making these braids are very varied. They include: (1) embroidered braids; (2) crochet braids; (3) tatted braids; (4) macrame braids; and (5) pillow lace braids.

(1) Embroidered braids. For articles requiring frequent washing, woven braids are often used. These can be of linen or soft canvas, and trimmed with a small design in cross stitch or satin stitch. They are very strong, and can be recommended for articles likely to be in constant use. Charming designs for such braids will be found in the chapter "Embroidery on Linen."

(2) Crochet braids. Furnishing braids can be imitated in crochet— using single and double crochet and trebles—to form rings and scallops on a foundation of closely woven braid. The work will be

Fig. 1117.
Macrame cord.

Fig. 1118. Crochet cord.

most effective if a well-twisted thread of medium thickness is used; see also the headings of the fringes in figs. 1127, 1129, and 1130, and the Bosnian crochet braids in figs. 519 and 520.

Fig. 1119. How to make the crochet cord in fig. 1118.

(3) Tatted braids. Tatting can also be used to make braids. Tatted braids are both dainty and strong. They can be further enriched with wheels or lace stitches in gold or silver thread. Even the simplest motifs, such as small connected rings, make charming braids, which can be further varied in different ways.

(4) Macrame braids. Macrame lends itself particularly well to the making of braids, and enables corners to be made without difficulty. We have already given several examples of braids in the chapter "Macrame." Those who have had some experience in this type of work will have little difficulty in converting most of the fringes and grounds into braids.

(5) Pillow lace braids. Narrow braids can be made with as few as four or six pairs of bobbins; the design called "eternal" is the one which lends itself best to this purpose. In the chapter "Pillow Laces," a series of grounds will be found which can be used as braids if the width comprises a single repeat of the design and a very strong thread is used for the work.

Fig. 1120.
Picot-edged braid made with lace bobbins.

Picot-edged braid made with lace bobbins (fig. 1120). For fine, delicate embroideries worked on a foundation of silk or velvet, the little braid shown in fig. 1120 is used, worked in gold thread. It consists of a plait in which, after each passée, one picot is made alternately on the right and on the left.

How to join braid. When a join in the braid cannot be avoided, it must be made as invisibly as possible. If the design contains large motifs, the join should be made at the point where a motif ends, so that the design shall be continued without a break.

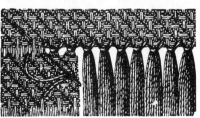

Fig. 1121. Small fringe made with the unravelled threads of the material.

How to miter corners. According to the angle to be made, the braid should be folded and sewn with a diagonal line of back stitching. When the stitching is finished, it is smoothed on the right side with the thimble and the superfluous braid is cut away.

Fringes. The most natural finish for a piece of work made in a woven fabric will always be a fringe, which can be prepared in various ways.

The simplest fringes are those made by drawing out the horizontal threads of the material, after securing the edge of the latter. The loose threads thus unravelled can be made more interesting in very simple ways: colored threads or tassels can be added, or the threads can be knotted to form patterns. Beside these fringes made from the material, there are also knotted fringes (see the chapter "Macrame"), fringes with crochet headings, and fringes made with lace bobbins.

We give here a series of various fringes, beginning with the simplest, that is to say, fringes made with the unravelled threads of the material.

Small fringes with various ornamentation (figs. 1121, 1122, 1123, 1124). Fig. 1121 shows a narrow fringe consisting solely of the threads of the material. The edge is secured with the stitch shown in fig. 763, after which the horizontal threads are drawn out. The same fringe, with the addition of red threads between the groups, appears in fig. 1122. The red

Fig. 1122.
Small fringe with colored threads added.

Fig. 1123. Small fringe knotted in two rows.

Fig. 1124. Small fringe with tassels.

threads are knotted over alternately one and two groups of threads of the material.

A fringe knotted in two rows is shown in fig. 1123. Each knot is made with two groups of threads. In the second row, the double groups formed by the first knotting are divided, and half are taken from the left and half from the right to make the knots of the second row, so that they shall alternate with those of the first row.

Finally, fig. 1124 shows a fringe with tassels. The edge is secured with the same stitch as in fig. 1121, and to it are fastened small tassels, at a distance of four groups of threads of the fringe, or eight of the material. As can be seen in the illustration, a thick bunch of floss thread is taken and fastened to the edge by means of a knot made with an auxiliary thread; the bunch is then folded in half and a thread of a contrasting color is wound round it half an inch below the edge of the material.

It goes without saying that when the work has been done the ends of thread are no longer all the same length as they were to begin with. Any inequalities in their length would spoil the appearance of the work and they must be carefully cut to make them even. For this part of the work, we refer our readers to the beginning of the chapter ''Macrame.''

Albanian fringe (fig. 1125). The edge of the linen is secured with a row of two-sided chain stitch, which serves at the same time as an ornamental stitch.

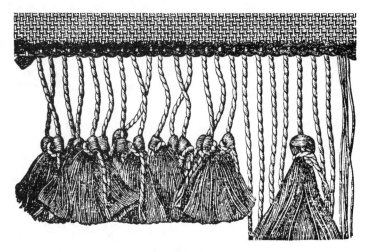

Fig. 1125. Albanian fringe.

When this row of chain stitches is finished, the material is frayed out to a depth of about six inches, and the threads are twisted together two by two to make little cords, to which tassels are fastened by means of a single knot; see fig. 1125. For these tassels we recommend a very soft, silky, floss thread, such as DMC special stranded cotton or DMC floss flax or flourishing thread; with either of these threads, very fine, rich tassels are obtained.

Tasselled fringes on canvas net (fig. 1126).   Fig. 1126 represents a very interesting fringe carried out on canvas net, ornamented with tassels attached to a grid of overcast bars which forms a continuation of the flat stitch design of the border.

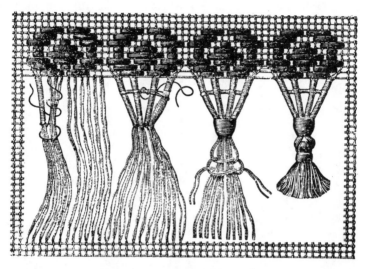

Fig. 1126. Tasselled fringes on canvas net.

To prepare the fringe, the necessary number of threads is drawn out, leaving, if the size of the material allows, a border of material about one inch wide, which will make the working of the overcast bars very much easier. When the material has been prepared, three double threads of the warp are very closely overcast to a depth of three-quarters of an inch (first detail on the left). Then the next group is firmly knotted to the first before being in its turn overcast from the top down.

The second detail of fig. 1126 shows three bars completed and the fourth begun, as well as the cross bars which are begun from the latter.

In the third detail the four bars are seen finished and joined by a few overcast stitches which form a collecting knot, below which, with two double threads, one double knot is made through which a bunch of threads is passed; this bunch is folded in half and secured with a few twists of thread. This tassel should be cut fairly short (detail four on the right).

For the little tassels and the flat stitch embroidery, DMC special stranded cotton is used, and for the overcast bars DMC pearl cotton.

How to make corners in fringes made from the fabric.   When the threads of the material are removed all round a square piece of work, empty spaces are produced at the corners; these spaces are filled with one or more bunches of the threads that have been drawn out, and the corners are ornamented in the same way as the rest of the fringe; finally, the corners are slightly rounded.

Fringe with two rows of tassels and crochet heading (figs. 1127 and 1128). DMC pearl cotton no. 3, used double, makes the foundation cord

Fig. 1127. Fringe with two rows of tassels and crochet heading.

for the heading of our crochet fringe, which is worked with DMC pearl cotton no. 5 in double crochet. The double threads form long and short loops, to which the little tassels are afterward added. The tassels are made with DMC special stranded cotton no. 25.

Fig. 1128 shows how the work is done, from right to left. Over the double thread of DMC pearl cotton, work 8 double crochet. Turn. 1 double crochet into each of the last 3 double crochet (each stitch is always worked into both loops of the stitch below and over the double thread), 5 double crochet over the double thread. * Turn. 1 double crochet into each of the last 3 double crochet, make a short loop with the double thread over a piece of card 1¼ inches deep, 1 chain. Turn. 1 double crochet into each of the last 3 double crochet, 5 double crochet over the double thread. Turn. 1 double crochet into each of the last 3 double crochet, 5 double crochet over the double thread. Turn. 1 double crochet into each of the last 3 double crochet, 5 double crochet over the double thread. Turn. 1 double crochet into each of the last 3 double crochet, make a long loop with the double thread over a piece of card 2½ inches deep, 1 chain. Turn. 1 double crochet into each of the last 3 double crochet, 5 double crochet over the double thread. Turn. 1 double crochet into each of the last 3 double crochet, 5 double crochet over the double thread. Turn. 1 double crochet into each of the last 3 double crochet, 5 double crochet over the double thread; repeat from * and continue making alternately one short and one long loop along one side of the close braid.

Each of these loops consists of two double threads; these threads have to be twisted separately from right to left, then the two ends are joined and they are twisted from left to right, thus making a cord; see fig. 1128. To each of these cords is attached, by means of a knot made with an auxiliary thread, a bunch of about thirty-two threads of DMC special stranded cotton, 3¾ inches long; this bunch is fastened exactly in the middle, folded in half, and secured with a few tight twists of thread, and the tassel is made.

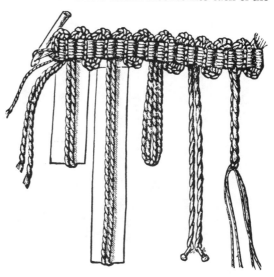

Fig. 1128. Method of making the fringe in fig. 1127.

Fig. 1129.
Fringe with one row of tassels and crochet heading.

Fringe with one row of tassels and crochet heading (fig. 1129). This example is made with two shades. The foundation cord for the heading consists of DMC pearl cotton no. 3 used double; the crochet is worked with DMC pearl cotton no. 5 in Moss green; the tassels and ornamental stitches require a floss thread, DMC special stranded cotton no. 25 in garnet red.

The close heading is worked backward and forward in rows of six double crochet with one chain to turn; the stitches are worked into both loops of the stitches below.

Along one side of this braid loops are made—over a card—half an inch long; along the other side, loops one and a half inches long.

The short loops are held along the top by a crochet chain made with DMC pearl cotton no. 5 in garnet red. Two double loops are taken on the

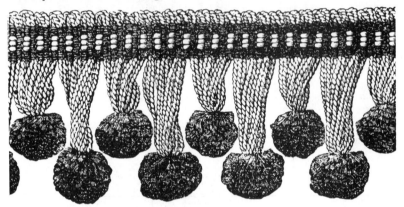

Fig. 1130. Ball fringe with crochet heading.

Fig. 1131. Knotted ball fringe.

hook and joined by 1 double crochet, 4 chain, 1 double crochet into the next two double loops, 4 chain, and so on. The long double loops on the other side are also taken two by two, and to them are attached the tassels, consisting of 25 to 30 red threads, knotted with green thread. Finally, the close braid of double crochet is embroidered with four complementary rows of running stitch.

Ball fringe with crochet heading (fig. 1130). For this fringe the foundation cord is DMC pearl cotton no. 3 in saffron used triple. The braid requires seven double crochet in DMC pearl cotton no. 5 in terra-cotta, worked backward and forward with one chain to turn. The stitches are worked into both loops of the stitches below.

The small triple loops at the top, formed by the yellow foundation cord, are a quarter of an inch long; the long loops which hang down are arranged in groups of three of the same length, alternately one and a quarter and one and three quarters inches. The three loops of each group are joined at the bottom by a ball or pompom made

Fig. 1132. How to make the small double knots.

Fig. 1133. How to make the large double knots.

with DMC special stranded cotton no. 25 in terra-cotta; see fig. 1149.

The small loops at the tops are left free.

The braid of double crochet is trimmed with three rows of running stitches, one above the other.

Knotted ball fringe (figs. 1131, 1132, 1133, 1134, 1135). The knotted fringe illustrated in fig. 1131 is, both in working and in effect, a type apart.

Fig. 1134. How to make the large tassel.

The motifs of this example are made up of knotted threads which are afterward cut and threaded like beads to make the details of the design.

In the present example, two kinds of knots can be distinguished: small double knots and large double knots. To make the small double knots, single knots are made with one thread, as shown in fig. 1132. These knots are cut two by two, each pair counting as one small double knot; the length of thread between the knots should be no greater than the space occupied by one knot.

Fig. 1135.
How to make the small double balls.

The large double knots are begun with one single knot, followed by three more single knots which are joined by a fourth knot, so as to make a single large knot (fig. 1133), which is then completed with one more single knot. Another double knot is made quite close to it, the thread is cut, and the large double knot is complete.

The heading of the fringe consists of a braid of flat knots, knotted over a quadruple knot-bearer, and it is to this braid that the knotted tassels are attached.

We advise beginning with the large single tassel. After a sufficient number of large and small double knots have been prepared with red and black thread, red thread is taken to make 1 small single knot; this thread is then threaded into a large crewel needle and drawn through 14 small double knots made of black thread, to which are added 8 large double knots made of

Fig. 1136. Fringe and heading made with lace bobbins.

red thread; all these knots are drawn very close together toward the bottom of the thread and the motif is ended with a small single knot. A space of $\frac{3}{8}$ of an inch is left and another small single knot is made, 6 small double knots in red are threaded on, drawn close together, and finished with another small single knot; then the completed tassel is fastened into the braid, leaving again $\frac{3}{8}$ of an inch of thread free. The next tassel is placed at a distance of 16 double knots along the braid.

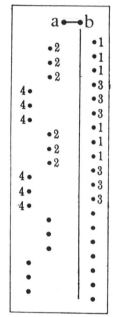

Fig. 1137.
Pattern for the fringe
and heading in fig. 1136.

The small motifs with double tassels which fill the spaces are also made with red thread. After making 1 large single knot, thread on 2 large double knots made with red thread and 5 small double knots made with black thread, draw them close, and finish with 1 small single knot. Leaving a space of $\frac{3}{8}$ of an inch, make 2 small single knots very close together and a third knot $\frac{3}{8}$ of an inch distant. Then thread on 5 small double knots of black thread and 2 large double knots of red thread, draw the knots close and complete the pompom with 1 large single knot, then cut the thread. To fasten this pompom to the braid, take another red thread, make 1 small single knot, and thread on 5 small double knots of red thread, pass the thread between the 2 single knots close together in the middle of the pompom, and end with 1 small single knot.

Finally the double tassel is attached to the braid, just halfway between the two large tassels, again leaving $\frac{3}{8}$ of an inch of thread free at the top. The little pompoms, consisting of 8 double knots of black thread, are placed between the large and small tassels. They are attached directly to the braid itself.

A moderately twisted thread should be used for this work, such as DMC pearl cotton nos. 1 and 3, and DMC special quality embroidery cotton nos. 8 and 12.

Fringe and beading made with lace bobbins (figs. 1136 and 1137). Three green floss threads are fastened on at *a* and three pairs of bobbins, one of each pair wound with yellow thread and one with pink, at *b,* on the pattern in fig. 1137.

* Twist the 1st pair from right to left, slip the green threads—twist the 2nd pair from right to left, slip the green threads—twist the 3rd pair from right to left, slip the green threads, stick a pin at 1—twist the 3rd pair

Fig. 1138. Scalloped fringe made with lace bobbins.

from right to left, slip the green threads—twist the 2nd pair from right to left, slip the green threads—twist the 1st pair from right to left, slip the green threads, stick a pin at 2 **; repeat twice from * to ** —*** twist the 1st pair from right to left, slip the green threads—twist the 2nd pair from right to left, slip the green threads—twist the 3rd pair from right to left, slip the green threads, stick a pin at 3—twist the 3rd pair from right to left, slip the green threads—twist the 2nd pair from right to left, slip the green threads— twist the 1st pair from right to left, slip the green threads, stick a pin at 4 ****; repeat twice from *** to ****; repeat from the beginning.

Scalloped fringe made with lace bobbins (figs. 1138 and 1139). Fasten on two yellow floss threads at *a,* and two pairs of bobbins (1 with yellow and 1 with mauve thread) at *b,* on the pattern in fig. 1139.

* Twist the 1st pair from left to right, slip the 2 yellow threads—twist the 2nd pair from right to left, slip the 2 yellow threads, stick a pin at 1—twist the 2nd pair from right to left, slip the 2 yellow threads—twist the 1st pair from left to right, slip the 2 yellow threads, stick a pin at 2 **; repeat six times from * to **; fasten on 2 green floss threads at *c*—twist the 1st pair from left to right, slip

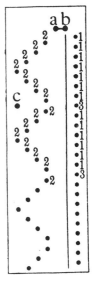

Fig. 1139.
Pattern for the scalloped fringe in fig. 1138.

the 2 yellow threads and the 2 green threads—twist the 2nd pair from right to left, slip the 2 yellow threads and the 2 green threads, stick a pin at 3—twist the 2nd pair from right to left, slip the 2 yellow threads and the 2 green threads—twist the 1st pair from left to right, slip the 2 yellow threads and the 2 green threads, stick a pin at 2 and set aside the 2 yellow threads; repeat six times from * to **—add the yellow threads—twist the 1st pair from left to right, slip the 2 green threads and the 2 yellow threads—twist the 2nd pair from right to left, slip the 2 green threads and the 2 yellow threads, stick a pin at 3—twist the 2nd pair from right to left, slip the 2 green threads and the 2 yellow threads—twist the 1st pair from left to right, slip the 2 green threads and the 2 yellow threads, stick a pin at 2—set aside the green threads and continue the fringe with the yellow threads.

When the whole of the fringe is finished, the connecting threads are cut quite close to the scallops.

Double scalloped fringe made with lace bobbins (figs. 1140 and 1141). Fasten on one dark yellow floss thread at *a*, two red floss threads at *b*, and 2 pairs of bobbins wound with light yellow thread at *c*, on the pattern in fig. 1141.

* Twist the 1st pair from left to right, slip the yellow thread and the red threads—twist the 2nd pair from left to right, slip the yellow thread and the red threads, stick a pin at 1—twist the 2nd pair from left to right, slip the yellow thread and the red threads—twist the 1st pair from left to right, slip the yellow thread and the red threads, stick a pin at 2 to hold the yellow thread

Fig. 1140.
Double scalloped fringe made with lace bobbins.

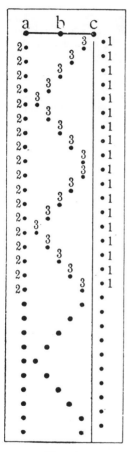

Fig. 1141.
Pattern for the double
scalloped fringe in fig. 1140.

and another at 3 to hold the red threads; repeat from * 8 times and continue in the same way.

When the fringe is removed from the lace cushion, the long loops of yellow thread are cut.

Double horizontal fringe made with lace bobbins (figs. 1142 and 1143). Fasten on four blue floss threads at *a*, and six pairs of bobbins (the 1st, 2nd, 5th, and 6th pairs wound with light yellow and the 3rd and 4th pairs wound with dark yellow) at *b*, on the pattern in fig. 1143.

Twist the 1st pair from right to left, slip the blue threads—twist the 2nd pair from right to left, slip the blue threads— twist the 3rd pair from right to left, slip the blue threads—twist the 4th pair from left to right, slip the blue threads—twist the 5th pair from left to right, slip the blue threads—twist the 6th pair from left to right, slip the blue threads, stick a pin at 1—twist the 6th pair from left to right, slip the blue threads—twist the 5th pair from left to right, slip the blue threads—twist the 4th pair from left to right, slip the blue threads—twist the 3rd pair from right to left, slip the blue threads—twist the 2nd pair from right to left, slip the blue threads— twist the 1st pair from right to left, slip the blue threads, stick a pin at 2 to hold the first two blue threads and another at 3 to hold the last two blue threads.

Repeat from the beginning.

Pompoms. Balls or pompoms are also used for trimming certain articles, like lampshades, on which, since they hang down freely, they show up to advantage.

Fig. 1142. Double horizontal fringe made with lace bobbins.

Soft pompoms are made with floss threads tied in the middle or plaited with a thick twisted thread. Hard pompoms consist of a crochet or plaited sheath covering a wooden mold. We give below examples of the various kinds of pompoms.

Pompoms made with floss threads (figs. 1144, 1145, 1146, 1147, 1148, 1149). To make this kind of pompom, a number of cardboard discs must first be prepared, with holes in their centers; see fig. 1144. Two of these are placed together and covered with close stitches passing through the hole in the center and over the outer edge, for which purpose DMC special stranded cotton, DMC pearl cotton no. 3, or DMC floss flax or flourishing thread is used. When the whole surface of the two discs is covered, scissors are inserted be-

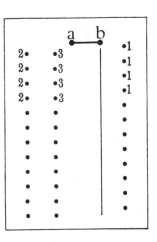

Fig. 1143. Pattern
for the double horizontal fringe
in fig. 1142.

tween the two discs and the threads are cut all round the outer edge (fig. 1146); then a thread is passed between the two discs, wound several times very tightly round the threads (fig. 1147), secured with a knot, and the ends left sufficiently long to make a tie with which the pompom can be fastened to the article it is to trim. When the threads are firmly tied, a slit is made in the discs (fig. 1148) and they are removed from the pompom, which is now finished and appears as in fig. 1149.

Pompom with crochet sheath (fig. 1150). Begin with 4 chain, close the ring with 1 single crochet into the 1st chain; 8 double crochet into the ring, * 2 double crochet into the 1st double crochet below, 1 double crochet into the next stitch, repeat from * nineteen times; then work 6 rounds in which 1 double crochet is worked into each stitch; insert a wooden mold

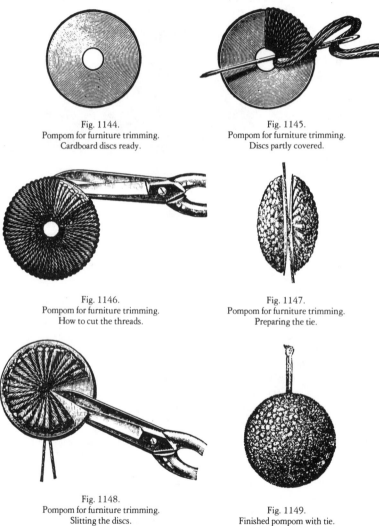

Fig. 1144.
Pompom for furniture trimming.
Cardboard discs ready.

Fig. 1145.
Pompom for furniture trimming.
Discs partly covered.

Fig. 1146.
Pompom for furniture trimming.
How to cut the threads.

Fig. 1147.
Pompom for furniture trimming.
Preparing the tie.

Fig. 1148.
Pompom for furniture trimming.
Slitting the discs.

Fig. 1149.
Finished pompom with tie.

about ⅜ of an inch in diameter into the little crochet pocket and continue working, decreasing gradually so as to end with 8 double crochet, whose upper horizontal loops are drawn very tight.

The pompom is suspended by a crochet chain. Sheaths can be made in the same way for molds of other shapes.

The thread used will depend on the materials used for the article which is to be trimmed; one or other of the following will be found suitable: DMC

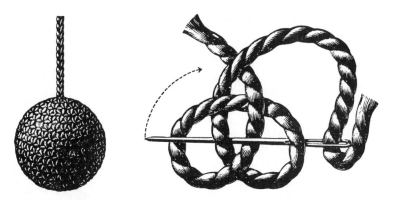

Fig. 1150.
Pompom with crochet sheath.

Fig. 1151. Plain plaited pompom.
Method of making the first loops.

pearl cotton, DMC shaded pearl cotton, DMC special stranded cotton, DMC special shaded stranded cotton, and DMC embroidery rayon.

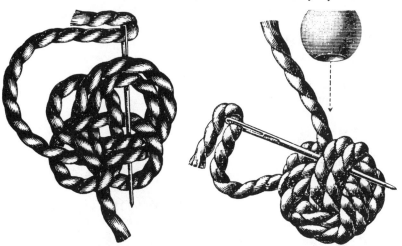

Fig. 1152. Plain plaited pompom.
Interlacing the second thread.

Fig. 1153. Plain plaited pompom.
Method of rounding the pompom.

Plain plaited pompom (figs. 1151, 1152, 1153, 1154). In spite of their complicated appearance, pompoms with plaited sheaths are easy to make.

The thread chosen should be very coarse and suited to the material of the article to be trimmed. Suitable threads are DMC pearl cotton nos. 1 and 3, DMC knotting cotton nos. 10 to 30, and DMC flax thread for knitting and crochet nos. 3 to 10.

Inside the pompom there must be a wooden mold or a pad of cotton wool round which the work is finished off.

The plaiting is begun with a Chinese knot, a figure formed by the interlacing of four loops; the detail in fig. 1151 shows the two lower loops finished, and the position of the needle for the third loop, while an arrow indicates the course to be followed by the needle to make the fourth loop.

Fig. 1152 shows how to make the second series of stitches, which must be made in the same direction and in the same way as the first. Before the third series is begun, the shape must be rounded with the fingers and the mold inserted into the center of the prepared sheath (see fig. 1153), then a fourth and fifth series of stitches are worked.

Fig. 1154.
Plain plaited pompom.

Fig. 1154 shows a plaited pompom made in DMC pearl cotton no. 1, which could be used to trim the corners of cushions, valances, or coverlets, as well as to finish the ends of all kinds of cord fastenings used with or without a running slot.

Fig. 1155.
Plaited pompom
with picots.

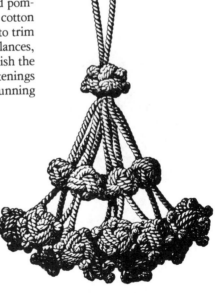

Fig. 1156. Tassel made of plaited pompoms.

Plaited pompom with picots (fig. 1155). Fig. 1155 shows a pompom plaited in three series of stitches and trimmed with knotted picots. For this we recommend DMC knotting cotton no. 10, which can be replaced, if preferred, by DMC flax thread for knitting and crochet nos. 3 and 4.

It is made like the pompom in fig. 1154, but without a mold inside; after the third series of stitches, knotted picots are added at the points where the threads cross—nine picots in all.

These picots are made as follows: bring out the thread with the needle at one of the points where the threads cross, twist the thread once round the needle to make a knotted picot (see fig. 606), and reinsert the needle at the point where it emerged, bringing it out again diagonally under three threads of the pompom, make another picot, and so on. If need be, the picots can be made with thread of a different color, which makes the pompom richer in appearance.

The materials used for this pompom were DMC knotting cotton no. 10, in ecru for the plaiting and turkey red for the picots.

Tassel made of plaited pompoms (fig. 1156). This graceful tassel is composed of eleven large and five small plaited pompoms.

Begin with a large pompom with picots, as shown in fig. 1155, then leave three inches of thread and make a second pompom exactly like the first; fasten off the beginning and end of the thread inside the pompoms. Fold the connecting thread in half, and over the fold slip and secure a small pompom without picots, made with two series of stitches. Make five of these pendants of three pompoms each, then an eleventh large pompom with eight picots round it, pass the threaded needle down through this last pompom, collect the five pendants and draw the thread up again through the large pompom.

For this tassel, use DMC knotting cotton no. 10 in ecru.

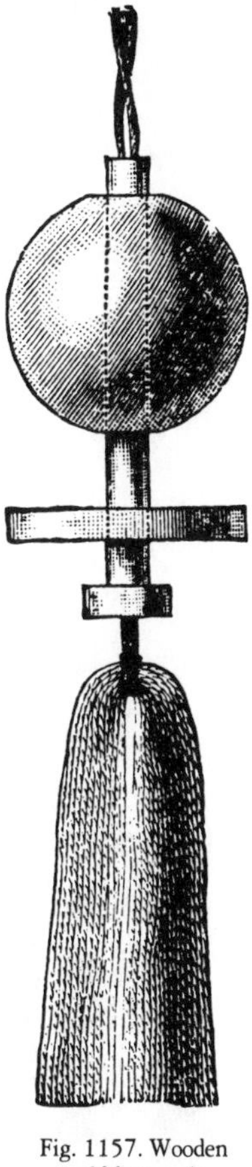

Fig. 1157. Wooden mold for tassels.

Tassels. The corners of certain articles are often ornamented with tassels. These tassels, whether they are simple or ornamental, should always harmonize with the main part of the work and its trimming. Small tassels are made with thread, without the help of any accessories, whereas larger tassels require a wooden mold. We give below a few specimens of more or less elaborate tassels made in different materials.

Plain tassel (figs. 1157, 1158, 1159, 1160). To make the plain tassel

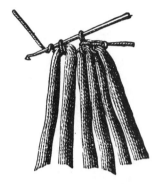

Fig. 1158. How to join the
bunches of threads.

Fig. 1159. How to make the tie of the tassel.

shown in fig. 1160, a wooden mold is used, over which the bunches of floss thread are knotted. This mold is composed of a ball and a disc, connected by a round rod, the whole perforated. At the bottom of the rod a thick bunch of thread is attached, which serves as body to the tassel.

The wooden ball is covered with bunches of threads, both ends of which hang down over the rod; they are joined by means of double crochet (see fig. 1158), and fixed to the head of the ball; see fig. 1159. When these bunches have been evenly distributed all round, they are tied between the ball and the disc, they are cut to the same length at the bottom, and the tassel is complete. To make it easier to attach the tassel to a piece of work, a cord of some kind is fastened to the head of the ball.

For the bunches of thread, a floss thread should be used, such as DMC special stranded cotton or DMC floss flax or flourishing thread; for the crochet, the cord, and the tie, use a moderately twisted thread, for instance DMC pearl cotton or DMC Alsatia, in a different color.

Tassel ornamented with crochet (figs. 1161, 1162, 1163, 1164). The body of the tassel is made with DMC special stranded cotton no. 25 in medium grey over a wooden mold. The tie, the trimming of the head of the tassel, and the hanging ornaments are made with silver thread of medium thickness.

The crochet is begun with the tie and consists of double crochet. Begin with 9 chain, then work backward and forward, 18 rows in one direction and 17 in the other, working 1 double crochet into the back loop of each stitch of the previous row. This tie is secured round the threads below the ball by means of small stitches.

The network which covers the ball is made in 10 rounds of looped chain stitch, the working of which is clearly shown in figs. 1162 to 1164.

Fig. 1160. Tassel completed.

Fig. 1161.
Tassel ornamented with crochet.

These looped chain stitches are made as follows: make 1 very loose chain stitch, then work 1 double crochet into the single thread at the bottom of the chain; 2 of these looped chain stitches form a small scallop which is joined by 2 double crochet to the first round of the band of double crochet; see fig. 1163.

Each round of nine scallops is begun with 2 double crochet and ended with 1 single crochet into the 1st double crochet. From the 2nd to the 10th round, the 2 double crochet are worked into the looped chain stitches of the previous round; see fig. 1164.

After the 10th round of scallops, a round of double crochet is worked, making 1 double crochet into each chain, therefore 18 double crochet in all. At the bottom of the band of double crochet 3 rounds of looped chain

Fig. 1162. How to make the looped chain stitches.
Detail of the tassel in fig. 1161.

Fig. 1163. How to work the first round of looped chain stitches.
Detail of the tassel in fig. 1161.

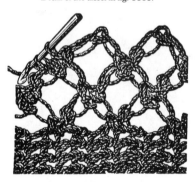

Fig. 1164. How to work the succeeding rounds of looped chain stitches.
Detail of the tassel in fig. 1161.

stitch scallops are added; each round should contain 10 scallops. In the 3rd round, after the double crochet of the 1st looped chain stitch, a sort of pendant is made as follows: 1 chain, 1 picot, 3 chain, 1 picot, 3 chain, 1 picot, 3 chain, 1 picot, 3 chain, 1 picot, 3 chain, 1 picot, 3 chain, 3 picots, 1 chain, 1 double treble into the 2nd of the preceding 3 chain, 1 chain, 1 picot, 1 chain, 1 treble into the 2nd of the next 3 chain, * 1 chain, 1 picot, 1 chain, 1 double crochet into the 2nd of the next 3 chain, repeat from * four times; at the last repeat work 1 single crochet into the double crochet which completes the looped chain stitch, then continue the scallops.

Macrame tassel (figs. 1165 and 1166). The ornamentation of this tassel, worked in gold threads of medium thickness, is begun with the pendants. Five long and five short pendants are required; they are joined at the top by a network of flat knots. The length of the threads for gold thread of medium thickness is between sixty and fifty inches.

The work is begun with the round figure at the bottom. A knot-bearer is fastened to the cushion, then a double bar is made by knotting 5 more threads to it. This bar is to be considered as the center; two similar bars are added on each side, then all the threads are taken and with the 6 middle threads 2 flat knots are made over 4 threads, then the 6 outer threads are added and 4 flat knots are made over the 10 threads; after the 2nd knot a looped picot is added on each side; see the explanatory illustration, fig. 1166. The threads are divided and joined on each side by 1 flat knot, then with each section of the threads two double bars are knotted, which are again finished with 1 flat knot.

When this is done, all the threads are collected with flat knots. After the 2nd, 5th, 8th, and 11th flat knots, 1 looped picot is added on each side. As the work proceeds, the number of threads is decreased by cutting the inner

Fig. 1165. Macrame tassel.

Fig. 1166.
Method of working a pendant for the tassel in fig. 1165.

threads one by one, until only 6 remain in all.

The short pendants consist only of the five-barred motif at the bottom, followed by 10 flat knots interrupted by 2 picots. When the pendants are finished, they are fastened to the macrame cushion, one long and one short pendant alternately, five-eighths of an inch apart; then the network, consisting of 10 rows of alternated flat knots, is worked over the tassel.

The latter is made over a wooden mold, without a tie, with DMC special stranded cotton no. 25 in golden yellow. After the 10th round of flat knots, 2 more rounds are worked, in which the knots are not alternated, then all the threads are fastened to the head of the tassel. Finally, with 4 threads a round cord of wave knots (fig. 602) is made; the other threads are fastened off invisibly on the inside.

Tassel with two rows of smaller tassels (figs. 1167 and 1168). This tassel, which is intended to finish articles trimmed with the fringes in figs. 1127 or 1128, requires a pear-shaped mold covered with a crochet sheath made with DMC pearl cotton no. 5 in grey-blue.

Fig. 1167. Tassel with two rows of smaller tassels.

This sheath is begun at the bottom of the mold with a ring of 5 chain into which 10 double crochet are worked, then the work continues, increasing or decreasing as the shape of the mold requires. The double crochet are always worked into the two upper loops of the stitch below. As the tassel gets thinner toward the top, the crochet sheath finally ends in a round cord, consisting of 6 double crochet. To fasten the small tassels to the mold, two rows of crochet loops, consisting of chain and single crochet, are worked. After the thread has been fastened onto the sheath at the spot indicated for the upper row of small tassels, make 12 chain, take a bunch of about 20 threads of DMC special stranded cotton no. 25, in hazelnut brown, lay it over the last 5 chain, miss these 5 chain and work 1 single crochet into each of the next 6 chain, so that the bunch of yellow threads, hanging in the loop of 5 chain, appears to be hanging from a cord; see fig. 1168. Finally, make 1 chain and 1 single crochet into the 2nd stitch of the sheath. Continue thus all round the mold.

Fig. 1168. How to fasten on the small tassels in fig. 1167.

In the original of our illustration, there are 16 small tassels in the upper row and 25 in the lower. The loops in the upper row are longer: they were made with 18 chain and 12 single crochet; the tassels are blue.

When these rows are finished, the bunches are folded in half and tied, the yellow with blue thread and the blue with yellow thread. Finally, a large pompom (fig. 1149) is made with DMC special stranded cotton no. 25 in hazelnut brown, and fastened to the little ring of crochet chain at the bottom of the mold. This pompom is to make the two rows of small tassels stand out well and make the tassel larger at the bottom.

Lace Trimmings. Fine embroideries on linen or cambric are usually trimmed with lace of all kinds which, according to their type and design, are either sewn on flat or gathered round the article to be trimmed. Needlemade lace and lace made with braid are joined to the fabric with overcasting; crochet lace and knitted lace are sewn on carefully stitch by stitch.

Turning corners. Knitted lace, crochet lace, needlemade lace, and pillow lace can be made in advance with corners; however, where the lace is in a straight piece, it must be gathered round the corners as much as may be necessary to make an even frame to the work.

Chapter heading, after Holbein.

CHAPTER XX

Miscellaneous Directions

Having dealt with all the subjects which formed the purpose of this publication, it now remains for us to add a few words about some methods of copying, arranging, and altering designs, and about various useful processes. The correct application of these processes is often an essential condition of the complete success of a piece of work.

Just as it is a good thing to know how to adapt designs to the space at one's disposal, so it is also useful to be able to give lace that suggestion of stiffness which is the hallmark of freshness, and, for embroideries which require pasting, to know which ingredients to use and how to prepare them.

Ordinary Tracing.   In order to reproduce a design, a sheet of tracing paper or linen is first laid over the paper on which the design is to be reproduced. The two sheets are fastened together at the four corners with small pins to prevent them from slipping during the work. If this happens, it may be difficult to replace them so that they fit exactly. This done, all the outlines of the design are followed with a pencil or, better still, with a paintbrush or pen dipped in ink.

If neither tracing paper nor tracing linen is available, a sheet of ordinary paper can be used, and the tracing is done against a window pane.

If the design of an actual piece of embroidery or lace is to be copied, the article is placed on a board and a sheet of glass or gelatin paper is laid over it; the tracing paper or linen is then fixed to the glass with a little glue at each corner, and the outlines of the model can be traced without any fear of injuring it.

Tracing by rubbing.   Another way of taking a tracing directly from a piece of embroidery is to proceed as follows: place the embroidery on the table and over it lay a sheet of fairly soft white paper. This paper must not be too thick to take a clear impression, nor so thin as to tear during the rubbing. The whole is then firmly secured with drawing pins and rubbed backward and forward with a tin spoon or a silver coin or, better still, with a piece of heelball, which can be obtained from any shoemaker.

By this process the design is reproduced on the paper in somewhat blurred black lines, which should afterward be gone over again with pen or pencil to make the copy of the original clearer. This process is very rapid, but has the disadvantage of flattening the relief of the embroidery which has been copied.

Tracing a design onto the material itself. The simplest way of transferring a design onto a transparent material is as follows: the original tracing is outlined in ink and then tacked with large stitches to the wrong side of the material; the whole is then spread out on a drawing board. Some very dark powdered indigo is then mixed with water in a dish, adding a pinch of sugar and the same quantity of gum arabic.

Using this preparation as ink, the outlines of the design, visible through the thin material, are traced with a mapping pen. The lines should be traced very lightly—if the material is left for some time before the work is done, they will bite into the material and cannot then be removed at the first washing; further, thick lines will make the work unpleasantly sticky.

Tracing by means of carbon paper. There is another fairly rapid way of tracing designs onto light-colored materials, especially those whose surface is smooth, by means of special carbon paper which is strongly impregnated with an oily, colored substance. This paper is laid between the design and the material, which has first been fastened down to a board. After the two layers of paper have been similarly secured, all the outlines of the design are followed with a blunt-pointed pencil or, better still, with the point of a bone crochet hook or the blade of a paper knife. Whichever implement is chosen, the pressure exercised on it should be moderate, for fear of tearing the paper which bears the design. The pressure on the two sheets of paper causes the colored substance on the carbon paper to come off on the material, and an imprint of all the lines which have been followed is left on the material.

This method of reproducing designs is suitable only for materials which are to be washed, for, however carefully the tracing is done, little spots of color are often left on the article; moreover, the carbon paper would dull the surface of velvet, satin, moiré, and any other silk material.

Ironing off designs. There are on the market pencils with greasy lead, and special inks, by means of which tracings can be made which can be transferred to the material with the help of a hot iron. The whole of the design to be transferred is drawn or traced with the special ink or pencil; it is then laid on the material, with the design down. When a fairly hot iron is passed over the pattern, the coloring matter is melted and marks the material. Small motifs may be simply laid on the material, but large designs should be tacked to it to prevent them from slipping during the ironing.

This very simple method of tracing may be recommended in preference to any other; we must, however, point out that the design is in this way reversed on the material. To avoid this, all asymetrical designs should first be traced with ordinary pencil or ink onto transparent paper; the paper is then turned the other side up and all the lines traced again with the special ink or pencil. The designs will thus, when transferred to the material, be the right way round.

Pouncing designs onto material. The methods already described cannot be used in every case; they are not suitable for thick materials such as velvet. For these the process of pouncing, which we are about to describe, must be used.

When the design has been reproduced on the tracing paper, the next step is to ''prick'' it. For this purpose it is laid on a thickly folded cloth, and with a special needle (see fig. 1037), following all the lines of the design, the complete outline is pricked. If several copies of the same design are required, these can be made at the same time by laying several sheets of paper together and pricking through them all in one operation. In this case, the paper should be fairly thin, so that all the copies will be quite clear. When the lines of the design are very fine, care should be taken to prick them with a fine needle.

It is advisable that the pricking should be done very regularly, with the holes close together, and following the lines accurately; otherwise the shapes of the outlines will be altered and the embroidery will be difficult to work successfully.

When the pricking is finished, the wrong side of the tracing paper is rubbed with emery paper to remove the rough edges round the little holes.

The two parts—the pricked paper and the material—are then secured with drawing pins to prevent them from slipping during the pouncing. Otherwise, the design may easily be reproduced double on the material, necessitating all kinds of expedients to remove the extra lines.

When the pattern has been firmly secured, a pouncing pad or ''baren,'' its base covered with cloth, is dipped in powder—of a light shade of the material is dark and dark for a light material—and the whole surface of the pricked paper is lightly rubbed with it. This rubbing causes the powder adhering to the cloth to pass through the little holes and leave visible traces on the material. When the design has been sufficiently pounced, the paper is removed; if the motif is to be repeated, the paper is replaced carefully where the pouncing leaves off and at the exact spot where the lines are to meet. This joining of the designs must be done with the utmost care so that the join shall not be visible.

When the pouncing is finished, the design is traced. The best medium for this is good watercolor, which can be obtained in any shade. Four colors are enough for all kinds of tracing on materials: black, blue, white, and yellow. On smooth materials, the tracing can be done with a pen; we advise, however, for all materials, the use of a small sable paintbrush. The rougher or more hairy the material, the finer the brush should be, so that the color penetrates well into the hairs. Before beginning to follow the lines of the pouncing with the brush, the article should be lightly blown upon, to remove any excess powder which may have passed through the holes.

Preparing Materials and Arranging Designs. We know many designers, skillful in the exercise of their craft on paper, who find themselves confronted with very real difficulties when transferring their compositions to material. We shall therefore point out, as far as possible, certain precautions to be observed in tracing designs, for which purpose we must return to one of the initial operations, that of pricking.

It is essential that the paper which is to be pricked should have a margin of one and a half to two inches outside the design itself so that the pad shall never touch the actual material. If the design is square and symmetrical, it can be folded in fourths and all four quarters pricked at the same time; if, on the other hand, it is a detached design, either one repeat, or the whole design will have to be pricked separately. The surface on which the design is to be traced should never be divided up beforehand with pencil lines, as it is almost impossible to remove these lines afterward and they may permanently spoil the effect of the work.

Before beginning the tracing, the material should be divided into quarters; then the width of the edge to be left beyond the design must be decided, allowing for a hem or other finishing, for the embroidery is very seldom carried right to the edge of the article.

When the design is to be transferred onto linen or cotton materials which will retain a fold, these are folded in fourths like the paper, and the fold is pressed so that it will remain until the tracing is finished. When the material has thus been divided in fourths, it is folded again diagonally to enable corner motifs, if there are any, to be accurately placed.

We are speaking of the division of the material into equal parts; in squares, the dividing line is the diagonal, which most readers will know how to draw with a ruler on paper, but not, perhaps, on material. This line is, nevertheless, very easy to find: it suffices to fold the material in such a way that the outside thread of the selvedge or cut edge lies along the weft thread which marks the corner of the fold.

By this double folding the foundation is divided into eight parts. It is an easy matter to decide the margin to be left if the article—a napkin, for instance—is to be finished with an openwork hem. In this case, the line produced by the drawing out of the threads will serve as a guide so that the design can be traced straight by the line of the threads. Often, however, it is preferable not to draw out the threads until after the design has been traced. If, therefore, the position of the design cannot be marked by the drawing out of threads, and the material is one in which the threads cannot be counted, the marking out should be done as shown in fig. 166.

Folding, as a method of dividing up the material, cannot be used for silks, velvet, and plush: certain kinds of silk will not retain a fold, others are spoiled by folding and become useless. The commonsense method of dealing with such materials is to mount them in a frame before beginning to trace. To mark the dividing lines, a fairly strong thread is taken and knotted at one end; a pin is passed through the knot, which is drawn tight upon it. One side of the material is then divided into two equal parts, and the pin, with the thread knotted to it, is inserted at the point which marks the middle. The same operation is repeated on the opposite side, and another pin inserted, by means of which the thread is stretched across the material; similar threads are stretched in the same way from the middle points of the other two sides and diagonally from corner to corner. In this way the material can be accurately divided up, and the dividing lines can be removed as soon as the pouncing has been completed, leaving no trace on the work.

Before the pouncing of a design is finished, the worker should ascertain that it fulfills the conditions necessary for the article it is to adorn. Suppose that a border with a corner is to be traced. The length of the design should be measured, and the points where the motif will have to be repeated should be marked by a light pouncing. It may happen that the repeats do not quite meet in the middle; if the gap is small, it can be filled, without altering the design, by bringing the whole a little further in, thus lessening the distance between the corners. If, on the other hand, the gap is too large to be filled in this way, it will be necessary to add a supplementary design of a suitable size. The same work will also be necessary if the design has to be shortened.

How to Transform Designs With the Help of Two Mirrors (fig. 1169). We have just stressed the need to adapt designs to the space available; these alterations, which sometimes cause difficulties

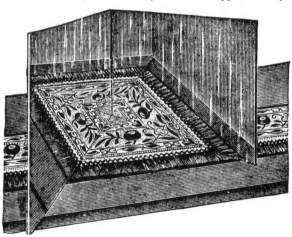

Fig. 1169. Transforming a straight design into a square design with the help of two mirrors.

only a designer can solve, are facilitated to a surprising extent, particularly in cross stitch embroideries, by the use of two frameless mirrors. When

placed carefully in accordance with the following instructions, they give truly astinishing results.

When only part of a design can be used, if it is to be enlarged or to be used
to form a center or a corner, the mirrors are placed, in the first two cases in
a straight line, in the last in a diagonal line, at the point where the design is
to be interrupted, whether it is to be repeated or reversed, and the design
will be reflected in the mirror in the required conditions. To form a square,
two mirrors are used, meeting at the point where the diagonal lines meet,

Fig. 1170. Design prepared for copying or alteration.

and the square appears, as can be seen in fig. 1169.

The portion of the design to be reproduced cannot be chosen arbitrarily.
It is only after some preliminary experimenting that the most suitable spot
can be found for the formation of a center or corners, since not all parts of
the design lend themselves to change. A few experiments with a mirror
before the work is begun will show the importance of these instructions better than a lengthy explanation.

How to Reproduce Designs, Modifying Their Size and Propor-

tions by Means of Squares (figs. 1170 and 1171). There are cases where more serious modifications have to be made to the design which is available. Suppose, for instance, that a running design is to be embroidered

Fig. 1171. Design reduced.

on a piece of material which is too small for the chosen design or, on the other hand, the design is too small for the material. Lacking a knowledge of drawing, one would seem obliged to have recourse to a designer or photographer, or be tempted to give up the intended work. Neither of these courses is necessary if the advice we are about to give is followed.

Take some squared paper, or if necessary prepare it yourself; reproduce the design on the squared paper, or draw the squares directly onto the pattern, as in fig. 1170. Then take a second sheet of paper and mark it out also in squares, but make them a quarter, a third, or half the size of those on the first sheet. Thus, if the side of one of the original squares is three-quarters of an inch long and you want to reduce the design by one third, the sides of the new squares must be half an inch long (see fig. 1171). In the same way, if the design is to be one third larger, the new squares will have to measure one inch. The lines of the design are then copied square by square, wider apart or closer together according to whether the design is to be enlarged or decreased.

If the design is to be copied directly from an embroidered model and at the same time enlarged or decreased, the following method should be used:

Fasten the embroidery to a board, stretching it evenly in all directions. Then with a tape measure gauge the length of the design; divide the inches by a number of units corresponding to the proportions you wish the modified design to have; if any fractions of an inch remain, divide them similarly. Then divide up the side of the work into the lengths thus obtained with the help of a pair of dividers: open the dividers so that the distance between the points is exactly the length of one division of the side and insert a pin, with a thread knotted to it, at the spot indicated by the dividers. Repeat this operation along the whole of one side of the embroidery, if possible a short distance beyond the actual embroidery, so as not to damage the latter. It then remains only to stretch the threads very straight across the work and then repeat the same process on the other two sides to complete the squaring.

It goes without saying that a mounted article cannot be stretched on a board, but with a little ingenuity some means can always be found of inserting the pins without damaging the article.

How to Modify the Length of a Design (figs. 1172, 1173, 1174). It is often necessary to enlarge a design in one direction only; in this case, the shape of the square is altered and rectangles, proportionate to the desired form of the design, are made.

Fig. 1172 shows a design to be worked in DMC superfine braid. In fig. 1173 the squares have been replaced by rectangles half as long again as the squares, and the design is proportionately longer; in fig. 1174 the width of the rectangles is only two-thirds that of the squares, and the design is proportionately shorter. These methods simplify all the difficulties of copying; they will enable even those who have no knowledge of drawing to undertake this kind of alteration.

How to Prepare Paste for Securing Embroidery and for Appliqué Work. It may appear strange that we should devote a special paragraph to such an apparently simple matter. It is, however, by no means so simple in reality. Badly prepared paste may completely ruin a piece of work begun under the best conditions, as well as waste a great deal of costly material.

To prepare paste, take some wheat—not rice—starch, and put in a double saucepan the amount you expect to require for the work to be done; add to the starch only just the quantity of water necessary to dissolve it and stir with a wooden spoon until all the lumps have disappeared.

In the meantime, boil some pure water and add to it some powdered resin or glue (a pinch about the size of a pea to every quarter of a pint); add the dissolved starch little by little, stirring well all the time. Allow it to boil a few seconds longer, remove from the heat, and continue to stir till the starch is only warm. Stirring is essential to prevent the formation of lumps. Paste made in this way does not stain, nor does it dull the brightest color, since it does not contain any trace of acid. In winter it will keep for several days—longer than in the heat of summer. As soon as it shows the least sign of deterioration, it should not be used. Gum arabic must never be used for fixing embroidery or for appliqué work: the substances used in its manufacture almost always stain materials.

How to Stiffen New Work. In the chapter "Needlemade Laces," we said that new work of this kind should always be ironed. The method of ironing is by no means a matter of indifference. After detaching it from its

Fig. 1172. Braid design.

Fig. 1173. Design kept the same width, but lengthened.

Fig. 1174. Design kept the same width, but shortened.

foundation, the lace is placed, right side down, on fine white flannel; then a piece of new, highly dressed organdy is dipped in water, removed as soon as it is thoroughly soaked, and squeezed gently to remove the excess moisture. The pad must be thoroughly damp but not dripping.

The lace is dabbed all over on the wrong side with the organdy, then ironed with a warm iron, which is passed over it slowly so that the moisture left by the organdy can evaporate. The lace must not be removed from the ironing board until it is completely dry.

We know of no better way of imparting to new lace that suggestion of stiffness which is often the only thing that distinguishes new from old. Water, by itself, does not stiffen the threads sufficiently, while starch, even diluted, is usually too thick: it is extremely difficult to obtain exactly the right consistency. But if organdy is used, there is no danger of producing the wrong degree of stiffening.

The same method can be used for embroidered net. It is damped with the organdy while it is still in the frame and left in the frame to dry. Openwork knitting and crochet are pinned out on the ironing board, damped with the organdy, and then ironed.

It is a good thing to treat articles embroidered on linen in the same way. If, however, the linen is very crumpled or badly creased, a piece of damp linen, preferably a napkin soaked in water and then well wrung, should be laid over it, and the ironing done over this.

How to Wash Ordinary Lace. Wind the lace round the cylindrical part of a bottle. When it has all been wound, cover it with a piece of white muslin and secure the muslin with a few stitches. Then the bottle is put in a pan with enough cold water to cover it completely and a small piece of good household soap. The water is brought to the boil and boiled for about an hour. The bottle can be prevented from moving about when the water is boiling by filling it halfway with sand.

When the water is dirty, fresh is substituted, and this process is repeated until the water remains clear. The lace is then clean, and after being rinsed several times in cold water—still on the bottle—to remove all trace of soap, it is unrolled and dried.

How to Wash Fine Lace. The process is the same as above, but as valuable lace is not washed so often, it is often yellower than ordinary lace and often, through lack of care, it is more fragile.

If, then, it is stained or greasy, it should first be put to soak for a few hours, or even a few days, according to the amount of cleaning necessary, in a bath of fine olive oil. The sole object of this bath is to restore the suppleness the lace has lost through use or washing. After the oil treatment, it is washed in the same way as other lace.

How to Starch Lace. When the washed lace is quite dry, a thin starch is prepared as follows: take some pure wheat starch and divide it into two parts; dilute both with cold water, then stir one part into boiling water. After boiling it for a short time, remove it from the heat and continue to stir until no steam rises from it. Once this part has cooled, mix the two parts together and add sufficient water to make the starch about the thickness of good milk. If the lace is to be tinted, add a few drops of coffee to the water, or replace the water which is used for the thinning by weak tea or an infusion of mallow. Coffee imparts a deep cream shade to the lace; tea a slightly greenish shade.

When the starch is prepared, the lace is dipped in it, and the excess liquid is gently squeezed out without wringing; the lace is then laid in one hand and beaten with the other to work the starch in; the lace is dipped twice more into the starch, and the same operation repeated each time. Then it is rolled in a fine linen cloth and left until it is to be ironed, or pinned out, according to the quality and type of lace to be renovated.

How to Iron Lace. When the lace has been left for an hour or two in the dry cloth, it is ironed if it is a plain lace or pinned out if it is a rich needlemade lace, pillow lace, or net guipure.

Before the lace is ironed, it is held in the left hand by the heading, while the right hand stretches each picot in turn along the whole length of the piece to be ironed. This done, the lace is laid on white flannel and ironed with a moderately hot iron. The iron is held on the lace as long as it is damp; when it is moved on to the next part, the part that has just been ironed should be quite dry. If creases are accidentally made in the ironing, a sponge should be dipped in a few drops of the starch that has been used for the lace, the creases are damped and ironed again. When the lace has been ironed once, it is stretched obliquely, bit by bit, first from left to right, then from right to left, and then ironed again. Stretching the lace in this way, in two opposite directions, removes the artificial stiffness caused by the first ironing.

How to Pin Out Lace. If lace is to be pinned out satisfactorily, a wooden drum is necessary, about twelve inches high and twenty-four inches in diameter, which rests upon the knees. The outer circumference of the wood is padded and covered with grey or white drill.

The pins to be used for pinning out the picots should correspond to these in size. Thus very fine pins should be used for Valenciennes and needlepoint laces, and coarser ones for other kinds of lace; but they should always be of white metal, never of steel, which would rust and ruin the lace. The drum is covered with blue paper (which is less tiring to the eyes than any other); then as much lace as can be pinned out before it dries is taken out of the cloth; the rest remains rolled in the cloth.

The heading is laid in a straight line and secured with pins placed at equal distances apart; then the picots of the edge are pinned one by one, taking care not to open them if they have retained their original shape and to straighten them if they have become twisted. If the pinning cannot be done quickly enough to be completed before the lace dries, the picots and the dry parts can be damped again slightly with a sponge, and the pins placed immediately. Completely dry parts should never be pinned, as there would be a danger of tearing the picots and thus spoiling valuable lace.

Certain kinds of lace, in which parts of the work are in relief, have to be pressed out on the wrong side with a lace awl, a kind of hook made of bone, made specially for this purpose. Some lace workers treat Valenciennes lace in this way, but in our opinion this is a mistake, as this kind of lace is entirely without relief when it leaves the worker's hands.

The pinning is continued round the cylinder without removing any of the lace until it stretches all round, if it is a length that is being renovated, or until the whole is dry, if it is only a piece being cleaned.

The lace should be carefully covered as it is pinned, and any parts that are finished and removed from the cylinder should be rolled up and put in a blue paper bag, so that it may all be equally clean.

Finally, our advice is to undertake the washing of lace at a time when one is sure not to be interrupted. Each operation should follow immediately after the preceding one, and the pinning in particular should never be interrupted.

Methods of Cleaning Colored Embroideries Worked in Cotton, Flax, and Rayon Threads.

1. Usual method of washing with soap.

Lathering. Dissolve in boiling water a quantity of good quality soap or soap flakes sufficient to make a good lather; do not use any soda or washing powders. Add cold water to reduce to a moderate temperature and wash the embroidery without rubbing it too much. Rinse, first in warm and then in cold water, until no trace of soap remains.

Restoring sheen. If, as sometimes happens through the use of unsuitable water, the sheen of the thread appears more or less dulled, it can be restored by using an acid bath after the rinsing. This is composed of a large tablespoonful of acetic acid (or half a glass of white vinegar) to a quart of water. The embroidery should be stirred in this solution for a few minutes and then well rinsed in water.

Drying. Squeeze out by hand and dry quickly, either by hanging up the embroidery, or by ironing it.

2. Method of removing stains (fruit, wine, iron, mold, black ink). Into a container made of wood, enamel, or earthenware (not iron), pour a sufficient quantity of cold bleaching solution and add the same quantity of boiling water. Immerse the embroidery, which should have previously been washed in hot water, in this solution, and leave it for half an hour, stirring occasionally. Rinse well in water, then proceed to wash with soap as described above.

How to prepare the bleaching solution (which does not keep). Dissolve half an ounce of salts of sorrel in a quart of water. When it is dissolved, add one and a half ounces of metasulphite (or a glass of bisulphate of soda); shake. These ingredients can be obtained from any chemist.

3. Lye washing. If all the stains are not removed by the preceding methods, the embroidery may, thanks to the excellent quality of most dyes, be subjected to lye washing as follows:

Dissolve in a copper basin some good quality soap, containing no soda, in the proportion of half an ounce to a quart of water. Boil the embroidery in this solution for ten minutes to an hour, according to the stains to be re-

700 / MISCELLANEOUS DIRECTIONS

moved. Rinse well in plenty of water, and, if necessary, immerse in an acid bath.

The use of soda and washing powders should be avoided; they would not, in any case, improve the cleaning.

4. Chlorinating. The three previous methods enable embroideries to be cleaned in every case with the certainty of success and without the disadvantages of cleaning with chlorine, with which there is always a risk of damaging threads and material. We would mention, however, that work executed with good quality colored threads will stand the following treatment:

Prepare a solution containing a tablespoonful of chlorine to a quart of cold water. Dip the embroidery in water and squeeze out the excess moisture, then immerse it in the chlorine solution. After about five minutes, remove it and rinse thoroughly in cold water; then proceed to the acid bath described above. Never leave the wet embroidery folded or heaped together.

Method of Cleaning Embroidery Worked in Real Silk. Use only a perfectly neutral soap, preferably white soap of the best quality; above all, soda and washing powders should be avoided. Dissolve in boiling water a sufficient quantity of this soap to make a good lather, add cold water to reduce it to a moderate temperature, and wash the embroidery quickly, without rubbing too much. Rinse well, first in warm water, then in several changes of cold water, until all trace of soap has been removed.

Squeeze out by hand without wringing, or by rolling in a soft cloth, and dry rapidly in the open air or by ironing on the wrong side with a warm iron; in the latter case, the embroidery should be laid, right side down, between two cloths. This is always best done with a calender. The wet embroidery should never be left folded or heaped together; nor should too hot an iron be used, as this would dull certain colors.